D0080046

APPLIED BEHAVIOR ANALYSIS

ANALYSIS

Principles and Procedures for Modifying Behavior

Edward P. Sarafino
The College of New Jersey

WILEY

JOHN WILEY & SONS, INC.

VICE PRESIDENT & EXECUTIVE PUBLISHER	Jay O'Callaghan
EXECUTIVE EDITOR	Christopher Johnson
SENIOR ACQUISITIONS EDITOR	Robert Johnston
ASSOCIATE EDITOR	Eileen McKeever
EDITORIAL ASSISTANT	Maura Gilligan
SENIOR MARKETING MANAGER	Danielle Hagey
SENIOR PHOTO EDITOR	Jennifer MacMillan
PHOTO RESEARCHER	Elle Wagner
SENIOR MEDIA EDITOR	Lynn Pearlman
SENIOR PRODUCTION MANAGER	Janis Soo
ASSOCIATE PRODUCTION MANAGER	Joyce Poh
ASSISTANT PRODUCTION EDITOR	Yee Lyn Song
COVER DESIGNER	Seng Ping Ngieng
COVER PHOTO CREDIT	Michael Newman/PhotoEdit (top photo)
	Relaximages/Cultura/Getty Images (bottom photo)

This book was set in 9.5/11.5 Novarese by Laserwords Private Limited and printed and bound by Courier Westford. The cover was printed by Courier Westford.

This book is printed on acid-free paper. ⊗

Founded in 1807, John Wiley & Sons, Inc. has been a valued source of knowledge and understanding for more than 200 years, helping people around the world meet their needs and fulfill their aspirations. Our company is built on a foundation of principles that include responsibility to the communities we serve and where we live and work. In 2008, we launched a Corporate Citizenship Initiative, a global effort to address the environmental, social, economic, and ethical challenges we face in our business. Among the issues we are addressing are carbon impact, paper specifications and procurement, ethical conduct within our business and among our vendors, and community and charitable support. For more information, please visit our website: www.wiley.com/go/citizenship.

Copyright © 2012 John Wiley & Sons, Inc. All rights reserved. No part of this publication may be reproduced, stored in a retrieval system or transmitted in any form or by any means, electronic, mechanical, photocopying, recording, scanning or otherwise, except as permitted under Sections 107 or 108 of the 1976 United States Copyright Act, without either the prior written permission of the Publisher, or authorization through payment of the appropriate per-copy fee to the Copyright Clearance Center, Inc. 222 Rosewood Drive, Danvers, MA 01923, website www.copyright.com. Requests to the Publisher for permission should be addressed to the Permissions Department, John Wiley & Sons, Inc., 111 River Street, Hoboken, NJ 07030-5774, (201)748-6011, fax (201)748-6008, website http://www.wiley.com/go/permissions.

Evaluation copies are provided to qualified academics and professionals for review purposes only, for use in their courses during the next academic year. These copies are licensed and may not be sold or transferred to a third party. Upon completion of the review period, please return the evaluation copy to Wiley. Return instructions and a free of charge return mailing label are available at www.wiley.com/go/returnlabel. If you have chosen to adopt this textbook for use in your course, please accept this book as your complimentary desk copy. Outside of the United States, please contact your local sales representative

Library of Congress Cataloging-in-Publication Data

Sarafino, Edward P.
   Applied behavior analysis : principles and procedures for modifying behavior / Edward P. Sarafino.
      p. cm.
   Includes bibliographical references and index.
   ISBN 978-0-470-57152-1 (pbk. : acid free paper)
1. Behavior modification. I. Title.
   BF637.B4S268 2012
1   2011025717

ACC LIBRARY SERVICES AUSTIN, TX

Printed in the United States of America

10 9 8 7 6 5 4 3 2 1

To Jim

ABOUT THE AUTHOR

Edward P. Sarafino received his PhD from the University of Colorado and immediately began his 32-year affiliation with the Department of Psychology at The College of New Jersey. His scholarship continues to combine areas of health and behavioral psychology, particularly in his study of asthma. In addition to having published dozens of research articles and chapters, he is the author of six books. He is a member of Division 25 (The Experimental Analysis of Behavior) of the American Psychological Association and is a fellow of Division 38 (Health Psychology). He served as an officer (secretary) of Division 38, and has been a member of several committees of the Division and the Society of Behavioral Medicine. When he is not working, he enjoys being with family and friends, traveling, hiking and other outdoor activities, and going to cultural events, especially music and visual arts.

TO CONTACT THE AUTHOR

I would be pleased to receive comments and suggestions about this book from students and instructors so that I may consider those ideas for future editions. You may contact me by e-mail at sarafino@tcnj.edu.
Edward P. Sarafino

PREFACE

Psychologists have discovered a great deal of information about human behavior, but not all of the knowledge we have gained can be applied to improve the way people behave and function in their everyday lives. The field of applied behavior analysis is unique in this respect, having developed a rich and varied system of methods, based on established principles of learning, that have been applied effectively toward improving people's behavior. Applications of behavior change techniques have been successful in almost all areas of psychology and in a wide variety of settings.

My goal in writing this book has been to create a clear and engaging teaching instrument that describes ways to analyze one's own specific behaviors in terms of the factors that lead to and maintain them and ways to manage those factors to improve the behaviors. I have drawn on research, theory, and my own and students' experiences to explain and provide examples of the concepts and methods of applied behavior analysis in a comprehensive text. The text is appropriate for several courses, especially those that focus on topics in *applied behavior analysis, behavior modification, behavior therapy, and psychology of learning*. These courses are likely to be offered in departments of psychology, special education, and speech pathology.

Two general features of the students' educational backgrounds shaped my writing. First, students who use this book are likely to come from a variety of fields. I have tried to make the material interesting and relevant to students from all fields by describing applications in psychology, education, counseling, nursing, and physical therapy. Second, students who use this book are likely to vary in their academic level and preparation. Although I aimed to make the content appropriate for upper-division students, especially juniors, I wrote with a straightforward writing style to make the content accessible to most sophomores, including those who've not taken an introductory psychology course.

The field of applied behavior analysis is enormously exciting, partly because of its relevance to the current lives of those who study it as well as to the individuals the students know or will work with in the future. The field is also exciting because its knowledge is applied in so many different settings and can be used to change one's own behavior. Creating a book that is comprehensive in its coverage of behavior change principles and up to date in each area of application is a challenge. I consulted thousands of articles and books in writing this text, which cites more than 1,000 references, over one-fifth of which were published in the last 10 years.

OBJECTIVES AND DISTINCTIVE FEATURES OF THIS BOOK

Several important objectives guided the content and organization of my writing. This text was designed to:

- Cover a large majority of tasks or concepts that the Behavior Analyst Certification Board (www.bacb.com) has identified as the field's essential content that should be mastered by all behavior analysts.

- Provide an understanding of the fundamental techniques of applied behavior analysis by presenting its concepts and procedures in a logical sequence and giving clear definitions and examples of each technique.

- Teach students how to pinpoint and define the behavior to be changed and how a response is determined by its antecedents and consequences.

- Teach usable, practical skills by specifically stating the purpose of each technique, describing how it is carried out, and presenting guidelines and tips to maximize its effectiveness.

- Describe why and how to design a program to change a behavioral deficit or excess by conducting a functional assessment and then selecting and combining techniques that can be directed at the behavior itself and its antecedents and consequences.

- Illustrate why and how to collect and analyze data.
- Provide students with a handbook to help them design and conduct interventions to modify behaviors when they enter professional careers.

It is my hope that this text will serve as a handbook for students who become behavior analysts to design and conduct interventions to change clients' behaviors.

Several features of this book and its companion website are seldom found in texts in applied behavior analysis or behavior modification. This book has:

- Case Study boxed material in almost all chapters, describing in some detail the application of behavior analysis methods with specific individuals to make behavior problems and the procedures to change them concrete.
- Close-Up boxed material in almost all chapters that presents theoretical or controversial issues and in-depth conceptual topics.
- Concept Check boxes, generally two per chapter, to test students' basic grasp of the concepts and procedures in the preceding sections. Some of the questions are "critical thinking" items that ask students to state an example from their reading or their own lives. Answers are given at the end of the chapter.
- Lists of key terms (which are defined in the text and the glossary) and essay-type review questions.
- Lists of tips in about half of the chapters on how to apply specific techniques.
- A whole chapter with detailed reasons, procedures, and data forms for doing a *functional assessment* of a behavior, enabling students to define a behavior and determine its antecedents and consequences. This material includes how to interpret data from a functional analysis with graphed examples.
- Material showing students how to graph data and do a *graphic analysis*.
- Chapters on biofeedback, token economies, and rule-governed and verbal behavior.
- A chapter that describes how to get additional training and certification in applied behavior analysis.
- An *online study guide* on its companion website.

HOW THIS BOOK IS ORGANIZED

I organized the chapters in this book so that the material within and across chapters occurs in an orderly sequence, establishing each conceptual foundation on which to add new information and principles. The chapters and material within them are organized to build upon relatively simple concepts and techniques toward increasingly complex and specialized methods. The book is divided into 28 relatively short chapters, each with a sufficient and manageable amount of information. The chapters are divided into the following seven parts:

- *Part I: Introducing Applied Behavior Analysis.* Chapters 1 to 4 describe basic behavioral concepts and processes, how to identify and assess target behaviors, graphic analysis and research methods, and how principles of applied behavior analysis have been applied effectively to improve a wide variety of behaviors in many settings.
- *Part II: Basic Operant Principles.* Chapter 5 discusses positive and negative reinforcement and describes their many types with examples from everyday life. Chapters 6 and 7 cover the processes and characteristics of extinction and punishment, describing types of and concerns about positive and negative punishers. Chapter 8 discusses the role of antecedents and stimulus control in producing specific behaviors. And Chapter 9 discusses motivating operations.
- *Part III: Methods to Establish New Operant Behaviors.* Chapters 10 to 12 discuss the process of shaping, methods for shortcut stimulus control (prompting and fading), and behavioral chains.
- *Part IV: Methods for Modifying Operant Behaviors.* Chapter 13 describes the need and procedures for functional assessments. Chapter 14 covers ways to manage antecedents. Chapters 15 and 16 discuss how to increase a behavior with basic and advanced reinforcement techniques. Chapters 17 to 19 focus on methods to decrease problem behaviors. And Chapter 20 covers ways to maintain improved operant behaviors.

- *Part V: Respondent Behaviors and Ways to Change Them.* Chapters 21 and 22 discuss respondent conditioning and methods to change respondent behaviors.

- *Part VI: Specialized Topics in Behavior Analysis.* Chapters 23 to 26 cover the topics of biofeedback, behavioral contracts, self-management, token economies, and verbal behavior.

- *Part VII. Current Concerns and Future Issues.* Chapters 27 and 28 discuss ethics and dilemmas in changing behavior, challenges for the field of applied behavior analysis, and careers and training in behavior analysis.

Some instructors may want to move some chapters, such as Chapter 10 on shaping, from the middle of the book to an earlier time in the course. Although I have tried to minimize references to material in intervening chapters, this isn't always possible when the goal is to build on earlier concepts when presenting advanced concepts. To help you identify possible problems with intervening material, I have created a table that is included in this preface with the brief table of contents. The table lists 10 chapters from Parts III, IV, and V and tells you the material each chapter refers to from earlier chapters of the book. I hope this table helps instructors decide whether to shift chapter locations and how to address the issue of references to intervening material.

LEARNING AIDS

This book contains many pedagogical features, including a *chapter contents* and *prologue* at the beginning of each chapter. These features give the student an overview of the chapter material and include an engaging, relevant vignette. The body of the chapters includes many *figures, tables, and photographs* to clarify concepts or research findings. For example, special figures were created to show how second-order conditioning occurs and how to collect data for a functional assessment. Dozens of graphs are presented to depict the effects of applied behavior analysis methods on performance. Important terms are printed in **boldface** type; *italics* are used liberally for other terms and for emphasis.

Three types of boxed material are incorporated throughout the text and identified with the corresponding icons. They are:

- *Concept Checks.* This type of box has the students apply concepts or techniques to specific questions or problems to check their basic understanding of the material they have just read. In some cases, a question is followed by the symbol ⇔ to identify this as a "critical thinking" item for which more than one answer could be correct. These questions are intended to promote students' analytical and creative thinking about the concepts and procedures they've just read about.

- *Case Studies.* The second type of boxed material describes actual cases in which behavior analysis techniques were applied. The person's behavior problem and the intervention are presented in rich detail, giving students an appreciation of how the procedures are conducted and their impact and utility.

- *Close-Ups.* The third type of box presents theoretical or controversial issues, in-depth conceptual topics and procedural steps, or important research.

Each chapter ends with a *summary*, a list of *key terms*, *review questions*, and a list of *related readings*. The key terms consist of all boldfaced items from the chapter and are redefined in the *glossary* at the back of the book.

INSTRUCTOR RESOURCES

Instructors who are using this text can access a companion website at www.wiley.com after registering and obtaining a password. It contains (a) an *instructor's manual* with information to help instructors present the subject matter effectively and design activities to enrich classroom discussion and (b) a *test bank*.

ACKNOWLEDGMENTS

Writing this book has been a big task. I am indebted to the researchers whose important and creative work I have cited. I also received a great deal of help and encouragement from a number of people whom I gratefully acknowledge. First, my thanks go to Chris Johnson, the acquisitions editor at John Wiley & Sons, who asked me to develop a plan for this book and signed it, and to the other Wiley personnel who helped establish my writing schedule, oversaw the review process, and coordinated the production process.

Second, the cover-to-cover review process generated many helpful suggestions. The resulting text has benefited greatly from this process and the ideas of the following colleagues:

Alicia Alvero, City University of New York, Queens College
Rafael Bejarano, Henderson State University
Glenn Carter, Austin Peay State University
Teresa Daly, University of Central Florida
Lisa Gurdin, Northeastern University
Brooke Ingersol, Michigan State University
Iver Iversen, University of North Florida
Lee Ann Mjelde-Mossey, Ohio State University
Anna Petursdottir, Texas Christian University
Oskar Pineno, Hofstra University
Kevin Thompson, University of Southern Florida

Very personal thanks go to the closest people in my life: family, friends, and colleagues encouraged and supported my efforts to write this book and tolerated my preoccupation.

TO THE STUDENT

When learning about principles of behavior change, you'll find two appealing features of the material that will probably make it interesting to you:

- The material is *personally relevant*. Many principles you learn can actually be applied in your everyday life.
- The methods described in this book will be *useful in your career*, particularly if you become a psychologist or teacher in special education or speech pathology settings.

Although taking a course in applied behavior analysis and reading this book will not make you an expert in changing people's behavior, you will learn skills to use in your own life. You will also acquire an understanding of what behavior analysis techniques are and how professionals use them. What you learn in this course will lay the foundation for gaining more training in applied behavior analysis, so that you may enter a career in which you can apply its techniques to help other people. If you pursue a career in applied behavior analysis, you can use this text as a handbook because it describes the most important, enduring, and well-established techniques in the field.

THE BOOK AND WEBSITE

This book was designed for you, the reader. First and foremost, it provides a thorough and up-to-date presentation of the major issues, theories, concepts, and research in applied behavior analysis. The material throughout the book is organized to build upon relatively simple concepts and techniques that lead to increasingly complex and specialized methods. Because some of the concepts are complex and technical, I have made special efforts to write in a straightforward, clear, and engaging fashion.

FEATURES OF THE BOOK

To help you master the course material and remember it longer, this book includes the following learning aids:

- *Chapter Outline and Prologue*. Each chapter begins with a list of the chapter contents—an outline—of the major topics in the order they are covered. This is followed by a prologue with a vignette that is relevant to the material ahead and gives an overview of the basic ideas you will read about.
- *Illustrations*. Figures and tables in each chapter are designed to clarify concepts and research findings and help them stick in your mind.
- *Concept Checks*. Each chapter contains boxed quizzes at appropriate intervals to check your basic understanding of the material you have just read. The symbol ⇔ identifies the question as a "critical thinking" item for which more than one answer could be correct. These questions are intended to get you thinking analytically and creatively about the concepts and procedures you've just read about.
- *Tips for Applying Methods*. About half of the chapters include a list of tips to consider when applying the methods discussed in that chapter.
- *Study and Review*. Each chapter has a Study and Review section that begins with a substantial *summary*. This is followed by a list of *key terms* from the chapter, arranged in order of their appearance, and a set of essay-type *review questions*.
- *Glossary*. The glossary at the back of the book gives definitions of all of the key terms. It will be useful when you are studying or reading and are not sure of the exact meaning of a term.

Each chapter also contains boxed material—Case Studies, Close-Ups, and Concept Checks, described earlier—that are identified with special icons and "Go to" instructions. These instructions will prompt you to read the nearby boxed material that has the same icon.

THE COMPANION WEBSITE

A companion website is available at www.wiley.com/college/sarafino. It contains an online *study guide* that you can use to prepare for exams and *links to websites* that are relevant for applied behavior analysis.

STUDY HINTS

You can use the features of this book in many ways to learn and study well, and you may want to "experiment" to find the best way for you. I will describe one method that works well for many students—it's called SQ3R: study, question, reflect, review, and reread.

1. *Survey* the chapter first as a preview. Start by reading the chapter contents list at the start of the chapter and the Study and Review at the end. Then browse through the chapter, looking at the figures, tables, and photographs. Then read the chapter.

2. *Question.* As you begin each new section of the chapter, look at its title and turn it into a question. Thus, the heading early in Chapter 1, "Relating Respondent and Operant Conditioning," might become "How are respondent and operant conditioning related?" Doing this helps you focus on your reading.

3. *Reflect.* After reading the section, reflect on what you have just read. Can you answer the question you asked when you reworded the title?

4. *Review.* When you have finished the body of the chapter, review what you have read by reading the summary. Next, define the items in the key terms. If there is an item you do not understand, look it up in the chapter or the glossary. Then develop in your mind an answer for each of the review questions.

5. *Reread* the chapter at least once, focusing on the important concepts or ideas.

You may find it helpful to underline or highlight selected material now that you have a good idea of what's important. If your exam will consist of "objective" questions, such as multiple choice, using this approach intensively should be effective. If your exam will have essay items, you will probably find it helpful to answer the review questions carefully, completely, and in writing.

I hope that you enjoy this book and learn a great deal from it. I also hope you will share my enthusiasm and fascination for applied behavior analysis by the time you finish the course.

BRIEF CONTENTS

NOTE: Some instructors may want to *move some chapters* from the middle of the book to an earlier time in the course. To help you identify possible problems with intervening material, the following table lists *ten chapters* from Parts III, IV, and V and tells you the *material each chapter refers to from earlier chapters*. The statement "requires material" from a chapter means that much of that chapter is needed; "refers to" means that a definition and some examples of the concept should be sufficient. With this information, you can decide whether you want to move a chapter and, if so, how and when to inform students where in the book they can find definitions or discussions of the intervening concepts, such as in the glossary or on specific pages in the chapters (found with the subject index). The table assumes that Chapters 1 and 2 contain required material for all subsequent chapters.

Chapter Number and Title	Material the chapter refers to from earlier chapters
10 Shaping	Refers to multiple-baseline design (Chapter **3**).
11 Shortcut Stimulus Control Methods	Requires and builds on material in Chapter **8**.
12 Chaining Behaviors	Requires material in Chapters **5, 8,** and **11**.
13 Functional Assessment and Program Design	Requires material in Chapter **5** and refers to alternative behaviors (Chapter **6**).
14 Managing Antecedents	Requires material in Chapters **8, 9,** and **11**; refers to material in Chapter **13** (functional assessment).
15 Using Basic Reinforcement Procedures to Increase a Behavior	Refers to concepts in Chapters **6** (alternative behaviors), **9** (establishing operations), **10** (shaping), and **14** (noncontingent reinforcement).
16 Using Advanced Reinforcement Procedures to Increase a Behavior	Refers to concepts from Chapters **6** (extinction) and **7** (response cost punishment).
17 Using Extinction, Differential Reinforcement, and Habit Reversal to Decrease a Behavior	Requires material in Chapters **5** and **6**.
21/22 Respondent Conditioning, Changing Respondent Behaviors	Refers to material in Chapter **13** (functional assessment).

CONTENTS

PART IV   Methods for Modifying Operant Behaviors   177

xxii Contents

1

WHAT IS APPLIED BEHAVIOR ANALYSIS?

PROLOGUE

"What do you think this study was about, Karen?" Joel asked a student who had participated in his psychology experiment. "I don't know—nothing much happened," she replied. Her tone suggested she was very curious to know the answer. Actually something important happened, but she didn't realize it. When she arrived at the laboratory an hour ago, Joel had her sit in a chair and instructed her simply to "say all the words you can think of. Say them individually. Do not use sentences or phrases. Do not count. Please continue until I say stop." Joel sat behind her and said nothing, except the sound "mmm-hmm" occasionally, while she recited words for

50 minutes. (The sound Joel made was pronounced, "mmm-HMM," the way an English speaker might simply acknowledge something a person said.)

What happened that was so important? Joel was very careful about when he said "mmm-hmm." He said it only when Karen said a plural noun, such as *chairs* or *books*. He never said it when she said anything else. Within just a few minutes, her behavior changed dramatically: She began saying lots of plural nouns and kept on saying them as long as Joel said "mmm-hmm"! But she didn't realize she was doing this, or that Joel's behavior was linked in any specific way to what she said.

This story, composed on the basis of a classic experiment by Joel Greenspoon (1955), illustrates that environmental events can modify specific behaviors substantially. This is true for almost all behaviors people perform, not just reciting plural nouns. For instance, a similarly conducted study found that individuals increase their reporting of unhappy experiences when a researcher shows interest in those statements—for example, by saying "mmm-hmm" or by just nodding or making eye contact with the person (Lam, Marra, & Salzinger, 2005). Our behavior in everyday life occurs in the context of events that are *external*, such as the behavior of other people or the weather in our environment, and *internal*, such as our thoughts and physiological processes. These events often occur naturally and influence how people behave, even when we are not aware of their effects. By using organized and systematic methods to regulate events in people's lives, professionals and others can help them change their behavior.

This chapter introduces you to the field of *applied behavior analysis*—the well-established and exciting approach to understanding and changing people's behavior. We first examine what behavior is and how it is acquired. Then we look at some defining characteristics and techniques of applied behavior analysis and chart its history.

WHAT DOES *BEHAVIOR* MEAN?

Because this book focuses on ways to change behavior, it needs to be very specific about what behavior is and is not. The term **behavior** refers to anything a person does, typically because of internal or external events. When Karen answered "I don't know" to Joel's question about what the study was about, her verbal behavior was in response to an external event: a verbal question. When you feel hungry and go to the kitchen to eat, you are responding to an internal event: feeling hungry. In each case, we can describe the individual's specific actions or responses. Sometimes the behavior to be changed is fairly simple, such as raising one's hand when a teacher asks a question, and sometimes it involves a sequence of actions, as in making a sandwich.

EXTERNAL AND INTERNAL BEHAVIORS

Not only are the events that affect behaviors external or internal, but so are our behaviors. The behaviors we've considered so far have been external or *overt*—that is, open to view or observation. Overt behaviors can be of two types, verbal and motor. *Verbal behaviors* are actions that involve the use of language. Karen's answering Joel's question and reciting words are examples of verbal behavior. *Motor behaviors* are actions that involve body movement, without requiring the use of language. Grasping a doorknob is an example of a motor behavior; and swinging a baseball bat, getting dressed, and walking up a flight of stairs are other examples. Some activities, such as filling out a crossword puzzle, require both verbal and motor components. *Overt behaviors have been and continue to be the main focus of applied behavior analysis.*

But not all behaviors we can change are overt (Homme, 1965; Scott et al., 1973). Some behaviors are internal or *covert*, not viewable or openly shown, and are sometimes called "private" events (Skinner, 1974). Suppose you see an advertisement on TV for your favorite sports team and it leads you to think about a game you went to some time ago with some friends. Thinking about that game is a response to seeing the ad, but the response is not viewable. Suppose seeing the ad also produces inside you some emotions, such as happiness if your team won or anger if they lost, and physiological changes, such as increased heart rate. These responses are also covert. A principal reason applied behavior analysis focuses on overt behaviors is that they can be observed and measured directly by another person. Covert behaviors can be observed or felt only by the person who is performing the behavior and must be measured either indirectly, perhaps through verbal or written reports, or with special equipment, such as a device to measure heart rate.

WHAT IS NOT BEHAVIOR?

If I asked you to describe your best friend's behavior, what would you say? Chances are, you wouldn't describe specific behaviors—you'd focus on the friend's prominent *traits*, or broad and stable characteristics. You might answer, for instance, "Oh, Nancy's really nice. She's considerate, honest, smart, and creative. But she's not very conscientious." We tend to focus on broad characteristics to describe a person's behavior because they provide a convenient and efficient way of communicating a lot of information. Although you may have chosen these traits, such as Nancy is smart, because of specific behaviors you've observed, "smart" is not a behavior. In fact, none of the adjectives in your answer describes a behavior.

One problem with using broad characteristics as if they were behaviors is that they can be misleading and inconsistent. For example, you may have decided that Nancy is "honest" because you saw her refuse to copy someone else's paper to use as her own and "considerate" because you heard her lie to save her friend some money. Aren't these observations inconsistent? Or are the terms *honest* and *considerate* misleading? Another problem with using broad characteristics is they are imprecise—they don't tell us specifically what we would need to change to improve a person's behavior. Consider Nancy's lack of conscientiousness. In all likelihood, she's conscientious in some ways, but not in others. Perhaps she almost always keeps promises to friends and gets to her part-time job on time, but she rarely cleans her room and often fails to finish her college assignments and studying on time. If we wanted to help improve her conscientiousness, we would focus on specific behaviors involved in cleaning her room and doing her schoolwork. The more precise we are in describing the behavior to be changed, the more successful we are likely to be in measuring and improving the behavior.

In clinical practice, therapists generally use *diagnoses* to classify clients. One client is diagnosed as having severe depression, and another client has schizophrenia. One child has mental retardation, and another has autism. The advantages and problems associated with using diagnoses are similar to those associated with using traits: Diagnoses are efficient for communicating, but they can be imprecise, and they do not always indicate what specific behaviors need to be changed. Therapists make diagnoses on the basis of behaviors that are common to individuals who have the condition. For example, children receiving the diagnosis of autism tend to have several of the following behavioral characteristics (Lovaas, 1977):

- Absence of speech or severely impaired speech with unusual patterns, such as echoing the speech of others.
- Lack of awareness of salient sounds and objects around them.
- Indifference to being liked; little or no affection.
- Frequent behaviors that seem to provide only self-stimulation: children rocking back and forth incessantly, for example, or fluttering their hands in front of their eyes.
- Absence or severe impairment of self-help behaviors, such as grooming and dressing themselves, and inability to protect themselves from physical danger.
- Frequent and severe self-injurious behaviors, such as biting their arms.

But most children with autism have only some of these characteristics and differ in the severity of the specific behavior problems they show. Knowing simply that a child has autism does not tell therapists how to help the child. They must assess and try to improve the child's specific behaviors.

Last, the *outcomes of behavior* are not behaviors. People who apply behavior change techniques to produce an outcome of, say, helping someone lose weight or get higher grades in school often misdirect their focus toward the outcome rather than the behavior change needed to reach the outcome. In the example of improving grades, the behavior generally involves spending more time on schoolwork and concentrating well when doing so. Getting higher grades is not a behavior—it is the outcome of the person's behavior. Individuals who focus their efforts toward the outcome often fail to identify and deal effectively with the specific behaviors that need to change.

HOW BEHAVIOR DEVELOPS

Human babies come into the world with only a small number of well-formed, inborn behaviors. These inborn behaviors are called *reflexes*. Several reflexes have obvious survival value for infants because they are useful in feeding, maintaining physiological functioning, and protecting the baby against injury (Sarafino & Armstrong, 1986). For example, two reflexes that are important for feeding are the *rooting reflex*, in which the baby turns its head toward an object that lightly touches its cheek, and the *sucking reflex*, in which the baby starts to suck when its lips are touched with any small rounded object, such as a nipple or finger. Inborn reflexive behaviors are inherited.

Virtually all other behaviors develop after birth, and their development depends on two processes: heredity and experience. Heredity affects behavioral development in at least two ways (Sarafino & Armstrong, 1986). First, it charts the course of the person's *maturation*, or physical growth, including growth of the muscle and nervous systems. In the earliest years, physical growth is fastest in the head and upper trunk of the body; it speeds up later in the lower trunk, arms, and legs. Growth and coordination of the muscle and nervous systems follow the same pattern, showing the fastest advances in the head and upper body in the earliest years and spreading down the arms and legs later. This is why typical 3-year-olds can put on a pullover sweater but cannot tie their shoelaces. Maturation determines when motor actions become possible. Second, hereditary factors provide the foundation for or tendency toward developing behaviors of certain types. For instance, studies have found that people's inheritance influences the likelihood that they will develop a wide variety of behavioral problems, including stuttering (Scarr & Kidd, 1983), severe anxieties (Roy-Byrne, 2004; Torgersen, 1983), autism (Cantwell & Baker, 1984), and alcoholism (Goodwin, 1986; Sarafino & Smith, 2011). The influence of heredity in developing some behaviors is moderately strong, but it is fairly mild for many other behaviors. Experience plays an important role—and is usually the dominant factor—in the development of almost all human behaviors. This role occurs through the process called *learning*. (Go to 📄—as noted in this book's preface, this instruction tells you to read the nearby boxed material that has the same icon.)

CONCEPT CHECK 1.1

Pause now to check your understanding of the concepts you've read about so far in this chapter. Answers to concept checks are given in the Study and Review section at the end of the chapter. A ⟷ following a question identifies a "critical thinking" item, one that encourages you to think analytically and creatively about what you've read and apply the material to your life. Correct answers to critical thinking questions can vary somewhat or take different directions—as a result, the answers the book gives are only suggestions; you may come up with different ones that are equally correct.

Here are five statements about people. In the space following each statement, write OB if it describes an overt behavior, CB if it describes a covert behavior, T if it describes a trait, or O if it describes an outcome of behavior.

1. Ellie was a very dependable student. _____
2. Jim laughed at the joke. _____
3. Devon developed strong biceps muscles at the gym. _____
4. Dolores dreamed about a spider last night. _____
5. Tony was a motivated employee. _____

HOW WE ACQUIRE AND CHANGE BEHAVIOR

People talk a lot about learning things. They say, for instance, "Ginny learned to brush her teeth a few months ago," or "Morry learned the multiplication tables in school," or "I learned to use my new computer software last week," or "I learned to like Japanese food when I was an exchange student in Tokyo." When we observe individuals, we decide that they have learned things when we see changes in their behavior—assuming we can rule out other influences on behavior, such as an injury that causes a person to walk differently. But what exactly do we mean by the term *learning*? A definition is difficult to frame because learning is an internal process that applies to such a wide range of behaviors, and people don't always display what they have learned. The definition we use takes these difficulties into account: **Learning** is a durable change in behavioral potential as a result of experience.

In the next sections, we'll see how different varieties of experiences lead to long-lasting changes in behavior. The types of learning we will consider are discussed briefly here and examined in more detail in later chapters. We begin with the type of learning called *respondent* (or "classical") *conditioning*.

RESPONDENT CONDITIONING

Let's first demonstrate an example of respondent conditioning in your life. Sit back, relax, and concentrate on the *name* of your favorite food. Does the name remind you of eating that food? If so, fine—you may let your imagination take over. Enjoy how tempting it looks and smells. Savor the delectable taste and allow it to linger in your mouth .... Are you salivating more now? If so, this illustrates your learned reaction to the *name* of a food. The flow of saliva is the result of prior respondent conditioning.

This example is a lot like the first laboratory demonstrations of respondent conditioning reported in 1927 by Ivan Pavlov, the Russian Nobel-Prize-winning physiologist. Pavlov was studying the role of salivation in dogs' digestive processes when he noticed that the dogs began to salivate before the food was actually in their mouths. From this observation he correctly concluded that the association between the *stimulus*, such as the sight of food, and the salivary *response* must have been learned. Moreover, he proposed that this learned relationship was formed through its association with the *reflexive*, or automatic, connection between food in the mouth and salivation. Pavlov later showed that virtually any stimulus, such as a light or tone, regularly associated with this reflexive connection could produce the salivary response.

In our demonstration you salivated in response to the *name* of your favorite food—say, chocolate. In the past, the name of that food has been frequently associated with eating it: "Oh, that's to-die-for chocolate," you'd think while eating it. The presence of food in one's mouth elicits, or produces, salivation reflexively—without prior conditioning. Thus food in the mouth is an example of an **unconditioned stimulus (US)**—an event that elicits a specific response automatically—and the automatic response to that stimulus is called the **unconditioned response (UR)**. Although this reflexive association was not learned, your associating salivation to the *name* of the food was learned through the experience diagrammed in Figure 1-1. We know it was learned, because you surely didn't salivate to the word *chocolate* before you had ever eaten any. Because you learned the name–salivation association, the learned stimulus (the food's name) is called the **conditioned stimulus (CS)**. Before conditioning, this stimulus was *neutral*—it didn't produce that response. And since there was no food in your mouth (that is, there was no US) in our demonstration, the salivation elicited by the name of the food is called a **conditioned response (CR)**. Notice that the UR and CR are essentially the same behavior: salivation. They are called *respondent behaviors* because they are elicited involuntarily by stimuli.

From this example, we can formulate the following definition: **Respondent conditioning** is a learning process in which a stimulus (the eventual CS) gains the ability to elicit a response through repeated association with a stimulus (the US) that already produces that response. The broad phrasing of this definition indicates that we can learn many things through respondent conditioning, and we do. For example, at one of Barbra Streisand's concerts in 1967, she forgot the words to songs in front of a huge audience. She developed severe

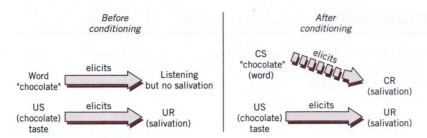

Figure 1-1   The respondent conditioning events. *Before conditioning*, the first couple of times your parents gave you chocolate, their saying, "Here's some chocolate" elicited some listening behavior from you, but no salivation. You didn't yet associate the word *chocolate* with the US, the taste of chocolate. *After conditioning*, you began to associate the word *chocolate*, now a CS, with having the taste in your mouth. The CS could then elicit salivation as a CR. Note that the dashed arrow indicates a learned association. Once conditioning has occurred, the CS can elicit the CR without the US being present, as we showed in our demonstration.

stage fright from this experience. "I was terrified. It prevented me from performing for all these years," she said in an interview (Seligmann, Namuth, & Miller, 1994). Performing on stage became a CS that began to elicit intense fear as a CR. Emotions, often negative ones, are some of the most important things we learn through respondent conditioning. Negative emotions are not always problematic, and they can be quite beneficial. For instance, a mild fear of heights leads to our being cautious when using a ladder. We also learn positive emotions and to like things through respondent conditioning. As an example, by watching comedian Tina Fey tell funny jokes, you probably learned to like her.

OPERANT CONDITIONING

In the story about Karen at the beginning of the chapter, why do you suppose her output of plural nouns increased? It was due to the consequences of her behavior. Each time she said a plural noun, but not other words, Joel said, "mmm-hmm." As long as he did this, Karen continued to say lots of plurals. Notice that Joel's saying "mmm-hmm" was *contingent* on—that is, depended on—Karen's saying plural nouns, and her saying plurals was affected by the contingent consequence of that behavior. This story gives an example of operant (or "instrumental") conditioning. **Operant conditioning** is the learning process by which behavior changes because of its *consequences*. The responses we acquire through this type of learning are called *operant behaviors*. The term *operant* indicates that these behaviors *operate* on the environment, producing consequences.

Consequences in Operant Conditioning

The scientist most prominently associated with operant conditioning is B. F. Skinner, who established the basic techniques and terminology for the study of operant behavior. Skinner (1938, 1953) distinguished between behavioral consequences of two types: reinforcement and punishment. In **reinforcement**, a consequence following a behavior *strengthens* that behavior, causing performance of the behavior to *increase*. We saw an example of reinforcement in the story about Karen: Her output of plural nouns increased in frequency as a result of Joel's saying "mmm-hmm," which was the consequence of her behavior. Reinforcement typically involves a consequence the person wants or finds pleasant, and perhaps Karen found Joel's "mmm-hmm" pleasant because she may have interpreted it to mean "That's good." In many cases, the consequence in the process of reinforcement is obviously desirable, something people often call a *reward* (such as praise, money, or candy). But our knowing why a particular consequence has an effect on behavior may be less important than knowing its results. If performance of a behavior increases when it is followed by a particular consequence, we can conclude two things: Reinforcement occurred, and the consequence was reinforcing.

In **punishment**, a consequence following a behavior leads to a *decrease* in performance of that behavior. In the experiment on which the story about Karen was based, Greenspoon (1955) tested other people using exactly the same procedure as we've seen, but the consequence of saying plural nouns was the researcher's saying "huh-uh" (pronounced "huh-UH," in a somewhat noncommittal way). For these subjects, the output of plurals *decreased*. Thus, "huh-uh" served to punish their saying plurals. Punishment generally involves a consequence the person does not want or finds unpleasant, and perhaps the people in Greenspoon's study interpreted "huh-uh" to mean "That's wrong." (If so, they were unaware of it. They, like the individuals who received "mmm-hmm," didn't realize that their behavior changed or that it was linked to what the researcher had said.) Once again, it isn't necessary to know *why* a particular consequence has an effect on behavior. If performance of a behavior decreases when it is followed by a particular consequence, we can conclude that punishment occurred and the consequence served as a punisher. When people try to apply punishment, they generally use events—such as spankings, reprimands, or reducing the person's privileges—that they *think* will work; but their thinking is not always correct. The best way to determine whether an event punishes a behavior is to observe the behavior over time: If it decreases when it is followed by the consequence, punishment has occurred.

Antecedents in Operant Conditioning

When you enter a room in your residence at night, the brightness of the lighting provides a cue that has a strong influence on your behavior. You see the lighting before you act: If it is bright enough, you just proceed into the room; if it is dark, you push the switch to turn on the light. Making these distinctions leads to reinforcement—being able to see where you're going—and helps you avoid punishment, such as bumping into objects or falling. Clearly, behavior is influenced not only by the consequences that follow it but also by the events and circumstances that precede it. These cues are called **antecedents** because they precede and set the occasion for your action. An important learning task in our lives involves discovering cues that help us determine the type of consequence our behavior will bring.

We can now diagram the process of operant conditioning, using the letters A, B, and C to stand for *antecedents*, *behavior*, and *consequences*:

$$A \Rightarrow B \rightarrow C$$

The boldly printed, solid arrow between the B and C means "produces"; that is, a behavior produces a consequence. All behaviors we perform produce consequences, regardless of whether we notice them. When you write a word correctly in your notes, the consequence includes being able to move on. You don't really notice this reinforcing event, but it is there. The diagram's open arrow between the A and B means "sets the occasion for"; that is, antecedents set the occasion for behavior. Whether the behavior occurs depends on many factors, including the strength of the link between the antecedent and the behavior. Being in a library or a place of worship presents a very strong antecedent for certain behaviors, such as whispering rather than talking loudly. At home, on the other hand, you have more latitude in how loudly you can talk and what you can say.

Operant conditioning can influence virtually any behavior, regardless of whether the behavior is verbal or motor, overt or covert. In subsequent chapters, we will see that programs to alter antecedents and consequences have been applied successfully to change essentially any behavior one can think of in people of all ages and with widely different backgrounds and abilities. (Go to 🐾.)

RELATING RESPONDENT AND OPERANT CONDITIONING

When books or instructors discuss learning, respondent and operant conditioning are usually presented as if they are separate, independent processes. To use looking at photographs as an analogy, it's as if you're being told: "Here's respondent conditioning in this picture, and here's operant conditioning in this other picture.

CASE STUDY

Using Operant Conditioning to Reinstate the Speech of a Man With Schizophrenia

This case study involves the use of operant conditioning to reinstate speech in an institutionalized 40-year-old man who had not spoken for the previous 19 years (Isaacs, Thomas, & Goldiamond, 1960). He had been diagnosed with schizophrenia, a condition characterized by major disturbances in thought, emotion, and behavior.

The therapist decided to try using chewing gum as a reward for speaking because of the interest the client had shown toward a package of gum that had fallen out of the therapist's pocket. The procedure progressed through five steps, each lasting a week or two with three meetings a week:

1. The therapist held a stick of gum in front of the client and waited. When the client looked at the gum, the therapist gave it to him. After several of these episodes, the client looked at the gum as soon as it appeared.

2. The therapist held up a stick of gum and waited until the client moved his lips before giving him the gum. After a few of these episodes, the client looked immediately at the gum and moved his lips.

3. The therapist held up the gum and gave it to the client if he made a vocal sound. After a few episodes, the client quickly looked at the gum and vocalized. The client's vocal sounds resembled "a croak."

4. The therapist held up the gum; said, "Say *gum, gum*"; and gave the reward to the client if his vocalizations progressed toward sounding more like "gum."

5. At a session in the sixth week, the therapist said, "Say *gum, gum*," and the client responded, "Gum, please." He also gave his name and age when asked.

At the time this case was published, the client had received very little additional therapy for his speech, which continued to be very limited. Still, this case provides a fascinating demonstration of the utility of operant conditioning.

See how separate and different they are?" This gives the impression that respondent and operant conditioning function separately or independently—as discrete units—in real life. Although the two types of conditioning are to some extent separate and different, they almost always happen together in real life—one type flows into the other (Allan, 1998). In terms of our analogy, real life is more like a videotape than a series of separate pictures. Let's consider some examples of the two types of conditioning occurring together.

The first example is of a newborn baby named Luisa who was being fed. Her behavior involved the UR of sucking on a nipple that provided milk. This was a situation in which respondent conditioning was likely to occur. That is, when the nipple touched Luisa's lips, she would begin to suck reflexively. Stimuli, such as the bottle or breast she noticed at the time her lips were touched (the US), were potential CSs. But the feeding sequence did not stop here. There was an operant component, too, because a baby's sucking behavior is not just a UR, it's also an operant motor behavior. Luisa's sucking produced a consequence, milk, that reinforced the sucking behavior. This sequence is diagrammed in Figure 1-2. In real life, the two components happen together.

Another real-life example of the two types of conditioning occurring together has the operant component preceding the respondent component. Ten-year-old Jim was in his room listening to a song he liked on the radio, which was plugged in a wall outlet. His curiosity led him to stick objects (an operant motor behavior) into the open outlet, which produced a painful shock to his hand (punishment for his behavior). For the respondent conditioning part, he was looking at the outlet (initially a neutral stimulus that will become the CS) when he heard a funny noise and felt the shock (US), which caused him to scream out in fear and pain (UR). For some months thereafter, Jim felt uneasy (CR) when he looked at that outlet (CS) or just heard the song (another CS) that had been playing on the radio when he received the shock (US). Operant and respondent conditioning

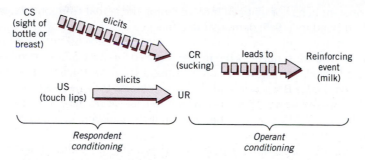

Figure 1-2   Respondent and operant conditioning functioning together in real life, using an example of a newborn infant's feeding experience. *Source*: Based on Sarafino & Armstrong (1986), Figure 4.13.

happen together in real life, and it's unlikely that experiences involving one type of conditioning do not include the other. (Go to .)

MODELING

Four-year-old Jo watches her father tie his shoelaces and tries to copy his movements. Jo is learning through the process of **modeling**, learning a behavior by watching someone else perform it. This method of learning involves the *observer* and a *model*—someone who demonstrates the behavior. Modeling is a useful and efficient way to acquire and change behavior, and we can learn virtually any operant motor and verbal behavior and respondent behavior through modeling. For instance, modeling can be used to teach simple operant responses, such as pulling open a drawer, and complex sequences of behavior, such as preparing scrambled eggs (Baer, Peterson, & Sherman, 1967; Griffen, Wolery, & Schuster, 1992). And people's existing operant behaviors are influenced by observation—for example, they increase their rates of drinking alcohol when others around them are drinking more than they are, and they decrease their drinking rates when others are drinking less (Caudill & Lipscomb, 1980; DeRicco & Niemann, 1980). Some cartoonists of well-known comic strips, such as *Blondie* and *Dennis the Menace*, increased their depiction of people in cars wearing seat belts after receiving letters explaining the importance of modeling this behavior (Mathews & Dix, 1992).

CLOSE-UP

A "Fishy" Application of Conditioning?

Here's an example of respondent and operant conditioning being applied in fish farming. A long-term study is under way in which farmed fish receive training to teach them to swim into a net and "catch" themselves after being released in the open sea (Lindsay, 2008). For the respondent conditioning part of the training, the researchers sound a loud tone (initially a neutral stimulus) and drop food (a US, which the fish could smell) into an enclosure, and the fish swim to and consume (UR) the food. Eventually, the fish should swim (CR) into the enclosure for just the tone (now a CS), without the food. For the operant part, swimming into the enclosure is a motor behavior, and it is reinforced with food during the training. (Notice how similar this situation is to Luisa's feeding experience.) After the training, the fish are released into the sea and will be lured back to the enclosure by sounding the tone. The bottom-line purpose of the training is to reduce industrial costs: The fish will live and feed most of their lives in the wild and will not have to be caught in usual, expensive ways. This research is testing whether the plan is viable.

Aggression is an operant behavior that can involve motor and verbal components, which people can learn through modeling. Albert Bandura (1965) demonstrated this in a classic study by showing children one of three films with a model performing a series of unusual aggressive acts, such as hitting a Bobo doll with a mallet and shouting, "Sockeroo!" The consequences the model received for these acts were different in the three films: The model either received punishment, rewards, or no consequences for the acts. The children were then taken individually to a room that had a Bobo doll and the other objects they had seen in the film. They were told they could play with the toys in any way they wished, and *no consequences* were promised or threatened for their actions. As expected, they copied the model's behavior, but the children who had observed the model being punished for aggression performed fewer of the model's aggressive acts than the other children did. Later, *all* the children were promised very attractive rewards if they would reproduce the aggressive behaviors they had seen the model do. Under this contingency, the children performed the same number of acts, regardless of the consequences they had seen in the film. These results indicate that children learn models' punished and rewarded aggressive acts equally. Seeing models punished for their acts merely *suppresses* the children's performance of those behaviors. These and other similar findings support the large body of research showing that watching violence on TV increases children's aggressive behavior (Friedrich-Cofer & Huston, 1986).

People also learn respondent behaviors—such as fears—through modeling. One study had children, with their parents' permission, watch a short film that portrayed a 5-year-old boy screaming and withdrawing when his mother simply showed him a plastic figure of a cartoon character, Mickey Mouse. But when his mother showed him a plastic figure of Donald Duck, he responded in a calm and undistressed manner (Venn & Short, 1973). After the children watched this film, they participated in a task that involved the Mickey Mouse and Donald Duck figures. At this time, they tended to avoid the Mickey Mouse figure (the one feared in the film) in favor of the Donald Duck. What's more, the researchers measured the children's physiological reactions while they watched the film. The children showed greater reactions during the Mickey Mouse (fearful) episode than during the Donald Duck. Although initially this fear was pronounced, a day or two later the children showed no avoidance or preference for either figure. Even though these effects were temporary, it is clear that observing fear in other people affects both internal and external behavior.

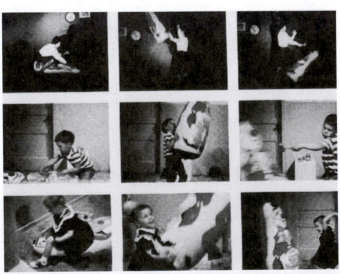

These photos show a boy and girl in Bandura's research performing the behaviors they saw an adult model (see top row) in a film. *Source:* Albert Bandura.

ARE COGNITIVE PROCESSES INVOLVED?

The term **cognition** refers to covert behaviors, particularly thinking and reasoning, that occur in the mind and are not observable to others. Thinking uses mental representations of our knowledge, mostly in the form of language or images; reasoning involves thinking in a logical manner, such as to make a plan or solve a problem. Cognitive processes can influence our learning and behavior, and we'll consider four examples. First, suppose a friend explains to you on the phone how to turn on your new MP3 player; even if you don't have the player with you at the time, you'll know the motor behaviors needed when it is there. Second, thoughts can serve as antecedents to our behavior, such as when you remember that you promised to call a friend and then do so. Third, evidence indicates that people can acquire respondent behaviors, such as fears of spiders or ghosts, by way of the scary statements other people make (Field & Lawson, 2003; Rachman, 1991). Fourth, in some cases, the main behavior individuals need to change is cognitive, such as when their thoughts (usually incorrect ones) make them severely and persistently depressed (Kring, Johnson, Davison, & Neale, 2010). Although cognitive processes affect overt behavior, we can change most overt behaviors without addressing covert events. (Go to .)

DEFINING APPLIED BEHAVIOR ANALYSIS

Now that we have seen what behavior is and how people can acquire and change it, we are ready to consider a definition: **Applied behavior analysis** is a field of practice and study that focuses on using principles of learning, particularly operant conditioning, to understand and improve people's socially significant behavior (Reitman, 2005). People who work in this field, practicing or studying its methods, are called **behavior analysts**. The name of the field includes two words that need clarification: The word *applied* is included to reflect behavior analysts' interest in discovering and practicing methods to improve people's lives; the word *analysis* is there to reflect behavior analysts' emphasis on understanding the functional relations between behaviors and their antecedents and consequences. With appropriate training, individuals can achieve certification as a behavior analyst through the Behavior Analyst Certification Board (see their website at www.bacb.com).

CONCEPT CHECK 1.2

Pause now to answer questions from the sections since the last concept check. Remember that items with the symbol ⇔ are critical thinking questions, and their answers can vary. The following questions are about learning processes.

1. The text mentions that you may have come to like Tina Fey by watching her tell jokes. What might be the **a.** US, **b.** UR, **c.** CS, and **d.** CR? ⇔
2. Anita's literature professor announced that a wonderful play was being performed on campus, and students who saw it and wrote a brief review would receive extra credit toward their final grades. Anita went to see the play and wrote a review, and she got the extra credit. Identify the **a.** antecedent, **b.** behavior, and **c.** consequence.
3. Learning by watching other people's behavior is called _____ .
4. People often use thoughts as covert _____ for behavior.

When professionals apply learning principles to change behavior, they can choose techniques of two types: behavioral and cognitive methods (Sarafino, 2001; Sweet & Loizeaux, 1991). Behavior analysts focus on using **behavioral methods**, techniques based on operant conditioning, respondent conditioning, and modeling, toward changing overt behaviors. *Cognitive methods* are geared for changing overt and covert behaviors by modifying people's thought processes—for example, by helping individuals recognize and alter their illogical beliefs. Some behavior change techniques make use of elements of both, as you would do if you practiced a modeled behavior in your mind. The process or time period in which efforts are made to change behavior is called an *intervention*.

RELATED TERMS AND FIELDS

Several fields that apply methods that are very *similar to and substantially overlap* those of applied behavior analysis emerged at about the same time period, the 1960s and 1970s. I will refer to these other fields as *adjuncts*, and we will consider three of them briefly:

1. *Behavior modification*: Behavioral and cognitive methods are applied mainly by professionals in a variety of applied settings, including institutions, schools, and industry, to improve almost any type of behavior.

2. *Behavior therapy*: Behavioral and cognitive methods are carried out mostly by professionals in a therapeutic setting to correct seriously maladaptive behavior, often involving emotional problems.

3. *Self-management*: Behavioral and cognitive methods are self-administered, or carried out mainly by the person whose behavior is being changed, often under the supervision of a professional.

Some professionals make distinctions among applied behavior analysis and these three adjuncts, but others do not. These views are not "official" or standard.

My approach for identifying distinctions among the four fields was to look at textbooks and journals with one of the four terms in their titles to compare the topics they include in the material they cover. These comparisons indicated that the four fields differ in several ways, especially two: the focus they give to (a) cognitive methods and (b) self-administration of techniques. Figure 1-3 diagrams the result of my comparisons of these books and journals, indicating that publications in applied behavior analysis give less focus to cognitive methods and self-administration than publications in the three other fields. Publications in all four fields discuss behavioral methods a great deal.

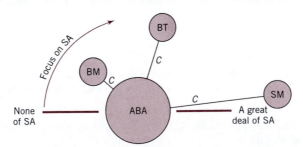

Figure 1-3   Conceptual diagram depicting the field of applied behavior analysis (ABA) and its relationship to three adjunct fields, behavior modification (BM), behavior therapy (BT), and self-management (SM). ABA publications focus on—that is, they discuss or present—cognitive methods and self-administration (SA) of techniques very little. Two dimensions in the diagram reflect the relation of each adjunct to ABA and each other: (a) the longer the spoke, C, leading from ABA, the more focus the adjunct gives to cognitive methods; and (b) the greater the radial distance from the left horizontal line, labeled *None of* SA, the more focus the adjunct gives to self-administration of its techniques. Of the three adjuncts, cognitive methods and self-administration are given the most focus by SM and the least focus by BM.

CHARACTERISTICS OF APPLIED BEHAVIOR ANALYSIS

Applied behavior analysis and the three related fields discussed earlier share several defining characteristics that make their basic approach unique (Baer, Wolf, & Risley, 1968; Kazdin, 1978; Wixted, Bellack, & Hersen, 1990). When professionals in these fields conduct studies of factors that affect people's behavior and use learning principles to modify behavior, they apply these characteristics, one of which is a focus on behavior.

Focus on Behavior

Because applied behavior analysis focuses on behavior, behavior analysts place a strong emphasis on:

- *Defining people's current status and progress in terms of behavior* rather than traits or other broad characteristics.
- Being able to *measure the behavior* in some way.
- *Whenever possible, assessing covert behaviors, such as fear, in terms of overt actions* the person makes so that objective and reliable measurements can be made.

Although emotional and cognitive events can be made accessible to study and change, assessing covert behaviors with only subjective measures, such as by having people rate their feelings of fear, provides weak evidence that efforts to change the behavior are succeeding.

The behaviors to be changed in an intervention are called **target behaviors**, and efforts to change them can be directed toward increasing or decreasing them, depending on whether the problem being addressed involves a deficit or an excess of the behavior. A **behavioral deficit** refers to a desirable behavior the person does *not* perform often enough, long enough, well enough, or strongly enough. Examples of behavioral deficits include not exercising often enough, not spending enough time studying, and not talking loudly enough. A **behavioral excess** is an undesirable behavior the person performs too frequently, too strongly, or for too long. Examples of behavioral excesses are performing aggressive acts too frequently, drinking alcohol too often, and experiencing too much fear when taking tests.

Importance of Learning and the Environment

For the most part, human behavior is *learned* behavior. We discussed earlier that genetic factors can influence behavior and its development, but learning and cognition provide the most substantial and pervasive processes by which people acquire and change almost everything they do. As a result, the application of behavior change techniques assumes behavior is generally malleable and can be modified by providing appropriate new experiences.

The new experiences used in modifying behavior involve altering aspects of the individual's *environment*, mainly by changing the antecedents and consequences of the behavior. Suppose a teacher wanted to reduce a behavioral excess, such as students being out of their seats too much. If an antecedent condition leading to the behavior was the children's being very far from one another while working on group projects, for instance, the teacher could rearrange the seating. If the consequences of students being out of their seats were more attractive than the consequences of being in their seats, the teacher could introduce rewards for students who stayed in their seats for appropriate amounts of time. The antecedents and consequences addressed in behavior change programs are usually in the person's external environment.

Although providing new learning experiences is highly successful in changing behavior, certain factors can limit these effects. For example, some behaviors are so severely disordered or so strongly determined by physiological processes—such as in certain pain conditions or the brain seizures in epilepsy—that behavior analysis methods may not be sufficient to change them, at least initially. In these circumstances, medication may be prescribed by a physician and used as an adjunct to environmental changes (Wilson & Simpson, 1990), and failing to include medication in the treatment may be unethical. The goal in using principles of behavior change in these cases often includes reducing or eliminating the use of medication over time.

Scientific Orientation

Applied behavior analysis has a strong scientific orientation—its core is the knowledge revealed through the methods of science. The *scientific method* basically involves conducting research by (a) carefully gathering data empirically—that is, by direct observation or measurement; (b) analyzing and interpreting the data; and (c) specifying the precise methods used to gather and analyze the data so that other researchers will know exactly what was done and can repeat the procedures. A hallmark and essential feature of research on and application of principles of behavior change is the careful and precise measurement of behavior. These methods have enabled researchers to discover ways by which learning and cognition influence behavior.

Pragmatic and Active Methods to Change Behavior

Applied behavior analysis takes a pragmatic approach in the methods it uses to change behavior. The term *pragmatic* means "practical, rather than theoretical or idealistic." Thus, professionals who use behavior change techniques emphasize finding and using *methods that work* to change behavior, regardless of whether the techniques fit into a particular theory or ideal. By taking this view, the discipline has incorporated and enhanced the effectiveness of many new and creative methods for changing behavior.

In addition, behavior analysts often require that clients or subjects be *active* participants in the process of modifying their behavior. In contrast to therapies in which clients or subjects just talk about their difficulties, behavioral and cognitive methods have clients or subjects *do* things to help. For instance, clients may help decide which techniques to use and how to implement them, perform behavior change methods under supervision, or apply some techniques on their own as "homework."

HOW BEHAVIOR ANALYSIS DEVELOPED

Although applied behavior analysis is a young discipline, practical applications of learning principles to influence behavior are by no means new in human history. For instance, psychologists were not the first to realize that rewarding a behavior tends to increase its frequency. What psychologists and other professionals did was to examine these methods, clarify what they are, and determine how to apply them most effectively. This section outlines highlights in the history of applied behavior analysis.

BEHAVIORISM: THE ORIGIN OF BEHAVIOR ANALYSIS

During the first half of the 20th century, the dominant theories—or systematic explanations—of why people behave the way they do proposed that behavior resulted from various internal "forces," such as drives, motives, conflicts, and traits. Some of these theories grouped several forces together, and the resulting constellation was called the *personality*. The well-known *psychoanalytic theory* of Sigmund Freud (1933, 1949), for example, views a person's behavior as an expression of his or her personality and its component forces, such as drives and conflicts. According to this theory, each person's personality develops through a maturationally determined series of stages, is strongly affected by early experiences, and becomes fairly entrenched in childhood. To change an individual's problem behavior, Freud believed that the person must talk with a therapist in depth to arrive at a comprehension of the behavior's underlying forces, such as conflicts and unresolved childhood experiences.

A different perspective, called *behaviorism*, began to emerge in the early 1900s. Psychologists John B. Watson (1913, 1930) and B. F. Skinner (1938, 1953) were two of its main proponents. **Behaviorism** is the theoretical orientation that emphasizes the study of observable and measurable behavior and proposes that nearly all behavior is the product of experience. As a result, behavior can be explained by principles of learning, particularly operant and respondent conditioning. This theory developed from two sources: philosophy and science. Certain philosophical views, which had been proposed more than 200 years earlier, had become widely accepted in England and the United States. For instance, the British philosopher John Locke had proposed that a baby's mind has no innate ideas and is essentially a blank tablet (called *tabula rasa* in Latin) on which experience "writes."

B. F. Skinner (1904–1990). *Source*: CSU Archives/Everett Collection/Alamy Limited.

John B. Watson (1878–1958). *Source*: Underwood & Underwood/Copyright © Corbis.

At the time behaviorism was introduced, psychology was already becoming a separate discipline from philosophy, and the scientific method was seen as the main feature permitting a distinction between the two fields. As a result, early behaviorists rejected philosophy's unobservable concepts, such as mind, consciousness, and soul. Instead, they used the scientific method to examine learning principles. Three lines of research were especially important. First, Edward Thorndike (1898, 1931) studied how "satisfying" and "annoying" consequences—reinforcement and punishment—affect learning. Second, Ivan Pavlov (1927) demonstrated in dogs the process of respondent conditioning. Third, B. F. Skinner (1938) named and defined two types of behavior, operant and respondent; designed an apparatus called an *operant chamber* (or more commonly, the Skinner box) to study the role of reinforcement on behavior; studied in detail the effects of consequences on behavior; and published these contributions in The *Behavior of Organisms*, which became a highly influential work.

Two important studies set the stage for applying learning principles to change behavior. In one of these studies, John Watson and Rosalie Rayner (1920) conditioned an 11-month-old boy they called Little Albert to fear a white rat. Albert was not afraid of the rat before conditioning began. On the contrary, he seemed to like it—he'd reach toward it and giggle. During conditioning, the researchers presented the rat along with a loud noise (the US) made by striking a steel bar with a hammer, which elicited distress (UR) in Albert. These pairings occurred several times during a week, after which the rat (now a CS) elicited distress and efforts to escape. This research demonstrated the *learning* of fear through respondent conditioning. Although Watson and Rayner had planned to reverse the conditioning with methods later shown to be effective, Albert's mother's job change may have made the child unavailable for this plan. The fear was not removed, and we don't know whether the fear persisted (Beck, Levinson, & Irons, 2009). (Note that a study like this one would not be conducted today, because the American Psychological Association has since developed ethical guidelines that restrict using potentially harmful procedures in research.)

A few years later, Mary Cover Jones (1924) published a report on a fear reduction procedure she used with a toddler named Peter. He had developed in his everyday life a fear that was a lot like Albert's—he was very fearful of white furry objects, such as rabbits. The procedure Jones used was conducted over many sessions in the course of several weeks: She would move a rabbit closer and closer while Peter ate favorite foods in the presence of a research assistant whom he liked. After this treatment, Peter no longer showed signs of fear in the presence of the rabbit and would seek it out and play with it. This dramatic reduction in Peter's fear demonstrated clearly the value of using learning principles to modify behavior.

The next few decades witnessed four important historical events (Bandura, 1969; Kazdin, 1978). First, psychology and philosophy became clearly separate disciplines, as illustrated by the humorous poem:

> *Alas, poor psychology, sad is her Fate!*
>
> *First she lost her Soul, and then she lost her Mind,*
>
> *And then she lost Consciousness.*
>
> *Now all that's left to her is her Behavior—*
>
> *And the less said of that, the better!*

(Anonymous; cited in Goldiamond, 1974, p. 38)

Second, researchers showed that principles of operant and respondent conditioning could be used effectively in many different settings to change a wide variety of behaviors. The case study we saw earlier of reinstating speech in a mute schizophrenic man is an example. Third, a research area called the *experimental analysis of behavior* developed to study basic theoretical processes in learning, usually without an emphasis on application. Fourth, psychologists became very dissatisfied with the lack of scientific evidence to demonstrate that traditional therapies, such as psychoanalysis, were effective in treating problem behaviors. Eysenck (1952) published a review of the literature indicating that people who received traditional forms of psychotherapy, especially psychoanalysis, were no more likely to show improved psychological functioning than individuals who receive no treatment at all. Although Eysenck's conclusions were somewhat exaggerated, they led psychotherapists to question the utility of traditional ways in treating psychosocial problems and to search for new approaches. Some of these new approaches involved the application of behavioral methods.

EMERGENCE AND GROWTH OF APPLIED BEHAVIOR ANALYSIS

The 1950s and early 1960s saw the emergence of an academic discipline to study and apply learning principles as an approach for changing people's behavior (Kazdin, 1978). B. F. Skinner continued to profoundly influence the development of this approach, mainly through his creative descriptions of ways to apply operant conditioning to modify behavior in education, business, government, and therapy. Other scholars contributed ideas and research findings that furthered the discipline during its emergent years—for instance, Joseph Wolpe (1958, 1973) developed highly effective respondent conditioning therapy techniques for reducing people's strong fears and anxieties.

By the late 1960s, applied behavior analysis had become a formal discipline. It established journals to publish research articles focusing on ways to apply behavioral methods to socially important problems, such as those relating to education, child rearing, crime, and mental illness (Baer, Wolf, & Risley, 1968; 1987; Kazdin, 1978; Wixted, Bellack, & Hersen, 1990). By that time, the fields of behavior modification, behavior therapy, and self-management had also emerged and were developing rapidly. Principles of behavior change are widely applied today. They are used by psychotherapists, teachers in regular and special education classrooms, parents of typically developing children, supervisors in business and industry, personnel in institutions for juvenile delinquents, and personnel who train children with intellectual and emotional disorders. A major reason for the wide acceptance of behavioral and cognitive methods is that professionals who use them, in both research and applied settings, measure the behavior they are trying to change and examine these data. Using these data, they can see and show others how well the methods work. (Go to 📖.)

CONCEPT CHECK 1.3

Check your understanding of the concepts in the last sections of this chapter. Remember: The symbol ⇔ means that various answers can be correct. The following fill-in-the-blank questions focus on the characteristics and development of applied behavior analysis.

1. An example of a behavioral deficit one of your friends has is _____ . ⇔
2. The four defining characteristics of applied behavior analysis are _____ .
3. A behavior change technique that uses operant conditioning would be classified as a _____ method.
4. "Little Albert" learned to fear a white rat by the process of _____ conditioning.

STUDY AND REVIEW

SUMMARY

Behavior is anything people do, usually in response to internal or external events. It can include overt actions that are observable by others or covert (private) activities that are not open to view. Our traits—broad and stable characteristics—are not behaviors, nor are psychological diagnoses or the outcomes of behavior, such as becoming more physically fit. Both heredity and experience affect behavioral development.

Experience affects behavior through learning. Behaviors are acquired and can be changed through respondent conditioning, operant conditioning, and modeling. In respondent conditioning, a potential conditioned stimulus (CS) gains the ability to elicit a conditioned response (CR) by being associated repeatedly with an unconditioned stimulus (US) that already elicits an unconditioned response (UR). The UR and CR are essentially the same behavior. In operant conditioning, antecedents set the occasion for behavior, which is affected by the consequences it produces: Reinforcement increases performance of a behavior, and punishment decreases its performance. Respondent and operant conditioning occur together in everyday life.

We can also learn operant and respondent behaviors through modeling, which involves observing other people's behavior. Cognition is mental activity, especially thinking and reasoning; and it is covert, not open to view. Expectations, beliefs, and rules can serve as covert antecedents to our behavior.

Applied behavior analysis is a discipline that uses principles of learning, mainly operant and respondent conditioning, to understand and change behavior. Professionals in this field are called behavior analysts; they focus on applying behavioral methods to change target behaviors. The discipline has four defining characteristics: (a) it focuses on behavior, trying to modify behavioral deficits and excesses; (b) it considers learning and the environment to be the main sources by which behaviors can be changed; (c) it has a strong scientific orientation; and (d) its approach to changing behavior is pragmatic and active.

The principles of behavior change used in applied behavior analysis developed from the perspective called behaviorism and associated research. These techniques are widely accepted and applied today, partly because professionals who have studied and applied them have collected data and conducted research showing their utility.

In addition to the concept checks you've already done, and the key terms and review questions that follow, an online study guide is available on this book's companion website at www.wiley.com/college/sarafino.

KEY TERMS

behavior
learning
unconditioned stimulus (US)
unconditioned response (UR)
conditioned stimulus (CS)
conditioned response (CR)
respondent conditioning

operant conditioning
reinforcement
punishment
antecedents
modeling
cognition
applied behavior analysis

behavior analysts
behavioral methods
target behaviors
behavioral deficit
behavioral excess
behaviorism

ANSWERS TO CONCEPT CHECKS (CCs)

CC1.1 *Answers:* **1.** T **2.** OB **3.** O **4.** CB **5.** T

CC1.2 *Answers:* **1.a.** funny joke **b.** laugh/feel happy **c.** Tina Fey's face/name **d.** feel happy **2.a.** professor's announcement **b.** see play and write review **c.** extra credit **3.** modeling **4.** antecedents

CC1.3 *Answers:* **1.** not exercising enough **2.** focus on behavior, importance of learning and environment, scientific orientation, and pragmatic and active methods to change behavior **3.** behavioral **4.** respondent

REVIEW QUESTIONS

1. Describe the research by Greenspoon (1955) on modifying verbal behavior, and explain why its results are important.

2. What do we mean by the term *behavior*? Give two examples each of overt and covert behaviors.

3. Why are traits, diagnoses, and outcomes of behavior not behaviors?

4. How is heredity involved in behavioral development?

5. Describe the components and process of respondent conditioning, and give an example from your own life.

6. Define the terms *reinforcement* and *punishment*, and give two examples of each from your own life.

7. Define the operant conditioning term *antecedent*. Give two examples of antecedents from your life.

8. How was reinforcement used in the case study of reinstating speech in a schizophrenic man?

9. Describe the research and findings of Bandura (1965) on the role of consequences on modeling.

10. Give two examples each of modeling and cognition affecting your behavior.

11. Define *behavioral methods* and *cognitive methods*.

12. Define the term *applied behavior analysis*. How do publications in that field differ in their coverage from those in behavior modification, behavior therapy, and self-management?

RELATED READINGS

- Baum, W. M. (1994). *Understanding behaviorism*. New York: HarperCollins.
- Kazdin, A. E. (1978). *History of behavior modification: Experimental foundations of contemporary research*. Baltimore: University Park Press.
- Skinner, B. F. (1974). *About behaviorism*. New York: Knopf.

IDENTIFYING AND ASSESSING TARGET BEHAVIORS

Goals and Target Behaviors
Identifying and Defining Behavioral Goals
Defining Operant Target Behaviors
Defining Respondent Target Behaviors
Prioritizing: Which Behavior to Address First

How To Assess Target Behaviors
Types of Data
Strategies for Assessing Behavior
Timing and Accuracy of Behavioral Assessments

Tips on Identifying and Assessing Behavior

Study and Review

PROLOGUE

The year was 1980. School counselors in the junior high and high schools in a medium-sized U.S. city became alarmed when they realized that drug use among their students had skyrocketed in the last decade and was approaching the levels seen in larger cities. The counselors decided that the way to prevent drug use was to address the students':

- Lack of knowledge about the negative effects of using drugs
- Low levels of self-esteem, which made them vulnerable to the appeal of drugs

The counselors then designed a drug prevention program for administration to eighth-graders. It addressed the lack of knowledge with readings, videos, and testimonials to describe how drugs can cause health problems or even death, lead to addiction and other criminal behavior, and ruin the user's life. Rewards were provided for learning the material. To deal with the self-esteem problem, the counselors included discussion groups in which the students could dispel negative ideas they had about themselves.

    To use personnel efficiently, the superintendent had the counselors conduct the program in half of the city's junior high schools in the fall semester and the remaining schools in the spring. When the program was finished, the results elated the counselors and superintendent. Comparisons made before and after the program revealed consistent outcomes: the students who received the program reported higher levels of self-esteem, scored much higher on knowledge about drugs, and reported much lower attitudes toward drugs, drug use, and drug abusers. A news release concluded that the program "was a complete success and accomplished everything the school officials had hoped for."

Was that conclusion correct? No. We'll see in this chapter why it was wrong, and we'll learn how to specify and assess behaviors we want to change. In this book, a person whose behavior is the target for change is usually called the *target person*, but is also called "the client" or just "the person" if being the target person is clear. We saw in Chapter 1 that behavior change programs focus on behavior and use data to decide whether it has changed. The first steps in this process include identifying and defining the goals and behaviors to focus on in the program.

GOALS AND TARGET BEHAVIORS

Suppose you are working in a personnel department: a supervisor comes to you for help in dealing with a difficult employee. You ask, "What's the problem?" The supervisor answers, "Well, Al's lazy, he doesn't have much initiative, and he's so negative all the time. He just doesn't seem to care about his work." This sounds bad, but the description doesn't yet help you decide how you can help. Why? So far all the information you have are broad characteristics of Al's behavior. As we saw in Chapter 1, broad characteristics don't specify the behaviors that need to change. So you ask the supervisor to be more specific—to pinpoint the behaviors with examples, and she does:

- Almost always when I talk to Al about a new project, he complains about his workload and looks only for difficulties in doing the project rather than trying to find solutions to these difficulties.
- He's come to work late in the mornings and after lunch several times this month and acts like I shouldn't think it's a problem when I call him on it.
- He turned in several reports late—2 or 3 days late—this month, and they were poorly prepared. One of them, for instance, contained data for the wrong month.
- When we have staff meetings, Al rarely contributes ideas that help move a project along. Instead, he verbally abuses the others, calling their ideas "stupid" or "silly," and distracts our work with jokes or irrelevant comments.

Now we can see what some of the target behaviors need to be: some involve *behavioral deficits*, such as in his late and poorly prepared reports, and some involve *behavioral excesses*, such as his joking at staff meetings.

A *good definition of the target behavior is objective and unambiguous* so that it identifies exactly what the person does that constitutes the behavioral excess or deficit you want to change. The definition is stated in such a way that someone who doesn't know the target person would understand what the behavior is and would identify the same instances of the behavior that you'd see if you were both observing the person independently. Here are some examples, with the name of the behavior followed by an objective and unambiguous definition:

- *Cuticle biting*: The person's finger is in his or her mouth, and the teeth are chewing on the skin beside the nail.
- *Exercising*: The person is jogging on a treadmill at 3.5 miles an hour at 5% incline for 30 minutes plus 3 minutes each of warm-up and cooldown at lower speeds and no incline.
- *Having a tantrum*: The person is crying, screaming, and being aggressive, such as by kicking or pounding on objects or surfaces.
- *Whining*: The person is expressing a complaint verbally in a high and wavering pitch.

Notice that each definition includes active verbs to describe the specific acts. Once the target behaviors are clear, we can identify and define specific goals for any program we design.

IDENTIFYING AND DEFINING BEHAVIORAL GOALS

The goals behavior analysts want to achieve by applying a behavior change program can be of two types: outcome goals and behavioral goals. *Outcome goals* are the broad or abstracted results we want to achieve. In Al's case, the outcome goals might be to help him be a more conscientious, cooperative, and productive employee. Outcome goals in behavior change programs usually are very obvious and straightforward, relating directly to the broad characteristics we've noticed about the person. Other examples of outcome goals might be enabling disabled children to do self-help skills and improving students' grades in school.

A **behavioral goal** is the *level of the target behavior* we hope to achieve in a program. For example, for the target behavior of jogging, the behavioral goal might be to increase jogging to three 1-hour sessions each week. Sometimes outcome and behavioral goals are the same; this can happen when both goals simply involve quitting a particular behavior, such as twirling one's hair. Very often, a program's outcome and behavioral goals are different; outcome goals are broader or less directly tied to the specific behaviors. Losing weight might be an outcome goal for a dietary target behavior, and the behavioral goal might be to reduce snacking to two servings per day.

Another example of the difference between these types of goals comes from an intervention to reduce cash-register shortages in a small restaurant (Marholin & Gray, 1976). The outcome goal was to have the cash in the register equal the register-tape totals at the end of each day, and the consequences introduced to change the cashiers' behavior were contingent on their meeting that goal. If a daily shortage exceeded 1% of daily sales, the cashier's salary was docked to cover the loss. The program succeeded in achieving the outcome goal—the average daily shortage dropped from about 4% to below 0.5%—but no target behavior or behavioral goal was identified. Not identifying a target behavior could present a problem because the cashiers could meet the goal in many different ways, including shortchanging customers and under-ringing sales on the register. To change behavior in a specific way, such as making cashier transactions more precise, we must identify the target behavior and behavioral goal and then make appropriate consequences contingent on the behavior.

Parents and teachers who want to improve students' learning often focus on an outcome goal, usually grades, rather than on the *behaviors* that enable attainment of the goal. There are two problems with this approach. First, although most people know that the "best" way to increase grades is to study for a longer time and with an emphasis on concentrating on and understanding the material, there are many other ways to increase one's grades. Some of these ways are unethical, such as cheating on tests or plagiarizing material for a report. And sometimes students will try to "boost" their study time and concentration with substances that make one more alert but can also lead to dangerous physiological events, such as cardiac arrest. Second, a student's low grades may involve a single skill, such as spelling or reading. Identifying that skill as the target behavior and working to improve it could increase his or her grades in several subjects.

Once each target behavior and behavioral goal for an intervention have been identified, we need to *define* them very clearly and in *measurable* terms. If we fail to do this, we will sometimes think the behavior occurred when it actually didn't, or we won't realize it occurred when it actually did. Defining the behavioral goal is also important: In trying to change Al's work performance, it wouldn't be enough to say, for instance, "By the end of the program, Al will come late to work much less than in the past." This is too vague. How will we know he achieved it? We must specify the level we want exactly, for example: "By the end of the program, Al should reduce his coming to work late from about 10 instances to fewer than 3 per month, and each instance of lateness should be less than 10 minutes." It's a good idea to indicate the starting level, "about 10 instances," in stating the behavioral goal. Another good idea in defining behavioral goals is to identify *behavioral subgoals*—intermediate levels of the behavior to be achieved by specific dates during the program. (Go to 🔍.)

CLOSE-UP

Deciding Whether a Program to Prevent Substance Abuse Worked

At the beginning of this chapter, we looked at a program school counselors designed and administered to prevent drug abuse and asked whether the program was a success. Let's see why the answer to this question is important.

The program focused on preventing substance abuse through drug education. This approach has been widely used in schools, and dozens of studies have been done to assess its effectiveness. An evaluation of these studies' findings was performed using a research technique called *meta-analysis*, which creates an overview of the findings by pooling data from many studies (Bangert-Drowns, 1988). Meta-analyses can clarify research results and arrive at an overall conclusion when the findings in some studies have been different from those in others, as has occurred in the field of substance abuse education. This meta-analysis revealed that "typical substance abuse education had its most positive effects on knowledge and attitudes, but was *unsuccessful in changing the drug-using behaviors* of students" (p. 243, italics added).

Did the counselors' program we discussed work? Probably not, because its purpose was to reduce drug use—the target behavior—but the counselors didn't measure this, and indeed, most similar programs have failed to reduce drug use. The counselors documented desirable changes only in the students' knowledge and attitudes about drugs. To tell whether a program to change behavior worked, it's necessary to measure the target behavior and compare it against a specified behavioral goal.

DEFINING OPERANT TARGET BEHAVIORS

To illustrate the importance of defining target behaviors clearly and in measurable terms, let's suppose you decided to change a young girl's diet and defined the target behavior as "to eat healthier." I would wonder, "What does *eat healthier* mean? Does it mean she should eat more vegetables and less fat; consume fewer calories; or, maybe, something else?" Eating is an operant behavior, and to change it, you'll need to alter its antecedents and consequences. If you define a target behavior vaguely, you'll be uncertain when, where, and how to introduce appropriate antecedents and consequences.

How much detail should your definition of the target behavior have? The answer depends on exactly what you're trying to achieve—the definition must match the goal. If your behavioral goal states or implies certain details of the behavior, such as the specific snacks she can or cannot eat, your definition of the target behavior must reflect those details. For instance, some evidence indicates that obese individuals who lose the most weight in a behavior change program chew each bite of food slower than those who are less successful in losing weight (Spiegel, Wadden, & Foster, 1991). If you wanted to modify how fast you chew each bite of food, you'd need to define *bite* and *slower*.

Overt and Covert Behaviors

In Chapter 1, we saw that behaviors can be overt or covert and that behavior analysts tend to focus on changing overt behavior. This is because we can usually define external behaviors more clearly and measure them more objectively than internal behaviors.

Think about the overt behavior of jogging on a treadmill—you could easily define and measure its occurrence accurately, couldn't you? Although you may have to work a little harder to define some other external behaviors, such as studying or being assertive, it can be done. However, defining and measuring covert behaviors—thoughts, feelings, and physiological changes—are more problematic, but still possible. For instance, having negative thoughts about oneself might be defined by including typical words or phrases the

"MY DAD SAID TO LISTEN TO MY CONSCIENCE.
MY CONSCIENCE SAYS, 'GO FOR IT!'"

Dennis' father described the boy's behavior far too broadly or vaguely, letting the boy decide what his "conscience" tells him. *Source*: Reprinted with special permission of King Features Syndicate.

person thinks, such as *stupid* or *lazy*. Still, measuring the behavior is a very subjective process. Without some independent way of substantiating the person's self-reports, any progress that is made will be unclear (Baer, Wolf, & Risley, 1968). This situation is less than ideal, but we will see later that there are ways to supplement the evidence from self-reports to make it more convincing.

Defining and measuring internal changes in physiology, such as increases in blood pressure or heart rate, often require special apparatus or biochemical analyses. Professionals in research or therapy may be able to make these assessments. One physiological measure you can make easily and fairly accurately is heart rate: When you take someone's pulse, you are counting heartbeats.

Complex Behaviors

Sometimes the operant target behavior we want to teach or improve involves a complex set of responses. If so, it is useful to determine what these responses are and whether they need to be performed in a certain sequence, as when we put on a shirt or pair of slacks. A motor activity that consists of a sequence of antecedents (stimuli) and responses is called a *behavioral chain*, and each antecedent–response pair making up the chain is called a *link* (Gagné, 1985). For instance, washing your hair might consist of the following links:

	Antecedents (stimuli)		Responses
1.	See shampoo bottle	→	Reach and grasp bottle
2.	See and feel grasp	→	Turn so spout is pointed down
3.	See pointed down	→	Pull off cap
4.	See cap off	→	Pour shampoo into hand
5.	See shampoo glob in hand	→	Replace cap
6.	See and feel cap is on	→	Return shampoo bottle to shelf
7.	See bottle on shelf	→	Spread shampoo glob across hands
8.	See shampoo is spread on hands	→	Mix shampoo vigorously into hair
9.	Feel suds mixed throughout hair	→	Rinse suds from hair

To perform a chain correctly, the links must be done pretty much in a particular order: In washing your hair, replacing the bottle cap and then trying to pour the shampoo won't work. Learning to perform a chain can be very difficult, especially if the task is extremely complicated or the person's learning abilities are very limited, as they are if the learner is a young child or has an intellectual disorder. Once the component links of a complex task are identified, a program can be designed to train the person to perform each component and put all the links together. We will examine how to identify the antecedent–response links that make up a sequence of behavior and to teach chains in Chapter 12.

DEFINING RESPONDENT TARGET BEHAVIORS

As we saw in Chapter 1, people learn through respondent conditioning to associate two previously unrelated events—a neutral stimulus and a response: The stimulus gains the ability to elicit a conditioned response (CR) by its being repeatedly paired with an unconditioned stimulus (US) that already elicits that response. Because we learn CRs—such as fears and dislikes—they can be targets of behavior change programs.

Like operant behaviors, respondent behaviors can be overt or covert. Often they are both: When we are anxious or afraid, we may show external signs of fear, such as in facial expressions or efforts to escape the situation, and experience internal behaviors, such as negative thoughts and increased physiological arousal. For example, a boy who is very anxious while giving a speech in class may show external fearful behaviors, such as a quivering voice and frequent moistening of his lips. He also may notice internal behaviors, such as nausea, fast heartbeat, and thinking that the audience can see he feels nervous. When designing a program to change a respondent behavior, we need to define the behavior in terms of its internal or external responses, or both. Some programs may need a dual focus to be fully successful. Reducing the person's covert feelings of fear while giving a speech will not necessarily reduce his or her overt signs of fear (Marshall, Presse, & Andrews, 1976). To reduce these overt signs of fear, programs probably need to include training in public speaking skills, too—for instance, by increasing the person's smiling at and eye contact with the audience (Fawcett & Miller, 1975).

PRIORITIZING: WHICH BEHAVIOR TO ADDRESS FIRST

Sometimes applied behavior analysis interventions are used with clients who have only one behavior they want to change, so no decision needs to be made about which behavior to address first. But often the target person has many behaviors that need to improve, and the behavior analyst needs to decide how to sequence the changes. Behavior analysts try to base these decisions mainly on the extent to which each changed behavior is likely to contribute to the person's behavioral and social functioning (Bosch & Fuqua, 2001; Hawkins, 1991). To make these decisions, the behavior analyst can try to answer the following questions, beginning with the phrase, *"Is the new or changed behavior likely to ..."*

- *Lead to reinforcement in the target person's everyday environment?* For example, let's consider a 4-year-old child named Pepe who is nonverbal and shows bizarre or extremely disruptive behaviors. If we taught him to communicate, he could ask for the things he wants and would be less frustrated; and if we reduced his bizarre and disruptive behaviors, other people would react more pleasantly to him and the behaviors that replace the maladaptive ones.

- *Reduce the occurrence of harm or damage?* Some behaviors, such as aggressive acts, can harm individuals or damage property.

- *Be a prerequisite for learning a skill that enables the person to function better?* For example, learning the finger positions to push a button into a hole is necessary before a child can learn to button clothing when dressing. And learning the names of numbers is necessary before learning to do arithmetic.

- *Affect in positive ways important individuals in the client's life?* Parents, teachers, spouses, and peers are important people who may benefit from behavior changes, such as a disabled person's learning self-care skills.

- *Be a behavioral cusp?* A *behavioral cusp* is a behavior that has benefits beyond its direct effects because it exposes the person to new and richer environments, learning opportunities, and consequences that would not be available otherwise (Rosales-Ruiz & Baer, 1997). Examples of behavioral cusps include a child's learning to crawl and read, each of which gives access to rich experiences that were previously unavailable.

- *Show response generalization?* In the phenomenon of *response generalization*, altering one behavior leads to similar changes in another, unaddressed response, usually one that is similar or related to the target behavior (Carr, 1988; Kimble, 1961). For example, 4-year-old girls who received rewards for changing the forms they made out of blocks in a preschool began to construct forms they had never made before (Goetz & Baer, 1973). Another example comes from the development of language skills: Children who've learned to add *-ed* to the ends of certain verbs to express past tense will do the same with other verbs (sometimes generalizing incorrectly, such as saying "sitted" instead of "sat"). A third example comes from behavior therapy: An adult whose fear of snakes was reduced said that the greatest benefit of the "treatment was the feeling that if I could lick [my fear of] snakes, I could lick anything. It gave me the confidence to tackle, also successfully, some personal stuff" (Bandura, Jeffery, & Gajdos, 1975). Response generalization is important because it can make behavior change processes more efficient.

- *Take the place of or interfere with performing a problem behavior?* For instance, rewarding students' raising their hands to ask a question instead of blurting it out reduces the latter behavior.

An answer of yes to these questions supports giving priority to changing the behavior in question. Two other factors behavior analysts consider are the likely degree of success in changing the behavior with the particular client and how much money or other resources the change will cost. Not all of the questions we've considered can be answered exactly and unambiguously, but even educated guesses can help in setting priorities. (Go to ▰.)

HOW TO ASSESS TARGET BEHAVIORS

Because applied behavior analysis focuses on changing behavior, as behavior analysts we need to be able to measure the target behavior at different points in the process to see whether our efforts are working. When the problem involves a behavioral deficit, we'll want the measure to show an increase; when the problem is a behavioral excess, we'll want the measure to decrease. Assessing behavior requires that we collect data, and there are several types of data we can use.

CONCEPT CHECK 2.1

Check your basic understanding of concepts presented so far in this chapter. Answers are given at the end. Remember that the symbol ⇔ following a question means it is a critical thinking item for which answers can vary or take different directions—the book's answers are suggestions, and you may have other, equally correct answers. The following questions are about goals and target behaviors.

1. A behavioral goal a college student might choose when modifying how much studying he or she does is _____ . ⇔
2. To tell if a behavior change program was successful, we need to assess the target behavior and compare it against a specified _____ .
3. A link in a chain you might perform when starting your car is _____ . ⇔
4. One factor that can influence the priority given for changing a particular behavior is whether an occurrence of the act can produce _____ .
5. A behavior that benefits the person by exposing him or her to new learning opportunities and consequences is called a(n) _____ cusp.

TYPES OF DATA

The data we collect must measure the target behavior and reflect any progress that has been made toward the behavioral goal. Because behavior can change in different ways—including how *often*, how *long*, and how *strongly* it occurs—we need to select the types of data that will best reflect how we want the target behavior to change (Dowrick, 1991). For example, if the behavioral goal is to increase the time the person exercises per week, the data must involve a measure of time. These data are commonly expressed as a *rate*—per unit of time—as in, "the number of hours a student studies *per week*" or "the number of aggressive acts a person makes *per session* (of standard length). Behavior analysts record their data on paper sheets or in a computer program designed for the particular types of data they are collecting. Let's look at the types of data we can use to assess behavior, beginning with how frequently it occurs.

Frequency

The **frequency** of a behavior refers to the number of times the response was observed. Frequency is an appropriate measure when the behavioral goal involves *changing how often* the behavior occurs, and each instance of the target behavior is *discrete*—that is, has a clear start and end—and takes about the *same amount of time* to perform. Collecting frequency data is fairly easy to do and is appropriate for most target behaviors.

What are some examples of behaviors assessed with frequency data? One study recorded the frequency of bed-wetting in a behavior change program to reduce how often that behavior occurred (Nordquist, 1971). Another study assessed the number of math problems computed correctly by underachieving fifth-graders after they participated in a program to increase their math skills (Pigott, Fantuzzo, & Clement, 1986). Other target behaviors that can be assessed with frequency data if they meet the criteria just described include exercising, turning homework in on time, saying a word correctly, nail biting, smoking cigarettes, cursing, being angry, saying "um" or "like" in sentences, and feeling unhappy.

Duration

Duration refers to the length of time each instance of the target behavior lasts from start to finish. This type of data is appropriate for assessing instances of a target behavior that last for *varying periods of time* and are subject to a *behavioral goal* that involves either *increasing or decreasing that time*. For example, the duration of social interaction was assessed in a program to increase the time two severely withdrawn children with mental retardation spent in simple social activities, such as rolling balls to each other (Whitman, Mercurio, & Caponigri, 1970). Other examples of target behaviors that can be assessed in terms of duration are studying, watching television, exercising, sleeping, sitting in one's seat, having a tantrum, playing computer games, spending time with one's children, and feeling anxious or "blue."

Magnitude

In a program to reduce someone's anger, wouldn't it be important to assess *how strong* the anger is? This would be an example of measuring behavior's **magnitude**—its intensity, degree, or size. Using this type of data is appropriate if the behavioral goal involves *changing the intensity, degree, or size* of an action or its product and if that measure *can or does vary*. For example, the magnitude of a girl's speech was assessed in a behavior change program to increase the loudness with which she spoke by measuring the volume with an electronic device (Jackson & Wallace, 1974). Before the program, her speech had been almost inaudible. As another example, many people who want to assess exercise intensity measure pulse or heartbeats or record the weights of barbells lifted.

It is usually important to use a magnitude measure when changing emotional behaviors, such as overt and covert expressions of anger, jealousy, fear, and depression. The most common way to measure emotion magnitude is to use a *rating scale* with discrete numerical values. In measuring anger, for example, we might use a 10-point scale ranging from 0 to 9, where 0 equals "no anger" and 9 equals "extreme anger." For other behaviors, such as grip strength in physical therapy or noise intensity in classrooms, a scale can be mechanical or electronic.

Data of Other Types

Other types of data are also useful in assessing behavior, and we consider a few of them briefly here. As we've seen before, you would use these measures if they are expressed in the behavioral goal. One measure is *latency*, or the amount of time a person takes to initiate the appropriate response to an antecedent. Assessing the quickness with which a child complies with a teacher's or parent's request would be an example of using latency to assess a target behavior. In another example of the use of a latency measure, progress in treating people's insomnia can be assessed by noting their latencies in getting to sleep after going to bed (Puder, Lacks, Bertelson, & Storandt, 1983).

If your behavioral goal involves improving *how well* the person performs a target behavior, you will assess its *quality*. For instance, a behavior change program was used to improve the quality of students' classroom discussions (Smith, Schumaker, Schaeffer, & Sherman, 1982). The students received training to use reasons, comparisons, and examples as discussion skills, and their statements in discussions were rated for quality based on the use of these skills. Quality is often assessed with a rating scale. Other target behaviors for which quality may be a useful measure include drawing pictures, playing a musical instrument, and performing athletic skills.

Another type of data behavior analysts use is *trials-to-criterion*, which involves tallying the number of trials the target person needed to achieve a specific level of performance. A *trial* is defined as "an opportunity to perform a particular behavior in a certain time period." The behavior analyst decides in advance what the required level of performance and the amount of time will be. So, if we were teaching a child to pronounce the "th" sound, we would count the number of trials until he or she said it correctly to a predetermined criterion, such as twice in a row. Trials-to-criterion data can evaluate some important issues—for example, a relatively low number of trials needed to reach the criterion can indicate that the target person's competence for a type of task, such as naming objects, has improved or that one training method is more effective than another.

The last type of data we'll consider for assessing behavior is the *percentage*—the proportion of behaviors, or individuals performing behaviors, that meet some criterion, multiplied by 100. Percentages are especially useful measures when people have *many opportunities to respond*, or when the *opportunities to meet a behavioral criterion vary* across time or circumstances. For example, percentage would be an appropriate measure of children's compliance with a teacher's requests because the number of requests each day is likely to vary. In this example, we'd calculate a percentage by dividing the number of compliant behaviors by the number of requests, and multiplying by 100. A similar situation exists when assessing driving behavior in traffic. Because the number of cars on the road varies with many conditions, such as the weather and time of day, we'd probably evaluate the success of a program to reduce speeding by looking for a reduction in the percentage of cars observed speeding, rather than just the frequency of speeding. A study recorded the percentage of cars speeding and found that it was reduced by posting the percentage of cars that did *not* speed during the day before and during the best day to date (Van Houten, Nau, & Marini, 1980).

There are two other issues to keep in mind about collecting data. First, it is often necessary to collect more than one type of data to reflect changes in a target behavior. For instance, in a behavior change program to reduce a child's tantrums, the behavioral goal might include reducing the frequency of these behaviors as well as their duration and magnitude. If so, three types of data should be collected. Second, it is typically useful to design and record data on carefully structured *data sheets*, like the one presented in Figure 2-1. Other data sheets can be simpler or more detailed—for instance, they can merely provide spaces for tick marks for frequency data, or they can incorporate a lengthy checklist of behaviors to be assessed with two or more types of data. Using data sheets makes recording and evaluating data much easier and faster. When designing a data sheet, it's a good idea to try it out by collecting some sample or "pilot" data so you can correct any design flaws before using it in a program. Sometimes computer software is available for recording data. (Go to 🐾.)

DATA SHEET: **Exercise**

Student: _____Bonnie_____   Observer: _____Mr. Armstrong_____

Date	Starting Time	Duration (entire session, in minutes)	Magnitude (pulse beats/min, while jogging)	Comments
9-1-10	3⁰⁰	30	120	She hasn't exercised before
9-9-10	3³⁰	35	125	
9-12-10	3¹⁵	40	130	
9-14-10	3⁴⁵	40	130	Feeling a little achy
9-16-10	3⁰⁰	45	140	Feeling better

Figure 2-1   Data sheet for use in an exercise program at school, with a physical education teacher as the observer. Each session includes general calisthenics and jogging and is assessed with two types of data: *duration* of the entire session and *magnitude*, as measured by the student's pulse rate taken for 1 minute during jogging.

CASE STUDY

Defining and Measuring Bob's Self-Talk

An institutionalized 31-year-old schizophrenic man named Bob had a history of *self-talk*; he talked to himself frequently and at varying levels of loudness (Wong et al., 1987). Many mental patients exhibit this speech pattern. In this case study, Bob's self-talk was defined and measured in the following way:

> Self-talk, defined as any vocalization not directed at another person, excluding sounds associated with physiological functions (e.g., coughing), was the target response for Bob. [His] vocalizations were monitored with a microcassette recorder (Sony model no. M-203) carried in a shirt jacket worn by the patient. The recorder received input from a tie-clip microphone (Radio Shack catalog no. 33–1058) attached to the jacket lapel. (p. 78)

The study's observers heard and scored the duration of Bob's actual self-talk from the recordings. The data showed that Bob's therapists reduced his self-talk by about 60% simply by providing recreational activities that would serve as antecedents for him to do other things.

STRATEGIES FOR ASSESSING BEHAVIOR

Assessing behavior always involves some form of *observation*, and the observer can be almost anyone—a therapist, teacher, coworker, relative, or even the person whose behavior is being changed, which is called *self-monitoring*, or *self-observation*. Overt target behaviors typically can and should be assessed directly, but covert behaviors are often assessed indirectly, supplemented with direct measures when possible.

Direct Assessment Methods

When using **direct assessment methods**, observers measure instances of the actual target behavior in a straightforward manner, usually by seeing or hearing them. For instance, a teacher may assess a student's hand-raising behavior by watching for instances of it and keeping a record of those instances. With direct assessment methods, observers may measure the behavior in three ways (Dowrick, 1991; Foster & Cone, 1986):

1. While in the same room or setting as the target person
2. By watching secretly from an adjacent room, perhaps through a one-way mirror
3. By making a video or audio recording of the behavior and scoring it later

This last approach was used in the case study about Bob's self-talk.

Sometimes direct assessments are made in a *structured test* of the behavior—that is, specific events are arranged to occur during the test (Bernstein, Borkovec, & Coles, 1986; Wixted, Bellack, & Hersen, 1990). For example, a client might be asked to perform a series of operant actions to see if a pain condition impairs movement. Structured tests can also be used with respondent behaviors. For instance, a client who is extremely afraid of snakes might be tested by having a therapist move a caged snake gradually closer. When the client feels uncomfortable, the test ends; then the distance between the snake and the client is measured and recorded. And clients with anxiety or assertiveness problems might be tested by having them role-play being in specified situations, such as asking for a date or for a raise at work, while the therapist rates their performance for specific behaviors, such as stammering or body tension.

Direct assessment methods often use devices to measure physical characteristics or dimensions of behavior. Professionals commonly use pedometers to keep track of a person's walking or running and tape measures to determine how close a target person will get to a feared object, how high an athlete can jump, and so on. In therapy or rehabilitation settings, the devices used can be quite specialized. For instance, medical patients with severe burns on their arms or legs must perform physical therapy exercises to stretch their limbs as far as they can so they will regain their range of motion. The degree of stretching can be measured with a *goniometer*, which has two arms joined by a pivot—one arm has a pointer and the other has a protractor scale (Hegel, Ayllon, VanderPlate, & Spiro-Hawkins, 1986). When the limb is stretched, the physical therapist positions the device on the limb and records the angle the limb forms.

Direct assessment methods *are the preferred approaches for collecting data* in applied behavior analysis programs to change overt behavior. But these methods have some drawbacks (Wixted, Bellack, & Hersen, 1990). For one thing, they can be time-consuming and expensive to use if it is necessary to train and employ paid observers. Also, these methods sometimes assess only a sample of the target behavior, and that sample may or may not be representative of the person's behavior in everyday life. One purpose of the indirect assessment methods we are about to examine is to document the occurrence of or change in a given behavior in everyday life.

Indirect Assessment Methods

Indirect assessment methods use abstract or roundabout ways to measure the target behavior, usually by having the client or others who know him or her well complete interviews, questionnaires, or rating scales.

Interviews are the most widely used assessment procedures in behavior therapy (Swan & MacDonald, 1978). They can serve three purposes (Ciminero, 1986; Gross, 1984; Turkat, 1986). First, interviews can identify the client's behavioral deficits and excesses, as well as existing antecedents and consequences for the problem behaviors and potential consequences to use in treatment. Second, interviews may also help in assessing related issues, such as important cultural norms that exist in the client's life and persons who will be affected by changes in the client's behavior. Third, therapists try to establish with interviewees a relationship of mutual trust, called *rapport*. Sometimes interviews are highly *structured*, asking a set of questions in a specific order; at other times they are *unstructured*, giving the interviewer leeway in posing questions and interpreting answers (Kring, Johnson, Davison & Neale, 2010; Turkat, 1986; Wixted, Bellack, & Hersen, 1990). Because interviews are retrospective—that is, the interviewee looks back at events that occurred in the past—therapists must watch for inconsistent answers that may reflect errors in memory.

Clients can report a great deal of clinically important information very efficiently by filling out *questionnaires* and *rating scales* (Jensen & Haynes, 1986; Wixted, Bellack, & Hersen, 1990). Some self-report instruments are constructed by individual therapists for their specific purposes, but many others have been developed for general use and are available to therapists through professional sources. Some self-report instruments provide information about the client's background, while other instruments help diagnose the problem and identify target behaviors (Jensen & Haynes, 1986). The questionnaires and rating scales listed in Table 2.1 are available to help therapists assess specific behavioral deficits or excesses. When used along with other assessment methods, data from self-report instruments can help select target behaviors and treatment approaches.

Useful information about an individual's behavior can also be obtained by having the target person's teacher, therapist, parents or spouse, friends, or coworkers fill out rating scales or checklists. For instance, a checklist is available that teacher-therapists can use to assess 20 dimensions of personal appearance and care in children with disabilities (McClannahan, McGee, MacDuff, & Krantz, 1990). Checklist items include whether a child's nose is clean and socks match. Totaling across dimensions gives an overall rating of the child's appearance. Other ratings scales are very simple and involve only a single class or dimension of behavior, such as in rating how effective psychiatric patients' social skills are (Frederiksen, Jenkins, Foy, & Eisler, 1976). Figure 2-2 presents a simple rating scale that could be used to measure jealousy/anger.

Physiological measures are the only objective approaches available to assess covert events, and these assessments can produce data on the frequency, duration, and magnitude of the target behavior. These measures can be useful if the target behavior is an internal physiological response, such as high blood pressure, or if it has a consistent physiological component to it, as when heart rate increases with a person's stress (Bernstein, Borkovec, & Coles, 1986; Kallman & Feuerstein, 1986). But physiological measures are often expensive to use because they generally require special equipment or biochemical tests, and they may not give a clearer picture of the current status of a covert behavior, such as anger or fear, than self-reports do (Kallman & Feuerstein, 1986).

TIMING AND ACCURACY OF BEHAVIORAL ASSESSMENTS

If you were going to assess a target person's responses, when exactly would you take your measures? How would you try to make sure that the data you collect accurately reflect the status of the behavior? These are the issues we examine next.

Table 2.1 *Questionnaires and Rating Scales to Measure Behavioral Excesses and Deficits*

Behaviors	References
Anger	Novaco, 1976
Assertiveness	Rathus, 1973
Binge eating	Hawkins & Clement, 1980
Depression	Beck et al., 1961; Carson, 1986
Fears and anxieties	Bernstein, Borcovec, & Coles, 1986; Cautela, 1981; Ollendick, 1983
Parent–child conflicts	Cautela, 1981; Frankel, 1993
Sexual dysfunctions, skills	Ackerman & Carey, 1995; Malatesta & Adams, 1986
Stress	Sarafino & Ewing, 1999; Sarason, Johnson, & Siegel, 1978
Substance abuse	Correa & Sutker, 1986

Figure 2-2   A rating scale to measure the magnitude of jealousy/anger experienced in various situations.

Timing Behavioral Assessments

A very common approach to collecting data in applied behavior analysis is **continuous recording**, which involves designating a specific period of time—such as a 1-hour therapy session, a half-hour play period at school, or an entire day at work—and trying to observe and record every instance of the target behavior during that time. The data we collect with continuous recording can include all of the types we've discussed: frequency, duration, magnitude, or latency. This approach can be difficult to use if the behavior occurs at extremely high rates or if the observer must monitor other events, such as other students' classroom activities, at the same time. In a variation of continuous recording, called *real-life recording*, the observer records the exact time each instance of a target behavior starts and stops. These records can be converted easily into frequency and duration data.

Another way to time behavioral assessments is **interval recording**, in which we'd designate a number of specific observation periods (say, 30 minutes each), divide each period into fairly short intervals of equal length (say, 15 seconds), and record whether the target behavior occurs in each interval. The data recorded for each interval is essentially the word *yes* or *no*; if more than one instance of the behavior occurs in a particular interval, the observer still records only one instance. Knowing when the intervals start and end is a problem that must be solved, perhaps by having a signal on a specific schedule, such as every 15 seconds; the signal might be the activation of a vibrating timer or the sound of a beeper through an earphone. The data used to evaluate the behavior would be either the number or the percentage of intervals in which the behavior occurred. In a study of children's distracting behavior on shopping trips with their parents, observers followed the family through a store and recorded on audiotape whether distracting behaviors occurred in each 15-second interval (Clark et al., 1977). A subsequent program of behavioral methods markedly reduced the percentage of intervals in which distractions occurred.

A third method used to time assessments is **time sampling**, in which we'd designate one or more observation periods of equal length, divide each period into subperiods of equal length (say, 1 minute), and designate a short interval (say, 10 seconds) at the start of each subperiod for collecting data. Several types of data can be collected during these intervals. For instance, researchers assessed the frequency and duration of an employee's in-seat behavior, recording whether she was in her seat for all, part, or none of each interval (Powell, Martindale, & Kulp, 1975). In another study, researchers collected a continuous record of nine social behaviors during each interval by jotting down a code for each response (Sarafino, 1985). As in interval recording, time sampling requires a way to signal the observer for the start and end of each interval. Figure 2-3 gives an example of a data sheet that could be used to keep time-sampling records of a child's disruptive behavior.

Accuracy and Validity of Behavioral Assessments

For assessments to be useful, they must be reasonably accurate and valid. A measure is *accurate* to the extent that the recorded value is the same as the true value, and it is *valid* to the degree that it reflects what it is intended to measure.

Direct assessment methods generally measure the actual target behavior they are intended to examine—for example, if the target behavior is saying "um" in sentences, we might count instances of it in a person's speech. The accuracy of these measures depends on how carefully the behavior has been defined, how thoroughly the observers have been trained, and how precise the measures are if scales and devices are used to assess

```
DATA SHEET: TIME SAMPLING ASSESSMENT OF DISRUPTIVE BEHAVIOR

Student: _____          Observer: _____

Start time: _____                   Day/date: _____ /_____

                                  Intervals

                 1          2          3          4          5
First 10 min   A O Y      A O Y      A O Y      A O Y      A O Y

Second 10 min  A O Y      A O Y      A O Y      A O Y      A O Y

Third 10 min   A O Y      A O Y      A O Y      A O Y      A O Y

         A = aggression, O = out of seat, Y = yelling, making loud noises
```

Figure 2-3   Data sheet for time-sampling assessment of disruptive behavior of a student in class. In this example, the complete observation period lasts 30 minutes, with fifteen 2-minute subperiods. During the short interval (say, 10 seconds each) at the start of each subperiod, the observer would circle the letter representing any of the three target behaviors that occurred in that interval. In this case, the data would be evaluated based on the number or percentage of intervals in which each type of behavior occurred.

the behavior. In contrast, indirect assessment methods, such as interviews and questionnaires, generally involve subjective estimates and rely on people's memories, which may impair the validity and accuracy of the assessment. We can enhance the validity of such measures by seeking corroboration from other people, such as family members. Family members can provide fairly accurate data if they know the target behavior well and have opportunities to observe it (McMahon, 1984). Also, the accuracy of indirect assessments is enhanced when questions are asked and answered clearly and when the person who administers interviews or physiological tests is highly trained.

Observing behavior can affect its performance—a phenomenon called **reactivity** (Bornstein, Hamilton, & Bornstein, 1986; Monette, Sullivan, & DeJong, 1990). As an example of reactivity, consider trying to assess students' cheating behavior during tests if they can see you are watching them intently. If they don't cheat during your observation, their behavior might reflect their reactivity rather than their honesty. Reactivity generally makes people's behavior more desirable or socially acceptable. The effects of reactivity on behavior can be short-lived if the observee "gets used to" being observed, doesn't want to behave in the new way, and finds that there are no new consequences for behaving that way. When *self-monitoring* techniques are used, the observee and the observer are the same person—and behavior therapists sometimes have clients use these techniques in order to take advantage of the beneficial effects of reactivity on behavior (Bornstein, Hamilton, & Bornstein, 1986).

Developmental and Normative Comparisons

Do people at 2, 10, 30, and 70 years of age behave the same? Of course not, and they're not expected to behave alike. What is "normal" or acceptable behavior changes with age. The strategies we use in assessing behavior and the way we interpret the data must be sensitive to the individual's developmental level (Edelbrock, 1984; Evans & Nelson, 1986; Ollendick & Hersen, 1984). And when we interpret data or set behavioral goals, we must consider what behavioral characteristics are normal for the person's age. For instance, many young children are fearful or wary of strangers, and this fear may increase the effects of reactivity. This problem usually can be overcome by having observers spend time playing with the children before trying to assess their behavior. Elderly people may have physical and cognitive conditions that limit their ability to comprehend instructions or perform certain motor actions.

Assessing Data Reliability

Reliability refers to the degree of consistency or dependability of the data a measurement procedure produces (Sarafino, 2005). If the data that one observer records are accurate and reliable, a second observer who watches simultaneously and independently for the same behavior should produce very similar records. The degree of consistency of the data independent observers record when measuring the same events is called **interobserver agreement (IOA)**. (This measure is also called *interrater reliability* or *interobserver reliability*). Observer consistency or reliability is not exactly the same as accuracy, but data are more likely to be reliable if they are accurate. To use this approach, the observers must collect data simultaneously and record their data independently, without being able to tell what is being recorded by another observer at any given time. Although there several ways to evaluate the consistency of the data different observers have collected, two methods are especially common (Foster & Cone, 1986).

In the *session totals method* for assessing IOA, all the data collected by each of two observers in an observation session or period are added, the smaller total is divided by the larger, and a percentage of agreement or consistency is obtained by multiplying by 100. For example, suppose Todd and Kim observed and recorded a worker's frequency of complimenting customers for an entire day at work. Todd recorded 40 compliments, and Kim recorded 36. We would divide 36 by 40 (which equals 0.90), and multiply by 100, which yields 90% agreement. What does this percentage mean?

IOA evaluated with the session totals method should be interpreted with caution. Although the percentage gives us a sense of the extent of overall agreement for the amount of complimenting Todd and Kim observed the worker perform, it does not necessarily mean that they both saw the same 36 compliments, with Todd seeing 4 additional ones that Kim missed. It is possible that Todd was mistaken about the 4 extra ones. And it is possible that the worker actually made 50 compliments, and only 30 of them were seen by both Todd and Kim. Still, a percentage as high as 90% gives us reason to believe that the total number of acts recorded is a reliable estimate of the actual behavior, even though the observers may have disagreed on some individual instances. This example used frequency data, but the session totals method can also be used with other types of data, such as duration or magnitude (Wysocki, Hall, Iwata, & Riordan, 1979).

The second commonly used approach for assessing IOA is the *point-by-point agreement method* (sometimes called the *interval-by-interval method*). We saw earlier that in interval recording, only one instance of the target behavior is recorded for each particular, specified time interval in an extended observation period even if many more instances occurred. Let's suppose Todd and Kim collected their data on the worker's complimenting by using the strategy of interval recording. They watched the worker for 30 minutes and were to record if an instance of complimenting a customer occurred during each 15-second interval. Their records might agree that complimenting occurred for some intervals and disagree with respect to other intervals. To calculate the IOA with the point-by-point agreement method, we would divide the number of intervals for which Todd and Kim agreed that a compliment occurred by the total number of intervals in which their records agreed and disagreed. Suppose that for eight of the intervals, both observers said that the worker complimented customers in each interval; but for two intervals, there was disagreement (Todd's records said complimenting occurred in one of the intervals, and Kim's said complimenting occurred in another interval). We would calculate the percentage of agreement by dividing 8 (agree intervals) by 10 (agree + disagree intervals) and multiplying by 100, yielding 80% agreement.

At this point, you may be wondering why all the intervals in which Todd and Kim recorded no complimenting are not included in the analysis. After all, they both seemed to agree that the behavior did *not* occur in those intervals. But many researchers do not include data for nonoccurrences of the behavior, because these data are more likely to be faulty or inaccurate than data for occurrences (Foster & Cone, 1986; Hawkins & Dotson, 1975). For instance, both records might show no complimenting—even though it actually occurred—if both observers missed seeing it because of a distraction in the environment. By including inaccurate records in assessing IOA, we would be biasing the evaluation. As a result, the interval-recording method generally excludes nonoccurrence data. One exception to this rule is when the target is a behavioral excess, such as an emotional reaction, and the observers need to determine if they agree that the behavior no longer occurs when the antecedent cues are present (Foster & Cone, 1986). In this case, they would use nonoccurrences in place of occurrences in the calculations.

Four additional points can be stated about assessing data accuracy and reliability. First, some evidence indicates that letting observers know their records will be checked against those of other observers appears to increase their accuracy (Foster & Cone, 1986). Second, methods to test IOA can be used in training observers before they begin to collect data for the research itself. In one study, observers received training until they showed 90% agreement during three consecutive observation periods (Zohn & Bornstein, 1980). Third, the general rule of thumb is that 80% agreement is the minimum acceptable level of reliability (Sulzer & Mayer, 1972). Fourth, data collected with indirect assessment methods can be compared for IOA in a similar manner.

Collecting reliable data is essential in evaluating changes in behavior. Without reliable data, research projects start out with weak foundations and produce ambiguous results that can have more than one plausible interpretation.

TIPS ON IDENTIFYING AND ASSESSING BEHAVIOR

Many chapters from this point on will end with a section giving a set of tips on how the techniques discussed in the text are usually applied by professionals when they design or conduct behavior change programs. Here is a list of helpful tips on specifying and assessing behavior:

1. Define the target behavior very carefully, giving details of its components.

2. If the target behavior is covert, look for overt signs to assess, too.

3. If the intervention will address a behavioral excess, try to find a behavior to strengthen in its place. If the program will address a behavioral deficit, such as not exercising, it helps for the person to decide how to make time for the behavior in his or her schedule.

4. Use direct assessment methods whenever possible.

5. If the target person will be using self-monitoring to keep track of his or her own behavioral excess that is performed absentmindedly or habitually, use special procedures to assure the accuracy of the collected data. People are usually unaware when they perform such responses; biting fingernails and swearing are two examples. One way to help people pay attention to these responses is to use a technique called *negative practice*, in which they deliberately perform the behavior over and over while paying close attention to every sensation it produces, such as the sounds they make or the exact position of their fingers.

6. Make sure that all data are *recorded immediately* or very close in time to when the behavior occurs.

7. Transfer data from data sheets to a table on a regular basis, at least daily, and check that no errors were made in this process.

(Go to 📖.)

STUDY AND REVIEW

SUMMARY

Target behaviors to be changed in applied behavior analysis programs must be defined in terms of specific, objective, and measurable actions. Pinpointing the behavior exactly makes it possible to specify a behavioral goal to be achieved by the end of the program. Some target behaviors are complex, requiring a sequence of antecedent–response links to be performed as a chain of behavior.

When a target person has many behaviors that need to be changed, behavior analysts decide which one to teach first on the basis of several considerations, such as whether the new or changed behavior is likely to

CONCEPT CHECK 2.2

Check your understanding of the preceding material. Remember that the symbol ⇔ means the answers can vary. Answer the following questions about assessing target behaviors.

1. A behavior not mentioned in the book that qualifies for using frequency data in its assessment is _____ . ⇔

2. Collecting ratings of a person's degree of self-esteem is an example of the type of data called _____ .

3. When opportunities to meet a behavioral criterion vary across time, it is useful to convert the data to _____ .

4. Having people assess their own target behavior is called _____ .

5. An example of an indirect assessment method is _____ . ⇔

6. The method of collecting data during a short segment of time at the beginning of each observation subperiod is called _____ .

7. Evaluating the degree of consistency in the data collected by two or more observers is called _____ .

8. If we examined two observers' data and divided the smaller number of responses by the larger number of responses they recorded, we'd be using the _____ method of assessing interobserver reliability.

9. The minimum level of reliability that is generally considered acceptable is _____ %.

lead to reinforcement in the person's everyday life, reduce harm or damage, or be a prerequisite for learning other important behaviors. Also, some changed behaviors can serve as behavioral cusps or may show response generalization.

We can assess a target behavior with data of several types, including frequency, duration, and magnitude. Observations of the behavior can be conducted by any of a variety of people, such as teachers or therapists, or by the target person, which involves self-monitoring. These observations can use any of several direct and indirect assessment methods. Timing behavioral assessments can involve continuous recording, interval recording, and time sampling. If people know their behavior is being observed, the accuracy and validity of behavioral assessments can be reduced by reactivity. We can evaluate the accuracy of our assessments through the interobserver agreement methods.

In addition to the concept checks you've already done, and the key terms and review questions that follow, you can prepare for exams with an online study guide that's available on this book's companion website at www.wiley.com/college/sarafino.

KEY TERMS

behavioral goal
frequency
duration
magnitude

direct assessment methods
indirect assessment methods
continuous recording
interval recording

time sampling
reactivity
interobserver agreement (IOA)

ANSWERS TO CONCEPT CHECKS (CCs)

CC2.1 *Answers:* **1.** studying 20 hours a week **2.** behavioral goal **3.** inserting the key in the ignition **4.** harm or damage **5.** behavioral

CC2.2 *Answers:* **1.** saying "like" in your speech **2.** magnitude **3.** percentages **4.** self-monitoring **5.** interviews **6.** time sampling **7.** interobserver agreement **8.** session totals **9.** 80

REVIEW QUESTIONS

1.   What are outcome goals and behavioral goals, and how are they different?

2.   Give two examples of alternative responses (that were not described in the text) and the behavioral excesses they might be helpful in reducing.

3.   Define the three main types of data—frequency, duration, and magnitude—one can use in assessing behavior.

4.   Distinguish between direct and indirect assessment methods, and give two examples of each.

5.   Define and give one example each of continuous recording, interval recording, and time sampling.

6.   Define the concept of reactivity, and give an example of it you saw in real life.

7.   Define the concept of interobserver agreement.

8.   In calculating interobserver agreement, how are the session totals and interval-recording methods different?

RELATED READINGS

- Ciminero, A. R., Calhoun, K. S., & Adams, H. E. (Eds.). (1986). *Handbook of behavioral assessment* (2nd ed.). New York: Wiley.

- Ollendick, T. H., & Hersen, M. (Eds.). (1986). *Child behavioral assessment: Principles and procedures.* New York: Pergamon.

3

USING DATA AND RESEARCH METHODS IN BEHAVIOR ANALYSIS

Using Data to Measure Changes
How We Use Data
Organizing Data
Graphing Data

Using Graphs and Basic Research Methods
Graphic Analysis
Basic Research Designs

Advanced Research Designs in Behavior Analysis
Multiple-Baseline Designs
Changing-Criterion and Alternating-Treatment Designs

Evaluating the Resulting Changes in Behavior
Dimensions of Evaluation
Preparing a Report

Tips on Using Graphs and Research Methods

Study and Review

PROLOGUE

Years ago, a student in a course I taught on behavior change methods came to me with a problem she wanted to correct. Her son Jeremy was a fifth-grader who was doing fairly well in all of his subjects, but was getting poor grades for the short speeches the students gave in class each day (on a 100-point scale, he was averaging 59.5). With the help of his teacher, we designed a tutoring program his mother would carry out at home.

Some of the behavioral deficits Jeremy's teacher identified involved the way he started and ended his speeches—for instance, he didn't smile or look at his classmates. So his mother encouraged him to do these acts. Another deficit was in his organization, so his mother taught him a few rules, such as ''Present an overview first'' and ''Cover the topics in the stated order.'' She also modeled ways to improve deficits and rewarded his improvements with praise and a snack at the end of a good session—the quality of the snack depended on how good his mother judged the speech. After just a few tutoring sessions, Jeremy's speech grades rose to above the class average (about 72 points) and continued to improve throughout the intervention.

Did Jeremy's improved grades result from his mother's intervention methods? Although it's tempting to think they did, other factors would need to be ruled out. For instance, maybe he already had good speaking skills, but his performance suffered because of family difficulties that existed and ended soon after. Or maybe he hadn't done any preparation during the first couple of weeks, but the individual attention he got in the sessions motivated him to work. But we can rule out one possible cause of the improved grades—that the teacher incorrectly perceived better skills because she knew Jeremy's mother was tutoring him—because we used an interobserver agreement method: A student teacher who didn't know about the mother's efforts graded the same speeches independently, and these grades matched the teacher's grades well.

This chapter examines how behavior analysts use data to measure changes in behavior, judge from graphs whether a behavior changed, and apply research designs to determine why the behavior changed.

USING DATA TO MEASURE CHANGES

By using the data we collect, we can determine whether our efforts to change a behavior worked. Although behavioral changes are sometimes obvious, usually they're not—an example comes from teachers' efforts at a preschool to stop a boy named Davey from pinching adults. They tried at first just to ignore his pinching, but Davey pinched:

> hard enough to produce at least an involuntary startle. Teachers next decided to develop a substitute behavior. They selected patting as a logical substitute. Whenever the child reached toward a teacher, she attempted to forestall a pinch by saying, "Pat, Davey," sometimes adding, "Not pinch," and then strongly approving his patting, when it occurred. Patting behavior increased rapidly to a high level. The teachers agreed that they had indeed succeeded in reducing the pinching behavior through substituting patting. Then they were shown the recorded data [which] showed clearly that although patting behavior was indeed high, pinching behavior continued at the previous level. (Harris, Wolf, & Baer, 1964, pp. 16–17)

Perhaps the teachers were so focused on the increase in patting that they didn't notice the pinching so much anymore; but whatever the reason, they wrongly evaluated the success of their efforts. Anytime applied behavior analysis is used, data must be collected and evaluated.

HOW WE USE DATA

Suppose you were a teacher, had a "Davey" in your class, and decided to try to stop his pinching. What data would you collect, and what would you look for to decide whether your intervention had worked? You'd probably want to keep track of exactly how often Davey pinched, perhaps by having the people he pinched record each instance on index cards they would carry all day. What would you look for in the data they collect?

One thing you'd want to see is that the frequency of pinching decreased during the intervention compared to its "baseline" level—that is, its level before you tried to change it. An **intervention** is a *program* or *period of time* in which action is taken to alter an existing situation, such as a target behavior. The term **baseline** has two meanings: it can refer to the *data* collected before the intervention begins or to the *period of time* during which those data were collected. If your intervention worked, the frequency of pinching during intervention would decline from its baseline level. You could see this pattern best in a graph, like the one in Figure 3-1, which depicts an obvious change.

Data tell us the current status and history of *variables*—characteristics of people, objects, or events that can *vary* or change. Behavior is a variable, and its antecedents and consequences are variables, too. The data we collect on these variables can clarify issues or concerns at different points in planning and conducting a program to change a target behavior, such as in choosing the best techniques to apply in changing the behavior. Baseline

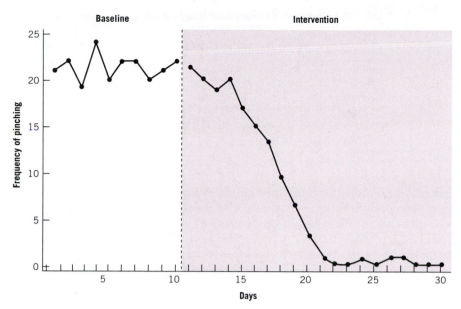

Figure 3-1   How a graph of "Davey's" pinching behavior might look if the intervention was successful. Although the graph assumes the baseline phase lasted 10 days and the intervention lasted 20, the durations of these periods can vary.

data give us a representative picture of the extent or severity of the problem behavior before the intervention begins. The main role of baseline data is to give a reference point for comparison during the intervention phase. By comparing baseline and intervention data, we can tell how well the behavior change program is working.

ORGANIZING DATA

To use data effectively, we need to organize them so that they present a clear picture of the behavior. Obviously, we'll need to organize the data chronologically to see whether the behavior has changed over time. Other ways to organize data are also used, and we'll consider how making arithmetic calculations and tables can help.

Using Arithmetic Calculations

Suppose we collected data on how often a pupil was out of her seat in class, and the data were as follows for 15 successive class days: 21, 31, 5, 9, 40, 7, 30, 4, 39, 8, 23, 38, 9, 3, and 22. By just looking at the data, can you tell how often she was out of her seat overall? Did the target behavior increase or decrease over time? It's hard to tell, isn't it? The picture these data present is not at all clear because they vary so much.

When our data vary a great deal, we can make the picture clearer by calculating the *mean*, or *average value*, for a set of data. In our example of the girl being out of her seat in class, we might separate the data by 5-day week and calculate a mean for each of the three weeks: 21.2, 17.6, and 19.0 instances of being out of her seat per day. Calculating the mean for each set smoothes out the record and gives the general level of the behavior. Grouping data by weeks is probably the most common approach in behavior analysis for calculating means because many behaviors fluctuate by day of the week.

Using Tables

A **table** is a systematic arrangement of data or other information in rows and columns for easy examination. It organizes the data visually, allowing us to see patterns and make comparisons in the data plainly and quickly.

Table 3.1   *Frequency of Cursing Each Day for 2 Weeks of Baseline*

Day of Week	Weeks	
	One	Two
Monday	27	18
Tuesday	21	34
Wednesday	33	25
Thursday	30	28
Friday	17	19
Saturday	9	11
Sunday	7	5

The rows and columns in a table can be divided on the basis of any variable we want to examine, such as different periods of time or different types of antecedents, behaviors, or consequences. Table 3.1 presents an example of tabular data that a student named Chris compiled for a 2-week baseline phase of a project to reduce his cursing.

Notice four features about this table. First, looking over the data, we get a sense of how much Chris cursed each day and a pattern: He cursed less on weekends than during the week (he went home on weekends). This is an example of how tables can help us see patterns and make comparisons. Second, an array of data like this one is called a *Table* and given a number that reflects the order in which it was first mentioned in the text material. Third, the text material refers to Chris's tabular material by number ("Table 3.1 presents … "). Fourth, the table has a descriptive title; always give each table a title, and refer to it by its number in the text material.

GRAPHING DATA

A **graph** is a drawing that displays variations within a set of data, typically showing how one variable changed with changes in another variable. Throughout this book, you'll see graphs to illustrate the effectiveness of different interventions in changing behavior. Data collection and precise records are essential parts of the scientific method and assessments of programs to change behavior. A carefully constructed graph gives the clearest picture of any changes that occurred in the target behavior over chronological time or when one or more techniques were applied.

Types of Graph

Graphs can take several forms, and we will discuss three: line graphs, bar graphs, and cumulative graphs. Each of these graphs is constructed with a *horizontal axis*, or "abscissa," and a *vertical axis*, or "ordinate." When behavior analysts construct graphs of data from behavior change programs, the vertical axis typically represents some measure of behavior, such as frequency or duration, and the horizontal axis represents another variable—usually chronological time, but sometimes the type of procedure applied.

Line graphs use straight lines to connect successive data points that represent the intersects of plotted values for the variables scaled along the horizontal and vertical axes. Line graphs are the most common type of graph used in applied behavior analysis, and the horizontal axis typically scales chronological time or sessions, spanning baseline and intervention phases of a program. That axis is usually divided into and labeled to indicate periods in which intervention techniques were used or not used. Figure 3-1, presented earlier, gives an illustration of a line graph for a boy's pinching behavior. Each data point in the graph reflects the number of pinches he made on a given day, and the graph shows that the number declined sharply during the intervention phase.

Bar graphs use vertically arranged rectangles to represent data points scaled along the vertical axis. The rectangles, or "bars," are usually spaced along and extend up from the horizontal axis to the appropriate point represented on the vertical axis. Each bar gives the data for a separate set of data that cannot be scaled on the

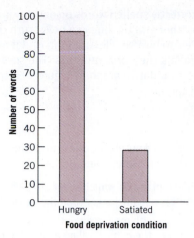

Figure 3-2   Number of correctly spelled words for food reward when a child was hungry (had not eaten for 5 hours) or satiated (had eaten a full meal 15 minutes earlier), presented in a bar graph. One session was carried out under each condition (hungry and satiated) on 10 successive days, and 10 words were tested in each session.

horizontal axis. For example, the bar graph in Figure 3-2 gives the number of correctly spelled words a student made for food rewards under two conditions: when hungry and when satiated. Sometimes the rectangles in bar graphs are arranged horizontally instead of vertically. If so, the axes are switched—the measure of behavior runs along the horizontal axis.

   Cumulative graphs, or *cumulative records*, are line graphs in which the measure of behavior accumulates across units scaled along the horizontal axis. Figure 3-3 presents two contrasting graphs—a regular line graph and a cumulative graph—for the same data, the frequency of correctly spelled words per day with food rewards when the child is hungry or satiated. The contrast allows you to can see how the graphs differ. Notice in the

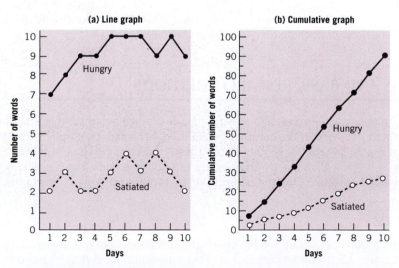

Figure 3-3   The same data presented in two contrasting graphs, a *line graph* (a) and a *cumulative graph* (b). Each graph gives the frequency of correctly spelled words for food rewards on 10 successive days in school, under two conditions: The child was either hungry or satiated. Notice how the cumulative graph accentuates the differential effects of hunger across days.

cumulative graph how the number of correctly spelled words on any day is added to the preceding total. Because the data accumulate, the graph is smoother and the line can never turn downward. If the number of responses declines, the cumulative graph just goes up by a smaller amount. And if no responses occur on a particular day, the line does not go up at all—it parallels the horizontal axis. The *steeper the slope* of the line in a cumulative graph, the *higher the response rate*. In the cumulative graph in Figure 3-3, the slope of the line is steeper for the hungry condition than for the satiated condition.

Preparing Graphs

Graphs can be prepared by hand or with computer graphics programs (see, for example, Carr & Burkholder, 1998; Dixon et al., 2009). For a graph to be complete, it should have five components:

1. *Axes*: There will be a vertical and a horizontal axis, which meet at the bottom left of the drawing. The horizontal axis of a line graph or cumulative graph is usually longer than the vertical axis.

2. *Axis scaling and labels*: Label each axis clearly with measurement units and a name that communicates what the axis represents. The vertical axis typically scales the behavioral measure. The horizontal axis scales chronological time in line and cumulative graphs; in bar graphs, it gives the separate conditions.

3. *Data points*: Correctly plotted data points are drawn at the intersects of the scaled values of the vertical and horizontal axes. In line and cumulative graphs, adjacent data points are connected by a straight line. The lines connecting a series of data points create a "path" depicting the level of the behavior and its trend over time.

4. *Phase lines and labels*: Line and cumulative graphs are usually divided into two or more phases, separated with vertical lines (usually dashed). The phases usually represent treatment and no-treatment periods, which are correspondingly labeled "Intervention" and "Baseline."

5. *Caption*: A figure caption begins with its figure number, which reflects the order in which the graph is referred to in the text material of the report or book. The number should be referred to (for instance, "Figure 1 presents …") in the text.

Each figure should create a clear, easy-to-read, and fair picture of what the data indicate, using distinct geometric forms, such as circles or squares, for data points. Don't use color to distinguish different sets of data. Look at the figures contained in this book as models. If the intervention is working, we should see a clear difference between the baseline and intervention data: For a behavioral excess, the target behavior should decline noticeably in the intervention; for a behavioral deficit, the behavior should increase. (Go to ▉.)

USING GRAPHS AND BASIC RESEARCH METHODS

When behavior analysts evaluate the success of a program to change behavior, they can have two purposes in mind. First, they want to know *whether* the behavior changed. We can inspect a graph of the data to determine the answer. This chapter examines how this is done. Second, if the behavior did change, they often want to know *why* it did. To find out why it changed, behavior analysts use research methods that can demonstrate that changes in a target behavior clearly resulted from the intervention's methods, rather than from some other factor.

GRAPHIC ANALYSIS

Graphs are wonderful tools: They can be used to assess the effectiveness of an intervention as well as to provide feedback as reinforcement for the target person during the intervention and thus increase his or her motivation. For instance, teachers can post and update a graph of their students' conduct or academic performance so that the teacher and the pupils can see how much progress has been made. In this section, we'll focus on a procedure

CONCEPT CHECK 3.1

Check your understanding of the preceding concepts. Remember that answers are given at the end of the chapter, and the symbol ⇔ following a question means that the book's answers are suggestions—you may have other, equally correct answers. Answer the following questions about using data to measure changes.

1. The time period and data collected before an intervention are called _____ .
2. The arithmetic approach to use if your data fluctuate a great deal from day to day is to calculate the _____ .
3. You can organize numerical data visually by arranging them in a(n) _____ .
4. The most common type of graph behavior analysts use in evaluating behavior changes is the _____ graph.
5. If a target person made 10 responses on the first day of baseline, 10 on the second day, and 5 on the third, the value of the data point for the third day in a cumulative graph would be _____ .
6. The five components of a completely prepared graph include _____, _____, and _____ . ⇔

called **graphic analysis**, in which behavior analysts inspect graphed data to evaluate whether the behavior changed substantially when intervention techniques were implemented (Sarafino, 2005). Although there is no widely accepted, specific criterion for deciding whether graphed data do or do not reflect "substantial" behavioral changes, there is agreement that the standards should be rigorous: The data should show very clear, marked changes for us to conclude that an intervention was successful. Well-trained behavior analysts show high agreement with one another in their graphic analyses of whether an intervention produced substantial changes in behavior (Kahng et al., 2010).

An Initial Graphic Analysis

As soon as we begin the intervention phase of a program to change a behavior, we'll be wondering if the program is working. In most cases, we can try to find out after a week or so of the intervention by drawing a graph and inspecting the data. Sometimes the change in behavior is dramatic—for example, a behavioral excess that occurred, say, 20 times per observation session in baseline drops by half right after the intervention starts and soon declines to near zero. The data for the opening story about Jeremy's giving speeches are not quite so dramatic, but the improvement was clear and marked in the first week of the intervention, as you can see in Figure 3-4 (disregard the dashed graph lines for now).

Judging whether the program is working after a week or so of an intervention involves assessing two *trends*—or general patterns of change in the behavior over time. One trend reflects whether the behavior *improved from baseline to intervention*, and the second trend reflects whether the behavior has continued to *improve across time during the intervention*. Figure 3-4 shows that Jeremy's speech grades were higher for the first days of the intervention than for almost all of baseline, and they continued to improve substantially. An initial graphic analysis is useful—if the program is working, no changes need to be made to the intervention methods; but if it is not working as well as we'd like, we would try to find out why and revise the methods it has been using. Later graphic analyses can be performed to see whether improvements continued and the behavioral goal was achieved.

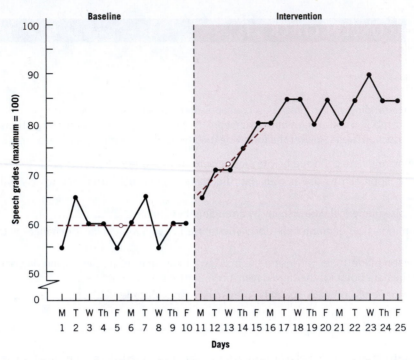

Figure 3-4   Line graph of Jeremy's baseline and intervention speech grades on a scale from 0 to 100. Each dashed line printed in color shows the trend for the set of data it spans, and the colored open circle on each of those lines represents the corresponding mean. Normally behavioral graphs do not use color; it's used here to help you see how to use trend lines.

Clarifying a Graphic Analysis

Sometimes graphic analyses do not show as large a change as we saw in Jeremy's data. We'll use the graph of Jeremy's data in Figure 3-4 to illustrate a three-step procedure that can make a graphic analysis clearer by adding a feature called *trend lines* to the graph:

1. Calculate the means for the baseline and intervention data we want to compare. In Jeremy's data, the mean speech grades were 59.5 for the 2 weeks (10 days) of baseline and 72.0 for the first week (5 days) of the intervention.

2. Place a data point on the graph for each mean halfway across the corresponding time period, using a geometric form that is different from any other forms we've used in the graph. Figure 3-4 uses small open circles, one between days 5 and 6 (halfway across the 10 days of baseline) and one at day 13 (halfway across the first 5 days of intervention).

3. For each time period we're comparing, draw a **trend line** —that is, a straight line that best "fits" or represents all of the data points in a time period—through or very near the data point for the corresponding mean; draw these lines in pencil lightly, so they can be changed if necessary. Darken the lines and distinguish them (such as using dashed lines) from other graph lines when finalizing the graph.

Keep in mind three issues about trend lines. First, if they are positioned correctly, each one looks like it carves the corresponding data points in half, with about the same number of points above and below the line. Second, you'll notice in Figure 3-4 that the vertical axis has a scale break between the values of 0 and 50 because we had no data points below 50. Occasionally, graphs have a scale break with data above and below the break; if this occurs, it's generally not appropriate to have a trend line that includes the break, because the slope of the line would be affected. Third, more complex procedures are available for constructing and interpreting trend lines if higher precision is needed (Fisher, Kelley, & Lomas, 2003; Stewart, Carr, Brandt, & McHenry, 2007; White, 2005).

A few other approaches can clarify the results of a graphic analysis. One way is to check the amount of overlap in the data points for baseline and intervention: The lower the overlap, the greater the intervention's effect (Parker & Hagan-Burke, 2007; Parker & Vannest, 2009). In the ideal condition, there is no overlap:

- For a behavioral excess, the lowest data point in baseline would have a higher value than the highest data point in intervention.

- For a behavioral deficit, the highest data point in baseline would be lower than the lowest data point in intervention.

In Figure 3-4, we see almost no overlap—only the first data point in the intervention (day 11) overlapped with any baseline data.

Data Problems in Graphic Analyses

Trends in the data from programs to change behavior can present problems, making a graphic analysis more difficult to interpret. Difficulties in evaluating trends can arise from data problems of three types: *excessive variability*, a *decreasing baseline trend* (for a behavioral excess), and an *increasing baseline trend* (for a behavioral deficit). Jeremy's data did not have these problems—the trend in baseline was level, and the data did not vary excessively. Figure 3-5 illustrates each of the three types of problem in graphs, using hypothetical data for 1 week of baseline and 1 week of intervention. As we look at these problems and examine the graphs, you'll see that the problems are compounded when data are collected for an insufficient amount of time.

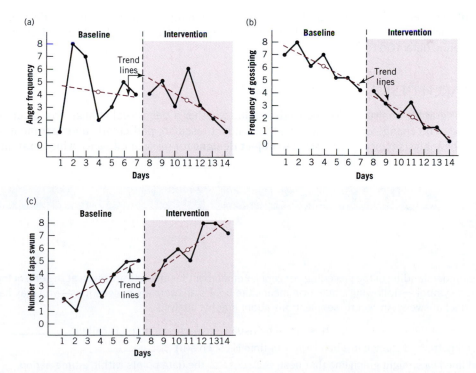

Figure 3-5   Graphs illustrating three types of problem data: (a) *excessive variability*, (b) *decreasing baseline trend* for a behavioral excess, and (c) *increasing baseline trend* for a behavioral deficit. The means (open circles) and trend lines (dashes) for each set of data are plotted. Each graph assumes that the evaluation of whether a program was working was undertaken 1 week after the start of the intervention.

Figure 3.5a presents data for a program to reduce the frequency of a person's anger episodes. The excessive variability in the baseline data makes it difficult to interpret whether any real change has occurred thus far in the intervention phase, even though the trend lines suggest that the number of anger episodes per day declined. This difficulty exists because the baseline data are very unstable, fluctuating sharply. Is the declining trend in anger frequency in the intervention just an extension of the baseline fluctuations, or has the behavior really decreased? Was the high baseline variability an unusual circumstance? If so, collecting baseline data for at least another week might have helped to stabilize the data.

In Figure 3.5b, the data represent a person's frequency of gossiping. Notice that the baseline data for this behavioral excess show a clear decreasing trend that existed before the intervention was introduced to reduce the gossiping behavior. Is the decrease in gossiping after baseline due to the intervention, or is it just a continuation of the existing trend? If the declining trend during the intervention phase had been much sharper than the trend in baseline, we could assume that the difference resulted from the intervention. But the two trends in this graph are very similar. As a result, we can't determine whether the program is working or whether the decreasing trends in both phases are due to some other factor, such as a temporary change in the person's general social experiences. Again, collecting baseline data for another week might have clarified the situation, perhaps by showing a reversal in the baseline trend.

Figure 3.5c presents data for a program to increase the number of laps a person swims in a pool each day. The problem in these data is similar to the one we just saw for the gossiping data. For the swimming behavior, the baseline data for this behavioral deficit depict a clear increasing trend before the intervention was introduced to increase swimming. Once again, the trends in both phases are not very different, so we can't tell whether the program is working or whether some other factor is responsible for the increases in swimming in both phases.

In general, whenever baseline data show excessive variability or an increasing or decreasing trend in relation to the behavioral goal, we should consider delaying the start of the intervention and collecting additional baseline data. (Go to .)

BASIC RESEARCH DESIGNS

We've seen that graphic analyses allow us to determine whether a behavioral change has occurred. But if we want to know *why* the change occurred, we need to conduct research, particularly an experiment. Research in applied behavior analysis typically uses **single-subject designs** (or *single-case designs*), which examine the target

---

CONCEPT CHECK 3.2

Check your understanding of the preceding concepts. Remember that answers are given at the end of the chapter and that the symbol ⇔ following a question means the book's answers are suggestions—you may have other, equally correct answers. Answer these questions about graphic analysis:

1. Assessment of the success of an intervention by visually inspecting a graph is called _____ .
2. A general pattern of change in a behavior over time is called a(n) _____ .
3. A trend line is a straight graph line that best _____ the data points within a time period.
4. An example of a set of data showing excessive variability for 5 days might be _____ , _____ , _____ , _____ , _____ . ⇔
5. An example of a set of data showing a decreasing baseline trend for 5 days might be _____ , _____ , _____ , _____ , _____ . ⇔

behavior of a person across time, while an intervention is either in effect or absent (Hilliard, 1993; Sarafino, 2005). In some cases, single-subject designs test more than one participant (subject), but the data collected for the target behaviors are usually evaluated for each participant separately, using graphic analysis methods.

Most research includes two types of variables: An *independent variable* is tested for its potential or suspected influence, and a *dependent variable* is assessed to see if its value corresponds to, or "depends on," variations in the independent variable. In applied behavior analysis research, the presence or absence of an intervention is the independent variable, and the target behavior is the dependent variable. When we examine why a behavior changed, we are seeking a *cause–effect* answer. Did an intervention cause the behavior to change? To answer this question, we must control all *extraneous variables*—factors, such as noise and lighting levels in the room, that could affect the dependent variable—by holding them constant across baseline and intervention conditions. If we don't rule out the action of extraneous variables, the effect of the independent variable will be unclear. When researchers find that a variable, such as reinforcement, causes a behavioral change, they demonstrate a *functional relation*—that is, the behavior changes as a function of the independent variable (Wacker, Berg, & Harding, 2005).

In our examination of single-subject designs, we'll see that researchers name and describe some types of these designs by using the first letters of the alphabet to signify different phases of the research. The letter A indicates a baseline phase in which the intervention was absent, and the letter B symbolizes a phase in which a specific form of intervention was in effect.

The AB Design

The **AB design** is the simplest type of single-subject research, consisting of one baseline phase and one intervention phase. We saw earlier an example of an AB design in which Jeremy's mother used several techniques to improve his public speaking skills. As we saw, we cannot know for sure that the mother's intervention was responsible for the boy's improved grades. This is because having just one baseline and one intervention phase doesn't allow us to rule out other factors in the person's life that may actually be responsible for the behavior changes observed. As a result, the AB design may be useful when the purpose of research is simply to determine the extent to which the behavior changed, but it is less than ideal when we want to isolate the cause of the change. For example, an AB design was sufficient to show that parent training in behavioral methods may aid treatment programs for children who are hyperactive (Erhardt & Baker, 1990).

The Reversal, ABA or ABAB, Designs

Reversal designs have a series of phases in which an intervention is alternately absent and present, usually with either three or four phases (Sarafino, 2005). The **ABA design** has three phases: baseline, intervention, and reversal—that is, the last phase withdraws the intervention, reinstating the baseline conditions. The reversal phase allows us to see whether the behavioral changes that occurred during intervention revert toward baseline levels when the intervention is absent. The **ABAB design** contains four phases: baseline, intervention, reversal (baseline), and intervention. By reinstating the intervention in the last phase, we can see whether the behavior responds again to the program's techniques. Reversal designs have a distinct advantage over AB designs—they can demonstrate increases and decreases in the behavior that correspond to the presence and absence of the intervention. Because the pattern of increases and decreases would be unlikely to result from factors other than the conditions in the research, they provide strong evidence for a functional relationship: The intervention *caused* the behavior to change. As a result, reversal designs show both that the behavior changed and why it changed.

To illustrate single-subject research using an ABAB design, we'll consider an intervention to reduce the excessive, loud, and abusive statements of a woman named Ruth, who was institutionalized with mental retardation (Bostow & Bailey, 1969). To reduce the frequency of her outbursts, the intervention applied two methods: punishment (moving her to a corner of the room when outbursts occurred and leaving her there for 2 minutes) and reward for *not* having an outburst for certain periods of time. As Figure 3-6 shows, the frequency of her loud vocalizations dropped sharply when the intervention was in force and returned to baseline levels during the reversal phase. These data clearly indicate that the consequences her outbursts received caused them to change.

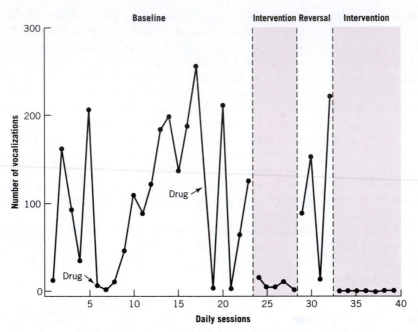

Figure 3-6 Number of loud verbal outbursts (vocalizations) made by a woman named Ruth in each 1-hour observation period in the baseline and intervention phases of a program using an ABAB design. On two occasions during the baseline phase (labeled "Drug"), Ruth was given a tranquilizer because her tirades had been so extreme. *Source*: From D. E. Bostow & J. B. Bailey (1969), Modification of severe disruptive and aggressive behavior using brief timeout and reinforcement procedures. *Journal of Applied Behavior Analysis*, 2, 31–37, Figure 1. Copyright © 1969 Society for the Experimental Analysis of Behavior. Used by permission.

Problems in Using Reversal Designs

Using reversal designs can present three problems for researchers. First, the effect of the intervention may not be fully or substantially reversible. That is, when the intervention is withdrawn, the behavior may not revert toward baseline levels. Under such conditions, our ability to interpret the results is impaired because we cannot be certain why the behavior changed during the first intervention phase. Why doesn't the behavior revert? One reason is that the behavior may have been changed permanently by the original intervention phase, as might occur if the target person learned a skill that he or she finds useful in a variety of settings. For instance, tennis players who learn effective strategies for performing excellent forehand and backhand strokes are not likely to stop using these strategies just because their trainers stopped reinforcing that behavior.

If we think that the target behavior we plan to change could not be expected to regress when the intervention is withdrawn, we should not use a reversal design. But it is not always possible to predict that an intervention will produce a quick and permanent change in a behavior. For example, an intervention consisting only of punishment with mild electric shock was used to reduce a 14-year-old boy's frequent and chronic cough (Creer, Chai, & Hoffman, 1977). The cough had become so severe that his classmates ridiculed the boy, and he was expelled from school at his teachers' request. Various other therapies had been unsuccessful, and the boy and his parents agreed to try the shock. The researchers planned to use an ABAB design. During the 1-hour baseline period, the boy coughed 22 times. In the initial intervention phase, the boy coughed once, which

> was followed immediately by a mild (5 mA) electric shock of 1 second duration to the forearm .... Because the boy did not cough again for the remainder of the hour or the next 2 hours, a reversal procedure could not be instituted. (p. 108)

The boy returned to school the next day and experienced no recurrence of the chronic cough in follow-up assessments over a $2^1/_2$-year period.

The second problem researchers can face with reversal designs is that they must decide what conditions would constitute a reversal of the intervention. For example, suppose an intervention consisted of reinforcing a behavior that had not been reinforced in baseline. To arrange a reversal, we could simply terminate the reinforcement, which is a common method and generally produces a very low level of responding. By terminating reinforcement, we would eliminate both the reinforcing stimulus and the contingency—performing the behavior leads to reward—learned during the intervention. Other ways to reverse a reinforcement condition involve continuing to provide reinforcers, but changing the contingency by providing them either *independently of the behavior* or only when the *behavior is not performed* for an amount of time. Because changing the contingency separates the effects of the contingency from presenting the reinforcing stimulus, it may be the best method for creating a reversal condition in research that has the goal of demonstrating a functional relationship between reinforcement and changes in the target behavior (Thompson & Iwata, 2005).

The third problem with reversal designs is that it may be undesirable or unethical to withdraw an intervention that appears to have produced a beneficial effect. Suppose, for example, an intervention successfully reduced harmful behaviors in disordered children. It would not be desirable or ethically appropriate for the researcher to withdraw the treatment to meet the needs of a research design. Fortunately, other single-subject research designs do not involve reversal phases and can be used in such situations, as we'll see next. (Go to 📄.)

ADVANCED RESEARCH DESIGNS IN BEHAVIOR ANALYSIS

Other research designs behavior analysts use are somewhat more complex than the ones we've seen so far. One group of designs uses multiple baselines to solve some problems with reversals.

MULTIPLE-BASELINE DESIGNS

In **multiple-baseline designs**, more than one AB design is conducted with all baselines starting at about the same time and proceeding together for a while (Sarafino, 2005). Each baseline continues for a different length of time before the intervention begins. As a result, multiple-baseline designs have two important characteristics.

CONCEPT CHECK 3.3

Answer the following questions about basic research methods. Remember: The symbol ⇔ means that the answer can vary.

1. Studies that examine changes in the behavior of individual subjects across time are examples of _____ designs.
2. Isolating the causes of changes in behavior is especially difficult in single-subject research when a(n) _____ design is used.
3. Experiments in which the intervention is withdrawn for a second baseline and then reinstated are using the _____ design.
4. A preschool child's behavior that might not regress when a reversal phase is in effect is _____ . ⇔

First, there are no reversal phases. This feature makes these designs useful when the behavior change is permanent or when withdrawing the intervention is undesirable. Second, introduction of the intervention is staggered across the separate AB designs so that a baseline phase in at least one AB design overlaps an intervention phase in at least one other AB design.

You can see the overlap of baseline and intervention phases in a diagram of a multiple-baseline design with three AB designs, where each column represents a period of time—say, one week—in either the baseline phase (which we'll label "A" and add no shading) or the intervention phase ("B" and add shading):

AB *Design* 1	**A**	**B**	**B**	**B**
AB *Design* 2	**A**	**A**	**B**	**B**
AB *Design* 3	**A**	**A**	**A**	**B**

Time moves from left to right. Notice how the baselines for designs 2 and 3 continue while the intervention begins for design 1; then the baseline for design 3 continues while the intervention operates for designs 1 and 2. This overlap enables us to compare the target behavior in baseline with the behavior in the intervention simultaneously *within and across* designs. Doing so allows us to see *whether* and *why* the behavior changed. If the behavior in intervention was markedly improved over baseline in each of the three AB designs, we can conclude that it changed. If the change in each AB design occurred *only after the intervention was introduced*, we can conclude that the changes resulted from the intervention and not some other factor.

Multiple-baseline research designs can be carried out across different *behaviors*, individual *subjects*, or *situations*. We discuss each of these types of multiple-baseline design in the next sections.

Multiple-Baseline-Across-Behaviors Design

The *multiple-baseline-across-behaviors design* uses separate AB designs for each of two or more different *behaviors* for a single individual in a particular setting. In using this research design, we would monitor simultaneously two or more different behaviors—for instance, a factory worker's daily number of items made and amount of time spent at his or her workstation and time in idle conversation—starting in baseline. Once the baseline data have stabilized for each behavior, we would apply the intervention techniques to only one of the behaviors. Soon, we should see in our graph that this behavior has changed. When the change is clear, we would apply the intervention to the next behavior, and so on. Assuming that the *only* behavior that changes at any given time is the one newly exposed to the intervention, we can infer with strong certainty that applying the techniques caused the change.

A multiple-baseline-across-behaviors design was used to examine the effects of an intervention to help children with asthma learn to use a device that sprays medication into their airways when an asthma episode has begun (Renne & Creer, 1976). Four 7- to 12-year-olds were having trouble learning to use the device and, after baseline, received training with reinforcement for three behaviors. The training for each child started with eye fixation behavior (looking constantly at the device), then facial posturing (inserting the device in the mouth at the right angle and with the lips and nostrils correctly formed), and then diaphragmatic breathing (using the stomach muscles correctly to breathe in the medication). Figure 3-7 depicts the sequencing of training for each behavior and the outcome of the intervention, as reflected in the mean number of inappropriate behaviors the children made. Notice three aspects in the graph. First, like all multiple-baseline designs, the baseline phases started together but lasted for different amounts of time (the baseline lengths increased from the first-, to the second-, to the third-trained behavior). Second, the children's inappropriate behaviors in facial posturing and diaphragmatic breathing did not diminish until each behavior was subjected to the intervention. Third, each behavior responded quickly once the intervention started.

The target behaviors of research using multiple-baseline-across-behaviors designs can vary in the degree to which they are related or unrelated. You can see different degrees of relatedness in the pairs of behaviors in

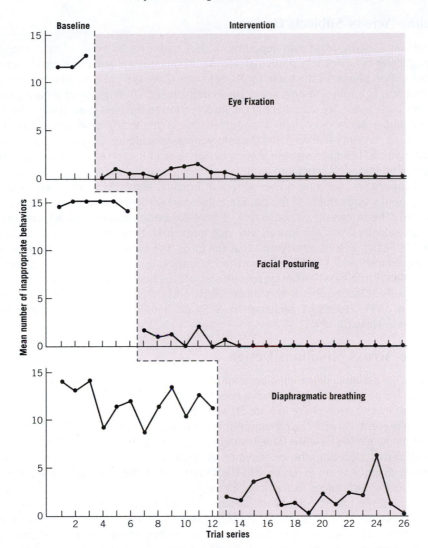

Figure 3-7   Mean number of inappropriate behaviors four children made in learning to perform the behaviors of eye fixation, facial posturing, and diaphragmatic breathing when using a device to control asthma episodes. The maximum number of inappropriate behaviors per trial was 15 for each behavior. In this multiple-baseline-across-behaviors study, the data for the four subjects were combined rather than presented for each child. *Source*: From C. M. Renne & T. L. Creer (1976), Training children with asthma to use inhalation therapy equipment. *Journal of Applied Behavior Analysis*, 9, 1–11, Figure 1. Copyright © 1976 Society for the Experimental Analysis of Behavior. Used by permission.

the following examples: Studies have examined the effects of interventions on articulation errors in producing "th" and "z" sounds (Bailey, Timbers, Phillips, & Wolf, 1971), classroom behaviors of being out of one's seat and making inappropriate statements or sounds (Calhoun & Lima, 1977), sleep problems of a child not going to sleep on time and entering her sister's bed (Ronen, 1991), and worksite safety behaviors, such as bending knees and keeping the back aligned when lifting a heavy object (Alvero & Austin, 2004). Some of these studies examined several behaviors, not just the two listed, and each specific behavior was observed in a baseline phase and an intervention phase.

Multiple-Baseline-Across-Subjects Design

The *multiple-baseline-across-subjects design* uses separate AB designs for each of two or more individual *participants* (subjects) for a particular behavior in a particular setting. In this design, each participant receives a baseline phase and an intervention phase for the same target behavior. Once the baseline data have stabilized for each subject, the intervention is applied to only *one* of these individuals. When graphed data indicate the behavior has changed for this participant, we would apply the intervention to the next participant, and so on. Assuming that the *only* subject whose behavior changes at any given time is the person newly exposed to the intervention, we can infer with strong certainty that applying the intervention techniques caused the change.

A study used a multiple-baseline-across-subjects design to examine the effects of an intervention to prevent HIV (the AIDS human immunodeficiency virus) infection among hospital nurses (DeVries, Burnette, & Redmon, 1991). The target behavior was wearing rubber gloves in hospital activities where there is a high probability of contact with a patient's body fluids. If the patient is infected with HIV, wearing gloves reduces nurses' risk of becoming infected. The intervention, consisting of biweekly performance feedback and encouragement to wear gloves in these activities, was introduced with one nurse first, then another nurse, and so on. Figure 3-8 illustrates the study's design and results. Notice that the target behavior improved in each nurse only after the intervention was introduced, which indicates that the feedback caused the behavior to change. Other studies have used this type of multiple-baseline design to demonstrate the beneficial effects of interventions to improve basketball players' skills (Kladopoulos & McComas, 2001) and school students' skills in math and spelling (Swain & McLaughlin, 1998; Truchlicka, McLaughlin, & Swain, 1998) and in recruiting teacher attention and feedback (Craft, Alber, & Heward, 1998).

Multiple-Baseline-Across-Situations Design

The *multiple-baseline-across-situations design* uses separate AB designs for each of two or more different *situations* (or *settings*), typically for a single individual and a specific behavior. In this design, the participant receives a baseline phase and an intervention phase in each of two or more situations—for example, in different places or with different people present. As with the other multiple-baseline designs, the baselines in all situations begin at much the same time. Once the baseline data are stable, the intervention is applied in only *one* of them. When the change is clear in that situation, the intervention is applied in the next situation, and so on. Assuming that the behavior *only* changes at any given time in the situation with the newly presented intervention, we can conclude that applying the techniques caused the change.

A study used a multiple-baseline-across-situations design to test the effects of an intervention of brief, mild punishment procedures on a young man's stuttering (James, 1981). In both the baseline and intervention phases, the client talked while a tape recorder was running in five situations: in a laboratory talking alone, in the laboratory conversing with a researcher, at home talking with an adult, on the telephone talking with an adult, and in various business settings talking with clerks or agents. The results demonstrated that his stuttering decreased in each situation, but only once punishment was applied there. Similarly, a study used a multiple-baseline, across-situations design to demonstrate the effectiveness of self-monitoring methods in improving students' on-task behavior in three different settings: language arts, reading, and computer classes (Wood et al., 1998). See graphs of data from other multiple-baseline-across-situations designs in Figures 7.3, 14.1, and 25.2.

A Limitation of Multiple-Baseline Designs

We hinted earlier at a potential problem in using multiple-baseline designs: A target behavior may begin to change during a baseline phase, before the intervention has been introduced. This occurred in a multiple-baseline, across-behaviors design to test the effects of an intervention to reduce a 29-year-old male patient's three delusional belief statements: that he was a woman named Amanda or had been Jesus Christ or Leonardo da Vinci in prior lives (Lowe & Chadwick, 1990). The beliefs were treated in the listed sequence. Although the man's statements that he had been Jesus and Leonardo in past lives did not change while the Amanda belief

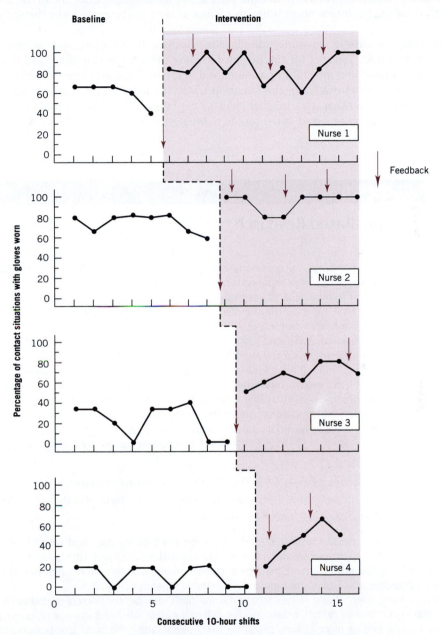

Figure 3-8   Percentage of occasions in which four nurses wore rubber gloves during 16 consecutive 10-hour shifts when contact with a patient's body fluids was likely. The intervention in this multiple-baseline-across-subjects design involved feedback about the nurses' recent use of gloves and encouragement to wear them more often. Arrows indicate points at which feedback was given by a nurse specializing in the control of the spread of infection in hospitals. *Source:* From J. E. DeVries, M. M. Burnette, & W. K. Redmon (1991), AIDS prevention: Improving nurses' compliance with glove wearing through performance feedback. *Journal of Applied Behavior Analysis, 24,* 705–711, Figure 1. Copyright © 1991 Society for the Experimental Analysis of Behavior. Used by permission.

declined, the Leonardo statements began to decline in baseline, paralleling the decline in the Jesus statements that was currently receiving the intervention. When this happens, we can't be certain why the untreated behavior has begun to decline.

Similar problems can arise in other multiple-baseline designs. In the multiple-baseline-across-subjects design, changes in the target behavior for the person receiving the intervention may lead to changes in the behavior of other individuals who are still in baseline. And in the multiple-baseline-across-situations design, changes in the target person's behavior in the situation where the intervention was introduced may lead to changes when the person is in other situations still lacking the intervention. These problems are probably not very common; but if they can be expected, other research designs should be used. (Go to .)

CLOSE-UP

Group-Based Research

Although we've focused so far on single-subject designs, important research on behavior analysis and behavior therapy can be *group-based*, which involves taking observations on many individuals instead of just one or a few and then combining the participants' data rather than examining each person's data separately. Combining data is usually accomplished by computing the average, or *mean*, across participants.

To evaluate whether two or more group means differ, researchers compute complex statistics to evaluate the "significance" of the difference. A *significant difference* indicates that given the pattern of data in each of the groups, the difference in the mean scores is sufficiently great that it probably didn't happen by chance or accident. Keep two things in mind about these statistical procedures. First, the term *significant* describes a mathematical concept and doesn't mean "important." It is possible to find a statistically significant difference between groups even if the outcome has little value. Second, the *average* response across a group of people may be very different from the behavior of any specific individual in the group.

Researchers use a variety of group-based methods to study variables in behavior analysis. When researchers use *experimental methods*, they use a high degree of control to examine differences in the effects of specific conditions by

- Manipulating an independent variable—that is, they determine or control the variable's level or presence.
- Monitoring a dependent variable, looking for changes that correspond to the level of the independent variable.
- Isolating or eliminating unwanted or extraneous variables.

When researchers use *nonexperimental methods*, they do not manipulate an independent variable or don't isolate or eliminate all unwanted or extraneous variables, leaving open the possibility that a factor other than the independent variable caused any observed changes in the dependent variable. Nonexperimental methods are used when it isn't possible or ethical to manipulate a specific independent variable.

Research with experimental and nonexperimental methods can be conducted as between-subjects or within-subjects designs. *Between-subjects designs* involve collecting data on the behavior of many participants who are separated into two or more groups (Sarafino, 2005). Separating the participants into groups can be accomplished in more than one way, and the strategy chosen can determine whether the research methods are viewed as experimental or nonexperimental. In experimental methods, the participants are typically separated into groups by assigning the individuals *randomly*. The term *random* indicates that the assignment of each individual is determined by chance alone; it does not mean "haphazard," which involves a lack of care and deliberation. *Within-subjects* designs test many individuals in more than one condition of the study (Sarafino, 2005). The data collected for all participants in each condition of between-subjects or within-subjects designs are combined, and the results can be revealed with statistics or by doing a graphic analysis.

CHANGING-CRITERION AND ALTERNATING-TREATMENT DESIGNS

Other single-subject research designs that can determine whether an intervention caused changes in behavior divide the intervention phase into subphases in which performance criteria are changed or different treatments are alternated.

Changing-Criterion Designs

A useful approach for demonstrating that intervention techniques caused changes in a behavior is called the **changing-criterion design**. As the name implies, the criterion for successful performance changes over time, usually becoming more rigorous. For instance, when we start the intervention, we may require a fairly lax level of performance for receiving a reward. After the behavior has stabilized at that level, we may raise the criterion to a higher level—and when the behavior stabilizes again, we may raise the criterion again, and so on. If the behavior increases or decreases in accordance with each change in the criterion, we can conclude that the reward is responsible for the behavioral changes.

An example of a changing-criterion design comes from a study of the effects of a token reinforcement system on exercising among 11-year-old obese and nonobese boys (De Luca & Holborn, 1992). Once each boy's pedaling rate on a stationary bicycle had stabilized in baseline, the researchers began to reinforce pedaling in each 30-minute exercise session. The number of pedaling revolutions each boy needed to make for each instance of reinforcement at the start of the intervention was set at about 15% above his average rate in baseline. Each subsequent increased criterion for reward was set at 15% above the average pedaling rate he achieved in the preceding phase. Whenever a boy met a criterion, earning "a point," a bell rang and a light turned on, announcing the success. The points could be exchanged later for material rewards. Figure 3-9 shows the data for two of the six boys in the exercise bicycle study. Notice how their pedaling increased in accordance with

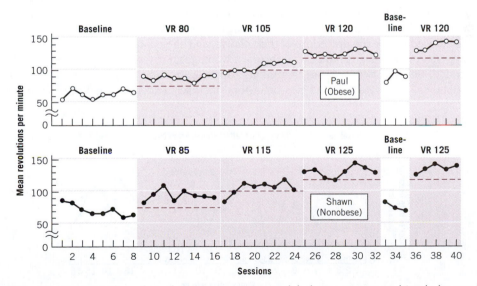

Figure 3-9   Mean (average) number of revolutions per minute pedaled on a stationary bicycle by two boys—Paul, who was obese, and Shawn, who was not obese. (Data for four other boys, not included here, showed similar patterns.) A changing-criterion design was used: Each increased criterion (dashed horizontal lines) was set at 15% above the average pedaling rate the boy achieved in the previous phase. For instance, Paul's criterion increased from 80 to 105 to 120 revolutions for each reward. The second baseline is a reversal phase. *Source:* From R. V. De Luca & S. W. Holborn (1992), Effects of a variable-ratio reinforcement schedule with changing criteria on exercise in obese and nonobese boys. *Journal of Applied Behavior Analysis, 25,* 671–679, Figure 1. Copyright © 1992 Society for the Experimental Analysis of Behavior. Used by permission.

each increase in the criterion for reinforcement. This pattern occurred for all six boys. Although a reversal phase was not essential in the design, the corresponding decrease in pedaling makes the effects of the reinforcement clearer.

Other researchers have used changing-criterion designs to study the effects of consequences introduced for meeting or not meeting specific criteria for smoking fewer and fewer cigarettes (Axelrod, Hall, Weis, & Rohrer, 1974; Belles & Bradlyn, 1987).

Alternating-Treatment Designs

Alternating-treatment designs (also called *simultaneous-treatment* or *multi-element designs*) examine the effects of two or more treatments, each of which is conducted within the same intervention phase with the same person. Although both treatments are applied in the same phase, they are separated in time and alternated. Thus, each treatment might be applied on different days or at different times during the day throughout the intervention phase. By examining graphs of the data, we can determine if one treatment is consistently more effective than another in changing the person's target behavior.

An example of an alternating-treatment design examined the tutoring behaviors of schoolchildren after they were trained in two tutoring procedures to help classmates in spelling (Kohler & Greenwood, 1990). The *standard tutoring procedure* involved having the tutor give the student reinforcers for correct spellings and provide corrective feedback when a word was misspelled. The *modified tutoring procedure* had the tutor use praise and other reinforcers for correct spelling and give corrective feedback as soon as a student gave an incorrect letter in a word. During the intervention phase, the tutors were told which procedure to apply in each tutoring session. The tutoring sessions in all phases were observed for instances of a type of tutoring behavior called *help*, which involved spelling a word *more than once* during corrective feedback for an error. The training the tutors had received had them spell the word only once. Figure 3-10 presents the number of help behaviors per tutoring session by Karen, one of the tutors. Notice that she rarely performed help behaviors in baseline and during the intervention phase when told to use the standard tutoring procedure. But her help behaviors occurred very frequently when she was told to use the modified tutoring procedure during intervention. In the "choice" phase, the tutors were allowed to use the procedure of their choice, and she continued to use help behaviors.

Alternating-treatment designs have two principal advantages. First, as in some other designs, no reversal phases are needed. Second, two or more treatments can be compared to see if one is more effective than another—for instance, a study alternated two behavioral methods to reduce disruptive classroom behaviors

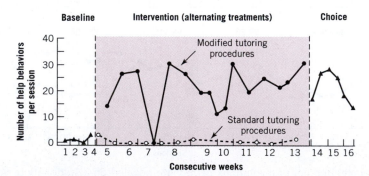

Figure 3-10   Number of "help" behaviors per 10-minute tutoring session by a tutor named Karen, as examined in an alternating-treatment design. Help behaviors were assessed in baseline, during training with two different tutoring procedures in the intervention phase, and later when Karen could use the tutoring procedure of her choice. (Data from two other tutors, not included here, showed similar patterns.) *Source*: From F. W. Kohler & C. R. Greenwood (1990), Effects of collateral peer supportive behaviors within the classwide peer tutoring program. *Journal of Applied Behavior Analysis*, 23, 307–322, Figure 2. Copyright © 1992 Society for the Experimental Analysis of Behavior. Used by permission.

and found that one was more effective than the other (Conyers et al., 2004). However, a problem can arise in alternating-treatment designs that cannot happen with other designs: The effects of the treatments may "interact"—the effect of one of the treatments may be influenced if the participant contrasts it with the second treatment (Barlow & Hayes, 1979; Hains & Baer, 1989). If only one of these treatments had been implemented during the intervention, its effects on behavior might have been different. (Go to .)

EVALUATING THE RESULTING CHANGES IN BEHAVIOR

Until now, we have focused on ways to evaluate the success of interventions in terms of whether and why the target behavior changed. Is that enough? In addition to seeing large graphical or statistical differences in behavior when the intervention was present and absent, we can evaluate the value of intervention techniques on other dimensions.

DIMENSIONS OF EVALUATION

Professionals commonly evaluate three practical dimensions that relate to the behavioral changes the intervention produced: the changed behavior's *generalization and durability*, the behavior's *amount and importance* to the person's everyday life and functioning, and the intervention's *costs versus benefits*.

Generalization and Durability of the Changes

For a behavior change intervention to be viewed as effective and useful, the improved behavior must generalize to the target person's natural environment and must be durable. Thus, people who have learned how to avoid antecedents that lead to an unwanted behavior, such as smoking or drinking, must continue to use these skills in their usual environment. We examine ways to maximize a changed behavior's generalization and durability in Chapter 20. For now, you should know that we can monitor the target behavior to assess the degree to

CONCEPT CHECK 3.4

Check your understanding of the preceding concepts. Remember: The symbol ⇔ means that the answer can vary. Answer the following questions about multiple-baseline, changing-criterion, and alternating-treatment designs.

1. A multiple-baseline design that examines the effects of an intervention to improve three different job skills in a single worker would be using a multiple-baseline-across- _____ design.
2. A multiple-baseline design that examines the effects of an intervention to improve one specific job skill in four workers would be using a multiple-baseline-across- _____ design.
3. A potential problem with multiple-baseline designs is that the behavior may begin to change during _____ .
4. In a changing-criterion design seeking to determine the effects of rewards on lifting weights in an exercise program, we might change the criterion by requiring more _____ . ⇔
5. A study that compares two or more treatments within the same intervention phase is called a(n) _____ design, which is also called a _____ or _____ design.

which each component of the program is critical for maintaining the behavior after the intervention has ended (Rusch & Kazdin, 1981). To evaluate the durability of a behavioral change, behavior analysts conduct follow-up assessments periodically after the intervention ends—if the behavior deteriorates, a posttreatment program may be needed to maintain the gains the intervention produced.

Amount and Importance of the Changes

The *amount of change* an intervention produces in the target person's problem behavior and the *importance of the changes* to the person's everyday life and functioning are critical dimensions in evaluating a program's effectiveness. We discussed earlier in this chapter that the amount of change—that is, the size of an intervention's effect—is greater when the amount of overlap in the data points for baseline and intervention phases is low. In Chapter 2, we saw that responses are especially important to change if they qualify as behavioral cusps, which expose the target person to rich environments, consequences, and learning opportunities. We can also assess these dimensions by considering two outcomes of the behavior change: its clinical significance and its social validity.

The concept of **clinical significance** refers to the degree to which the change in behavior is *meaningful* to the target person's life and functioning; meaningful change is usually defined as *large*, and bringing the behavior into the *normal range* (Jacobson, Follette, & Revenstorf, 1984; Jacobson, Roberts, Berns, & McGlinchey, 1999; Kendall, Marrs-Garcia, Nath, & Sheldrick, 1999; Speer, 1992). As an example, let's consider a hypothetical case of an 8-year-old boy who stutters, on average, about 10% of the syllables he speaks. Suppose that an intervention reduces his stuttering to 6% of his spoken syllables. This would be a large change, but the behavior would not yet be in the normal range. Now suppose that the intervention were continued or strengthened and reduced his stuttering to 3% of his spoken syllables. This level would represent a clinically significant change because it is both large *and* the behavior is within the normal range (Gagnon & Ladouceur, 1992). Determining the normal range can be accomplished in two ways. First, research may have previously identified a *norm* for the behavior—that is, its usual level among a large population of individuals of the same age and gender (Trull, Neitzel, & Main, 1988). Second, the researcher may identify and test a comparison group to assess their average level of the behavior (Dush, Hirt, & Schroeder, 1983).

The second outcome of behavior change that indicates the amount or importance of the change is its **social validity**, the utility and adaptiveness of the change for the target person's everyday functioning (Foster & Mash, 1999). We can evaluate the social validity of a behavior change by collecting data to answer three questions (Wolf, 1978):

1. Are the behavioral goals of the program desired by society and appropriate for the target person's life?
2. Are the target person and significant individuals in his or her life—such as relatives, teachers, or coworkers—satisfied with the amount and utility of the behavioral changes the program has produced?
3. Are the treatment techniques and procedures acceptable to the target person, significant individuals in his or her life, and the community at large?

Answers to these questions can be obtained in several ways (Foster & Mash, 1999). For instance, we can ask for assessments or opinions from relevant individuals—the target persons and significant people in their lives who might be affected by the behavioral changes the program produces (Schwartz & Baer, 1991). We can also have independent judges make evaluations of the person's behavior after the intervention and other aspects of the program (Fawcett & Miller, 1975). And we can examine measures of the outcome that show a clear social impact of the changes, such as improved communication and friendships after reductions in stuttering. For a program to modify delinquent behavior, we might assess social impact in terms of the person's future use of drugs or arrests for criminal activity (Bank et al., 1991). By evaluating the clinical significance and social validity of behavioral changes, we can get a sense of the degree to which the intervention has made a real difference for target persons and people in their lives. (Go to 🐾.)

CASE STUDY

Assessing Social Validity in Reducing a Boy's Tics

Hugh had developed multiple tics at the age of 3 and was 11 years old when he entered a behavioral program to treat this problem (Finney, Rapoff, Hall, & Christophersen, 1983). In the months before beginning the program, there had been an increase in the frequency and intensity of four tics: head shaking, head jerking, mouth grimacing, and eye blinking. The program produced dramatic reductions in the tics within several weeks; follow-up assessments revealed that these improvements continued over the next year.

People commonly seek treatment for tics because of the unusual appearance and social embarrassment these motor behaviors produce. To evaluate the program within a social validity framework, the researchers made videotapes of Hugh during baseline and intervention phases of the treatment. These tapes were rated by two groups of judges: 12 teachers from a junior high school and 36 graduate students in pediatric fields, such as nursing and special education. These judges did not know Hugh, but were chosen because of their regular contact with children of Hugh's age. When the panel rated his tics, using a 7-point scale (1 = not distracting; 7 = very distracting), the average ratings were as follows: about 6.5 for the baseline tapes and 1.6 for the intervention tapes. This assessment of social validity suggests that Hugh's tics became far less embarrassing as a result of this treatment.

Costs and Benefits in Producing the Changes

Lastly, we can evaluate the value of an intervention by assessing its **cost–benefit ratio**, or the extent to which the costs of providing the treatment are outweighed by the money saved in the long run (Jospe, Shueman, & Troy, 1991; Kaplan, 1989). In medical settings, for example, studies have shown that providing behavioral interventions to reduce anxiety enables surgery patients to recover more quickly and use less medication than patients who do not receive these interventions (Sarafino & Smith, 2011). The financial savings in medical costs far exceed the costs of administering these interventions.

PREPARING A REPORT

After an intervention has been completed, the professionals who supervised the project usually write a report to describe the target behaviors, intervention techniques, and outcomes of the program. Often, these reports are published in professional journals; in other cases, they are kept on file in counseling offices or institutions. The outcomes of an applied behavior analysis program are presented in words and graphically, showing data from baseline and intervention phases. When possible, the outcomes should provide data on follow-up assessments, too.

TIPS ON USING GRAPHS AND RESEARCH METHODS

When performing and evaluating an intervention, keep in mind the following helpful tips on using data and conducting research:

1. When collecting data, use interobserver reliability methods (see Chapter 2) for as much of the data as possible—at least 25% is desirable. Let all observers know in advance this will be done.

2. If you are collecting data for research, use a practice period before actual records will be collected. This provides training for the observer and reduces reactivity by the target person.

3. In doing research, use a design that allows you to make a cause–effect conclusion.

4. Before moving from baseline to the intervention, wait for the behavior to stabilize, or reach a fairly constant level, if possible.

5. Keep track of any unusual circumstances, such as sickness, that may have affected the target person's performance. If necessary, add footnotes to the graph to explain peculiar data.

6. Look for problems in the data, such as excessive variability and increasing or decreasing baseline trends.

7. Make sure all tables and graphs that are constructed are neat and accurate. Don't draw any lines freehand—use a ruler.

8. When constructing a graph, sketch it out freehand on scratch paper first to see what it will look like. For the final version, be sure each graph has a vertical axis and a horizontal axis, the axes are scaled and labeled, all data points are in place and accurate, all phases are separated with vertical lines and are labeled, and a caption is included with a figure number.

9. After the intervention has been in force for about a week, do a graphic analysis with trend lines.

(Go to ▤ .)

STUDY AND REVIEW

SUMMARY

To evaluate the success of a behavior change program, behavior analysts compare data from intervention and baseline phases. We can clarify patterns in the data by organizing them in tables, line graphs, bar graphs, and cumulative graphs. Line graphs are the most common way of presenting data from programs in applied behavior analysis because the horizontal axis typically scales units of chronological time, such as days. Graphs should have vertical and horizontal axes, axis scaling and labels, data points, phase lines and labels, and captions. Graphic analysis is a procedure for visually inspecting a graph to determine whether a target behavior changed substantially in an intervention. When the behavioral change is not very obvious, we can clarify the inspection by drawing trend lines and by checking the amount of overlap in baseline and intervention data points. Problems in

CONCEPT CHECK 3.5

Answer the following questions about group-based research and ways to evaluate resulting changes in behavior. Check your understanding of the preceding concepts. Remember: The symbol ⇔ means that the answer can vary.

1. Studies that use _____ methods manipulate an independent variable, eliminate extraneous variables, and randomly assign participants to groups or conditions.

2. An independent variable that might be used in a between-subjects design in applied behavior analysis is _____ . ⇔

3. An example you have seen in everyday life of a person being randomly chosen might be _____ . ⇔

4. A norm for infant or child motor development might describe the age at which most children _____ . ⇔

5. Determining whether an intervention's treatment procedures are acceptable to the person can be part of an evaluation of a program's _____ .

graphic analyses include excessive variability and a baseline trend showing a decrease (for a behavioral excess) or an increase (for a behavioral deficit).

Research using single-subject designs examines behavioral changes over time in one subject at a time, while interventions are either in force or absent. Single-subject designs include the AB, ABA, and ABAB types. AB designs, which consist of a baseline phase and an intervention phase, do not indicate unequivocally whether the intervention caused changes in the behavior. Reversal designs and multiple-baseline designs yield strong evidence for functional relations between an intervention and changes in behavior.

Multiple-baseline designs start baselines for two or more AB designs at about the same time but begin the interventions in sequence, thereby showing patterns of behavior change that correspond to the introduction of the intervention. Multiple-baseline designs can be applied across behaviors, across subjects, and across situations. In changing-criterion designs, the criterion for success changes, generally by becoming increasingly rigorous. When using changing-criterion designs, we can conclude that the intervention is responsible for behavioral changes if the behavior increases or decreases in accordance with criterion changes. Alternating-treatment designs allow the comparison of two or more treatments presented in the same intervention phase. Group-based research collects data on many participants and then combines and compares the data by computing means and complex statistics and by graphic analysis.

Applied behavior analysis interventions can be evaluated also for three practical dimensions. First, the improved behavior should generalize to the person's everyday environment, and it should be durable. Second, the amount and importance of the change in behavior should be substantial, which can be evaluated by assessing the clinical significance of the change and the social validity of the program and its outcomes. Third, programs should strive to have a favorable cost–benefit ratio, saving more money in the long run than they cost.

To prepare for exams, use the following key terms and review questions and the online study guide that's available on this book's companion website at www.wiley.com/college/sarafino.

KEY TERMS

intervention	graphic analysis	multiple-baseline designs
baseline	trend line	changing-criterion design
table	single-subject designs	alternating-treatment designs
graph	AB design	clinical significance
line graphs	reversal designs	social validity
bar graphs	ABA design	cost–benefit ratio
cumulative graphs	ABAB design	

ANSWERS TO CONCEPT CHECKS (CCs)

CC3.1 *Answers*: **1.** baseline **2.** mean **3.** table **4.** line **5.** 25 **6.** axis and scaling labels, phase lines and labels, caption

CC3.2 *Answers*: **1.** graphic analysis **2.** trend **3.** fits/represents **4.** 9, 2, 0, 7, 3 **5.** 9, 8, 6, 6, 5

CC3.3 *Answers*: **1.** single-subject **2.** AB **3.** ABAB **4.** learning to play with others

CC3.4 *Answers*: **1.** behavior **2.** subjects **3.** baseline (before the intervention) **4.** weight or repetitions **5.** alternating treatments, simultaneous-treatment, multi-element

CC3.5 *Answers*: **1.** experimental **2.** amount of reinforcement **3.** a lottery drawing **4.** start to walk without being supported **5.** social validity

REVIEW QUESTIONS

1. What is a data table, and how is it useful?
2. What are line graphs, bar graphs, and cumulative graphs? How are they similar and different from one another?
3. Describe the axes used when presenting graphical data for a behavior change program.
4. Describe in detail how to do a graphic analysis using trend lines. What do we look for in the graphs to decide whether the behavior changed in the intervention?
5. How can we clarify a graphic analysis when the change in behavior is not stark?
6. Define ABAB designs. How are they superior to AB designs in research?
7. What problems can occur with reversal designs?
8. Define the term *multiple-baseline designs*, and indicate how these designs can be carried out across behaviors, subjects, and situations.
9. Describe the research design and results of the study by DeVries, Burnette, and Redmon (1991) to decrease the risk of HIV infection in nurses.
10. Define the term *changing-criterion designs*, and give an example of how such designs might be used in an intervention to improve a child's spelling skills.
11. Define the terms *clinical significance*, *social validity*, and *cost–benefit ratio*.
12. Describe the three questions by which one can assess the social validity of a behavior change program.

RELATED READINGS

- Ciminero, A. R., Calhoun, K. S., & Adams, H. E. (Eds.). (1986). *Handbook of behavioral assessment* (2nd ed.). New York: Wiley.
- Monette, D. R., Sullivan, T. J., & DeJong, C. R. (1990). *Applied social research: Tool for the human services* (2nd ed.). Fort Worth, TX: Holt, Rinehart & Winston.
- Sarafino, E. P. (2005). *Research methods: Using processes and procedures of science to understand behavior.* Upper Saddle River, NJ: Prentice Hall.
- Schwartz, I. S., & Baer, D. M. (1991). Social validity assessments: Is current practice state of the art? *Journal of Applied Behavior Analysis, 24,* 189–204.
- Wolery, M., & Gast, D. L. (1990). Re-framing the debate: Finding middle ground and defining the role of social validity. In A. C. Repp & N. N. Singh (Eds.), *Perspectives on the use of nonaversive and aversive interventions for persons with developmental disabilities.* Sycamore, IL: Sycamore.
- Wolf, M. M. (1978). Social validity: The case for subjective measurement *or* how applied behavior analysis is finding its heart. *Journal of Applied Behavior Analysis, 11,* 203–214.

4

SOME AREAS OF EFFECTIVE APPLICATION

PROLOGUE

Ken was 7 years old when he entered behavior therapy for problems at home and school that were associated with his attention deficit hyperactivity disorder (Oltmanns, Neale, & Davison (1991). His most serious problem behaviors at home were mealtime disruptions, such as kicking his sister under the table and leaving the table during a meal; at school, he was out of his seat far too often. The main behavioral method used in therapy involved a reward system in which, if Ken met the criteria for a day, he could choose from three reinforcers:

playing a game with his parents, extra time watching TV, and a favorite dessert. Ken's teacher and parents kept records of his behavior. In just a few days, his behavior improved markedly, and the program was extended to several less frequent behaviors, such as temper tantrums and fighting.

In this chapter, we discuss some effective, commonly used applications of applied behavior analysis. The interventions were conducted in many settings—such as at home, in school, at jobs, or in therapy—by psychologists and other professionals and have focused on a variety of individuals and behaviors. As you read this material, you'll notice three things. First, the potential for applying behavioral and cognitive methods is almost limitless. Second, some details of how applications were conducted were left out so you could see an overview of each program. We examine the details of behavior change programs in later chapters. Third, behavior change techniques have a promising future built on solid research support developed mainly with single-subject designs like those discussed in Chapter 3. Our overview begins with a look at how methods of applied behavior analysis can improve parenting and parent–child relationships.

PARENTING AND PARENT–CHILD RELATIONSHIPS

Suppose 4-year-old Tim's mother will not buy the junk food he wants while they're shopping, so he sasses her. How will she respond? She may react constructively to dampen his hurtful behavior, or she can aggravate it. She can dampen it by talking with him calmly to explain why she won't buy the food and why his behavior is unacceptable, or she can escalate the encounter by responding in a *coercive*, or dominating, manner—such as by snapping, "You really are a brat today," which can develop into a *coercive pattern* and come to characterize family interactions with one another (Patterson, 1982, 2005). How can parents acquire the skills they need to promote constructive family environments?

TRAINING IN GENERAL PARENTING SKILLS

Teaching parents behavior analysis skills can help change their behavior, which, in turn, fosters improvements in their children's behavior. Parents who learn behavioral methods, such as how to use reinforcement and modeling, are often surprised at how effective these techniques can be. Research has shown that training parents in behavioral methods enables them to deal with a variety of child-rearing concerns, such as getting their children to do household chores or reduce TV watching (Christophersen, Arnold, Hill, & Quilitch, 1972; Wolfe, Mendes, & Factor, 1984).

Modeling and discussion are useful strategies for teaching parents behavior change methods to improve their child-rearing practices; this was demonstrated in research with mothers and their 3- to 5-year-old children (Webster-Stratton, 1982a, 1982b). The mothers received training for 4 weeks, with four 2-hour sessions each week. The training sessions consisted of watching and discussing short, videotaped vignettes of parent models who portrayed either positive or negative social behaviors toward children. Direct observations and surveys after the training revealed substantial improvements in mother–child social interactions and in the children's general behavior. Additional assessments a year later showed that the gains had persisted.

CORRECTING A CHILD'S EXISTING DIFFICULTIES

When parents postpone getting professional help until their child's behavior has become a problem, training parents in behavior change techniques often occurs as part of an effort to correct problems that have already developed. Parent training in these circumstances is very effective in treating many childhood problems, and we'll consider two: children's oppositional behavior and bed-wetting (TFPDPP, 1993).

Oppositional behavior refers to acting in a hostile and contrary manner, such as a child's frequent arguing and fighting, ignoring of rules, and failing to comply with others' requests (Wahler & Dumas, 1984). Oppositional behavior is very distressing and frustrating for parents. Parent training in behavioral methods helped reduce a variety of serious behavior problems in three boys (Wahler, Winkel, Peterson, & Morrison, 1965). We'll discuss the oppositional behavior of a 4-year-old named Eddie who would ignore requests of the parents, who claimed that pleas, threats, or spankings were ineffective in changing his behavior. Observations of Eddie and his mother during 20-minute play sessions revealed two findings. First, the boy made over 200 oppositional responses and only about 30 cooperative responses per session! Second, his mother reacted to his oppositional behavior with disapproval, but she rarely engaged him in positive social activities. The researchers trained her to respond enthusiastically and with a smile (intended as reinforcement) when Eddie was cooperative and to isolate him in an empty room (punishment) for a few minutes each time he showed oppositional behavior. After several play sessions, Eddie's behavior had changed markedly: He now showed over five times as many cooperative responses as oppositional ones.

Subsequent research has shown that the benefits of training parents to apply behavioral methods at home appear to be broad and durable. For instance, studies have found that when parents used behavior change methods to reduce disruptive behavior at home, the children behaved better in other settings, too—such as when shopping, visiting relatives, or in school (McNeil et al., 1991; Sanders & Glynn, 1981). Comprehensive programs to train parents in a variety of skills in managing antecedents and consequences to prevent and correct oppositional behavior in their children have been developed, and evaluations have shown that the benefits of these programs are broad and can last for many years (Long, Forehand, Wierson, & Morgan, 1993; Webster-Stratton, 2005).

Bed-wetting—technically called *nocturnal enuresis*—is defined as wetting the bed at least twice a month after reaching 5 years of age (AMA, 2003; Houts, Berman, & Abramson, 1994). About 15% of American 6-year-olds and 1% of 18-year-olds have bed-wetting problems; only about 15% of children diagnosed with enuresis "outgrow" the problem in a year (Houts, 2003). Although all children start out wetting the bed, most stop by 3 or 4 years of age. Normally, people awaken from sleep when bladder tension reaches a certain limit. If a physical examination of a bed-wetting child shows nothing organically wrong, the enuresis is usually assumed to result from a failure to learn the response of awakening to the antecedent, bladder tension. Two approaches that apply learning principles appear to be effective in helping parents eliminate their children's bed-wetting (Doleys, 1977; Houts, 2003). One approach uses a **urine alarm apparatus** consisting of a liquid-sensitive sheet electrically connected to a loud battery-powered bell or buzzer (Mowrer, 1938). No shock is involved. When urine is released, the bell rings, waking the child. This technique incorporates both operant and respondent conditioning components, as Figure 4-1 diagrams. Treatment success using this apparatus without any other behavioral methods is fairly high: About 75% of children who receive this treatment stop wetting the bed within a few months (Houts, 2003).

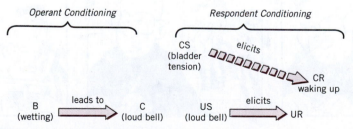

Figure 4-1   Operant and respondent principles applied in a urine alarm apparatus to reduce bed-wetting. In the *operant conditioning* component (left diagram), wetting the bed leads to the sound of a loud bell, which is an aversive consequence that punishes the release of urine. Parents can also provide praise and other rewards for improvement. In the *respondent conditioning* component (right diagram), the child learns to wake up (the CR) when the bladder is tense (the CS), but *before* urine is released. Responding to the CS prevents wetting and enables the child to avoid the aversive bell. *Source:* Based on Sarafino & Armstrong (1986), Figure 7.10.

The second approach for eliminating bed-wetting uses a program of operant conditioning techniques, having the child be an active participant with the parents in the process (Azrin, Hontos, & Besalel-Azrin, 1979; Azrin & Thienes, 1978; Houts, 2003). The operant program includes having the parents wake the child from sleep periodically during the first week or two to prevent "accidents." At each awakening, they provide praise if the bed is dry and encouragement for him or her to use the toilet at that time. If the bed is wet, they make sure the child remakes the bed and changes pajamas. This approach can be quite effective in helping children stop wetting the bed—for instance, one study found that children with enuresis wet the bed an average of over 90% of nights in baseline and less than 25% in the intervention. There is some evidence that combining operant methods and the urine alarm apparatus may be more successful than using either method alone (Doleys, 1977; Houts, Berman, & Abramson, 1994). (Go to .)

CLOSE-UP

Are Rewards Bribes?

Many people think that providing reinforcement for performing appropriate behavior is "bribery." But two arguments can be made against this view. First, dictionary definitions of *bribery* either imply or state that the behavior thus rewarded is unethical or illegal. As psychologists John and Helen Krumboltz have noted:

> Our language contains many words to represent the exchange of services, products, or money. Wage, salary, commission, honorarium, fee, prize, reward, reparation, bribe, ransom, tip, blackmail, pay, and compensation all refer to the exchange of one valuable for another. However, each different word connotes different circumstances. Only if you wish to pervert the judgment of a child or corrupt the conduct of a child could it be said that you are bribing him by offering him some reinforcer. (1972, p. 26)

Second, the reinforcers we apply are not necessarily material things, such as money, that we usually think of as bribes. They can be praise, smiles, or fun activities, too. The cartoon in Figure 4-2 nicely illustrates the distinction between rewards and bribes.

Figure 4-2   The "good-grade incentive money" promised to Funky Winterbean (striped shirt) was intended as a *reward*, probably for studying hard. Funky is proposing to use part of that money as a *bribe* to get Monroe to help him cheat, which is unethical behavior. Note also that the good-grade incentive money was contingent on reaching outcome goals (grades), not on performing the appropriate behavior (studying) for achieving good grades. This illustrates why it is important to make reinforcers contingent on the behavior you're trying to change. *Source:* Funky Winkerbean. Copyright © 1994 Batam, Inc. North American Syndicate, reprinted with special permission of King Features Syndicate.

EDUCATION

Principles of behavior change have been applied effectively in educational settings to improve instructional methods and classroom conduct. Let's see how.

ENHANCING INSTRUCTIONAL METHODS

Angela was sitting at a computer in her kindergarten class and wrote the following story: "I like sprang. Sprang brangs flowers. Berds seng in sprang. I git days off. That is wi I like sprang" (Asbell, 1984). Not a perfect job, but quite remarkable for a 5-year-old! Computers are being used to teach kindergartners language skills, usually by showing them how to spell sounds or syllables, put these together as words, and combine the words into sentences.

The use of computers in classroom instruction has its roots in B. F. Skinner's (1954) concept of **programmed instruction**, a self-teaching process in which students actively learn material presented step-by-step as a series of discrete items with corrective feedback in textbooks or with technological devices. The items build toward overall learning goals, such as being able to spell a body of words or to recite multiplication tables. A more advanced form of programmed instruction, called **computer-assisted instruction (CAI)**, uses a computer to coach students through a series of lessons, much as a human tutor might do. CAI programs explain concepts, give examples, ask questions, give feedback for students' answers, and provide additional explanations if needed. Newer forms of computerized training use CD-ROM and Internet technologies to present material in a highly *interactive* manner. Studies have shown that these teaching methods are very effective, especially when computerized training requires students to be highly active participants, rather than only moderately active or passive participants (Kritch & Bostow, 1998; Ormrod, 1990).

Psychologist Fred Keller (1968) applied behavioral principles to develop an alternative approach to teaching students at the college level. This approach, called the **personalized system of instruction (PSI)**—sometimes called the Keller Plan—divides the course content into units called *modules*, has students study independently the modules presented in textbooks and guides, tests students on each unit when they feel ready, and gives immediate feedback on test performance. Students must master each module, getting a high score—such as 80% correct—on the test, or they must take another test on the same material. Advanced student "proctors" provide tutoring, administer tests, and give feedback, under supervision. Using students as tutors is an important innovation of the PSI approach that has been used effectively in primary and secondary school classrooms (Kohler & Strain, 1990). Peer tutoring is a practical way to give extra help to specific students, individualize the focus of instruction, and enhance the academic and social skills of both the tutee and tutor (Greenwood, Carta, & Kamps, 1990; Greer & Polirstok, 1982). Although the PSI approach has problems, such as mastery criteria and student procrastination, it is gaining popularity in distance learning courses offered on the Internet (Eyre, 2007).

IMPROVING CLASSROOM CONDUCT

Student conduct problems disrupt the class and upset the teacher, such as when students are out of their seats without permission, making noises, fighting, or refusing to follow a teacher's request. What can a teacher do about conduct problems? The answer can be seen in the operant sequence of antecedent, behavior, and consequence.

Researchers examined the role of antecedents on kindergartners' on-task behavior at a preschool during story reading and demonstration activities (Krantz & Risley, 1977). "On-task behavior" was essentially paying attention to the activities and not being disruptive. Two antecedent conditions were studied: the amount of activity the children showed in the periods preceding the activities and the degree of crowding in the seating arrangements during the activities. The researchers found that on-task behavior was far lower when the activities followed a vigorous play period rather than a rest period and when seating during the activities was crowded rather than uncrowded. Antecedents are not always obvious events that appear suddenly before the behavior.

Peer tutoring can enhance the academic and social skills of both parties. *Source:* Stock Foundry/Photolibrary.

Teachers need to watch carefully for antecedents in the classroom that lead to off-task and disruptive behavior so that they can try to alter those antecedents.

Consequences also have strong effects on behavior, and teachers can deploy them quite effectively. One consequence that teachers can employ easily is social attention to students: Teachers can increase students' on-task behavior by praising or paying attention to it, and they could decrease disruptive behavior by not giving it the attention it had received in the past (Becker, Madsen, Arnold, & Thomas, 1972; Madsen, Becker, & Thomas, 1968). A teacher can also improve classroom conduct by using as rewards the opportunity to engage in free-choice activities, such as playing with toys or crafts, when students meet conduct goals (Wasik, 1970).

Using principles of behavior change to reduce classroom misconduct enhances the school environment and has other positive side effects. Teachers who use behavioral methods come to provide more reinforcement and less punishment than other teachers do, and their students show greater gains in academic achievement (Rollins, McCandless, Thompson, & Brassell, 1974). Also, students with conduct problems who participate in a behavior change program to improve their conduct continue in school longer than those who do not participate in such a program (Heaton & Safer, 1982).

INSTRUCTION FOR PEOPLE WITH DEVELOPMENTAL DISABILITIES

The term *developmental disability* refers to significant and broad limitation in learning or performing mental, physical, or social activities that is evident in childhood and continues throughout life (AMA, 2003; Pellegrino, 2007). Although many different disorders may result in developmental disability, the term in this book is used mainly for individuals who were diagnosed with mental retardation or autism. People with mental retardation and autism share many characteristics, particularly a great difficulty in learning almost all skills—motor, cognitive, language, and social. These characteristics greatly influence the choice of target behaviors and behavioral goals, and these individuals need highly structured and well-planned training to learn even simple tasks. Since the 1950s, behavioral methods have provided this kind of training for people with developmental disabilities of all ages and offer the only psychological techniques with well-established success in treating individuals with these disorders (Didden, Duker, & Korzilius, 1997; TFPDPP, 1993).

TRAINING PEOPLE WITH MENTAL RETARDATION

Two respected professional organizations, the American Association on Intellectual and Developmental Disabilities and the American Psychiatric Association, define mental retardation on the basis of two main characteristics: subaverage intellectual functioning and deficiencies in adaptive behavior, such as literacy, interpersonal skills, and personal care (AAIDD, 2011; Kring, Johnson, Davison, & Neale, 2010). In actual practice, people are most often classified as retarded on the basis of IQ—"intelligence quotient"—scores and clinical judgment because tests of adaptive behavior have only recently been fully developed. People's IQ scores are determined by their performance on a standardized intelligence test, usually either the *Wechsler Intelligence Scale for Children* or the *Stanford-Binet Intelligence Scale*. The average IQ score in the general population is 100.

About 3% of individuals in the United States population have mental retardation (Kring, Johnson, Davison, & Neale, 2010), which has four levels:

1. *Mild* (IQ from about 53 to 69): This category includes the large majority—about 85%—of people with retardation. They are sometimes labeled "educable" because they can benefit from special education programs and are usually able to function at about a sixth-grade academic level in adulthood and maintain unskilled jobs.

2. *Moderate* (IQ from about 38 to 52): These individuals constitute about 10% of those with retardation and are sometimes called "trainable." They often have poor motor coordination and are unlikely to advance beyond a second-grade academic level by adulthood.

3. *Severe* (IQ from about 22 to 37): People classified as having severe retardation can learn only very simple tasks and often have serious physical handicaps, too. They are likely to remain very dependent on the help of others throughout life, but many acquire habits of personal cleanliness and perform simple self-help skills.

4. *Profound* (IQ below about 22): These individuals usually have severe physical deformities as well; they require lifelong care and have short life spans.

Many factors can lead to mental retardation. The more serious levels of retardation often stem from abnormal brain development due to genetic disorders, prenatal damage, or diseases. At the less serious levels, particularly among the mildly retarded, there is no detectable brain damage. Because these individuals frequently come from culturally alienated, poverty-stricken families with neglectful and socially immature parents, their retardation may result mainly from environmental deprivation.

Training the mentally retarded requires intensive effort, particularly at the more serious levels of retardation. The behavior analyst must break down tasks into small steps, introduce the antecedents and monitor each student's performance carefully, and provide rewards for correct responding. Using these behavioral methods, these students can learn tasks that are appropriate to their ages and levels of ability (Azrin & Foxx, 1971; Guess, Sailor, Rutherford, & Baer, 1968; Whitman, Mercurio, & Caponigri, 1970). For example, many adult mothers with mental retardation can learn basic child-care skills, such as bathing their babies, cleaning baby bottles, and treating diaper rash (Feldman et al., 1992). (Go to 🐾.)

TRAINING CHILDREN WITH AUTISM

Autism is a developmental disorder characterized by an early onset, severe deficits in social and language behaviors, and excesses in disruptive and attentive behaviors. Its symptoms appear in the child's first three years; the disorder afflicts about 1 in 750 children and is much more common among boys than girls (Kring, Johnson, Davison, & Neale, 2010; Lovaas & Smith, 2003). For children like Sam in the case study, behavior analysts begin training with the simplest of tasks, building skills from one task to the next (Lovaas, 1977; Lovaas & Smith, 2003). Children with autism learn slowly and with great difficulty. Tasks must be presented many, many times. Individual instruction, a great deal of structure, and immediate feedback with rewards for correct performance are necessary.

In Sam's case, training for his many behavioral deficits started with developing eye contact with the teacher (Oltmanns, Neale, & Davison, 1991). A teacher might have begun by saying, "Look at me," and rewarding a

CASE STUDY

Sam—A Child With Autism

Although Sam seemed to be developing normally in his first year or so, by his second birthday his parents were becoming concerned (Oltmanns, Neale, & Davison, 1991). For instance, Sam's motor development slowed (his sister's had been more rapid) and

> seemed uneven. He would crawl normally for a few days and then not crawl at all for awhile. Although he made babbling sounds, he had not developed any speech and did not even seem to understand anything his parents said to him. Simple commands such as "Get the ball," "Come," or "Do you want a cookie?" elicited no response. (p. 248)

At first, his parents thought Sam might be deaf. They consulted his pediatrician, who suggested mental retardation as a possibility. When Sam was nearly 3 years old, his

> parents also began to notice him engaging in more and more behavior that seemed strange and puzzling. Most obvious were his repetitive hand movements. Many times each day he would suddenly flap his hands for several minutes. Other times he rolled his eyes around in their sockets. He still did not speak, but he made smacking sounds and sometimes he would burst out into laughing for no apparent reason. (pp. 248–249)

Sam's social and play behavior were also worrisome to his parents. For instance, he would let them hug him, but acted indifferently to their attention and wouldn't look at them. He didn't play with his sister, and his solitary play also seemed deviant. If he had a toy car, for example, he wouldn't pretend to drive it around, as other children do. He'd turn it over and spin its wheels incessantly.

After a physical and neurological examination revealed no detectable defect, a psychiatrist examined Sam, diagnosed him as having autism, and recommended that he attend a special school for treatment. Like many schools for severely disordered children, the school he attended used behavioral methods to provide training.

primitive response that improves over time, becoming more and more like the requested act. After Sam learned eye contact, his training during his first year involved learning to imitate simple behaviors ("Sam, stretch your arms up like this."), point to named objects in pictures ("This is an orange. Point to the orange."), imitate simple speech sounds ("Say this, *ah*."), use the toilet, and dress and undress himself. Progress for children with autism usually is very slow. By the end of the first year, Sam could point correctly to only 38 named objects when presented in pairs, such as an orange and a cat.

Children with autism also exhibit many behavioral excesses that must be reduced or eliminated to make treatment accessible (Schreibman, Charlop, & Kurtz, 1992). One of these behaviors is called *repetitive/ritualistic behaviors* (or *self-stimulation*), which may consist of rocking back and forth, flapping the hands, spinning objects with the fingers, and so forth for long periods of time. The reason for these behaviors is unknown, but one possibility is that they produce internal perceptual stimuli that are reinforcing (Lovaas, Newsom, & Hickman, 1987). Behavioral methods have been successful in reducing self-stimulation in autistic children (Lovaas, Koegel, Simmons, & Long, 1973). Another behavioral excess many of these children show is *self-injurious behavior*, in which they engage in activities that are destructive to their bodies, such as smashing their heads against a wall or biting their arms. A third behavioral excess is called *echolalia*, which consists of mimicking what others say. For instance, if asked, "Do you want some candy?" they'd respond, "Do you want some candy?" Table 4.1 presents a list of common behavioral deficits and excesses that programs for children with autism must address. Some of these children display virtually all of these behavioral problems, and some show only some.

Table 4.1   *Common Behavioral Deficits and Excesses Among Children With Autism at the Start of Treatment*

Behavioral Deficits	Behavioral Excesses
Show no interest in other people, including parents or peers	Repetitive/ritualistic acts
Reject physical affection or play, such as tickling	Self-injurious behavior
Avoid eye contact	Echolalia
Poor or nonexistent language development	Tantrums
Poor cognitive skills; low IQ	Aggression
Lack of attention to surroundings	
Lack of normal play behaviors	
Lack of self-care skills, such as dressing	

Sources: Kring, Johnson, Davison, & Neale (2010); Lovaas & Smith (2003); Rutter & Garmezy (1983).

A Model Intervention for Children With Autism

Interventions using applied behavior analysis for children with autism advance through a series of stages. One such program was established at the University of California, Los Angeles (UCLA) by O. Ivar Lovaas, a pioneer in treating autism. Most of the children receive one-to-one training sessions for 40 hours a week for about 3 years (Lovaas & Smith, 2003). The program follows five stages; the early stages provide the foundation for later ones, as you'll see in the next paragraphs.

Stage 1 establishes a teaching relationship, which usually takes 2 to 4 weeks. The first session is almost always very difficult because these children typically have learned to avoid challenging interactions with people, such as teaching situations, by attending to other things or performing tantrums or self-injurious behavior when pressed to continue in the session. The behavior analyst cannot allow the session to be disrupted and, instead, requests that the child perform a simple action he or she can probably do successfully, such as to put a block in a pail. By guiding the action and reinforcing its completion each time, the behavior analyst maintains control and increases the child's attentiveness and compliance. In subsequent sessions, the program adds requests for other actions the child can do and reinforces each one. Once the child attends to the teacher and complies fairly consistently in each session, the program advances to the next stage.

Stage 2 teaches foundation skills, which usually takes 1 to 4 months. The skills include imitating simple actions, such as clapping or waving, that the behavior analyst models; matching and sorting objects according to simple features, such as color or size; completing puzzles; and performing self-care actions, such as putting on a shirt. Then the child learns to perform these behaviors on command and to discriminate among requests, such as waving only when the behavior analyst says, "Wave," or approaching when the request is, "Come here," and not confusing the commands.

Stage 3 focuses on simple communication skills (usually taking 6 months or more). In this stage, the children continue to learn foundation and self-care skills, but they begin to work on speaking: imitating speech sounds, full words, and short phrases. Mastery of verbal imitation is a major predictor of these children's eventual level of achievement, and only half of them master this skill in the first few months. Children in this stage also learn to name everyday objects, such as saying "Ball" when one is shown to them, and retrieve a requested object.

Stage 4 expands communication skills and begins peer interaction (about 1 year). The children learn abstract concepts, such as big/little, and learn to speak in grammatically correct sentences. They also begin attending preschool classes with normally developing children; this introduction is gradual, often starting with only several minutes a day. To prepare for this introduction, the children are taught some games and activities, such as "Ring Around the Rosie," they will encounter in school.

Stage 5 promotes advanced communication and adjustment to school (about 1 year). The children learn to use pronouns, prepositions, and past tense in their speech and to comprehend stories. They also learn how to make appropriate requests for help and to converse with and understand the perspective of others. Although much of the instruction is still carried out on a one-to-one basis, the children are taught how to work more and more independently and to learn while in the group settings of classrooms.

How Effective Are Interventions for Autism?

The effectiveness of interventions for autism depends on how intensive the training is. For individuals with autism who get little or no training, almost all have poor prognoses for functioning in adulthood, and many are confined to hospitals (Kring, Johnson, Davison, & Neale, 2010). But the prospects are much better for children who receive intensive training, particularly those who learn to speak by 6 years of age. Research comparing children in the UCLA program we just described with other children with autism who received either minimal training (less than 10 hours a week) or only special education classes showed that IQ scores increased substantially for most of the children in the UCLA program but did not increase at all for the children who received less intensive treatment (Lovaas & Smith, 2003). Most individuals diagnosed with autism who show substantial gains with intensive treatment will not require residential care as adults, and some will be able to attend college, hold jobs, and support themselves (Kring, Johnson, Davison, & Neale, 2010). (Go to 🖥.)

HEALTH AND SPORTS

Since the late 1970s, psychologists have become increasingly involved in efforts to promote physical health, treat illness, and improve athletic performance. Let's look at the basis for this involvement and some methods that help.

HEALTH PSYCHOLOGY

If you became really sick, what would you do to get better? One thing you might do is see your physician—that certainly would be a good idea. We typically think of illness as an affliction of the body that results from injury, biochemical imbalances, or bacterial or viral infection that physicians can treat.

In recent years, we have become aware that psychological and behavioral patterns can also affect whether we get sick and how quickly we recover from an illness. For instance, we know that our health can be harmed if we experience long-term intense stress, smoke cigarettes, have a physically inactive lifestyle, eat diets that are

CONCEPT CHECK 4.1

Check your understanding of the preceding concepts. Remember that answers are given at the end of the chapter, and that the symbol ⇔ following a question means the book's answers are suggestions—you may have other, equally correct answers. Answer the following questions about applications to improve parent–child relationships, education, and training children with developmental disabilities.

1. An example of a child's oppositional behavior is _____ . ⇔
2. The urine alarm apparatus uses _____ conditioning to stop children's bed-wetting.
3. A behavioral instructional approach that divides class material into small units and gives immediate feedback on test performance is called _____ . ⇔
4. A person who is described as "trainable" is probably classified at the _____ level of mental retardation.
5. A behavioral deficit and a behavioral excess in the case study of Sam that might have suggested he had autism are, respectively, _____ and _____ .

high in fat and low in fiber, have unsafe sex, drive when intoxicated, and fail to perform treatments a physician prescribes. These examples illustrate that health and illness result from the interplay of biological, psychological, and social aspects of life. This perspective is called the *biopsychosocial model* of health and illness (Engel, 1977, 1980). The idea that medicine and psychology are linked led to a combined field; **health psychology** is a field of psychology that examines the causes of illness and ways to promote and maintain health, prevent and treat illness, and improve health-care systems (Sarafino & Smith, 2011). Two similar fields are called *behavioral medicine* and *psychosomatic medicine*.

Principles of behavior change have been applied effectively to *promote health and prevent illness or injury* in an enormous variety of ways, and we'll look at three. First, we all know that smoking, heavy drinking, and drug abuse can harm our health. One method that helps people quit using a substance is providing rewards for stopping. Compared to treatments that don't use reinforcement, treatments that do are more successful in reducing the use of tobacco, alcohol, and a variety of drugs (Higgins, Heil, & Lussier, 2004). The rewards have been mainly monetary based—for instance, vouchers that could be exchanged for desirable items. Second, programs have been conducted to increase people's physical activity, which benefits health. Interventions implemented to promote exercise are especially effective when they include behavioral methods to modify the antecedents and consequences of physical activity (Sallis & Owen, 1999).

The third application we will consider is a behavior change program to reduce the risk of infection with the AIDS human immunodeficiency virus (HIV) among nurses in high-risk hospital situations (DeVries, Burnette, & Redmon, 1991). The target behavior was wearing rubber gloves in hospital activities where there was a high likelihood of contact with a patient's body fluids. If the patient is infected with HIV, wearing gloves reduces nurses' risk of becoming infected. The intervention consisted of giving nurses biweekly feedback regarding when they had and had not worn the gloves in the prior 2 weeks, praising them for using gloves, and encouraging them to wear gloves in the future. This program produced a large increase in nurses' use of protective gloves in high-risk hospital situations. But programs like this one need to be repeated periodically because their effects fade over time (Vincent, 2003). Many other interventions using behavioral methods for health promotion have also been successful—for example, by helping many people improve their diets, use seat belts, and reduce stress in their lives (Sarafino & Smith, 2010).

Not only can behavior change techniques help in promoting health when people are well, they also can *enhance the medical treatments* patients receive when they are ill. For instance, many patients do not adhere to their physician's recommendations as closely as they should, and behavioral methods have been applied effectively to increase patients' *adherence* to their medical treatment (Sarafino & Smith, 2011). Some of these methods involve altering the behavior's antecedents—for instance, patients are more likely to take their medication if they have reminders or cues, such as an alarm, to do it and if taking medicine coincides with their habits and rituals, as when pills are taken at meals. Adherence to treatment also improves when reinforcers are contingent on performing the behavior. Behavioral methods have improved treatment adherence in patients with many different medical conditions, including asthma (Sarafino, 1997) and diabetes (Lowe & Lutzker, 1979).

Principles of behavior change can also enhance medical treatment by reducing the anxiety of hospitalized patients who are awaiting surgery; those with high anxiety tend to stay in the hospital longer and use more medication for pain during recovery than patients with less preoperative anxiety (Anderson & Masur, 1983). A study demonstrated the benefits of modeling techniques for children who were awaiting surgeries that were not life threatening (Melamed & Siegel, 1975). One group of children saw a film that showed the experiences of a hospitalized boy, and the other group saw a film about a boy going on a trip to the country. The children who saw the film about the hospitalized boy had less anxiety before and after surgery than those who saw the other film. Children who receive this kind of intervention before surgery recover more quickly than children who do not receive it (Pinto & Hollandsworth, 1989).

SPORT PSYCHOLOGY

Sport psychology is a discipline that examines relationships between psychological factors and athletic activities and skill (May & Meyers, 2004). Research has shown that using behavioral methods enhances athletic performance (Gee, 2010). For instance, having coaches provide feedback on specific skills and praise for good performance improves the skills of athletes in martial arts and basketball (Harding et al., 2004; Kladopoulos & McComas, 2001). Modeling and reinforcement for better performance are effective in improving a wide range of athletic skills among individuals who do and do not already possess good skills (Donahue, Gillis, & King, 1980; Scott, Scott, & Howe, 1998; Whelan, Mahoney, & Meyers, 1991). Technical advances in video and computer equipment can make modeling and feedback more precise (Franks & Maile, 1991).

EMPLOYMENT AND COMMUNITY SETTINGS

Edward Feeney (1972) was working for an air freight business as a vice president when he introduced praise and other reinforcers for good worker performance and saved the company millions of dollars. Applying behavioral methods at worksites—such as business firms and human service agencies—is called *organizational behavior management* (Frederiksen & Lovett, 1980).

Organizational behavior management focuses on changing behavior by altering its antecedents and consequences and by teaching new actions through instructions and modeling (Brown, 1982; Luthans & Kreitner, 1985). One frequent outcome goal in using these methods is to save money, either by reducing losses or by increasing productivity. For example, a large grocery store used behavioral methods to reduce thefts (Carter, Holmström, Simpanen, & Melin, 1988), and factories reduced tardiness (Hermann et al., 1973) and absenteeism (Pedalino & Gamboa, 1974). Improving worker safety is another goal that has been addressed successfully by modifying employee behavior to decrease accidents and exposure to toxic chemicals (Alvero & Austin, 2004; Hopkins et al., 1986; Komaki, Barwick, & Scott, 1978; Nielsen, Sigurdsson, & Austin, 2009).

In the general community, behavioral methods are often applied to benefit large portions of the population. For example, changing the antecedents and consequences of target behaviors has reduced electric energy use (Becker, Rabinowitz, & Seligman, 1980) and improved motorists' seat belt use in vehicles (Ludwig & Geller, 1991) and stopping and caution at stop signs (Van Houten & Retting, 2001).

Applications of behavior analysis at worksites can use convenient parking spaces and public recognition of good work as rewards. *Source*: Ilene MacDonald/Alamy Limited.

SELF-MANAGEMENT: CHANGING ONE'S OWN BEHAVIOR

Do you wish you could study more, or eat a healthier diet, or stop biting your nails, or stop complaining so much? If you have tried to change these or other behaviors in the past and failed, you probably lacked the skills to help you succeed. We learn behavior change skills, and applying these skills to modify one's own behavior is called **self-management**, or *self-modification* (Malott, 2005; Sarafino, 2011). The techniques used in self-management derive from those used in applied behavior analysis and behavior modification, such as changing the antecedents and consequences of the target behavior, and include both behavioral and cognitive methods.

BENEFITS OF SELF-MANAGEMENT

By learning self-management techniques, people can strengthen two general abilities:

1. *Self-control* is the ability to *exercise restraint* over our emotions, impulses, or desires. For instance, people with self-control can resist temptation or delay gratification when they want something.

2. *Self-regulation* is the ability to *direct* and *modulate* our own actions and behave appropriately even when our actions are not being monitored by someone else.

Chances are, you called your lack of these abilities "no willpower" when you didn't succeed in changing your behavior in the past. These two abilities often overlap, but self-regulation involves a broader set of skills that may require the person to have strong skills in self-control. That is, people who can control their impulses, such as deciding not to socialize the night before a big exam, are better able to modulate their actions and behave appropriately, such as staying home and studying.

Self-management has been applied extensively and with considerable success. When used in behavior therapy, the therapist and client design the self-management program together, and the client carries it out. For example, self-management programs helped several men reduce their hard-driving, Type A behavior and increase the time they spent relaxing after dinner (Nakano, 1990). What's more, students have learned and applied behavior change techniques successfully in college courses for many years, achieving the goals of their self-management projects (Hamilton, 1980) and being satisfied with the behavioral changes they achieve (Barrera & Glasgow, 1976). The behaviors people can change in self-management projects are quite diverse—for example, they have increased exercising (Kau & Fischer, 1974) and reduced tooth grinding (Pawlicki & Galotti, 1978).

SELF-MANAGEMENT FOR CHILDREN WITH DEVELOPMENTAL DISABILITIES

Efforts are being made to train children with developmental disabilities in skills to self-manage their own behavior under parental supervision. For children with autism, for example, the parents (Schreibman & Koegel, 2005):

*   Help the child to choose and define a target behavior and to identify a reinforcer for appropriate behavior.
*   Teach the child to identify when a behavioral excess has occurred, or when a behavioral deficit did not occur but should have.
*   Teach the child to record data for the behavior, giving reinforcement for accurate recording.
*   Phase out their direct involvement, allowing the child more and more independence in self-managing the behavior.

To carry out these steps, the parents receive careful training in procedures for teaching their child self-management skills. The parents' training continues until they have carried out the steps with their child for two target behaviors. For the next 12 months, periodic assessments are made to determine whether the children are continuing to use the self-management procedures successfully. (Go to ▮.)

CONCEPT CHECK 4.2

Answer the following questions about applications in health and sports, employment and community settings, and self-management.

1. The idea that health and illness result from the interplay of biological, psychological, and social processes is called the _____ model.
2. The text discusses how behavioral methods can increase patients' adherence to doctor-prescribed behaviors, such as taking medicine. A prescribed behavior not discussed in the text that might respond to behavioral methods is _____ . ⇔
3. Applying behavioral methods in business and industry is called _____ .
4. A 16-year-old's behavior that would be an example of self-control is _____ . ⇔
5. True or false: Students' self management projects generally succeed in changing their behavior. _____

STUDY AND REVIEW

SUMMARY

Principles of behavior change can be applied effectively to improve behavior in many spheres of everyday life. Parents can be trained in behavioral methods to improve their parenting skills and reduce behavior problems of their children. For instance, by altering antecedents and consequences, they can decrease their children's oppositional behavior; and by using a urine alarm apparatus and operant conditioning techniques, they can decrease their children's bed-wetting.

In educational settings, behavioral methods can make instruction more effective through the techniques of programmed instruction, computer-assisted instruction (CAI), and the personalized system of instruction (PSI). These educational approaches divide course material into small units and give immediate feedback on test performance. Behavioral methods are also useful in helping teachers decrease class disruptions and increase students' attention to class activities.

The target behaviors and behavioral goals used in training the developmentally disabled are geared to each individual's abilities. Many of these individuals are classified into one of four levels of mental retardation: mild, moderate, severe, and profound. Other people with markedly impaired learning abilities are classified as autistic. The training these individuals receive stresses the use of behavioral methods to help these people acquire basic self-help skills, language and social behaviors, and, sometimes, vocational skills.

Professionals in the field of health psychology apply behavioral methods toward the promotion of human health—such as in helping people to increase their physical activity and to stop smoking or using drugs—and enhancing medical treatment. In other effective behavior change applications, professionals in sport psychology have used behavioral methods to improve athletes' skills, and employers have used behavioral methods to improve workers' productivity and safety in organizational behavior management programs. People can apply behavioral and cognitive methods in a self-management program to change their own behavior and improve their self-control and self-regulation.

To prepare for exams, use the following key terms and review questions and the online study guide that's available on this book's companion website at www.wiley.com/college/sarafino.

KEY TERMS

urine alarm apparatus
programmed instruction
computer-assisted instruction (CAI)

personalized system of instruction
   (PSI)
autism

health psychology
sport psychology
self-management

ANSWERS TO CONCEPT CHECKS (CCs)

CC4.1 *Answers:* **1.** disobeying rules **2.** operant and respondent **3.** programmed instruction, CAI, or PSI **4.** moderate **5.** no speech at all [and] self-stimulation behavior (spinning wheel)

CC4.2 *Answers:* **1.** biopsychosocial **2.** reducing dietary fat **3.** organizational behavior management **4.** refusing to have sex, particularly without using a condom **5.** true

REVIEW QUESTIONS

1. In the study (Wahler et al., 1965) on oppositional behavior with a boy named Eddie, he performed about seven times more oppositional than cooperative responses when playing with his mother. In terms of operant conditioning, why did he do this?

2. Describe the operant and respondent conditioning processes in the urine alarm apparatus reducing bed-wetting.

3. What are the processes and characteristics of programmed instruction?

4. Describe the four levels of mental retardation.

5. Name five self-help skills one would probably need to teach a 7-year-old girl with autism or moderate mental retardation who had received little special training.

6. Describe three types of reminders or cues, other than alarms, health psychologists might suggest as antecedents to help patients' adherence in taking medication.

RELATED READINGS

* Karoly, P., & Kanfer, F. H. (Eds.). (1982). *Self-management and behavior change: From theory to practice.* New York: Pergamon.

* Krumboltz, J. D., & Krumboltz, H. B. (1972). *Changing children's behavior.* Englewood Cliffs, NJ: Prentice-Hall.

* Luthans, F., & Kreitner, R. (1985). *Organizational behavior modification and beyond: An operant and social learning approach.* Glenview, IL: Scott, Foresman.

* Sarafino, E. P. (2011). *Self-management: Using behavioral and cognitive principles to manage your life.* Hoboken, NJ: Wiley.

* Sarafino, E. P., & Smith, T. W. (2011). *Health psychology: Biopsychosocial interactions.* (7th ed.). Hoboken, NJ: Wiley.

* Sulzer-Azaroff, B., Drabman, R. M., Greer, R. D., Hall, R. V., Iwata, B. A., & O'Leary, S. G. (Eds.). (1988). *Behavior analysis in education.* Lawrence, KS: Society for the Experimental Analysis of Behavior.

5

REINFORCEMENT: POSITIVE AND NEGATIVE

PROLOGUE

In the 1890s, Edward L. Thorndike (1898) conducted a study comparing the learning processes in animals, including 13 cats and 3 dogs. For each trial, he placed an animal in an enclosed apparatus called a "puzzle box" that had a latch that would open a door, enabling release from the box. The animals were hungry, and food was placed outside that they could see and maybe smell. By observing each animal's actions very carefully, Thorndike noticed two aspects of their learning to escape the box that were consistent for each species.

What did he notice? First, unlike the dogs, the cats seemed more interested in gaining release to escape confinement than to get food. Second, the behavior of the cats and dogs appeared to follow a pattern of "trial and error" across trials: the time it took each animal to escape decreased *gradually* from trial to trial. They didn't suddenly "discover" a solution. Even after several successful escapes, the animals would not run to and trigger the latch immediately on being put in the box, but seemed to trigger it eventually while engaging in other activities. From findings in this and other research, Thorndike (1911) later proposed the Law of Effect: "satisfying consequences," such as rewards or escape from unpleasant circumstances, strengthen stimulus–response connections gradually in the process of learning.

B. F. Skinner (1938) later studied learning processes in animals with an apparatus, often called the Skinner box, that had partway up a wall a lever projecting out and a tray below. When a hungry rat depressed the lever, a pellet of food dropped into the tray, which the animal could access. The food was used as a reward, which Skinner called a "reinforcer," for the behavior of pressing the lever. Using this procedure and apparatus, Skinner demonstrated many features of reinforcement and its importance in learning.

This chapter describes what reinforcement is and its importance in learning and changing behavior. We'll discuss the main types of reinforcers and factors that affect how effective they are in modifying behavior.

DEFINING REINFORCEMENT

To *reinforce* means to strengthen, increase, or make more pronounced. In operant conditioning, **reinforcement** refers to the process in which a consequence of a behavior strengthens that behavior, making it more likely to occur in the future. The consequence is *contingent on* the behavior—that is, the consequence occurs if the behavior does. The object or event that serves as the consequence in reinforcement is called a **reinforcer**, a stimulus that is introduced or changed when the behavior occurs. Because reinforcement strengthens a behavior, measurement of that behavior in the future should show reduced latency or increased frequency, duration, or magnitude. If we provide a consequence for a behavior and the person does not perform it at least as quickly, frequently, persistently, or intensely, we have no evidence that our consequence was a reinforcer.

Loosely speaking, a reinforcer is something the person (or animal) "wants" or finds "pleasant" or "satisfying." Although we previously used the terms *reinforcer* and *reward* as synonyms, which they usually are, *reward* is a less precise term with excess meanings. For instance, we tend to think of a reward as an obvious event, such as a prize or special payment for doing something extraordinary, such as giving authorities information that leads to an arrest in a crime. But reinforcers can be very subtle events we may notice fleetingly or not at all, as when we push a switch to illuminate a room, say a series of words that matches our intention, or smile at an attractive person who then starts to converse with us. We probably wouldn't call the consequences of our behavior in these examples "rewards." Also, objects or events we call rewards are usually stimuli most people find pleasant or satisfying, but this isn't true of all reinforcers. The type of music called polkas is not very popular in most of the world and might not be a reinforcer for your turning on a radio, but some people like it, and their turning on a radio would be reinforced if they heard it. Because *reinforcer* is a more precise term, it is used more frequently than *reward* in the rest of this book.

NATURAL AND PROGRAMMED REINFORCEMENT

If you think about the reinforcers mentioned so far in this book, you'll notice that some of them occur in our everyday lives without being planned or contrived to influence our behavior, such as when pushing a switch illuminates a room or smiling at someone leads to a desired conversation. The consequences—illumination and conversation—are not provided for the purpose of increasing our switch pushing or smiling behavior. Such consequences are called **natural reinforcers** because they happen spontaneously as a normal part of everyday events and are *not planned and given systematically* to affect a behavior, even though they do. Thus, to the extent that our smiling at someone results in desired conversation, we will continue or increase that behavior in the future. Here are some other examples of natural reinforcers:

- Telling a joke is reinforced by the enjoyment other people express.
- In a sequence of movements, such as writing a word, actions are reinforced by sensory feedback that we are doing it correctly and the ability to move on to the next task when this one is done.
- Reading labels on file folders is reinforced by accessing needed material.
- Eating food is reinforced by its good taste and hunger reduction.

A special case of natural reinforcement is **automatic reinforcement**, in which a behavior produces a reinforcer directly, without other people playing a role (Piazza et al., 2002; Vollmer, 1994). Examples include scratching an itch and making a sound that is pleasing to oneself, as babies seem to do when they babble while alone. Some evidence suggests that automatic reinforcement can maintain the repetitive/ritualistic behavioral excesses, such as flapping the hands, of children with autism as well as the "nervous habits," such as nail biting and hair pulling, of other people (Iwata et al., 1982; Rapp et al., 1999).

In contrast, other reinforcers in our lives are provided deliberately with the goal of influencing our behavior. We saw an example of deliberate reinforcement in the opening story of Chapter 3: Jeremy's mother provided praise and snacks when his public speaking skills showed improvements in tutoring sessions. Consequences we'll call **programmed reinforcers** are provided within a program of reinforcement with the goal of increasing or strengthening specific behaviors. Everyday examples of programmed reinforcers are high grades for good work in school and wages for satisfactory work on a job. Other examples of programmed reinforcers are the rewards behavior analysts use in teaching social skills to children with autism, health psychologists provide in stop-smoking interventions, employers use to promote worker safety, or you might provide yourself in a self-management project to increase your studying.

POSITIVE AND NEGATIVE REINFORCEMENT

Reinforcement involves a sequence of events: A behavior is followed by a consequence, and the sequence can take two patterns, *positive* and *negative*. In **positive reinforcement**, the consequence involves presenting or *adding* a stimulus, called a **positive reinforcer**, after the individual has performed the response. Almost all the rewards mentioned so far in this book have been examples of positive reinforcers, including hearing songs we like by turning on a radio, social reactions to our telling a joke, and the praise and snacks Jeremy's mother gave him for his improvements in public speaking.

When the *negative* pattern occurs, a stimulus is *subtracted*—for example, if a boy has a tantrum in a store because his mother refused to buy him candy, and she relents, the tantrum *stops*. In this example, both people's behavior received reinforcement. The boy's tantrum behavior resulted in positive reinforcement (candy), but the mother's behavior of relenting also got reinforced: The tantrum, an *aversive stimulus*, stopped (was subtracted). The mother's relenting received negative reinforcement, making her more likely to relent for future tantrums. In **negative reinforcement**, the consequence of the behavior—in this case, relenting and buying candy—involves *decreasing* or *removing* an aversive stimulus, the tantrum. Here are some other examples of behaviors that receive negative reinforcement:

- Drinking alcohol to reduce unpleasant feelings
- Taking aspirin to decrease physical pain, such as from headaches or arthritis
- Eating food to reduce feelings of hunger
- Employing an umbrella while outside to stop getting wet when rain begins falling

In the opening story about Thorndike's research with the puzzle box, the cats' behavior of using the latch to open the door was probably negatively reinforced by gaining release from the box.

Many people have a hard time understanding negative reinforcement; sometimes they confuse it with punishment. One reason for the confusion is that negative reinforcement and punishment both involve aversive stimuli, which we tend to link with some types of punishment. But in punishment, the aversive stimulus, such as a scolding, occurs *after* the behavior on which it is contingent; in negative reinforcement, the aversive stimulus is present *before* the behavior that removes it. Another reason for confusions about negative reinforcement is that the word *negative* could suggest the process or the behavior is undesirable, but it doesn't: The words *positive* and *negative* are used in the arithmetic sense—that is, *positive* means plus (+) and *negative* means minus (–). Thus, in describing reinforcement, *positive* indicates that a stimulus is *added* and *negative* means a stimulus is *subtracted*, or removed. Positive and negative reinforcement each result in a relatively desirable state of affairs for the recipient: In our tantrum example, the child got candy, and his mother got an end to the tantrum. Unfortunately, both of them learned things that make the child's tantrums and the mother's relenting more likely in the future.

UNCONDITIONED AND CONDITIONED REINFORCEMENT

Some consequences can serve as reinforcers as a result of inborn processes, probably because they promote survival of each individual and the species. These consequences are called **unconditioned reinforcers** (or *primary reinforcers*) because they function as reinforcers even when the individual has had no learning history with them. Examples of unconditioned reinforcers include food, water, warmth, and the reduction of pain when the individual is, respectively, hungry, thirsty, cold, or in pain.

In contrast, **conditioned reinforcers** (or *secondary reinforcers*) are stimuli that did not have the ability to strengthen behavior until they became reinforcing as a result of learning. This learning involves a stimulus–stimulus relationship that develops when the nonreinforcing stimulus is paired repeatedly with an existing reinforcer (Kimble, 1961). For example, animal trainers often develop conditioned reinforcers to make rewards more easily and quickly available when teaching tricks. They do this by repeatedly presenting a nonreinforcing stimulus, such as a sound, together with an unconditioned reinforcer, such as food, when the animal responds correctly in training. Eventually, the sound itself becomes a reinforcer—a conditioned reinforcer. Money is an example of a conditioned reinforcer, and it probably developed its ability to strengthen behavior for you by being associated with other stimuli that were already reinforcing, such as when you or your parents paid for food or clothing. Other examples of conditioned reinforcers include praise, television shows or music we like, good grades in school, fashionable clothing, access to the Internet, games, hobby activities, and jewelry. (Go to 🔍 and then 🗐.)

TYPES OF POSITIVE REINFORCERS

Reinforcers have a powerful impact on a person's behavior if they are carefully chosen. To choose reinforcers for an intervention to change operant behavior, we must be aware of the types of reinforcers available. In this section, we'll consider several different but somewhat overlapping categories of positive reinforcers. Most potential rewards belong to one or more of these categories.

TANGIBLE AND CONSUMABLE REINFORCERS

If I asked you to give some examples of reinforcers, you'd probably include items that are *tangible*—that is, material objects we can perceive, such as toys, clothing, or musical recordings—or *consumable*—that is, things we can eat or drink, such as candy, fruit, or soft drinks. Tangible and consumable rewards include unconditioned and conditioned reinforcers. When you go to a store to buy a new novel, the book is a tangible reinforcer for your shopping behavior. When children at mealtime obey their parent's instructions to wash their hands before they may sit at the table and eat, food is the reinforcer for their behavior.

Although food can be a powerful reinforcer, it isn't used as often as you might expect in applied behavior analysis interventions, for at least three reasons. First, food is most effective as a reinforcer when the individuals

CLOSE-UP

Why Are Reinforcers Reinforcing?

Theories have been offered to explain why reinforcers strengthen behavior. One theory is that reinforcers have the ability to *reduce drives*. Learning theorist Clark Hull (1943) proposed that biological needs produce unpleasant internal drives, such as hunger, that can be reduced directly by performing behavior that leads to a relevant unconditioned reinforcer—in this case, food. This reduction in drive and biological need strengthens the connection between the successful behavior and its antecedents. Conditioned reinforcers, such as money, work indirectly through their associations with unconditioned reinforcers, such as food.

Although drive reduction seems to be an important property that enables some consequences to reinforce behavior, not all reinforcers reduce drives. As you read the following research examples with animal subjects, ask yourself if the reinforcer could have reduced any *biologically based drive* directly or indirectly:

- *Visual exploration as a reinforcer*: Butler (1954) placed a series of monkeys individually in a cage that was enclosed in a box that prevented the monkeys from seeing out. There was a small door in the box, however, and Butler trained the monkeys to open it, and the only consequence was that they could see an empty laboratory room for a short time. Later tests with different stimulus conditions in the room showed that door opening occurred at an even higher rate when they could see in the room a moving toy train or another monkey in a cage.

- *Saccharin as a reinforcer*: Saccharin is an artificial sweetener (like brand names Splenda or Equal) that has no calories or nutritional value. Researchers examined saccharin as a reinforcer with rats that had been fed entirely on an unsweetened grain mash and had water always available in their home cages (Sheffield, Roby, & Campbell, 1954). The subjects, which were hungry but not thirsty, were trained to run from one end to the other in a runway; some got plain water for running, and others got a water–saccharin solution. In the last few days of testing, the rats trained with the water–saccharin reinforcer ran six times faster than those trained with just the plain water.

- *Brain stimulation as a reinforcer*: Olds and Milner (1954) implanted very thin electrodes deep in rats' brains to deliver tiny pulses of electrical current to specific locations. The researchers then trained the subjects to press a lever and receive an electrical pulse to the brain with each press. Not only did the subjects learn this operant task, but they would then perform the response at extremely high rates if the pulses were to a particular region (the septal area)—for instance, one rat made 1,920 responses in a 1-hour period for this reinforcer.

Although the reinforcing effects of at least some of these reinforcers may seem intuitively reasonable, the problem is that reinforcement occurred without reducing a biologically based drive directly or indirectly. This means that other properties of consequences must also enable them to strengthen behavior.

Three other properties of consequences may also make them reinforcing. First, they usually provide *sensory stimulation*. You've probably experienced two extremes of stimulation, feeling bored with nothing to do and feeling overwhelmed with too much stimulation. Both feelings are unpleasant. Some evidence suggests that the effectiveness of sensory stimulation as a reinforcer is greatest between these extremes, when there is enough going on to keep your interest and when the stimulation has some variety and meaning to it (Baldwin & Baldwin, 1981; Fiske & Maddi, 1961; Schultz, 1965). Second, some consequences involve performing *high-probability behaviors*, which may make them reinforcing (Premack, 1959; 1965). High-probability behaviors are responses the person performs frequently or for long periods of time when free to choose what he or she will do. Some common high-probability behaviors are eating, watching TV, having sex, dancing, and playing games. For the most part, these behaviors are ones the person enjoys doing. Third, reinforcers of all types have specific *physiological effects*—for example, the release of a chemical called dopamine in the brain (Blum, Cull, Braverman, & Comings, 1996; White & Milner, 1992).

CONCEPT CHECK 5.1

Check your understanding of the preceding concepts. Remember that answers are given at the end of the chapter, and that the symbol ⇔ following a question means the answer can vary. Answer the following questions about defining reinforcement.

1. Reinforcement always _____ the behavior on which it is contingent.
2. In positive reinforcement, the consequence is _____ after the behavior occurs.
3. If you stubbed your toe, a behavior you could perform that would produce negative reinforcement might be _____ . ⇔
4. The terms *positive* and *negative* to describe reinforcement are analogous to _____ and _____ in arithmetic.
5. A reinforcer with high reward value for a typical child might be _____ . ⇔
6. Another term for primary reinforcer is _____ .
7. One property reinforcers often have that may enable them to strengthen behavior is that they involve _____ . ⇔

receiving it are hungry. Because depriving people of food can raise ethical and legal concerns, programs often reserve using food until just before mealtime. This limits its utility, as does the fact that hunger will weaken as the individuals consume their rewards. Second, consumable reinforcers are often difficult and messy to carry around and dispense in everyday settings, such as at work, in classrooms, or in stores. This problem is compounded by the great differences in food preferences from one person to the next and for the same person from one time to the next. Thus, to use food effectively as a reinforcer, we would need to have a sufficient variety of foods with us at all times when the target behavior could occur. Third, people who receive and consume food as a reward for each instance of a target behavior are likely to be distracted from the behaviors they're trying to learn. For example, suppose we were trying to improve children's concentration while studying. Giving them food reinforcers every several minutes would disrupt their efforts.

Still, using food reinforcers is sometimes reasonable and practical. For instance, a parent or teacher could use food rewards for children's meeting specifically identified behavioral goals. An example of this approach would be a teacher providing snacks at specified times if students keep their disruptive behavior below a certain level. And food rewards often are used when few or no other reinforcers are effective. For instance, some children with mental retardation may respond only to edible reinforcers in the early phases of an intervention (Lancioni, 1982). In addition, a study found that using highly preferred foods as reinforcers was helpful in getting children to eat a wider range of foods after they had become malnourished because they refused to eat almost all other foods (Riordan et al., 1984).

ACTIVITY REINFORCERS

"You may draw pictures with crayons at the table in the back of the room after you finish your arithmetic problems," the teacher promised. The teacher was using an activity as a reinforcer for students' doing arithmetic problems. Drawing pictures is one of many activities children often enjoy and do frequently when they have a free choice. We saw earlier that these kinds of activities are called high-probability behaviors. Premack (1959, 1965) proposed that one reason consequences are reinforcing is that they involve performing high-probability behaviors, and these activities will work as reinforcers only for less frequent behaviors. This rule is called the **Premack principle**.

The Premack principle appears to have some validity—studies have shown that having the opportunity to engage in high-probability behaviors can increase people's performance of infrequent behaviors. Here are some example research results:

- Adults with mental retardation increased the number of repetitions they performed of physical exercises, such as knee bends and toe touches, when researchers made the opportunity to participate in games contingent on increased exercising (Allen & Iwata, 1980).

- Toothbrushing at a summer camp increased when the campers' opportunity to go swimming was contingent on brushing their teeth (Lattal, 1969).

- Children's classroom conduct improved when their teacher made the opportunity to play with toys, games, and crafts contingent on increasing desirable behaviors and decreasing undesirable ones (Wasik, 1970).

How can we identify potential activity reinforcers to apply? We can monitor people's naturally occurring activities and see which ones they choose most often when they have a free choice. This approach is usually effective and easy to use, but deciding how to assess and compare different behaviors can be tricky (Allison, 1989). For instance, if two of the activities under consideration were watching TV and text messaging, would you compare them for their frequency or their duration? Suppose TV watching occurred, say, twice a day for an average of 2 hours each time, and text messaging occurred 15 times for an average of 20 seconds each. Would the best measure be frequency or duration? And suppose you decided that frequency is the best measure for one behavior, but duration is best for the other. If so, how would you determine whether one activity involves a higher-probability behavior than the other? Problems like these are not common and can usually be solved (Allison, 1989). But they make the Premack principle a little harder to apply than you might have guessed.

Although using high-probability behaviors, such as playing a game, usually works to reinforce the performance of low-probability behaviors, we're not entirely sure why. Timberlake and Allison (1974) have proposed an explanation called the *response deprivation hypothesis*. According to this view, using a high-probability behavior (for instance, playing a game) as a reward makes that activity contingent on performing an infrequent behavior (doing chores), thereby restricting or depriving the person of his or her usual opportunities to perform the high-probability behavior. So, if we used activities to reinforce a person's doing chores, the person would increase doing chores to overcome the restricted opportunities to do the restricted behavior, playing a game. A number of studies have found evidence supporting this explanation (Konarski, Johnson, Crowell, & Whitman, 1981).

SOCIAL REINFORCERS

Social reinforcers are consequences consisting of interpersonal acts that strengthen one's behavior, as when our behavior receives praise, attention, or a smile, nod, or affectionate touch. These acts can be given directly to the person or indirectly, such as in a letter of appreciation or commendation at work. Social reinforcers usually are very subtle in our everyday lives, but they can have very powerful effects on people's actions. Oftentimes we strengthen undesirable behaviors inadvertently with social reinforcers. As an example, a parent or teacher who pays attention to children's misbehavior by trying to correct or "punish" it—saying, "Stop that," for instance—without attending to their desirable acts often increases their conduct problems (Harris, Wolf, & Baer, 1964; Madsen et al., 1970; Wahler, Winkel, Peterson, & Morrison, 1965). In a study at a preschool, researchers found that teachers were unknowingly reinforcing children's excessive crying, whining, and solitary play activities (Harris, Wolf, & Baer, 1964). The teachers were then instructed to ignore such behaviors and give social reinforcers for other responses, such as playing with other children. Figure 5-1 presents the substantial effect the teachers' attention had on a 4-year-old girl's social interactions with other children.

Using social reinforcers to improve people's behavior has three main advantages over other rewards. First, social reinforcers can be administered easily and quickly in almost any setting, thereby disrupting ongoing behavior very little. Second, they can be given immediately after the target behavior, which enhances their effectiveness. Third, social reinforcers occur "naturally" in people's everyday lives for most kinds of behavior. As a result, social consequences may continue to reinforce a target behavior after the intervention ends. (Go to 🐾.)

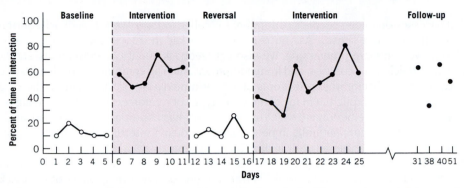

Figure 5-1   Daily percentages of time a 4-year-old socially impaired girl spent in social interaction with other children during 2-hour morning sessions. In the intervention phases, she received social reinforcement from teachers for playing with other children in her nursery school. The follow-up data on the right indicate that the increased social interaction was durable.   *Source:* From F. R. Harris, M. M. Wolf, & D. M. Baer (1964), Effects of adult social reinforcement on child behavior. *Young Children,* 20, 8–17, Figure 2. Copyright © National Association for the Education of Young Children. Used by permission.

CASE STUDY

Using Social Reinforcers to Overcome a Man's "Pain Behavior"

People in pain behave in characteristic ways, such as by moaning, grimacing, moving in a guarded or protective manner, or stooping while walking. These actions are called *pain behaviors*. Regardless of why these behaviors start, they often receive reinforcement, such as attention and care from family and friends. They also get certain benefits, called *secondary gains*, like not having to go to work or do chores around the house. If these reinforcing conditions persist too long, the person who was in pain may continue to perceive or anticipate pain and show pain behaviors when little or no physical basis for pain exists. The person gets caught in a vicious circle of others' solicitous behavior leading to more pain behavior, which elicits more solicitousness, and so on. But don't misunderstand this phenomenon—the person and his or her family and friends are seldom aware this is happening.

   This phenomenon may have led to the condition of a 42-year-old man who was admitted to a medical center in a wheelchair after having experienced years of medical treatment, including surgery, for back pain that had no medically detectable cause (Kallman, Hersen, & O'Toole, 1975). He had retired from work 5 years earlier, and his wife was supporting the family. At admission, he was unable to walk or straighten his body, which was bent at the waist. The behavioral methods applied were very simple: A female assistant paid three 10-minute daily visits to his room, each time chatting with him and then asking him to stand and walk as far as possible. She assessed these behaviors and provided social reinforcers, saying, for instance, "You're standing straighter now," and "I'm very proud of you." During the first few days, the social rewards had little noticeable effect, but soon his standing and walking began to improve. After 18 days, he was walking normally and was discharged from the center. A month later, he was readmitted to the center, showing severe pain behaviors again. Because his family had socially reinforced these behaviors after the intervention, they got training to ignore his pain complaints and praise his motor activities. Follow-up assessments in the 12 weeks after he was discharged from the center again revealed no further problems.

FEEDBACK

Information that assesses or guides people's performance is called *feedback*. We get feedback continuously about our motor actions through our senses: As you reach to put a key in a lock, you see and feel through your muscles how the movements are progressing. We also get feedback about our movements and learning from other people, such as teachers or coaches, and from equipment, such as computers. This feedback can be either "positive," indicating our behavior was correct or is being performed well, or "negative," indicating corrections are needed. Feedback is often implicit in many of the other types of reinforcers we get. Receiving praise or a gift for something we did tells us we performed well. Using feedback has essentially the same advantages as using social reinforcers: Feedback occurs naturally in people's lives, doesn't interrupt ongoing behavior, and can be administered easily, quickly, and immediately in almost any setting.

Although feedback alone can be sufficient to strengthen or maintain a behavior, combining feedback with other rewards, such as praise, usually works better. The greater reinforcing effect of feedback plus praise was demonstrated in an intervention to decrease home heating-oil consumption (Seaver & Patterson, 1976). Heating-oil customers were divided into three groups. A feedback group received a form with information about their rate of oil use during the current delivery period, their rate for a comparable period in the preceding year, and what the difference in these rates means in dollars their household saved or lost. A feedback/praise group got the same type of feedback, but if their rate of oil use had declined, the information form had a decal that read, "We are saving oil," in red letters and a note commending their efforts. The third group got no special information at all. Assessments at the next oil delivery revealed that the feedback/praise group used 10% less oil than either of the other groups, which did not differ.

A special feedback technique called *biofeedback* helps people gain voluntary control over body processes by using equipment to give them continuous and specific information about the current functioning of a physiological process, such as heart rate or muscle tension. This technique has been used effectively in helping individuals reduce chronic headaches and asthma attacks (Sarafino & Smith, 2011). We will examine biofeedback in greater detail in Chapter 23.

TOKENS

Tokens are conditioned reinforcers that are like money because they can be accumulated and exchanged for goods or privileges, which are called *backup reinforcers*. The tokens can take several forms, such as tickets, small chips or buttons, check marks or stars on a chart, or points recorded in a log. The backup reinforcers are generally some form of tangible, consumable, activity, or social rewards. So, for example, someone who has earned enough tokens can exchange them for a snack or the opportunity to listen to a favorite music CD as a backup reinforcer. If one were to receive tokens for good performance without being able to trade them in for backup reinforcers, the tokens would just constitute feedback or social reinforcement.

To use token reinforcers, we must determine in advance the specific behavioral criteria to earn them, what the backup reinforcers will be, and how many tokens will be needed to buy each backup reinforcer. For example, a simple token system was used as part of a program to reduce the frequent tantrums of an 8-year-old elementary school student named Diane (Carlson, Arnold, Becker, & Madsen, 1968). Her teacher gave

> Diane a star (on the board) for each half-day of non-tantrum behavior. When four stars *in a row* were received there would be a little class party, with Diane passing out the treats. The latter provision was designed with the thought of increasing Diane's acceptance by her peers. (p. 118)

Although she had several tantrums in the first couple of weeks of the program, she had only three more in the remaining 2½ months before summer recess. Having the tokens buy a backup reinforcer that Diane and her classmates could share seems to be a useful approach. Another study found children's earning tokens to provide backup reinforcers for all students in their class is more effective than earning tokens to buy rewards for themselves alone (Kazdin & Geesey, 1977).

Token reinforcement systems can be much more complicated than the one used with Diane. They can involve more than one behavior, offer different numbers of tokens for different behaviors or levels of performance, and have many backup reinforcers from which to choose. Using tokens as reinforcers has many of the advantages we've seen for social and feedback reinforcement, such as being administered easily, quickly, and immediately in almost any setting. What's more, tokens have the advantages of:

- *Bridging the delay* between performing the target behavior and getting tangible, consumable, or activity reinforcers for it.
- Offering the possibility of *a variety of backup reinforcers*, thereby maintaining the tokens' value at a consistently high level.

Tokens have no reinforcing value of their own—they become reinforcers because of the backup reinforcers they can buy. Simply explaining the token system is sufficient for most people to establish the link to the backup reinforcers. But individuals who are either very young or have severe learning impairments may need a little training to establish the value of the tokens.

When designing a token reinforcement system, keep in mind that the criteria for earning tokens should be neither too easy nor too difficult, and the number of tokens needed to buy backup reinforcers should be reasonable. Individuals should get attractive backup reinforcers when they perform at acceptable levels. Chapters 16 and 25 discuss in detail how token reinforcement systems are applied and can be used in a single setting to modify many target behaviors for many individuals, as occurs in institutions. (Go to 📖.)

FACTORS THAT INFLUENCE THE EFFECTIVENESS OF REINFORCEMENT

Several factors determine how powerful the effect of reinforcement will be in changing a target behavior, and we'll discuss some of them, beginning with reward value and timing.

REWARD VALUE AND TIMING

The degree to which an individual *values* a specific consequence determines how likely it is to reinforce a behavior (Trosclair-Lasserre et al., 2008): up to a point, the *greater its value, the greater its strengthening effect* on a behavior. What aspects of a reinforcer determine its value? Reinforcers can vary in their *quantity*—for example, the amount

CONCEPT CHECK 5.2

Answer the following questions about types of positive reinforcers.

1. A favorite consumable reward of people you know is _____ . ⇔
2. Parents saying to a teenager, "You can go out tonight if you finish your chores," is an example of using a(n) _____ as a reinforcer.
3. An advantage of using feedback or social reinforcers is _____ . ⇔
4. Providing continuous information about the functioning of a person's physiological processes is called _____ .
5. A backup reinforcer for tokens might be _____ . ⇔

of ice cream the person receives for good behavior—and *quality*, or character—for instance, ice cream comes in different flavors.

To understand how these factors affect reward value, we need to consider positive and negative reinforcement separately. In *positive reinforcement*, the quantity and quality of a reinforcer determine its value. A large piece of chocolate candy generally has more reward value than a small piece, and chocolate candy may have more reward value for many people than the same amount of licorice candy. Studies of positive reinforcement have found that reinforcers with greater value produce stronger responding than lesser reinforcers do, as reflected in the frequency or magnitude of the behavior (Crespi, 1942; Flaherty & Caprio, 1976; Green, Reid, Canipe, & Gardner, 1991). Reward value *in negative reinforcement* seems to be determined mainly by two factors:

1. Quantity—that is, the amount by which the aversive situation is reduced (Campbell & Kraeling, 1953). For instance, we are more likely to take aspirin to relieve a headache in the future if doing so in the past stopped most or all of the pain rather than just a little of it.

2. Intensity of the aversive condition—negative reinforcement is more effective when the behavior reduces a very aversive stimulus than when it reduces a milder one (Piliavin, Dovidio, Gaertner, & Clark, 1981).

Some reinforcers are at least moderately effective for almost all people, as with money as a positive reinforcer and pain reduction as a negative reinforcer. But for most specific reinforcers, our preferences usually differ from one person to the next—a case of "different strokes for different folks"—and can change from one time to the next. For instance, getting tickets to the latest Harry Potter movie as a reward for studying might be very reinforcing for you, but a friend who studies with you might prefer tickets to a more serious movie as a reward. And these preferences can change: If you are "in the mood" for a serious movie, Harry Potter might be less appealing. What's more, to get a highly valued reward, such as going to a good movie or a large reduction in very intense pain, you may even be willing to endure unpleasant situations—traffic jams to get to the movie or major surgery to reduce the pain, for example.

When we are helping someone change an existing behavior or learn a new one, we can maximize the effect of reinforcement by delivering it *immediately after each and every correct response*. This is an important rule, and it applies to both positive and negative reinforcement (Chung, 1965; Michael, 1986; Weiss, Cecil, & Frank, 1973). The longer the reinforcer is delayed, the less effective it will be.

MOTIVATION

Some circumstances can make certain consequences more (or less) reinforcing than they might be otherwise. For instance, food is an especially effective reinforcer when the person is hungry. Circumstances can increase or decrease a person's motivation and the reward value of a reinforcer. In interventions to change behavior, we can sometimes manipulate circumstances that affect reinforcement. **Motivating operations (MOs)** are procedures that temporarily alter the (a) effectiveness of a consequence on behavior and (b) performance of behaviors that normally lead to those consequences (Laraway, Snycerski, Michael, & Poling, 2003). Although the consequence can be either a reinforcer or a punisher, we'll focus for now on using MOs in positive reinforcement, continuing with our example of food as a reinforcer.

What MOs can we use for food as a positive reinforcer? The two main ones are *deprivation* and *satiation*. In deprivation, we would restrict access to food or just wait enough time after the individuals have eaten, which increases their hunger and the reward value of food. In satiation, we would make sure the individuals have eaten a large amount of food, thereby decreasing the reward value of food. An intervention to help individuals lose weight might use satiation: One approach is called *preloading*, in which they eat enough of low-calorie foods, such as vegetables, to reduce their appetite just before going out to dinner, enabling them to eat less. Deprivation and satiation work especially well for altering the effects of unconditioned reinforcers, such as food or water, but can also affect the reward value of some conditioned reinforcers. For instance, you might opt not to turn on your MP3 player to listen to your favorite music if you had already listened to it for several hours that day.

MOs can also affect the reward value of negative reinforcement, for example, in pain reduction. We saw earlier that the greater the intensity of an aversive situation, the greater the reward value in reducing it. Several psychological factors affect people's perception of pain, such as from arthritis (Sarafino & Smith, 2011). For instance, anxiety and boredom increase the perception of pain, and distraction and relaxation reduce it. To alter the reward value of pain reduction, we might manipulate the amount of distraction or boredom the person experiences. We'll examine MOs in more detail later in this book, especially in Chapter 9.

NEGATIVE REINFORCEMENT IN ESCAPE AND AVOIDANCE

One of the reasons heavy drinkers drink so much is the negative reinforcement they get from it. Drinking relieves their feelings of stress and other negative emotions, at least temporarily (Baker et al., 2004; Chapman, Gratz, & Brown, 2006). The nicotine in cigarettes has similar effects, triggering the body to release chemicals that reduce a variety of negative emotions in a matter of seconds (Pomerleau & Pomerleau, 1989). Thus, substance use and abuse develop partly because users rely on the substance to escape or avoid negative emotional states.

ESCAPE AND AVOIDANCE

The aversive stimuli we try to reduce in negative reinforcement can be *covert*, as in anxiety or depression, or *overt*, as when noisy neighbors keep us from sleeping. In these situations, we learn to perform behaviors that help us escape from the aversive stimuli.

Escape Conditioning

Escape conditioning involves learning to make a response that reduces or eliminates an aversive stimulus we are currently experiencing. A response that succeeds is strengthened through the process of negative reinforcement. For example, when you feel cold, you put on a sweater or coat—becoming warmer reinforces that behavior. Escape conditioning is clearly useful when the aversive stimuli we experience can harm us and when the behaviors we learn enable us to adapt well in our lives.

But escape conditioning can lead to maladaptive behaviors, too. For example, children may learn that having a tantrum can help them escape from chores at home or a class they don't like in school. Evidence also indicates that self-injurious behavior, such as that seen in children with developmental disabilities, leads to negative reinforcement by relieving negative emotions temporarily (Chapman, Gratz, & Brown, 2006). This process was studied in children who frequently performed self-injurious behaviors, such as banging their heads or biting their arms (Iwata et al., 1990). The researchers introduced various antecedents and consequences to see whether they affected the behavior, which revealed two relevant findings. First, self-injurious behaviors were especially frequent when the children were asked to perform a behavior they were being trained to do, such as a self-help skill. Second, self-injurious behavior became more frequent when it resulted in the behavior analyst stopping the training activity, removing the training materials, and turning away from the child. These findings indicate that training procedures can be unpleasant to children with developmental disabilities and that stopping the training when self-injury occurs negatively reinforces the escape behaviors.

How can we eliminate maladaptive escape behaviors? One way requires ending the negative reinforcement: In the research by Iwata and his coworkers, they no longer stopped the training when self-injurious behavior occurred; instead, they helped the child perform the task. This approach almost entirely eliminated the self-injurious behavior during training sessions. A similar method stops negative reinforcement and includes positive reinforcement for good behavior, which was used with children who were very disruptive during dental treatment (Allen, Loiben, Allen, & Stanley, 1992; Allen & Stokes, 1987). The children's disruptive behavior decreased markedly when the dentist praised them and gave them "a little rest break" when they were quiet and still but did not stop the treatment when disruptive behavior occurred.

Avoidance Conditioning

Suppose children who have successfully disrupted dental treatments in the past learn that they have a new appointment for dental treatment. How might they react? They may do something to avoid the unpleasant experience (Ayres, 1998). In **avoidance conditioning**, people learn to respond in ways that prevent them from experiencing aversive events. So, the children may have a tantrum upon learning of the appointment or when they enter the dentist's office, for instance. Not all avoidance conditioning is maladaptive: We learn to carry an umbrella when rain is likely, for instance. But avoidance conditioning can prevent people from acquiring useful skills, such as when they give an excuse if asked to do something they find threatening, such as giving a speech.

"GOTTA GO. MY MOM'S USIN' THAT 'BOY-ARE-YOU-IN-TROUBLE-NOW' VOICE!"

Dennis has learned that the "voice" his mother is using is a signal for trouble he can avoid by going home quickly. *Source:* Reprinted with special permission of King Features Syndicate.

Learning to avoid aversive events appears to involve both respondent and operant conditioning, as outlined in *two-factor theory* (Mowrer, 1947). Let's use as our example a young girl who successfully used disruptive acts to terminate dental treatments and now has a tantrum when she learns of a dental appointment. Respondent conditioning played a role: The term *dental appointment* is paired with the unpleasant experience, an unconditioned stimulus, making *dental appointment* a conditioned stimulus. Because *dental appointment* now elicits distress, an aversive situation, she tries to reduce the distress by having a tantrum. If the tantrum leads to canceling the appointment, operant conditioning is involved: Her avoidance behavior receives negative reinforcement.

A good deal of evidence supports the combined roles of respondent and operant conditioning in learning to avoid aversive events (Stasiewicz & Maisto, 1993; Williams, 2001). But some researchers believe two-factor theory may not fully explain avoidance behavior. One reason is that people often learn to avoid events without having direct experience with these events, as children do when they stay away from a house they've heard is "haunted." In addition, research has shown that avoidance behavior that was learned by direct experience can be extremely persistent even though the aversive event has not occurred since the original experience (Herrnstein, 1969; Solomon, Kamin, & Wynne, 1953). Other researchers disagree and have proposed ways in which conditioning can account for these situations (McAlister & McAlister, 1995; Williams, 2001).

PROBLEMS USING ESCAPE AND AVOIDANCE CONDITIONING

Although negative reinforcement occurs frequently in our everyday lives and influences much of our behavior, it isn't used very often in applied behavior analysis programs. To use negative reinforcement, an aversive situation must be present. This can happen when punishment is used. Professionals who design and administer interventions to change behavior typically try to minimize the use of aversive events, partly for humanitarian reasons and partly because of undesirable side effects in the person's behavior. Often when aversive events are used, the target person becomes physically aggressive and makes efforts to escape or avoid the program and the staff involved in it. In addition, the behaviors rewarded through negative reinforcement are often undesirable or superficial. For example, to escape or avoid punishment, the person may lie about the situation or apologize verbally for having been bad. But the lie is dishonest, and the apology may be insincere—in which case, dishonest or insincere verbal behavior is reinforced. When negative reinforcement must be used, the person should receive clear instructions about the link between making the escape or avoidance response and reducing the aversive stimulus, and positive reinforcement should be provided for performing the appropriate behavior. (Go to 📄.)

STUDY AND REVIEW

SUMMARY

Reinforcement is a process in which consequences strengthen the behaviors on which they are contingent—this rule is true for all types of reinforcement—and a reinforcing consequence is called a reinforcer. Natural reinforcers, including automatic reinforcers, occur spontaneously in daily life, and programmed reinforcers are applied deliberately to influence behavior. Positive reinforcement is a process in which a consequence—a positive reinforcer, or reward—is introduced after a behavior; negative reinforcement involves a reduction in an existing aversive event contingent on a behavior. Both positive and negative reinforcement result in a desirable state of affairs and strengthen the target behavior.

Unconditioned reinforcers satisfy basic physiological needs without having to be learned, but we learn to value conditioned reinforcers as they become associated with stimuli in our lives that are already reinforcing. Evidence suggests that reinforcers can strengthen behavior for any of four reasons: They reduce biologically based drives directly or indirectly, they provide sensory stimulation, they involve performing high-probability behaviors (as in the Premack principle), and they have biochemical effects. The many types of positive reinforcers include tangible or consumable items, activities, social reinforcers, feedback, and tokens.

The effectiveness of reinforcement is highest in three circumstances: The reward value of the reinforcer is high, the reinforcer is delivered immediately after the behavior, and motivating operations are manipulated to enhance the value of the reward for the person. Negative reinforcement is involved in escape and avoidance conditioning, which appear to be responsible for developing and maintaining self-injurious behaviors among children with developmental disabilities.

CONCEPT CHECK 5.3

Answer the following questions about reinforcement effectiveness and escape and avoidance conditioning.

1. The greater a consequence's _____ , the more likely it will reinforce behavior.
2. A reinforcer that could bridge a delay between the target behavior and its main reinforcer is _____ . ⇔
3. Manipulating circumstances, such as food deprivation or satiation, to alter the effectiveness of reinforcement is called _____ .
4. Escape and avoidance conditioning are strengthened by the process of _____ .
5. According to two-factor theory, the first step in learning to avoid an aversive stimulus involves _____ conditioning.

To prepare for exams, use the following key terms and review questions and the online study guide that's available on this book's companion website at www.wiley.com/college/sarafino.

KEY TERMS

reinforcement	positive reinforcement	Premack principle
reinforcer	positive reinforcer	tokens
natural reinforcers	negative reinforcement	motivating operations (MOs)
automatic reinforcement	unconditioned reinforcers	escape conditioning
programmed reinforcers	conditioned reinforcers	avoidance conditioning

ANSWERS TO CONCEPT CHECKS (CCs)

CC5.1 *Answers*: **1.** strengthens **2.** added **3.** rub the toe **4.** adding, subtracting **5.** candy **6.** unconditioned reinforcer **7.** drive reduction, stimulation, or high-probability behavior

CC5.2 *Answers*: **1.** chocolate **2.** activity **3.** they are administered immediately/easily and quickly **4.** biofeedback **5.** watching TV

CC5.3 *Answers*: **1.** reward value **2.** praise/tokens **3.** motivating operations **4.** negative reinforcement **5.** respondent

REVIEW QUESTIONS

1. Define *positive* and *negative* reinforcement, and indicate how they are different. Give two examples of each.
2. Define *natural*, *automatic*, and *programmed* reinforcers. Give an example of automatic reinforcement from your life.
3. What is the difference between unconditioned and conditioned reinforcers?
4. Describe two research examples suggesting that not all reinforcers directly or indirectly reduce biologically based drives.
5. What are tangible and consumable reinforcers? Give two examples of each.
6. Describe two examples of the Premack principle in your own life.
7. Give two examples each of teachers using social reinforcement and feedback in the classroom.
8. What are tokens and backup reinforcers?
9. What determines the reward value in positive and negative reinforcement?
10. How do timing and motivating operations affect the effectiveness of reinforcement?
11. Describe the two-factor theory of avoidance conditioning, and give an example of how these processes may have happened in your own escape or avoidance behavior.

RELATED READINGS

- Laraway, S., Snycerski, S., Michael, J., & Poling, A. (2003). Motivating operations and terms to describe them: Some further refinements. *Journal of Applied Behavior Analysis, 36*, 407–414.
- Michael, J. (1975). Positive and negative reinforcement, a distinction that is no longer necessary; or a better way to talk about bad things. *Behaviorism, 3*, 33–44.
- Premack, D. (1965). Reinforcement theory. In D. Levine (Ed.), *Nebraska Symposium on Motivation*. Lincoln: University of Nebraska Press.

6

EXTINCTION

PROLOGUE

Helen was a psychiatric patient who had been hospitalized for several years before Teodoro Ayllon and Jack Michael (1959) conducted a simple intervention to reduce her problem behavior of "psychotic talk," which refers to making statements based on delusional (false) beliefs. In Helen's case, she would talk mainly about an illegitimate child she claimed to have and men who pursued her constantly. She had been making these untrue statements for 3 years or more. What really made her psychotic talk a problem was that it constituted almost all of her speech—91% of her baseline talking—and it

> had become so annoying during the last 4 months prior to treatment that other patients had on several occasions beaten her in an effort to keep her quiet .... Some of the nurses reported that, previously, when the patient started her psychotic talk, they listened to her to get to the "roots of her problem." A few nurses stated that they did not listen to what she was saying but simply nodded and remarked, "Yes, I understand." (p. 327)

Observations of Helen's behavior suggested that people's seeming to pay attention to the psychotic talk was reinforcing it.

So the intervention simply consisted of *extinguishing* the psychotic talk by having the nurses stop paying attention to those statements and *reinforcing* appropriate speech by paying attention whenever Helen made sensible statements. With these new consequences, her psychotic talk declined rapidly, constituting only about 50% of her speech after 2 days and 25% after another week. Interestingly, her psychotic talk then began to increase again; probably other individuals at the hospital had begun to reinforce it: One time when Helen wasn't getting attention from a nurse, she said, "Well you're not listening to me. I'll have to go and see ... [a social worker] again,' 'cause she told me that if she would listen to my past she could help me."

In this chapter, we focus on the method of extinction to decrease behavioral excesses. We'll examine what extinction is, its advantages and disadvantages, and the factors that affect its effectiveness in decreasing undesirable behavior.

WHAT IS OPERANT EXTINCTION?

When discussing operant behavior, the term **extinction** actually has two meanings. It is a *procedure* or *condition* in which a previously reinforced response no longer receives reinforcement, and it is a *process* whereby the rate and force in performing the no-longer-reinforced response decrease. The verb form for extinction is *extinguish*. So, we talk about a therapist extinguishing Helen's psychotic talk and that the behavior has been extinguished when it rarely or no longer occurs. In reducing Helen's psychotic talk, the nurses used the procedure of extinction when they stopped paying attention (the past reinforcer) to her delusional statements.

Extinction can occur as a haphazard condition in everyday life or as a careful and deliberate procedure in an intervention. In everyday life, for example, if children have parents who are quite indifferent toward or uninvolved in their parenting roles, many of the appropriate social behaviors children observe in school and elsewhere may not receive sufficient reinforcement to be maintained. At the same time, negative social behaviors, such as aggression, may produce quick rewards. These reinforcement patterns help explain why children with indifferent, uninvolved parents tend to be aggressive, disobedient, and disagreeable (Sarafino & Armstrong, 1986). In contrast, extinction procedures in interventions are planned to accomplish certain behavioral goals. To start an extinction procedure for a target behavior, we must identify what the reinforcement is and be able to control its source. If we don't control the source of reinforcement very carefully, extraneous reinforcers may occur and reinstate the behavior.

Extinction can apply to behaviors that have received either positive or negative reinforcement. In either case, reinforcement is terminated and the behavior on which reinforcement was contingent now declines.

EXTINCTION FOR POSITIVE REINFORCEMENT

If the consequence of the behavior was *positive reinforcement*, such as receiving tangible or social reinforcers, the extinction procedure involves making sure those rewards are no longer provided.

An example of an extinction procedure for a target behavior that had received positive reinforcement comes from an intervention to reduce arithmetic errors of an 8-year-old pupil named Bob (Hasazi & Hasazi, 1972). Although the boy would add the numbers correctly, he usually reversed the digits in a two-digit sum. The behavior analysts determined that the reinforcer for the digit reversal was teacher attention: When the teacher marked Bob's 20-problem work sheets, she marked each correct answer with a C and each incorrect (reversed digits) answer with an X, which appeared to provide the attention that served as a reinforcer for the reversals. During the intervention phases of the study, the teacher continued to mark each correct answer with a C and would also pat his back and say "This one is *very* good," but did not mark or comment on any incorrect item. As shown in Figure 6-1, Bob's baseline digit reversals occurred at very high levels, but declined dramatically during the intervention phases.

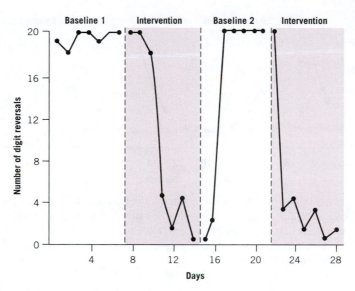

Figure 6-1   Daily number of digit reversals in a student's answers to 20 arithmetic problems with two-digit sums. In baseline, almost all answers contained the reversals; but in the two intervention phases, incorrect answers declined quickly to very low levels. *Source*: From J. E. Hasazi & S. E. Hasazi (1972), Effects of teacher attention on digit-reversal behavior in an elementary school child. *Journal of Applied Behavior Analysis*, 5, 157–162, Figure 1. Copyright © 1972 Society for the Experimental Analysis of Behavior. Used by permission.

EXTINCTION FOR NEGATIVE REINFORCEMENT

If the consequence maintaining the behavior was *negative reinforcement*, the extinction procedure involves preventing the individual from escaping or avoiding the unpleasant situation. Because reducing the unpleasant situation provides negative reinforcement, that consequence must be stopped in order to use extinction to decrease the behavior. For example, children who do not want to be in school sometimes develop tantrums when they arrive there, leading their parents to take them home (Sarafino, 1986). Extinguishing their tantrums requires that these children not be allowed to escape or avoid school.

An intervention that used extinction to decrease a target behavior maintained with negative reinforcement was implemented for a boy named Drew, who had been diagnosed with autism and mental retardation (Anderson & Long, 2002). The problem behaviors the behavior analysts addressed occurred during speech training and included aggression and self-injurious behavior; observations indicated that these behaviors were reinforced by Drew's escape from the task he was learning. The intervention used only extinction, consisting of stopping the behavior's negative reinforcement: When a problem behavior occurred, the speech therapist simply continued the session and physically guided Drew's completing the task. Figure 6-2 shows that the boy's problem behavior occurred at high levels in baseline and decreased markedly during the intervention phases. (Go to 🔍.)

THE PROCESS AND CHARACTERISTICS OF EXTINCTION

Picture this scene. You're running late on your way to class one morning and had to skip breakfast. You expect from the many other times this has happened in the past that you'll be able to buy a snack from a conveniently located vending machine to take the edge off your hunger. You get to the machine, insert the correct change,

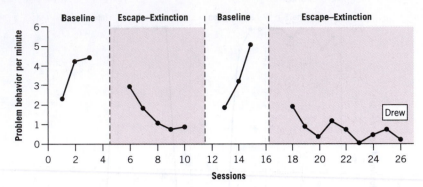

Figure 6-2   Mean frequency of Drew's problem behavior per minute during baseline and intervention phases. Problem behaviors of two other boys were also markedly reduced with extinction plus other methods, but the data are not presented here. *Source:* Adapted from C. M. Anderson & E. S. Long (2002), Use of a structured descriptive assessment methodology to identify variables affecting problem behavior. *Journal of Applied Behavior Analysis*, 35, 137–154, Figure 5. Copyright © 2002 Society for the Experimental Analysis of Behavior. Used by permission.

and pull the lever for the snack you want; but nothing comes out. How will you react to not having your behavior reinforced? Chances are, you'll react initially by pulling the lever once again. When that produces the same result, you might pull the lever several times in rapid succession and very strongly. And when that doesn't work, you might kick the machine or pound on it.

EXTINCTION BURST AND AGGRESSION

The vending machine example illustrates two phenomena of the extinction process. For one thing, when reinforcement fails to occur, the response often increases temporarily in its frequency and magnitude—for example, pulling the vending machine lever rapidly and strongly (Skinner, 1938). This phenomenon is called an

CLOSE-UP

Extinction: Is It Forgetting?

We know that behavior declines when reinforcement that maintained it is terminated, but does extinction "erase" the original learning, making the person forget how to perform the behavior? No, it doesn't. After the response has been extinguished, the individual's memory retains at least part of what was learned in the original conditioning and in extinction (Bouton & Swartzentruber, 1991).

Whether the person ever performs the behavior after extinction seems to depend on whether antecedent stimuli activate the person's memory for performing the behavior or memory for extinction of the behavior. For instance, people who have quit smoking are much more likely to start smoking again if antecedents occur that are like those that were present when they smoked in the past. These antecedents can be overt, such as seeing a pack of cigarettes, or covert, such as feeling tense. This means that behavior change programs need to prevent the return of an extinguished behavior by incorporating techniques to modify the impact of antecedents. And so, programs to stop smoking need to make antecedents associated with extinction as strong as possible, and antecedents associated with smoking must be weakened or avoided when the program ends. We'll discuss ways to manage antecedents in Chapter 14.

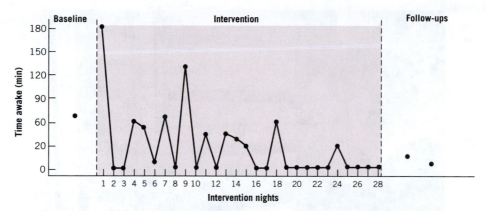

Figure 6-3   Number of minutes an infant was awake after having gone to sleep at night. Each data point for baseline and follow-up periods represents the average time awake across 14 nights for one infant (child 2 in the study). The intervention was conducted with seven 8- to 20-month-old infants who had been referred by nurses for treatment because of long-term sleep disturbances. The infant whose data are presented in the graph was sick only once (night 9) during the intervention. *Source*: Data abstracted from France & Hudson (1990), Figure 2.

extinction burst, which may result from frustration. Figure 6-3 gives an example of an extinction burst for the first night in an intervention to decrease the amount of time an infant was awake after having gone to sleep at night (France & Hudson, 1990). On that night, the infant was awake almost three times longer than the baseline average. The sole technique used in the intervention was extinction: The parents put the child to bed and did not return if the infant woke up unless the child was sick or might be injured. A target person's behavior in extinction does not always show a burst; but when it does, people who want to change the behavior but don't expect a burst may think that extinction does not work.

The other phenomenon illustrated in the vending machine example is aggression: Extinction often increases the target person's aggression and other emotional behaviors (Kelly & Hake, 1970; Kimble, 1961; Todd, Morris, & Fenza, 1989). If extinction-induced aggression or emotion occur when we try to extinguish an undesirable behavior, it can present problems in carrying out the extinction procedure, particularly if someone may be harmed physically or if the behavior is very annoying, such as the screaming of a child in a tantrum. Although aggression and extinction bursts occur in a substantial proportion of cases when extinction is used alone, these problems can be reduced markedly (Lerman, Iwata, & Wallace, 1999). Two ways to curb these problems are to instruct the person of the new contingencies in advance and to combine extinction with other methods, such as reinforcement for other actions.

What other actions would we reinforce? When using extinction, behavior analysts often reinforce actions of two types: competing responses and alternative behaviors. A **competing response** is an action that is incompatible or interferes with performance of a target behavior. For example, in this chapter's opening story about Helen, extinction was applied to her psychotic talk and reinforcement was given for the opposite behavior of making sensible statements. Similarly, children with autism can't engage in repetitive hand flapping if their hands are folded on their laps or in their pockets. An **alternative behavior** is dissimilar to and can take the place of the target behavior as a desirable act, but the two actions aren't necessarily incompatible and could occur together. An example would be students raising their hands to ask a question as an alternative behavior for just blurting it out. If the reinforcer for blurting out questions was receiving attention from the teacher, blurting out would be placed on extinction (withholding attention) and raising hands would receive immediate attention. Ordinarily, behavior analysts try to provide the same or very similar reinforcers for alternative behaviors as those that the target behavior had received, but this isn't essential—any strong reinforcer can strengthen an alternative behavior. To the extent that an alternative behavior or competing response occurs, the target behavior is less likely to be performed.

This angry man is reacting with aggression to an instance of extinction, the failure of the vending machine to deliver the item (reinforcer) he expected for performing the behavior that has led to reinforcement in the past. *Source:* Bernd Vogel/Corbis Cusp/Alamy Limited.

GRADUAL DECLINE AND REAPPEARANCE OF THE BEHAVIOR

Extinction has two other characteristics that are quite typical of the process. For one thing, the behavior tends to decline gradually or irregularly rather than immediately and smoothly. You can see this in Figure 6-3: Notice how the infant's awake time had a generally decreasing trend but fluctuated a lot during the first couple of weeks of the intervention. Although the awake times of the infants treated in that intervention didn't all show so much fluctuation, they all declined in a fairly gradual pattern, and some were extinguished in just a few days (France & Hudson, 1990). Looking back at Figures 6-1 and 6-2, we see that the declines were more gradual and not as fast in the first intervention phase in each study as they were in the second intervention phase.

The other characteristic of the extinction process is that an extinguished behavior can reappear temporarily, even though reinforcement is not given for the behavior. This effect is generally seen across sessions or periods of extinction (Bouton, 2000; Hulse, Deese, & Egeth, 1975). Reappearance of an operant behavior can occur in more than one way. In **spontaneous recovery**, the main factor seems to be the passage of time between periods of extinction. Two conditions can lead to spontaneous recovery. First, placing another behavior on extinction can cause a previously extinguished response to recur (Volkert, Lerman, Call, & Trosclair-Lasserre, 2009). Second, spontaneous recovery may happen because antecedents that were present when the behavior had been reinforced in the past are present again (Bouton & Swartzentruber, 1991). When an extinguished response "recovers" without being reinforced, its strength—as reflected in its frequency, duration, or magnitude—usually is weaker than it was before extinction. Referring again to Figure 6-3, the infant's fairly brief durations of being awake during the follow-up assessments probably reflect spontaneous recovery. Some evidence indicates that spontaneous recovery is less likely to occur when extinction is carried out along with reinforcement of an alternative behavior or competing response (Lerman, Kelley, Van Camp, & Roane, 1999).

Two processes that are like spontaneous recovery can also lead to reappearance of an extinguished operant behavior (Bouton, 2000). In *renewal*, the main factor is the context in which conditioning and extinction occur: If conditioning occurs with certain external and internal stimuli present, and extinction is carried out in a context without these stimuli, the behavior may reappear if extinction sessions switch to a context that has stimuli that are either like those present in conditioning or are new. Why? Because the context now is unlike that used in extinction, it may not call up the individual's memory of the extinction process. In *reinstatement*, the main factor leading to the reappearance of the extinguished behavior is that, without performing the behavior, the individual is exposed to the same stimuli that had originally reinforced the behavior. (Go to ▰.)

WHAT FACTORS AFFECT EXTINCTION EFFECTIVENESS?

Several factors affect how quickly and completely extinction procedures will extinguish a behavior. When any of these conditions is less than ideal in an extinction program, the behavior will show more **resistance to extinction**—or take longer to extinguish. We've already mentioned some of these factors. That is, extinction is especially effective in stopping a target behavior when we've carefully identified the reinforcers that maintained the response in the past, withheld all these reinforcers when the behavior occurs, and added to these procedures reinforcement for other actions. We'll look at these and other factors that affect extinction, starting with identifying and withholding a target behavior's reinforcers.

KNOWING AND CONTROLLING ALL RELEVANT REINFORCERS

Consider this example: Valerie is an elementary school student who blurts out statements in class, which get reprimands from the teacher and lots of laughs from her classmates, and each of these consequences is a reinforcer for her behavior. The teacher decides to use extinction by withholding the reprimands, but doesn't try to stop the laughing. How effective will the teacher's efforts be? Probably not very effective—the target behavior will still get the laughs, which will help maintain it and raise its resistance to extinction.

CONCEPT CHECK 6.1

Check your understanding of the preceding concepts. Remember that the symbol ⇔ means the answer can vary. Answer the following questions about the definition and process of extinction.

1. Terminating reinforcement for a previously reinforced response is called _____ .
2. Before introducing an extinction procedure, we should identify all of the _____ for the behavior so we can withhold them.
3. A temporary increase in a target behavior at the start of extinction is called _____ .
4. A behavior that is incompatible or interferes with a target behavior is called a(n) _____ .
5. The reappearance of a previously extinguished response simply after the passage of time is called _____ .
6. The decline in a target behavior in extinction is usually _____ rather than immediate.

To conduct extinction very effectively, we must know what all of the reinforcers are that maintain the behavior and then stop them all. Withholding only some of the relevant reinforcers is not ideal, because the remaining ones may be sufficient to impair the extinction process. How do behavior analysts determine what the reinforcers are for someone's behavior? Methods that use careful and systematic observation of the person's target behavior can identify the reinforcers, and we'll examine these methods in Chapter 13. Automatic reinforcement, such as a sensory consequence that the behavior produces directly, is often more difficult to identify and control than other types of reinforcement are. (Go to 🐾.)

PAST PATTERN OF REINFORCEMENT

Let's consider the vending machine example again. Before your encounter with the faulty machine, your past experiences had been with reliable vending machines: You put in your money, made your choice, and out popped the desired item, *always* or nearly so. This pattern in which individuals receive an external (nonautomatic) reinforcer virtually every time they perform a particular behavior is called **continuous reinforcement**. But not all our behaviors receive continuous reinforcement—some are reinforced some of the times they're performed, but not other times, in a pattern called **intermittent reinforcement** (or *partial reinforcement*).

As an example of intermittent reinforcement, think about having problems with the reception of a cell phone. As you dial a number, you notice that the reception has dropped to one bar—so you walk a few steps and twist your body. In the past you've noticed that this action usually improves reception, but often it doesn't. Your actions have received intermittent reinforcement. But suppose your past experiences had been different: Your walking and twisting had almost always improved reception, giving you continuous reinforcement. Now suppose you have moved your residence to a region where reception is really poor and you try to make a call. After which of the patterns of past experience we just described, intermittent or continuous reinforcement, are you likely to persist in your efforts to improve cell phone reception? The answer is that you are more likely to persist in this situation after having received intermittent reinforcement for your efforts.

In general, when a behavior has almost always been reinforced in the past—that is, it received continuous reinforcement—and then reinforcement is terminated (in our example, cell phone reception is virtually nonexistent), the behavior extinguishes fairly quickly, showing little resistance to extinction. When a behavior has been reinforced only some of the times it was performed in the past—that is, with an intermittent pattern—and then reinforcement is terminated, the behavior persists longer, showing more resistance to extinction (Kimble, 1961; Lewis, 1960; St. Peter Pipkin & Vollmer, 2009). For instance, a study was conducted in which two male adults with mental retardation were instructed that they could earn reinforcers if they conversed with other individuals (Kazdin & Polster, 1973). During a 5-week period, reinforcers for conversing were given to one man on a continuous schedule and to the other on an intermittent schedule. Later when reinforcement was withdrawn, conversing during the next 5 weeks continued at a high rate in the man who received intermittent reinforcement but declined rapidly in the man who received continuous reinforcement.

The reinforcement history of a behavior can also affect its resistance to extinction in two other ways. First, the more times the behavior was reinforced in the past, the longer it is likely to take to become extinguished (Siegel & Foshee, 1953). Second, the greater the reward value of the reinforcers the behavior produced in the past, the longer it is likely to take to be extinguished (Lewis & Duncan, 1957).

COMBINING EXTINCTION WITH REINFORCING OTHER ACTIONS

We've seen that by reinforcing alternative behaviors or competing responses while implementing extinction for a target behavior, we can reduce the problems of extinction burst, aggression by the client, and spontaneous recovery. There's another benefit to reinforcing other actions while extinguishing a target behavior: We can increase the effectiveness of the extinction procedure (Lerman & Iwata, 1996). So, if we want to reduce a child's oppositional behavior, we could withhold reinforcement for hostile or contrary acts and provide reinforcers for cooperating, which is likely to make extinction occur more quickly and be more durable. If we decide to reinforce alternative behaviors or competing responses, we should define them fully, just as we would target behaviors.

CASE STUDY

Reducing Reggie's Self-Stimulation

We saw in Chapter 4 that a common and unusual class of behavior of children with developmental disabilities is repetitive/ritualistic behavior—also called self-stimulation—which generally seems to be maintained by automatic reinforcement. This type of behavior was targeted for reduction in an intervention for a 9-year-old boy named Reggie who was diagnosed with autism (Rincover, Cook, Peoples, & Packard, 1979). The boy

> persistently twirled objects, such as a plate, on a hard surface. When he twirled an object, however, he also leaned toward it, seeming to listen to the object as it was spinning. (p. 223)

This observation led the behavior analysts who worked with Reggie to conclude that the sound of the spinning plate on a hard surface was the reinforcer. To stop reinforcement during the intervention, they had him spin plates on a table covered with a carpet that was hard enough to allow the plate to spin but eliminated the sound.

The baseline and intervention sessions occurred five days a week and were 30 minutes long. Data were collected using a time-sampling method, and the percentage of intervals in which his plate-twirling behavior was observed in baseline and intervention sessions was recorded. These data are presented in Figure 6-4, showing that the twirling behavior occurred at high levels during baseline phases but dropped dramatically during the intervention phases. Equally successful extinction methods were used with three other children with different repetitive/ritualistic behaviors—for instance, the hand flapping of a boy named Larry was extinguished by attaching small vibrators to his hands to mask his feeling of the flapping sensation during intervention sessions. Sometimes, procedures for stopping reinforcement require a lot of creativity!

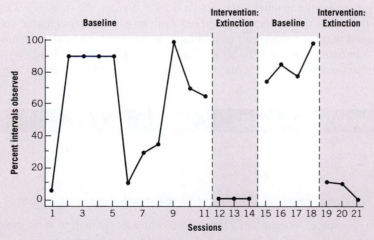

Figure 6-4 Percentage of intervals in which Reggie performed the repetitive/ritualistic behavior of plate twirling during baseline and intervention (extinction). Sessions were 30 minutes in length. *Source:* Adapted from A. Rincover, R. Cook, A. Peoples, & D. Packard (1979), Sensory extinction and sensory reinforcement principles for programming multiple adaptive behavior change. *Journal of Applied Behavior Analysis*, 12, 221–233, Figure 1. Copyright © 1979 Society for the Experimental Analysis of Behavior. Used by permission.

INSTRUCTION IN THE NEW CONTINGENCIES

Another factor that can affect how quickly extinction procedures will eliminate a behavior is instruction in the new contingencies. People's behavior often extinguishes faster when they are told their responses will no longer be reinforced than when reinforcement simply ceases to appear (Weiner, 1970). For instance, when teachers use small group projects in class, they can provide instructions that while they are working with a particular group, questions from students in other groups will be ignored; instead, students should save their questions until the end of the teachers' session with a group, when all students will have an opportunity to ask their questions. It may also help to give the students a way to help them remember their questions—for example, they could state the question in an audio recording or have paper and a pencil to write it down.

    The factors that affect the effectiveness of extinction lead to a couple of basic rules about using extinction procedures. Remember that the behavior we want to reduce may show an extinction burst and may fluctuate early in the process. If we have identified the reinforcers carefully and eliminated them, we *shouldn't conclude from just a burst or fluctuation that the extinction process isn't working.* Behaviors sometimes get worse for a while before they get better. If we stop the extinction procedure and allow the behavior to be reinforced again, however, we'll reinforce the behavior's getting worse—that is, we'll fuel the burst. Keep in mind that most behaviors in everyday life receive reinforcement intermittently, making them harder to extinguish. As a result, we'll need to be patient when using extinction. (Go to .)

STUDY AND REVIEW

SUMMARY

In the procedure or condition of extinction, the reinforcers that maintained an operant behavior are terminated, and the behavior eventually declines. To conduct extinction effectively, we must first determine all of the reinforcers that maintain the behavior so we can terminate those sources of reinforcement; these sources can involve positive or negative reinforcement. Extinction does not erase the memory of the behavior. At the beginning of extinction, the behavior may increase temporarily in an extinction burst, and sometimes behaviors that have been extinguished reappear as a result of spontaneous recovery, renewal, or reinstatement.

    A behavior's decline in extinction tends to be gradual, but the process can lead the target person to be aggressive. The target behavior's reinforcement history can affect its resistance to extinction. Behavior that has

---

CONCEPT CHECK 6.2

Answer the following questions about factors that influence the effectiveness of extinction.

1. Behaviors previously reinforced intermittently rather than continuously tend to show greater _____ to extinction.
2. The more times a behavior was reinforced in the past and the greater the reward _____ , the more _____ it is likely to take to become extinguished.
3. Suppose a teacher terminated the social reinforcement that previously maintained a child's habit of blurting out questions in class. An alternative response the teacher might reinforce is _____ . ⟺
4. An example of an instruction parents might give to a child that would increase the effectiveness of the extinction technique they are about to start for their child's whining behavior is _____ . ⟺

a history of having received intermittent reinforcement is likely to take longer to extinguish than behavior that almost always received continuous reinforcement.

When we use extinction, we can enhance its success and reduce problems, such as extinction burst, by also reinforcing alternative behaviors or competing responses and instructing the target person that the target behavior will not receive the reinforcers it has gotten in the past.

> To prepare for exams, use the following key terms and review questions and the online study guide that's available on this book's companion website at www.wiley.com/college/sarafino.

KEY TERMS

extinction
extinction burst
competing response

alternative behavior
spontaneous recovery
resistance to extinction

continuous reinforcement
intermittent reinforcement

ANSWERS TO CONCEPT CHECKS (CCs)

CC6.1 *Answers:* **1.** extinction **2.** reinforcers **3.** extinction burst **4.** competing response **5.** spontaneous recovery **6.** gradual

CC6.2 *Answers:* **1.** resistance **2.** value, time **3.** hand raising **4.** "You know how sometimes when you would whine like that I would give you what you want? Well, that won't happen anymore."

REVIEW QUESTIONS

1. What is extinction?

2. Describe how extinction is conducted when the operant behavior has been maintained with positive and negative reinforcement.

3. Discuss the incorrect idea that extinction erases the person's memory of the target behavior.

4. Describe an undesirable operant behavior of someone you know and state its likely reinforcers. Outline how you could or why you couldn't extinguish that behavior.

5. Define and give an example of an extinction burst of an operant behavior.

6. Define and give an example of spontaneous recovery of an operant behavior.

7. What is resistance to extinction, and how is it affected by the behavior's history of having received continuous or intermittent reinforcement?

8. Describe a behavior that you think you could extinguish in someone you know. What do you think the reinforcers are? What alternative behaviors could you reinforce? Why do you think instructing the person of the new contingencies would or would not help?

RELATED READINGS

- Bouton, M. E., & Swartzentruber, D. (1991). Sources of relapse after extinction in Pavlovian and instrumental learning. *Clinical Psychology Review, 11,* 123–140.

- Lerman, D. C., & Iwata, B. A. (1996). Developing a technology for the use of operant extinction in clinical settings: An examination of basic and applied research. *Journal of Applied Behavior Analysis, 29,* 345–382.

7

PUNISHMENT

Defining Punishment
Natural and Programmed Punishment
Positive and Negative Punishment
Unconditioned and Conditioned Punishment

Types of Punishing Events
Physically Aversive Stimuli
Reprimands
Aversive Activities
Time–out
Response Cost

Advantages and Disadvantages in Using Punishment
Advantages of Punishment
Disadvantages of Punishment

Study and Review

PROLOGUE

Sandra was a 6-month-old girl who entered a university hospital emaciated, weighing less than her birth weight, and unresponsive to the world around her (Sajwaj, Libet, & Agras, 1974). She was lethargic, showing no broad movements and seldom grasping objects. Medical examination didn't reveal an organic basis for her condition. Her malnutrition appeared to result mainly from her own behavior of *chronic rumination*: Immediately after feeding, she would

> open her mouth, elevate and fold her tongue, and then vigorously thrust her tongue forward and backward. Within a few seconds milk would appear at the back of her mouth and then slowly flow out. This behavior would continue for about 20 to 40 min until she apparently lost all of the milk she had previously consumed. No crying or evidence of pain and discomfort was observed during this behavior. (p. 558)

These bouts could be interrupted, such as by poking or touching her, but would resume soon after. Although chronic rumination is a rare condition, many cases in infants have been reported and an alarming number of them have died of it. Clearly, this behavior must be stopped.

One approach that stops rumination is punishment. The behavior analysts working with Sandra used a form of punishment called "lemon-juice therapy"—as soon as she began the vigorous tongue movements she would use in bringing up food, they squirted a small amount of unsweetened lemon juice into her mouth. This punishment was carried out any time of day that the tongue movements occurred, and the juice was given every 30 to 60 seconds if the movements persisted. Sandra's rumination declined dramatically in the first couple of days and reached near zero in a couple of weeks, and her weight increased markedly. Other mild punishers that have succeeded in treating rumination include smelling a pungent odor, such as ammonia, and mild electric shock (Altman, Haavik, & Cook, 1978; Cunningham & Linscheid, 1976). Figure 7-1 shows an infant who, like Sandra, had chronic rumination that was corrected with punishment therapy.

DEFINING PUNISHMENT

"Punishment doesn't work with Brian," his parents told a neighbor who complained of the child's daily racket. "We've scolded him and spanked him for making so much noise. That stops him for the moment, but he starts making noise again in a while." Did Brian's parents punish his making noise when they scolded and spanked him? Probably not. Let's see why we should doubt it.

In operant conditioning, **punishment** is a process whereby a consequence of a behavior *suppresses* that behavior, decreasing its frequency, duration, or magnitude. The consequence that suppresses the behavior in punishment is called a *punisher*. Punishers are stimuli or conditions the person finds aversive—loosely speaking, they're undesirable or unpleasant. Brian's behavior didn't seem to be affected by the consequences his parents applied. If a consequence must suppress behavior to be considered a punisher, it isn't likely that scolding or

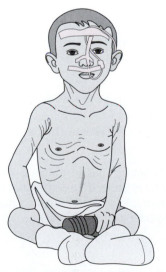 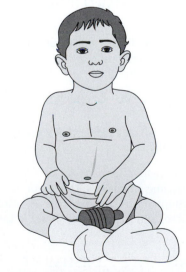

Figure 7-1   These drawings are of a real infant boy. On the left, his chronic ruminating (vomiting after feeding) had reduced his body to skin and bones (the tape on his face was used for holding a tube to feed him through his nose). After punishment was used to suppress his ruminating, his weight increased by 26% in less than 2 weeks, and his face, body, arms, and legs had filled out, as shown on the right. Before using a behavioral method for this type of problem a medical examination should rule out possible physical causes, such as acid reflux disease, that may be corrected with medical procedures. *Source:* Based on Photographic Media Center, University of Wisconsin-Madison Archives.

spanking punished Brian's making noise. If it had been a punisher, the behavior would have decreased. From casual reports like Brian's parents gave, we can't be sure whether a given behavior actually declined because parents typically don't assess their children's behavior carefully, and their impressions may be wrong.

You may be thinking, "But everyone finds scolding and spanking unpleasant!" Well, maybe Brian doesn't agree. If we're going to define *punishers* as "consequences people find unpleasant," we must be sure to assess the unpleasantness from the *viewpoint of the person who will receive these consequences*, not our point of view. Studies have shown that conditions parents and teachers ordinarily think of as punishers, such as scolding, can sometimes *reinforce* the behavior they're intended to decrease (Madsen et al., 1970; Wahler, Winkel, Peterson, & Morrison, 1965). What's more, we know that some people dislike stimuli or conditions most other people like, and vice versa. For instance, people usually dislike pain and think of it as a punisher, but some people seem to like physical pain—at least under some, usually sexual, situations—and are called *masochists*. It may be that pain becomes a conditioned reinforcer for these people through the process of respondent conditioning—that is, by participating in or viewing activities that associate pain with pleasure in a sexual context (Wincze, 1977).

There are two other reasons for not being certain whether scolding and spanking are punishers for Brian. First, if these consequences were applied poorly, their effects may have been weakened. We will see in a later chapter that several factors influence how effective punishment is likely to be. Second, scolding and spanking may be punishers for Brian, but the reinforcement he gets from making noise may be much stronger than the punishment being applied. As a result, his noisemaking wouldn't change much after the scolding or spanking. These problems in knowing which events are punishers are like those we've discussed for reinforcement: We need to assess carefully the consequences for a behavior we want to change. Hunches of what consequences may increase or decrease a behavior are helpful, but not sufficient.

As part of our definition of punishment, we are about to see that we can make distinctions in its types that are similar to those we made for types of reinforcement in Chapter 5. That is, punishment can be natural or programmed, positive or negative, and unconditioned or conditioned.

NATURAL AND PROGRAMMED PUNISHMENT

Natural punishers are consequences that decrease a behavior, happen spontaneously as a normal part of everyday life, and are not planned and given systematically to affect the behavior (Azrin & Holz, 1966; Vollmer, 2002). Hitting your finger while hammering a nail would be a natural punisher. Here are some other examples of natural punishers and their effects:

- A friend berates you for saying something that's offensive; in the future, you are wary of and refrain from saying similar things.
- You hurt your leg in a fall off a ladder that you positioned in a wobbly manner; in the future, you steady ladders and climb carefully.

In contrast to natural punishers, *programmed punishers* are consequences that are planned and used systematically with the goal of decreasing a behavior. The lemon-juice therapy in the opening story that was used to decrease an infant's chronic rumination is an example. An everyday example of a programmed punisher would be our getting a speeding ticket and then driving slower in the future (at least for a while).

POSITIVE AND NEGATIVE PUNISHMENT

Reinforcement in which a stimulus or condition is *added* following a behavior has the label *positive*; reinforcement in which a stimulus or condition is *subtracted* is called *negative*. The same "adding" versus "subtracting" distinction exists in punishment. As Figure 7-2 outlines, punishment can be delivered in two ways:

1. In **positive punishment**, an aversive stimulus or condition is *added* as a consequence of the behavior. This is the kind of punishment used in the lemon-juice therapy to stop Sandra's ruminating.

	Positive	Negative
Reinforcement	"Pleasant" stimulus or condition **added** (increases target behavior)	Aversive stimulus or condition **subtracted** (increases target behavior)
Punishment	Aversive stimulus or condition **added** (decreases target behavior)	"Pleasant" stimulus or condition **subtracted** (decreases target behavior)

Figure 7-2 Four types of behavioral consequences: positive reinforcement, negative reinforcement, positive punishment, and negative punishment. Notice that "positive" and "negative" refer to whether the stimulus or condition is *added* to or *subtracted* from the situation following a response.

2. In **negative punishment**, a stimulus or condition the person already has at the time the behavior occurs is *subtracted* as a consequence of performing the behavior. This stimulus or condition typically is something "pleasant" or valued—that is, receiving it for doing something would reinforce that behavior.

An example of negative punishment is a late fee imposed when we failed to pay a bill on time. The money to pay the fee is something we already had and was probably obtained as reinforcement for an earlier behavior, such as working.

We discussed in Chapter 5 that many people confuse the processes of punishment and negative reinforcement. An example may help you distinguish between these types of consequences. Suppose 2-year-old Fran is curious about electrical outlets and keeps trying to pull plugs out of and stuff things into the little holes. This behavior justifiably frightens her parents, and they scold her each time. Scolding has helped—she stops immediately and has been playing with outlets less and less. Scolding in this case is positive punishment for Fran's behavior, but it is also an *escape* behavior for her parents since it stops her behavior, thereby reducing their fright. The parents' scolding behavior is negatively reinforced by reducing their fright.

UNCONDITIONED AND CONDITIONED PUNISHMENT

Like reinforcers, punishers can be classified as unconditioned or conditioned. Aversive stimuli called *unconditioned punishers* typically decrease behavior on which they are contingent even though they were not learned to function that way. The punishment function of these stimuli appears to be inborn, probably promoting survival of each individual and the species. Examples of stimuli that generally serve as punishers for most people without having been learned are pain, certain strong tastes and odors, electric shock, very intense or harsh sounds, and physical restraint. *Conditioned punishers* are stimuli that did not have the ability to suppress behavior until they developed this function as a result of learning. This learning involves a stimulus–stimulus relationship that develops when the not-yet-punishing stimulus is paired repeatedly with an existing punisher (Dorsey, Iwata, Ong, & McSween, 1980; Hake & Azrin, 1965). For instance, a child may learn his or her parent's sternly saying "No" as a punisher by the word being paired repeatedly with a slap to the child's hand.

TYPES OF PUNISHING EVENTS

All sorts of stimuli and conditions can serve as punishers to suppress behavior (Azrin & Holz, 1966; Matson & Taras, 1989; Van Houten, 1983). Most punishers can be classified into several categories that may overlap somewhat. The first few types of punishers we'll consider involve positive punishment, and the last types involve negative punishment. Ways to apply these types of punishers are covered more fully in Chapters 18 and 19.

PHYSICALLY AVERSIVE STIMULI

I visited a stop-smoking clinic years ago and tried out a device that gave a mild electric shock to my finger. It was used to punish cigarette smoking to help people quit. The shock didn't hurt, but it produced a very unpleasant sensation, and I wanted it to stop. **Physically aversive stimuli** are events that cause physical pain, discomfort, or other unpleasant sensations. These stimuli are mainly unconditioned punishers—for example, hitting someone and administering electric shock, loud noise, certain odors and tastes. To be punishers, they must suppress behavior.

Physically aversive stimuli are very common consequences of behavior in our everyday lives. These consequences may be provided deliberately with the intention of correcting behavior—for instance, when parents and other adults hit children or animals for behaving in inappropriate or undesirable ways. But physically aversive stimuli can also be naturally occurring events that happen in our environments as consequences of our behavior (Azrin & Holz, 1966). Natural punishers that come to mind most easily involve careless behavior. Examples include bruising your head by walking into a post because you were looking at a physically attractive person, burning your hand by spilling hot coffee because you moved too quickly, and getting scratched by a pet because you played with it too roughly. If these consequences decreased your careless behavior, they are punishers.

Using physically aversive stimuli as punishers in therapy is usually avoided for humanitarian reasons and because of their side effects on behavior, which we consider later in this chapter. When punishers are strongly aversive, their use is very controversial. One controversial form of punishment is strong, painful electric shock (Goodman, 1994). The use of painful electric shock as a punisher in behavioral methods was tested in the 1960s in interventions for children with developmental disabilities, mainly to eliminate self-injurious and self-stimulatory behaviors (Corte, Wolf, & Locke, 1971; Lovaas, Schaeffer, & Simmons, 1965; Lovaas & Simmons, 1969). Although this method had some success, it is rarely used today and is reserved for situations in which all other approaches have failed and the behavior must be suppressed quickly, as in cases of self-injury. Other punishers to stop self-injury and self-stimulation that are usually successful and more acceptable include using *mild*, brief electric shock as punishment (Linscheid et al., 1990) and withdrawing negative reinforcement for these behaviors while giving positive reinforcement for alternative behaviors or competing responses (Iwata et al., 1990; Repp, Felce, & Barton, 1988). Using mild electric shock is less controversial than strong shock, but behavior analysts still avoid it.

Lemon-juice therapy uses a mild punisher, and an example of its use is the case of a 7-year-old boy with severe retardation who had begun masturbating publicly when he was living in an institution and continued to display this behavior for the nearly 2 years since returning to live at home (Cook, Altman, Shaw, & Blaylock, 1978). The behavior would occur at home and at school and other public places, causing his parents great embarrassment to the point that they were considering placing him in an institution again. Before the intervention, the boy's parents or teachers had tried to stop his public masturbating by shouting, "No!" and spanking his hand, but this didn't seem to work. Because the parents were not concerned with his private masturbation in his bedroom or a bathroom, the intervention punished occurrences in all other places. Whenever he put his hand in his pants at the crotch, his parent or a teacher would squirt into his mouth some unsweetened lemon juice. Data on the boy's target behavior were collected during four phases: a baseline in which the prior method ("No" plus hand spanking) was continued, a second baseline in which the target behavior was simply ignored, the intervention with lemon-juice punishment, and a follow-up. As Figure 7-3 shows, the boy's masturbatory behavior occurred at very high rates during both baseline periods, was almost completely eliminated quickly when the lemon-juice intervention was used, and was totally absent in 6 months of follow-up assessments.

REPRIMANDS

Reprimands are disapproving statements—such as "No! That's bad."—or feedback that sharply criticize a behavior. Because these statements are added after the behavior, they provide positive punishment when they reduce operant behavior. Reprimands are very common, naturally occurring events in people's everyday lives. Studies have found that teachers use reprimands more than praise with their students, particularly after second grade (Bear, 1998; Thomas, Presland, Grant, & Glynn, 1978; White, 1975). Classmates also use reprimands, sometimes to the detriment of other students' learning: Some students claim that they avoid

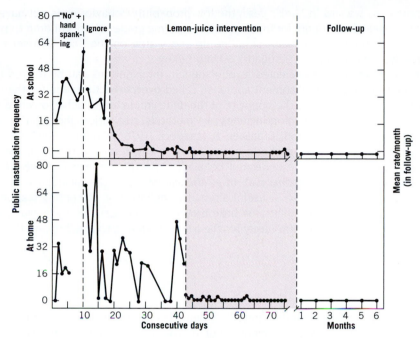

Figure 7-3   Public masturbation frequency in a multiple-baseline-across-situations design—at school (top panel) and at home (bottom panel)—during four phases: "No" plus hand spanking, ignoring, lemon-juice therapy intervention, and follow-up. Assessments were taken during six 5-minute observation periods in a day. For the first three phases, the data represent daily frequencies during the observation periods. For the follow-up phase, the data represent the mean frequency per day for each of 6 months. *Source:* From J. W. Cook, K. Altman, J. Shaw, & M. Blaylock (1978), Use of contingent lemon juice to eliminate public masturbation. *Behaviour Research and Therapy*, 16, 131–134, Figure 1. Copyright © 1978 Elsevier Ltd. Used by permission.

speaking up in class because they've been ridiculed in the past for giving *correct* answers (Herbert, 1997). One problem with applying reprimands by themselves to change behavior is that their effects appear to be more variable than those of other consequences. For instance, we've seen that reprimands by parents and teachers sometimes serve as reinforcers for a child's undesirable behavior, *increasing* the behavior instead of decreasing it.

AVERSIVE ACTIVITIES

An 11-year-old boy named Mark who lived at a residential institution during the week used swearwords about 11 times per dinner period (Fischer & Nehs, 1978). He went home on weekends. His "cottage parents" at the institution had been unsuccessful in trying to convince Mark to stop swearing, so they conducted an intervention requiring him to spend 10 minutes washing windows for each instance of swearing during dinner. His swearing declined sharply within a few days and remained infrequent during follow-up assessments taken in the 15 days after the intervention ended.

This example illustrates that aversive activities can serve as positive punishers. When we discussed the Premack principle and reinforcement in Chapter 5, we saw that engaging in high-probability behaviors can reinforce performing infrequent responses. Using aversive activities as punishers is essentially the other side of this coin—that is, being required to engage in a *low*-probability behavior as a consequence of performing a target response that occurs too frequently, such as Mark's swearing, can reduce the person's performance of the frequent response. As we saw in Mark's case, the low-probability behavior does not have to be related to the target behavior. Researchers found, for instance, that requiring grade-school children to perform arbitrarily chosen motor activities, such as repeatedly standing up and sitting on the floor, can serve as punishers to reduce their aggressive behavior (Luce, Delquadri, & Hall, 1980).

Of course, the aversive activities selected as punishers in interventions can be related to the behavioral excesses we're trying to reduce. A punishment approach called **overcorrection** requires the person to engage in aversive activities that correct or are the opposite of the undesirable target behavior when that misbehavior occurs (Foxx & Azrin, 1972). Overcorrection includes two methods, restitution and positive practice, that can be used together or separately (Axelrod, Brantner, & Meddock, 1978; Donohue, 2005; Ollendick & Matson, 1978). *Restitution* refers to correcting the effects of misbehavior and restoring the environment, usually to a condition better than it was before the undesired behavior. For example, a person who wrote graffiti on a wall might be required to paint the entire wall. In *positive practice*, when the misbehavior occurs, the person must repeatedly perform an appropriate or useful alternative behavior or competing response to that of the misbehavior. For instance, a girl who pushes her little brother down to get the toy he was playing with might have to practice over and over asking him nicely for the toy and offering to give him another toy in exchange. (Go to .)

TIME-OUT

"Go to your room!" the parent commanded, intending punishment. Being sent to your room from someplace more reinforcing can provide negative punishment if your room is not very stimulating and does not provide many opportunities for reinforcement. The reinforcing situation you had is taken away, contingent on misbehavior. Punishing a behavior by converting or moving the person's environment from one that is relatively reinforcing to one that is less reinforcing is called **time-out** (Brantner & Doherty, 1983; Van Houten, 1983).

How long should the time-out last? After reviewing the results of many studies, Brantner and Doherty (1983) concluded that time-out periods can be fairly short, lasting a matter of minutes rather than hours or days. Periods from 1 to 15 minutes are usually effective in suppressing a behavior. One study compared the punishing effects of three time-out period lengths: 1, 15, and 30 minutes (White, Nielsen, & Johnson, 1972). The time-out procedures were applied with individuals at an institution for mental retardation to reduce their deviant behaviors, such as aggression and tantrums. The results indicated that all of the time-out periods

CONCEPT CHECK 7.1

Check your understanding of the preceding concepts. Remember that the symbol ⟺ means the answer can vary. Answer the following questions about the definition of punishment and types of positive punishment.

1. Punishment is a process whereby a consequence _____ the behavior on which it is contingent.
2. Stubbing your toe because you were walking carelessly is an example of a _____ punisher.
3. An example of positive punishment from your life is _____ . ⟺
4. An example of negative punishment from your life is _____ . ⟺
5. Washing a child's mouth out with soap for swearing is an example of using a(n) _____ stimulus as a punisher.
6. Overcorrection consists of two methods: _____ and _____ .

reduced deviant behavior, but the 15- and 30-minute lengths reduced it the most and were equally effective. Generally speaking, time-out periods should be as short as possible while still reducing the target behavior markedly. Sometimes just a minute or two is sufficient.

Brantner and Doherty (1983) have described three types or levels of time-out. The most restrictive level is called *isolation time-out*: The target person is removed from the relatively reinforcing environment and placed in a separate, substantially less reinforcing environment. Being sent to your room would be an example of isolation time-out if it is a less reinforcing environment. Some schools or institutions have set up special "time-out rooms" where individuals are sent or taken when they misbehave (Barton, Guess, Garcia, & Baer, 1970). But using isolation time-out can have disadvantages and is not advisable in some cases. For instance, individuals who might harm themselves if left unattended may require a staff member to monitor their behavior in isolation. And isolating children who are developmentally disabled may provide them with opportunities to perform self-stimulation or self-injurious behaviors that are undesirable and dangerous.

In *exclusion time-out*, target individuals are removed from opportunities for reinforcement without isolating them—for instance, by moving the persons to a separate part of the same environment and not allowing them to participate in any reinforcing activities that are going on. Researchers used this method in a day-care center to reduce the children's disruptive behavior, such as being aggressive or damaging toys or other objects (Porterfield, Herbert-Jackson, & Risley, 1976). When an instance of disruptive behavior occurred, the caregivers described to the child both the misbehavior and an alternative behavior. "No, don't take toys from other children," the caregiver might say, "Ask me for the toy you want." Then the time-out would be started: The target child had to sit on the floor with no toys at the periphery of the other children's activities and watch as they interacted. After the child watched quietly for a minute or so, he or she was allowed to rejoin the other children. Misbehavior occurred during the intervention with time-out punishment at a rate that was only about 37% of the rate resulting when the children were only told the behavior was wrong and given another activity to do. Similar exclusion time-out procedures have been applied in interventions that effectively reduced oppositional behavior in preschoolers and disruptive behavior in adults with mental retardation (Bostow & Bailey, 1969; Roberts, Hatzenbuehler, & Bean, 1981).

This girl has been placed in exclusion time-out for misbehavior in class. *Source:* Copyright © Myrleen Pearson/The Image Works.

In *nonexclusion time-out*, individuals who misbehave are not removed from the ongoing activities at all, but receive a signal indicating a period in which they cannot earn reinforcers that would have been available if the misbehavior hadn't occurred. An intervention using a nonexclusion time-out procedure was conducted to reduce disruptive behaviors, such as aggression and yelling, of five boys with mental retardation in a special education class (Foxx & Shapiro, 1978). During usual classroom activities, the boys could earn social and consumable reinforcers every few minutes for working quietly. Each child who was eligible for these reinforcers wore a colored ribbon around his neck to signify this status. When a boy misbehaved, the teacher removed the ribbon from his neck for 3 minutes. Thus, when the teacher gave the next reinforcers, he could not receive any. This procedure reduced disruptive behavior in all of the boys, and the two boys who had been most disruptive during baseline were misbehaving only about 5% as often by the end of the intervention.

In addition to being a punishment technique, time-out can be extended to become extinction or negative reinforcement procedures, too. For example, suppose we sent Len to his room for hitting his sister, and he began to have a tantrum. Maintaining the time-out conditions until the tantrum ends would serve as extinction of that behavior. Or if we required Len to apologize to his sister to gain release from time-out, apologizing would be negatively reinforced.

Time-out punishment appears to be effective in reducing unwanted behavior and may be a very good alternative to punishers of other types, especially those that apply physically aversive stimuli (Brantner & Doherty, 1983). Exclusion and nonexclusion time-out methods seem to be as effective as isolation time-out procedures in most situations, while having fewer disadvantages. Time-out punishment is likely to be most effective in suppressing behavior if the amount of reinforcement in the original environment is much greater than that in the time-out environment (Solnick, Rincover, & Peterson, 1977; Van Houten, 1983). (Go to 🔍.)

RESPONSE COST

Losing money as a result of misbehavior is an example of a type of punishment called **response cost**, a negative punishment procedure in which a behavior results in the person losing a valued item or privilege (Rapport & Begolli, 2005; Van Houten, 1983). Although the person usually has the item or privilege already, perhaps having received it as a reinforcer for an earlier behavior, it can also be something he or she has earned but not yet received. Response cost in everyday life often involves having to pay money—for instance, as a fine for underpaying income taxes, writing a check that bounces, or returning a library book late. But response cost can take away things other than money, such as a favorite music recording or article of clothing, or a privilege the person ordinarily has, such as using a cell phone or the Internet. Of course, the response cost procedure is carried out only when the unwanted target behavior has been performed.

Interventions have used response cost punishment in a variety of settings, usually as fines in the form of money or tokens. One example comes from the treatment of a man's alcohol abuse in behavior therapy (Miller, 1972). The client and his wife agreed that he should drink no more than three drinks per day and must consume all drinks in her presence. They also agreed to the following response cost procedure. If he drank outside the agreed upon conditions—which his wife might determine by smelling liquor on his breath or by his appearing drunk—he had to pay her a large amount of money that she would spend very frivolously, which he claimed would be very unpleasant for him. His drinking decreased from baseline levels by 60% in less than 2 weeks and stayed at three drinks a day during follow-up assessments over the next 6 months. Although this simple approach effectively reduced this man's drinking, response cost would not be sufficient by itself to control drinking in most alcohol abusers.

Response cost has been applied very effectively in classrooms. One intervention used response cost to reduce off-task, distracted behaviors in children with conduct and learning problems (Sullivan & O' Leary, 1990). In this program, teachers would scan their classes periodically, checking to see whether individual children were working on class activities or performing off-task behaviors. In some classes, response cost was used in

CLOSE-UP

A Penny Lost and a Penny Earned—Are Their Effects Equal?

One way we can be punished is to *lose* money, such as having to pay a fine; but *receiving* money generally serves as a reinforcer—money can be the medium for reinforcement and punishment. Do punishers and reinforcers have equal but opposing impacts on behavior? That is, does losing money suppress the behavior on which it is contingent to the same degree as receiving the same amount of money strengthens the behavior?

Researchers examined this issue in an ingenious study that tested college students in a computer task (Rasmussen & Newland, 2008). Instructions told the students that they would see on the monitor two moving targets and that:

Clicking the mouse on these targets can cause you to earn or lose money. When this happens, a flashing message will show how many cents you gained or lost. The two targets differ in terms of how clicking affects your earnings. (p. 160)

The students' task was to figure out how to earn as much money as possible, but they weren't given information at any time on the amount of money they had accumulated. The two targets on the monitor were small boxes of different colors; one was on the left side of the screen, and the other was on the right. The students participated in the task for several hours that were divided into sessions. In any session, clicking on one target would result in reinforcement: A light would flash "+4¢" to indicate that they had earned four cents. In some sessions, clicking on one target would lead to punishment: A light would flash "–4¢" to indicate a loss of four cents. Reinforcement and punishment were given on a random intermittent schedule, meaning that not all the clicks received a consequence, and the students could not predict which clicks would.

What did this research find? Based on the pattern of responses (clicks) made to each of the targets and the number of reinforcers and punishers received, the researchers reached two conclusions. First, as we would expect, monetary gain and loss functioned, respectively, as reinforcers and punishers. Second, even though the monetary value, 4¢, was identical for each instance of reinforcement and punishment, the punisher had a much larger impact on the behavior—that is, it suppressed clicking substantially more than the reinforcer strengthened it.

---

a way that punished performing *off*-task behavior during the scan with the loss of a token, which was worth 1 minute of recess. In other classes, reinforcement was used instead of punishment: Performing *on*-task behavior was reinforced with a token that was worth 1 minute of recess. Both conditions improved the children's working on class activities, and using response cost was at least as effective as using reinforcement. Other classroom interventions have used fines in tokens that reduced:

- Off-task behavior in hyperactive children (Rapport, Murphy, & Bailey, 1982).
- Stealing in second-graders (Switzer, Deal, & Bailey, 1977).
- Disruptive behavior in fourth- to sixth-graders (Barrish, Saunders, & Wolf, 1969; Harris & Sherman, 1973).
- Spelling errors in adolescents (Truchlicka, McLaughlin, & Swain, 1998).

Response cost punishment is fairly easy to apply, especially when it is part of a token reinforcement program.

Here's something to keep in mind about the response cost approach: Taking away something people value as a consequence of their misbehavior is not the same as withholding reinforcement until they perform an appropriate behavior. Many students confuse the two situations. The former applies to decreasing a behavioral excess—that is, the person *has performed* an unwanted act; the latter applies to increasing a behavioral deficit—the person *has not yet performed* the desirable target behavior. (Go to 🐾.)

CASE STUDY

Response Cost to Stop "Lady Mary's" Blurting Out

A 29-year-old woman with psychiatric and mental retardation disorders who worked in a sheltered workshop had a habit of blurting out statements that were false or didn't make sense in the context (Kazdin, 1971). For instance, she would suddenly say, "You can't take that away from me," when no one had tried to take anything; or "My name is Lady Mary," which it wasn't.

A response cost intervention was designed to reduce the frequency of "Lady Mary's" blurting out. To implement this intervention, a response cost procedure was added to a token reinforcement system that had already been in effect for 6 months to increase her job production rate, which was only 20% of the minimum industrial rate. She was informed that her blurting out would now cost her tokens. But during the first week, no tokens were taken for the target behavior in order to see if the threat would be sufficient to reduce the behavior. It wasn't—her blurting out continued at the baseline rate of about 40 instances a week. Once the response cost procedure was actually in force, her blurting out plummeted to about 3 per week. What's more, it remained at that level during the 4-week follow-up period when the response cost consequences were no longer applied.

ADVANTAGES AND DISADVANTAGES IN USING PUNISHMENT

We've seen that there are many varieties of punishers and that punishment can suppress behavior effectively. But using punishment is very controversial, especially when the punisher is a physically aversive stimulus. These controversies focus on the advantages and disadvantages of using punishment in applied behavior analysis—in behavior therapy, everyday parenting, education, business and industry, and so on (Brown, 1982; Singh, Lloyd, & Kendall, 1990; Walters & Grusec, 1977). Let's see what the issues are.

ADVANTAGES OF PUNISHMENT

One of the main advantages of using punishment techniques lies in the *rapid results* it achieves in suppressing the undesired behavior (Dinsmoor, 1998). This advantage is especially important if the behavior is dangerous, as in the cases we discussed earlier of self-injurious behavior and infant ruminative vomiting. Physically aversive stimuli have been applied to stop these behaviors, and *mild* stimuli are frequently sufficient to suppress them very quickly, sometimes with just a few applications (Cunningham & Linscheid, 1976; Linscheid et al., 1990). These effects are especially impressive because the target behaviors in these interventions had occurred for months or years before aversive stimuli were applied, and other methods had been tried to stop the behaviors without success.

Rapid results are also important when the target behavior is very embarrassing, as in the case we considered earlier of a boy who masturbated in public. Using lemon juice as a punisher dramatically reduced this boy's public masturbation (see Figure 7-3) in just a few days and virtually eliminated it in a couple of weeks (Cook, Altman, Shaw, & Blaylock, 1978). Interventions using time-out and overcorrection punishment methods have quickly and substantially decreased aggressive and self-stimulation behaviors, too (Marholin & Townsend, 1978; Wilson, Robertson, Herlong, & Haynes, 1979). Speed in reducing all three of these behaviors is desirable.

Another advantage in using punishment is the *positive side effects* it sometimes produces in nontarget behaviors. In the mild shock intervention Linscheid and his colleagues (1990) applied to decrease the long-standing self-injurious behaviors of individuals with autism and mental retardation, only certain types of self-injurious behaviors were targeted for punishment. Yet specific assessments indicated that several of the nontarget behaviors improved, too. And anecdotal information suggested that social behaviors and independent feeding improved in some individuals. Other studies using other kinds of punishment have found positive side effects on such nontarget behaviors as individuals' greater attentiveness when aggressive behavior was suppressed and increased play behavior when self-stimulation was suppressed (Van Houten, 1983).

The last advantage in using punishment we'll consider is that it often leads to a *complete suppression* of the unwanted response (Dinsmoor, 1998; Van Houten, 1983). For most of the studies of punishment effects we examined earlier, the data presented verbally in the text or graphically (see Figure 7-3) depict long-lasting, complete or near-complete suppression of the target behaviors. This durability is important for two reasons. First, when the target behavior is dangerous, the most appropriate behavioral goal is to stop it entirely. Although other behavioral methods frequently can reduce dangerous responses substantially, they may not eliminate them. Second, behaviors that have been strongly suppressed are less likely to recover and become problems again in the future.

DISADVANTAGES OF PUNISHMENT

Researchers have described several negative side effects punishment may sometimes produce. Here we examine these disadvantages of punishment within three broad categories: emotional and escape/avoidance reactions, aggressive behaviors, and future use of punishment.

Emotional and Escape/Avoidance Reactions

People don't like to be punished—they don't like to receive unwanted or unpleasant consequences for their behavior. As a result, being punished sometimes produces negative emotional reactions, causing the person to cry or have tantrums, for instance. These reactions are not limited to punishment techniques that involve physically aversive stimuli, such as painful events, but may also occur with other methods, such as overcorrection (Axelrod, Brantner, & Meddock, 1981; Carey & Bucher, 1981). We might be concerned about causing negative emotions for many reasons, but one relates to the likely success of our intervention: Negative emotions interfere with therapy and learning processes.

A related side effect of punishment is that the unpleasantness of the aversive stimuli may cause the target person to try to escape from the situation, even when the punisher is fairly mild (Azrin & Holz, 1966; Dinsmoor, 1998). What's more, associations the person is likely to make between the aversive stimuli and the therapy or training situation may lead him or her to try to avoid the situation or the people dispensing the punishment (Morris & Redd, 1975).

Aggressive Behavior

Sometimes individuals become physically aggressive toward the people who dispense punishment and other individuals in the environment (Azrin & Holz, 1966; Dinsmoor, 1998; Hutchinson, 1977; Mayhew & Harris, 1978; Oliver, West, & Sloane, 1974). In therapy sessions, this may take the form of hitting, kicking, or throwing objects at the therapist—behavior that disrupts the session, at least temporarily, and may cause injury. To the extent that the target person's aggression leads to escape from the therapy or training session, that behavior will be negatively reinforced by virtue of the reduced discomfort from getting out of the session.

Future Use of Punishment

I remember seeing a cartoon years ago depicting a boy across his father's lap, being spanked. The caption read, "This will teach you to hit your sister." Although the father was using punishment to reduce the boy's physical aggression, he was also modeling the undesired type of behavior for his son to learn. Children often imitate the punishing acts they see, and the punishment can be physical or nonphysical, as in response cost (Gelfand et al., 1974; Walters & Grusec, 1977).

A dramatic example of the likely role of modeling in children's using physical punishment comes from a study of disadvantaged toddlers in four day-care centers that focused on helping battered children and nonabused children from "families under stress" (Main & George, 1985). The researchers observed the children for incidents in which a child showed distress by crying or behaving fearfully and assessed the reactions of the other children toward the distressed child. How did the abused and nonabused children react? Nonabused children tended to respond in a concerned or sad manner. In contrast, the abused boys and girls showed little or no concern—instead, they often reacted with physical attacks or anger. The following example describes one such episode:

> Martin [an abused boy of 32 months] tried to take the hand of the crying other child, and when she resisted, he slapped her on the arm with his open hand. He then turned away ... and began vocalizing very strongly, "Cut it out! CUT IT OUT!", each time saying it a little faster and louder. He patted her, but ... his patting became beating, and he continued beating her despite her screams. (p. 410)

Although these observations can't pinpoint why the abused children reacted this way, the similarity to their parents' abusiveness is both disturbing and provocative, suggesting a role of modeling. We know also that abusive parents often were abused or neglected as children (Kempe, 1976).

But the recipient of punishment is not the only person in the aversive situation who can learn to use punishment more in the future—the person dispensing it can, too. For example, parents or teachers who use punishment are likely to find that it stops the current misbehavior immediately and tends to reduce future instances of the response rapidly. When this happens, their punitive acts are reinforced, and they become more likely to use aversive consequences in the future.

Should We Use Punishment?

Controversies over using aversive stimuli with people who are developmentally disabled led to the design of a training approach called *Gentle Teaching* (McGee & Gonzalez, 1990; McGee, Menolascino, Hobbs, & Menousek, 1987). What is this approach? Gentle Teaching uses no punishment in training; the only consequences the teacher (called a caregiver) applies are social reinforcers—such as praise, hugs, and smiles. When inappropriate behaviors occur, the teacher withholds social reinforcement in an effort to extinguish them and tries to redirect the behaviors toward a desirable activity by using new task materials. If self-injurious behavior begins, the teacher tries to block the act, perhaps by deflecting the person's arm in the act of hitting, and then conveys calming messages, such as "Everything's fine. No one will hurt you."

Is Gentle Teaching effective? Research on the success of the Gentle Teaching approach with individuals who are developmentally disabled has yielded mixed results (Barrera & Teodoro, 1990; Jones, Singh, & Kendall, 1990; Jordan, Singh, & Repp, 1989; McGee & Gonzalez, 1990). For instance, studies using this approach to decrease self-injury and self-stimulation have found that Gentle Teaching either fails to decrease the behaviors or is less effective in decreasing them than are behavioral methods that include a wider range of reinforcers and some mild punishers.

The negative side effects of using punishment in changing behavior are serious concerns when they occur, but they don't appear to happen very often (Linscheid & Meinhold, 1990; Matson & Taras, 1989; Van Houten, 1983). For instance, children are not likely to become abusive individuals from having received punishment occasionally, even if some of it was fairly intense and physically aversive. The more excessive the punishment is in its frequency, duration, and intensity, the more likely long-lasting negative side effects will develop. Still, whenever we consider using punishment in interventions to change behavior, we should move cautiously and examine the likely advantages and disadvantages carefully. We should also determine whether using a form of punishment we are considering, such as physically aversive stimuli or isolation time-out, violates the law or institutional policies. And if we use punishment and don't begin to see improvements in the target behavior quickly—usually in a matter of hours or days—we should reassess the situation and, perhaps, discontinue these consequences. (Go to 📖.)

CONCEPT CHECK 7.2

Answer the following questions about methods of negative punishment and the advantages and disadvantages of punishment.

1. The length of time-out periods usually doesn't need to exceed _____ to be effective.
2. Having a student sit facing a rear corner of his or her classroom is an example of _____ time-out punishment.
3. The research on the relative effects of monetary gain and loss in a computer task showed that punishment has a _____ impact on behavior than reinforcement does.
4. Losing something of value as a result of misbehavior is called _____ punishment.
5. An advantage of using punishment is _____ . ⇔
6. A disadvantage of using punishment is the target person's _____ . ⇔

STUDY AND REVIEW

SUMMARY

Punishment suppresses the behavior on which it is contingent; if a consequence intended as a punisher does not decrease the behavior, it is not a punisher. Natural punishers occur spontaneously in life, and programmed punishers are administered systematically with the intention of reducing a behavior. In positive punishment, a consequence is added after misbehavior occurs; in negative punishment, a valued stimulus or condition is taken away after misbehavior. Unconditioned and conditioned punishers serve to decrease behavior, but the latter were learned to function that way.

Some types of punishment involve physically aversive stimuli or reprimands. Other punishers consist of aversive activities—as in the method of overcorrection, which includes the procedures of restitution and positive practice. These consequences are examples of positive punishment. Examples of negative punishment methods include imposing a time-out from opportunities for reinforcement or applying response cost after the target behavior. Time-out can take three forms: isolation, exclusion, and nonexclusion time-out.

Punishment methods have several advantages and disadvantages that influence decisions on whether to use them and which types of punishers to select. The advantages are that they sometimes produce desirable side effects and often achieve rapid results with a complete suppression of the target behavior. The disadvantages are that they may produce undesirable emotions, escape or avoidance behavior, and aggression in the target person and make him or her more likely to administer punishment to others in the future.

To prepare for exams, use the following key terms and review questions and the online study guide that's available on this book's companion website at www.wiley.com/college/sarafino.

KEY TERMS

punishment
positive punishment
negative punishment

physically aversive stimulus
reprimands
overcorrection

time-out
response cost

ANSWERS TO CONCEPT CHECKS (CCs)

CC7.1 *Answers:* **1.** suppresses **2.** natural **3.** a scolding **4.** interest paid for not paying a credit card bill on time **5.** physically aversive **6.** restitution, positive practice

CC7.2 *Answers:* **1.** 15 minutes **2.** exclusion **3.** greater **4.** response cost **5.** behavior declines rapidly **6.** aggression

REVIEW QUESTIONS

1. Describe the intervention and findings of Sajwaj, Libet, and Agras (1974) to eliminate an infant's chronic rumination.

2. What is punishment, and how do positive and negative punishment differ?

3. What are physically aversive stimuli? Give four examples.

4. How could you determine if a stimulus, such as a reprimand, is a punisher for a specific person?

5. Define the term *overcorrection*, and give an example of how a parent might use this method to decrease a child's misbehavior.

6. Distinguish among the three types of time-out punishment.

7. Define *response cost punishment*, and give an example of it from your own life.

8. What are the advantages and disadvantages of using punishment?

9. What is the Gentle Teaching approach? Is it effective in reducing problem behaviors in individuals who are developmentally disabled?

RELATED READINGS

- Axelrod, S., & Apsche, J. (Eds.). (1983). *The effects of punishment on human behavior.* New York: Academic Press.

- McGee, J. J., Menolascino, F. J., Hobbs, D. C., & Menousek, P. E. (1987). *Gentle teaching: A nonaversive approach for helping persons with mental retardation.* New York: Human Sciences Press.

- Repp, A. C., & Singh, N. N. (Eds.). (1990). *Perspectives on the use of nonaversive and aversive interventions for persons with developmental disabilities.* Sycamore, IL: Sycamore.

- Walters, G. C., & Grusec, J. E. (1977). *Punishment.* San Francisco: W. H. Freeman.

8

ANTECEDENTS: STIMULUS CONTROL

PROLOGUE

Think back to your driving history regarding stop signs. Have you ever driven through a stop sign because you were preoccupied, or did you fail to look left and right or come to a full stop because you were in a hurry? These acts create great risks and occur all around the world. In the United States alone, hundreds of thousands of accidents occur at stop signs each year, producing tens of thousands of incapacitating injuries and about 3,000 deaths (NHTSA, 2004). What can be done to increase safe driving practices and reduce accidents at stop signs?

Ron Van Houten and Richard Retting (2001) conducted a study to examine ways to manage antecedent stimuli to increase cautious driving behavior at stop signs. Here's what they did: At the bottom of stop signs at three intersections where there had been at least four crashes in a 3-year period, they installed either a sign saying "LOOK BOTH WAYS" or a sign that used LED (light-emitting diode) technology to create animated eyes scanning to the left and right (with no words) when a vehicle approached. Across 4 months, researchers videotaped over 6,000 vehicles passing through the intersections and scored the tapes for whether the driver made a full stop, looked right before proceeding, and started to enter the intersection but encountered a "conflict" with another vehicle in which one of them made a sudden stop. Interobserver reliability methods revealed very good agreement between observers, particularly for the conflict and full-stop measures.

Did using the signs as antecedents improve traffic safety? During baseline, only a little more than half of the drivers made a full stop and over three quarters looked right; conflicts occurred in less than 10% of the cases. During the intervention, although the LOOK BOTH WAYS sign had little effect, the LED sign with animated eyes noticeably increased drivers' coming to a full stop and decreased conflicts; the LED sign increased looking right only modestly, perhaps because it was already occurring at fairly high levels in baseline. These findings show that antecedents affect behavior and vary in the degree to which they are effective.

In this chapter, we'll focus on the role of antecedent cues in operant behavior and examine how they set the occasion for behavior to take place, how we acquire these cues, and what kinds of events can serve as cues.

SETTING THE OCCASION FOR BEHAVIOR

We've seen that **antecedents** are cues that precede and set the occasion for a behavior—they lead us to do, think, or feel something. What are some examples? If you notice that you are *thirsty* and see a *water fountain*, these two cues set the occasion for you to use the fountain to get a drink. In the past, getting a drink of water when these antecedents were present quenched your thirst. As another example, when you hear a radio announcer say that one of your favorite recordings is about to be played, you stop what you were doing and turn up the volume. In the past, hearing this recording gave you great enjoyment. We learn cues that tell us when and where to perform or not perform certain responses by linking the cues with the behavior and its consequences.

TYPES OF ANTECEDENTS

Our behavior happens in a *context* that includes objects, other people, and internal events, such as feeling hungry; anything in the context that arouses behavior is a *stimulus*. We can learn to use almost any stimulus—any event, person, object, or place—as an antecedent for performing or not performing an operant behavior. Consider the behavior of telling an off-color joke: A teenager might learn that telling the joke among friends leads to laughter and praise, but telling the joke at a family dinner does not. Here are some other examples of antecedents influencing behavior:

- A teacher asking a question sets the occasion for students to raise their hands.
- Seeing your dog leads you to call its name.
- Smelling freshly made coffee persuades you to pour a cup.
- Hearing someone call your name gets you to look at the person.
- Feeling someone you like caress your neck leads you to hug him or her.
- Being in a bar sets the occasion for ordering a drink.
- Thinking about a past stressful event makes you act like a grouch.
- Saying in your mind, "I hate to exercise," leads you away from physical activity.
- Feeling tired induces you to stop studying.

As you can see in this list, antecedents can involve any of our senses. You probably also expect that the effects of particular antecedents can differ from one person to the next, and you're correct (Wahler & Fox, 1981). For instance, some students never raise their hands when a teacher asks a question, and some students raise their hands only when they are sure they know the answer. We learn when and when not to respond.

Overt and Covert Antecedents

Antecedents can be *overt*—that is, open to or directly observable through our senses—or *covert*, internal and not open to observation. In the list of antecedents you just read, the first several are examples of overt antecedents, such as seeing a dog or smelling coffee, and the last ones are examples of covert antecedents, such as saying something in your mind or feeling tired. A study of people who buy things compulsively found that covert antecedents involving negative emotions, such as feeling angry or depressed, are the most common events that lead them to buy (Miltenberger et al., 2003). What's more, the most common consequence of compulsive buying involved negative reinforcement, such as by gaining relief from the negative emotions that led them to buy.

Immediate and Distant Antecedents

Most antecedents are present shortly before the behavior occurs and are called *immediate antecedents*, such as when you hear someone in a building yell, "Fire!" and you head toward an exit right away (Groden, 1989; Wahler & Fox, 1981). Other immediate antecedents are less dramatic but still effective—for instance, traffic lights are antecedents to behavior. Making it through a signal without having to stop is reinforcing for most drivers (some may even feel "victorious" at times), and having to stop for a long time can be unpleasant, or punishing. To reduce drivers' zipping through a signal when it is yellow or has just turned red, traffic engineers could alter the antecedents and/or consequences. Researchers did this at an intersection in Chicago after collecting baseline data showing that more than half of the drivers approaching yellow or red lights at that intersection went through without stopping (Jason, Neal, & Marinakis, 1985). By altering the timing sequence of the two signals so that the second signal's yellow light came on sooner and the red stayed on for a shorter period, the researchers made driving safer: Over 90% of the drivers now stopped for the yellow or red lights, and the accident rate declined by more than 36% at that intersection. This example describes a clearly successful application of behavior analysis.

In a sports example of applying antecedents to improve behavior, Ziegler (1987) trained beginning tennis players to use cues to help them hit balls projected from a machine. Simply saying "Concentrate" and "Keep your eye on the ball" brought no improvement. But the players' skills in hitting the balls—with both forehand and backhand strokes—improved substantially when they were taught to give themselves four verbal cues. The cues were to say "Ready" when the machine was about to project the next ball, "Ball" when the ball shot out of the machine, "Bounce" when the ball hit the surface of the court, and "Hit" when they saw the racquet meet the ball. Training can help people learn the cues they fail to learn on their own.

Most of the antecedents we've described are discrete events, such as saying a word, that have a start and end, usually in a short period of time. But antecedents can be continuing or ongoing conditions, too. Here are two examples of interventions in which people's behavior improved after ongoing antecedent conditions were changed:

1. A study found that elderly patients in a mental institution communicated more frequently with each other and staff when the institution made two environmental changes: The staff rearranged furniture on the wards so that the patients sat around small tables rather than along walls, and they served meals and snacks buffet style so the patients would serve themselves rather than being given their food on individual trays (Melin & Götestam, 1981).
2. Researchers found that students on a school playground waiting for the building to open engaged in half as much aggression when they were encouraged to play organized games, such as rope jumping and foot races (Murphy, Hutchison, & Bailey, 1983). This approach is being used today in schools to curb bullying (Graham, 2010).

In these two cases, the original antecedents set the occasion for solitary behavior in the elderly patients and aggressive behavior in the children. The changes that were made to produce the new immediate antecedents make sense.

Not all antecedents occur just before the behavior they influence. Sometimes antecedents precede the behavior by several minutes, hours, or much longer amounts of time, and are called *distant antecedents* (Groden, 1989; Wahler & Fox, 1981). Distant antecedents often continue to affect behavior for a long time after the occurrence of the actual antecedent because they have strong emotional and covert components. Thus, the behavior of a woman who has been physically abused at home might be influenced for weeks or years by the emotion and frequent thoughts about these events.

When behavior analysts design an intervention to change a target behavior, they usually need to identify the behavior's existing antecedents. Not all stimuli that precede a behavior set the occasion for the person to respond. Some stimuli may just happen now and then to coincide in time and place with the actual antecedents. The procedures we can use to identify antecedents involve making systematic observations of the target behavior, looking for the circumstances or events that regularly precede it. Antecedents that are *overt and immediate* are usually fairly easy to identify because they are present and observable just before the target behavior occurs. Antecedents that are *covert* or *distant* can be relatively difficult to identify. Covert antecedents are not directly observable and consist of thoughts, feelings, and physiological states. Often the person whose target behavior is to be changed isn't aware of these cues. Chapters 13 and 14 examine the procedures for identifying antecedents.

ANTECEDENT FUNCTIONS

Antecedents can have two types of functions. For instance, in a hypothetical example of antecedents we considered earlier, you were thirsty and saw a water fountain. This example includes antecedents with two different functions—one function is motivational, and the other is discriminative (Michael, 1982). The *motivational function* relates to your thirst, which affects the effectiveness of a consequence for a behavior: In our example, if you are thirsty and not hungry, water is likely to be a more effective reinforcer than food for the behavior you make—that is, using the fountain. The *discriminative function* relates to seeing the water fountain, a stimulus that you can distinguish from many other objects, such as a lamp, and you have learned in the past that using it leads to a particular type of consequence: water as reinforcement. Because of this function, psychologists would call the water fountain a discriminative stimulus.

Discriminative Stimuli

Suppose a 7-year-old girl named Carrie is talented in music and has already learned to sight-read music scores pretty well. When she sees in a score the symbol for the note A in the middle of the piano scale, she presses the correct piano key to sound that note. The symbol for the note is a stimulus for her response of pressing the correct key. That is, the symbol is a **discriminative stimulus (S^D)** (pronounced "ess-DEE"), a cue that sets the occasion for a particular response and signals that the response will be followed by a particular type of consequence. In Carrie's case, the S^D is the symbol, and the consequence is reinforcement: hearing the correct note or being told it is correct. If she were to play an A note for any other symbol, she would not receive reinforcement, and may even receive punishment, such as criticism.

Silhouettes as discriminative stimuli, telling people that both genders may use this restroom. *Source:* iStockphoto.

When we learn a discriminative stimulus, the behavior tends to occur in the future in accordance with the condition—that is, the presence of the S^D—that existed when it was reinforced or punished in the past. Thus, in the presence of the S^D, the behavior is likely to continue or increase if it was reinforced in the past or to occur less frequently if it was punished. Here are some other examples of S^Ds you may have learned:

- You hear a dial tone (S^D) from your home phone and dial the number you want to call. In the past, you learned that dialing on that type of phone works (is reinforced) only if the dial tone sounds.
- You see a light (S^D) on your electric range indicating that a burner was turned off but is still hot, so you avoid touching that burner. In the past, you were punished for touching the burner when the light was on.
- You double-click your mouse on an icon (S^D) on your computer desktop to start an application. In the past, you learned that launching an application by double-clicking on the desktop works (is reinforced) only when the icon is present.
- Someone asks, "Please spell your last name" (S^D), and you do so. In childhood, you were reinforced, such as with praise, for spelling your name correctly when asked to do so. Today, spelling your name when asked still receives reinforcement, such as allowing you to complete an interview quickly.

In many cases, the discriminative function of an antecedent is the main determinant of its effect on behavior, but in other cases, the motivational function is critical. Think back, for instance, to the water fountain example we discussed. Without your being thirsty, it's not likely that you would use the fountain (S^D), even though you saw it. Chances are, the discriminative function wouldn't suffice to induce the behavior when you are "satiated with respect to the type of reinforcement relevant to that S^D" (Michael, 1982, p. 150). Discriminative and motivational functions of antecedents have two features in common: Both functions exist before the target behavior occurs and increase the likelihood that the behavior will occur. When making a response depends strongly on people's motivation, behavior analysts may try to increase that motivation by applying establishing operations.

Establishing Operations

An **establishing operation** is a procedure that increases the effectiveness of a particular consequence—a reinforcer or punisher—on performance of a target behavior, which enhances the motivational function of the antecedent conditions (Laraway, Snycerski, Michael, & Poling, 2003; Michael, 1982). In everyday language, establishing operations determine what an individual "wants or needs" as a reinforcer at a given time. For instance, a person who has not eaten in several hours is hungry, making food a more effective reinforcer than it was soon after a meal.

A common establishing operation in interventions is *deprivation*—presenting the S^D when the person has been without a specific reinforcer, such as food or water, for a suitable amount of time. The deprivation procedure can either restrict access to the reinforcer or simply wait until shortly before the normal or scheduled access, such as lunchtime. Research with adults who are developmentally disabled demonstrated that the effectiveness of various reinforcers—food, music, and social attention—on behavior increases with deprivation from those stimuli and decreases with satiation (Vollmer & Iwata, 1991). Chapter 9 examines establishing operations in more detail when we discuss motivational processes and procedures. (Go to 📖)

LEARNING ANTECEDENTS

As a child, you learned to spell your last name when asked to do so, correcting a behavioral deficit and achieving a behavioral goal. Your parent said, "Spell your last name" (the S^D), you recited the correct letters in the right order (the target behavior), and you got a hug and were told enthusiastically, "That's right!" Your correct behavior was reinforced. To accomplish this feat, you had learned previously to distinguish among a large number of stimuli. For instance, your parents also may have been teaching you to spell other words, such as *dog* or *cat*. So, you needed to respond differently to different S^Ds: "Spell your last name," "Spell dog," and "Spell

CONCEPT CHECK 8.1

Check your understanding of the preceding concepts. Remember that the symbol means the answer can vary. Answer the following questions about the types and functions of antecedents.

1. An example of a fragrance or smell as an antecedent that leads to a behavior is _____ . ⇔
2. Antecedents for a specific behavior are relatively easy to identify if they are _____ and _____ .
3. The two types of functions of antecedents are _____ and _____ .
4. A cue indicating that performing a specific behavior is likely to lead to a particular consequence is called a _____ stimulus.
5. Deprivation is a common way to introduce a(n) _____ operation.

cat." What's more, to respond correctly to each of these requests, you must have learned to distinguish among letters of the alphabet.

STIMULUS DISCRIMINATION

A teaching procedure in which a consequence is administered for a particular behavior when a specific stimulus is present but not when another stimulus is present is called **discrimination training** (Strand, 2005). This procedure teaches people to distinguish between different stimulus conditions and respond differently toward them. For example, we learned as toddlers to say "doggie" when we saw a dog, but not when we saw a cat or bird. In early childhood, we learned to say "bee" when we saw the letter *b*, but not when we saw the number 6 or the letters *p* or *d*. Seeing these items and being asked of each, "What is this?" constituted antecedents for our behavior as we learned to discriminate among letters and words in our growing verbal skills. Once children have learned to label objects and events with words, they are able to use *mands*, or requests for items they want. Teaching mands is discussed in Chapter 26.

Discrimination training can also be applied to improve classroom conduct, such as in dealing with students trying to get the teacher's attention too often or at inconvenient times. An intervention instructed elementary school students in a new rule: The teacher will be available to answer questions when she is wearing a green lei but not when she wearing a red lei, and the teacher did her best to follow the rule (Cammilleri, Tiger, & Hanley, 2008). The students acquired the rule quickly; the rate at which they approached the teacher with questions was about one third as high when the teacher wore the red lei than the green lei. Discrimination training is likely to proceed smoothly and quickly if the different S^Ds are clearly distinctive, such as by a parent or teacher annunciating them slowly and precisely or making them visually very different.

We learn to discriminate through an operant process in which responding in a certain way (such as by saying "Mommy") to a particular stimulus (mother) leads to a rewarding consequence (in this case, lavish attention and praise). But responding in the same way to other stimuli (aunts, teachers) does not. This process involves antecedent stimuli of two types:

1. An S^D: A discriminative stimulus; discrimination training teaches us that this antecedent leads to a particular type of consequence.

2. An S^Δ: A stimulus that is associated with *not* being reinforced for making a given response is called an **S-delta** (S^Δ) (Δ is the fourth letter in the Greek alphabet). Thus, the S^Δ becomes a cue for *not* performing that particular behavior.

As examples of an S^D and S^Δ from everyday life, suppose you wanted to borrow some money for a day or so. People you encounter could be the S^D or S^Δ for the behavior of asking for a loan: A close friend or family member who has lent you money in the past (that you've paid back!) might be an S^D, and a stranger might be an S^Δ. Close friends or family are likely to reinforce (give you the money) your request, but strangers are not. For children in school, their regular teacher is usually an S^D for their paying attention; a substitute teacher is an S^Δ for paying attention, all too often!

A study demonstrated how people who dispense rewards can become (S^Ds) for the behavior of others (Redd & Birnbrauer, 1969). The study was done with 12- to 15-year-old boys with mental retardation who received praise and sweets (candy, bites of ice cream, or sips of cola) every minute or so in a playroom with toys and other boys. Two adults who provided the praise and sweets as rewards became the S^Ds. One of these adults was a woman who dispensed the rewards to the boys only when they engaged in cooperative play, moving or manipulating a toy with another boy. The other adult, a man, provided the same rewards, but at certain time intervals that had no relation to what the boys were doing. Because the man's rewards were not contingent on any particular behavior, playing cooperatively was unlikely to receive rewards very often from him. In later tests, the children showed much more cooperative play when the woman entered the playroom than when the man entered, indicating that the woman had become an S^D for cooperative play and the man had not. Then when the adults switched the ways they gave rewards, the man eventually became an S^D for cooperative play and the woman lost her influence on the boys' play behavior.

Another study showed a similar effect when the consequence was punishment (Rolider, Cummings, & Van Houten, 1991). The participants were an adolescent and an adult who were developmentally disabled. Two teachers were present during training sessions, but only one reprimanded the participants for misbehaviors. Later tests showed that the participants' misbehaviors decreased only if the reprimanding teacher, the S^D, was present. These findings indicate that teachers and other individuals can also become antecedents for the withholding or suppression of inappropriate behaviors. The effect of antecedents on behavior depends on the consequences they have been associated with in the past. (Go to 🔍.)

STIMULUS GENERALIZATION AND EQUIVALENCE

As we learn to make a particular response to a specific S^D, a phenomenon called **stimulus generalization** occurs: We also learn to respond in the same way to *other stimuli that are similar to the S^D we learned*. The more similar

CLOSE-UP

Discriminative Stimuli for Punishment

Although we've focused on S^Ds as antecedents for behaviors that lead to reinforcement, a similar process operates when the consequence is punishment. Thus, we can learn a *discriminative stimulus for punishment* (abbreviated as S^Dp; O'Donnell, 2001). A behavior that receives punishment when a particular antecedent is present will tend to decrease, and perhaps stop entirely, in the future when that S^Dp is present. For example, a child who doesn't know that a signal light on an electric range means that a burner that was turned off is still hot may notice the light and touch the burner. If this happens again, perhaps a few times, or someone explains the meaning of the light, that light will become an S^Dp, indicating that touching the burner when the light is on will lead to punishment. As you would expect, research has shown that after discrimination learning is carried out for punishment, the response is less likely to be performed when the S^Dp is present (O'Donnell, Crosbie, Williams, & Saunders, 2000).

the other stimuli are to the S^D we learned, the more likely we are to make the response to those stimuli. Thus, children who have learned to say "dee" when they see the letter *d* may also say "dee" when they see a *b* or even a *p*, but they are less likely to say "dee" when they see an *m* or an *s*. Because *d* and *b* are similar to one another, we may be tempted to think that generalization simply reflects a failure to discriminate carefully (Rilling, 1977). But stimulus generalization seems to be more than that. Consider these examples. When children learn to raise their hands to ask questions in kindergarten, they continue to use this convention when they enter first grade; similarly, when they learn to say "please" to request something from their parents, they tend to do the same with other people. These behaviors probably aren't mistakes, but they show stimulus generalization.

Stimulus generalization is an important process: Behavior analysts who teach a skill usually want the person to use that behavior with similar antecedents in everyday life. Let's consider a couple of examples, one where generalization occurred readily and one where it did not. First, a study demonstrated that adult martial arts students used the skills, such as how to avoid punches and counterstrike, they had learned in training drills when they were tested later in sparring sessions (Harding et al., 2004). This is the kind of effect teachers usually want. Second, suppose a child has mastered using mands (requests for wanted items) with a teacher; will the child readily generalize the use of mands with other people? Children with developmental disabilities may not. Researchers taught a repertoire of mands to children with autism and tested for generalization in real-life situations with parents, siblings, and peers (Pellecchia & Hineline, 2007). Although the children generalized the use of mands to their parents, they only generalized the mands to siblings or peers after they were trained to use mands with children.

In a phenomenon related to generalization and called *stimulus equivalence*, two or more physically different stimuli come to serve the same purposes and be used interchangeably (Sidman & Tailby, 1982; Tierney & Bracken, 1998). For instance, suppose no one told you the numbers 4 and IV mean the same thing, but you had the following two experiences in childhood. First, when your father taught you about numbers, he showed you four dots and wrote next to them, "There are 4." Then, when your teacher taught you about Roman numerals, she drew four dots on the board and wrote next to them, "There are IV." If you remembered both experiences, wouldn't you have assumed that, or at least wondered if, 4 and IV are interchangeable? If someone at that time asked you count out 4 fingers on one hand and IV fingers on the other hand, you'd have counted four on each hand. Stimulus generalization and stimulus equivalence involve learning processes that allow us to connect a variety of antecedent stimuli to a single response without actual training for each stimulus. (Go to 🐾.)

CASE STUDY

From Pigeons' Generalization to Val's Self-Injury

The less similar other stimuli are to the S^D, the less likely the target behavior will occur in the presence of these stimuli. This relationship can be depicted as a *generalization gradient*, a graph showing response strengths produced by stimuli of varying degrees of similarity to the S^D. Guttman and Kalish (1956) trained pigeons in an apparatus to peck at a key that was illuminated with a colored light—if the pigeons pecked when the key was a specific color (yellow-green, the S^D), they received reinforcement. After extensive training, the pigeons were tested for generalization under an extinction procedure (no reinforcement was given) with the key at the yellow-green color (a measured wavelength of 550 millimicrons, or mμ) and at other colors with a range of wavelengths. An illustration of the findings in Figure 8-1 shows that key pecking was greatest for colors most similar to the S^D and, as the color (wavelength) became less similar to the S^D, correspondingly less pecking occurred.

(Continued)

(*Continued*)

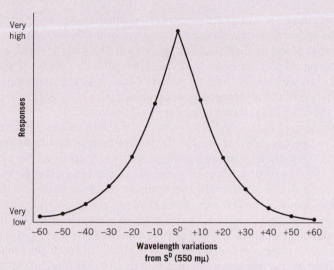

Figure 8-1 Representation of generalization gradients based on data across many graphs in Guttman and Kalish (1956). Stimulus generalization declined as the difference in color from S^D increased.

The relevance of these findings for humans can be seen in a study of self-injurious behavior—repeated head hitting with the fist—of Val, a girl with mental retardation (Lalli, Mace, Livezey, & Kates, 1998). Through observations, the researchers determined that the presence of an adult was the S^D, and her head hitting was reinforced by attention adults would give her when she engaged in that behavior. Stimulus generalization was tested by having an adult positioned at various distances from her, ranging from 0.5 meter (about 20 inches) to 9 meters. Figure 8-2 shows the generalization gradient: The farther away the adult was from Val, the fewer self-injurious behaviors she performed; 65% of her head hitting occurred when the adult was within 1.5 meters (5 feet) of her.

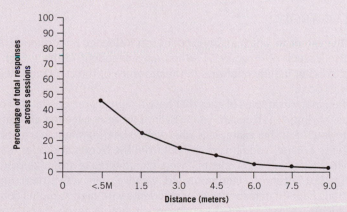

Figure 8-2 The percentage of total self-injurious behaviors (head hitting) made by a 10-year-old girl named Val when an adult was positioned at various distances from her during generalization tests. Note: The gradient extends in only one direction, because distances along the horizontal axis cannot be less than zero. *Source:* From J. S. Lalli, F. C. Mace, K. Livezey, & K. Kates (1998), Assessment of stimulus generalization gradients in the treatment of self-injurious behavior. *Journal of Applied Behavior Analysis*, 31, 479–483, Figure 1, upper panel. Copyright © 1998 Society for the Experimental Analysis of Behavior. Used by permission.

CONCEPT FORMATION

Concepts help us make sense out of the enormous amount of information we find in our worlds. In childhood, we begin to acquire concepts by learning relationships among two or more distinguishable objects, events, or ideas and classify them together based on their common properties. Think of the word *car*, for example. We can identify and discriminate among all sorts of items that are cars—different brand names, models, and colors. Obviously they are different, but we classify them all as cars because of their commonalities in appearance and function. Thus, we will define the term **concept** as a cognitive category by which we group *noticeably different* objects, events, or ideas on the basis of their concrete or abstract *commonalities*.

The processes of stimulus generalization and discrimination are both involved in forming a concept. Given that the grouped items are noticeably different, we clearly can distinguish one from another: a Buick from a Jaguar from a Toyota. If we could not discriminate among them, we'd see them as all the same and wouldn't need to bring their commonalities into the picture. Stimulus generalization is involved in forming a concept because the commonalities among items in the group make them similar in appearance or function. Some concepts are *concrete*—for example, *chair*. Many of the features of "chair-ness" are perceptible and physical: Chairs tend to have four legs, a back, and are wide enough to accommodate one person in the seated position. Other concepts are *abstract*—for instance, *love* or *honesty*. They can't be materially defined, and their commonalities are not concrete, although we may be able to describe instances of them. To teach people a concept, we need to make sure they can discriminate among relevant items and help them to identify the critical commonalities that the items share.

STIMULUS CONTROL

When we hear a telephone ringing, we're very likely to answer it, even if we have an answering machine. And our answering the phone—that is, picking up the receiver and saying "Hello"—happens only when the phone rings. We don't go around answering the phone when it hasn't rung! After we learned to associate a response with an S^D as an antecedent, this cue came to exert stimulus control over the behavior. The S^D of a phone ringing is an antecedent with a high degree of stimulus control over our phone-answering behavior.

WHAT IS STIMULUS CONTROL?

Stimulus control refers to the extent to which an antecedent can influence performance of a specific behavior (Albin & Horner, 1988; Luiselli, 2005; Rilling, 1977). When an antecedent exerts a high degree of stimulus control, the behavior tends to occur mainly or always in the presence of the cue; and when the cue is present, the response is highly likely to occur.

Our everyday lives contain many examples of cues that have a high degree of stimulus control. For instance, suppose someone greets us, saying, "Hi. How are you?" Even if we're not feeling all that well, we're likely to reply, "Fine, thanks. How are you?" Another example is when you're heating water in a teapot with a whistle that sounds, telling you the water is boiling. You remove the pot from the burner and pour hot water into a cup to make your tea. Many behaviors for which antecedents have a high degree of stimulus control are habitual and automatic, such as writing the last letters of a common word. We give them very little thought, or no thought at all. Habitual, automatic actions happen in response to antecedents with high stimulus control.

The examples of antecedents we've considered were generally simple, involving only one stimulus. But our everyday lives often have much more complex antecedents, consisting of several relevant stimuli. For example:

> if you are driving on a two-lane road and you come up behind a slow-moving vehicle, you only pass when the center line is broken on your side *and* there are no oncoming cars in the opposite lane. [The antecedent] consists of at least three elements: (1) the slow-moving vehicle ahead, (2) the broken center line, and (3) the clear opposite lane. If any one of those elements were absent, you would be unlikely to pass. The combination sets the *context*. (Baum, 1994, p. 89; emphasis added)

Oftentimes the antecedent for a behavior is the overall context, rather than a collection of stimuli (Baer, Wolf, & Risley, 1987; Michael, 1982; Wahler & Fox, 1981). When this is the case, stimulus control is described as *contextual control* (Haring & Kennedy, 1990).

Principles of stimulus control have been used effectively in treating people with insomnia (Morin, Culbert, & Schwartz, 1994). An intervention was conducted with men and women who were over 60 years of age and had experienced insomnia for at least the past 6 months (Puder, Lacks, Bertelson, & Storandt, 1983). The treatment consisted of teaching these individuals to re-associate the bed and bedroom with going to sleep quickly by having them (a) go to bed only when sleepy, leave the bed if they are awake for 10 minutes, and return to bed only when drowsy again; and (b) if not ready to sleep, go to another room to engage in activities that are incompatible with sleep, such as reading, watching TV, and worrying. This treatment was effective for most of the clients, and the data across all clients showed that the average latencies in getting to sleep declined from over an hour per night to about half an hour.

PROMOTING STIMULUS CONTROL

Several factors influence the development of stimulus control for a behavior. When engaging in methods to develop an effective antecedent, behavior analysts should make sure that:

- The person is paying attention to the stimuli we are training as the S^D.
- The training stimulus is prominent, or easily noticed; it should be different from other stimuli in its size, color, sound, or location.
- The task is straightforward enough so that the person is likely to make few errors, such as not responding to the S^D or responding when an S^Δ is present.
- The contingencies are stated in words the person can understand. For example, if we were teaching a child to dial a phone with the dial tone as the S^D, we might say, "Remember, if you start to push the buttons after you hear the tone, you can make the call. Don't push the buttons until you hear the tone."

(Go to .)

CONCEPT CHECK 8.2

Answer the following questions about learning antecedents and stimulus control.

1. We learn to respond differently to different stimuli through _____ training.
2. An example of discrimination training of an S^D in learning a sport skill is _____ . ⇔
3. In your last answer, the S-delta (S^Δ) might be _____ . ⇔
4. A child who uses a key to open a padlock after having learned only how to open a door lock is showing stimulus _____ .
5. The condition in which two or more different stimuli come to serve the same purposes is called stimulus _____ .
6. An example of an antecedent with a high degree of stimulus control in a high school classroom might be _____ . ⇔

STUDY AND REVIEW

SUMMARY

Any stimulus—a person, event, object, or place—can serve as an antecedent for operant behavior. Antecedents can be overt or covert; immediate antecedents are present shortly before the behavior occurs, and distant antecedents precede the behavior by a period of time. Distant antecedents generally have strong emotional or covert components.

Antecedents often have discriminative and motivational functions. Discriminative functions link an antecedent, called a discriminative stimulus (S^D), with the consequences of a specific behavior. Motivational functions affect the effectiveness of a consequence in changing behavior and can be altered through establishing operations. People learn antecedents through discrimination training in which responding to an S^D is regularly associated with reinforcement and S-delta (S^Δ) stimuli are not. In this way, people who are regularly associated with reinforcement of particular behaviors can become antecedents for those behaviors. Although individuals can learn to make fine discriminations and to make a certain response only when specific stimuli are present, the behavior often shows some degree of stimulus generalization. Stimulus discrimination and generalization form the basis for learning concepts.

To the extent that a stimulus has the ability to affect performance of a specific behavior, it exerts stimulus control. Some antecedents exert a great deal of stimulus control: The behavior typically occurs only when the S^D is present, and when that antecedent is present, the behavior is very likely to occur. When the antecedent involves the overall context in which behavior occurs, the stimulus control is called contextual control.

> To prepare for exams, use the following key terms and review questions and the online study guide that's available on this book's companion website at www.wiley.com/college/sarafino.

KEY TERMS

antecedents	discrimination training	concept
discriminative stimulus (S^D)	S-delta (S^Δ)	stimulus control
establishing operation	stimulus generalization	

ANSWERS TO CONCEPT CHECKS (CCs)

CC8.1 *Answers:* **1.** the smell of food gets you to go to the kitchen **2.** overt, immediate **3.** discriminative, motivational **4.** discriminative **5.** establishing

CC8.2 *Answers:* **1.** discrimination **2.** rewarding a baseball batter for swinging at a "strike" pitch **3.** a pitch that is "high and outside" **4.** generalization **5.** equivalence **6.** the end-of-class bell

REVIEW QUESTIONS

1. Describe the research by Van Houten and Retting (2001) on increasing safe driving behavior at stop signs.
2. Describe an antecedent that might set the occasion for each of the following behaviors: calling a plumber, turning down the heat at home, and going shopping.
3. Define the term *establishing operation*, and state its relation to motivational functions of antecedents.
4. What is discrimination training, and how is it involved in children's learning letters of the alphabet?
5. Define and give the abbreviations for the terms *discriminative stimulus* and *S-delta*.
6. Describe the study by Redd and Birnbrauer (1969) on how people can become discriminative stimuli.

7. Define and give the abbreviation for the term *discriminative stimulus for punishment*.

8. Define *stimulus generalization*, and give an example of it in the names children use for different flowers.

9. Describe the research by Lalli, Mace, Livezey, and Kates (1998) on stimulus generalization in Val's self-injurious behavior.

10. How are stimulus discrimination and generalization involved in learning concepts?

11. What is stimulus control? Give two examples of it from your current life.

RELATED READINGS

- Rilling, M. (1977). Stimulus control and inhibitory processes. In W. K. Honig & J. E. R. Staddon (Eds.), *Handbook of operant behavior*. Englewood Cliffs, NJ: Prentice-Hall.

- Shiffman, S. (1984). Coping with temptations to smoke. *Journal of Consulting and Clinical Psychology*, 52, 261–267.

9

MOTIVATION

Defining Motivation
Traditional Views
A Behavior Analytic View

Motivating Operations
Establishing and Abolishing Operations for Reinforcement
Establishing and Abolishing Operations for Punishment
Unconditioned and Conditioned Motivating Operations

Applying Motivating Operations
Deprivation and Satiation
Altering the Consequence Itself
Chemical Methods

Study and Review

PROLOGUE

"Oh," the teacher said, "Tommy's a popular student and quick with jokes, but he's not very motivated academically. He doesn't do his homework on time, comes to class late, daydreams a lot in class, and doesn't do well on tests. He's very different from Jack, who is very motivated—he pays attention in class, always does his homework, and does well on tests." People in everyday life use the idea of motivation frequently to:

- Explain differences in people's behavior, particularly in its care and vigor.
- Account for people's preferences for different activities.
- Assign responsibility for people's actions.
- Explain why people persevere despite obstacles and adversity.

Most often, people think of motivation as an internal state, which they can't see or otherwise sense physically, and infer its status on the basis of behavior: Jack's teacher thinks he's motivated because he behaves in certain ways and believes Jack's motivation is at least partly the cause of his academic behavior and success. People also tend to think that motivational states are not easy to change.

In this chapter, we examine what motivation is—considering traditional views briefly and then focusing on behavior analytic views. We'll also discuss procedures by which we can alter motivation, enabling us to correct behavioral deficits and excesses more efficiently.

DEFINING MOTIVATION

If you were to consult a dictionary for a definition of motivation, you would find a complex array of interconnected terms. The first definition of *motivation* in the 11th edition of *Merriam Webster's Collegiate Dictionary* is "the act or process of motivating." So I checked the verb form, and found that *to motivate* means "to provide with a motive," and *motive* means "something (as a need or desire) that causes a person to act." These definitions seem to "dance around" the concept, without clarifying it enough. Let's see whether traditional psychological views help.

TRADITIONAL VIEWS

Over the years, introductory psychology textbooks have viewed motivation as a process that initiates, directs, and maintains physical and psychological activities of people and other organisms (Hilgard, 1962; Huffman, 2002; Myers, 1998; Zimbardo, 1985). Psychologists often divide the concept of motivation into two parts: *drives*, which are mainly unconditioned and biologically based, such as hunger and thirst, and *motives*, which are at least partly learned and psychologically or socially based, such as the desire for money and the things it buys.

Broad Motives

Some motives are fairly specific, such as thrill or adventure seeking, and others are much broader, such as the *achievement motive*—the desire to succeed and make significant and valuable accomplishments (McClelland, Atkinson, Clark, & Lowell, 1953). An example of someone who fits the definition of a strong achievement motive is Thomas Edison. He had over a thousand patents for his inventions, including the light bulb, microphone, and phonograph. Broad motives, such as for achievement, are like personality traits (Maddi, 1996), and after decades of study, we still don't have a clear understanding of how traits and motives develop or ways to alter them. Many developmental psychologists believe that achievement motives are learned and that the more that children experience pride in accomplishments and shame in failure, the stronger the achievement motive will become (Dweck & Elliott, 1983). But these beliefs have little practical value, beyond the obvious and commonsense parenting advice: Help your children have lots of success experiences. Knowing that Tommy in the opening story has low achievement motivation does not help his teacher or parents improve his academic behaviors much.

Desire and Readiness to Change

Because this book's focus is on changing behavior, it is useful to consider the role that the person's desire and readiness to change play in this process. In general, people who want to improve their behavior are more likely to participate successfully in interventions for making changes (Cautela & Upper, 1975; Kanfer & Grimm, 1980; Perri & Richards, 1977). The *desire* to change is considered a motive, and assessing it can be important in therapy, especially if the client will be applying self-management techniques, such as reinforcement. This motivation can be assessed by having a client fill out the Scale of Motivation to Change Behavior given in Figure 9-1.

A theory called the *stages of change model* describes a series of five stages through which people's motivation and intention to modify a specific behavior, such as exercising, progress in *readiness* to change (Prochaska & DiClemente, 1984; Prochaska, DiClemente, & Norcross, 1992). At the lowest stage, the person has no interest in changing the behavior; at the highest stage, the person has completed the change and is working to maintain it. People at an intermediate stage called *preparation* have made the commitment to modify the behavior, such

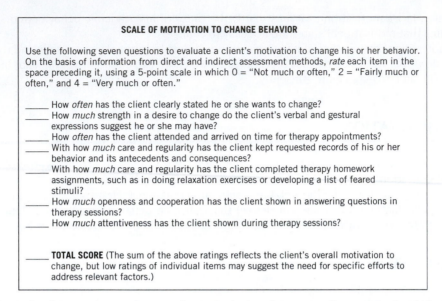

SCALE OF MOTIVATION TO CHANGE BEHAVIOR

Use the following seven questions to evaluate a client's motivation to change his or her behavior. On the basis of information from direct and indirect assessment methods, *rate* each item in the space preceding it, using a 5-point scale in which 0 = "Not much or often," 2 = "Fairly much or often," and 4 = "Very much or often."

_____ How *often* has the client clearly stated he or she wants to change?
_____ How *much* strength in a desire to change do the client's verbal and gestural expressions suggest he or she may have?
_____ How *often* has the client attended and arrived on time for therapy appointments?
_____ With how *much* care and regularity has the client kept requested records of his or her behavior and its antecedents and consequences?
_____ With how *much* care and regularity has the client completed therapy homework assignments, such as in doing relaxation exercises or developing a list of feared stimuli?
_____ How *much* openness and cooperation has the client shown in answering questions in therapy sessions?
_____ How *much* attentiveness has the client shown during therapy sessions?

_____ **TOTAL SCORE** (The sum of the above ratings reflects the client's overall motivation to change, but low ratings of individual items may suggest the need for specific efforts to address relevant factors.)

Figure 9-1 The Scale of Motivation to Change Behavior is designed to assess client motivation in individual therapy, but similar items could be rated for other types of interventions. *Source:* Based on Cautela & Upper (1975).

as starting to exercise, and are in the process of planning the efforts they will use to achieve that goal in the near future. Studies have confirmed that people at higher intermediate stages, such as preparation, are more likely than those at lower stages to succeed in making the change toward healthful behaviors, such as stopping smoking (Spencer, Pagell, Hallion, & Adams, 2002).

A BEHAVIOR ANALYTIC VIEW

Traditional views of motivation provide little guidance in trying to increase people's motivation to change their behavior. Although it may be useful to know how ready a person is to change a behavior, and the stages of change model offers ways to encourage movement to higher stages, the behavior analytic view is more useful: It focuses mainly on ways to *manipulate motivation as an antecedent*. This focus relates to practical issues in applied behavior analysis: We want to enhance the motivation of individuals in interventions to modify their behavior. Enhanced motivation increases the likelihood of behavior change. Because behavior analysts try to maximize the effects of antecedents and consequences, the motivational functions of the antecedents need to make as effective as possible the specific consequences we will use in our efforts.

Although the basic behavior analytic ideas on motivation were discussed decades ago, the current approach began with a journal article by Jack Michael (1982) in which he outlined a set of ideas on motivational functions of antecedents. These ideas included a preliminary version of the concept of *establishing operations*, which he defined as environmental manipulations that alter the effect of a stimulus, such as water, as a reinforcer and increase the frequency of all responses that have been reinforced with that stimulus in the past. By the end of the 20th century, this concept became widely accepted among behavior analysts, who found it "increasingly helpful in describing, studying, and arranging antecedent influences over behavior" (Iwata, Smith, & Michael, 2000, p. 411). During those years, Michael refined his views of establishing operations; and in 2003, he joined colleagues in presenting a more thorough and complex picture of motivational processes that is the basis for the behavior analytic view of motivation presented in this book (Laraway, Snycerski, Michael, & Poling, 2003).

We've discussed parts of the behavior analytic approach on motivation earlier in this book, introducing you to basic aspects of the concepts of motivating operations and establishing operations. Now we'll present a larger picture and more detail. (Go to .)

MOTIVATING OPERATIONS

In Chapter 5, we defined **motivating operations (MOs)** as procedures that temporarily alter the (a) effectiveness of a reinforcer or punisher on behavior and (b) performance of behaviors that normally lead to those consequences. Now we can expand this concept in three ways. First, we can name the two effects of MOs: Changing the effectiveness of a consequence is called the **value-altering effect**; changing the performance of behaviors that normally lead to those consequences is called the **behavior-altering effect**. These effects can be diagrammed as:

MOs ➜ value-altering effects + behavior-altering effects

Although the behavior-altering effect is measured most often as the frequency of a behavior, the effect also applies to other measures, such as the duration and magnitude of the behavior.

Second, there are two types of behavior-altering effect: It is an **evocative effect** if it increases the behavior and an **abative effect** if it decreases the behavior. Third, MOs can be of two types:

1. **Establishing operations (EOs)** *increase* the effectiveness of a reinforcer or punisher (the value-altering effect) and lead to corresponding changes in behavior (the behavior-altering effect): If an EO applies to a reinforcer, it increases the behavior (an evocative effect); if an EO applies to a punisher, it decreases the behavior (an abative effect).

2. **Abolishing operations (AOs)** *decrease* the effectiveness of a reinforcer or punisher on behavior: If an AO applies to a reinforcer, it decreases the behavior (an abative effect); if an AO applies to a punisher, it increases the behavior (an evocative effect).

Figure 9-2 diagrams and organizes the relations among these concepts and clarifies their meanings. We'll refer to this diagram as we examine the procedures and processes of establishing and abolishing operations for reinforcement and for punishment.

CONCEPT CHECK 9.1

Check your understanding of the preceding concepts. Remember that the symbol ⇔ means the answer can vary. Answer the following questions about defining motivation.

1. An example of a drive is _____ and of a motive is _____ . ⇔
2. The Scale of Motivation to Change Behavior assesses people's _____ to change, which may be important to measure if they are applying _____ techniques.
3. The behavior analytic view of motivation focuses on ways to _____ motivation as an antecedent to behavior.
4. The current behavior analytic view of motivation is based on the concept of _____ that Jack Michael described in the early 1980s.

Motivating Operations →	Value-Altering Effect		and	Behavior-Altering Effect	
	Reinforcement	Punishment		Reinforcement	Punishment
Establishing operations (EOs) →	Increase effectiveness	Increase effectiveness		Increase behavior (evocative effect)	Decrease behavior (abative effect)
Abolishing operations (AOs) →	Decrease effectiveness	Decrease effectiveness		Decrease behavior (abative effect)	Increase behavior (evocative effect)

Figure 9-2 Diagram of the types of motivating operations (MOs) and the value-altering and behavior-altering effects they produce for reinforcement and punishment. Notice, for example, that when EOs increase the effectiveness of a reinforcer, they have an evocative effect, increasing the behavior that normally leads to that reinforcer. But when EOs increase the effectiveness of a punisher, they have an abative effect, decreasing the behavior that normally leads to that punisher.

ESTABLISHING AND ABOLISHING OPERATIONS FOR REINFORCEMENT

Let's start with a straightforward example of EOs and AOs for positive reinforcement. When we haven't eaten for a few hours and are hungry, food becomes a strong positive reinforcer for behaviors, such as food seeking and preparation, that normally lead to food as a reinforcer. But after we have eaten a substantial meal, food is for a while a far less potent reinforcer. Food-seeking and preparation behaviors increase with deprivation and decrease with satiation.

Food deprivation and satiation are MOs for food serving as a reinforcer: Being deprived of food is an EO, and consuming food is an AO. The changes in reinforcer strength are value-altering effects, and the changes in behavior are behavior-altering effects. Looking back at Figure 9-2 in the columns for reinforcement, we see that the EO (deprivation) should have the value-altering effect of increasing reinforcer effectiveness and the evocative behavior-altering effect. In contrast, the AO (satiation) should have the value-altering effect of decreasing reinforcer effectiveness and an abative behavior-altering effect. Research has confirmed that food deprivation and satiation have the expected value-altering and behavior-altering effects (Gottschalk, Libby, & Graff, 2000; Vollmer & Iwata, 1991). What's more, research has demonstrated similar effects of EOs and AOs with conditioned positive reinforcers, such as toys, music, and social attention (McAdam et al., 2005; Vollmer & Iwata, 1991).

EOs and AOs should also have similar effects with negative reinforcement—the reduction of an uncomfortable condition, such as a high or low room temperature in your home. Let's consider the behavior of adjusting the thermostat, assuming you had gone away on vacation and had lowered the temperature (the EO) to conserve energy before leaving. If the room temperature was very low when you arrived home, the reinforcer effectiveness of making the room warm and the evocative behavior-altering effect would both be very strong. In contrast, if the temperature had not been lowered while you were away, an AO would be in effect, decreasing the reinforcer effectiveness and the behavior of adjusting the thermostat (the abative effect). These effects can be seen in Figure 9-2 in the columns on reinforcement.

We saw in Chapter 5 that people often try to escape from aversive conditions, as some children do when receiving training for a difficult task, such as by engaging in self-injurious or destructive behavior. To the extent that their escape behavior gets them out of the training, it is negatively reinforced. Researchers used careful observations of three boys with autism to identify the aspect of the training that constituted an EO, increasing the reinforcer effectiveness and the evocative effect for their destructive escape behavior (McComas, Hoch, Paone, & El-Roy, 2000). For instance, the EO for Ben was his having to perform the same tasks over and over, which led to his hitting and punching behaviors that disrupted the training. When the researchers modified the training so that tasks would not be repeated (an AO), Ben's aggression dropped almost to zero. (Go to 🔍.)

CLOSE-UP

Abolishing Operations for Substance Abuse

Using substances such as tobacco or opiate drugs provides the user with positive reinforcement by producing pleasant feelings, such as a "buzz" or "rush," and negative reinforcement by removing unpleasant feelings, such as anxiety (Sarafino & Smith, 2011). And once the person has become dependent or addicted to the substance, deprivation is an EO that increases the reinforcer effectiveness and the performance of behavior involved in using the substance (evocative effect). Are there AOs for reducing the behavioral excess of substance use? Yes, and one approach involves having the person take medication that blocks the reinforcing effects of the substance. For example, a chemical called *methadone* prevents opiates from producing euphoria, and *varenicline* blocks the pleasant effects of nicotine in cigarettes (Mattick, Kimber, Breen, & Davoli, 2003; NLM, 2011). These chemicals are useful in treating substance use, but they are most effective when combined with behavioral methods of applied behavior analysis (Sarafino & Smith, 2011).

ESTABLISHING AND ABOLISHING OPERATIONS FOR PUNISHMENT

So far, we've focused on value-altering and behavior-altering effects of EOs and AOs when the consequence for a behavior is reinforcement. Looking again at Figure 9-2, we see that MOs also apply when the consequence is punishment. That is, EOs should increase the effectiveness of a punisher and have an abative effect, decreasing the associated behavior, and AOs should decrease the effectiveness of a punisher and have an evocative effect, increasing the behavior. For example, pain and other physically aversive stimuli can serve as punishers for a behavior on which they are contingent. Increasing the intensity of the pain or stimulus should be an EO, and decreasing its intensity should be an AO.

In Chapter 7, we discussed a variety of punishers, including the use of physically aversive stimuli in "lemon-juice therapy," in which concentrated lemon juice is squirted into the person's mouth. This method can be justified if the behavior is very problematic and other techniques have been tried without success. Making the lemon juice highly concentrated would be an EO, and watering it down or adding sweetener to it would be an AO. Other types of punishers we discussed are time-out (moving the offending person to a less reinforcing setting) and response cost (losing a valued item or privilege). An EO with time-out punishment might involve increasing the reinforcement the person could be receiving in the original setting while he or she is in time-out, and an EO for response cost might involve increasing the value of the lost item, such as the money to be paid as a fine.

UNCONDITIONED AND CONDITIONED MOTIVATING OPERATIONS

We saw in Chapter 5 that we can distinguish between unconditioned and conditioned reinforcers: Unconditioned reinforcers function as reinforcers without our having had a learning history with them; conditioned reinforcers function as reinforcers because of our prior learning with them. A similar distinction can be made for MOs (Michael, 2002). **Unconditioned motivating operations (UMOs)** have inborn value-altering effects on consequences; that is, these effects were not learned. For example, the EOs of food and water deprivation are UMOs—they increase the effectiveness of food and water as reinforcers without having been learned to do so. And the AOs of food and water satiation are UMOs, decreasing the effectiveness of food and water as reinforcers without prior learning. Other EOs that are UMOs include:

- Oxygen deprivation
- Sex deprivation

- Sleep deprivation
- Body becoming too cold or too warm
- Increase in painful stimulation

Removing these conditions, such as by falling asleep or becoming warmer or cooler, would constitute AOs that are UMOs.

Conditioned motivating operations (CMOs) alter a consequence's effectiveness; that is, they have value-altering effects, as a result of prior learning. For example, most people value large amounts of money more than small amounts of money because they have learned that more of it is "better." Getting a raise in pay at work is an EO that is a CMO. Keep in mind that the pattern of value-altering and behavior-altering effects shown in Figure 9-2 remain the same, regardless of whether the EOs or AOs are unconditioned or conditioned MOs. And these effects apply with reinforcement and punishment just as they did before. In the case of response cost punishment, for instance, if communities were to increase the fine for jaywalking, they'd be applying an EO that is a CMO. In Figure 9-2, the effectiveness of the punishment should increase and jaywalking behavior should decrease (abative effect).

APPLYING MOTIVATING OPERATIONS

To consider ways to apply MOs in interventions, it is useful to distinguish again between discriminative stimuli (S^Ds) and MOs, particularly after having discussed CMOs. We saw in Chapter 8 that an S^D is a cue that signals that a specific behavior is likely to lead to a particular consequence—for instance, the S^D of hearing a dial tone tells you that dialing a phone number now will register the call you want to make. An MO is a procedure that alters the value of a particular consequence, increasing or decreasing its effect. In the phone call example, variations in the purpose of the call alter its importance: If you learned something exciting to tell a friend, this is a CMO, increasing your wanting to complete the call. Now, let's look at procedures for applying MOs.

DEPRIVATION AND SATIATION

Because deprivation and satiation are such basic procedures in motivation, we've already discussed them when giving examples of EOs and AOs. The effects of food and water deprivation on behavior have been studied extensively and have been well known for a long time (Kimble, 1961). Within limits, the greater the deprivation, the more effective the reinforcer becomes in strengthening behavior. This rule applies to most unconditioned reinforcers and probably many conditioned reinforcers.

A study of EOs for an unconditioned reinforcer and two conditioned reinforcers tested adult males with profound retardation during training sessions (Vollmer & Iwata, 1991). The procedures the researchers used in creating the EOs were:

- For *food reinforcement*, testing began within 30 minutes before each man's scheduled lunch time.
- For *music reinforcement*, testing began after an observer had seen that the man had not heard music for at least 30 minutes.
- For *social attention reinforcement*, testing began after an observer had seen that the man had not had social interaction with anyone for at least 15 minutes.

During the training sessions, these reinforcers were then used to reward correct behavior: Food consisted of nuts and dried fruit, music rewards consisted of playing taped songs for several seconds, and social attention consisted of praise, such as "Good job, [name]! You are a hard worker." To create satiation (the AOs), the researchers made sure the man received food, music, or social attention before testing. With all three reinforcers, higher rates of correct responding occurred under deprivation than satiation.(Go to .)

ALTERING THE CONSEQUENCE ITSELF

Another procedure for creating MOs is to change the value of the consequence itself. One way to do this is to alter what the person can do with the item received as a reinforcer. Suppose you are an American traveling in a foreign country and the currency there was suddenly devalued by half relative to the dollar; your dollars would be worth much more now. You could buy things you couldn't afford before. This would be an example of an EO: There would be a value-altering effect because the effectiveness of each dollar as a reinforcer for you would increase while you were in that country. How might this relate to applied behavior analysis? In Chapter 5 we discussed a type of reinforcer called tokens, which can be exchanged for or buy goods or privileges, called *backup reinforcers*. If an intervention was using tokens as reinforcers, one way to carry out an EO would be to revalue the tokens so that each one buys more of the backup reinforcers.

Another way to alter the value of consequences is to publicly post performance information, especially if the consequences involve feedback or praise. For example, a study was conducted with five linebackers on a college football team who were not performing certain skills, such as tackling, well (Ward & Carnes, 2002). The linebackers were asked to select goals for percentage correct skill performance with the restriction that the goals must be higher than their baseline levels. The players were then told that each one's percentage of correct skill performances in practice would be posted on a locker-room wall along with a statement, yes or no, of whether he had met his goal. The performance of all five players improved dramatically. Having the athletes select performance goals and posting their progress are EOs—they appear to increase the effectiveness of feedback as a reinforcer (value-altering effect) and improve their skill performance (behavior-altering effect).

CASE STUDY

Daniel's Reinforcer Preferences in Deprivation and Satiation

We know that deprivation and satiation alter reinforcer effectiveness, but do these MOs change a person's *preferences* for those particular items or experiences? Research has shown that MOs do affect preferences for the related reinforcers (Gottschalk, Libby, & Graff, 2000). The researchers tested four children with developmental disabilities for their preferences for food items, and we'll focus on the data for a boy named Daniel.

Before starting the study, initial preference assessments were made by presenting eight candies and snacks in pairs to Daniel (and each other child) and allowing him to take one and eat it. After many pairs were presented, the items in the mid-range of those he chose were selected for subsequent testing—for Daniel, these items were jelly beans, popcorn, Cheez-Its, and crackers. Preference assessments were then made by presenting pairs of items from the four under the MO conditions: Deprivation involved no access for 48 hours to only one of the four items, and satiation involved free access to only one of the items for 10 minutes before testing. Because preference assessments occurred across several days, each food item could be tested under deprivation and satiation. Daniel's data showed that for each food item, his preference for it was several times higher when it was tested under deprivation than under satiation. Similar effects were found with the other children.

Publicly posting performance information on a chart is a conditioned motivating operation that can increase the value and effect of a reinforcer. *Source:* Robin Sachs/PhotoEdit.

CHEMICAL METHODS

We saw earlier that medications can be used as AOs in helping people stop using certain substances, such as opiates and tobacco, by blocking the pleasant effects these substances have. Other medications can be used for alcohol abuse: *Disulfiram* produces nausea if the person drinks, and *naltrexone* blocks the "high" feeling from alcohol (Sarafino & Smith, 2011). Chemical methods for creating MOs to stop substance use should be done under the direction and supervision of a physician.

As a general rule, using chemicals—even over-the-counter drugs—for any reason with clients may benefit from supervision by a medical practitioner. Behavior analysts' employers can probably provide advice or rules on this issue. (Go to ▤.)

STUDY AND REVIEW

SUMMARY

The traditional view of motivation includes biologically based drives and psychologically or socially based motives, such as for achievement. These ideas have had little practical value. The motivational concept of people's readiness to change can be useful in behavior change programs, especially if they include self-management methods, because people who want to improve their behavior are more likely to start and succeed in the program.

Motivating operations (MOs) change the effectiveness of a specific reinforcer or punisher (the value-altering effect) and the individual's current performance of behaviors that normally lead to that reinforcer (the behavior-altering effect). MOs can be of two types: Establishing operations (EOs) increase the effectiveness of the consequence, and abolishing operations (AOs) decrease the effectiveness of the consequence. There also are two types of behavior-altering effect: In the evocative effect, performance of the behavior increases; in the abative effect, the behavior decreases. EOs and AOs can have value-altering effects for positive reinforcers, negative reinforcers, and punishers.

CONCEPT CHECK 9.2

Answer the following questions about motivating operations (MOs).

1. Procedures that temporarily alter the effectiveness of specific consequences and the performance of related behaviors are called _____ .
2. Altering the effectiveness of a consequence is called the _____ .
3. The two types of behavior-altering effects are the _____ and _____ effects.
4. An MO is called an _____ if it increases the effectiveness of a consequence and an _____ if it decreases the effectiveness of a consequence.
5. Two commonly used MOs for reinforcement are _____ and _____ .
6. An example of a chemical that serves as an abolishing operation in treating substance abuse is _____ . ⇔
7. MOs that have value-altering effects that were learned are called _____ MOs.
8. An example of an unconditioned motivating operation is _____ .

Some MOs are called unconditioned motivating operations (UMOs) because they alter the effectiveness of reinforcers without having been learned to do so; others were learned and are conditioned motivating operations (CMOs). We can apply MOs by using deprivation and satiation procedures, altering the consequence itself, or using chemical methods—for instance, as AOs to help people stop using opiates, tobacco, and alcohol.

To prepare for exams, use the following key terms and review questions and the online study guide that's available on this book's companion website at www.wiley.com/college/sarafino.

KEY TERMS

motivating operations (MOs)
value-altering effect
behavior-altering effect
evocative effect

abative effect
establishing operations (EOs)
abolishing operations (AOs)

unconditioned motivating
  operations (UMOs)
conditioned motivating operations
  (CMOs)

ANSWERS TO CONCEPT CHECKS (CCs)

CC9.1 *Answers:* **1.** hunger, achievement **2.** desire, self-management **3.** manipulate **4.** establishing operation

CC9.2 *Answers:* **1.** motivating operations (MOs) **2.** value-altering effect **3.** evocative, abative **4.** establishing operation, abolishing operation **5.** deprivation, satiation **6.** methadone, varenicline, or naltrexone **7.** conditioned **8.** food or water deprivation

REVIEW QUESTIONS

1. Describe the traditional view of motivation expressed in introductory psychology textbooks.
2. What are motivating operations (MOs), and what two effects do they have?

3. Define the term *establishing operation* (EO), and give one example each of EOs that should produce an evocative effect and an abative effect.

4. Define the term *abolishing operation* (AO), and give one example each of AOs that should produce an evocative effect and an abative effect.

5. Describe an EO and an AO for negative reinforcement from your life.

6. Describe how chemicals can be used to treat substance use, and explain why they should help in terms of MOs.

7. What are unconditioned motivating effects (UMOs) and conditioned motivating effects (CMOs)? Give two examples of each.

8. Describe the research of Vollmer and Iwata (1991) that examined the effects of EOs and AOs for three different reinforcers.

9. Describe the research of Ward and Carnes (2002) in which football players who had their progress on improving poorly performed skills publicly posted.

RELATED READINGS

* Laraway, S., Snycerski, S., Michael, J., & Poling, A. (2003). Motivating operations and terms to describe them: Some further refinements. *Journal of Applied Behavior Analysis, 36*, 407–414.

* Mook, D. G. (1987). *Motivation: The organization of action.* New York: Norton.

10

SHAPING

PROLOGUE

Here's a "when I was your age" story: I got my first chance to apply operant principles while I was an undergraduate. I was a psychology major taking a course on the topic of learning, and the course had a lab section each week. One of the tasks each small group of students was assigned to do in the lab was to train a rat to press a lever positioned a few inches up a wall in a Skinner box that had a floor about 1 square foot in area. The rats had never been in a Skinner box before, so we were starting from scratch. Two good circumstances helped the process. First, rats tend to wander around looking at and sniffing new environments. Second, we had used a motivating operation—the animals were deprived of food for hours before each lab session, and we were using pellets of dry food as reinforcers. Our behavioral goal was to get the rat to press the lever (a behavioral deficit) at a moderately high rate when placed in the apparatus.

Our instructor recommended a *starting response*, an initial behavior that was not like pressing the lever but one we should look for and reward because it would be a good point to begin. Let's assume that the starting response was something like "Rat moves to within 6 inches of the lever." As soon as that happened, we pressed

A Skinner box (operant chamber). *Source:* Mimi Forsyth/Age Fotostock America, Inc.

a button that released a pellet of food from a dispenser to a trough just below the lever. Although the dispenser made a clicking sound, the rat showed no sign of associating it with food delivery or being aware of the pellet in the trough. Then we waited until the rat found the pellet, consumed it, and started moving about. From that point on, we used basically the same reinforcement procedure; but for successive pellets, we gradually required behaviors closer and closer in form to a lever-pressing response. No reinforcers were given for responses that were inferior to the last one. Let's assume that the sequence of behaviors for subsequent pellets consisted of requiring that the rat:

1. Moves to within 4 inches of the lever.
2. Is within 4 inches of the lever and facing it.
3. Has nose within 2 inches of the lever.
4. Rises up on its hind legs near the lever.
5. Rises up and moves a paw toward the lever.
6. Touches the lever with a paw.
7. Presses the lever hard enough to trigger release of a pellet.

From this point on, the rat would trigger the pellet release on its own, and pretty soon it reached the behavioral goal of pressing the lever at a moderately high rate. This approach can be used to teach all animals and humans new behaviors.

This chapter discusses a procedure called *shaping* that applied behavior analysts use to teach people (and animals) new operant behaviors and to improve ones that are not performed as well as desired. We'll examine various ways to structure shaping processes, examples of how shaping occurs in everyday life, and tips for using shaping.

WHAT IS SHAPING?

Shaping is a procedure by which performance of a specific behavior improves because higher and higher criteria are required for successive instances of reinforcement for that behavior (Gaynor & Clore, 2005). This means that for the target behavior to keep being reinforced, it must advance through a series of successively better approximations to the behavioral goal.

SUCCESSIVE APPROXIMATIONS

A sequence of behaviors in which the responses become closer and closer to the form and quantity of a well-performed target behavior is called **successive approximations**. Each of these approximations is called a *step*. In the opening story about my group's shaping a rat to press a lever, the list of behaviors that we reinforced gives the steps we used after the starting response. The progression of these steps can be seen in Figure 10-1. Two points should be made about the steps. First, notice in the figure that once the behavior moved from one step to another, the response in a lesser step was no longer reinforced (nlr), as shown in the shaded portion of the diagram. Second, our group would sometimes allow the behavior to stay at a step for a while, reinforcing that specific response more than one time before requiring movement to the next step.

People's behavior can be shaped with a similar deliberate process, but it is also shaped naturally. For instance, babies on their way to learning to talk will start to babble, seemingly "playing" with vowel and consonant sounds, such as repeatedly saying "gaga" or "a-bah-bah." Smiling and attentive parents appear to elicit vocal sounds by the baby (Bloom, 1979). Studies have shown that if specific vocal sounds are reinforced, such as with tickling or praise, infants make more of those sounds; if reinforcement is no longer given (a procedure called *extinction*), these sounds decline (Routh, 1969; Wahler, 1969). In everyday life, parents listen to their baby's vocalizations and reward those that are like words in their language—especially "mama" and "papa," which receive effusive praise.

Later, as the child is beginning to learn to print block letters with a pencil, parents may initiate casual training sessions to teach printing. For example, suppose 3-year-old Erin is learning to print the first letter of her name, and her father is looking for better and better approximations to well-formed Es and giving social reinforcers when he sees them. Even though her first attempt is a very distant or primitive approximation to an E, the initial attempt would receive praise as a good starting response. But then the standards for printing an E would begin to increase, and Erin would need to make successively better approximations to receive continued praise. Figure 10-2 presents an illustration of Erin's successive approximations in printing an E.

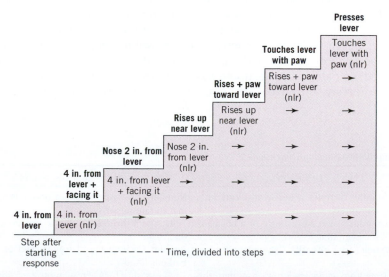

Figure 10-1   Steps after starting response in successive approximations for rat lever pressing. Shaded areas represent behaviors that are no longer reinforced (nlr).

Figure 10-2   Illustrations of Erin's successive approximations in printing a well-formed E.

Although shaping is often used to train a behavior the person hasn't performed before, it can also be applied to improve existing skills—improving a good tennis backhand stroke to make it excellent, for example.

QUALITATIVE "TOPOGRAPHIC" SHAPING

Shaping can be applied to improve qualitative and quantitative features of the behavior. In *qualitative shaping* (or "topographic" shaping), the successively higher standards for performance pertain to the degree to which the responses look, sound, or feel like the well-formed behavior. Erin's printing better and better Es is an example of qualitative shaping. Virtually any operant behavior can be qualitatively shaped.

An application of qualitative shaping was used with Dicky, a preschool-age boy with autism, to get him to wear his glasses (Wolf, Risley, & Mees, 1964). When people tried to get him to wear them, he would pull them off and throw them on the floor. The lenses were very powerful, and it may be that the degree to which they changed his visual field was aversive. After a variety of efforts failed, the researchers decided to try shaping methods that they conducted during breakfast so that Dicky would be hungry when they used food reinforcers. The successive approximations began with the starting response of touching the glasses. After this behavior was established, the steps moved on to picking up the glasses, putting them up to his face, and then putting the glasses on in their proper position. Later, he was required to wear the glasses for activities, such as at meals and on walks, or the activity would be terminated. By the end of the study, Dicky was wearing the glasses about 12 hours a day.

QUANTITATIVE SHAPING

Quantitative shaping refers to setting criteria for reinforcement to increase or decrease the quantity of the behavior, generally by changing its frequency, duration, or magnitude. An example of quantitative shaping can be seen in a study that used biofeedback methods to increase a 20-year-old man's heart rate by 17 beats per minute above baseline levels (Scott et al., 1973). The man could hear the audio portion of television programs at all times during the intervention, but the video portion remained on only if he kept his heart rate at certain levels. The initial criterion was 5 beats above baseline to keep the video portion on, but the criteria were raised once each level had been achieved. An older man's heart rate was decreased by 16 beats per minute in a similar fashion. These changes were temporary, of course. Other examples of quantitative shaping can be seen in Table 10.1. (Go to 🐾 and then 📖.)

Table 10.1   *Quantitative Shaping Dimensions of Behavior*

Dimension	Definition	Example Behaviors
Frequency	Number of times a behavior occurs in a given time	Number of potatoes washed or words spelled correctly in a 10-minute session
Duration	Length of time an instance of a behavior lasts, beginning to end	Time spent exercising on a treadmill or reading a textbook
Magnitude	A behavior's intensity, degree, or size	Amount (in volume) of fruit picked or the weights of barbells lifted
Latency	Time from an antecedent's onset until the behavior starts	Time elapsing between going to bed and falling asleep or being told to be seated in class and doing so

CASE STUDY

Teaching Alice to Speak Louder

An example of quantitative shaping comes from an intervention to induce a girl named Alice to talk louder and louder (Jackson & Wallace, 1974). Alice was a 15-year-old with mild mental retardation who rarely spoke at an audible level. The behavior analysts used a device to measure the loudness of her speech—if her speech reached a preset volume, the apparatus would dispense a token. Alice's task was to read individual words that were printed on cards; the volume of her speech had to increase for her to continue receiving reinforcers. At the beginning of shaping, she was told that she would need to talk loudly to earn tokens, and at the start of each session she was reminded of this contingency. Then, following each session,

> the tokens were counted and the number was recorded on a ledger sheet. Alice could earn enough tokens in one session to buy a small item (e.g., a hair brush), or she could save them up until she had enough to buy a larger item (e.g., a book or photo album). (p. 463)

The decision to move up a step in the volume required for reinforcement was made on the basis of the following rule: If 80% of the words Alice spoke by midway in a session were louder than the preset value, the researchers reset the required loudness to a "slightly" higher level at that time. After nearly 40 sessions of gradual improvement, the loudness of her speech began to increase sharply, and soon she was talking louder than her peers. A similar shaping procedure was used with two young socially withdrawn children; their data are presented in Figure 10-3 (Fleece et al., 1981).

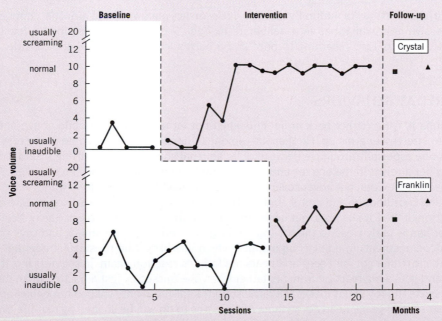

Figure 10-3   Average voice loudness levels in a classroom setting for two children during baseline, intervention, and follow-up phases in a multiple-baseline design. *Source*: From L. Fleece, A. Gross, T. O'Brien, J. Kistner, E. Rothblum, & R. Drabman (1981), Elevation of voice volume in young developmentally delayed children via an operant shaping procedure. *Journal of Applied Behavior Analysis*, 14, 351–355, Figure 1. Copyright © 1981 Society for the Experimental Analysis of Behavior. Used by permission.

CONCEPT CHECK 10.1

Check your understanding of the preceding concepts. Remember that the symbol ⇔ means the answer can vary. Answer the following questions about the process of shaping.

1. The first behavior we choose to reinforce in shaping is called a _____ response.

2. The responses chosen in shaping that are closer and closer to the well-formed target behavior are called _____ .

3. An example of an intermediate successive approximation in teaching a child how to lock a door might be _____ . ⇔

4. Using shaping to teach a new behavior so that it looks, sounds, or feels like the well-formed act is called _____ .

5. Using shaping to improve the frequency or magnitude of an existing behavior is an example of shaping _____ .

6. An example of quantitative shaping used in this text is _____ . ⇔

SHAPING IN REAL LIFE

Events in real life shape behavior naturally. There's little or no planning, and no one chooses the steps constituting successive approximations in a deliberate manner. We've already described a few examples of shaping in real life, such as Erin's learning to print and a baby's learning to talk. Let's consider a few more examples.

SHAPING EVERYDAY BEHAVIORS

One-month-old Alma is lying on her back in her crib when her father installs a mobile above her and within reach if she were to stretch her arms up. He then lifts up one of her arms to jiggle some of the toys hanging on it, and Alma finds one especially attractive because of its unusual shape and the rattling sound it makes when jiggled. He notices her interest in the one toy and lifts her arm to jiggle it again, and she's hooked. At this point he leaves her to her own devices, but hovers over the crib to watch what she does for a while.

Alma's eye–hand coordination and motor ability with her arms are not yet well developed. She reaches both hands in the direction of the toy she likes, but her hands are off to the side of the object. She notices two things: Her reach puts her hands fairly close to the toy (but "no cigar"), and her father smiles and says something (it was praise and encouragement) in a singsong manner, which she likes. She tries again, gets her hands a bit closer, notices how close she got, and sees and hears her father's reaction again. In the next few tries she gets closer and closer and gets a big reaction from her father when she misses by just a fraction of an inch. Her next try succeeds: She swats the toy and it makes the rattle sound! Real-life events shaped her behavior.

During the next several years, nearly everything Alma learns to do will be shaped by real-life events. As she learns to eat with a spoon, her aim at her cereal and her face will get better and better, giving her more cereal on her spoon and in her mouth. When she learns to throw a ball to her mother, her aim will improve gradually until she hits her target almost every time. When she gets the guitar she wanted for her sixth birthday, one of the first skills she'll learn is to tune it, which will get better and better as she listens for the tones of the strings strummed in sequence and gets feedback from other people. In a similar way, her guitar playing will improve gradually as she requires of herself higher and higher standards for acceptable performance.

SHAPING PROBLEM BEHAVIORS

Three-year-old Zev is lying on the floor, flailing his arms and legs about, and screaming. Temper tantrums are a common occurrence of early childhood, and parents dread them. How do children develop tantrums? One factor is that they have associated crying with reinforcers, such as getting attention and items or activities they want. Before Zev had any language to express what he wanted, he just cried, which got attention and often other things he wanted.

At 2 or 3 years of age, children are acquiring mands, phrases to request what they want. If they don't know the words yet or say the correct mand but don't get what they want, they feel frustrated and begin to cry, partly out of frustration but also because crying had worked in the past. So, when Zev's parents didn't comply quickly, the child cried louder until they gave him what he wanted—saying, for instance, "OK. OK. You may have a cookie. Stop your screaming." In the future, when his parents would try not to "give in," Zev would cry louder and louder, and perhaps add some flailing, which made the parents concerned he might hurt himself. So they gave in again. This kind of parental response reinforces the behavior and teaches the child that such outbursts are an effective means of getting his own way. As you can see, Zev's tantrum behavior was shaped over time. Children who are rewarded for their tantrums have more and more outbursts.

Shaping can also increase the frequency and magnitude of aggressive behavior children perform against other people. For example, suppose a 2-year-old girl wants a toy her parent is using with her younger brother. If she takes the toy, the parent may decide to let her have it and use another toy with the brother instead. At day care, she may try to take a toy from a younger child, get a little resistance, and pull the toy with a little force, which succeeds. If she gets a little more resistance she may pull harder and push on the other child's hand, which succeeds. In subsequent similar situations, she may find more resistance and apply more force, perhaps even hitting the other child. To the extent that her behavior continues to get reinforced with greater and greater force, she is likely to be more and more aggressive toward others when she wants something they have. Children who receive rewards for being aggressive increase their aggression in the future (Walters & Brown, 1963). (Go to 🔍.)

ASPECTS OF SHAPING METHODS

Before starting to conduct a shaping procedure, three tasks must be completed. First, we should describe the behavioral goal—the final level and form of the target behavior that we want the person to achieve. Be sure that the goal is reasonable and useful for the person to achieve. Second, we should identify the starting response, or the first step that will receive reinforcement in the successive approximations. This behavior may be a very primitive approximation to the target behavior. Third, we should develop a tentative and flexible plan for the steps we expect to apply.

SHAPING "STEPS"

Because the behavior that undergoes shaping is a behavioral deficit and usually new to the person, it generally starts as a very primitive approximation to the desired action—and it often is so primitive that its relationship to the desired behavior may be hard to see. In the earlier example of Erin's first attempt to print an E, she started by writing squiggly lines that have little resemblance to the letter. But as a first approximation, it was worth reinforcing.

CLOSE-UP

Is Self-Injurious Behavior Shaped by Real-Life Events?

I remember the first time I worked with children with developmental disabilities while I was an undergraduate, and I saw a boy—I think his name was Kenny—engage in self-injurious behavior, smashing his head against a block wall so hard that he bled. Why would Kenny do this? How could he have developed this behavior?

A possible answer to these questions is that Kenny's self-injurious behavior was shaped by real-life events. Because he was developmentally disabled, he may have been more prone to accidents, such as falling and hitting his head. Perhaps an accident of this type occurred, and his parents saw it, ran to him, and gave him a lot of attention and care. He may also have engaged sometimes in a form of self-stimulation, such as tapping his head with his hand, which his parents might attend to as well. As his parents got used to his head tapping, they may have stopped reinforcing it with attention. So, he may have begun to tap harder, to which they responded. Over time he may have tapped with more and more force and had additional accidents in which his head hit the floor or furniture, and his parents reinforced these behaviors with attention.

For ethical reasons, we cannot demonstrate the shaping of self-injurious behavior with children. But researchers have shaped potentially self-harmful behavior in animals. One study used food as a reinforcer for two rats to shape the behavior of leaning farther and farther over the edge of a platform until they fell off, landing in a safety net (Rasey & Iversen, 1993). Another study shaped head hitting with paws in two monkeys—an act that is very similar to self-injurious behaviors performed by many children with developmental disabilities (Schaefer, 1970). Reinforcers consisted of food (banana pellets, slices of fruit); the animals had been deprived of food for many hours at the start of a training session. The shaping involved three steps: raising a paw, positioning the paw above the head, and bringing the paw down to hit the head. Each time the correct action occurred in a step, reinforcement was given. This training was completed in one session, which ended when the animal had hit its head 30 times.

How big should the gap between steps be? There's no hard-and-fast answer to this question, because the gap sizes depend on the difficulty of the task and the person's abilities. But a very general rule can be given: Gaps between steps should be large enough to produce some challenge and fairly quick progress, but small enough to allow the person to succeed. If a gap is too large, the person will fail. Here are three guidelines we can follow:

1. Do not try to advance to the next step until the person has mastered the current one. If we do, the gap is likely to be too big.

2. If the person's behavior begins to deteriorate because we tried to advance too quickly, reinforce an earlier approximation to build from there again.

3. Try not to make the gaps too small, either. If we do, the task may become boring, the training will be inefficient and unnecessarily expensive, and the person may become "stuck" at a level of behavior that has produced inordinate reinforcement.

Conducting shaping—especially qualitative shaping—is something of an art that requires the judgment and flexibility you will gain with experience.

Sometimes the shaping steps you will use can be outlined fairly straightforwardly in advance, particularly for quantitative shaping. This is because the form of the behavior already exists, and we are trying to improve only some dimension of it, such as its latency or magnitude. An example of a rule governing the steps used in quantitative shaping comes from a study on preparing children to remain still during a medical and research procedure called magnetic resonance imaging, or MRI (Slifer, Koontz, & Cataldo, 2002). Each of four children was placed headfirst in a simulated MRI apparatus while lying on a platform; the goal was to have them keep their heads as still as possible during eight 7-minute sessions, including baseline. At the end of intervention sessions, the children received a prize they had selected if they met a specific criterion: a decrease in head motion of at least 0.1 millimeter per minute as compared to their preceding session, which was the rule governing movement to a more rigorous step in the successive approximations. All of the children showed dramatic reductions in head movement during intervention.

Perhaps the best advice in shaping behavior is to *be flexible* enough to speed up or slow down the shaping process as needed, particularly in qualitative shaping. Being able to shape behavior effectively is a skill that requires knowledge of the person's abilities and experience in training different people to perform various tasks. For individuals with very severe learning difficulties, such as children with profound retardation, we may even need to train them to retrieve, use, or consume the reinforcer. Computer programs are available that simulate important features of the shaping process and help train many skills behavior analysts need to administer reinforcement effectively (Acker, Goldwater, & Agnew, 1990; Shimoff & Catania, 1995).

SHORTCUTS TO SHAPING

A limitation to using shaping is that the process can be time-consuming and expensive. For complex behaviors and clients who have great difficulty learning, many steps may be needed in carrying out the successive approximations. Are there ways to deal with this problem?

While you were reading the material on shaping, you may have recognized that there are ways to shortcut the process of shaping. One way to shortcut shaping is to use *physical guidance*, manually moving the person's body through the desired movements. For instance, Erin's father could have put his hand on hers and helped her write the letter she was working to learn. Another method involves using *pictures* of the behavior or its product, such as the printed letter. Her father would probably show her an example of a well-formed E, the letter she was learning to write. The third approach is *modeling* the behavior: Her father could have written the letter, pointing out what he was doing. And the fourth way to shortcut shaping is to use *instructions* to describe how to perform the responses. Only this last approach requires that the learner have good language skills. We examine these methods in detail in Chapter 11 when we discuss ways to shortcut stimulus control.

COMPUTER-AIDED SHAPING

Because shaping is a complex process and requires experience to perform it well, procedures have been developed that can simplify it by automating parts of the process with two components. First, a method called *percentile schedules* applies a mathematical formula to determine the criteria for reinforcement and decide whether each instance of the behavior has met the current criterion (Galbicka, 1994). Second, software on a handheld computer can process data for the formula continuously and report whether an instance of the behavior has met the needed criterion. Using a handheld computer to conduct shaping with percentile schedules, researchers increased the amount of time four students with learning disabilities spent on task (Athens, Vollmer, & St. Peter Pipkin, 2007).

TIPS ON USING SHAPING

The tips on using shaping listed here have been applied by behavior analysts in a wide variety of behavior change interventions.

1. Decide whether shaping is an appropriate procedure: It is used to teach people a behavior they don't already know how to do or to improve a behavior gradually. Shaping is a time-consuming procedure. There's no need to use it if the target person can perform the behavior if simply given a description of it or if the shortcut methods, such as physical guidance, would be sufficient.

2. Choose the steps in successive approximations based on what you think the person can do; don't make the gaps between steps too small or too hard. Don't advance to the next step until the person has mastered the current

one. Define what "mastery" will consist of for any step: For example, you could define it as performing the action within 1 minute of the antecedent's presentation on four of the last five trials.

3. Select appropriate reinforcers, and describe to the target person as clearly as possible that the reinforcers are contingent on and consequences for making progress toward performing the target behavior.

4. Don't reinforce the response at any one step too often. Doing so makes the person "fixate" on that response, preventing him or her from advancing to the next step.

5. Be flexible and follow the needs of the target person to determine how big each step should be and how long to stay at any step.

6. If the target person stops working or seems to be having difficulty at a particular step, check whether he or she still wants the reinforcer and consider whether you may have tried to advance too quickly. To correct the former problem, replace the reinforcer or introduce a motivating operation; for the latter problem, reinforce an earlier approximation to build from there again, and design an easier step to follow it.

7. Make sure that after the target behavior is mastered, it continues to receive either natural or programmed reinforcement.

(Go to .)

STUDY AND REVIEW

SUMMARY

The process of shaping begins with a starting response, which receives reinforcement like all of the successive approximations to the target behavior. Each approximation is called a *step*, and once the process advances to a new step, inferior behaviors no longer receive reinforcement. This procedure can be used to develop entirely new responses—a process called *qualitative shaping*—or to improve qualitative and quantitative aspects of existing behaviors. Training someone to speak louder is an example of quantitative shaping.

Shaping can be conducted deliberately in a training program, but it also occurs naturally with everyday events. In real life, it can lead to the development of appropriate behaviors, such as learning to read or to

---

CONCEPT CHECK 10.2

Answer the following questions about shaping in real life and aspects of shaping.

1. When children develop new behaviors in real life without planning or choosing successive approximations, shaping occurs _____ with everyday events.
2. An example of the shaping of an appropriate behavior in real life used in this text is _____ . ⇔
3. An example of the shaping of a problem behavior in real life used in this text is _____ . ⇔
4. True or false: Once you've designed the successive approximations for shaping someone's behavior, you should stick with the planned steps even if the person is having trouble learning _____ .
5. An example of a shortcut to shaping used in this text is _____ . ⇔

feed oneself, and problem behaviors, such as tantrums or self-injurious behaviors. Before starting a shaping procedure, we should describe the behavioral goal, identify a starting response, and develop an outline of the planned successive approximations. Each time the approximation occurs at the current step, it should be reinforced; try not to reinforce the behavior either too much or too little at any step. The gaps between steps should be small enough that the response will occur, but not so small that the person becomes bored. Shortcuts to shaping can speed the process, and computer-aided methods with percentile schedules can simplify it.

> To prepare for exams, use the following key terms and review questions and the online study guide that's available on this book's companion website at www.wiley.com/college/sarafino.

KEY TERMS

shaping   successive approximations

ANSWERS TO CONCEPT CHECKS (CCs)

CC10.1 *Answers*: **1.** starting **2.** successive approximations **3.** reach toward the doorknob **4.** qualitative shaping **5.** quantitative **6.** training someone to speak louder

CC10.2 *Answers*: **1.** naturally **2.** tuning a guitar **3.** tantrums or aggression **4.** false **5.** modeling or instructions

REVIEW QUESTIONS

1. Define the term *shaping*. Pick a behavior you learned as a child that was not used as an example in this text; describe how it may have been shaped.
2. What tasks should you complete before starting to shape a behavior?
3. Explain what successive approximations are. Give an example of how you could use them in a shaping program with a young child for a behavior not described in this text.
4. Name and define the four dimensions of behavior that can be quantitatively shaped.
5. Give an example of a friend's undesirable behavior not discussed in this text, and speculate on how it might have been shaped naturally.
6. Describe the study by Jackson and Wallace (1974) in which they shaped the loudness of Alice's speech.
7. What problems arise in shaping when the gaps between steps are too large or too small?
8. Under what conditions is shaping not the best way to develop a behavior?
9. Why is it important not to reinforce a behavior at any one step too much or too little?

RELATED READINGS

- Acker, L. E., Goldwater, B. C., & Agnew, J. L. (1990). Sidney Slug: A computer simulation for teaching shaping without an animal laboratory. *Teaching of Psychology*, 17, 130–132.
- Rasey, H. W., & Iversen, I. H. (1993). An experimental acquisition of maladaptive behavior by shaping. *Journal of Behavior Therapy and Experimental Psychiatry*, 24, 37–43.
- Shimoff, E., & Catania, A. C. (1995). Using computers to teach behavior analysis. *The Behavior Analyst*, 18, 307–316.

11

SHORTCUT STIMULUS CONTROL METHODS

Prompting
Response Prompts
Stimulus Prompts

Transferring Stimulus Control
Response Prompt Fading
Stimulus Prompt Fading
Sizes of Fading Steps
Increasing Assistance and Delay Approaches

Tips on Using Prompting and Fading

Study and Review

PROLOGUE

Jan was a 3-year-old with a neurological disorder that made it difficult for her to perform motor activities. Tests had shown that she had mild retardation; she understood simple instructions and spoke in a somewhat slurred manner. A behavior analyst named Ty was beginning a program to teach her to eat with a spoon. It was lunchtime, and she had not eaten for a few hours. Ty started by telling and showing her a couple of times the name of the task ("eating") and what it consists of—he:

- Said, "Look at what I do."

- Scooped some food with a spoon, saying, "Scoop some food" as he made the act.

- Lifted it to his mouth, saying, "Put it in my mouth" as the spoon neared his mouth.

Then he grasped Jan's hand with one of his, put the spoon in that hand, and, while still grasping her hand, guided her to imitate his eating behavior, saying, "Scoop some food" and "Put it in your mouth" just before she did those acts. When she puts the food in her mouth, her feeding behavior receives two forms of reinforcement: the food and Ty's praise, "Good job eating!"

Ty had decided that Jan's ability would enable her to learn this behavior without having to use time-consuming shaping methods. Instead, he used shortcut methods that introduce antecedents that have a high degree of stimulus control. We saw in Chapter 8 that *stimulus control* refers to the ability of an antecedent to influence a behavior—if the stimulus control is high, the response is very likely to occur. The present chapter describes in detail several shortcut stimulus control methods behavior analysts use to make training new behaviors or improving existing ones more efficient. As we'll see, these methods involve the use of prompts.

PROMPTING

Prompts are stimuli that supplement the desired or normal discriminative stimulus (S^D) for a correct behavior, increasing the likelihood that the response will occur and receive reinforcement. It functions either by *reminding* us to perform a behavior we already know how to do or by *helping us to perform* a behavior we don't do often or well. Our everyday lives contain many prompts, such as when a teacher points at a chalkboard or when a baseball coach describes how to swing a bat to hit a pitched ball. Most prompts are learned S^Ds. Using prompts to remind or help people to perform a behavior is called *prompting*.

When behavior analysts use a prompt, it is typically presented along with S^Ds that should themselves set the occasion for the behavior in the future, minus the prompt. The behavioral goal for Jan in the opening story involved having her eventually use a spoon to feed herself with only the normal antecedents, no longer needing Ty's helpful acts. Prompting serves an important purpose: It forms the basis for stimulus control to be transferred or "shifted" from the prompt to the desired or normal S^D. Prompts can be grouped into two categories—response prompts and stimulus prompts (Alberto & Troutman, 1990). The type of prompt behavior analysts use in a given situation will depend on their judgment of the learner's ability and the method's likely success.

RESPONSE PROMPTS

In **response prompts**, the behavior analyst makes a response as a supplement to the S^D to induce performance of the target behavior. There are several types of response prompts.

Physical Guidance Prompts

In our opening story, Ty grasped Jan's hand and guided her use of the spoon to scoop food and lift it to her mouth. Manually moving part of the person's body through the desired action or sequence is called a **physical guidance prompt**.

This prompting method is often used in teaching simple tasks to children who have not yet developed very much language. For instance, infants who are physically guided to shake a rattle and hear its sound soon learn to perform that behavior on their own to produce the reinforcing sound. Older children with retardation, autism, or other learning impairment also benefit from manual prompts for basic tasks, such as using a toilet or rolling a ball to one another (Kazdin & Erickson, 1975; Lovaas, 1977; Strain, Shores, & Kerr, 1976).

Physical guidance is also very useful with older children and adults who are trying to learn or improve complex skills, such as golfing, playing a violin, or dancing. A violin teacher might put the violin in the playing position and manually move the child's head so the chin clamps the instrument in place, position the hand to grasp the violin fingerboard correctly, position the hand to grasp the bow, and move the bowing arm back and forth. Elderly people in nursing homes are often unoccupied, even when recreational activities are available. Research has shown that placing recreational equipment in their hands and helping them to use it can increase their involvement in these activities, as Figure 11-1 depicts (McClannahan & Risley, 1975).

Verbal Prompts

When Ty in the opening story said to Jan, "Scoop some food" and "Put it in your mouth" before she did those actions, he used **verbal prompts**—words that induce a specific behavior. Parents and teachers use verbal prompts a lot with children: When teaching a child to read a new word, *dog*, for example, they might point to

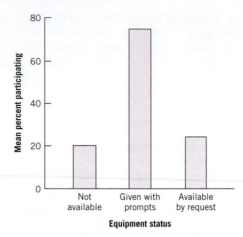

Figure 11-1   Mean percent of nursing home residents participating—that is, engaged with recreational equipment, materials, or other people—while in a communal lounge. Data were taken on days when recreational equipment was either not available, given directly to individuals with prompts to encourage participation, or available only on request. *Source:* Data from McClannahan & Risley (1975).

the word and say, "Dog." Then they might point to the word again and ask, "What's that word?" If the child doesn't respond correctly, they'd say, "It's dog." Eventually the child's just seeing the word, the normal S^D, will be sufficient. These prompts are useful with individuals who can understand the words in the prompt and can be very helpful when learning new skills, particularly in speaking. As another example, a director of a dramatic play might give the first few words of an actor's lines in rehearsal when the actor can't recall them. In such a case, the actor usually hasn't mastered the lines fully yet and simply needs a reminder.

A more elaborate form of verbal prompts are *instructions*, oral or written information that is designed to *describe how* to perform the target behavior. For instance, a manual for a video recorder describes how to set the device to record a program you won't be there to watch. Modeling and instructions occur very frequently in our everyday lives because they are easy to use and enable people to learn behavior with few or no errors.

Verbal prompts function as statements or descriptions of the behavior to be performed and have been used effectively in many different ways, for instance:

- Researchers had a passenger in a car flash a sign that read, "Please buckle up—I care" to drivers of stopped cars who were not using their seat belts (Geller, Bruff, & Nimmer, 1985). Of the nearly 900 drivers who looked at the sign, 22% buckled up before driving on.

- Four brain-injured adults were able to modify their behavior to avoid accidents at home by using checklists that described potential hazards, such as a drinking glass near the edge of a table, and included steps to eliminate each hazard (O'Reilly, Green, & Braunling-McMorrow, 1990).

- Customers at an employee cafeteria were given the opportunity to play a game to make their diets healthier (Zifferblatt, Wilbur, & Pinsky, 1980). While they stood in the serving line, they got cards that had verbal prompts, such as "The idea is valid—have a salad." At the end of 6 weeks, the customers could use the cards they collected to win prizes. Even though winning prizes did not depend on the foods the customers bought, their diets improved during the intervention.

Verbal prompts don't have to be as direct as those we've considered so far. Sometimes they're less direct, as in the question, "What is the next thing you need to do?" Notice that the question doesn't say what the specific behavior should be, but it still serves to encourage the person to make the response.

Instructions have been used effectively in changing a wide variety of behaviors. Researchers used instructions to help preschoolers keep working on a task of copying X and O letters on a sheet of paper when they could be distracted by a Clown Box that contained a tape recorder that invited the children to play a game (Patterson & Mischel, 1975). Two of the instructions the children received to resist the invitations were:

When Mr. Clown Box says to look at him and play with him, you can just look at your work, not at him, and say, "No, I can't; I'm working." And when you say it, do it. That's Number One: he says "look" and you say, "No I can't; I'm working." The second thing you can do is … say to yourself, "I'm going to keep working so I can play with the fun toys and Mr. Clown Box later." (p. 371)

Not all children were given instructions on how to resist the invitations, but all were promised that they could play with the fun toys and Clown Box if they finished their work quickly while the researcher was out of the room; otherwise, they could play only with broken toys. Those children who were given instructions on how to resist the invitations worked far longer on the task than the other children.

Gestural Prompts

Behavior analysts and other professionals also use **gestural prompts**—physical motions that the target person previously learned as S^{D}s for specific behaviors. For example, a teacher putting a finger to his or her lips means "Be quiet," and a frown in certain contexts means "Stop that." In the opening story, if Ty had lifted his hand while pointing to the spoon as Jan scooped some food, his gesture would have meant "Now lift it."

Here are a few other examples of gestural prompts. An orchestra conductor signals to musicians to play louder by using gestures, such as turning his or her palms up and moving the hands in a high and upward direction. Teachers use pointing as a gesture to direct students' attention toward material on the chalkboard or in a diagram to enable students to learn the material and study it better on their own. Or a parent who is teaching a child to discriminate between printed words might present *cat* and *dog* on cards, say "Point to the word *cat*," and then nod toward the correct card. The nod is a gestural prompt.

Modeling Prompts

Modeling is another shortcut method of using antecedents with a high degree of stimulus control to help a person learn and perform new or infrequent responses. We saw in Chapter 1 that modeling is a process by which people learn behaviors by watching what other individuals do. In **modeling prompts**, the antecedent is the modeled action, which *demonstrates how* and *induces* the person to perform the behavior. For example, Ty in the opening story showed Jan how to use a spoon to eat, which induced her to perform that act. As another example, a woodshop teacher might show students how to install a new bit in an electric drill and then take out

Hand signals of this traffic officer provide clear gestural prompts. *Source:* David Grossman/Alamy Limited.

the bit, start the procedure again, and have the students perform the rest of the procedure, imitating what they had seen. When modeling prompts are used in behavior change programs, the target person usually sees and learns *when* to perform the behavior and *what consequences* are likely to follow it.

Models do not need to be adults. Studies have found that children can provide very effective modeling to help other children learn and perform appropriate behaviors (Kohler & Strain, 1990; Lancioni, 1982; Strain, Shores, & Kerr, 1976). How practical it is to use children as models depends on the circumstances. For example, if students in a classroom are expected to serve as models or tutors to teach specific skills to certain classmates, they will need to be trained to do this and monitored to see that they are applying these methods correctly (Kohler & Strain, 1990). If the classroom has, say, 20 or 30 students and only one teacher, it can be difficult or impossible for the instructor to monitor and provide feedback for several models.

Behavior analysts often combine modeling and instructions in a training program. As an example, three 10- to 13-year-old students with moderate retardation were trained to prepare foods, such as scrambled eggs, by providing instructions to one student, the model, while the others watched (Griffen, Wolery, & Schuster, 1992). The instructions were provided to the model verbally and with a printed recipe consisting of words and pictures. Rewards were also provided to the model for correctly performing the responses making up each food preparation activity and to the other students for paying attention and for performing actions they had seen the model do. The model learned the instructed skill, and the observers learned most of what they had seen. Similar approaches are also used in business and industry to teach workers new skills. (Go to 🐾.)

STIMULUS PROMPTS

Stimulus prompts involve altering the normal antecedent in some physical way, either by changing something about the S^D itself (called a *within-stimulus prompt*) or by adding another stimulus to it (called an *extra-stimulus prompt*), to increase the likelihood that the person will respond correctly. Behavior analysts usually apply within-stimulus prompts temporarily to make the antecedent, or just some aspect of it, more noticeable or obvious until the normal S^D is sufficient. Stimulus prompts can involve pictures, sounds, or environmental alterations.

CASE STUDY

Three–Step Prompting With Ned

Sometimes behavior analysts use prompts in a progressive manner, such as by applying a *three-step prompting* procedure—starting with a verbal prompt and moving to modeling and then physical guidance prompts if the client does not respond correctly. Notice that the prompts become increasingly intrusive or controlling: Physically moving the client's body is more controlling than prompting with words. The three-step procedure was used with 8-year-old Ned, who had autism, and two other boys with other disorders to improve their compliance with teacher or parent requests (Tarbox, Wallace, Penrod, & Tarbox, 2007). The researchers had parents and teachers list some of the boys' behavioral deficits, tasks they consistently failed to do when asked. The lists included writing, dressing, and self-care tasks.

Ned was tested initially by his teacher. In baseline, the teacher simply asked him to do tasks from his list; but during the intervention, the three-step prompting procedure was used: The teacher asked him to do these same tasks; if he didn't comply, the same prompt was used again; if he continued not to comply, the teacher modeled the behavior and then physically guided it. Ned rarely complied in baseline, but after training with three-step prompting, Ned's compliance increased to 87% and usually required only one request. When he was later tested for generalization with a new set of tasks, Ned's compliance was at 100%, usually with only one request. His compliance also generalized to another teacher and a teacher's aide when they tested him.

Pictorial Prompts

Pictorial prompts use pictures—such as drawings, paintings, photographs, or video images—to alter the normal antecedent. Many buttons on your computer have drawings representing their functions: For example, ✉ means e-mail. These icons make it easier to learn how to operate the computer. A teacher gave me an example of using pictorial prompts temporarily: She wanted to learn the names of the students in her class at the start of the year and made this process easier with extra-stimulus prompts—on a piece of paper, she had their names with their pictures pasted beside them. When checking attendance, she used the photos to help her find each child and call the name. Eventually, she didn't need the photos and could discard them.

Pictures can also be used for within-stimulus prompts. For instance, sometimes a pictorial prompt involves accentuating just an element in an S^D, such as part of a letter of the alphabet, to make it more distinctive so that children can learn to discriminate one letter from another more easily (Gibson & Levin, 1975). Figure 11-2 illustrates how this might be done for the capital letters P and R. Other ways by which we can present a within-stimulus prompt—that is, make an S^D more noticeable—are to change its location or one of its dimensions, such as its size or color.

Although pictorial prompts usually consist of a single picture to induce the person to perform a specific response, they can also show a sequence of pictures to prompt each link in a complex behavioral chain. An example of this method comes from the training we described earlier of students with moderate retardation learning to prepare foods, such as scrambled eggs, by watching a student model the acts (Griffen, Wolery, & Schuster, 1992). The researchers prompted the model with instructions that included words and a series of pictures (extra-stimulus prompts). The other students watched and learned the behaviors. (Go to 🔍.)

Auditory Prompts

Auditory prompts are sounds other than words the person previously learned as S^Ds for particular behaviors. A within-stimulus prompt for an auditory stimulus, such as the ring of your alarm clock, might involve changing the location of the clock or the loudness of the alarm or its sound, such as a buzz instead of a ring. Changes like these can make the alarm more noticeable.

Sounds can also be used as extra-stimulus prompts. An example would be an alarm beeping on your cell phone during the first weeks after starting a new part-time job to remind you to check your work schedule so you will not be late. Another example of extra-stimulus prompts comes from an intervention demonstrating that auditory prompts can help incontinent children who are moderately to severely retarded learn toileting behaviors (Mahoney, Van Wagenen, & Myerson, 1971). The procedure involved presenting an auditory signal through an electronic device repeatedly with each link the children practiced in the behavioral chain of toileting responses (walking to the toilet, lowering their pants, and so on). Once each child learned to perform the chain in response to the signal, that same sound was used in a urine alarm apparatus (like the one we described in Chapter 4) that was placed in the child's pants. When the child released urine during regular activities, such as playing, the first drops triggered the signal, thereby prompting the child to perform the chain of toileting responses. This toilet training procedure was effective in eliminating "accidents" for four of the five children.

Figure 11-2   A pictorial prompt designed to accentuate the feature that distinguishes two stimuli children often find hard to discriminate. In this case, the distinctive feature is the diagonal leg of the R. Similar prompts can be made to help children discriminate between other letters, such as E and F, *c* and *e*, and *b* and *d*.

CLOSE-UP

Can Pictorial Prompts Sometimes Impair Learning?

When teaching children to read individual words, behavior analysts sometimes present with the word, such as *house*, a picture of the object as a pictorial prompt. Using an extra-stimulus prompt in this way seems reasonable, especially if the children have a hard time learning to read. Is this procedure a good idea?

Researchers examined this issue with 7- to 9-year-olds with moderate mental retardation who could read only a few words (Didden, Prinsen, & Sigafoos, 2000). Of the several research conditions the children experienced, some involved presentation of the printed word alone and the others involved presentation of the picture together with the word. Before the intervention, all of the children could name the pictures but none could name any of the words. The results showed that five of the six children learned to read the words correctly faster with a word-alone procedure than with the word and extra-stimulus pictorial prompt. This suggests that the children's prior learning of the names for the pictures may have "blocked" their learning the names of the printed words when the extra-stimulus prompt was given. Future research needs to determine why pictorial prompts impair learning to read words and whether this effect occurs also for children with stronger intellectual ability.

Environmental Prompts

In **environmental prompts**, alterations are made to the physical surroundings in which the normal S^D is presented; these alterations increase the likelihood that the desired act will occur. Consider the classroom as a normal S^D for "on-task behavior," such as paying attention to academic activities and not being disruptive. If the seating arrangements for a particular activity are crowded, on-task behavior is lessened. An environmental prompt in this situation would be to spread the students apart more, which increases the likelihood of on-task behavior (Krantz & Risely, 1977). This would be an example of a within-stimulus prompt, and the seating could be moved somewhat closer after the students were engaged consistently in on-task behavior. Another example of a within-stimulus prompt would be keeping fruits and vegetables in plain view (and hiding junk foods!) in your residence when you are trying to eat a healthier diet.

Environmental alterations can also be extra-stimulus prompts. For example, if you wanted to jog outdoors regularly but have failed to do so, you might keep on your bed the clothes you use when you jog to remind you to exercise (and not nap!). Once you get in the habit of jogging and become pleased with your fitness, and maybe have lost weight, you can probably phase out this prompt. (Go to 📖.)

TRANSFERRING STIMULUS CONTROL

When the target behavior is well established and stable, the prompts can be phased out so that the S^D that should normally elicit the behavior will become sufficient. In effect, the stimulus control for the behavior is transferred, or "shifts," from the prompt to the S^D. By phasing out the prompt gradually, we reduce the person's reliance on it while maintaining the stimulus control. Behavior analysts usually reduce a person's reliance on a prompt by applying a procedure called **fading**—gradually removing or changing a prompt so that it becomes more and more like the normal antecedent for the behavior (Danforth, 2005; Deitz & Malone, 1985; Demchak, 1990; Rilling, 1977). Most often, fading involves a process of *decreasing assistance* (also called the *most-to-least* strategy) in which the frequency or magnitude of the prompt's presentation is gradually reduced.

CONCEPT CHECK 11.1

Check your understanding of the preceding concepts. Remember that the symbol ⇔ means the answer can vary. Answer the following questions about prompts.

1. A stimulus that supplements the normal S^D to elicit a behavior is called a _____ .
2. There are two categories of prompts: _____ prompts and _____ prompts.
3. A father who manually moves his daughter's fingers to help her learn to tie her shoelaces is using a _____ prompt.
4. An example of a verbal prompt you could use to remind yourself to take medicine before going to bed might be _____ . ⇔
5. Examples of pictorial prompts that are often used to designate men's and women's restrooms are _____ . ⇔

Typically, therapists and teachers who help individuals acquire new skills intend for these people to function without prompts in their everyday lives. Fading not only reduces people's reliance on prompts but also appears to enhance performance of target behaviors and generalization to new situations (Karlsson & Chase, 1996; Krantz & McClannahan, 1998). There are several ways to transfer stimulus control, and we'll first consider approaches used with response prompts.

RESPONSE PROMPT FADING

To fade response prompts, we remove the prompt gradually over time while we continue to present the normal S^D and reinforce correct responding. To reduce a prompt's frequency, we would simply present it less and less often, while still presenting the S^D, until the person responds consistently to the S^D alone. This approach can be used for any type of response prompt—physical guidance, verbal, gestural, or modeling. For instance, a program that used physical guidance and other prompts to train women with profound retardation to stamp return addresses on envelopes faded the prompts by gradually reducing the number of occasions on which the trainer helped the women perform parts of the task (Schepis, Reid, & Fitzgerald, 1987).

Reducing a response prompt's magnitude can be accomplished in two ways. First, we could alter the type of prompt from one that is very direct, such as physically guiding a child's printing the letter C on a sheet of paper, to one that is less direct, such as gesturing the shape of a C on the paper. Second, we can lessen the completeness or strength of the response prompt. For instance, suppose a mother was physically guiding her son's printing with her entire hand. She could reduce this prompt by (a) beginning to guide with only two of her fingers, (b) then using only one finger, and (c) eventually following, or "shadowing," the child's actions with her hand but not touching the child.

For a verbal prompt, its magnitude could be reduced by saying the words softer or saying only parts of them. As an example of saying only parts of the words, if you were teaching a child to read from a flashcard the word *blueberry*, you might start prompting by saying the whole word and then progress to "blueber–, " "blue–, " and "b–. " Similarly, it is possible to reduce the completeness or strength of gestural or modeling prompts.

STIMULUS PROMPT FADING

Fading stimulus prompts—pictorial, auditory, or environmental—also involves removing them gradually by reducing their magnitude or frequency (presenting them less and less often). If we wanted to reduce the magnitude of a pictorial prompt, such as a drawing of the letter that a child has to trace, the materials could weaken the lines in the drawing, as Figure 11-3 illustrates, thereby decreasing its completeness. Teachers in a school for children with retardation used this fading approach to help 8-year-old Danny match digits he could already name, such as 5, with the number of objects each digit represented (Murrell, Hardy, & Martin, 1974). A digit and its corresponding number of circles were printed on a page, and Danny had to identify the digit and place circle cutouts on the printed circles. The lines of the circles were weakened over time until no circles were on the page, but Danny could still place on the page as many circles as were represented by the digit.

Reducing the magnitude of an auditory prompt, such as an alarm, might simply involve decreasing its volume. An environmental prompt mentioned earlier for the behavior of eating healthier was keeping fruits and vegetables in plain view. To reduce the magnitude of this stimulus prompt, we might decrease the number of fruits and vegetables we used.

SIZES OF FADING STEPS

You may have noticed in Figure 11-3 that the sizes of the steps as fading progresses from one level to the next are fairly easy for the individual to handle. This is done to promote *errorless learning*—fading is introduced gradually enough so that the person makes few or no errors while performing the task (Deitz & Malone, 1985; Rilling, 1977). Thus, the child in the figure would draw a C correctly at each of the six steps. In general, we want to design the steps so that the person continues to perform the target behavior correctly and receive reinforcers as the prompts are faded.

Designing an effective and efficient fading procedure for a particular person is more of an art than a "science" and requires some experience, skill, and, often, creativity. An important concern is the choice of "steps"—where a *step* is the movement from one level to the next—particularly with respect to the *sizes of the steps*. If the steps are too large, the person will make many errors, and the usefulness of the prompts will be impaired. But if the steps are too small, the person may become too dependent on the prompts, and the learning process will become inefficient and tedious. Psychologist O. Ivar Lovaas, who has worked extensively with children with autism, has recommended that the child's ability should determine the rate of fading:

> In some cases, very rapid, almost sudden, fading is appropriate and possible. In other cases, for certain children performing certain behaviors, fading is a slow process. The rule is to use the minimal number of prompts necessary to obtain the desired response. (1977, p. 20)

The same recommendation probably applies to all fading methods with all individuals. We can cite a few guidelines that can enhance the design of fading procedures:

- List the steps that are planned for the fading procedure and the criteria for advancing from one step to the next.
- The steps should be small enough to keep errors to a minimum.

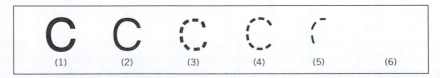

Figure 11-3   Illustration of how fading a pictorial prompt is presented as a child is asked to "Make a C." The child starts with the drawing that is darkest and most complete—the level marked (1)—and traces the letter with a marker pen. Once the child has mastered that level of prompt magnitude, he or she can progress to the next level, and so on to the last level—marked (6)—where no prompt is given.

- Monitor the person's performance carefully. When errors begin to occur, try going back to the previous step for a while and then advance again to the step at which errors occurred. If more errors occur at that step, consider revising the size of that step and perhaps others that were planned.

INCREASING ASSISTANCE AND DELAY APPROACHES

We've focused on approaches for transferring stimulus control that gradually reduce the frequency or magnitude of the prompts we use after the behavior is well established. But approaches other than fading with decreasing assistance can also be used to transfer stimulus control.

Another technique used in fading, called *increasing assistance* (or the *least-to-most* strategy), takes a very different approach (Demchak, 1990). For each trial of the target behavior, the behavior analyst starts by presenting just the normal S^D to see if the person will respond correctly. If the individual does not respond correctly, a minimal prompt is given—as an example, for a verbal prompt, the behavior analyst might whisper only part of the word. If the individual still does not respond correctly, stronger and stronger prompts are introduced until the correct response occurs. The stronger prompts can be of the same type, such as a louder verbal prompt, or ones that are more controlling or intrusive, such as physical guidance. For each subsequent trial, the behavior analyst starts again with just the S^D and then uses a minimal prompt and stronger prompts only when necessary. Although the level of assistance increases when individuals do not respond correctly, they require less and less assistance over time. This is why the method of increasing assistance is applied as a fading technique. Increasing assistance can be applied for response and stimulus prompts.

The last method we will consider for transferring stimulus control is *delayed prompting* (or *time delay*), in which a normal S^D for the behavior and a response prompt are presented together initially; thereafter, the prompt is delayed following presentation of the S^D (Demchak, 1990; Touchette & Howard, 1984). The delay can be *constant*, such as always 3 seconds across trials, or *progressive*, such as increasing by 1 second with each trial. If a delayed prompting procedure is designed appropriately, the person will begin to respond correctly during the delay period, before the prompt occurs, and will make few or no errors in learning the task. Technically, delayed prompting is not really a fading method, because the prompt is not actually changed or removed (Deitz & Malone, 1985).

TIPS ON USING PROMPTING AND FADING

Use the following guidelines in designing prompting and fading methods for a target behavior you want to train someone to do. Keep in mind that if the person has mastered the behavior and performed it well in the past with the normal S^D, you shouldn't need to teach the behavior or use prompting; your efforts should be to get him or her to comply. Use prompting only when the person hasn't already learned to perform the behavior with the normal S^D. The following tips assume that you've already determined that prompting is appropriate.

1. Response prompts are most useful to teach a specific action or sequence, such as how to hold a pencil or tie shoelaces. Stimulus prompts are mainly useful for helping someone learn to discriminate between stimuli, such as letters of the alphabet.

2. When the target person's abilities are very limited, as occurs with children with retardation or autism, behavior analysts often need to apply prompts that provide more structure or control, such as modeling and physical guidance.

3. When presenting S^Ds and prompts, make sure the person is paying attention to them.

4. When the person can understand instructions as a prompt, try to *describe reasons* for the behavior in terms of their natural consequences, as in "If you share your toys with her, she'll be nice to you" or "If you play with matches, you may get burned."

5. When using modeling prompts, use models who perform the responses reasonably well. Try to use more than one model, and make sure they all perform the target behavior in a consistent manner.

6. Fading methods to transfer stimulus control can be applied with response and stimulus prompts, but delayed prompting is typically used only with response prompts.

7. Sizes of steps in fading or delay should be small enough to avoid errors in responding and should be smaller for people with limited abilities than for individuals with stronger abilities.

8. Reinforce all correct responses the person makes during prompting and fading. Try to assure that reinforcement will continue after stimulus control has been transferred.

(Go to .)

STUDY AND REVIEW

SUMMARY

Many shortcut stimulus control methods can be used in applied behavior analysis. These methods include a variety of prompts, which are stimuli introduced to supplement the normal S^D to elicit the appropriate behavior, which is then reinforced. Prompts are presented with the S^D during training.

There are two categories of prompts, response prompts and stimulus prompts. Response prompts can be of several types: physical guidance (moving the target person's body through the desired action), verbal (stating words or instructions), gestural (making movements that direct the person's actions), and modeling (performing the act for the person to see) prompts. Stimulus prompts can be pictorial (such as drawings or photos), auditory (sounds, such as an alarm), and environmental (changes in the target person's surroundings).

Prompts are typically removed in a gradual manner once the behavior has been learned and is well established. This allows stimulus control to be transferred to the S^D. Fading of response and stimulus prompts can be done through decreasing assistance and increasing assistance methods; delayed prompting is used only for response prompts and can involve constant or progressive delays across trials. The steps in the fading process are usually small so that the person will make few or no errors.

CONCEPT CHECK 11.2

Answer the following questions about transferring stimulus control.

1. The process of gradually removing or changing a prompt to reduce someone's reliance on it is called _____ .

2. The fading strategy in which a prompt's frequency or magnitude is gradually reduced is called _____ .

3. One way we can reduce the magnitude of a verbal prompt might be _____ . ⟺

4. The sizes of fading steps are usually kept small to prevent _____ , which is especially important for target persons with _____ abilities.

5. Beth's special education teacher had trained her with prompts to use a spoon to eat. To fade the prompts, he first pointed to the spoon—and when this didn't work, he asked her to use the spoon. Then he placed it in her hand. He was using the fading method called _____ assistance.

6. In delayed prompting, the amount of time to wait before presenting the prompt after presenting the S^D can be _____ or _____ across trials.

To prepare for exams, use the following key terms and review questions and the online study guide that's available on this book's companion website at www.wiley.com/college/sarafino.

KEY TERMS

prompts
response prompts
physical guidance prompt
verbal prompts

gestural prompts
modeling prompts
stimulus prompts
pictorial prompts

auditory prompts
environmental prompts
fading

ANSWERS TO CONCEPT CHECKS (CCs)

CC11.1 *Answers:* **1.** prompt **2.** response, stimulus **3.** physical guidance **4.** put a sign saying "Take meds" with your toothbrush **5.** silhouettes of a man and a woman

CC11.2 *Answers:* **1.** fading **2.** decreasing assistance **3.** saying only part of a word or saying it softer **4.** errors, limited **5.** increasing **6.** constant, progressive

REVIEW QUESTIONS

1. What is a response prompt, and how is it different from a stimulus prompt?

2. Define the terms *within-stimulus prompts* and *extra-stimulus prompts*. How are they different?

3. Describe how you might use physical prompts to teach a dog to respond correctly to the command, "Give me your paw."

4. Describe two gestural prompts a baseball coach might make.

5. Give one example each of a verbal prompt and a modeling prompt that were not presented in this book.

6. Give one example each of a pictorial prompt and an environmental prompt that were not presented in this book.

7. What is three-step prompting?

8. Describe the research and findings of Didden, Prinsen, and Sigafoos (2000) on using pictorial prompts when teaching children with mental retardation to read words.

9. Define the term *fading*, and give an example of how you might fade (a) a verbal prompt to improve first-graders' classroom conduct and (b) a pictorial prompt to help a child discriminate between the numbers 3 and 8.

10. Discuss the issue of the sizes of fading steps.

11. Describe the delayed prompting procedure, and explain how constant and progressive delays can be used.

RELATED READINGS

- Demchak, M. (1990). Response prompting and fading methods: A review. *American Journal on Mental Retardation, 6,* 603–615.

- Gibson, E. J. (1969). *Principles of perceptual learning and development.* New York: Appleton-Century-Crofts.

12

CHAINING BEHAVIORS

PROLOGUE

Think about the task of toothbrushing. Chances are you see it as a simple activity that consists of only a few actions, such as opening the tube and squeezing toothpaste onto the brush, brushing back and forth, and rinsing the mouth and the brush. Your view of toothbrushing as a simple activity stems from the fact that you do it well and probably learned it easily. But for individuals who have difficulty learning, either because they are very young or have an intellectual disorder, toothbrushing can be a complicated task.

In Chapter 2, we considered briefly the concept of behavioral chains—complex sequences of actions that consist of antecedent–response pairs, called *links* or *steps* (Gagné, 1985). Toothbrushing is an example of a behavioral chain, and for all of us, it was a behavioral deficit when we were very young. An intervention taught this chain to eight 9- to 17-year-old individuals with mild to moderate retardation by breaking down the activity into 15 links (Horner & Keilitz, 1975). The chain started with:

1. Turning on the water and picking up the toothbrush.
2. Wetting the toothbrush.

3. Removing the cap from the toothpaste tube.
4. Applying the toothpaste to the brush.
5. Replacing the cap on the tube.

Then there were three links of actual brushing, such as "brush the outside surfaces of the teeth," followed by seven steps for rinsing and finishing up. Each action was described in detail: For instance, the last action, "discard the disposables," was defined as "Any used paper cups and tissues should be placed in a waste receptacle" (p. 303). The training procedure involved teaching all of the links, and learning the entire chain took from 18 to 30 sessions.

When we brush our teeth, put on a shirt, or place a phone call, we are performing a behavioral chain with responses that need to be carried out in a certain sequence. This chapter discusses in detail what behavioral chains are, how to identify their links, and methods for training chains.

FORMING AND ANALYZING BEHAVIORAL CHAINS

When an operant target behavior we want to teach or improve involves a complex set of responses, it is useful to determine what these responses are and whether they need to be performed in a certain sequence. If the behaviors should occur together in a sequence, they constitute a chain.

WHAT IS A BEHAVIORAL CHAIN?

A **behavioral chain** is a complex activity with links that occur in a certain order and usually include motor responses. Each step consists of a discriminative stimulus (S^D) and a response (R), and:

*   Each response (except the very last one) results in an S^D for the next R.
*   Each S^D (except the first one) serves as a reinforcer for the last R.

Suppose we wanted to help Ray, a boy with mental retardation, learn to dress himself, and we were teaching him to put on his sock while seated. This chain consists of four links, each containing an S^D and an R. The responses are (1) *grasp* the sock at the hole with one hand, making sure the toe points down; (2) *spread* the hole with the fingers of both hands; (3) *position* the foot up at the hole; and (4) *insert* the foot into the sock all the way. Seeing the outcome of each completed response, such as the grasp, serves as the S^D ("see grasp") for Ray in the next step, as depicted in the following diagram:

$$S^{D1} \rightarrow R_{(1)} \rightarrow S^{D2} \rightarrow R_{(2)} \rightarrow S^{D3} \rightarrow R_{(3)} \rightarrow S^{D4} \rightarrow R_{(4)} \rightarrow \text{Reinforcer}$$

| see sock | grasp | see grasp | spread | see spread | position | see position | insert | |

And each S^D, such as "see grasp," serves as a reinforcer for the preceding R ("grasp").

So much of our behavior is composed of behavioral chains. Turning on your computer and opening an application is one example, and others are making coffee for breakfast, washing your hair, tying your shoes, putting on a coat, and starting your car. Each of these activities consists of a sequence of links, each with an S^D and an R. So it's no wonder that behavior analysts spend a lot of their time and effort in teaching chains. Once the component responses of a behavioral chain are identified, a program can be designed to train the person with the behavioral goal of performing all of the steps together in the correct sequence.

This woman's going to a refrigerator, opening the door, finding the food she wants, reaching in to grasp it, pulling it out, and closing the door constitutes a behavioral chain for getting food. *Source:* UpperCut Images/Age Fotostock America, Inc.

DOING A TASK ANALYSIS

The process of identifying the antecedents and responses and all required sequences that make up a behavioral chain is called a **task analysis**. The objective in this process is to identify the component responses that are required to perform the chain and the order in which they should be carried out. A record of this information should be made, such as in words or pictures, so you can refer to it for the rest of the analysis. Another important step is to identify the S^D for each R so that you can try to determine whether the target person can discriminate between the S^D and other stimuli and is paying attention to the S^D in each link as you provide training in the chain.

To identify the responses and sequences in the task analysis, behavior analysts can choose from three strategies. They can:

1. Perform the task themselves, paying attention to each action and S^D.
2. Watch someone else who does the task well perform it, paying attention to each action and S^D.
3. Ask someone who is expert in the task to describe its component actions and S^Ds.

With each strategy, each action and its antecedent would be written down. For the training in toothbrushing in our opening story, the researchers videotaped three staff members as they brushed their teeth and then viewed those tapes to produce the task analysis (Horner & Keilitz, 1975).

Behavior analysts have developed and applied task analyses for a wide variety of complex skills and populations, and Table 12.1 describes two task analyses conducted for people in the general population and

Table 12.1   *Examples of Behavioral Chains and Links Taught for Variety of Skills in Two Populations, General and Developmentally Disabled*

Skill	Sample Link in Chain	Reference
Population: General (adult employees and schoolchildren)		
Lifting and transferring disabled clients	Lock wheelchair brakes.	Alavosius & Sulzer-Azaroff (1986)
Sports (executing football plays)	On the correct count, the center "snaps the ball."	Komaki & Barnett (1977)
Population: Developmentally disabled (usually with mental retardation)		
Apartment upkeep, such as refrigerator care	Remove food from freezer compartment.	Williams & Cuvo (1986)
Bed making	Pull top of blanket to headboard.	McWilliams, Nietupski, & Hamre-Nietupski (1990)
Janitorial activities, such as cleaning a sink	Spray entire sink with back-and-forth sweeping motions.	Cuvo, Leaf, & Borakove, (1978)
Menstrual care	Pull tab off clean sanitary napkin.	Richman, Reiss, Bauman, & Bailey (1984)
Pedestrian (crossing street)	Look left and right for traffic while crossing.	Page, Iwata, & Neef (1976)
Telephone use (coin phone)	Put receiver to left ear and listen for dial tone.	Test, Spooner, Keul, & Grossi (1990)

several for individuals who were developmentally disabled. All of these task analyses included large numbers of steps in the behavioral chains. (Go to .)

HOW TO TEACH BEHAVIORAL CHAINS

After having conducted a task analysis, we are ready to teach the behavioral chain. Keep in mind that the links identified in the task analysis may need to be revised, depending on how the training goes. It's important to be flexible with the training plans we develop from a task analysis. Two types of revisions are common. First, if the target person has difficulty with one of the steps, we may need to divide the behavior into two or more smaller links. For instance, in the list of steps for toothbrushing we saw in the opening story, the first link was "Turning on the water and picking up the toothbrush." This step actually mentions two behaviors, and a target person with retardation may not be able to keep track of both initially. Other links in the list may not express the component behaviors in enough detail: Although "Replacing the cap on the tube" states only one behavior, it actually requires more than that, such as reaching for the tube, grasping the cap, putting the cap in place, and either screwing or pressing the cap on.

CONCEPT CHECK 12.1

Check your understanding of the preceding concepts. Remember: The symbol ⇔ means that the answer can vary. Answer the following questions about forming and analyzing behavioral chains.

1. A link in a chain you might perform to start a computer is _____ . ⇔
2. Each response, except the last one, in a chain serves as a(n) _____ for the next _____ .
3. We would do a _____ to break down a complex act into its component responses.
4. One way to identify the antecedents and responses for a task analysis of a chain is to _____ . ⇔

Second, the steps may be too simple for some learners, leading to boredom. We may need to combine two or more of the listed links to reduce the person's boredom and make the training more efficient. Regardless of whether the revisions involve combining steps or dividing originally planned links into smaller components, each new step will be composed of an S^D and an R.

Three main approaches are used to teach behavioral chains: forward chaining, backward chaining, and total-task presentation. In each of these training methods, the behavior analyst may use prompts of all kinds, as needed. In contrast to total-task presentation, forward- and backward-chaining methods teach each step individually and then connect it to an adjacent one. When links are taught separately, reinforcers are given for performance of each link, but the criterion for reinforcement will eventually require that the entire chain be performed.

FORWARD CHAINING

Forward chaining involves teaching one link at a time in sequence, beginning with the first step in the behavioral chain. Performing the first link leads to reinforcement. After the target person has learned the first step, he or she must perform it to begin work on the second link. Prompting, such as modeling or physical guidance, is commonly used to teach each step and is generally faded before starting on the next link.

In our example of Ray learning to put on a sock, if we used forward chaining, he would first learn to grasp the sock correctly ($R_{(1)}$ in the diagram above) as a response to S^{D1} ("see sock") and a prompt, and the reinforcer would be given just for that response. After Ray mastered the first link and the prompt is faded, he would need to add the second response (spread the hole with the fingers) to the first to get the reinforcer. Thus a trial would begin with the S^{D1} ("see sock") again, and once Ray grasped the sock, a prompt would be given to help him spread the hole of the sock open ($R_{(2)}$). Then the next link in the behavioral chain is added, and so on, until the complete chain, with all steps included, is required for the reinforcer.

An intervention used forward chaining to teach adolescents with moderate mental retardation to make beds (McWilliams, Nietupski, & Hamre-Nietupski, 1990). A task analysis indicated that the entire sequence of bed making could be divided into five subtasks (such as one dealing with bed preparation and another dealing with putting on the blanket), and each subtask would contain four or five links. For each training trial, the adolescents were presented with the S^D: They were shown a messed-up bed and asked to make it. Then training followed a forward-chaining pattern, starting with the first link in the first subtask, bed preparation. The steps in this subtask were:

1. Remove pillow from bed.
2. Pull bedspread to foot of bed.
3. Pull blanket to foot of bed.
4. Pull flat sheet to foot of bed.
5. Smooth wrinkles of fitted sheet.

The adolescents first mastered "Remove pillow from bed," and then each of the other links in turn; they eventually performed the entire subtask to receive the reinforcer. After mastering this subtask, they moved to the next subtask with forward-chaining methods. At the end of this training, the adolescents were able to make the bed with little or no assistance when asked to do so, and the skill generalized to their beds at home.

BACKWARD CHAINING

Backward chaining consists of teaching one link at a time in the reverse sequence, beginning with the last one in the behavioral chain. On each training trial, performing the last link in the chain always leads to reinforcement. Referring again to the diagram for teaching Ray to put on a sock, the behavior analyst would do $R_{(1)}$, $R_{(2)}$, and $R_{(3)}$ for him, and Ray would first learn to insert his foot correctly, $R_{(4)}$ to the S^{D4} ("see position") and any prompts that were needed. The reinforcer would be given for that response. After Ray mastered the last step and the prompt was faded, his training would progress by adding the next-to-last response ($R_{(3)}$, "position" the foot at the hole) to the last response ($R_{(4)}$) to get the reinforcer, and so on, until the chain is complete.

An intervention used backward-chaining methods to teach three adult males, two with autism and all with mild mental retardation, to use the Internet (Jerome, Frantino, & Sturmey, 2007). A task analysis produced a list of 13 links, beginning with pressing the power buttons for the computer and then for the monitor. The last six steps were:

8.   Type in the search topic of interest.
9.   Place hand back on mouse.
10.   Move cursor to the box labeled "search."
11.   Single-click the box.
12.   Move the cursor with the mouse down to the website of choice.
13.   Single-click the website of choice.

In conducting the backward chaining, physical guidance prompts were used as needed for each response and then faded with a decreasing assistance (most-to-least) approach. An edible item, such as a jelly bean, was given as a reinforcer after each correct response.

Training started with link 13: A behavior analyst did the first 12 actions and then had the client do $R_{(13)}$, clicking on the website of choice. Performing $R_{(13)}$ always received an additional reinforcer—access to the chosen website for 5 minutes. After mastering $R_{(13)}$, the client worked on $R_{(12)}$, moving the cursor with the mouse to the website of choice. After performing $R_{(12)}$ and receiving the edible reward, he would do $R_{(13)}$ and receive access to the Internet. When each step was mastered with the prompts faded, training would move to the preceding link in the sequence, and so on. Each man learned the behavioral chain fairly quickly: Two men took only one 40-minute session and the third took five sessions, and the skills generalized to using another computer.

TOTAL-TASK PRESENTATION

Total-task presentation involves teaching all of the links together as a full sequence, rather than teaching the links separately and putting them together. To teach Ray to put on a sock, from the start of training he would be required to make the entire series of responses from beginning to end to receive the reinforcer. The behavior analyst provides prompts or other assistance for any response the person cannot do independently, and the prompts are faded. Suppose Ray needed prompts for each link initially; as he learned a particular step, the prompts for that response would be faded until he could do it on his own. He would receive a reinforcer every time he completed the chain whether or not the prompts were used. Eventually, he'd learn to perform the entire chain without help. (Go to 🐾.)

CASE STUDY

Total-Task Presentation to Teach Larry Toothbrushing

The opening story for this chapter described an intervention to teach eight individuals with mild to moderate mental retardation to brush their teeth (Horner & Keilitz, 1975). A boy named Larry was one of the individuals who received the intervention.

A task analysis divided the behavioral chain into 15 links—the first step involved turning on the water and picking up the toothbrush, and the last one involved discarding paper cups and tissues in a waste receptacle. Total-task presentation was used in teaching this chain, and rewards—tokens and praise with pats on the

(Continued)

(Continued)

back—were given for correct performance of each step. Larry could exchange his tokens for sugarless gum at the end of each session (five tokens for one piece of gum). For each link, the behavior analysts began by providing no help. If Larry did not make the response, help was given in the following progression: verbal prompt (for example, "Wet the toothbrush"), modeling plus a verbal prompt, and physical guidance plus a verbal prompt. Training sessions were given once a day.

In baseline, Larry could perform about six of the links without help. Mastery of the entire behavioral chain was defined as performing all 15 steps correctly without help during two of three consecutive training sessions. Larry achieved this criterion within 24 sessions; Figure 12-1 depicts his performance and that of another boy, Russell. Although most of the individuals mastered the chain within 30 intervention sessions, two did not.

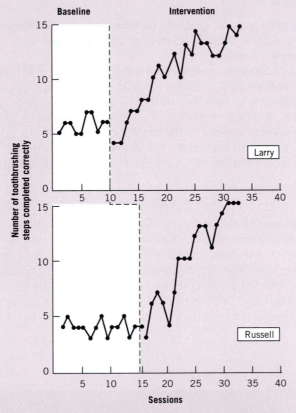

Figure 12-1   Number of the 15 toothbrushing steps Larry performed correctly without prompts in baseline and training sessions. Data in this multiple-baseline design are also presented for another boy, Russell, who also mastered the task. The data for six other individuals who received training showed similar baseline abilities and improvements across training, but two of them did not reach mastery in 30 sessions. *Source:* Adapted from R. D. Horner & I. Keilitz (1975). Training mentally retarded adolescents to brush their teeth. *Journal of Applied Behavior Analysis, 8*, 301–309, Figure 1. Copyright © 1975 Society for the Experimental Analysis of Behavior. Used by permission.

IS ONE TRAINING METHOD BEST?

Let's begin our discussion to answer the question of which method is best for teaching behavioral chains by thinking logically and making hypotheses. For one thing, we'd expect that the answer would depend on two factors: the ability of the target person and the complexity, or number of links, in the chain. Specifically, our hypotheses are as follows:

- Forward or backward chaining should work better than total-task presentation for teaching people with intellectual disabilities, such as autism or mental retardation, because the latter approach involves all of the links on each trial, making it more complex than the other methods. For people with stronger learning abilities, total-task presentation should work at least as well, maybe better, than forward or backward chaining.

- Forward or backward chaining should work better than total-task presentation for behavioral chains that are very complex; for simple chains, such as ones with fewer than 10 steps, total-task presentation should work at least as well, maybe better, than forward or backward chaining.

By "work better" we mean that the person would learn the chain in fewer trials and with less assistance and fewer errors.

What has research found when comparing the three methods for teaching chains? The results have been mixed and do not support the hypotheses we stated. Let's look first at two studies that compared all three methods when teaching college students to perform complex chains. One study taught musical keyboard chains to undergraduates with no prior musical training and examined a variety of performance measures, such as melodic errors during training and memory of the chains a week later (Ash & Holding, 1990). Forward chaining was the most effective method, and total-task presentation was the least effective method. Another study taught college students two different motor chains, each with more than 100 links (Smith, 1999). For one of the tasks, students with total-task presentation made *more* errors than those with forward- or backward-chaining methods; but for the other task, students with total-task presentation and forward chaining made *fewer* errors than those with backward-chaining methods.

The outcomes of studies of individuals with mental retardation have been more consistent but do not support our hypotheses regarding which of the three methods should work best. These studies found that total-task presentation methods teach behavior chains at least as quickly as backward- or forward-chaining methods, and that the superiority of total-task methods applies even when the chain has much more than 10 steps (Kayser, Billingsley, & Neel, 1986; Spooner, 1984; Spooner, Weber, & Spooner, 1983; Yu et al., 1980).

Although the results of research comparing methods for teaching behavioral chains do not support our expectations and are not fully consistent, a tentative conclusion can be given: Total-task presentation is often the most effective method and is likely to work best when the target person can already perform many of the links in the chain. But three reservations about this conclusion should be mentioned. First, some evidence suggests that individuals who are severely retarded show more disruptive behavior, such as aggression, when trained with total-task methods than with methods that break the task down (Weld & Evans, 1990). Second, for chains in which the last link is particularly difficult, using backward-chaining methods may be the best approach (Ash & Holding, 1990). Third, for some chains it may be important to use backward chaining if being able to perform one of the last links will enhance the success of the learning or the safety of the target person. For instance, when teaching children to ride a tricycle, you'd want to be sure they could use the brakes to stop. (Go to 🔍.)

TIPS ON CHAINING BEHAVIORS

Regardless of which method we use to teach a behavioral chain, we can enhance training effectiveness by following several guidelines.

1. Do a task analysis of each chain, and make sure that all links it identifies are likely to be simple enough for the person to learn without too much difficulty.

CLOSE-UP

Self-Prompting Methods to Learn Behavioral Chains

When you get a new electronic device, such as an MP3 player or cell phone, it comes with a manual that tells you how to use it and its features. The manual allows you to learn behavioral chains, such as in accessing particular songs on the MP3 player, on your own. If the manual is written clearly and completely, it gives you a *written task analysis* (also called *textual prompts*) for each of the chains it describes, which is an efficient teaching approach because it uses *self-prompting* with verbal prompts and doesn't require as much supervision from a teacher. Anyone who can read and carry out the steps in written task analyses can use them to learn a chain. For example, researchers used written task analyses with adults who had mild retardation or learning disabilities and were receiving training in skills for independent living (Cuvo et al., 1992). These people got a detailed list of steps needed to clean a stove and a refrigerator, and when they finished each chain, they received praise and descriptive feedback as reinforcers. All of these individuals learned the skills to a criterion of 100% correct performance for three consecutive trials.

What if the target person doesn't read well or has a different primary language—can we still use self-prompting methods? Yes, and two types are useful: self-instructions and pictorial prompts. *Self-instructions* consist of a sequence of verbal prompts people can recite overtly or covertly to direct their actions. When you tell yourself at a supermarket, "I need to get milk, bread, and orange juice," you are providing self-instructions that prompt the steps in a behavioral chain to get these items. Researchers trained adults with severe mental retardation to recite self-instructions as they performed a vocational task: a behavioral chain for packaging combs (Salend, Ellis, & Reynolds, 1989). Self-instructions increased the productivity and decreased the error rates of these people on the task.

Pictorial prompts (also called *picture prompts*) can be used to guide people's performance of a behavioral chain. Researchers demonstrated the utility of using drawings to prompt students with mild mental retardation to perform each step in chains to use two software programs on a computer (Frank, Wacker, Berg, & McMahon, 1985). The pictures were bound into separate books, one with a sequence of 32 drawings and one with 23 drawings. In training, the students were first asked to describe the behavior each picture represented, receiving praise for correct answers and corrective feedback for incorrect answers. Then the students were given one of the books and asked to use the pictures to perform the behavioral chain, again receiving praise for correct actions. The students' performance improved quickly during training and had no errors after 8 to 13 sessions. All three of the self-prompting methods we've considered can help people learn behavioral chains and enhance the efficiency of the training.

2. Consider whether self-prompting methods would be sufficient for training.

3. Design the training approach to ensure that to receive reinforcement, the person must perform all the links he or she has learned, and always in the correct order.

4. Use a baseline procedure to assess whether the person can already perform some of the steps in the chain.

5. When using forward or backward chaining or total-task presentation, apply and then fade prompts to help the person learn each step in a chain.

6. Early in training, provide programmed reinforcement for each correct response, especially when the final link in a chain is made. As the person learns more and more of the chain, you can gradually decrease reinforcement for individual links.

7. Make sure reinforcement continues for performing the chain after training ends.

(Go to 📖.)

CONCEPT CHECK 12.2

Answer the following questions about teaching behavioral chains.

1. An example of a behavioral chain not mentioned in this book is _____ . ⇔
2. If we were teaching the chain in item 1 using forward chaining, the first link we would train would be _____ . ⇔
3. If we were teaching that chain in item 1 using backward chaining, the first link we would train would be _____ . ⇔
4. The method of teaching a behavioral chain in which the person performs the entire chain in each trial is called _____ .
5. Although the evidence comparing chaining methods is somewhat mixed and not fully _____ , it appears that _____ is usually the most effective method to teach chains.
6. One self-prompting method discussed in this book is _____ . ⇔

STUDY AND REVIEW

SUMMARY

A behavioral chain is a complex sequence of links or steps, each consisting of a discriminative stimulus (S^D) and a response. Each response, except the very last one in the chain, results in an S^D for the next response; and each S^D, except the first one in the chain, serves as a reinforcer for the last response. A task analysis is performed to identify the links and their component S^Ds and responses.

Three approaches are used to teach behavioral chains. In forward chaining, each step is trained in order, starting with the first step. In any trial, an S^D is presented with a prompt, and each time the person makes a correct response, reinforcement is given. After the person masters that link and the prompt is faded, training moves to the next step, and so on for the remaining links. In backward chaining, each step is trained in the reverse order, starting with the final link in the chain. The S^D is presented with a prompt, and each time the person makes a correct response, reinforcement is given. After the person masters that link and the prompt is faded, training moves to the preceding step, and so on for the remaining links. In total-task presentation, training requires the person to perform the entire chain on each trial, which is followed by reinforcement. Prompts are given and faded for each link. Although the research evidence is somewhat inconsistent, the total-task presentation method is often more effective than forward or backward chaining.

Self-prompting methods can be efficient in teaching behavioral chains. One of these methods is written task analyses, in which the person reads a list describing each of the steps in the chain. The self-instructions method involves having target persons learn and recite overtly or covertly each of the links before they perform it. A third method, pictorial prompts, provides a picture of each response in the correct order required to perform the chain.

To prepare for exams, use the following key terms and review questions and the online study guide that's available on this book's companion website at www.wiley.com/college/sarafino.

KEY TERMS

behavioral chain   forward chaining   total-task presentation
task analysis   backward chaining

ANSWERS TO CONCEPT CHECKS (CCs)

CC12.1 *Answers:* **1.** see "on" button (S^D) and press it (R)   **2.** S^D, response   **3.** task analysis   **4.** watch someone do the chain

CC12.2 *Answers:* **1.** open a locked door   **2.** see lock (S^D), reach in pocket for key (R)   **3.** feel doorknob fully turned (S^D), push doorknob (R)   **4.** total-task presentation   **5.** consistent, total-task presentation   **6.** written task analysis, self-instructions, or pictorial prompts

REVIEW QUESTIONS

1. Define the term *behavioral chain*, and give two examples from your life that are not mentioned in this chapter.

2. Pick a link from a chain you identified in question 1, and describe the S^D and R.

3. Define the term *task analysis*, and describe the strategies behavior analysts use to develop one.

4. Construct a task analysis of making a peanut butter and jelly sandwich, identifying any chains and links within them.

5. Compare the procedures of forward chaining, backward chaining, and total-task presentation.

6. Describe the forward-chaining method used in the intervention by McWilliams, Nietupski, and Hamre-Nietupski (1990) to teach bed making.

7. Describe the backward-chaining method used in the intervention by Jerome, Frantino, and Sturmey (2007) to teach Internet skills.

8. Describe the total-task presentation method used by Horner and Keilitz (1975) to teach Larry toothbrushing.

9. Describe in detail the total-task presentation method you could use to teach a very young child how to perform one of the chains you identified in question 1.

10. Discuss the question of whether one training method is best for teaching chains.

11. Describe how you could train a young child to perform the chain you described in question 4 for making a sandwich by using the self-prompting methods of written task analysis, self-instructions, and pictorial prompts.

RELATED READINGS

*   Frank, A. R., Wacker, D. P., Berg, W. K., & McMahon, C. M. (1985). Teaching selected microcomputer skills to retarded students via picture prompts. *Journal of Applied Behavior Analysis, 18*, 179–185.

*   Gagné, R. M. (1985). *The conditions of learning and theory of instruction* (4th ed.). New York: Holt, Rinehart & Winston.

*   Spooner, F. (1984). Comparisons of backward chaining and total task presentation in training severely handicapped persons. *Education and Training of the Mentally Retarded, 19*, 15–22.

13

FUNCTIONAL ASSESSMENT AND PROGRAM DESIGN

PROLOGUE

An 11-year-old boy of normal intelligence and with no apparent organic disorder often showed disruptive classroom behavior that was unusual for a child his age. He would speak baby talk, voice irrelevant comments and questions, and have several temper tantrums each week (Zimmerman & Zimmerman, 1962). For instance, when he refused to go to class, attendants would drag him down the hall as he

screamed and buckled his knees. On several of these occasions, the boy threw himself on the floor in front of the classroom door. A crowd of staff members inevitably gathered around him. The group usually watched and commented as he sat or lay on the floor, kicking and screaming. Some members of the group hypothesized that such behavior seemed to appear after the boy was teased or frustrated in some way. However, the only observable in the situation was the consistent consequence of the behavior in terms of the formation of a group of staff members around the boy. (p. 60)

This description suggests two possible reasons for this boy's tantrums: the *antecedents*—being frustrated or teased—and the *consequences*, receiving attention. The possible role of the tantrums' consequences was based on observing the actual situation. When the staff was instructed not to attend to the boy's tantrums, his problem behavior disappeared gradually over several weeks. Because the staff hadn't realized that the function of the tantrums was to get their attention, they had been rewarding the behavior unknowingly.

Determining the functions of behavior usually requires careful observation. In this chapter, we examine the procedure of functional assessment that behavior analysts apply to identify the antecedents and consequences of a target behavior. We'll also see how they use that information to design a program to change that behavior.

WHAT IS A FUNCTIONAL ASSESSMENT?

A critical part of designing a program to change behavior is answering the question, "What functions does the behavior serve?" (Groden, 1989; O'Neill et al., 1997). We've seen in earlier chapters that behavior is influenced by its antecedents and consequences. Thus, to determine the functions of a behavior requires that we know the situations, such as the places and times, in which the behavior does or does not occur and how the person benefits from his or her current pattern of behavior. When people who want to change a target behavior do not analyze its functions, they frequently make the situation worse without realizing they are doing so. Conducting a functional assessment improves the success of behavior change programs (Didden, Duker, & Korzilius, 1997).

FUNCTIONAL ASSESSMENT: A DEFINITION

A **functional assessment** is a set of procedures by which we can identify connections between a behavior and its antecedents and consequences (Cone, 1997; Freeman, Anderson, & Scotti, 2000; O'Neill et al., 1997). Some functional assessments are highly rigorous, detailed, and complete in the way they are carried out, as they are in carefully conducted research (for example, Borrero et al., 2002; Cooper et al., 1992; Iwata et al., 1982; Johnson et al., 1995; Mueller, Sterling-Turner, & Scattone, 2001; Piazza et al., 2003; Sasso et al., 1992). Oppositely, people in everyday life do very informal functional assessments when they try to figure out why people behave the way they do (O'Neill et al., 1997). Most interventions to change behavior in school settings probably aim for moderately rigorous and complete functional assessments (McConnell, Cox, Thomas, & Hilvitz, 2001). These assessments are usually sufficient and should have three outcomes—they should:

1. Define the target behavior exactly and clearly.
2. Determine which antecedents function to produce the behavioral excess or deficit.
3. Reveal how the person's behavior functions to produce reinforcement.

Although the antecedents and consequences in functional assessments are usually overt, they can be covert, too. Keep in mind that an antecedent is not necessarily a discrete event, such as someone calling your name; it can be a situation, such as the time and place, or another person who is present when the target behavior does or does not occur.

WHAT FUNCTIONS CAN BEHAVIOR SERVE?

A main purpose of conducting a functional assessment is to identify the consequences of the target behavior. Evidence from thousands of studies shows that operant behavior is learned and maintained because of its consequences—that is, the reason people learn and persist in a behavior is that it results in reinforcement. If the behavior leads to positive reinforcement, the individuals *get something they want*, such as a toy or favorite food;

if it leads to negative reinforcement, they *get out of something they don't want*, such as an unpleasant task. Thus the function of the behavior is to get something or get out of something, either of which strengthens the behavior that accomplishes the goal.

Researchers examined over 500 published data sets from studies that assessed the functions of 12 types of problem behaviors, such as self-injury, aggression, disruption, and noncompliance (Hanley, Iwata, & McCord, 2003). All 12 behaviors were behavioral excesses. Overall, the studies identified four types of reinforcement—*escape, attention, automatic,* and *tangible*—as maintaining the problem behaviors, and sometimes multiple reinforcers were involved. Figure 13-1 shows the percentages of cases in which each type of reinforcement or multiple types was the reason for the behavior. Let's look at these types of reinforcement.

Escape as Reinforcement

Escape is a form of negative reinforcement: We learn many behaviors because they end or postpone aversive circumstances. Escape gets us out of something we don't want. We all learn many everyday behaviors that function to get us out of disliked situations. If you dislike a song you hear on the radio or a show you see on TV, you change the station or channel. When roommates or neighbors are making too much noise, you ask them to quiet down. Both of these examples involve escape.

What about problem behaviors? A commonly disliked situation for children with developmental disabilities is being in training, where they're asked to learn something they find difficult and face teacher demands to pay attention and keep on task. They often want out of that situation. What gets them out? They find that self-injury, aggression, disruption, and noncompliance seem to work, often very quickly: The training stops for at least a little while and sometimes much longer. To the extent that a problem behavior gets the child out of training, that behavior is negatively reinforced.

Attention as Reinforcement

Getting attention from other people is often an effective positive reinforcer. The type of attention we get that serves as a reinforcer is usually intended to compliment us or make us feel better. The attention can include a look that says, "Wow, you look great," for example; or a statement of praise for work we've done; or just a hug to soothe us when we look distressed. Sometimes even a reprimand is attention enough to serve as a social reinforcer, particularly for a problem behavior (Kodak, Northup, & Kelley, 2007). Misbehavior that is maintained by the reactions of others, whether the reactions are meant to praise or reprimand, often occurs when the target person normally gets too little attention or lacks the desirable behaviors that would receive praise.

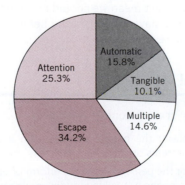

Figure 13-1   Percent of cases in which certain types of reinforcement served to maintain problem behaviors. Most of the participants (70.0%) were children up to 18 years of age, and the great majority (91.3%) was diagnosed with a developmental disability. *Source:* Data from Hanley, Iwata, & McCord (2003), Table 5.

Automatic Reinforcement

In automatic reinforcement, the behavior produces a reinforcer directly, such as when we massage an aching muscle to make it feel better. Automatic reinforcement can be of the positive or negative types:

- In automatic positive reinforcement, the behavior directly leads to a reinforcing stimulus being introduced or added. For instance, if you sketch a picture and like what it looks like, you've received automatic positive reinforcement for your sketching.
- In automatic negative reinforcement, the behavior directly leads to the reduction or removal of an aversive situation. Massaging a sore muscle or taking aspirin to relieve a headache are examples.

In each of these situations, the reinforcement is not provided by someone else. In fact, to conclude that reinforcement is automatic, we typically need to rule out all other sources of reinforcement, especially social sources. For instance, if the behavior persists even when the person is alone, we have evidence that the reinforcement is automatic.

Automatic reinforcement can also maintain problem behaviors (Hanley, Iwata, & McCord, 2003; Lovaas, Newsom, & Hickman, 1987). For example, a usual function of repetitive/ritualistic behaviors that children with autism often display, such as spinning objects or flapping their fingers, is apparently to provide sensory stimulation as automatic positive reinforcement. And automatic negative reinforcement appears to maintain binge-eating and compulsive-buying behaviors in people by reducing their unpleasant emotions, such as depression or anxiety (Miltenberger, 2005). For example, individuals with binge-eating problems are likely to eat excessively when they feel these emotions, and binging relieves these feelings for a while.

Tangible Reinforcement

Tangible items are material objects, such as toys or articles of clothing. If receiving a tangible item for performing a behavior strengthens that behavior, that item is a tangible reinforcer. Many of our behaviors result in access to tangible reinforcers. For example, we learned in childhood how to shop for clothing; and for the clothing we now have, we learned how to find a particular item in a dresser or closet so we can wear it.

Sometimes problem behaviors produce tangible reinforcers (Hanley, Iwata, & McCord, 2003). For instance, a child may have a tantrum because he or she wants a toy and can't find or reach it. If someone gets the toy for that child, tantrum behavior receives tangible reinforcement. In some cases tangible items are given to children to soothe or distract them after they performed a problem behavior, especially self-injurious behavior: A well-meaning adult may give the item and say, "Oh, you hurt yourself. Let's play with this game to make you feel better." If problem behaviors consistently lead to tangible reinforcers, those behaviors are likely to occur in the future in similar situations. This doesn't mean we should never act compassionately when people injure themselves, but if our reactions appear to have reinforced the behavior and made it worse, we need to find another way of handling these circumstances.

PERFORMING A FUNCTIONAL ASSESSMENT

We saw in Chapter 1 that a target behavior can be one of two types:

1. Behavioral excess—undesirable behavior the person performs too frequently, too strongly, or for too long. Examples include someone having tantrums or smoking cigarettes.
2. Behavioral deficit—desirable behavior the person does not perform often enough, long enough, well enough, or strongly enough. Examples include someone not talking loudly enough or not exercising.

This distinction is important when we design and conduct a functional assessment. If the assessment involves a *behavioral excess*, we focus on instances of the behavior occurring too much and try to determine its antecedents and consequences. If the assessment deals with a *behavioral deficit*, we focus on instances when the behavior *could have* or *should have* occurred, but didn't. If the behavior was physically possible to perform and/or the antecedents that usually work for other people were present, we can assume the person could have or should have performed the behavior.

A functional assessment can apply any or all of three approaches that differ in how rigorously the assessments are made. From least to most rigorous, the approaches for identifying antecedents and consequences are as follows: *indirect methods,* which use questionnaires and interviews; *direct methods,* in which instances of the behavior are carefully observed in their natural settings; and *experimental methods* (or *functional analysis*), in which behavior analysts manipulate antecedents and consequences to see their effects on the behavior. We'll describe these methods in order of increasing rigor.

INDIRECT METHODS: INTERVIEWS AND QUESTIONNAIRES

With indirect methods for functional assessment, information about the behavior and its antecedents and consequences is obtained from the target person or from other people who know the client well, such as family, friends, or teachers, through *interviews* or *questionnaires*. Interviews with clients and others are routinely done as a part of most therapy processes and behavior change interventions. When they are used for functional assessment, they focus on trying to identify and define the target behavior and determine its antecedent conditions and consequences (O'Neill et al., 1997). These interviews often use a structured set of questions that typically ask for or about the following:

- A detailed description of the target behavior: What are its frequency, duration, and intensity?
- What factors in the person's general life, such as diet and sleep, could be involved in the behavior?
- Antecedent conditions: When, where, with whom, and with what activities is the behavior most likely and least likely to occur?
- What does the person get or get out of (avoid or escape) by performing or not performing the behavior?
- What items or experiences does the person like—that is, what could serve as reinforcers to change the behavior?
- What efforts have been tried in the past to address the problem behavior, and what was the outcome?

Notice that the questions ask about conditions related to the person's performance and nonperformance of the target behavior, which means that they can assess antecedents and consequences for behavioral excesses and deficits. Lists of structured interview questions have been published to provide a standard format for collecting relevant data for a functional analysis (for example, O'Neill et al., 1997).

Questionnaires can be used to collect similar information, and some of them ask about most of the issues listed earlier and can be used for a variety of behaviors and populations (for example, the Functional Assessment Interview of O'Neill et al., 1997). Other questionnaires are more specific in the scope of questions they ask. For example, the Motivation Assessment Scale (Durand & Crimmins, 1988) assesses the consequences for self-injurious behavior in individuals with developmental disabilities, and a survey called Questions About Behavioral Function (Matson & Vollmer, 1995; Paclawskyj et al., 2000) assesses five possible functions—that is, reinforcers, such as attention and escape—for problem behaviors individuals with mental retardation often show.

Although the value of data from indirect methods is limited because they do not involve direct observation of the behavior and rely on people's memories, such methods can be useful. For one thing, they are easier and more convenient to carry out than more rigorous methods of functional assessment. And they can provide tentative information that can support and be confirmed by data from more rigorous methods. In many cases, functional assessments that combine indirect methods with direct observation can provide sufficient information to formulate useful hypotheses and design an effective program to change behavior (Arndorfer et al., 1994). (Go to 🔍.)

CLOSE-UP

A Questionnaire to Assess the Functions of Nail Biting

Nail biting is a curious behavior. Why do people bite their nails? Researchers conducted an experiment and developed a questionnaire to answer this question (Williams, Rose, & Chisholm, 2006). The experiment videotaped undergraduates in one of four research conditions lasting 10 minutes: being alone in a room, having to calculate 20 math problems, being engaged in casual conversation, and receiving reprimands if they bit their nails while watching a video recording. The average number of times the students bit their nails was about $6^1/_2$ times in the alone condition, 3 times in the math calculation condition, and almost not at all in each of the two other conditions.

These same students also filled out a questionnaire that the researchers composed by modifying the items in the Questions About Behavioral Function survey (discussed earlier) to fit the new purpose of assessing the functions of nail biting in college students. Here are some of the items in the questionnaire that the students linked strongly with their nail biting:

- When you are bored.
- When there is something bothering you.
- To get out of homework or chores.
- Because it feels nice.

The questionnaire data coincided with the experimental data. For instance, being alone is probably boring, and doing math problems is like homework and may be somewhat distressing or uncomfortable.

DIRECT METHODS: OBSERVATION OF THE BEHAVIOR

When using direct methods of functional assessment, someone has the job of watching for and describing the *actual target behavior and its antecedents and consequences in its natural environment*. The person who does the observations should know the behavior well enough to recognize when it does or does not happen and be trained to *detect the antecedents and consequences* and *record relevant data* immediately. This person can be almost anyone: a behavior analyst, the target person's parents or teacher, a hospital staff member, or even the target person him- or herself, such as when using self-management approaches. Direct methods are designed to *describe* the behavior and its antecedents and consequences, and they can use either of two strategies (English & Anderson, 2006; Freeman, Anderson, & Scotti, 2000):

1. **Unstructured descriptive assessment**, in which observations are done without altering natural events in the environment in any way.
2. **Structured descriptive assessment**, which involves observations in the natural environment while specific antecedent events are manipulated systematically, but the behavior's consequences are allowed to happen as usual and are not altered.

The purpose of structuring the assessment is to make sure the behavior occurs and that it and its antecedents and consequences are observed. The manipulated antecedents are events that were previously shown to evoke the target behavior. Structuring assessments may be expected to enhance the accuracy and efficiency of the observations.

Making the Observations

The procedures we use to make observations of the target behavior depend on whether we are using unstructured or structured descriptive assessments. For the unstructured strategy, we would use procedures like those called *continuous recording*, which we examined in Chapter 2. We would designate periods of time, such as parts of a day or even an entire couple of weeks, when we would be on the lookout for the behavior and record every instance of it and its antecedents and consequences.

If we are using the structured strategy, we would set up opportunities to observe by presenting one or more antecedents and recording how the person behaved and the consequences that occurred. In each case, we would make the observations in the person's natural environment, as mentioned earlier. Behavior analysts know more about conducting unstructured than structured descriptive assessments because the latter strategy is fairly new, having been introduced around the turn of the 21st century (English & Anderson, 2006). As a result, the information we will discuss pertains mainly to unstructured descriptive assessments, which have been used for a few decades.

One question about making observations is, how long should we observe? When we conduct an unstructured descriptive assessment to address a *behavioral excess*, we must make observations of the target behavior until the behavior has occurred often enough to reveal patterns in the connections between the target behavior and its antecedents and consequences. In an unstructured descriptive assessment to address a *behavioral deficit*, we'll need to look for instances when the behavior *could have* or *should have* occurred, but didn't. Generally, useful patterns in people's everyday behavior tend to emerge after about 2 to 5 days of observation, after *about a dozen or more instances* of occurrences (for a behavioral excess) or nonoccurrences (for a behavioral deficit) of the target behavior have been recorded. The amount of observation time depends on the rate at which instances happen: The higher the rate of occurrences or nonoccurrences, the shorter the time until useful patterns emerge.

When descriptive assessments are conducted under highly structured conditions, the observation period can be shorter (Kahng & Iwata, 1999; Watson & Sterling, 1998). A study using structured descriptive assessment for behavioral excesses in children with developmental disabilities found stable functional patterns for the behaviors after, perhaps, two dozen 10-minute sessions (English & Anderson, 2006). And each child had displayed the problem behaviors dozens of times across the sessions.

Recording the Data

When we conduct a descriptive assessment, we must maintain detailed records of our observations of the target behavior on forms. For instance, we may need separate forms giving data for each observation of the target behavior and giving a summary of the observational data. Gerald Groden (1989; Groden, Stevenson, & Groden, 1996) and Robert O'Neill and his coworkers (1997) have written excellent guides for conducting functional assessments and developing forms to record and organize the data. I used these guides as main sources in preparing the material for this section and constructing the two forms we will examine.

Figure 13-2 presents a form for an **A-B-C Log**—a chronological record of the target behavior's occurrences and nonoccurrences, along with the antecedents and consequences of each instance. This form has been filled out for a boy's tantrum behaviors. When we conduct a descriptive assessment, we use an A-B-C Log to record data regarding the target behavior. For each instance of the behavior's occurrence or nonoccurrence, we record its *day, date, time,* and *place*. The place would be specified as precisely as necessary—for example, if the behavior tends to occur in certain rooms in the house, such as the bedroom or kitchen, we would use special codes for those places.

The A-B-C Log also includes three other sets of codes that should be recorded for each occurrence or nonoccurrence of the behavior. Column 6 (from the left) in Figure 13-2 records the codes for the *type of data* used to assess the behavior, and column 8 records the codes for the *types of consequences* the behavior produced. The codes in column 4 specify the conditions that preceded the behavior, classified into the following seven *antecedent types*:

1. *Activity*: What specifically was the person doing immediately before the behavior, such as giving the name of a game the person was playing?

2. *Social*: Which people were in the environment, and what specifically did they do or say immediately before the behavior occurred?

3. *Covert*: What was the person thinking or imagining just before the behavior? Sometimes this can be determined by asking the person or noticing what he or she said before the behavior.

4. *Emotion*: What type of emotion did the person seem to experience just before the behavior?

A-B-C Log for _____Tantrum_____ behavior
Person: _Ray_ Age: _4_ Observer(s): _Ms. Ashcroft, Mother, Father_

Day/ Date/ Time	Place[1]	Antecedents Description	Type[2]	Behaviors Description	Data[3]	Consequences Description	Type[4]	Thoughts/ Comments
Mon/ 9-26-11/ 11:50 Am	H	Drawing trees Ashcroft told him favorite food on table for lunch, parents had big argument before leaving for work, Ray sulked	A, S, D, E	Screaming, crying, hitting.	11 min D	Ashcroft made Ray another lunch	+	Ray had been upset all morning
Mon/ 9-26/ 7:00Pm	H	Watching Tv, mother told Ray it was time take bath, Ray seemed anxious at dinner	A,S E	Screaming, crying, Kicking.	15 min D	Parents let him watch TV longer	+	
Tues/ 9-27/	H			No tantrum				No family problems
Wed/ 9-28/ 9:30 Am	H	Ray and Ashcroft reading picture book, she told him it was time to practice his printing (he dislikes)	A,S	Screaming, crying	4 min D	Ashcroft said maybe he would print later, continued reading	– +	No family problems Ray seemed OK before

[1] Place: C = classroom, H = home, __ = _____, __ = _____,__ = _____
[2] Type: A = activity, S = social, C = covert, E = emotion, P = physical events, O = other, D = distant
[3] Data: record with F = frequency, D = duration, M = magnitude, Q = quality, or L = latency
[4] Type: + = get or obtain desirable or wanted object or activity
    – = escape, avoid, or reduce something unpleasant
    U = unpleasant consequence

Figure 13-2 An A-B-C Log. Use this form to keep a chronological record of the behavior(s) in a descriptive assessment. This log uses hypothetical data for 4-year-old Ray's tantrum behavior, with his babysitter and parents as the observers. Although the format used in the log would work well for many behaviors, it can be modified for others. Codes are provided for place, antecedents, behaviors, and consequences; other codes can be added as needed.

5. *Physical events*: What nonsocial stimuli occurred or did the person notice, such as a loud noise or an object that came in view, immediately before the behavior?

6. *Other*: What immediate antecedents that do not belong to the above categories occurred?

7. *Distant*: Did any conditions or events happen minutes, hours, or more before the behavior occurred that you think may be related to the behavior's occurrence or nonoccurrence (Groden, 1989)? Even though you are speculating about distant antecedents, they can sometimes be useful in functional assessments.

Other forms with the same purpose as the A-B-C Log vary in their format and degree of detail—for example, sometimes they are in the form of a *checklist* of likely antecedents, behaviors, and consequences. Checklists are appropriate when the range of items in the list is fairly limited, such as with children with autism or mental retardation in a special education class or institution. Functional assessment forms to collect data are essential in designing a careful behavior change program and should be detailed enough to identify the main links between the target behavior and its antecedents and consequences.

After having observed a sufficient number of occurrences or nonoccurrences of the behavior during a period of a few days or more, we use the data collected to fill out a **summary record** form. This form organizes, collates, and summarizes the data, allowing us to see patterns among the factors examined and the behavior. Figure 13-3 presents a summary record of Ray's tantrum behavior during a 2-week period, during which time he had 12 tantrums. As you examine this summary record, you'll probably notice several patterns, the clearest of which is that after a tantrum, the boy always got his way.

Interpreting the Data

The patterns we see between the target behavior and its antecedents and consequences in the summary record data should give us information about two important relationships. First, they should enable us to predict when the target behavior is likely to occur or not occur—that is, the days and times, the places, and the immediate and distant conditions that are associated with the likelihood that the behavior will or will not happen. Second, we should be able to see how different consequences relate to the behavior. From these relationships, we should understand *why the behavior does or does not occur*. All of this information will be useful in designing a program to change the behavior. If the patterns of relationships are clear, we can proceed to design the program.

What if the relationships are not clear? If we conduct a descriptive assessment and the summary record of a dozen or so instances of the behavior does not reveal sufficiently clear patterns, we can do two things (O'Neill et al., 1997):

1. Check the data collection process for flaws, such as poorly defined behaviors, and determine whether the observers did the observation and recording correctly. If we find problems with the process, we'll need to correct the problems and collect the data again.

2. If there were no problems in the data collection, observe another dozen or so instances of the behavior. Doing so can clarify the patterns.

Sometimes a thorough functional assessment produces data that are inconclusive because the target behavior either occurs frequently in or is quite variable across all antecedent and consequence situations. Such outcomes are called *undifferentiated* and do not seem to occur often. An undifferentiated outcome may mean that the behavior is maintained by automatic reinforcement, but the data may not reflect this possibility very clearly.

EXPERIMENTAL METHODS: FUNCTIONAL ANALYSIS

A **functional analysis** uses methods of scientific experiments by conducting *systematic environmental manipulations*—that is, introducing or altering likely antecedents or consequences—to see how they affect the target behavior (Truax, 2005). The procedure is generally conducted in a laboratory or other contrived setting and includes a control condition in which antecedents are not manipulated and reinforcement is freely available. When assessments are done for a behavioral excess, such as self-injury or oppositional behavior, the control condition engages the target person in play with toys or other activities and is expected to elicit infrequent problem behaviors. Undifferentiated outcomes in functional analyses occur rarely—in, perhaps, less than 5% of cases (Hanley, Iwata, & McCord, 2003)

Functional Assessment

SUMMARY RECORD of A-B-C Log of _____*Tantrum*_____ behavior

Person: *Ray*   Period covering: *9-26 to 10-9-11*   Observer(s): *Ms. Ashcroft, Mother, Father*

Factors Examined	Behavior Frequency (Magnitude)	Factors Examined	Behavior Frequency (Magnitude)
Day		**Immediate antecedents** (continued)	
Monday	*4 (12 min. avg)*	Social (describe):	
Tuesday	*2 (6 min. avg)*	*Asking him to do*	*8 (7:25 min avg)*
Wednesday	*1 (8 min)*	*something he dislikes*	
Thursday	*3 (7 min. avg)*	*Asking him to do*	*4 (11 min avg)*
Friday	*0*	*something he likes or*	
Saturday	*1 (3 min)*	*is neutral*	
Sunday	*1 (10. min)*		
Time AM PM			
12:00 – 1:59	*1 (6 min)* (PM)	Covert (describe):	
2:00 – 3:59	*2 (9. min avg)* (PM)	*None clear*	
4:00 – 5:59	*1 (9 min)* (PM)		
6:00 – 7:59	*1 (4 min)* (AM) *3 (12 min. avg)* (PM)	Emotions (describe):	
8:00 – 9:59	*3 (6 min. avg)* (AM)	*Upset*	*4 (12 min avg)*
10:00 –11:59	*1 (11 min)* (AM)		
		Physical events (describe):	
Place		Other (describe):	
Home	*12 (8.5 min. avg)*		
Other places	*Never*	**Distant antecedents** (describe):	
		Parent arguments	*3 (11 min. avg)*
Immediate antecedents		**Consequences**	
Activities when behavior occurs (describe)			
Playing	*2 (10 min avg)*	Positive reinforcement (+), describe:	
Watching TV	*3 (11 min avg)*	*Got food he wanted 2 times*	
Reading	*1 (4 min)*	*Got to continue playing, reading,*	
Awakening from nap . . .	*2 (45 min avg)*	*or watching TV 7 times.*	
Printing or other	*4 (9 min. avg)*	Negative reinforcement (–), describe:	
academic training		*Avoided academic training 5 times.*	
Activities when it doesn't occur (describe):		Punishment/unpleasant (U), describe:	
Seems to happen regardless of activities he's doing		*Scolded at each tantrum, but that didn't help*	

Figure 13-3   A summary record form with hypothetical data for Ray's tantrums. When doing a descriptive assessment, use a form like this one to summarize the A-B-C Log data and see patterns between the behavior and its antecedents and consequences more clearly. This form can be modified to suit the needs of other programs.

The Functional Analysis Procedure

To manipulate antecedents, we could make certain requests of the person, place the individual in particular settings, or give him or her access to certain objects or activities, for example. To manipulate consequences, we could vary whether positive or negative reinforcement occurs for the target behavior. For instance, two common reinforcers that behavior analysts test with behavioral excesses, such as tantrums, are:

1. *Attention* as a positive reinforcer for the problem behavior is manipulated, such as by withholding all forms of attention, including soothing and reprimands, whenever the behavior occurs.
2. *Escape* as a negative reinforcer for the problem behavior is manipulated, such as by not allowing a break from an activity whenever the behavior occurs.

The target person is also tested while *alone*, and behavior under these conditions is compared with behavior during *play*, the control condition. Functional analyses are done after indirect and direct assessments have been made, and the choice of antecedents and consequences to use is based on data from those assessments. By manipulating selected events, we can test their effects by seeing whether the behavior changes—if it changes in a consistent manner, we will know how these events influence the behavior.

There are two reasons for doing a functional analysis: to confirm the data and hypotheses from a descriptive assessment and to clarify patterns of relationships that are not yet clear. Functional analyses are usually conducted under controlled conditions, such as in a laboratory, rather than in a natural environment to prevent extraneous factors, such as noises, from influencing the tests. Because functional analyses manipulate the behavior's antecedents and consequences, these events are not exactly the same as those that happen naturally. For this reason, these observations are called *analog* assessments. Whether the degree of control used in analog assessments is necessary is controversial: Two studies have produced conflicting results on whether functional analyses of problem behavior conducted in a natural setting (classroom) or with an analog procedure yield the same outcomes (Lang et al., 2008; Noell, VanDerHeyden, Gatti, & Whitmarsh, 2001). Still, functional analyses appear to produce more accurate outcomes than descriptive assessments (Thompson & Iwata, 2007).

Researchers have performed functional analyses to discover why children with autism repeatedly perform behaviors that cause self-injury—for example, biting their arms hard enough to draw blood. These studies have found that these behaviors often function to gain *escape* from certain activities, such as toothbrushing or learning a new skill (Carr, Taylor, & Robinson, 1991; Sasso et al., 1992; Steege et al., 1990). It may be that the children dislike these activities or just find them unpleasant momentarily—for instance, a child may feel overwhelmed by the cognitive demands of a task. Studies have also used functional analyses to find out how self-injurious behavior can be stopped. One study found that self-injury can be reduced by identifying and rewarding a noninjurious alternative behavior that allows the children to escape from these activities for brief periods of time (Steege et al., 1990). (Go to 🐾.)

CASE STUDY

A Functional Analysis of Jim's Body Rocking

What factors influence repetitive/ritualistic behaviors, such as body rocking or hand flapping, in persons with developmental disabilities? Researchers examined this issue in a series of experiments with four boys, one of whom was 11-year-old Jim (Durand & Carr, 1987). Observations of Jim's behavior had suggested that he would engage in these acts often when he was in training sessions, and it appeared that their function was to escape classroom work. He would start to rock his body back and forth; and if this didn't get him out of the task, he would take it up another notch with screaming and self-injurious behavior, such as hitting his head and face. One hypothesis the researchers developed from observations of these boys' repetitive/ritualistic behaviors was that task difficulty influenced these acts: The harder the task, the more these behaviors would occur.

The researchers tested this hypothesis in a straightforward manner with all of the boys, but we'll focus on Jim. In the first experiment, the researchers manipulated two variables, *task difficulty* (a possible antecedent)

(Continued)

(*Continued*)

and the amount of *social attention* (a possible reinforcer) the trainer gave to the boy. One of the training tasks these children often encountered was *receptive labeling*: The trainer would show Jim four pictures pasted on cards and ask him to point to one—for instance, to "Point to the brush." The researchers had pretested pictures and divided them into two sets—pictures the children always chose correctly and pictures they chose correctly only 25% of the time.

After conducting baseline assessments, the researchers tested Jim in a series of phases, each with 3–5 sessions. Figure 13-4 presents his data in the top panel and data for the three other boys below. As you can see, the phases alternated conditions of increased task difficulty, baseline, and decreased attention. Notice how Jim's body rocking responded to these conditions: It occurred very frequently in the increased task difficulty condition and very little in decreased attention and baseline conditions, indicating that high task difficulty causes the body rocking. Data for the other boys were very similar.

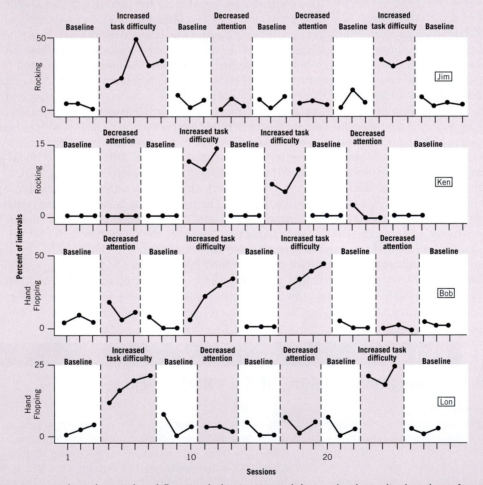

Figure 13-4   Body-rocking or hand-flapping behavior Jim and three other boys displayed as a function of three conditions: baseline, increased task difficulty, and decreased attention. The data represent the percentage of session intervals in which the target behavior was observed. *Source*: From V. M. Durand & E. G. Carr (1987), Social influences on "self-stimulatory" behavior: Analysis and treatment application. *Journal of Applied Behavior Analysis*, 20, 119–132, Figure 1. Copyright © 1987 Society for the Experimental Analysis of Behavior. Used by permission.

(*Continued*)

(*Continued*)

One of the other experiments the researchers did followed up on this finding by teaching Jim (and the other boys) to ask the trainer to "Help me" when a task was too difficult. The data for this study showed that Jim used the "Help me" request often, and his body rocking decreased compared to baseline, as did the target behaviors of the other boys.

Functional Analysis Variations and Data Interpretations

The factors behavior analysts manipulate in functional analyses and the structure of the research can vary. In the case study of Jim's body rocking, the target behavior's likely antecedents were manipulated, but not its consequences; and these manipulations were alternated across phases. Manipulating only the antecedents seems to be less successful in identifying reinforcers that maintain the behavior than procedures that manipulate both events (Potoczak, Carr, & Michael, 2007). Instead of alternating manipulations across phases, we can alternate them within the same phase, as an alternating-treatment design. Researchers used the alternating-treatment approach in a functional analysis of self-injurious behavior in nine individuals with mental retardation and showed that self-injury was controlled by different factors in different individuals (Iwata et al., 1982).

What do the data from a functional analysis with an alternating-treatment design look like, and how do we interpret them? Behavior analysts construct a graph of the data and inspect it to see whether one or more conditions are linked to the problem behavior. Figure 13-5 presents graphs showing what the data might look like if they indicated that the factor maintaining a problem behavior, such as self-injury or tantrums, was positive reinforcement (social attention), negative reinforcement (escape), automatic reinforcement, or undifferentiated. Notice in the graphs that each condition, such as play or escape, is applied in separate sessions. Also, if you divide the sessions sequentially into blocks of four, each condition appears once in each block and in different orders across blocks. This is done to make sure the condition's effect on behavior results from the condition and not the order in which the condition occurred. As we saw earlier, the play condition is used as a comparison—a control condition—because no reinforcer is expected to act on the problem behavior during play. The level of the problem behavior is usually fairly low during the play condition.

Let's examine the graphed data. Figure 13-5 presents four graphs, one for each potential outcome regarding the function the behavior may serve.

1. The top left graph shows heightened problem behavior in sessions when the behavior receives social attention, such as attempts to soothe or reprimand the person, but not in other sessions. These data suggest that the behavior is maintained by attention as a positive reinforcer.

2. The lower left graph shows heightened problem behavior in sessions when it leads to escape from an unpleasant situation, such as being asked a difficult question, but not in other sessions. These data suggest that the behavior is maintained by escape as a negative reinforcer.

3. The top right graph shows heightened problem behavior in sessions when the target person is alone and receives little attention or environmental stimulation. These data suggest that the behavior is maintained by automatic reinforcement, such as sensory stimulation.

4. The bottom right graph shows the problem behavior occurring at moderate levels in all of the conditions. These data are viewed as *undifferentiated*, or not conclusive. Sometimes undifferentiated data reflect the operation of automatic reinforcement, but often we can't tell this for sure.

If a functional analysis reveals that the level of the problem behavior is relatively high in more than one condition, such as attention and escape, this probably means the behavior serves multiple functions, such as to gain both positive and negative reinforcement.

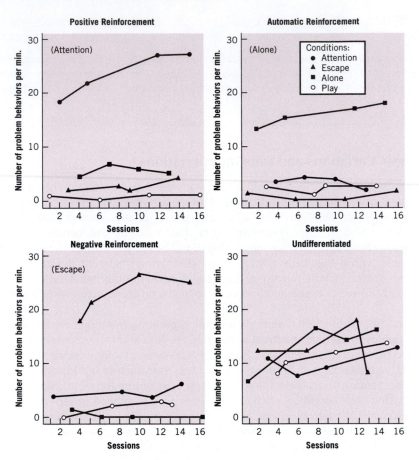

Figure 13-5 Four graphs with hypothetical data to illustrate potential outcomes from a functional analysis of a problem behavior, such as self-injury or tantrums. The functional analysis suggests that the problem behavior is maintained by positive reinforcement in the top left graph, negative reinforcement in the bottom left graph, and automatic reinforcement in the top right graph. The data in the bottom right graph do not identify a clear function and so are undifferentiated.

Is Doing a Functional Analysis Hard to Learn?

When students read about doing functional assessments, some of them worry that they would not be able to do one because the procedure seems complicated. If you're one of those students, you'll see evidence here that may allay your fears.

A study examined how hard it is to learn the skills needed to do a functional analysis (Iwata, Wallace et al., 2000). The participants were 11 upper-level undergraduate students who had previously completed a course in behavior analysis. These students were tested in baseline and performed about 70% of the requested skills correctly. They then received training in providing specific behavior analytic methods and took a quiz. Students who scored below 90% on the quiz received another training session. How did they do? All of the students displayed improved performance after training, and now 97.5% of the skills were correctly performed. Clearly, undergraduates could learn the skills to a high level with a modest amount of training. Another study provides additional evidence of the ease in learning the skills for doing a functional analysis (Najdowski, Wallace, Doney, & Ghezzi, 2003). The researchers trained the mother of a boy with autism to perform a functional analysis on his behavior of refusing, sometimes violently, any foods outside a very restricted set, such as candy and chicken nuggets. The mother completed the functional analysis, and a subsequent intervention based on her data successfully increased the range of foods the boy would accept. (Go to .)

FROM FUNCTIONAL ASSESSMENT TO PROGRAM DESIGN

To design a behavior change program, we should first do a functional assessment—and it generally should use methods that are at least moderately rigorous. It is rarely sufficient to use only indirect methods for the assessment. To understand the antecedents and consequences well that are responsible for initiating and maintaining a behavior, we need to observe the behavior carefully. After we've done the functional assessment, how do we decide what the data mean?

INTERPRETING FUNCTIONAL ASSESSMENT DATA

The big question we want to answer with a functional assessment is, "Which antecedents and consequences seem to be responsible for the target behavior's occurrence, for a behavioral excess, or nonoccurrence, for a behavioral deficit?" How we answer this question depends on the type of functional assessment we do.

Using Data From Unstructured Descriptive Assessments

If we use direct methods and perform an unstructured descriptive assessment, we would examine the completed summary record form to see which antecedents and consequences are most strongly associated with the target behavior's occurrence or nonoccurrence. For example, the summary record in Figure 13-3 shows that Ray's tantrums seem to happen when he is doing academic tasks or when he is asked to do something, either because he dislikes it or he's already engaged in an activity he enjoys, such as watching TV. His tantrums brought

---

CONCEPT CHECK 13.1

Check your understanding of the preceding concepts. Remember: The symbol ⇔ means that the answer can vary. Answer the following questions about the purposes and types of functional assessments.

1. In the opening story of the 11-year-old boy's tantrums, observations indicated that _____ served as the antecedents and _____ was the reinforcer for the behavior.
2. The set of procedures by which we can identify the antecedents and consequences that control a behavior is called _____ .
3. The four types of reinforcers that typically maintain problem behaviors are _____ , _____ , _____ , and _____ .
4. An example of an indirect method for collecting data for a functional assessment is a(n) _____ . ⇔
5. Observing a target behavior in its natural environment to collect data for a functional assessment can involve two strategies, _____ and _____ descriptive assessments.
6. The two forms used in collecting and organizing data from direct observations of a target behavior are the _____ and the _____ .
7. The functional assessment approach that uses experimental methods to manipulate antecedents and consequences is called a _____ .

him rewards: He got out of the academic task or got to continue his enjoyable activities. Because summary records combine and organize the data, they are more likely than A-B-C Logs to reveal patterns like these as clearly. Carefully done, unstructured descriptive assessments provide a moderately rigorous analysis of a target behavior's functions and are very useful in designing a program to change it. In fact, interventions designed on the basis of data from descriptive assessments are about as effective as those based on functional analyses (Delfs & Campbell, 2010).

Using Data From Structured Descriptive Assessments and Functional Analyses

Because structured descriptive assessments manipulate antecedents, and functional analyses can manipulate both antecedents and consequences, we would graph the data in either of two ways. First, if we manipulated the target behavior's consequences, we could make a graph like those in Figure 13-5 to determine the behavior's reinforcers. Second, we could make a graph showing comparisons of the target behavior in baseline and the manipulated condition. A graphic analysis of these graphs would enable us to develop an interpretation of the role of the antecedents and consequences in maintaining the problem behavior. Although, as we saw earlier, the outcomes can be undifferentiated, unclear findings from functional analyses seem to be rare.

We saw an example of graphed data from a functional analysis in Figure 13-4 of Jim's body-rocking behavior. The interpretation of it was clear: Difficult learning tasks were a strong antecedent for his problem behavior. What's more, we can see in the graph that reducing social attention for his body rocking had no effect on it. These effects were basically the same for all of the boys in the study. This finding is especially important because prior research had found that repetitive/ritualistic behaviors are maintained by automatic reinforcement in the form of sensory stimulation. Probably both automatic reinforcement and task difficulty have a great deal of control over these behaviors, and it may be that these behaviors in some individuals are affected much more by one of these factors than the other. Other researchers have found that the reinforcers that affect self-injurious behavior in children with developmental disabilities differ for different children (Iwata et al., 1982). The reinforcers appear to be attention for some, escape for others, and sensory stimulation for still others.

These findings highlight the importance of doing functional assessments. If the researchers who worked with Jim had assumed from the prior studies that automatic reinforcement was the only important factor, they might have tried to decrease his body rocking by reducing the sensory stimulation he received from the behavior. And they might not have done the functional assessment that discovered the effect of task difficulty or found that providing an alternative behavior ("Help me") can reduce its impact. Each person is different; functional assessments allow us to take individual differences into account.

USING A FUNCTIONAL ASSESSMENT

A functional assessment is typically carried out before the baseline phase in a program to change behavior, but sometimes direct observations of the behavior can overlap baseline. If we follow up a descriptive assessment with a functional analysis, we can choose which specific manipulations to try by looking at interview and observational data and then generating hypotheses about why the target behavior does or does not occur.

Once we have completed the functional assessment and identified the antecedents and consequences that affect whether the person does or does not perform the target behavior, we can design a program, selecting the most appropriate methods of applied behavior analysis to improve the behavior. This is what the researchers working with Jim did, as we discussed earlier: They identified task difficulty as a factor in his body rocking and designed a program to teach him to ask for help with difficult tasks (Durand & Carr, 1987). When we find antecedents are involved in initiating the problem behavior, we can consider methods to change or eliminate the motivating operations or discriminative stimuli (S^Ds) that promote the behavior. When we identify consequences that maintain the current target behavior, we can consider ways to eliminate the existing reinforcers or introduce punishment for the behavior, or we can provide reinforcers for alternative behaviors. Although we've discussed these methods to some extent in earlier chapters, the next several chapters describe how to combine and apply them in a program to change operant behavior.

After we have a design, we introduce the intervention and carry it out until the behavioral goal is achieved. Ideally, the program also should have a follow-up phase to determine the degree to which improvements in the target behavior are maintained after the intervention ends. Although follow-up phases usually extend for several months, they sometimes cover much shorter or longer time periods.

STRENGTHS AND LIMITATIONS OF FUNCTIONAL ASSESSMENTS

There are several advantages to performing functional assessments, particularly because they can identify important antecedents and consequences that control target behaviors. But there are also some important difficulties in using these methods. We'll start this discussion with two major advantages of functional assessment—that is, we can now provide better treatment and early treatment for problem behaviors.

BETTER AND EARLY TREATMENT

Due to the increasing use of functional assessment procedures, programs to change problem behaviors have become better in two ways. First, the application of behavior analysis methods has become more effective and efficient. An extensive review of research in school settings on children with and without disabilities found that using functional assessments was "valuable for determining the causes for problem behaviors" and that the programs "were overwhelmingly effective in producing improvements in target behaviors" (Ervin et al., 2001, pp. 206, 208).

Second, the intervention techniques used in applied behavior analysis are now more humane. Behavior analysts years ago relied on using punishment, including painful stimuli, to treat severe cases of self-injurious and aggressive behaviors; these methods were often very effective (Pelios, Morren, Tesch, & Axelrod, 1999). But with the increased use of functional assessment procedures, behavior analysts have developed new, more effective reinforcement-based methods and are more inclined to apply these methods instead of punishment to correct these behaviors.

With the development of functional assessment methods, we can detect and treat effectively serious problem behaviors, such as self-injury, early in a child's life, before they have a long history of reinforcement and become entrenched. Because studies had found that self-injurious behavior tends to begin before 5 years of age, often before 2, researchers conducted functional assessments on 30 children from 10 months to 4 years 11 months of age who had already received medical attention for the injuries they had caused (Kurtz et al., 2003). Although most of the children had developmental disabilities, some did not. Head banging was the most prevalent self-injurious behavior, occurring in 83% of the children, and other serious acts included aggression (87%), tantrums (77%), and disruption (60%). Assessment and treatment were carried out across 12 to 16 weeks in 2- to 3-hour sessions, 2 or 3 days a week. Functional analyses were conducted in 10-minute sessions either by behavior analysts or by caregivers who were trained in the skills. These analyses revealed that the most common reinforcers for the self-injurious behaviors were attention and tangible rewards, and the operant functions of the problem behaviors overall were determined in over 87% of the children. Treatment with applied behavior analysis methods succeeded in reducing self-injurious behavior by 95% and the problem behaviors overall by 87%. These findings are very important because they show that we can identify the functions of serious problem behaviors in very young children and correct them early.

FEASIBILITY ISSUES

An important limitation to functional assessments is that sometimes conducting them is not feasible, particularly if they involve doing a functional analysis. We'll consider a few examples.

First, functional assessments may require a great deal of resources—mainly time, expense, and space—that may be prohibitive in some settings, such as schools (Ervin et al., 2001). Second, some problem behaviors may be serious but occur at very low frequencies, such as stealing, which would require a great deal of time for observation, exacerbating the issue of resources. One way to deal with the problem of resource burden is to do a *brief version of functional analysis*, having only a few sessions and keeping them short; this often produces useful information for designing interventions (Ervin et al., 2001; Ishuin, 2009; Northup et al., 1991; Tincani, Castrogiavanni, & Axelrod, 1999). Sometimes brief functional analyses don't identify the controlling factors well. If that happens, the procedure can be extended to four phases: If an early phase doesn't identify the factors, the analysis would progress to the next phase (Vollmer, Marcus, Ringdahl, & Roane, 1995). Third, some medications clients take may affect their behavior during a functional assessment, thereby making the data less useful (Dicesare, McAdam, Toner, & Varrell, 2005).

A fourth issue affecting the feasibility of doing functional assessments is the danger presented by some target behaviors, such as self-injurious and aggressive acts. This issue has been addressed in two common ways: having the target person wear protective equipment, such as headgear, during assessments and restricting the amount of time individuals are exposed to these behaviors (Ervin et al., 2001). But protective gear can create a problem in a functional assessment: It can suppress self-injurious or aggressive acts, impairing the ability to identify the controlling factors (Borrero et al., 2002). An approach that may solve this problem in some cases is to perform a functional assessment and treatment on a *precursor behavior*—that is, an act the person generally performs immediately before the target behavior—such as yelling just before hitting (Najdowski et al., 2008).

METHODOLOGY ISSUES

Other limitations to functional assessments relate to their methodologies. When using indirect methods, behavior analysts face two issues of concern. First, data from interviews and surveys are suspect because they rely on the respondent's memory of events that occurred in the past, sometimes the distant past, and people sometimes give biased reports. Second, the questionnaires used in functional assessments often do not have strong evidence of their reliability (ability to produce essentially the same scores consistently when nothing has changed) and validity (ability to measure what they claim to measure).

When behavior is being directly observed, descriptive assessments indicate events that are associated with the behavior; but they don't necessarily assure that the events are, in fact, functioning as antecedents and consequences. That is, observing an association does not provide evidence of cause–effect. The purpose of using experimental methods in functional analyses is to provide that evidence. But functional analyses have drawbacks, too. For instance, they are usually not conducted in natural settings, and the manipulated events are contrived. Does the target person respond to these events in the same way as in everyday life? To the extent that the outcomes from a functional analysis are the same as those from a prior descriptive assessment, the person probably does.

TIPS ON DOING FUNCTIONAL ASSESSMENTS

Functional assessments have become an essential element of applied behavior analysis since the early 1980s. In this section, we'll list several guidelines to follow when doing functional assessments:

1. Although behavior analysts can use a variety of methods in functional assessments, indirect methods are the least rigorous and typically should not provide the only information for planning an intervention. Use direct methods as part of the assessment if at all possible.
2. Start by defining the target behavior carefully so it will be easy to monitor.
3. Watch carefully for the target behavior, and try to identify immediately after each instance what the antecedents and consequences were. Record these data immediately.

4. Before using a data sheet or an A-B-C Log, compose a draft of it and try it out to find "bugs" to correct.

5. If at all possible, do a functional analysis—even a brief version—to confirm the data from the descriptive assessment and clarify relationships between the behavior and its antecedents and consequences.

6. Interpret unstructured descriptive assessment data by looking in the summary record for associations between the target behavior and likely antecedents and consequences. If you do a structured descriptive assessment or functional analysis, graph the data and look for evidence that the manipulated variables cause changes in the behavior.

(Go to .)

STUDY AND REVIEW

SUMMARY

Functional assessments are conducted to identify the antecedents and consequences that influence target behaviors. These assessments can vary in their rigor, and most should try to be at least moderately rigorous. The consequences that maintain problem behaviors tend to include escape, social attention, and tangible items as reinforcement; automatic reinforcement is also important. Functional assessments can be applied with behavioral excesses and deficits.

Three approaches can be used to collect data on the target behavior and its antecedents and consequences in functional assessments—in order of increasing rigor, they are indirect methods, direct methods, and functional analysis. In indirect methods, we collect these data with interviews and questionnaires. In direct methods, we observe the behavior and look for the controlling variables in the person's natural environment. Direct methods can use an unstructured descriptive assessment strategy or a structured descriptive assessment strategy; the latter manipulates possible antecedents to see their effect and to watch for the behavior's consequences. Observational data are collected in an A-B-C Log and later consolidated in a summary record.

CONCEPT CHECK 13.2

Answer the following questions about the utility of functional assessment in designing behavior change programs as well as its strengths and limitations.

1. We interpret the outcome of an unstructured descriptive assessment by looking in the _____ form for relationships between the behavior and its antecedents and consequences.

2. We interpret the outcome of a structured descriptive assessment and functional analysis by looking at a _____ of the data.

3. A strength of using functional assessments is _____ . ⇔

4. A limitation of functional assessments that relates to the feasibility of using them is _____ . ⇔

5. A limitation of functional assessments that relates to the methodology in doing them is _____ . ⇔

The third approach for conducting a functional assessment is the functional analysis, a procedure that uses experimental methods to demonstrate causal relationships between the behavior and its antecedents and consequences. These methods involve manipulating antecedents and consequences to see their effects on the target behavior. The skills for doing a functional analysis are not hard to learn.

The way we interpret the outcome of a functional assessment depends on the methods we used to gather the data. If we used direct observation of the behavior in its natural environment, we examine data in the summary record looking for associations between the behavior and possible antecedents and consequences. If we used a functional analysis or structured descriptive assessment, we would graph the data and look for variations in the behavior that correspond to the manipulations of antecedents and consequences.

Functional assessment procedures enable behavior analysts to provide better and early treatment for problem behaviors, such as self-injury and aggression. Sometimes these assessments are not easily feasible or have methodological issues that affect the usefulness of the data or how we interpret them.

> To prepare for exams, use the following key terms and review questions and the online study guide that's available on this book's companion website at www.wiley.com/college/sarafino.

KEY TERMS

functional assessment
unstructured descriptive assessment

structured descriptive assessment
A-B-C Log

summary record
functional analysis

ANSWERS TO CONCEPT CHECKS (CCs)

CC13.1 *Answers:* **1.** being frustrated or teased, attention **2.** functional assessment **3.** escape, attention, automatic, and tangible **4.** interview or questionnaire **5.** unstructured, structured **6.** A-B-C Log, summary record **7.** functional analysis.

CC13.2 *Answers:* **1.** summary record **2.** graph **3.** better treatment **4.** burden on resources **5.** interviews and questionnaires rely on the respondent's memory.

REVIEW QUESTIONS

1. What is a functional assessment, and what does it tell you?
2. Describe the four types of reinforcers that usually maintain problem behaviors, and give an example of each.
3. What are unstructured descriptive assessments?
4. How are A-B-C Logs and summary records used in functional assessments?
5. Describe the types of antecedents one can assess with an A-B-C Log.
6. What are structured descriptive assessments and functional analyses, and how are the procedures different?
7. How do we decide which specific manipulations to use in a functional analysis?
8. Describe the research by Durand and Carr (1987) on Jim's body-rocking behavior.
9. Describe the procedures behavior analysts use to interpret data from unstructured descriptive assessments and from structured descriptive assessments and functional analyses.

10. What evidence would you give to someone's question, "Is doing a functional analysis hard to learn?"

11. Describe the process of using a functional assessment to design a program to change a behavior.

12. What strengths do functional assessments have in changing behavior? Include a description of the research by Kurtz and colleagues (2003) on problem behaviors of very young children.

13. What feasibility problems occur sometimes in doing a functional assessment, and what possible solutions have been used?

14. What methodological issues limit the utility of specific methods in functional assessments?

RELATED READINGS

- Groden, G. (1989). A guide for conducting a comprehensive behavioral analysis of a target behavior. *Journal of Behavior Therapy and Experimental Psychiatry, 20,* 163–169.

- O'Neill, R. E., Horner, R. H., Albin, R. W., Sprague, J. R., Storey, K., & Newton, J. S. (1997). *Functional assessment and program development for problem behavior: A practical handbook* (2nd ed.). Pacific Grove, CA: Brooks/Cole.

14

MANAGING ANTECEDENTS

PROLOGUE

In the early 1970s, American nursing homes were not providing sufficient activity programs for their residents, mostly elderly people. As a result, researchers decided to assess the activities residents participated in at a Kansas skilled-care facility in a middle-income neighborhood and try to improve the activities if needed (McClannahan & Risley, 1975). Observations were conducted hourly for 12 hours a day, one weekday a week, for 8 weeks and revealed that on average the residents spent about 36% of the time—seldom more than 40% or less than 30%—engaged with other people, equipment, or materials that were available. Because of the residents' low level of participation in suitable activities, the researchers implemented an intervention to improve participation.

The intervention focused on managing antecedents for engagement in activities in the following way: If residents entered the lounge area and did not seek out activities that were available, a staff member would go to them, place a piece of recreation equipment in their hands, invite them to use it, and show them how. Additional prompting was given if they stopped using the equipment or asked for something else to do. This approach was both simple and very effective in changing the residents' behavioral deficits—it increased their participation in activities to an average of 74% of the time.

The title, and the focus, of this chapter is "Managing Antecedents." To manage antecedents, we must identify existing cues, select the most appropriate stimulus control techniques, and administer them carefully to change existing antecedents or introduce new ones.

IDENTIFYING AND MODIFYING EXISTING ANTECEDENTS

The first step in managing antecedents to change behavior is to identify the existing cues through observational methods as part of a functional assessment.

IDENTIFYING ANTECEDENTS

Not all events or conditions that precede a behavior set the occasion for the person to respond—some of them may just happen to coincide now and then in time and place with the actual antecedents. To identify the antecedents for a behavior, behavior analysts need to make systematic observations in a functional assessment of the behavior. Although it's useful to have hunches about which stimuli are antecedents for the target behavior, *hunches should not be conclusions*. Sometimes our hunches are based on antecedents we know operate for a particular behavior in people other than the target person. But here's the rub: The antecedents for a behavior, such as children's noncompliance, are often idiosyncratic—specific to the individual (Call et al., 2004). We need to *assess the antecedents for each person*. The ease with which we can identify antecedents depends on whether they are overt or covert and/or immediate or distant, and whether the problem is a behavioral excess or deficit.

Antecedents for Behavioral Excesses

When dealing with behavioral excesses, antecedents that are *overt and immediate* are usually fairly easy to identify in a functional assessment because they are present and observable just before the target behavior occurs. But sometimes overt, immediate antecedents are not easily noticed. For instance, we saw in Chapter 1 that children in a classroom become distracted from their studies when they are seated too close together. Although this antecedent is overt and immediate, we might not notice it.

Antecedents for a behavioral excess that are *covert* or *distant* are usually difficult to identify because they are not directly observable and consist of thoughts, feelings, and physiological states. In some cases, the person whose target behavior is to be changed isn't even aware of these cues. But probably in most cases, the person is aware of them—for instance, many people who bite their nails report that boredom is an antecedent for this behavioral excess (Williams, Rose, & Chisholm, 2006). To identify covert and distant antecedents, we can use two approaches: careful direct observations and indirect assessment methods, such as interviews or questionnaires.

Antecedents for Behavioral Deficits

When dealing with behavioral deficits, we need to identify cues that set the occasion for a behavior *not* occurring, such as exercising by someone who's an extreme "couch potato." We saw in Chapter 13 that functional assessments for behavioral deficits look for antecedents and consequences that are linked to *nonoccurrences* of responses that could have or should have occurred. Knowing what cues usually precede people's *not* performing the behavior when they could or should do so can help us decide how to alter those antecedents to make the behavior occur more frequently. For instance, a student who could and should study more may fail to do so partly because friends interrupt her reading when she tries to study in her dorm room. She might study more if she could change her venue for studying, such as reading in a library.

WAYS TO ALTER THE ANTECEDENTS

Procedures to manage antecedents involve manipulating the target person's physical or social stimuli to encourage the desired behavior or discourage an undesired behavior. In general, there are four basic ways to manipulate these stimuli—we can:

1. Develop or introduce new cues (discriminative stimuli; S^Ds).
2. Modify existing cues (S^Ds).
3. Manipulate motivating operations.
4. Manipulate the effort needed to make responses.

We'll look at a brief overview of these approaches first and then examine the methods in more detail in the rest of the chapter.

Developing or Introducing New S^Ds

Developing new antecedents involves teaching individuals S^Ds that they don't already know, by using the discrimination training procedures we discussed in Chapter 8. In this approach, we provide a consequence, such as reinforcement, for a particular behavior when a specific stimulus, the S^D, is present but not when some other stimulus, the S^Δ, is present. Although discrimination training can be a time-consuming process, we can speed it up by applying shortcut methods of response prompting, such as physical guidance and instructions, and transferring stimulus control, which we examined in Chapter 11. For example, if your roommate wanted to reduce TV watching, you could post a sign on the TV that says, "Don't watch."

These shortcut methods are generally used temporarily to build stimulus control to the normal S^Ds. But in some cases, response prompts can become a permanent part of the normal antecedents, especially if the person cannot perform appropriately without them. When we manage antecedents in an intervention, we need to keep in mind that the desirable behavior that the S^D elicits must be reinforced during the intervention and in the natural environment later.

Modifying Existing S^Ds

Another way to manage the antecedents is to modify the normal cues. Chapter 11 describes two approaches that use stimulus prompts to do this: altering an S^D physically or adding another stimulus to it. The former approach is called a *within-stimulus prompt*, and the latter is called an *extra-stimulus prompt*. Stimulus prompts can involve pictures, sounds, or environmental alterations and are especially useful when trying to correct a behavioral deficit.

When dealing with a behavioral excess, two techniques are useful: eliminating the S^Ds for the target behavior and encouraging a desirable alternative behavior. A variant of eliminating S^Ds involves reducing them—for example, if your roommate watches TV too much and the antecedent includes the time or places that this behavior occurs, you might suggest that he or she "narrow" the range of these cues—for instance, restricting the times to between 9:00 and 11:00 p.m. and the place to a specific room.

Manipulating Motivating Operations and Response Effort

We've seen in earlier chapters, especially Chapter 9, that motivating operations (MOs) are antecedent procedures that alter the effectiveness of specific reinforcers and punishers and the performance of acts that normally lead to those consequences. For example, when people have not eaten for some hours, food becomes a more powerful reinforcer to them; and after they have eaten, food is now a less powerful reinforcer. Similarly, MOs can increase or decrease a punisher's effect on a behavior. By manipulating MOs, we can increase a behavior that occurs too little or decrease a behavior that occurs too much.

You probably know that people tend to follow the "law of least effort"—they are more likely to make responses that are easy to do than hard to do. Sometimes we can manage antecedents by making problem behaviors more difficult to do or making desirable behaviors easier to do. In the latter case, for instance, people might be more likely to exercise if they can do their workouts at home rather than at a gym that is miles away. They choose the behavior that takes less effort.

MANAGING DISCRIMINATIVE STIMULI (S^{D}s)

Two approaches for managing S^{D}s involve eliminating or reducing existing antecedents for a problem behavior and developing or introducing antecedents for a desirable act, such as a competing response or alternative behavior. We'll examine these methods now.

ELIMINATING EXISTING S^{D}s FOR A PROBLEM BEHAVIOR

An important approach for dealing with a problem behavior is to eliminate or reduce the S^{D}s that encourage it. For the behavioral excess of drinking too much alcohol, for instance, staying away from places where liquor is available, such as bars, would help a lot. Similarly, someone who must eat out often and goes a lot to restaurants that serve too much fatty food can find other restaurants with healthier fare. For a behavioral deficit, a college student who fails to study because there are too many distractions in the dorm could study in the library.

Another way to eliminate an existing S^D is to turn it into an S$^\Delta$, signaling that the associated behavior won't be reinforced. We can do this by presenting the S^D repeatedly while preventing it from being associated with rewards, thereby turning it into an S$^\Delta$. For instance, seeing or smelling alcoholic beverages can be a strong antecedent for drinking. Some research has found that presenting S^{D}s that heavy drinkers of alcohol associate with drinking and simultaneously preventing reinforcement (consuming alcohol) of the behavior can help them quit drinking (Blakey & Baker, 1980). (Go to 🐾.)

MANIPULATING S^{D}s FOR A DESIRABLE BEHAVIOR

We can manipulate S^{D}s to promote desirable behavior in two ways: We can correct a behavioral deficit or increase a competing response or alternative behavior to replace a problem behavioral excess, such as aggression. Recall

CASE STUDY

The "Betrayed" Husband

A 29-year-old graduate student began therapy in an effort to save his marriage 2 years after his wife had committed the "ultimate betrayal" with his best friend (Goldiamond, 1965). This event was especially distressing to him because he

> had suggested that the friend keep his wife company while he was in the library at night. Since that time, whenever he saw his wife, [he] screamed at her for hours on end or else was ashamed of himself for having done so and spent hours sulking and brooding. (p. 856)

The antecedents that set the occasion for his behavior were probably both immediate (seeing his wife) and distant (the betrayal). Part of the therapy program to change this behavior involved altering the cues. For instance, to decrease the activity of sulking, the husband was told to sulk as much as he wanted; but not in the rooms at home where he usually sulked, and not in the presence of his wife. When he finished sulking, he could leave his sulking place and join his wife. This method helped decrease his sulking duration to about half an hour per day for the first couple of weeks, after which it stopped entirely. Similarly, individuals who worry chronically can successfully restrict their worrying to certain times or places (Borkovec, Wilkinson, Folensbee, & Lerman, 1983).

from Chapter 6 that a *competing response* is a desirable act that is incompatible or competes with a target behavior, and an *alternative behavior* is an action that is different from and can take the place of the target behavior, but it isn't necessarily incompatible with it. Research we discussed in Chapter 13 used the latter approach to replace a boy's problem behavior, body rocking, with his asking for help (Durand & Carr, 1987). The boy would rock back and forth when he was asked to perform a difficult training task. To teach him the alternative behavior—saying, "Help me"—the behavior analyst would use verbal and modeling prompts, saying to him "Say, help me," when he was having a hard time with a task and answered incorrectly. The verbal prompt ("Say") was then faded and delayed to transfer stimulus control so that he would ask for help without being prompted when he was told (the S^D) that his answer on a task was not correct.

To correct a behavioral deficit, we can teach a new S^D by way of discrimination training or by using shortcut stimulus control methods, particularly prompting. Recall from Chapter 11 that response prompts include verbal, gestural, modeling, and physical guidance prompts. Researchers have applied verbal prompts to improve safety behavior in a variety of settings. For example, a study used verbal prompts to increase seat belt use in a supermarket and a large retail store that had shopping carts available with seats and belts for young children (Barker, Bailey, & Lee, 2004). When adults came into the stores with a child, a greeter asked if they wanted a cart; if they did and didn't buckle the belt before proceeding, the greeter simply said, "Don't forget to buckle up." During baseline sessions, no verbal prompt was given. Figure 14-1 presents the data for the two settings and shows that the percentage of shoppers who buckled the seat belts was about twice as high when they received the prompt than in baseline. Other research using verbal prompts with automobile drivers has found increased seat belt use and decreased cell phone use when they were prompted to do the safety behaviors (Clayton, Helms, & Simpson, 2006; Geller, Bruff, & Nimmer, 1985; Gras et al., 2003). (Go to ▉.)

ALTERING MOTIVATING OPERATIONS (MOs)

In Chapter 9, we examined MOs in some detail. The critical issue to recall at this time is that MOs can be of two types:

1. *Establishing operations* (EOs) increase the effectiveness of a reinforcer or punisher—we've seen, for example, that deprivation increases the power of food as a reinforcer.

CONCEPT CHECK 14.1

Check your understanding of the preceding concepts. Remember: The symbol ⇔ means that the answer can vary. Answer the following questions about identifying antecedents and managing S^Ds.

1. Because antecedents are often idiosyncratic, we need to conduct a _____ to identify the antecedents for each person's target behavior.
2. Antecedents for a target behavior are relatively easy to identify if they are _____ rather than if they are _____ .
3. Two of the four ways to alter antecedents are _____ and _____ . ⇔
4. One way to eliminate an existing S^D is to turn it into a(n) _____ .
5. Presenting an S^D for a(n) _____ response sets the occasion for the person to make a response that is incompatible with making a problem behavior.

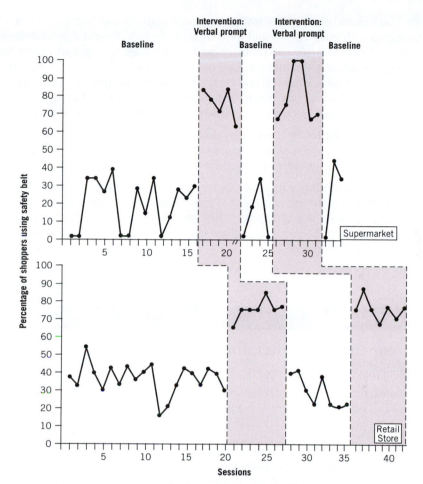

Figure 14-1   Percentage of shoppers buckling safety belts for children in shopping carts at a supermarket and a retail store during baseline and verbal prompt phases of a multiple-baseline design. Observation sessions were conducted over a 3-month period on separate days and lasted about 2 hours each. Not all of the data at the two settings were collected concurrently. *Source:* From M. R. Barker J. S. Bailey, & N. Lee (2004), The impact of verbal prompts on child safety-belt use in shopping carts. *Journal of Applied Behavior Analysis, 37,* 527–530, Figure 1. Copyright © 2004 Society for the Experimental Analysis of Behavior. Used by permission.

2.   *Abolishing operations* (AOs) decrease the effectiveness of a reinforcer or punisher—for example, someone who overeats at restaurants or parties can snack on low-fat foods before going out to eat.

In both types of MOs, there are corresponding changes in the associated behavior, which are shown on the right side of Figure 9.2. The behavior should increase if we apply an EO for a reinforcer or an AO for a punisher; it should decrease if we apply an AO for a reinforcer or an EO for a punisher. (Go to 🔍.)

REDUCING OR REVERSING MOs THAT HELP MAINTAIN A PROBLEM BEHAVIOR

We've seen that MOs can increase the effectiveness of reinforcers that maintain problem behaviors, such as aggression and self-injury. For example, these problem behaviors can lead to escape, a negative reinforcer, when the antecedent involves requiring children to perform tasks they find very difficult. Requiring engagement in difficult tasks is an MO that makes escape, such as through noncompliance, a more powerful reinforcer for some children (Call et al., 2004).

An intervention that focused on reducing MOs that maintained problem behavior, such as aggression and self-injury, was conducted with three 20-year-old individuals with developmental disabilities (Kennedy, 1994). A functional assessment had found that the problem behaviors tended to occur when the teacher made task demands, such as "Put the dish away," at high rates (about four per minute), but not at low rates (about one per 2½ minutes) or when the teacher made general comments. For the intervention, the teacher presented demands and comments in 10-minute sessions once or twice a day for each participant, starting at a low rate of demands (one per 2½ minutes) and a high rate (six per minute) of general comments. Then, when a participant displayed

a low frequency of problem behavior, demands were gradually increased across sessions. As long as problem behavior remained at a low frequency, task demands continued to be increased across sessions. If an increase in problem behavior occurred, the frequency of task demands was decreased. (p. 164)

Across dozens of sessions with this procedure, task demands increased gradually to about four per minute; but problem behaviors were at near-zero levels for all three participants, and two of them showed high levels of positive social affect, such as in smiling or saying, "I like you." What's more, follow-up tests months later still showed very low levels of problem behavior. Using low rates of demands and then gradually increasing them served as an AO for escape as a reinforcer.

CLOSE-UP

Noncontingent Reinforcement as an Antecedent

Noncontingent reinforcement is a procedure in which a known reinforcer for the target behavior is delivered on a periodic schedule that is independent of the occurrence of that behavior (Poling & Ehrhardt, 2005). This procedure is an antecedent manipulation that can reduce problem behavior and can be used with positive or negative reinforcers.

Social attention is a positive reinforcer that has been applied in noncontingent reinforcement procedures. An intervention using this procedure was conducted with three women with developmental disabilities who engaged in severe self-injurious behavior (Vollmer et al., 1993). A functional analysis had identified attention as a reinforcer that maintained the problem behaviors. During the intervention, 10- or 15-minute sessions were carried out, two to four sessions a day on five days per week. In each session, the researchers provided 10 seconds of social attention on a fixed schedule, beginning at a very high rate; across sessions the rate was decreased gradually until attention was given only once every 5 minutes. For all three women, self-injurious behavior declined in the intervention by more than half from baseline levels, and for one woman the behavior dropped to near zero almost immediately. Giving frequent noncontingent attention apparently served as an AO, decreasing the effectiveness of attention as a reinforcer for self-injury. Another study produced similar findings with noncontingent attention for noncompliance in children who were not disabled (Call et al., 2004).

Escape is a negative reinforcer that has been used in noncontingent reinforcement procedures. An intervention was conducted with two boys, 18 and 4 years of age, with developmental disabilities who displayed self-injurious behaviors during training sessions; a functional analysis determined that these behaviors were maintained by escape from the sessions (Vollmer, Marcus, & Ringdahl, 1995). In each session, the researchers gave the boys "breaks" (escape) lasting 20–30 seconds on a fixed schedule, beginning at a very high rate; across sessions, the rate was decreased gradually to low rates. For both boys, self-injurious behavior dropped by more than half from baseline levels and quickly reached near-zero levels. Giving frequent noncontingent breaks apparently served as an AO, decreasing the effectiveness of escape as a reinforcer for self-injury. Another study had similar outcomes with five children in dental visits, using brief noncontingent escape for disruptive behavior, such as body movements or crying (O' Callahan, Allen, Powell, & Salama, 2006). Figure 14-2 presents their data.

(Continued)

(*Continued*)

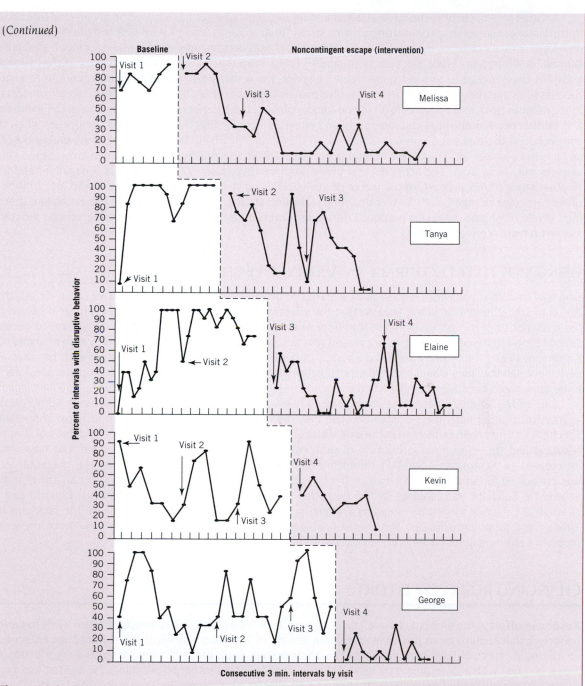

Figure 14–2 Percentage of 15-second intervals containing disruptive behavior assessed during consecutive 3-minute periods of treatment for five children across four visits to the dentist. Some visits were in baseline and some in intervention (noncontingent escape) using a multiple-baseline design. All children showed marked reductions in disruptive behavior. *Source*: From P. M. O'Callahan K. D. Allen S. Powell, & F. Salama (2006), The efficacy of noncontingent escape for decreasing children's disruptive behavior during restorative dental treatment. *Journal of Applied Behavior Analysis*, 39, 161–171, Figure 1. Copyright © 2006 Society for the Experimental Analysis of Behavior. Used by permission.

Another approach for reducing MOs that maintain problem behavior has focused on giving students choices in curricular decisions in school settings. In one study, three students, two 11-year-olds and one 5-year-old, with developmental disabilities engaged in problem behaviors, such as tantrums and aggression, at high levels (Dyer, Dunlap, & Winterling, 1990). Because prior studies had shown that giving students choices in the classroom activities they engage in reduces undesirable behavior, the researchers trained the three children to express their choices and then alternated in three to five phases the opportunity to choose or not choose from three or four available tasks and reinforcers. In the no-choice phases, the teacher made selections from the same tasks and reinforcers. For all three children, problem behaviors were far less frequent during the phases when they could choose the tasks and reinforcers than when they couldn't. Giving the students choices probably served as MOs in two ways: (a) The choice of reinforcers served as an EO, making them more effective; (b) the choice of tasks may have made the activities less unpleasant, serving as an AO for escape as a negative reinforcer. Another study found support for the use of choice in reducing student problem behaviors and also found that other curricular changes, such as breaking long tasks into shorter ones, reduced these behaviors and that the high levels of on-task behavior produced during the intervention were maintained during several months of follow-up tests (Kern et al., 1994).

USING MOs THAT ENCOURAGE AN ALTERNATIVE BEHAVIOR

One way to curb a behavioral excess is to replace the problem action with an alternative behavior, which we can encourage by manipulating MOs so that the effectiveness of the reinforcers for the problem behavior is reduced. For example, an intervention was done with three 16- to 18-year-old boys with autism to decrease several problem behaviors, such as aggression and tantrums, they would perform while in supermarkets (Carr & Carlson, 1993). The intervention used a variety of methods to deal with six behaviors for each boy that were severe enough that they would result in expulsion from the store. In baseline, almost all shopping sessions had to be terminated because of problem behavior.

One of the problem behaviors would occur while waiting on line at checkout: The boys would become aggressive to other customers or staff because they didn't like being there and wanted to leave immediately. This behavior had been reinforced in the past with escape. During baseline, almost all of the dozens of shopping sessions had to be terminated because of problem behavior. To deal with this situation, the intervention introduced an AO for the negative reinforcement of escaping: As the boys approached the checkout, an S^D was presented for an alternative behavior the boys liked to do. For one boy, the S^D was a magazine, and the alternative behavior was reading; for the two other boys, the S^D was snacks they had just bought, and the alternative behavior was eating. Reading and eating are behaviors they could do while on the checkout line. After several treatment sessions, the boys were able to complete almost all shopping trips without any serious problem behaviors across dozens of subsequent trips.

CHANGING RESPONSE EFFORT

Response effort is the amount of work it takes to perform a behavior. Because people are less likely to perform behaviors that require more response effort than behaviors that take less effort, we can manage antecedents by making problem behaviors more difficult to do or making desirable behaviors easier to do. For instance, a 3-year-old boy with a developmental disability who would hit his mother to get things he wanted was taught to use two mands (verbal requests) instead (Richman, Wacker, & Winborn, 2001). Because the boy didn't speak recognizable words, the mands involved his using the word *please* by presenting it either on a card or in sign language. Using the card took more effort because it consisted of a longer chain of responses. The mands did replace the boy's aggression, and he came to use the "please" sign more than the card. What's more, he eventually began to *say* "please" as he signed it.

INCREASING THE EFFORT NEEDED TO MAKE A PROBLEM BEHAVIOR

If we can increase the *response effort* needed to perform a problem behavior, the frequency of the behavior should decline. This effect has been demonstrated in several studies of hand mouthing, which involves persistently placing at least part of a hand in the mouth to the point that it can cause tissue damage, scarring, or other self-injuries (Cannella, O'Reilly, & Lancioni, 2006). Functional assessments have found evidence indicating that hand mouthing is maintained by automatic reinforcement, but it is also maintained sometimes by attention or other reinforcers.

One study used increased response effort to curb hand mouthing in four 33- to 51-year-old women with profound mental retardation (Zhou, Goff, & Iwata, 2000). The researchers found evidence that automatic reinforcement maintained the behavior: The behavior was observed more frequently in functional analysis sessions when the women were alone with no leisure materials than when they were with staff who gave them social attention and had them work on learning tasks. During intervention sessions, the procedure for increasing response effort involved wrapping the arms from mid-forearm to mid-biceps in a tight cloth sleeve, making it difficult for the arms to bend. This procedure was very effective—hand mouthing declined quickly to near-zero levels and stayed there for dozens of sessions. Despite this success during sessions, some questions remain about the ethics and long-term effectiveness of the procedure. For example, are less restrictive methods available that would work? And because the problem behavior was reinforced automatically, will it return after the response effort (sleeve) is gradually faded? Will the improved behavior generalize to other settings? If the problem behavior does return or doesn't generalize, would reapplying the increased response effort reduce the behavior quickly?

DECREASING THE EFFORT NEEDED TO MAKE AN ALTERNATIVE BEHAVIOR

Another approach for reducing a person's problem behavior is to decrease the response effort needed to perform a desirable, alternative behavior. For instance, if you would like to eat healthier snacks at home or in your room instead of eating the high-calorie, high-fat snacks you usually eat, keep handy the healthy snacks, not the unhealthy ones. Keeping healthy snacks handy decreases the effort you would need to expend to get that snack.

Recycling trash is an important ecological process, and it was the subject of a study on the manipulation of response effort to decrease the amount of office paper that was thrown in regular trash cans and increase the paper thrown in recycling containers (Brothers, Krantz, & McClannahan, 1994). The study was conducted at a treatment center for children with autism that had 25 employees who worked in offices and instructional and general areas of the facility. Recyclable and nonrecyclable paper was separated and weighed in a central utility room. After the baseline phase, a high response effort condition began: All employees got a memo defining recyclable and nonrecyclable (glossy paper, hardboard boxes, etc.) paper and stating that they could deposit recyclable paper in a container at a central location. After from 1 to 3 weeks, a low-response-effort condition began: Small recycling containers were placed on each employee's desk and on all counters in the dining room and classrooms. Because these containers were placed where paper was used, they served as an S^D to recycle and as a low-response-effort place to put recyclable paper. The results showed that compared to baseline, the amount of recyclable paper in the regular trash was 40% lower in the high-response-effort condition and 89% lower in the low-response-effort condition. What's more, the increased paper recycling was maintained during several months of follow-up assessments. Clearly, manipulating antecedents was successful and offers a simple way to encourage recycling.

Having well-marked, conveniently-located recycling bins makes it easy for this woman to recycle items. *Source*: Datacraft/Age Fotostock America, Inc.

ALTERING ANTECEDENT CHAINS

Suppose your friend asked you to help her cut back on the amount of money she spends on clothes and other items she buys, mainly at shopping malls. Spending money in stores requires a behavioral chain of antecedent responses that begins when she decides to go to a mall. Once she's there, the spending chain proceeds when she decides to go into a particular store "just to browse," finds something nice, and takes it to the checkout counter. The final part of the chain is paying for the item: reaching into a pocket, pulling out a wallet, pulling out a credit card, handing it to the cashier, signing the receipt, grabbing the package, and walking away. In a *behavioral excess*, it becomes harder and harder to stop from performing the final, undesirable behavior with each advance through the antecedent chain. It would be easiest to decide not to go to the mall in the first place; once she's there and has found something "nice," it would be easier to stop herself from taking it to the counter than to cancel the process once she's already pulled out the credit card.

A good way to reduce the likelihood of performing undesirable acts that occur at the end of an antecedent chain is to change the sequence of events in some way (Beneke & Vander Tuig, 1996). This approach, called *altering antecedent chains*, is especially effective if it is used *early* in the chain. How can we alter chains? There are two ways:

1. *Build pauses into the chain.* For instance, in trying to reduce the amount of money she spends, your friend can pause before deciding to go to the mall, into a store, or to the counter with the nice item. During the pause, she can think about her goals and whether the behavior is a good thing to do.

2. *Reorder the links.* For instance, before taking the nice item to the counter, your friend can reach for her wallet. Doing this can help break down the antecedent chain's stimulus control.

Whenever the target person performs the alteration of an antecedent chain, she or he should receive a reinforcer—in your friend's case, not the opportunity to buy something!

Can the technique of altering antecedent chains be used when the target response is a *behavioral deficit*? When someone has not yet learned the behavior, the deficit doesn't result from performing a behavioral chain. In this case, altering antecedent chains is not useful, and training in the behavior with the normal S^Ds would be appropriate. But other behavioral deficits involve target behaviors the person can do, yet doesn't. In this case, the failure to perform the behavior can result from an antecedent chain in two ways:

1. The initial links don't occur, so the chain doesn't get started.
2. A chain is performed but ends in responses that make the target behavior unlikely. For instance, a student might get materials ready to study and then think, "I'm too tired."

In either scenario, the chain's stimulus control needs to be increased using shortcut stimulus control methods we saw in Chapter 11, such as response or stimulus prompts. For many people, exercising is a behavioral deficit. To start a chain leading to exercise or keep one going, they could use verbal, environmental, or auditory prompts. Verbal and environmental prompts might include signs in the person's room or exercise clothing in plain view. An auditory prompt might be an alarm tone to initiate the chain (Azrin & Powell, 1969). The alarm can be turned off manually or automatically in a few seconds. In either case, the prompt can be faded later.

TIPS ON MANAGING ANTECEDENTS

Here are several tips for managing antecedents in behavior change programs.

1. Look for antecedents carefully. Don't rule out particular stimuli in immediate antecedents simply because they don't *seem* to be important. Preconceived "hunches" are useful, but they can be misleading.
2. If possible, ask the client's friends and relatives to help observe the target person's behavior to identify antecedents in everyday life.
3. Be creative in finding ways to manage antecedents, especially for reducing or avoiding antecedents, narrowing antecedent control, and turning S^Ds into S^Δs.
4. Look for alternative behaviors or competing responses to reinforce, especially if they would serve the same function as the target behavior it would replace.
5. Look for motivating operations to introduce that can be manipulated to change the effectiveness of reinforcers or punishers to improve the target behavior.
6. Look for ways to manipulate response effort needed to make the target response or an alternative behavior.

(Go to ⬛.)

STUDY AND REVIEW

SUMMARY

To manage antecedents to change a target behavior, we first need to identify the existing conditions that maintain it. We can manipulate antecedents in four ways: develop or introduce new cues (S^Ds), modify existing cues, alter motivating operations, and change the effort needed to make responses. We can manage S^Ds by eliminating the ones that lead to a problem behavior and by teaching new ones to correct a behavioral deficit or to increase an alternative behavior or competing response.

CONCEPT CHECK 14.2

Answer the following questions about altering MOs, changing response effort, and altering antecedent chains.

1. When manipulating MOs, applying an AO to the problem behavior's reinforcer or an EO for its punisher should get the behavior to _____ in frequency.

2. When manipulating MOs, applying an EO to a desirable behavior's reinforcer or an AO for its punisher should get the behavior to _____ in frequency.

3. A procedure for decreasing a target behavior by delivering a reinforcing stimulus periodically and independently of a target behavior is called _____ .

4. An example of a reinforcer that was applied noncontingently to reduce a problem behavior is _____ . ⇔

5. If we increase the response effort needed to perform a problem behavior, the behavior should _____ in frequency.

6. The method of altering antecedent chains is especially effective if it is used in a link that occurs _____ in the chain.

Altering motivating operations (MOs) involves manipulating the effectiveness of reinforcers or punishers by applying establishing operations or abolishing operations. We can reduce MOs that help maintain a problem behavior, develop ones that encourage alternative behaviors, or apply noncontingent reinforcement. Two other approaches can be used to alter antecedents and improve behavior. First, we can increase the response effort needed to make a problem behavior or decrease the effort to make an alternative behavior. Second, if the problem behavior occurs at the end of a chain, we can use the method of altering antecedent chains by building pauses into the chain or reordering the links.

To prepare for exams, use the following key terms and review questions and the online study guide that's available on this book's companion website at www.wiley.com/college/sarafino.

KEY TERMS

noncontingent reinforcement   response effort

ANSWERS TO CONCEPT CHECKS (CCs)

CC14.1 *Answers:* **1.** functional analysis **2.** overt and immediate, covert and distant **3.** modify existing cues, manipulate motivating operations **4.** S^Δ **5.** competing

CC14.2 *Answers:* **1.** decrease **2.** increase **3.** noncontingent reinforcement **4.** attention **5.** decrease **6.** early

REVIEW QUESTIONS

1. What are the four basic ways to alter antecedents for a target behavior?

2. Describe how you might turn an S^D into an S^Δ for someone who wants to quit smoking cigarettes.

3. What are establishing and abolishing operations, and what effects do they have on reinforcers for a target behavior?

4. Describe the research by Kennedy (1994) on reducing MOs that maintained the problem behaviors of aggression and self-injury. State how AOs were involved.

5. Describe the research by Dyer, Dunlap, and Winterling (1990) on using curricular manipulations to reduce problem behaviors in classroom settings. How were EOs and AOs involved?

6. What is noncontingent reinforcement? Describe the research by Vollmer and his colleagues (1993) on using this method to reduce self-injurious behavior.

7. Describe the research by Carr and Carlson (1993) on manipulating MOs to encourage alternative behaviors in teens with autism who performed serious problem behaviors when shopping.

8. Describe how you might increase response effort for individuals who want to reduce the amount of high-fat, high-calorie foods they eat.

9. Describe the research by Brothers, Krantz, and McClannahan (1994) on increasing paper recycling in a workplace.

10. Describe how you could help a friend stop smoking cigarettes with the methods of building in pauses and reordering links in altering antecedent chains.

RELATED READINGS

• Brothers, K. J., Krantz, P. J., & McClannahan, L. E. (1994). Office paper recycling: A function of container proximity. *Journal of Applied Behavior Analysis, 27*, 153–160.

• Cannella, H. I., O'Reilly, M. F., & Lancioni, G. E. (2006). Treatment of hand mouthing in individuals with severe to profound developmental disabilities: A review of the literature. *Research in Developmental Disabilities, 27*, 529–544.

15

USING BASIC REINFORCEMENT PROCEDURES TO INCREASE A BEHAVIOR

PROLOGUE

Try to envision the work schedule of a creative person, such as a famous novelist. Do you believe that people can't be creative "on call" or at will because creativity happens spontaneously, from a rush of inspiration? Actually, creative people generally work on regular schedules, and many keep track of their progress—for instance, American novelist Ernest Hemingway kept a chart of the number of words written per day (Wallace & Pear, 1977). He would write about 500 words a day, plus or minus 50 or so. Probably his main rewards for writing were self-administered, such as seeing that he had met a daily goal, completed a chapter, or produced writing he evaluated as "high quality." These rewards are examples of automatic reinforcement.

Can feedback from other people reinforce writing in fiction authors, increasing their productivity? An Internet-based intervention showed that it can (Porritt, Burt, & Poling, 2006). Researchers recruited 10 fiction writers who claimed to be dissatisfied with their progress on a current manuscript. Each writer submitted that manuscript and daily updates and writing goals by e-mail to the researchers, who made sure that the new material was thematically related to the prior manuscript. During the intervention, the writers received several forms of reinforcement. First, they could access a personal web page for a graphic display of their progress relative to their goals. Second, each week all writers received a public e-mail acknowledging those who had achieved their goals, and those who met their goals for three successive weeks received special recognition. Third, the writers could also access each others' writing and give critiques—doing so gave them the opportunity to receive critiques of their own work. The study found that the number of words submitted per day was much greater during the intervention than it had been in baseline.

Programmed reinforcement is the cornerstone of methods for changing operant behavior, and using it effectively is essential to the success of interventions. In this chapter, we examine how to identify potential reinforcers and enhance their effectiveness. Then we consider how to administer positive reinforcement and the conditions when negative reinforcement is sometimes used.

IDENTIFYING AND STRENGTHENING POSITIVE REINFORCERS

People differ in their reinforcer preferences, which can change to some degree from one time to the next. Some items or experiences are reinforcers for virtually all people—an example is food or liquid when they are hungry or thirsty. Other reinforcers work for some people, but not for others—this is true mainly for conditioned reinforcers, such as money and social attention. We need to identify positive reinforcers that we can apply to change a person's behavior and use a functional assessment to identify the reinforcers that have maintained the target behavior in the past (Groden, 1989; Iwata et al., 1982; O'Neill et al., 1997). For behaviors that are maintained by more than one reinforcer, we can assess the relative reward value of each reinforcer through functional analysis methods (Lalli & Kates, 1998; Piazza et al., 1998). We can determine what reinforcers to apply in our program and what existing reinforcers we must overcome or eliminate to change the target behavior.

Sometimes the actual consequences that reinforce behavior are surprising and would not be discovered if we simply asked the person or someone else. For example, one study had a woman named Peg, who was profoundly retarded, learn the behavior of placing a marble in a box when prompted to do so (Favell, McGimsey, & Jones, 1978). The only consequence used in teaching the response was placing her arms in splints for 30 seconds after each correct response. When this reinforcer was discontinued, Peg's performance deteriorated sharply; when it was reintroduced, her performance improved quickly and dramatically. If being placed in splints is reinforcing for children who engage in self-injury, it may be that placing their arms in splints to restrain them when they start to harm themselves could increase their self-injurious behavior.

Generating hunches about what consequences will have high reward value can be a useful *first step* in identifying potential reinforcers for a particular individual. We develop these hunches through our everyday observations, noticing, for instance, that many of the things people seem to like are related to broad demographic factors, such as their gender and age. For instance, Americans' reinforcer preferences change with age: Although kindergarten children tend to prefer tangible or consumable reinforcers, such as candy or trinkets, over social reinforcers, such as praise, this preference is reversed by third grade (Witryol, 1971). And survey data on spending patterns suggest that teens value entertainment, clothing, and music recordings as reinforcers (Minton, 1999). But hunches are not sufficient to decide what reinforcers to use in changing a person's behavior. To the extent that the everyday connections we observe between demographic factors and reward value are valid, they reflect overall trends and not necessarily what *a particular person* will value. How can we assess what consequences will serve as strong reinforcers for a given individual?

Table 15.1 *Types of Positive Reinforcers*

Type of Reinforcer	Definition
Tangible and consumable reinforcers	Items that are material objects, such as toys or musical recordings, or that we can eat or drink.
Activity reinforcers	Opportunities to engage in activities we would choose to do when we have a free choice.
Social reinforcers	Interpersonal acts, such as praise or a smile, by other people.
Feedback	Information that assesses or guides our performance of a behavior.
Tokens	Conditioned reinforcers that can be exchanged for a backup reward, such as a tangible or activity reinforcer.

IDENTIFYING POTENTIAL REINFORCERS

Recall from Chapter 5 that we distinguished between *natural reinforcers*, which happen as a normal part of everyday events, and *programmed reinforcers*, which are deliberately provided with the goal of increasing specific behaviors. In that chapter, we also described several types of positive reinforcers; Table 15.1 recaps that information to refresh your memory. As we discuss ways to identify potential rewards we can use to improve a target behavior, *our focus will be on programmed reinforcers*. But keep in mind that motivating operations can influence preference assessments (Gottschalk, Libby, & Graff, 2000; McAdam et al., 2005). For instance, if individuals have had free access to and are satiated for a particular reinforcing stimulus, they may not show a strong preference for that item or event even though it may actually be a strong reinforcer when establishing operations are in effect. As a result, it is important to monitor the person's access to the items or events you are assessing as potential reinforcers and take that information into account.

Interviews and Questionnaires

A straightforward way to identify potential reinforcers is to ask individuals what items or experiences they like or find pleasurable. We can do this by asking probing questions in an interview or by having the person fill out a survey, such as the Preferred Items and Experiences Questionnaire (PIEQ) presented in Figure 15-1. This questionnaire assesses adolescents' and young adults' preferences for dozens of potential reinforcers that are appropriate for that age group and that can be controlled and administered efficiently and ethically. Research findings indicate that the PIEQ has high degrees of reliability and validity (Sarafino & Graham, 2006). And it provides some flexibility to the assessment process by allowing the person to add potential reinforcers that were not listed and clarify the information he or she gives. Other surveys have been developed to assess reinforcer preferences for other age groups, such as students in grades 2 to 5 (Fantuzzo, Rohrbeck, Hightower, & Work, 1991).

Using indirect assessment methods to identify reinforcers has some limitations. First, like all self-report measurements, they may be less accurate than direct methods might be (Northup, 2000). Second, individuals whose verbal abilities are very limited, such as young children and people with developmental disabilities, may be unable to answer the questions even when the items are read to them. And third, people who are extremely depressed may feel that nothing gives them pleasure. When the latter two limitations arise, people who know the individual may be able to answer some of the questions, but it would be better to use direct assessment methods.

Direct Assessment Methods

A good way to determine what consequences will reinforce a person's behavior is through *direct assessment methods*: observing and recording the individual's reactions toward the stimuli when they occur or are available. Direct assessment methods can be carried out in two ways. First, we can use *naturalistic observations*—observing the person in his or her natural environments and recording the frequency and duration of each behavior displayed. This approach identifies high-probability behaviors to serve as activity reinforcers (Premack, 1959, 1965). The

---

PREFERRED ITEMS AND EXPERIENCES QUESTIONNAIRE (PIEQ)
for Adolescents and Adults

Age _____ Sex _____
Ethnic background/race (circle):
Caucasian/White   African American   Hispanic   Other (specify): _____

This questionnaire is designed to find out how much you like or get pleasure from various *items and experiences* in your life. The questionnaire contains lists of items and experiences many people enjoy, and each list has spaces in which *you may add other things* you like that the list left out. Assume that each type of item or experience is *about as good as it could get* for you. For example, if you like "sports or hobby supplies" only a little, assume that the item is one that you would choose at a store if you would get it for free. For each item or experience, *rate* how much you like *to receive, have, or do it*. Use the following scale:

0	**1**	**2**	**3**	**4**
Not at all	A little	A fair amount	A lot	Very much

Items/Experiences	*Ratings*	*Items/Experiences*	*Ratings*
1. *General items:*		5. *Friends'/relatives'* actions toward you:	
New clothes	_____	Praising your	
Sports or hobby supplies . . .	_____	appearance	_____
Games (including software)	_____	competence	_____
Tools or appliances	_____	personality	_____
Jewelry	_____	Giving affection	_____
Beauty supplies	_____	Socializing with you	_____
Music recordings	_____	Inviting you for	
Video recordings	_____	a date	_____
Other: _____	_____	a party or dinner . . .	_____
Other: _____	_____	Other: _____	_____
2. *Snack foods:*		6. *Leisure activities (active participation):*	
Ice cream	_____	Hobbies/arts/crafts	_____
Candy	_____	Gardening	_____
Fruit	_____	Going to museums	_____
Pastry	_____	Hiking/camping	_____
Cookies	_____	Playing athletics	_____
Popcorn or pretzels	_____	Exercising	_____
Potato chips/nachos, etc. . . .	_____	Playing board/table games . .	_____
Pizza	_____	Playing computer games	_____
Other: _____	_____	Playing musical instrument . .	_____
Other: _____	_____	Reading	_____
3. *Beverages:*		Shopping	_____
Milk	_____	Talking on phone to friends . .	_____
Soft drinks	_____	Using Internet/e-mail	_____
Shakes	_____	Spending time with friends . .	_____
Juices	_____	Other: _____	_____
Coffee	_____	Other: _____	_____
Tea (iced or hot)	_____	7. *Leisure activities (inactive/passive):*	
Water	_____	Watching TV	_____
Other: _____	_____	Watching movies	_____
Other: _____	_____	Attending performances of	
4. *Outcomes* for work, chores, or skills		sports	_____
at work, school, or home:		music	_____
Money	_____	drama	_____
Praise/feedback/grades	_____	dance	_____
Input in decisions	_____	Listening to music	_____
Flexible duties	_____	Lying in sun	_____
Special privileges	_____	Taking leisurely bath	_____
Other: _____	_____	Taking a nap/sleeping	_____
Other: _____	_____	Other: _____	_____
		Other: _____	_____

Figure 15-1   The Preferred Items and Experiences Questionnaire (PIEQ) for adolescents and adults to identify potential reinforcers.   *Source:* From E. P. Sarafino & J. A. Graham (2006), Development and psychometric evaluation of an instrument to assess reinforcer preferences: The Preferred Items and Experiences Questionnaire. *Behavior Modification, 30,* 835–847, Appendix. Used by permission.

activities that the person performs most frequently or for the longest amounts of time are likely to be good reinforcers.

The second direct assessment method involves conducting *structured tests*—that is, presenting a previously selected set of stimuli and assessing which ones the person prefers. The stimuli can be presented in two ways: (a) one at a time, while collecting data on how soon the person approaches or reaches for the stimuli, or (b) two or more at a time, while collecting data on which ones the person chooses (Fisher et al., 1992, 1994; Green et al., 1988; Green, Reid, Canipe, & Gardner, 1991; Pace et al., 1985). The 1988 study by Green and her coworkers demonstrated that reinforcers identified through structured tests are more effective in changing children's behavior than ones identified by asking staff who work with the children. Structured tests are especially useful when we try to identify reinforcers for individuals who have severe learning or motor disabilities.

ENHANCING REINFORCER EFFECTIVENESS

It is often useful to strengthen the effectiveness of potential reinforcers, such as by using deprivation as an establishing operation (EO) when food is the reinforcer. We'll consider several other types of EOs that can help enhance reinforcer effectiveness.

One of these EOs involves presenting a small or brief sample of the consequence *before* the behavior occurs to increase the likelihood that the person will make the response and get the reinforcer. This method is called *reinforcer sampling* (Ayllon & Azrin, 1968a). For instance, to encourage a child with mental retardation to repeat a word you say, you might show the child a small bit of candy that he or she will receive after saying the word. Stores selling food sometimes use a similar method, displaying the food or allowing customers to sample items they can buy in larger quantities.

Modeling is another useful EO for increasing reinforcer effectiveness. Individuals who see others receiving and enjoying pleasant consequences for their behavior tend to increase the value they place on these consequences and copy the behavior they saw the other people do. This effect was demonstrated with elementary schoolchildren who had mild retardation (Kazdin, 1973). The researcher had the teacher praise some children in the classroom when they were in their seats and paying attention to their work. Praising attentive behavior in these children increased the attentive behavior of the children who were praised *and* of classmates who were sitting near them.

Explaining or demonstrating the value of a reinforcer is an especially useful EO for token reinforcers, which have no value in their own right. An explanation of a token reinforcement system can work with individuals who can understand it; but if they can't, they'll need to have the tokens associated repeatedly with the backup reinforcers. We can do this by giving these people tokens either for desirable behaviors they already perform readily or for no particular behavior at all and then exchanging the tokens immediately for backup reinforcers.

Public posting of performance data is an effective EO, especially if the reinforcer is feedback or praise. In the opening story of this chapter, we considered the use of public e-mails to writers acknowledging those who had achieved their goals; those who had met their goals for 3 successive weeks received special public recognition (Porritt, Burt, & Poling, 2006). Other studies have shown that public posting of sports skills performance data relative to self-selected goals enhances the effectiveness of feedback for athletes, such as football players (Smith & Ward, 2006; Ward & Carnes, 2002).

Using varied reinforcers is an EO because the potency of a single reinforcer often declines with frequent use. This decline can be because of satiation or because the person habituates to—that is, gets "used to" or "tired of"—a particular reinforcer (Murphy, McSweeney, Smith, & McComas, 2003). For example, children who always receive the opportunity to listen to a snippet of their favorite song as a reward for doing tasks may become less interested in hearing that music, and performance may decline. To overcome this problem, we can have a variety of songs presented in a random order or a "menu" of different reinforcers, such as songs, candy, and watching a video, from which they could choose. (Go to 🔍 and then 📖.)

CLOSE-UP

The Role of Choice in Reinforcement

Do people prefer to have a choice in the reinforcer they receive, and what role does the opportunity for choice play in the reinforcement process? Researchers investigated these questions in a series of studies that tested all or just some of six 3- to 5-year-old boys and girls at a university-based preschool (Tiger, Hanley, & Hernandez, 2006). In each testing session, the children were asked to complete training tasks they had not yet mastered that involved letters, numbers, or words printed on colored worksheets. All reinforcers used were candies (such as M&Ms) or snacks (such as Goldfish) that had been identified with structured tests as being highly preferred by the specific child.

At the start of each session, the children were asked to choose one of three worksheets of different colors that indicated the reinforcement condition—choice, no-choice, or control—under which the child wanted the session to run:

1. *Orange* (choice) indicated that the child would receive praise and get to choose one candy or snack from five identical ones after performing the task correctly.
2. *Blue* (no-choice) indicated that the child would receive praise and one candy or snack item after performing the task correctly. The reinforcer was identical to the ones in the choice condition.
3. *Yellow* (control) indicated that the child would receive praise but no candy or snack after performing the task correctly.

The meanings of the different colors were explained and demonstrated to the children in advance of each session.

The first study in the series simply examined whether the children preferred the choice condition. The number of sessions each of the six children participated in ranged from 8 to 18. Three of the children showed a clear preference for the choice condition across virtually all sessions; two children preferred the choice condition during the first several sessions but not thereafter; and one child showed a clear preference for the no-choice condition across virtually all sessions.

The second study tested only the three children who clearly preferred the choice condition in the first study, but this time the number of reinforcers they could choose from was varied, ranging from 4 to 16 items, across sessions. This study showed that the greater the number of reinforcers the children could choose from, the more they preferred the choice condition.

The last study in the series tested the same three children, and for each child, the number of reinforcers he or she could choose from was set at the number that had produced his or her greatest preference for the choice condition in the second study. But this time, the number of tasks the children needed to complete to receive reinforcement with the opportunity to choose a reinforcer was increased from 2 to 32 across sessions to assess the reward value of the opportunity to choose. In general, the children continued to show a preference for the choice condition until the number of completed tasks reached about 8 for each reinforcement; beyond that point, the children preferred the no-choice condition, which still required only one completed task to receive the reinforcer.

The results of these studies suggest that having the opportunity to choose a reinforcer may have two roles: Choice may be a reinforcer in itself, or it may serve as an EO for the programmed reinforcer, such as candy or snacks.

CONCEPT CHECK 15.1

Check your understanding of the preceding concepts. Remember: The symbol ⇔ means that the answer can vary. Answer the following questions about identifying and strengthening positive and negative reinforcers.

1. An example of a tangible or consumable reinforcer kindergartners tend to prefer over social reinforcers is _____ . ⇔

2. When trying to identify potential reinforcers, we should monitor the target person's access to items and events we are assessing to take into account _____ that may affect preferences.

3. The Preferred Items and Experiences Questionnaire assesses the preferences of individuals in the _____ and _____ age ranges regarding dozens of appropriate potential reinforcers.

4. Two direct assessment methods for identifying potential reinforcers are _____ and _____ .

5. One way other than deprivation to enhance reinforcer effectiveness is _____ . ⇔

HOW TO ADMINISTER POSITIVE REINFORCEMENT

Once we have decided which reinforcers to use in changing someone's behavior, we need to consider exactly how and when to provide these consequences. This section examines a variety of procedures for administering reinforcement.

REDUCE EXTRANEOUS COUNTERPRODUCTIVE REINFORCERS

Picture this scenario. Almost every day for the past month, Ms. Wu, the teacher of a sixth-grade class, has shown her displeasure when one student, Jeff, has come to class late and disrupted ongoing activities. When he arrives, the other students giggle, which reinforces his behavior of arriving late. Ms. Wu will want to eliminate that reinforcement to help stop Jeff's lateness.

Three approaches can stop people from reinforcing someone's problem behavior. One way is simply to describe the situation to them and *ask them to stop reinforcing* the problem behavior. The second approach is to *reinforce them for not reinforcing* the target person's problem behavior. This method was used in the program to reduce the classroom tantrums of a girl named Diane (Carlson, Arnold, Becker, & Madsen, 1968). In addition to giving Diane tokens for nontantrum behavior, the teacher attempted to reduce the social reinforcers she might receive from other students for disruptive behavior. If Diane had a tantrum, she was taken to the back of the room so her classmates couldn't watch her, and the classmates were given candy treats if they didn't turn around. The third approach involves having the *other people share in the rewards* the individual earns for improved behavior. In the intervention for Diane's tantrums, the whole class would have a party if she did not have a tantrum for four half-days in a row. Similar approaches have reduced conduct problems in larger numbers of classroom students by providing token reinforcers to classmates for not socially reinforcing the problem behaviors (Broussard & Northup, 1997; Walker & Buckley, 1972). The backup reinforcers in these programs included snacks, watching cartoons, and taking field trips.

Often behavior analysts have enough control over the target person's environment to eliminate a counterproductive reinforcer. This usually occurs in training sessions with children who have used their problem behaviors, such as oppositional and self-injurious behavior, to escape the sessions. Eliminating escape involves the process of extinction—that is, ending the negative reinforcement from escaping the session. What can we do when we can't control the existing reinforcement? One useful approach is to provide a strong positive reinforcer for an alternative behavior. For instance, a study examined the preferences of five children with developmental disabilities for different reinforcers in training sessions that were conducted before lunch or more than an hour after a meal (Kodak, Lerman, Volkert, & Trosclair, 2007). After complying with training requests, the children could choose their reinforcement: a break from training for 30 seconds (negative reinforcement) or a favorite food item (positive reinforcement). Four of the five children preferred the food—but when the positive reinforcement involved a less desirable food, most of the children tended to choose the break.

WHO WILL ADMINISTER REINFORCEMENT?

In most of the interventions we've discussed so far, reinforcement was administered by teachers, therapists, or parents. If the target person is a young child or severely disabled, this is typically the best arrangement. But many behavior change programs have used peer-administered or self-administered reinforcement when the individuals were able to do so physically and intellectually. How well do these approaches work?

Peer-Administered Reinforcement

Studies have shown that by about 8 to 10 years of age, children who can perform the target behavior can monitor other children's acts and provide reinforcement for correct responses. As an example, an intervention was introduced to improve arithmetic skills in underachieving fifth-grade students, whose classmates served as tutors (Pigott, Fantuzzo, & Clement, 1986). The tutors' jobs included keeping score of the number of math problems each target student completed correctly, comparing that number with the current goal, and deciding whether the student had earned any backup reinforcers. During baseline, the students who were to receive the intervention had averaged only about half as many correct math problems as their classmates. But their performance improved dramatically, equaling that of their classmates by the end of the 3-week intervention and during the next 12 weeks of follow-up assessments. Other studies have shown that programs with same-age children serving as tutors and administering reinforcement can improve on-task behavior in 10-year-old students with attention deficit hyperactivity disorder, reading skills in ninth-graders, and social skills in children with mental retardation (Flood, Wilder, Flood, & Masuda, 2002; Greer & Polirstok, 1982; Lancioni, 1982).

Using peers as tutors and administrators of reinforcement has some advantages. For one thing, the individuals requiring the intervention can receive more frequent and individualized help than is available with standard teaching procedures. Second, the peers who serve as tutors often gain from the experience themselves. For instance, the same target behaviors they are helping others improve, such as socialization with classmates, also tend to improve in themselves (Dougherty, Fowler, & Paine, 1985; Fowler, Dougherty, Kirby, & Kohler, 1986). In addition, the general social relationships among the tutors and tutees also tend to improve as a result of the intervention experiences (Fantuzzo & Clement, 1981; McGee, Almeida, Sulzer-Azaroff, & Feldman, 1992; Pigott, Fantuzzo, & Clement, 1986; Sanders & Glynn, 1977). A potential disadvantage of using peers to administer reinforcement with children is that they appear to be much more liberal than teachers in giving reinforcers. A study found that although child peers correctly gave reinforcers that were earned, they often provided reinforcers that were *not* earned, too (Smith & Fowler, 1984). When children administer reinforcement, the professional who supervises them should monitor their decision making periodically and try to improve it when needed.

Self-Administered Reinforcement

Administering reinforcement to oneself is a cornerstone of self-management programs and is often used as a supplemental method in behavior therapy. This technique has been used in a variety of settings and to change many different behaviors, such as college students' studying and psychotherapy patients' feelings of anxiety (Gross & Drabman, 1982; Jones, Nelson, & Kazdin, 1977).

Several studies have examined the use of self-administered reinforcement in classroom settings. In an intervention to improve third-graders' story writing, the children wrote a story in class each day and assessed it for the number of sentences, verb variations, and modifying words (adjectives and adverbs) it contained (Ballard

& Glynn, 1975). The children had been taught how to use verbs and modifying words, and these features were listed on a chart they could see while they scored their stories for the number of points they earned. Later, they could choose and exchange points for backup reinforcers, such as opportunities to have their stories displayed publicly or to play games or read. Self-reinforcement more than doubled the stories' number of sentences, verb variations, and modifying words over baseline levels. What's more, ratings of the stories by English instructors who knew nothing about the study revealed that the stories written when self-reinforcement procedures were in effect were of higher quality than those written during baseline.

One problem with using self-administered reinforcement is that sometimes people take unearned rewards (Gross & Drabman, 1982; McReynolds & Church, 1973; Santogrossi, O'Leary, Romanczyk, & Kaufman, 1973). It's difficult to know how deliberate these errors are. Although it may seem that the individuals must know they have not performed the behavior, oftentimes these reinforcement errors appear to result from the person simply using very lenient standards in assessing their behavior. Three approaches can help reduce these errors. First, training by using modeling and instruction methods can teach the person to apply more rigorous or accurate standards in assessing personal behavior (Gross & Drabman, 1982; O'Brien, Riner, & Budd, 1983). Second, having the person make his or her target behavior and goals public appears to increase accuracy in self-reinforcement (Hayes et al., 1985). Third, using an accuracy-checking procedure in a behavior change program increases the person's accuracy, especially if there are consequences for inaccuracies (Hundert & Batstone, 1978; McLaughlin, Burgess, & Sackville-West, 1982).

USE EASY CRITERIA INITIALLY

When trying to increase or decrease a behavior, it's tempting to identify the final level of a behavior—the target behavior, alternative behavior, or competing response—you want and expect the person to perform at that level from the beginning of the intervention, using that level as the criterion for each instance of reinforcement. If you are sure the person can perform at that level, this approach may be fine and efficient. However, if you are not sure the person can perform at that level, it is a mistake to use that criterion: doing so may preclude the person's experiencing the reinforcer and its connection to the target behavior.

A better approach is to treat most behaviors we want to increase as if they need some *shaping*, the process we considered in Chapter 10 of identifying an easily achieved *starting response*, which gets reinforced, and gradually raising the criterion for reinforcement. Suppose we wanted to change the frequency of a target behavior—a good way to choose the starting response level is to use the person's baseline performance:

- For a behavioral deficit, the level of the starting response might be higher than the average baseline frequency but lower than the highest frequency.
- For a behavioral excess, the level of the starting response might be lower than the average baseline frequency but higher than the lowest frequency.

There are two common complications to this rule. First, a behavioral deficit may involve a behavior that didn't occur at all in baseline, as often happens when the target behavior is to start a program of regular exercise. Second, a behavioral excess may involve a highly frequent behavior that is dangerous or destructive, which we may not want to allow at any level. In these cases, we need to use our best judgment in selecting the level of the starting response. Once we have implemented the initial reinforcement criterion, we would increase it as quickly as possible without allowing the person to fail to achieve the criteria very often.

IMMEDIATELY REINFORCE EACH INSTANCE OF THE TARGET BEHAVIOR

Whether we are helping someone change an existing behavior or learn a new one, we can maximize the effect of reinforcement by delivering it *immediately after each and every correct response* (Chung, 1965; Michael, 1986; Weiss, Cecil, & Frank, 1973). This is an important rule. The longer we delay giving reinforcement, the less effective it will be in strengthening the behavior.

For positive reinforcement, a delay of just several seconds can reduce its effectiveness. Think, for example, of your telling a joke: If your friends waited several seconds before they laughed, how reinforcing would their social reinforcement be? Sometimes the reinforcers we're using cannot be given immediately—for instance, we are using prizes for improved performance throughout a whole school day. When this happens, we should find ways to *bridge the delay* in time between the behavior and the reinforcer. The best way to bridge the delay is to use additional reinforcers, such as tokens or praise, that can be delivered immediately and then describe instances of the target behavior when we give the prizes. (Go to .)

GRADUALLY THIN AND DELAY REINFORCEMENT

During an intervention to change or teach behaviors, we monitor the person's responses and provide immediate reinforcement. We also try to "schedule" the reinforcement so that it occurs for each and every correct response—a pattern called a **continuous reinforcement (CRF)** schedule. This approach is ideal and produces the fastest progress in modifying behavior. But we cannot monitor people's behavior and provide continuous reinforcement forever, and fortunately, that isn't necessary. We can actually help people maintain the target behavior by phasing out our use of programmed reinforcement after the behavioral goal has been achieved and the target behavior is well established.

How can we phase out the programmed reinforcers we use? We can gradually change the **schedule of reinforcement**—that is, the rule that determines which instances of a response, if any, will be reinforced. Most of our everyday behaviors do not receive natural or programmed reinforcers from other people each time they occur; sometimes people give reinforcement, and sometimes they don't. If you clean your room, people notice and praise you only sometimes.

Thinning the Reinforcement Schedule

At the end of behavior change programs, we try to copy everyday life by employing a procedure called **thinning**, whereby we gradually reduce the *rate* at which the behavior receives programmed reinforcement. For example,

---

CASE STUDY

Walsh's Multiply Controlled Problem Behaviors

How should behavior analysts reduce behavioral excesses that are maintained by more than one reinforcer? Researchers examined this issue with a 7-year-old boy named Walsh who had mental retardation (Borrero & Vollmer, 2006). The target behaviors were aggression, which included hitting and kicking other people, and disruption, such as property destruction. A functional analysis revealed that these behaviors occurred at very high rates, about three to six times per minute, and were maintained by three reinforcers: attention, escape, and tangible items. Multiple reinforcers are not unusual—they're found in about 15% of functional analyses of problem behavior (Hanley, Iwata, & McCord, 2003).

To reduce Walsh's problem behaviors, the researchers implemented methods to deal with each reinforcer. These methods consisted of eliminating each of the reinforcers (the process of extinction), reinforcing alternative behaviors (Walsh making requests and complying with demands), and providing noncontingent attention on a periodic schedule that was independent of the problem behaviors' occurrence. The methods were phased in for each reinforcer separately, and as each reinforcer was addressed, the associated behaviors declined. Eventually the frequency of aggression and disruption was reduced to near zero. These results indicate that to reduce multiply controlled problem behaviors, it is important to eliminate all of the reinforcers for a problem behavior and use other methods that address antecedents and encourage alternative behaviors.

we might start by reinforcing, say, 80% of the correct responses for a few days and then slowly reducing the rate to 60%, 40%, 20%, and 10%. These reductions make the reinforcement schedule progressively "thinner." Reinforcing only some instances of a behavior is called **intermittent reinforcement** or *partial reinforcement*. There are several types of reinforcement schedules, and we'll discuss them and their effects in detail in Chapter 16.

An example of thinning a schedule of reinforcement comes from an intervention to improve the arithmetic skills of a 13-year-old boy named Tom (Kirby & Shields, 1972). Each day, the researchers gave Tom a set of 20 math problems to do in 20 minutes. They reinforced Tom's correct arithmetic answers with simple statements of praise, such as "Good work" or "Great, you got 14 right today." Every couple of days, they doubled the number of problems Tom needed to complete to receive praise, until eventually he was required to produce 16 correct problems. As you can see in Figure 15-2, by the end of this program, the speed at which he correctly computed math problems tripled as compared to his original baseline level. What's more, Tom's on-task behavior increased during the intervention, even though that aspect of his conduct was not specifically reinforced.

A major benefit of thinning the reinforcement schedule at the end of an intervention is that the *target behavior usually becomes even stronger*—that is, it occurs at a higher rate than it did under continuous reinforcement and persists longer when programmed reinforcement is no longer provided. This is one of several ways we'll discuss in Chapter 20 to help maintain appropriate behavior after an intervention ends.

Delaying Reinforcement

Another way to phase out a person's reliance on programmed reinforcers and maintain a target behavior after the intervention ends is to increase the delay between the occurrence of the response and its reinforcer (Stromer, McComas, & Rehfeldt, 2000). As in thinning schedules of reinforcement, delaying reinforcement is begun after the behavior is well established and proceeds in gradual "steps." This approach was used in an intervention to increase elementary schoolchildren's following rules of good classroom conduct, such as working quietly on assignments and following their teachers' instructions (Greenwood, Hops, Delquadri, & Guild, 1974). The

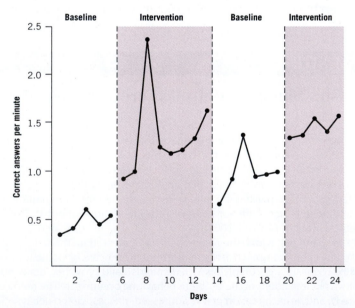

Figure 15-2 Number of correct arithmetic answers Tom achieved per minute during daily sessions in school. *Source:* From F. D. Kirby & F. Shields (1972), Modification of arithmetic response rate and attending behavior in a seventh-grade student. *Journal of Applied Behavior Analysis, 5,* 79–84, Figure 1. Copyright © 1972 Society for the Experimental Analysis of Behavior. Used by permission.

students received continuous feedback regarding their conduct during reading and mathematics sessions, and activity reinforcers were given immediately after each session if their behavior met certain criteria. When the students' good conduct was well established, the activity reinforcers were delayed more and more, so that the students behaved well for longer periods of time before engaging in the reinforcing activities. Follow-up assessments taken a few weeks after the intervention ended showed that the children's good conduct remained at high levels.

SWITCH TO NATURAL REINFORCERS

After we have improved a target behavior in an intervention that included programmed reinforcers, we will want the person's natural environment to take over the reinforcement function. For example, if we use programmed reinforcers to teach children to use mands to ask for things they want, they will use the mands in their everyday lives and get those things. Using the mands will receive natural reinforcement. But most behaviors children learn in interventions don't lead to obvious rewards in everyday life. For instance, a child who learns in school to discriminate among different letters and is publicly awarded a star on a chart for doing so may not receive a reward at home that's so noticeable for making those discriminations there. The reinforcers he or she may receive might be a smile or a bit of praise or feedback, such as "Yes, that's a J." One thing behavior analysts can do at the end of training a task to help maintain the behavior is to anticipate the likely natural reinforcers the person will experience and use them when phasing out the programmed reinforcers.

USING NEGATIVE REINFORCEMENT

Negative reinforcement occurs frequently in our everyday lives and influences much of our behavior. But behavior analysts don't apply it very often to change behavior, because it requires them to place the person in an aversive situation that he or she can reduce by making a specific response. Behavior analysts typically try to minimize the use of aversive events, partly for humanitarian reasons and partly because of undesirable side effects in the person's behavior. When aversive events are used, the target person may become physically aggressive and make efforts to escape or avoid the program and the staff involved in it. In addition, the behaviors rewarded through negative reinforcement are often "superficial." For example, a child may apologize verbally for having been bad, thereby escaping or avoiding punishment, but the apology may be insincere. If it is, insincere behavior is reinforced.

WHEN NEGATIVE REINFORCEMENT IS USED

Behavior analysts sometimes apply negative reinforcement when the aversive situation is not very severe, the target behavior is dangerous or destructive, and other methods to change the behavior have not worked. When aversive conditions are used, the person should receive clear instructions about the link between making the escape or avoidance response and reducing the aversive stimulus, and that response should also receive positive reinforcement. An example of a mild aversive situation is being hungry after being without food for a few hours. We've seen that behavior analysts will use food as a reinforcer before mealtime, which provides negative reinforcement by reducing hunger and positive reinforcement if it tastes good.

An example of the application of negative reinforcement methods comes from a program applied with three young children about 3 years of age to correct a problem behavior called *food refusal* in which a person rejects consuming almost all food items (Ahearn et al., 1996). To illustrate the severity of the behavior, one child named Donna had required tube or intravenous feedings for much of her first 2 years, and the primary nutrition for all three children was formula or milk given from a bottle or cup. In baseline, the children were presented with spoons of food—if they displayed *acceptance* of the food by independently opening the mouth, they received social attention and access to liked toys or activities (positive reinforcement) for a while; if they didn't accept it, the spoon was removed and no positive reinforcement was given.

During the intervention, each child received in separate sessions at mealtimes one of two types of aversive situation—a therapist would:

1. Place a spoon of pureed food at the child's mouth, say "open," and leave the spoon there until the child independently opened his or her mouth enough to accept the food. The child was told at the start of the session, "You have to stay in the chair until you take all of the bites."

2. Physically guide the child's mouth to open by using fingers to apply gentle pressure to the junction of the upper and lower jaws if he or she did not accept the spoon of food when asked to open the mouth. The child was told at the start of the session, "If you do not take a bite, I will have to help you."

Acceptance of the food ended the aversive situation (negative reinforcement) and resulted in the children's receiving positive reinforcement. If a child expelled the food, the therapist either scooped up that food and presented it again or replaced it with another spoon of food. This intervention was quite successful: Food acceptance increased quickly—it soon occurred on nearly 100% of trials and stayed at that level for the remaining dozens of sessions.

HOW TO ADMINISTER NEGATIVE REINFORCEMENT

Several factors can affect how effective negative reinforcement will be in changing behavior. One factor is the *reward value* of the negative reinforcement, which appears to be determined by how much the escape or avoidance behavior reduces the aversive stimulus. The greater the degree to which the behavior removes the aversive event, the more effective the negative reinforcement is (Campbell & Kraeling, 1953). Another factor is how strong the aversive stimulus is: Negative reinforcement is more effective when the behavior reduces a very aversive stimulus than when it reduces a milder one (Piliavin, Dovidio, Gaertner, & Clark, 1981). The last factor we'll consider is delay of reinforcement: The more quickly the behavior results in removing the aversive stimulus, the more effective the negative reinforcement will be (Weiss, Cecil, & Frank, 1973).

TIPS ON USING REINFORCEMENT

The following tips on using reinforcement have been applied by professionals in a wide variety of behavior change interventions. They would be useful in designing almost any program to change operant behavior.

1. Monitor the target person's activities before assessing potential reinforcers so you can take into account the effects of EOs that may affect the results.

2. Use more than one assessment method whenever possible to identify potential reinforcers.

3. Be sure to select reinforcers with strong reward value, and apply them consistently when the person performs the operant target behaviors.

4. Don't use reinforcers that could work against the behavioral or outcome goals. For instance, it's not a good idea to use the opportunity to buy clothing as a reward for reducing the target behavior of spending too much money. This may seem obvious, but I've seen students do things like this.

5. Make sure the person whose behavior is to be changed is aware that the reinforcers are contingent on and are consequences for the target behavior.

6. Use a variety of reinforcers whenever possible, such as allowing the target person to select from a menu the item he or she wants when it has been earned.

7. Be sure to maintain a high degree of reward value during the intervention. If the program is using consumable reinforcers, be careful not to let the target person become satiated on them before a training session is over. To prevent this problem, either switch to other types of reinforcers periodically or give small portions of the food or drink for each instance of reward.

8. Use naturally occurring reinforcers, such as praise, whenever possible, especially near the end of the intervention.

9. Make sure that some kind of reinforcement can be presented immediately after the appropriate behavior and will not disrupt ongoing desirable responses very much.

10. Give reinforcement on a CRF schedule initially, and then thin the schedule after the behavior has become well established.

11. Look for and try to eliminate counterproductive extraneous reinforcers.

12. Check the behavior periodically to make sure the reinforcer is improving it (or maintaining it if it is a desirable act that occurs at an appropriate level).

(Go to .)

STUDY AND REVIEW

SUMMARY

Programmed reinforcement is a critical component of behavior change programs. People differ in their reinforcer preferences, and we need to identify strong positive reinforcers specifically for each person whose behavior we try to change. The various types of positive reinforcers include tangible or consumable items, activities, social reinforcers, feedback, and tokens. We can identify potential reinforcers by using indirect assessment methods, such as self-report instruments like the Preferred Items and Experiences Questionnaire, and direct assessment methods, such as naturalistic observations and structured tests.

The effectiveness of reinforcers can be enhanced by using deprivation as an establishing operation (EO) and the techniques of reinforcer sampling, modeling the reinforcement process, explaining or demonstrating the value of a reinforcer, public posting of feedback, and using varied reinforcers. Giving the person the opportunity to choose a reinforcer may serve as a reinforcer itself or provide an EO for the programmed reinforcer.

Several procedures are available for administering reinforcement. When the target person is a young child or severely disabled, his or her teachers, therapists, or parents administer reinforcement. But with older, more able individuals, reinforcement can be administered by peers or self-administered, especially in self-management programs. Initially in an intervention, it is generally best to reinforce the target behavior immediately after each occurrence on a continuous reinforcement schedule and to apply easy criteria, gradually increasing the standards

CONCEPT CHECK 15.2

Answer the following questions about administering positive reinforcement.

1. When administering reinforcers, we need to _____ extraneous counterproductive rewards.
2. One way to stop other people from reinforcing inappropriate behavior is to _____ . ⟷
3. Self-management programs generally have the _____ person administer reinforcement.
4. Providing reinforcement for each and every correct response is called _____ .
5. Providing reinforcement for only some instances of a behavior is called _____ .
6. Near the end of an intervention, we should switch from using programmed reinforcers to _____ reinforcers.
7. The degree to which escape removes an aversive stimulus affects the _____ value in negative reinforcement.

for reinforcement. After the behavior is well established in the intervention, we should try to reduce the person's reliance on the programmed reinforcer by delaying reinforcement, thinning the schedule of reinforcement by using intermittent reinforcement to reduce the rate at which the behavior is reinforced, and switching to natural reinforcers.

Negative reinforcement can be used to increase an operant behavior, particularly when the aversive situation applied to the person is not severe and the target behavior is dangerous or destructive. The success of negative reinforcement in changing behavior is heightened when the aversive situation is intense and the target behavior reduces the aversive situation a great deal and quickly.

To prepare for exams, use the following key terms and review questions and the online study guide that's available on this book's companion website at www.wiley.com/college/sarafino.

KEY TERMS

continuous reinforcement (CRF)   thinning   intermittent reinforcement
schedule of reinforcement

ANSWERS TO CONCEPT CHECKS (CCs)

CC15.1 *Answers:* **1.** candy or trinkets **2.** motivating operations **3.** adolescent, young adult **4.** naturalistic observations, structured tests **5.** reinforcer sampling

CC15.2 *Answers:* **1.** reduce **2.** ask them to stop **3.** target **4.** continuous reinforcement **5.** intermittent reinforcement **6.** natural **7.** reward

REVIEW QUESTIONS

1. Discuss the example of Peg's surprising reinforcer, and explain why this is important with regard to identifying potential reinforcers.

2. Describe the Preferred Items and Experiences Questionnaire (PIEQ), and discuss how it can be useful in designing an intervention in a high school.

3. Describe the structured tests procedures you could use to identify potential reinforcers for a child with little language skills.

4. What are some ways to enhance reinforcer effectiveness?

5. Describe the research of Tiger, Hanley, and Hernandez (2006) on the role of choice in reinforcement, and explain what the findings mean.

6. What are some ways to reduce extraneous counterproductive reinforcers?

7. What are the pros and cons of using peer-administered and self-administered reinforcement?

8. Discuss the importance of using easy criteria for reinforcement initially in an intervention and providing immediate continuous reinforcement.

9. Describe the research by Borrero and Vollmer (2006) with a boy named Walsh. What do the results mean for designing programs to change behaviors that are maintained by more than one reinforcer?

10. Describe the procedures and utility of thinning and delaying reinforcement.

11. Describe the research by Ahearn and his coworkers (1996) on using negative reinforcement to correct three children's problem behavior of food refusal.

12. What factors affect the effectiveness of negative reinforcement?

RELATED READINGS

- Bellamy, G. T., Horner, R. H., & Inman, D. P. (1979). *Vocational habilitation of severely retarded adults: A direct service technology*. Baltimore, MD: University Park Press.

- Jones, R. T., Nelson, R. E., & Kazdin, A. E. (1977). The role of external variables in self-reinforcement. *Behavior Modification*, 1, 147–178.

16

USING ADVANCED REINFORCEMENT PROCEDURES TO INCREASE A BEHAVIOR

Token Reinforcement Systems
Tokens as Conditioned Reinforcers
Pros and Cons of Using Token Reinforcers
Setting Up and Administering Token Systems

Lottery and Group Contingency Systems
Lotteries
Group Contingencies

Using Intermittent Positive Reinforcement
Intermittent Reinforcement Schedules
Effects of Intermittent Reinforcement
Variations on Reinforcement Schedules

Tips on Using Advanced Reinforcement Procedures

Study and Review

PROLOGUE

The reinforcement systems we've discussed so far have been fairly simple—for instance, a child might receive a bite of a snack or a statement of praise after responding correctly in a training task. Probably most reinforcement systems in applied behavior analysis are straightforward and relatively simple to administer.

But reinforcement systems can be more complex. As an example, an intervention was implemented on the Internet to reduce cigarette smoking in 14 adults who smoked from 15 to 40 cigarettes a day and wanted to quit (Glenn & Dallery, 2007). To confirm the self-reports of the number of cigarettes smoked each day, twice a day the participants also hooked themselves up to a device that measured the amount of carbon monoxide (CO) in their breath, which reflects their smoking status, and e-mailed to the researchers a video clip they made of that measurement.

Part of the intervention's reinforcement system provided vouchers for money for each submitted "negative" CO sample—that is, one having a reading low enough to suggest abstinence. In this system, the first negative CO sample a participant submitted

> resulted in a $3 voucher. The value increased by $0.25 for each successive negative sample. Bonus vouchers ($5) were delivered for every third consecutive negative sample. If a participant failed to provide a sample or submitted a positive sample, the value of the next voucher was reset to $3. After three consecutive negative samples following a reset, the value of the next voucher returned to the highest value previously obtained. (p. 5)

In this phase of the study, the participants could earn as much as $56.25 if they abstained from smoking continuously during that time.

The study had four phases, each lasting 5 days. The first and last phases collected baseline data, when no intervention was used. The two middle phases used interventions, either the voucher system we just discussed or treatment simply with a nicotine patch; half of the participants received the voucher phase before the nicotine patch phase, and half received the reverse order. The results compared the percentages of negative samples received in the two intervention phases: 24% were negative during the voucher phase, and 5% were negative in the nicotine patch phase. Other research has shown that programs combining the nicotine patch and behavioral methods are more effective in helping smokers quit than using either approach alone (Alterman, Gariti, & Mulvaney, 2001).

In this chapter, we examine reinforcement systems that are relatively advanced, having more complicated structures and requiring more planning and administrative effort than the simpler systems we've seen before. We'll start by examining systems of token reinforcement; then we'll consider systems that involve lotteries and group contingencies. We'll end by discussing systems that apply intermittent reinforcement.

TOKEN REINFORCEMENT SYSTEMS

We've seen in earlier chapters that tokens are conditioned reinforcers that can be exchanged for backup items, such as snacks or opportunities to engage in liked activities, and that tokens are not reinforcing in themselves until the person learns to value them. In a **token reinforcement system**, token rewards and backup reinforcers are selected and applied with detailed rules and procedures to change a target behavior.

TOKENS AS CONDITIONED REINFORCERS

Tokens can take many different forms. For instance, they can be poker chips, stars or stamps attached to a chart, check marks in a table, data entries in logs that are like bankbooks, or specially printed paper money. Tokens can be color-coded to reflect some important dimension, such as their value or the type of behavior for which they were earned. Because tokens function like money, they serve as points or credits toward the exchange cost for backup reinforcers.

Since tokens were not originally reinforcing for the person and came to function as reinforcers through learning, they are conditioned reinforcers. Almost any stimulus can become a conditioned reinforcer if it is paired repeatedly with an established conditioned or unconditioned reinforcer. This process happens by way of respondent conditioning: The previously established reinforcer is the unconditioned stimulus, and the originally neutral token becomes the conditioned stimulus. (Go to 🔍.)

PROS AND CONS OF USING TOKEN REINFORCERS

Some reinforcers are fleeting, such as the feedback we get in the movements we make or praise someone gives us. This isn't the case for tokens. Like money, tokens last and can be accumulated, usually enabling us to exchange them for better backup reinforcers. This is one of several advantages of using token reinforcers over using rewards of some other types. Here are some other advantages of using tokens:

Can Modeling Establish Tokens as Reinforcers?

Researchers conducted a study with six preschoolers to determine whether children can learn through modeling to value tokens—small colored plastic discs and short lengths of string—as reinforcers (Greer & Singer-Dudek, 2008). Tests were first done by having the children perform tasks, such as matching identical pictures of common items, using food or the tokens as the consequence for correct responses, which demonstrated that food strengthened their performance but the tokens did not. Thus, initially the tokens were not reinforcers.

The children then experienced a modeling condition in which they could see that a peer was engaged in a task, such as matching pictures of different colored shapes, while they engaged in the same task. The participants and peers had previously mastered these tasks. Although a partition blocked the participants' view of the peer's performance, they could see that the peer received discs or strings for correct responses. The participants did not receive tokens for their performance and did not know that the peers could exchange the tokens for reinforcers. The modeling condition continued until the participant asked for tokens or tried to take some of the peer's discs and strings. Later tests were conducted using the same tasks the children engaged in initially, before the modeling condition, and the participants received the tokens for correct performance. Compared with their original performance, they now responded correctly at far higher rates. Clearly, the tokens were now reinforcers.

- Tokens can be given immediately after a desirable behavior to bridge the delay between performing the behavior and getting the tangible, consumable, or activity reinforcer that has been earned.
- Token reinforcers don't disrupt ongoing activities as much as several other types of reinforcers do.
- Token reinforcers can be applied more easily than other rewards with groups of individuals.
- Because tokens can be exchanged for a variety of attractive backup reinforcers, their reward value is likely to remain high and not highly dependent on a specific establishing operation that currently exists.
- It is possible to build into the system the type of punishment called *response cost*, in which the person loses something of value (tokens earned but not yet spent) after performing an inappropriate behavior.

Advantages like these have made token reinforcers very popular in behavior change programs.

What disadvantages does using tokens have? Because the reinforcement system is complex, staff members need extra training and must keep track of more details than with most other types of reinforcers. Also, tokens that the person actually receives as material objects, such as poker chips, need to have certain practical characteristics: They should not be hazardous—for example, not likely to be mouthed and lead to choking—and should be durable, convenient to store and handle, easy to carry around and dispense, and difficult to steal or counterfeit. Stealing tokens can be a major problem in some settings and must be prevented. It is a good idea to provide some way for each person to store the tokens he or she earns, such as in a purse or wallet, and mark them to identify ownership. Last, children who are very young or have poor cognitive abilities may not be able to understand or keep track of tokens and their connection to backup reinforcers.

SETTING UP AND ADMINISTERING TOKEN SYSTEMS

Three tasks must be carried out before setting up and administering a token reinforcement system. First, we must identify whether each target behavior is a behavioral deficit or an excess and define it clearly. Second, we should conduct a functional assessment to identify existing antecedents and consequences of each behavior. Third, any staff members who will implement the system must receive training so that they will know when a target behavior has or has not occurred and how to administer the consequences. To set up and begin to administer the token system, we need to design various features of the program, starting with deciding the nature of the tokens and the backup reinforcers.

Choosing the Tokens and Backup Consequences

We've seen that tokens can take many different forms, such as poker chips and stars or stamps attached to a chart. They should be easy for staff to dispense, easy and readily available for the target person to accumulate or tally, and secure against loss and theft.

Deciding which backup reinforcers and punishers to include in a token reinforcement system can be accomplished by using material we discussed in Chapter 15. To identify potentially strong backup reinforcers, we use *direct assessment methods*, such as observing the target person's preferences in naturalistic or structured tests, and *indirect assessment methods*, such as by asking the person probing questions in an interview or having the person fill out a questionnaire, like the Preferred Items and Experiences Questionnaire (see Figure 15-1). The larger the variety of reinforcers available for exchange in the token system, the greater the chance that the tokens will maintain their effectiveness and provide strong reinforcement. A related issue to keep in mind is that token reinforcement is more effective when target individuals can select their reinforcers from an array of items rather than having items assigned (Karraker, 1977).

A type of punishment that can dovetail easily into token systems is response cost: The person pays fines, in tokens, for instances of a behavioral excess (behavioral deficits are best handled by withholding reinforcement until the behavior occurs, rather than applying punishment for not performing the behavior). Although problems can arise if a person runs out of points or credits to lose, the reinforcement system can be designed to provide enough credits for appropriate behavior so that the person will almost always have enough to cover any amount of misbehavior he or she performs. Some research findings suggest that punishment by losing tokens is at least as effective in changing behavior as receiving tokens as rewards (Rasmussen & Newland, 2008; Sullivan & O'Leary, 1990). However, punishment methods can create negative feelings in clients, and token systems can be effective without including response cost.

Deciding How to Manage the Consequences

Once we have decided what reinforcers and punishers to include in the program, we will need to keep a large supply of backup reinforcers available and devise a system for managing the distribution of the consequences. To manage the consequences effectively, we should follow a few important guidelines:

- Specify clearly to everyone involved the behavioral criteria for earning tokens and the exchange rates for backup reinforcers. Post the criteria and rates prominently, if possible.
- Be sure to award tokens as soon as possible after the desired behavior occurs.
- Use natural reinforcers, such as praise, in conjunction with dispensing tokens.
- Keep careful and accurate records of the target behaviors performed and the reinforcers dispensed.
- Provide bonus rewards for high-level performance, if possible.

In addition, we need to arrive at answers for certain critical questions in advance. These questions begin each of the next few paragraphs.

Who will administer consequences?   Administering consequences in a token system involves delivering and keeping track of the tokens each target person earned or lost and the backup reinforcers or punishers received. The individuals bearing these responsibilities will need to monitor the target behaviors closely, record data carefully, and deliver tokens promptly. Staff members of the organization or institution—for example, attendants, teachers, or supervisors—usually have these responsibilities. When more than one staff member can administer consequences, each member should have a separate role in the process and know what that role is (Ayllon & Azrin, 1968b). Otherwise they may duplicate each other's actions or fail to act, thinking that another staff member will do it. If the token system includes self-management methods, there must be ways to check the accuracy of the data and the judgments the target person makes regarding consequences (Hundert & Batstone, 1978; McLaughlin, Burgess, & Sackville-West, 1982).

How many tokens will a behavior earn?   Several factors should be taken into account when deciding the number of tokens a behavior will earn. First, the laws of supply and demand are relevant (Ayllon & Azrin, 1968b). Behaviors or chores that are less attractive than others—perhaps because they are relatively time-consuming, strenuous, fearful, or tedious to do—may require more tokens to enhance the reward value of the reinforcer. And there is a fairness issue, too. People tend to feel that they deserve more pay for performing less attractive behaviors. So, for example, in a token system in which college students earned tokens for doing chores in their residence, the number of tokens each student received for completing a task was directly related to the amount of time the chore took per week to do (Johnson, Welsh, Miller, & Altus, 1991). Second, target individuals with lesser abilities to learn or perform the needed behaviors may be given more tokens per behavior or more opportunities to exchange them for backup reinforcers. Third, it is sometimes useful to reinforce the behavior with more tokens in the first few days of a person's participation in a token system than later in the program. Fourth, after the behaviors have become well established, the schedule of reinforcement can be thinned to an intermittent schedule (Stainback, Payne, Stainback, & Payne, 1973).

What will the exchange rates be?   Decisions about the number of tokens needed to buy each backup reinforcer depend on four factors. First, one factor is the number of tokens target individuals can earn for each behavior. If the number of tokens earned per behavior is small, the cost of the backup reinforcers should be low—and vice versa. Second, some reinforcers cost the program money to buy. The number of tokens needed to get a particular reinforcer should be related to the monetary cost of that item. Third, the laws of supply and demand may apply again. Some reinforcers are in greater demand than others; those with high demand and low supply can cost more than those with low demand and high supply. Fourth, some backup reinforcers may have more therapeutic relevance than others. Charging a relatively small number of tokens for these reinforcers can encourage individuals to choose them. For example, an activity reinforcer of going on a shopping trip might cost only a few tokens if a target person can learn valuable skills from that experience.

How often will backup reinforcers be available?   At the start of a token system, exchanging tokens for backup reinforcers should occur frequently enough to establish the power of the token system. When deciding how often and when tokens can be redeemed for backup reinforcers, one factor to consider is the intellectual ability of the target individual. Very young children and low-functioning individuals, such as people with mental retardation, will probably need to have the backup reinforcers available at least twice a day, especially when they first enter the program. For other children, token exchanges for backup reinforcers can occur once or twice a day initially; but after the first few days, reinforcer availability can be reduced gradually toward the goal of allowing the children to redeem their tokens infrequently, in some cases only once a week. The frequency with which tokens can be redeemed should be based on the characteristics of the individuals who receive them and on the rate that maintains the target behavior best.

Phasing Out the Token Program

After the behavior is well established, we can phase out the token program in the same ways we've discussed with other reinforcement systems. First, we can switch to natural reinforcers. Second, we can delay opportunities to redeem tokens. Third, we can decrease the number of tokens a target behavior earns or increase the number of tokens required to buy backup reinforcers. These approaches can be used separately or in combination.

LOTTERY AND GROUP CONTINGENCY SYSTEMS

Most of the interventions we have seen so far in this book have involved *individual contingencies*—that is, the reinforcers received were contingent on the learner's own behavior and did not depend on the performance of other individuals. But it is possible to arrange contingencies in ways that involve the performance of groups of people. We'll discuss some of these approaches in this section.

LOTTERIES

In a **lottery**, all eligible individuals are entered in a drawing to determine one or more prizewinners on the basis of chance. In behavior change programs, eligibility to enter lotteries is based on behavior, and the lottery can apply to an individual or a group of people. Entering individuals into a lottery is often a simple process, such as giving one entry to each person whose behavior meets a certain criterion. But methods to enter people into a lottery can be more complicated—for example, by allowing more than one entry per person on the basis of the number of points (tokens) he or she earned and whether or not the behavior improved since the last lottery (Sarafino, 1977). Lotteries are useful to thin reinforcement schedules or when constraints, such as costs, make it difficult to provide attractive rewards to all eligible people.

Lotteries can be used in many different settings, including schools, psychiatric hospitals, and workplaces. For instance, a lottery intervention was introduced to improve the courteousness of human service staff when they interacted with clients (Johnson & Fawcett, 1994). The staff first received training in ways to be courteous, such as by addressing clients by name and stating reasons for requesting information. In the lottery, assessments of the staff members' courteousness determined how many entries they had in a weekly drawing for a $10 cash prize. As Figure 16-1 shows, the training alone increased courteous behavior substantially, and the lottery increased it a good deal more and made it more consistent. Other lottery interventions have reduced employee absenteeism and unnecessary use of automobiles at workplaces (Foxx & Schaeffer, 1981; Pedalino & Gamboa, 1974; Wallin & Johnson, 1976) and cocaine use by drug abusers (Ghitza et al., 2008).

A potential problem with lotteries is that the likelihood of winning a reinforcer may be set too low, causing performance to suffer. Because very little research has addressed this issue, we can't give specific guidelines on setting the chances of winning. One study found, for example, that reducing the chance of winning to 25% impaired the performance of 9- and 10-year-old children in an intervention to improve their math skills in school (Martens et al., 2002). It's likely that low chances of winning are tolerated well by individuals who are older and have high intellectual ability, and when the reinforcers given for winning are strong and the chances are not reduced too quickly.

GROUP CONTINGENCIES

In a **group contingency**, whether *members of a group* receive consequences depends on the performance of all or some of the members (Massetti & Fabiano, 2005). A common example is when restaurant workers who use a group contingency share in pooled tips. Another example is a trash recycling program in some regions of the United States where residents can earn points based on the amount of trash the whole community recycles (Bauers, 2009). The points can be redeemed for gift cards and other items. The structures of group contingencies can vary; here are three types (Litow & Pumroy, 1975):

1. *Independent*, which provides reinforcement only to the members who meet a behavioral criterion.
2. *Dependent*, in which rewards given to the entire group depend on performance of one or some members.
3. *Interdependent*, which requires that the group as a whole or each and every member meet a criterion before rewards are given to all of them.

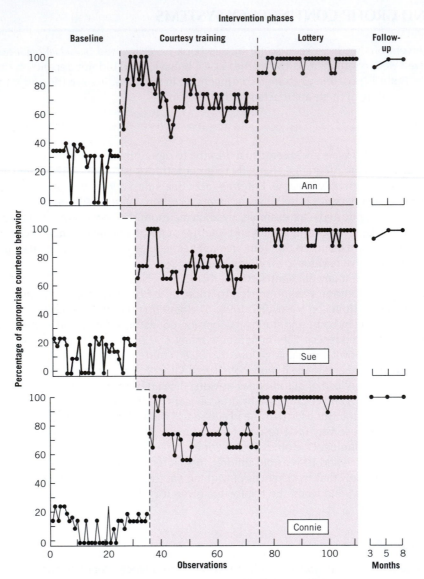

Figure 16-1 Performance of courteous behaviors by three staff members during interactions with clients, as reflected in the percentage of the 30 behaviors they received training to use in the courtesy training phase. The data for the baseline, courtesy training, and lottery phases were collected over a 5-month period in a multiple-baseline design. *Source*: From M. D. Johnson & S. B. Fawcett (1994), Courteous service: Its assessment and modification in a human service organization. *Journal of Applied Behavior Analysis*, 27, 145–152, Figure 1. Copyright © 1994 Society for the Experimental Analysis of Behavior. Used by permission.

An intervention that used a group contingency for reinforcement was conducted with boys whose prior behavior indicated they were at risk for becoming habitual delinquents (Alexander, Corbett, & Smigel, 1976). The boys were living at a treatment center and were supposed to go to a high school during the day, but they skipped nearly half of their classes. To increase the boys' class attendance, lunch money was used as a reinforcer. They had been accustomed to receiving lunch money from the center with no strings attached. But a few weeks before the intervention began, the center started packing sack lunches for them instead. Then the boys were told that they could get lunch money instead of sack lunches if they attended all their classes. At first this reinforcer was on an individual contingency: If a boy attended all his classes for the day, he received the money for the next day. Later, the lunch money was offered on an interdependent group contingency: The boys would receive the money only if *all* the boys attended *all* their classes for the preceding day. Under the individual contingency, attendance increased to an average of about 80% of the classes; but with the group contingency, the boys' average attendance increased to nearly 100%.

Another way group contingencies can be used is to divide the individuals into *teams* that compete with one another for reinforcers. This approach has been used with employees (Kortick & O'Brien, 1996) and schoolchildren (Swain, Allard, & Holborn, 1982). The school intervention was implemented to improve first- and second-grade schoolchildren's toothbrushing. Each class was divided into teams to play the "Good Toothbrushing Game," in which four children from each team were chosen randomly each day to have their oral hygiene assessed with a standardized procedure. All members of the class team with the best oral hygiene score got "scratch 'n' sniff" stickers and had their names posted. The children's oral hygiene scores improved markedly during the intervention and remained quite good at a follow-up assessment 9 months later.

Advantages and Disadvantages of Group Contingencies

Group contingencies have three main advantages over individual contingencies in behavior change programs. For one thing, for programs that apply to more than a few people, group contingencies are easier to administer—it's simpler to monitor and keep records on behavior and to dispense reinforcers for a group as a whole than to carry out these tasks for each person in the group. Second, group contingencies have built-in incentives to prevent members of the group from reinforcing one another's inappropriate responses.

Third, group contingencies often promote desirable side effects in the social behaviors of the group members (Greenwood & Hops, 1981). For example, a program was implemented in which elementary school classmates were assigned to teams that were divided into pairs of students to tutor each other in spelling (Kohler & Greenwood, 1990). After the children received training in tutoring, they earned points for practicing these skills. The only reinforcer the teacher provided for tutoring was announcing at the end of each day which team, having earned the most points that day, was the winner. With this contingency, the children not only performed the tutoring skills they were trained to do, but some students added helpful techniques they had not been trained to use, such as spelling the word more than once when correcting a teammate's errors. In a similar vein, another study found that, among elementary schoolchildren, group contingencies for candy rewards produced greater cooperation than individual contingencies did (Williamson, Williamson, Watkins, & Hughes, 1992).

But two cautions should be pointed out. First, contingencies that use the overall group's performance to determine consequences need to guard against a few individuals accounting for almost all of the group's score and some individuals receiving rewards while performing very poorly. Second, group contingencies can sometimes have negative effects—for instance, by leading to negative peer-pressure tactics, such as threats or scolding (Greenwood & Hops, 1981; Romeo, 1998). Although it isn't entirely clear why these negative tactics occur, they are probably more likely when the program consequences include group *punishment* if behavioral criteria are not met. Some research indicates that design features of the program can minimize these negative behaviors, such as if the reinforcers and goals are selected randomly from sets of acceptable ones (Popkin & Skinner, 2003). Keep in mind also that a program can be a hybrid: Some behaviors can be rewarded under group contingencies and others under individual contingencies.

Setting Up and Administering a Group Contingency

To set up an effective group contingency, we must identify and clearly define the target behaviors and determine and apply strong reinforcers, using procedures we discussed in this and earlier chapters. We must also decide whether the group members will all receive the same reward or individual ones—a single reinforcer may not have high reward value for some individuals. The next step is to set reasonable performance criteria, making sure that each member of the group can achieve them and be reinforced. Then we need to select the most appropriate type of group contingency—for instance, a dependent group contingency may be most appropriate if the program goal is to improve the performance of one or a few individuals, and an interdependent group contingency may be best when the goal is to improve the behavior of all group members. Keep in mind that the overall design of the program can include methods to manage antecedents and consequences to increase some behaviors and decrease others. (Go to .)

USING INTERMITTENT POSITIVE REINFORCEMENT

We saw in Chapter 15 that once a target behavior is learned and well established under a *continuous reinforcement* (CRF) schedule, we can introduce procedures for *thinning* (sometimes called *fading* or *leaning*) the schedule of programmed reinforcement. Thinning is generally done *gradually* rather than suddenly, to guard against deterioration of the behavior. If reinforcement is reduced too quickly, the behavior may decline rapidly, necessitating the reintroduction of a CRF schedule to reestablish the behavior. How gradual should the thinning be? There are no fixed rules. Sometimes the reinforcement schedule can be thinned very quickly; at other times, the process takes weeks (Sulzer & Mayer, 1972). Chances are, thinning can progress rapidly for people who can understand the need to reduce the rate of reinforcement and have some control—perhaps through negotiations—over how quickly these reductions take place.

Probably the most common approach for thinning a schedule of programmed reinforcement is to reduce the percentage or *ratio* of correct responses that receive rewards. In a CRF schedule, 100% of correct responses receive reinforcement. In a program to teach a child to name various items in a set of objects, researchers thinned the reinforcement schedule, starting

> by *skipping* reinforcement for about one correct response out of four. As time went by, more and more trials went unreinforced until eventually the child had to label the whole set before the … reinforcer was delivered. (Sulzer & Mayer 1972, p. 109)

CONCEPT CHECK 16.1

Check your understanding of the preceding concepts. Remember: The symbol ⇔ means that the answer can vary. Answer the following questions about reinforcement systems involving tokens, lotteries, and group contingencies.

1. An example of a type of token that could be used in a token reinforcement system is _____ . ⇔
2. People can learn to value tokens as reinforcers through _____ and _____ processes.
3. Two problems that can occur with token reinforcement systems are _____ and _____ .
4. Two of the several features that must be decided to set up and administer a token reinforcement system are _____ and _____ . ⇔
5. A _____ is a reinforcement system in which a person's likelihood of receiving a reward for a correctly performed behavior is determined by chance.
6. An employer who gives special privileges to an entire department if they all come to work on time is using a type of reinforcement system called a(n) _____ group contingency.

This thinning process began by reducing reinforcement to about three of every four correct responses, or 75%, by skipping one reward. When the schedule was thinned to 50%, the child had to name two objects correctly to get a reinforcer. Gradually, the child had to name more and more objects correctly for each instance of reinforcement. Other strategies can also be used to thin reinforcement schedules, and here are two examples:

1. *Decreasing days when rewards are available.* An intervention trained children to identify and request nutritious snacks, such as fruit, to receive reinforcers of various types on a CRF schedule (Baer, Blount, Detrich, & Stokes, 1987). In the process of thinning, the children continued to get reinforcement on a CRF schedule on days when rewards were made available; but the percentage of *days* when rewards were available was reduced from 100% of the days to 67% and then to 33%.

2. *Decreasing frequency of assessment.* An intervention was conducted to discourage a boy from stealing the belongings of other students in his classroom (Rosen & Rosen, 1983). Initially, token reinforcers and punishers were administered by assessing his stealing every 15 minutes, but this schedule was thinned by increasing the *interval* between assessments to once every 2 hours.

Decreasing the rate of reinforcement is a flexible process that can progress at different speeds and follow different strategies. To determine whether the thinning procedure we are using is advancing too quickly, we monitor the person's performance carefully and frequently. If the behavior seems to be regressing, we may be reducing the reinforcement rate too quickly and hence may need to slow the pace.

INTERMITTENT REINFORCEMENT SCHEDULES

Thinning a reinforcement schedule means that only some instances of the behavior will be reinforced, and the schedule of programmed reinforcement is *intermittent* or *partial*. The rule governing which instances of the behavior are reinforced is called an **intermittent reinforcement schedule** or *partial reinforcement schedule*. For example, a rule in many workers' lives specifies that they will be paid every Friday. Although the rules governing intermittent reinforcement schedules in our everyday lives are sometimes stated or clear, often they are not. The matrix in Figure 16-2 outlines the four basic intermittent reinforcement schedules; the two in the top row are *ratio schedules*, and the two in the bottom row are *interval schedules*. Let's examine these types of reinforcement schedules.

Ratio Schedules

In **ratio schedules**, the rule for administering each instance of reinforcement is based on *the number of correct responses* made since the last reinforcer was given. This rule can describe one of two *patterns*: The number of responses required for reinforcement can be *fixed*, or constant, for every instance of reinforcement; or it can be

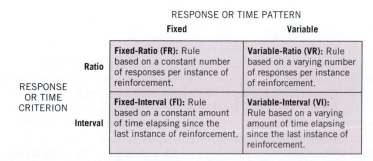

| | | RESPONSE OR TIME PATTERN | |
		Fixed	Variable
RESPONSE OR TIME CRITERION	Ratio	**Fixed-Ratio (FR):** Rule based on a constant number of responses per instance of reinforcement.	**Variable-Ratio (VR):** Rule based on a varying number of responses per instance of reinforcement.
	Interval	**Fixed-Interval (FI):** Rule based on a constant amount of time elapsing since the last instance of reinforcement.	**Variable-Interval (VI):** Rule based on a varying amount of time elapsing since the last instance of reinforcement.

Figure 16-2   Four basic types of intermittent reinforcement schedules: fixed ratio, variable ratio, fixed interval, and variable interval. Each reinforcement schedule is defined by a rule based on two factors: (a) the response or time *criterion* (the number of responses or elapsed time) since the last instance of reinforcement, and (b) the response or time *pattern* (fixed or variable) required for the criterion.

variable, changing from one instance to the next. For variable schedules, the number of responses needed for each instance of reinforcement is determined with a random or near-random process, such as by using a table of random numbers or a lottery procedure.

In a **fixed-ratio (FR)** schedule of reinforcement, the criterion for the individual's receiving each instance of reinforcement is performance of a constant number of correct responses. Typically, the reinforcer is given immediately after the individual makes the last response in the fixed criterion. An everyday example of an FR schedule is the practice of factories to pay employees on a piecework basis—garment workers might have to sew five pullover shirts to earn one dollar. Although these workers are not paid immediately, they probably keep track of their earnings. In school, a child might receive a token reinforcer after spelling five new words correctly. In these examples, the ratio of the number of responses (shirts sewn or words spelled) for each reinforcer is 5:1, which is abbreviated as FR 5; a CRF schedule is an FR 1, but it isn't intermittent. People's rate of responding for FR intermittent reinforcement is usually very high because the more rapidly they respond, the more rewards they'll get.

The process of thinning reinforcement to an FR schedule was used in an intervention to improve a boy's arithmetic skills by providing praise, such as "Good work," for correctly solved math problems (Kirby & Shields, 1972). The number of correct math problems required for each statement of praise was doubled every couple of days, until an FR 16 schedule was reached. In FR schedules, the rule governing when reinforcement is given is often stated explicitly or is easy for the person to detect after many instances of reward. Of course, people with low intellectual ability may not notice the pattern or understand it when told; still, the schedule seems to affect their behavior.

In a **variable-ratio (VR)** schedule, the rule governing when reinforcement will be given requires an unspecified and changing number of correct responses for each instance of the reward. As with FR schedules, the reinforcer is typically given immediately after the individual makes the last response in the varying criterion. Thus, for a series of six instances of reinforcement, the person might be required to perform the following number of responses: 4, 12, 23, 8, 11, and 2, respectively. This is an example of a VR 10 schedule because the *average* number of responses required for reinforcement is 10. Notice that the required number of responses varies from one instance of reinforcement to the next. VR schedules keep the person guessing about whether or when a payoff will happen because instances of reinforcement are unpredictable. But responding rapidly increases the frequency of reward. As a result, people usually respond at high rates for VR reinforcement.

Gambling pays off on VR schedules. When you are playing a slot machine for a few hours, for instance, the number of times you need to perform the behavioral chain of dropping a coin into the slot and pulling the lever varies from one jackpot to the next—the machine is programmed to ensure this. Telemarketing work provides another example of behavior being reinforced on a VR schedule: Telephoning people to sell products or services earns a commission for each sale, but the number of calls the person has to make before selling something varies; which call will lead to a sale is unpredictable.

Interval Schedules

In **interval schedules**, the rule for administering each instance of reinforcement is based on the *elapsed time* since the last reinforcer was dispensed. A reinforcer is given for the *first correct response* following some period of time since the last reinforcement occurred. In other words, reinforcement is not available for a period of time after each reward is given. But when reinforcement becomes available, the first correct response is reinforced. As with ratio schedules, the specific rule for an interval schedule can describe one of two *patterns*: The amount of time when reinforcement is not available can be *fixed*, or constant, for every instance of reinforcement; or it can be *variable*, changing from one instance to the next. For variable schedules, the timing when reinforcement is unavailable is determined with a random or near-random process, such as by using a table of random numbers or a lottery. To compare interval and ratio schedules, refer to Figure 16-2. Thinning reinforcement to an interval schedule is generally done by gradually extending the time when reward is not available.

A **fixed-interval (FI)** schedule makes reinforcement unavailable for a constant amount of time after each instance of reinforcement. The first correct response the individual makes after that time has elapsed is reinforced immediately, and the next interval begins. Because the time period is fixed, people and animals usually can learn to predict fairly accurately when reinforcement will be available again. They come to respond slowly or not at all early in the interval and then increase their rate of responding toward the end of the interval. FI schedules are typically not used for behaviors that should occur at high and stable rates.

There are many examples of FI schedules in everyday life. For instance, checking my (snail) mail is rewarded on an FI schedule because it is delivered at the same time every weekday (getting mail I want is a reward). An employee going to work on paydays is rewarded for doing so by getting paid in cash or by check. These are examples of FI 24-hours (or 1-day) and FI 1-week schedules. Notice that with interval schedules, the abbreviation must specify the time units, such as seconds, minutes, or days. Another everyday example of an FI schedule entails watching TV. If you're watching a show you enjoy and don't enjoy the commercials, reinforcement for looking at the TV is not available during the time commercials are aired. Because commercial interruptions tend to have a somewhat standard duration, you can leave the room or engage in some other activity for about that amount of time and start looking at the TV again toward the end of the interval.

In a **variable-interval (VI)** schedule, the rule governing when the reinforcer will not be available involves an unspecified and changing amount of elapsed time after each instance of the reward. As with FI schedules, the reinforcer is given immediately after the individual makes a single correct response after reinforcement is again available, and the next interval begins. Thus for a series of, say, six instances of reinforcement, the reward might be unavailable for the following amounts of time: 4, 12, 23, 8, 11, and 2 minutes. This would be an example of a VI 10-minutes schedule because the *average* time that reinforcement was unavailable is 10 minutes. VI schedules, like VR schedules, make instances of reinforcement unpredictable and keep the person guessing about whether or when a payoff will happen. But in VI schedules, responding at a continuously rapid rate will not speed up the reinforcement. As a result, people tend to respond at a steady, moderate rate when this type of schedule is in effect.

Behavior analysts used a VI reinforcement schedule in an intervention to increase grade-schoolers' sitting in their seats in class (Wolf et al., 1970). The teacher set a kitchen timer for varying amounts of time on a VI 20-minutes schedule and provided token reinforcement for students who were in their seats when the timer sounded. An everyday example of a VI schedule can be seen in grilling steaks on a barbecue. The amount of time needed to cook steak to the desired doneness can vary a lot, depending on how hot the coals are, how cold the meat was before it went on the grill, and how thick the steak is. Another everyday example of a behavior being reinforced on a VI schedule is looking to see when a red traffic light turns green. If you arrive at an unfamiliar light or a familiar light after it has already turned red, you don't know when it will change. And looking at it a lot won't make it turn green faster! When it turns green, looking at it is reinforced by being able to proceed.

EFFECTS OF INTERMITTENT REINFORCEMENT

So far, we have considered the effects of intermittent reinforcement on behavior rather broadly. Next we'll look at the effects of the four basic intermittent reinforcement schedules in more detail, examining them first while the schedules are in force during an intervention to correct a behavioral deficit and then after reinforcement has been discontinued—that is, after the intervention ends. Our discussion of the effects of various schedules of reinforcement on behavior during interventions assumes that the target responses have progressed to the point of being well established and the reinforcement schedules have been thinned. In general, all intermittent reinforcement schedules produce higher rates of responding than CRF schedules do while they are in force.

Effects of Ratio Schedules During an Intervention

Ratio schedules produce very high rates of responding while they are in force. Response rates are often higher under VR than FR reinforcement schedules, as Figure 16-3 illustrates. The two cumulative graphs present hypothetical data contrasting the usual kinds of effects of FR and VR schedules, as we might find in an intervention to increase a child's performance in reading words from a list.

Notice three features of these graphs. First, the two reinforcement schedules are calibrated to equalize the average number of responses, 20, required for reinforcement. By equating the two schedule types in this way,

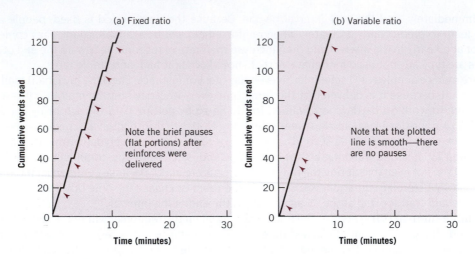

Figure 16-3 Illustration of hypothetical *cumulative graphs* of the number of words a child might read correctly in interventions using (a) a *fixed-ratio* (FR 20) reinforcement schedule or (b) a *variable-ratio* (VR 20) reinforcement schedule. The arrowheads pointing at the plotted lines indicate instances of reinforcement.

we can compare their effects without being concerned that one schedule provides more reinforcement than the other. Second, although the slope is steep in both cases, the VR graph is somewhat steeper than the FR graph. In cumulative graphs, the steeper the slope, the higher the response rate. Third, individuals receiving reinforcement on FR schedules tend to pause briefly in their responding, usually just after obtaining the reward (Schlinger, Derenne, & Baron, 2008). These **post-reinforcement pauses** tend to be longer when many responses are required for each reward than when few responses are required. Although it's tempting to think that these pauses result because the individual is using the reinforcer, such as eating a food reward, there are two reasons to think other factors must be involved. First, the pauses don't usually happen with VR schedules. Second, pauses also occur with reinforcers of other types, such as praise and money. It's as if the individual sees completing each fixed number of responses for a reward as a "goal" and "takes a break" after achieving each one.

Research using ratio schedules has shown that increasing the number of responses required for each instance of reinforcement increases people's response rates, within limits (Schroeder, 1972; Stephens, Pear, Wray, & Jackson, 1975). But at some point, the number of responses may become too large, and the behavior may begin to deteriorate. This is called **ratio strain** because the ratio of responses to reinforcement has become so large that the behavior isn't reinforced enough to be maintained (Miller, 1980). Although we can't predict exactly when ratio strain will happen, it appears to depend on several factors, such as the reward value, how gradually the thinning procedures advanced, and how much effort the response requires. Still, individuals often will perform at very high rates for fairly modest reinforcers. For instance, researchers used VR token reinforcement to increase exercising on a stationary bicycle on the part of obese and nonobese 11-year-old boys (De Luca & Holborn, 1992). The backup reinforcers included a kite, a model car, a flashlight, and comic books. The schedule of reinforcement was thinned for each boy to at least a VR 100 schedule, in which the boy earned one point for every 100 pedal revolutions on the bicycle, with no deterioration in the behavior. What's more, when the 30-minute exercise sessions were over, the boys often asked if they could continue exercising to "get more points."

Effects of Interval Schedules During an Intervention

Figure 16-4 illustrates that interval schedules produce moderately high response rates that are stronger and more constant with VI than with FI schedules. Like the graphs for ratio schedules, these two cumulative

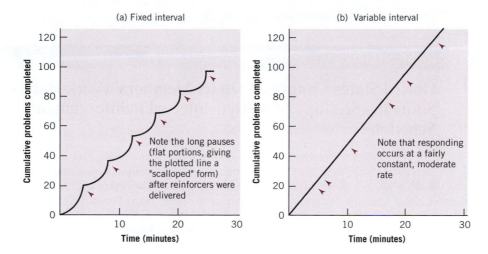

Figure 16-4   Illustration of hypothetical *cumulative graphs* of the number of arithmetic problems a teenager might complete correctly in interventions using (a) a *fixed-interval* (FI 4 minutes) reinforcement schedule or (b) a *variable-interval* (VI 4 minutes) reinforcement schedule. The arrowheads pointing at the plotted lines indicate instances of reinforcement. Notice in graph (a) that the scallops produced by not responding become more pronounced over time as the individual learns that responding early in an interval will not lead to reinforcement.

graphs present hypothetical data contrasting the usual effects found with FI and VI schedules. In this case, the intervention involves increasing the number of arithmetic problems a teenager completed in half-hour sessions. Notice that the two reinforcement schedules are calibrated to equalize the average interval length, 4 minutes, when reinforcement is not available. Once again, equating the two schedule types in this way enables us to compare effects without being concerned that one schedule provided more reinforcement than the other.

An important phenomenon tends to occur with FI schedules. As the cumulative record in Figure 16-4a shows, FI schedules produce a prolonged pause in responding after each instance of reinforcement, causing the graph to resemble a series of *scallops*, or arcs. These pauses occur because the individual learns that the response will not lead to reinforcement soon after a reward was received. But after a while, responding begins to accelerate because the end of the interval is approaching and reinforcement will be available again. You've surely seen this in school: Students are assigned to write a paper or prepare for a test and wait to do the work until the deadline approaches; then, they work at a faster and faster rate. The pauses in response rate with FI schedules make them less desirable than VI schedules in many interventions. And although VI schedules don't produce response rates that are as high as those produced with ratio schedules, they have a practical advantage for use in certain settings, especially in classrooms: Administering the schedule doesn't require us to keep track continuously of all instances of the target behavior. Keeping track of more than one person's behavior simultaneously and continuously is difficult and time-consuming. (Go to ❧.)

Effects of Reinforcement Schedules After the Intervention Ends

After an intervention ends and the programmed reinforcement given in the behavior change program ends, the everyday life of the person may provide little or no natural reinforcement for the target behavior. If this happens, ratio strain or extinction may cause the improved behavior to deteriorate. We saw in Chapter 6 that giving reinforcement on an intermittent schedule rather than a CRF schedule makes the behavior more persistent, more *resistant to extinction*. This effect has been found in a large body of research with animal and human participants (Kazdin & Polster, 1973; Kimble, 1961; Lewis, 1960; Lewis & Duncan, 1956; but see Nevin, 1988). What's more,

CASE STUDY

United States Congress—Do Its Members' Work Habits Show the Scallops of a Fixed-Interval Reinforcement Schedule?

Members of the U.S. House of Representatives are elected for a 2-year term in each even-numbered year, and there are two major reinforcers for their work: completing a body of legislation by the end of each year and getting reelected to office. Each of these reinforcers is on an FI schedule—the first is an FI 1-year schedule, and the second is an FI 2-year schedule. Do graphs of the frequency of bills being enacted by Congress show the scallops that are characteristic of FI schedules?

Researchers examined this question by looking at annual data published in the *Congressional Record* from 1971 to 2000 (Critchfield et al., 2003). Figure 16-5 presents those data graphically, revealing two patterns: The enactment of bills in each year starts out slowly and speeds up later—showing the scallops—and the number of bills passed was consistently higher in election years than in nonelection years. The first of these patterns reflects the effects of the FI 1-year schedule, and the second pattern reflects the FI 2-year (election) schedule.

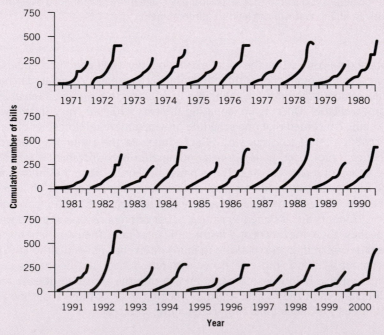

Figure 16-5   Cumulative graphs of the number of bills enacted per month by the U.S. House of Representatives in each of 30 consecutive years. *Source*: From T. S. Critchfield, R. Haley, B. Sabo, J. Colbert, & G. Macropoulis (2003), A half century of scalloping in the work habits of the United States Congress. *Journal of Applied Behavior Analysis, 36*, 465–486, Figure 2. Copyright © 2003 Society for the Experimental Analysis of Behavior. Used by permission.

studies have found that behaviors reinforced on variable schedules rather than on their fixed counterparts appear to be especially resistant to extinction (Shaw, 1987).

VARIATIONS ON REINFORCEMENT SCHEDULES

Although most examples of intermittent reinforcement schedules from everyday life probably fit into the four basic types, not all do. For instance, the so-called *duration schedules* require that the person engage in the target behavior for certain amounts of time before being reinforced. Being paid an hourly wage is an example because work behavior is required during each hour. Sometimes interval schedules have an extra requirement that the person must respond within a certain amount of time after reinforcement becomes available or lose the chance. This added requirement is called a *limited hold* because reinforcer availability is "held" for a limited time. Consider a train that has a regular, FI schedule. The "limited hold" aspect of the rule is that the train will wait at the station for only a limited amount of time.

Other everyday reinforcement schedules involve combinations of the types we've discussed. For example, taking full advantage of a department store's weekly sales requires that you arrive there when they open, and arriving much earlier probably won't matter. So far, this is just an FI schedule. Once you're in the store, a VR schedule will apply: The number of rummaging behaviors you'll need to perform in finding items you want at bargain prices will vary from one item to the next.

TIPS ON USING ADVANCED REINFORCEMENT PROCEDURES

The following tips apply to the use of token reinforcement systems, lotteries and group contingencies, and intermittent reinforcement.

1. Choose tokens that are not hazardous, that can be administered immediately and easily, and that the target person can accumulate securely.

2. Initially in an intervention using a token system, make criteria to receive tokens easy to achieve and opportunities to exchange them for backup reinforcers fairly frequent. Gradually make the criteria more stringent and the backup reinforcers less frequently available.

3. For reinforcement procedures that involve lotteries, guard against having a very low chance for the person to win.

4. For reinforcement procedures with group contingencies, match the type of contingency with the goal of the program. Also guard against competition and peer pressure that can lead to undesirable social behaviors.

5. When planning to use intermittent reinforcement, choose a schedule that can be administered easily and conveniently, preferably using devices (counters or timers) to keep track of the number of responses made or the elapsed time.

6. Gradually thin the reinforcement, staying at each level long enough to ensure that the behavior has remained strong. To avoid ratio strain, don't make the schedule too lean.

7. Variable schedules of reinforcement generally lead to higher frequencies of the behavior than fixed schedules, and FI schedules lead to lower frequencies than FR schedules.

8. The schedules used for variable-ratio or interval reinforcement are difficult to design and administer. The design process for variable schedules can be made easier by using computer programs, such as Microsoft Excel (Bancroft & Bourret, 2008).

9. Before implementing an advanced reinforcement system, explain it to the person in language he or she can understand.

10. Consult also the tips given in Chapter 15 on using reinforcement.

(Go to 📖.)

CONCEPT CHECK 16.2

Answer the following questions about intermittent reinforcement.

1. The most common procedure for thinning a schedule of reinforcement is to reduce the _____ of correct responses that receive rewards.

2. When we apply a rule for administering intermittent reinforcement that is based on the number of correct responses since the last reward, we are using a _____ schedule.

3. When we give rewards immediately after the person makes the last response in a constant criterion requiring 10 correct responses for each reinforcer, we are using a schedule that is abbreviated as _____ .

4. The abbreviation for a reinforcement schedule in which the reward is unavailable for 2 minutes after each reinforcer is given is _____ .

5. The reinforcement schedule that produces the highest response rate is the _____ schedule.

6. Temporary halts in responding after receiving rewards are called _____ .

7. Compared to a CRF schedule, an intermittent reinforcement schedule is likely to result in greater _____ to extinction after an intervention ends.

STUDY AND REVIEW

SUMMARY

A token reinforcement system uses a complex process of planning, setup, and implementation. People can learn to value tokens through respondent conditioning and modeling. Using tokens as reinforcers has several advantages; for example, they can be given immediately after the target behavior. A disadvantage is that certain types of tokens can be stolen. To set up a token reinforcement system, we need to choose the tokens and backup reinforcers and decide how to manage the consequences, such as the number of tokens a behavior will earn and the exchange rates for backup reinforcers.

A lottery determines by chance whether someone will receive a reward. It can be used to administer reinforcement when we are thinning a reinforcement schedule or it is difficult to provide attractive reinforcers for the target persons. In a group contingency, the consequences that members of a group receive depend on the performance of all or some of the members. Although using group contingencies has advantages, it sometimes has the disadvantage of leading to negative peer pressure.

An intermittent reinforcement schedule provides rewards for only some instances of a target behavior. In ratio schedules, the occurrence of reinforcement is based on the number of correct responses made. For each instance of reinforcement, a fixed-ratio (FR) schedule requires a constant number of responses, but a variable-ratio (VR) schedule requires an unspecified and changing number of responses. Responding under FR schedules generally shows post-reinforcement pauses. Ratio schedules of reinforcement produce very high rates of response while the schedules are in force, especially if the ratio is variable. If the number of responses required in a ratio schedule becomes too large, ratio strain may occur, causing the behavior to deteriorate. In interval schedules, rewards are given following the first correct response after an interval of time has elapsed. For each instance of reinforcement, a fixed-interval (FI) schedule sets a constant length of time when the reward is not available, but a variable-interval (VI) schedule makes rewards unavailable for an unspecified and changing period of time. Interval schedules produce moderate response rates, and cumulative graphs of responses with FI schedules show a scalloping pattern. Thinning reinforcement from a CRF to an intermittent schedule tends to make the behavior more persistent, or more resistant to extinction after an intervention ends.

To prepare for exams, use the following key terms and review questions and the online study guide that's available on this book's companion website at www.wiley.com/college/sarafino.

KEY TERMS

token reinforcement system
lottery
group contingency
intermittent reinforcement schedule

ratio schedules
fixed-ratio (FR)
variable-ratio (VR)
interval schedules

fixed-interval (FI)
variable-interval (VI)
post-reinforcement pauses
ratio strain

ANSWERS TO CONCEPT CHECKS (CCs)

CC16.1 *Answers:* **1.** poker chips **2.** respondent conditioning, modeling **3.** they are difficult to set up and administer, tokens can be stolen **4.** choosing the backup reinforcers, deciding who will administer consequences **5.** lottery **6.** interdependent

CC16.2 *Answers:* **1.** percentage or ratio **2.** ratio **3.** FR 10 **4.** FI 2-minutes **5.** variable-ratio **6.** post-reinforcement pauses **7.** resistance

REVIEW QUESTIONS

1. Describe the method and results of the Internet intervention by Glenn and Dallery (2007) to help people stop smoking.

2. Describe the research by Greer and Singer-Dudek (2008) demonstrating that children can learn to value tokens through modeling.

3. Describe the research of Johnson and Fawcett (1994) and its findings on using a lottery to administer rewards at a workplace.

4. Define the term *group contingency*; describe its three types and its advantages.

5. Describe three ways to thin a CRF schedule to an intermittent reinforcement schedule.

6. What is an intermittent reinforcement schedule, and how are ratio schedules different from interval schedules?

7. Define *fixed-ratio* (FR) *schedule* and *variable-ratio* (VR) *schedule*. For each type of schedule, give an example that was not in this book.

8. Define *fixed-interval* (FI) *schedule* and *variable-interval* (VI) *schedule*. For each type of schedule, give an example that was not in this book.

9. What are the effects of ratio schedules during an intervention? Include a description of post-reinforcement pauses and ratio strain.

10. What are the effects of interval schedules during an intervention?

11. What do scallops in the graphs of FI data represent? Describe the research of Critchfield and coworkers (2003) on the work habits of the United States Congress.

RELATED READINGS

- Ayllon, T., & Azrin, N. H. (1968b). *The token economy: A motivational system for therapy and rehabilitation.* Englewood Cliffs, NJ: Prentice-Hall.

- Greenwood, C. R., & Hops, H. (1981). Group-oriented contingencies and peer behavior change. In P. S. Strain (Ed.), *The utilization of classroom peers as behavior change agents* (pp. 189–259). New York: Plenum.

- Lattal, K. A., & Neef, N. A. (1996). Recent reinforcement-schedule research and applied behavior analysis. *Journal of Applied Behavior Analysis, 29,* 213–220.

17

USING EXTINCTION, DIFFERENTIAL REINFORCEMENT, AND HABIT REVERSAL TO DECREASE A BEHAVIOR

PROLOGUE

Here's an admission that may suggest I need to "get a life": Sometimes I watch reruns of *America's Funniest Home Videos* on TV. One of the videos they aired showed a young boy, probably 2 or 3 years old, having repeated tantrums. Some characteristics of his behavior and that of a woman I assume was his mother are relevant to a topic in this chapter—the method of extinction. The video started with the boy falling to the floor, screaming and crying as if he were in a terrible situation. What did his mother do? She, followed by a dog, ignored his tantrum and simply walked to a nearby room. What did the boy do? He stopped the tantrum abruptly, got up, and calmly looked for his mother. When he found her, he immediately fell to the floor and resumed his tantrum. His mother ignored the tantrum again and walked to another nearby room. He stopped the tantrum abruptly, found her again, and resumed his tantrum. This same sequence repeated over and over.

   What was going on here? Although I don't know for sure, here's what it looked like. First, the boy was not in a terrible situation, and although his initial tantrum episodes looked convincing, they looked more and more

247

contrived with repetitions. Second, this behavior had surely led to reinforcement in the past, which his parents may have provided; the rewards probably involved social attention and, maybe, a tangible or consumable item. Third, his mother seemed to be using the method of extinction: If she had reinforced his tantrum behavior in the past with attention and items, she was withholding them now quite consistently. Good job, Mom!

Unfortunately, although the video showed several repetitions of the tantrums, it did not continue long enough to see whether the mother's methods worked. When the reinforcers that maintain a behavioral excess are consistently withheld, the behavior should begin to subside and eventually stop. In this chapter, we examine how to decrease operant behaviors with three procedures: extinction, differential reinforcement, and habit reversal.

IDENTIFYING AND CONTROLLING REINFORCEMENT IN EXTINCTION

Chapter 6 defined **extinction** as a procedure or condition in which reinforcement is ended for a behavior and described the process of extinction as having certain characteristics:

- *Extinction burst and aggression*—when the target behavior occurs and no longer results in reinforcement, its frequency and magnitude may increase temporarily, and the person may make aggressive acts.

- *Gradual decline and reappearance*—the target behavior's decline usually occurs gradually or irregularly, and an extinguished behavior can reappear after a while.

- *Resistance to extinction* is stronger when the target behavior was reinforced in the past on an intermittent schedule than on a continuous reinforcement schedule.

We also saw that extinction for behavior that was maintained with positive reinforcement involves terminating those rewards, and extinction for behavior maintained with negative reinforcement involves preventing the escape or avoidance that the response previously produced from an aversive situation. Automatic reinforcement is often more difficult to terminate than other types of reinforcement; the procedure generally involves blocking the experience of the sensory stimulation the behavior produces. One of the first steps to take before applying extinction is to identify the behavior's existing reinforcers.

IDENTIFYING A BEHAVIOR'S REINFORCERS

Before the 1980s, many professionals who tried to apply extinction simply ignored inappropriate behaviors (Lerman & Iwata, 1996). Maybe they thought that ignoring the behavior was the same as withholding its rewards, which might be correct if social attention was, in fact, the reinforcer. But they couldn't be sure what the reinforcer was because functional assessment procedures had not yet been developed.

To apply extinction effectively, we must determine the reinforcers for the target behavior and terminate them. The best way to identify a behavior's reinforcers is to conduct a functional assessment, which we discussed in Chapter 13. Doing a functional assessment is essential for five reasons. First, trying to implement extinction based just on assumptions about a behavior's reinforcer rather than performing a careful functional assessment is very unlikely to succeed (Iwata, Pace, Cowdery, & Miltenberger, 1994). Second, researchers have demonstrated that the reinforcers for a specific behavior, such as self-injury, can differ from one person to the next. For instance, a study found that the reinforcers for self-injurious behavior in children with developmental disabilities were social attention for some children, escape from aversive situations for others, and sensory stimulation for yet others (Iwata et al., 1982).

Third, the consequences that influence a problem behavior, such as repetitive body rocking, can be different in different contexts—during training sessions and during leisure activities, for instance (Haring & Kennedy, 1990). Fourth, sometimes a problem behavior is maintained by multiple reinforcers (Hanley, Iwata, & McCord, 2003). When multiple reinforcers are involved, it's important to eliminate all of them to reduce the target behavior (Borrero & Vollmer, 2006). Fifth, studies indicate that identifying the reinforcers with functional assessment procedures has made extinction methods more effective in reducing target behaviors (Lerman & Iwata, 1996).

ELIMINATING A BEHAVIOR'S REINFORCERS

By definition, using the method of extinction requires that we eliminate the behavior's reinforcers. Once we've determined what the reinforcers are, we must assess whether we have control over their occurrence. If we can't control them, we can't use extinction to reduce the behavior.

Can You Control the Reinforcement?

In two circumstances, it can be very difficult to control the reinforcers a functional assessment has identified. One circumstance is when the consequence for the target behavior is automatic reinforcement, such as the stimulation a person gets from spinning objects or flapping hands repeatedly. The other is when people other than the individual who is trying to modify the behavior provide the reinforcers. The challenge is to get the control we currently lack.

We saw in Chapter 6 that some creativity may be needed to control automatic reinforcement that maintains a problem behavior. For instance, when the reinforcer for a child was the sound a plate made when he would spin it on a table, the behavior analysts covered the table with carpeting (Rincover, Cook, Peoples, & Packard, 1979). And when the reinforcer was the sensation a child felt when flapping his hands, they attached small vibrators to his hands to mask the feeling.

The circumstance of other people providing reinforcers for problem behavior is very common. These other people can be the target person or his or her family, friends, classmates, or workmates. For example, in the Chapter 6 opening story, therapists were trying to use extinction for Helen's psychotic talk, but she claimed a social worker would listen to her statements. Similarly, children who whine when their parent doesn't let them watch certain TV shows may get their other parent to let them. Or a disruptive student in class may receive favorable comments or laughs from other students for that behavior. If we wanted to apply extinction to change these behaviors, we would need to stop these people from providing counterproductive rewards. Sometimes we can stop the rewards by explaining to the people what they are doing and how it promotes undesirable behavior. Another approach is to give them rewards for *not* providing reinforcers for the target person's problem behavior.

But getting control of the reinforcer is not always possible, and we'll consider an everyday example: Teenagers may play an electric guitar very loudly and enjoy the sound, which serves as automatic reinforcement. If the teens' parents wanted to decrease the loudness, it's not likely that they could stop the reinforcement unless they could convince the teens to lower the volume. Maybe they could install an electronic device that prevents the music from being so loud, but the teenager would probably find a way to disconnect it. Yes, the parents could then apply punishment either for playing the music loudly or for disconnecting the device, but they would not be using extinction any longer. In some cases, the solution would be to get earphones for the teens so the music would be loud, but it would not bother others in the house. Of course, if part of the parents' concern is that the music is so loud as to damage the teens' hearing, earphones would not be a good solution.

Enhancing the Effectiveness of Extinction

Once we have identified a problem behavior's reinforcers and determined that we can eliminate them, we should consider a few guidelines that can affect the effectiveness of extinction. First, we need to *withhold all of the target behavior's reinforcers consistently*. Although it's important to apply all behavior change methods in a consistent manner, being consistent is especially important with extinction because occasionally failing to withhold the reinforcers means that reinforcement is occurring intermittently. We saw in Chapter 16 that reinforcing a behavior intermittently increases its resistance to extinction. Thus, all individuals who could reinforce the problem behavior—behavior analysts and significant others, such as parents, teachers, classmates, or workmates—should withhold reinforcement whenever the target behavior occurs.

Second, whenever possible we should *reinforce appropriate acts that are alternative behaviors or competing responses for the problem behavior*. For instance, if a girl acts aggressively to get things she wants, such as toys, we would make sure she doesn't get those things when she's aggressive and reinforce her when she asks or negotiates for the things instead. Asking and negotiating are appropriate acts that are alternative behaviors or competing responses for her aggression. Although reinforcing appropriate other behaviors works especially well when those behaviors result in the same types of rewards that the problem behavior had produced, any strong reinforcer can work.

Third, we can provide *instructions regarding the new contingencies:* The problem behavior will not result in reinforcers as it had in the past. And if we'll also be reinforcing alternative behaviors or competing responses, we should explain what those acts are and what their consequences will be. It also helps if the instructions explain why the new contingencies are needed. For example, if a teacher separates pupils in a class into small groups and then visits each group for several minutes, he or she can tell the students to hold their questions until he or she visits their group so as not to disrupt the teaching in the other groups.

Fourth, it's a good idea to *link extinction to a variety of conditions* in which the target behavior can occur. Extinction should be carried out in a variety of settings and with more than one person withholding reinforcement. By doing this, we can promote generalization of the improved behavior to many different circumstances—that is, the problem behavior will stop virtually everywhere it could occur—and maintain the change over time.

PROBLEMS IN APPLYING EXTINCTION

Problems can occur in applying extinction that may make the technique inappropriate to use or difficult to continue.

What If Extinction Creates Danger?

Some problem behaviors, such as aggression and self-injury, are destructive to property or could harm the target person or someone else in that person's environment. If we apply extinction as the only method to reduce the problem behavior, that behavior will not be reinforced and will decline over time, but it may still produce damage before it stops entirely. In such cases, using extinction by itself creates danger, raises ethical concerns, and is generally not recommended. Behaviors that are dangerous must be reduced with methods that work rapidly while still being humane. We discuss more appropriate approaches later in this chapter and in the next two chapters.

Dealing With the Characteristics of Extinction

The extinction process has three characteristics—extinction burst, extinction-elicited aggressive behavior, and reappearance of the target behavior—that make the method difficult to use or mislead people into thinking it is not working. In this section, we examine ways to plan for and minimize the effects of these characteristics.

We've seen that behaviors undergoing extinction may show an extinction burst—a temporary increase in frequency or magnitude—or produce aggressive behavior when the usual reinforcement is not forthcoming. An example of these phenomena comes from an intervention by Goh and Iwata (1994) for the self-injurious behavior of Steve, a man with profound mental retardation. The target behavior involved Steve's banging his head against hard surfaces and hitting his head or face with his hand or fist. A functional analysis had revealed that these behaviors were maintained by negative reinforcement, in the form of escape from training sessions. The intervention consisted solely of extinction: When self-injurious behavior occurred during training sessions, the trainer did not suspend the trial and simply physically guided Steve to complete the task. When extinction of self-injury was introduced, Steve became aggressive, slapping or kicking the trainer; the trainer blocked these actions to prevent injury, but otherwise ignored them. Figure 17-1 presents two graphs of Steve's behavior, one for self-injury and one for aggression. Notice four features of the data. First, Steve showed little or no aggression during baseline phases. Second, the frequency of self-injurious behavior shows extinction bursts soon after each extinction phase started, especially the first one. Third, aggression also increased after each extinction phase started. Fourth, self-injurious and aggressive behaviors declined gradually and irregularly across sessions

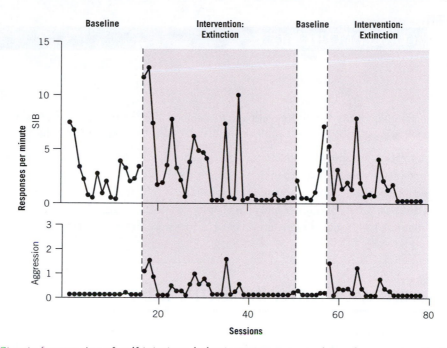

Figure 17-1   Steve's frequencies of self-injurious behaviors (SIB, top graph) and aggression (bottom graph) per minute of training sessions during baseline and intervention phases. The intervention consisted of extinction only. *Source:* From H.-L. Goh & B. A. Iwata (1994), Behavioral persistence and variability during extinction of self-injury maintained by escape. *Journal of Applied Behavior Analysis, 27,* 174. Copyright © 1994 Society for the Experimental Analysis of Behavior. Used by permission.

in extinction, sometimes occurring at very high frequencies, which is why using extinction by itself is no longer recommended to reduce dangerous behaviors.

A temporary reappearance of an extinguished behavior can occur. A graph presented in Figure 6-3 depicts this phenomenon in an intervention to reduce an infant's awake time after being put to bed. It is important to know about the possibility of an extinguished behavior's reappearance because its occurrence can mislead people, such as teachers or parents, to think that the process of extinction didn't succeed, and this belief may lead them to stop withholding reinforcement for the target behavior. If the behavior reappears, allowing it to be reinforced even just a few times will make it much more resistant to extinction.

The most essential element in dealing with these characteristics of the extinction process is to be aware that they can occur so that you can plan for their occurrence and interpret them correctly. When a target behavior shows an extinction burst or a temporary reappearance, it is important to maintain the extinction procedure, which will eventually decrease the behavior. In fact, these phenomena are typically short-lived if reinforcement does not occur. If we expect extinction-elicited aggression, we should plan in advance how to handle it—for instance, by being prepared to block the aggressive acts or wearing protective gear, such as padded clothing. Sometimes the aggression involves only verbal abuse, which we can opt to tolerate until it is extinguished if it is not reinforced.

We discussed earlier two methods for enhancing the effectiveness of extinction. These methods can also minimize the problems of extinction bursts, extinction-elicited aggression, and reappearance: We can give the target person instructions regarding the new contingencies and combine extinction with other methods, particularly reinforcing appropriate alternative behaviors or competing responses for the target behavior (Lerman, Iwata, & Wallace, 1999; Lerman, Kelley, Van Camp, & Roane, 1999). (Go to 📄.)

CONCEPT CHECK 17.1

Check your understanding of the preceding concepts. Remember: The symbol ⇔ means that the answer can vary. Answer the following questions about applying extinction to decrease an operant behavior.

1. Before using extinction, we should conduct a _____ to identify the reinforcers.
2. It is not appropriate to use extinction when _____ . ⇔
3. To make extinction effective, it is critical that all reinforcers be withheld _____ .
4. Linking extinction to a variety of settings and people promotes its _____ .
5. Two ways to minimize the problems of extinction burst, aggression, and reappearance are _____ and _____ .

DECREASING A BEHAVIOR WITH DIFFERENTIAL REINFORCEMENT

Although behavior analysts use reinforcement most often to correct behavioral deficits, it can also be used to decrease undesirable behaviors if the reinforcement is applied in a "differential" manner. The term *differential reinforcement* has more than one meaning. It can mean reinforcing a response in one situation but not in another or reinforcing one type or category of response but not another. When we use differential reinforcement to decrease a target behavior, the procedure involves reinforcing one response category (an alternative behavior or competing response) while withholding reinforcement—mainly by using extinction—for another response category (the problem behavior). Differential reinforcement distinguishes between different classes of response.

This section examines a variety of ways to structure differential reinforcement to decrease a behavior. Although most interventions that apply differential reinforcement methods to decrease behaviors use positive reinforcement, negative reinforcement has also been applied. For example, a study found that children's self-injurious behavior during training sessions can be reduced by allowing them to escape these activities (negative reinforcement) if they perform noninjurious alternative behaviors instead (Steege et al., 1990).

DIFFERENTIAL REINFORCEMENT OF INCOMPATIBLE OR ALTERNATIVE BEHAVIOR

In the procedure called **differential reinforcement of incompatible behavior (DRI)**, pronounced by spelling "d-r-i," we withhold reinforcers for the target behavior and systematically provide reinforcers for performing a competing response (M. K. Bonem, 2005). The competing response can be any incompatible behavior—any action that is impossible or very difficult to make simultaneously with the target behavior. For example, a teacher might eliminate reinforcers for a student's wandering around the classroom and provide rewards for completing academic tasks; wandering and completing tasks are incompatible. Allen and Stokes (1987) used a DRI procedure to reduce 3- to 6-year-old children's disruptive behavior, such as crying or body movements, during dental visits. The children received explanations of the intervention contingencies: withholding reinforcement (extinction) of disruptive behavior and positive and negative reinforcers for staying still and quiet, which are competing responses for disruption. Staying still and quiet for certain amounts of time resulted in praise, stickers, and prizes for being a "big helper" and short stoppages of the procedures (negative reinforcement). These procedures reduced disruptive behavior in all of the children, and the decreases were rapid and large in most of them.

A similar approach, **differential reinforcement of alternative behavior (DRA)**, pronounced "d-r-a," involves withholding a target behavior's reinforcers and rewarding a dissimilar desirable behavior that is not necessarily a competing response. The DRA approach was used with three girls in a preschool to increase their production of diverse forms, such as ramps or arches, in block building (Goetz & Baer, 1973). When the girls produced a novel form, their teacher showed approval and enthusiasm; but when they made a form they had made before, the teacher showed little interest (extinction). Over time, the girls' novel forms increased and nonnovel forms decreased. Sometimes the alternative behavior can be quite arbitrary—for instance, researchers had a child place a plastic block in a bucket as an alternative behavior to the problem behavior of screaming (Roane, Lerman, & Vorndran, 2001). Although extinction plays an important role in the DRA method, it may not always be possible to carry out, such as if it leads to extinction-elicited aggression by a large target person. When extinction is not possible, DRA can still be successful if the reinforcers for the alternative behavior have much more reward value than the rewards for the problem behavior (Athens & Vollmer, 2010).

The DRI and DRA approaches were mentioned but not named before when we discussed combining extinction of a target behavior with reinforcing a competing response or alternative behavior. These methods are fairly straightforward, and parents can be trained to apply them at home to decrease their child's problem behaviors. For instance, parents have used DRI procedures to curb disruptive behaviors and sibling conflicts in their children (Friman & Altman, 1990; Leitenberg et al., 1977). (Go to .)

DIFFERENTIAL REINFORCEMENT OF OTHER BEHAVIOR

Another way to use reinforcers to decrease operant behaviors is called **differential reinforcement of other behavior (DRO)**, pronounced "d-r-o." This method involves withholding reinforcement when the problem behavior occurs (extinction) and giving reinforcement when the behavior does *not occur at all* during a certain time period, such as a minute, an hour, or a whole day (LaVigna & Willis, 2005). In a sense, the person receives reinforcement for doing anything except the target response, which is why the name of the method mentions "other behavior." Because reinforcement is given if the target behavior is absent, the method is sometimes called *differential reinforcement of zero responding*.

CLOSE-UP

Functional Communication Training: A Type of DRA

Carr and Durand (1985) have noted that problem behaviors can often be placed into two categories: behaviors that function to gain *social attention*, providing positive reinforcement, or to *escape* from unpleasant—usually difficult—tasks, providing negative reinforcement. They hypothesized that teaching target persons alternative behaviors, such as asking for attention or assistance, would give them appropriate behaviors that have the same function as and reduce their need to perform the problem behavior. They then applied an intervention to decrease problem behaviors, such as aggression and self-injury, in four children with developmental disabilities. After determining that the function of the problem behaviors was to communicate the need for help or feedback, the researchers had the children's teachers use a procedure they called **functional communication training**. The procedure has three components:

1. Extinction—withholding reinforcement for the problem behaviors.
2. Prompting or shaping an alternative behavior—one or more mands (requests), such as saying, "I don't understand" or "Am I doing good work?"
3. Reinforcing the mands—providing attention when the children communicated their needs verbally with the mands.

Functional communication training is a DRA procedure, and it was effective in reducing high levels of problem behavior to near zero in all four children. It is now a commonly used and highly effective approach for treating problem behavior, such as self-injury in very young children (Kurtz et al., 2003).

A DRO reinforcement contingency can be structured in either of two ways: In an *interval* DRO, reinforcement is given if the behavior was absent throughout the entire time period; in a *momentary* DRO, reinforcement is given if the behavior was absent at a specific moment after a time period has elapsed (Lindberg, Iwata, Kahng, & DeLeon, 1999). Both approaches are carried out across a sequence of time periods. In addition, the time periods in either structure can be *fixed*, or constant across many instances of reinforcement, or *variable*, changing from one instance to the next. These types of DRO approaches are outlined in Figure 17-2. Most applications of DRO procedures use the fixed-interval DRO approach, which is our focus for the rest of this section.

Before carrying out a DRO method, four tasks should be completed. First, we must do a functional assessment to identify the past reinforcers for the target behavior so we can eliminate them in the extinction component of the procedure. Second, we must choose one or more reinforcers to provide when the behavior is absent for the designated time. Third, we need to choose the initial time interval for the interval or momentary DRO criterion for reinforcement; this interval can be lengthened later. The initial time interval should be based on baseline data for the problem behavior: This interval should be shorter than the average amount of time that elapsed between baseline instances of the behavior. This approach makes it likely that the person will meet the criterion for not performing the behavior and will receive the reward. Fourth, we should explain to the person as clearly as possible the new contingency—for instance, that a reward will be given when he or she has not performed the target behavior for specific amounts of time.

The most complicated aspect of the DRO procedure is keeping track of the time intervals. We'll consider the procedure for the fixed-interval DRO approach, which is the simplest. The process involves resetting a stopwatch under two conditions:

1. When the person performs the behavior before the interval ends.
2. When a reinforcer is delivered because the person successfully completed an interval without making the target behavior.

Let's suppose that the initial time interval was 5 minutes (the schedule is referred to as DRO 5 minutes). If the target behavior occurs before the end of the 5-minute interval, the time is reset immediately to 5 minutes. If the behavior doesn't occur during the interval, the reinforcer is given and the time is reset for another 5-minute interval. When the target person masters this interval length—that is, the behavior is absent in almost every interval—we begin to increase the interval length slowly, perhaps moving to 6 minutes at first. As each new interval length is mastered, we move to longer and longer lengths at a faster and faster pace, always making sure that the behavior never regresses very much. For most clients, we can eventually increase the intervals to span hours or days, and for many we can eliminate the DRO procedure entirely when the target behavior declines to the behavioral goal, usually near zero.

DRO methods can successfully reduce a variety of operant behaviors, including sibling conflict at home, classroom misconduct, thumb sucking, and tantrums (Leitenberg et al., 1977; Repp, Deitz, & Deitz, 1976; Wilder et al., 2006). However, some evidence suggests that they may be less effective than DRA methods and punishment procedures, such as time-out or response cost, for performing the behavior (Conyers et al., 2004; Didden, Duker, & Korzilius, 1997; LeGray et al., 2010; Whitaker, 1996). (Go to 🐾.)

| | DRO REINFORCEMENT CONTINGENCY | |
	Interval	Momentary
Fixed	Fixed-Interval (FI DRO)	Fixed-Momentary (FM DRO)
Variable	Variable-Interval (VI DRO)	Variable-Momentary (VM DRO)

TIME PERIODS

Figure 17-2 Four variations of DRO methods, depending on whether the reinforcement contingency is based on an interval or momentary criterion and whether the time periods are fixed or variable.

CASE STUDY

Reducing Bridget's Self-Injurious Behavior With DRO Methods

An intervention using DRO methods was performed to decrease self-injurious behavior in three women with profound mental retardation (Lindberg, Iwata, Kahng, & DeLeon, 1999). One of the women was 50-year-old Bridget, who engaged in severe head banging and body hitting. A functional analysis determined that the main reinforcers for her self-injurious behaviors involved social attention. During the intervention, social attention was not given to the target behavior but was given on a variable-momentary DRO schedule: Bridget received a few seconds of social attention if she was not performing a self-injurious behavior at the end of each interval, which varied randomly in length. The initial average interval length was 15 seconds, but it could be as short as about 8 seconds or as long as 22 seconds.

As Figure 17-3 shows, the intervention was applied in two phases: In the first VM DRO phase, her self-injurious behavior dropped to near zero; the second VM DRO phase followed a new baseline phase, and the behavior declined again, eventually to near zero. Because the decline during the second VM DRO phase was not so rapid, the interval lengths remained the same for many sessions and were then lengthened, averaging 300 seconds in the last sessions.

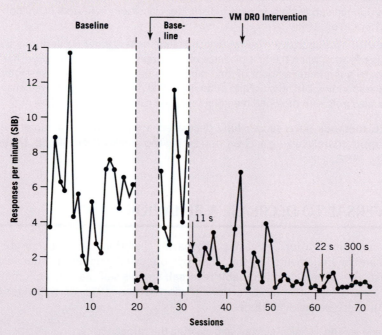

Figure 17-3 Bridget's frequency of self-injurious behaviors (SIB) during two phases each of baseline and VM DRO intervention. For the first intervention phase, the initial average interval length was 15 seconds; but in the second intervention phase, it was 11 seconds (at session 61, the average interval length was doubled to 22 seconds; at session 68, it was increased to 300). *Source*: From J. S. Lindberg, B. A. Iwata, S. W. Kahng, & I. G. DeLeon (1999), DRO contingencies: An analysis of variable-momentary schedules. *Journal of Applied Behavior Analysis, 32*, 123–136, Figure 4. Copyright © 1999 Society for the Experimental Analysis of Behavior. Used by permission.

DIFFERENTIAL REINFORCEMENT OF LOW RATES OF BEHAVIOR

The last way we'll consider to use reinforcers to decrease a target behavior is to give rewards contingent on the behavior occurring below a certain frequency per unit of time. In this approach, called **differential reinforcement of low rates (DRL)**, pronounced "d-r-l," a reinforcer is given only when the undesirable behavior falls below a certain rate—for example, a teacher might reinforce students if they are out of their seats fewer than three times in an hour. Using the DRL method, we don't reinforce the *absence* of the target behavior; we give reinforcement for a *reduced rate* of performance than the behavior had in the past (E. Bonem, 2005). A usual goal for applying DRL is to reduce but not eliminate the behavior. Reaching the behavioral goal is usually achieved by requiring lower and lower rates of performance for earning reinforcement across intervention sessions.

The description of DRL methods so far seems simple, but there are actually three variations in the way the procedure is carried out (Deitz, 1977):

1. **Full-session DRL**. In this approach, reinforcement is given at the end of a session if the target behavior occurred at a level below a predetermined criterion. Suppose the sessions last half an hour—a behavior analyst might require for the reinforcer that the person perform fewer than two disruptive behaviors during the entire half hour. Full-session DRL was used in separate studies involving a specific student and an entire class to decrease the behavior of talking in class without permission (Deitz & Repp, 1973).

2. **Interval DRL**. The behavior analyst divides a full session into a set of equal time intervals, sets a criterion for a reduced level of the behavior, and delivers a reward at the end of each interval in which the target persons performed the target behavior at a level below the criterion. If the persons exceed the criterion before the end of an interval, that interval is ended at that time and a new one is started. Although the interval DRL approach is not often used, it was applied successfully to reduce disruptive classroom behaviors of an individual student and a group of students (Deitz et al., 1978).

3. **Spaced-responding DRL**. This approach requires that the target behavior not occur during a specific interval of time; reinforcement is provided when the first instance of the target behavior occurs *after* that time. It separates or "spaces" responses by a minimum amount of time, which can be increased across sessions, thereby reducing the behavior. Spaced-responding DRL was used to attain a marked decrease of repetitive behaviors, such as body rocking, in three teenaged girls with profound mental retardation (Singh, Dawson, & Manning, 1981).

Interventions using DRL methods have successfully decreased a wide variety of target behaviors, such as sleeping, aggression, inappropriately talking in class, and eating too quickly (Deitz, Repp, & Deitz, 1976; Lennox, Miltenberger, & Donnelly, 1987).

USING HABIT REVERSAL TO DECREASE A BEHAVIOR

This section describes an approach for decreasing a behavior that does not concentrate on providing or withdrawing reinforcers and is implemented by the target person, usually under the supervision of a behavior analyst or other therapist. This approach, called **habit reversal**, applies self-management methods to decrease habitual behavior, particularly repetitive motor actions (Azrin & Nunn, 1973; de Kinkelder & Boelens, 1998; Donohue & Farley, 2005). These behaviors include:

- Motor tics, such as head jerking, facial grimacing, and clearing the throat.
- Stuttering, such as repeating syllables or prolonging sounds when trying to speak.
- Nervous habits, such as skin picking, nail biting, and hair twirling.

In many cases, the behavior occurs automatically, without the target person's awareness.

The three main methods used in habit reversal are awareness training, competing response training, and social support. In *awareness training*, the target person is taught to describe the problem behavior and then to watch for and notice when it occurs or is about to occur. In *competing response practice*, the person engages for a while in a response that is the opposite of the target behavior. For example, to reduce skin picking or nail biting, clients might be instructed to place their hands by their sides and clench their fists for a while when they notice that the target behavior has begun or is about to happen. The ideal amount of time each instance of competing response practice should last appears to be between 1 and 3 minutes (Twohig & Woods, 2001a). In the *social support* method, family members or other people who are frequently with the target person point out when the behavior is happening or about to occur, prompt the use of the competing response, and reinforce the competing response practice and improvements in the behavior. Several studies have found that habit reversal procedures often decrease highly frequent habits greatly or almost entirely (Azrin & Nunn, 1973; Azrin, Nunn, & Frantz, 1980; Azrin & Peterson, 1990; Finney, Rapoff, Hall, & Christophersen, 1983; Miltenberger, Fuqua, & Woods, 1998; Townsend et al., 2001).

An example of the application of habit reversal comes from an intervention to decrease chronic skin picking in two adult male siblings, Stan and Drew, who had no other problem behaviors (Twohig & Woods, 2001b). Their skin picking had begun in childhood and involved digging their fingernails into the skin at the tip of their fingers, causing bleeding and scarring. Awareness training consisted of having each man:

- Describe skin picking of fingers and its antecedents, such as rubbing the fingers.
- Recognize the therapist's simulation of the antecedent and problem behaviors.
- Acknowledge his own antecedent and picking behaviors.

The competing response involved clenching the fist for 1 minute when picking or an antecedent behavior occurred. Training in the competing response used two techniques: The therapist modeled the behavior, and the men practiced it after each simulation of the picking or antecedent behavior until they correctly and consistently applied the response. During the 2- to 3-week intervention, periodic "booster sessions" were given to shore up or refresh the awareness and competing response training. The men monitored their own skin-picking behavior and reported daily skin picking in baseline, which averaged at 11 instances for Stan and 26 for Drew. For both men, skin picking decreased dramatically in the intervention—particularly for Drew, whose picking dropped by 90%. At a follow-up assessment months later, Stan had maintained his improvements; but Drew reported increased picking (his picking was still substantially lower than in baseline), and photos showed much less damage to the men's fingers than existed in baseline.

TIPS ON USING EXTINCTION, DIFFERENTIAL REINFORCEMENT, AND HABIT REVERSAL

The following tips apply to the use of extinction, differential reinforcement, and habit reversal.

1. When using extinction, remember that extinction bursts, extinction-elicited aggression, and reappearance of the target behavior can occur. Plan for these phenomena in advance.

2. After extinction has begun to decrease the target behavior, watch for new sources of reinforcement that may cause the behavior to rebound. Make sure that all individuals who could reinforce the behavior do not do so.

3. If you will use extinction, identify and plan to reinforce a desirable alternative behavior or competing response.

4. If you will use extinction or differential reinforcement to decrease a behavior, tell the target person exactly what the behavior is and what the new reinforcement rules are.

5. When planning to use differential reinforcement, decide which approach is best. Use DRI, DRA, or DRO methods if the behavioral goal is to reduce the behavior to zero or nearly so; for DRI, you must identify a competing response to reward. Use DRL if some low level of the behavior is desirable or acceptable. Also keep in mind that DRL methods work more slowly than other differential reinforcement approaches.

6. When using DRO, base the length of the initial time interval on baseline data: It should be shorter than the average amount of time that elapsed between baseline instances of the behavior.

7. When using DRO methods, gradually increase the length of the intervals so that that the behavior becomes less and less frequent. With DRL, require lower and lower rates of performance for earning reinforcement across intervention sessions.

8. In habit reversal, the target person's awareness of when the behavior occurs or is about to occur is critical and can be enhanced by training and by enlisting other people to point out when the behavior happens or is about to occur.

(Go to 📄.)

STUDY AND REVIEW

SUMMARY

Before conducting extinction for a target behavior, behavior analysts need to identify its reinforcers with a functional assessment so that we can eliminate them. After identifying the reinforcers, we need to determine whether we can control them; if not, we can't use the method of extinction. We can enhance the effectiveness of extinction by withholding all of the target behavior's reinforcers consistently, reinforcing alternative behaviors or competing responses, telling the target person about the new contingencies, and linking extinction to a variety of conditions. Using extinction is not recommended if it creates a dangerous situation that we cannot prevent. We can minimize occurrences of extinction burst, extinction-elicited aggression, and the reappearance of the target behavior by explaining the new contingencies to the target person and reinforcing alternative or competing responses.

It is possible to decrease a target behavior by using differential reinforcement, whereby we withhold the behavior's reinforcers and reward another response category, such as an alternative behavior or less frequent occurrences of the target behavior. There are four types of differential reinforcement procedures:

CONCEPT CHECK 17.2

Answer the following questions about using methods of differential reinforcement and habit reversal to decrease a behavior.

1. An example of differential reinforcement in learning a sport skill in baseball is _____ . ⇔
2. A commonly used competing response for swearing with the word *f__king* is _____ . ⇔
3. If we withhold reinforcement for a behavior and give rewards for performing a different, but not competing, response, we are using the _____ method.
4. Functional communication training is a form of the _____ method.
5. If we withhold reinforcement for a behavior and give rewards for not performing at all during a certain period, we are using the _____ method.
6. If we provide reinforcement for a target behavior only when its occurrences drop below a certain level, we are using the _____ method.
7. The three main methods used in habit reversal procedures are awareness training, _____ , and social support.

1. Differential reinforcement of incompatible behavior (DRI)—reinforcers are withheld for the target behavior but given for a competing response.

2. Differential reinforcement of alternative behavior (DRA)—reinforcers are withheld for the target behavior but given for another behavior that is not necessarily a competing response.

3. Differential reinforcement of other behavior (DRO)—reinforcers are withheld for the target behavior and given when the behavior does not occur for some period of time (which is called interval DRO) or only at the end of a period of time (called momentary DRO). DRO intervals can be a fixed length or variable.

4. Differential reinforcement of low rates (DRL)—reinforcement is given when the target behavior falls below a certain rate (frequency per unit of time). This approach can be implemented with one of three procedures: full-session DRL, interval DRL, and spaced-responding DRL.

Functional communication training is a variation of DRA in which reinforcers for the target behaviors are withheld and a mand is taught and reinforced to serve the same function, or get the same reinforcers, as the problem behavior. The approach called *habit reversal* uses awareness training, competing response practice, and social support to help clients reduce repetitive, annoying behaviors they perform unintentionally.

To prepare for exams, use the following key terms and review questions and the online study guide that's available on this book's companion website at www.wiley.com/college/sarafino.

KEY TERMS

extinction
differential reinforcement of
    incompatible behavior (DRI)
differential reinforcement of
    alternative behavior (DRA)

functional communication training
differential reinforcement of other
    behavior (DRO)
differential reinforcement of low
    rates (DRL)

full-session DRL
interval DRL
spaced-responding DRL
habit reversal

ANSWERS TO CONCEPT CHECKS (CCs)

CC17.1 *Answers*: **1.** functional assessment **2.** you can't control the reinforcers or it creates danger **3.** consistently **4.** generalization **5.** instructing the person of the new contingencies, rewarding an alternative or competing response

CC17.2 *Answers*: **1.** withholding reinforcement for swinging the bat at a pitch that is out of the ideal area and reinforcing swinging at one that is in the area **2.** freaking **3.** differential reinforcement of alternative behavior (DRA) **4.** DRA **5.** differential reinforcement of other behavior (DRO) **6.** differential reinforcement of low rates (DRL) **7.** competing response practice

REVIEW QUESTIONS

1. Why is it important to conduct a functional assessment before using extinction?

2. Is a teacher applying extinction if he or she simply ignores a student's problem behavior? Explain your answer.

3. Describe four ways to enhance the effectiveness of an extinction procedure.

4. Describe the procedure and findings of the intervention of Goh and Iwata (1994) that used extinction to decrease self-injurious behavior and aggression.

5. What characteristics of the extinction process can make the method difficult to apply, and how can we minimize their effects?

6. What are the two components of the process of differential reinforcement?

7. Define and distinguish among DRA, DRO, and DRL procedures for reducing an undesirable behavior.

8. Describe the procedure of functional communication training, and give an example of how it might be used by a parent of a child who has frequent tantrums.

9. Describe how to choose the initial time interval to use in the DRO method and how to track the intervals when you implement the method.

10. Describe the intervention of Lindberg, Iwata, Kahng, and DeLeon (1999) and the outcome for Bridget's self-injurious behavior.

11. Distinguish among full-session DRL, interval DRL, and spaced-responding DRL methods.

12. Describe the method of habit reversal and the types of behavior for which it is generally used.

13. Describe the habit reversal intervention of Twohig and Woods (2001b) to reduce skin picking in two brothers.

RELATED READINGS

• Deitz, S. M. (1977). An analysis of programming DRL schedules in educational settings. *Behaviour Research and Therapy*, 15, 103–111.

• Lerman, D. C., & Iwata, B. A. (1996). Developing a technology for the use of operant extinction in clinical settings: An examination of basic and applied research. *Journal of Applied Behavior Analysis*, 29, 345–382.

18

USING TIME-OUT AND RESPONSE-COST PUNISHMENT TO DECREASE A BEHAVIOR

Deciding Whether to Use Punishment
Advantages and Disadvantages of Using Punishment
When to Consider Using Punishment

Negative Punishment: Time-Out and Response Cost
Using Time-Out
Using Response Cost

Considerations in Using Negative Punishment
Issues With Time-Out
Issues With Response Cost

Tips on Using Negative Punishment

Study and Review

PROLOGUE

Some of you may remember the days when telephone companies didn't levy a direct charge for using directory assistance to find a local phone number. An example of the effect of charging for directory assistance on behavior was reported for the Cincinnati, Ohio, area (McSweeny, 1978). In the early 1970s, the number of these calls increased from about 64,000 to 87,000 per average business day. When a system of charges was approved but not yet initiated in mid-1973, the number of calls declined to about 55,000 in February of 1974, just before the system's introduction in March. The system of charges allowed three complementary directory assistance calls per month from a particular line, after which a charge of 20 cents per call was levied. In March of 1974, the calls plummeted to about 17,000 a day, after which they increased very slowly over the next couple of years to about 24,000.

Because the charge for using directory assistance is levied contingent on the behavior of placing a call, it qualifies as response cost, a type of punishment that we considered in Chapter 7. After telephone users were charged for using directory assistance, their behavior of making those calls decreased. Chances are, they then used an alternative behavior: finding phone numbers in the local phone directory, which the telephone company had asked people to do for years without success.

All effective forms of punishment suppress the behavior they are contingent on. In this chapter, we examine the punishment techniques of time-out and response cost, look at examples of ways to use these procedures, and consider how to apply them effectively to decrease operant behaviors. We'll start by discussing whether to use punishment to correct a behavioral excess and when to consider doing so.

DECIDING WHETHER TO USE PUNISHMENT

Recall that the various types of **punishment** can be grouped into two categories: *positive punishment*, in which an aversive stimulus or condition (such as a reprimand) is added as a consequence of a behavior; and *negative punishment*, in which a stimulus (such as money or a condition the person already has at the time the behavior occurs) is taken away. Time-out and response cost are types of negative punishment—our focus in the present chapter. In Chapter 19, we discuss positive punishment methods.

ADVANTAGES AND DISADVANTAGES OF USING PUNISHMENT

Using punishment has some important advantages: It achieves rapid results in suppressing a problem behavior, and it often eliminates the behavior entirely or reduces its frequency to near zero (Dinsmoor, 1998). These advantages are particularly significant when the problem behavior is dangerous or destructive, such as self-injurious behavior or aggression, or very embarrassing for the target person or his or her family. But using punishment also has some disadvantages, especially because it can lead the target person to have strong emotional reactions that can involve escape, avoidance, or aggressive behaviors. These behaviors are counterproductive because they interfere with therapy and learning processes.

WHEN TO CONSIDER USING PUNISHMENT

Some people think, "Wouldn't it be nice if punishment occurred little or not at all in life?" Punishment, like all forms of reinforcement, is a common and natural part of people's lives. It teaches us not to repeat behaviors that lead to unpleasant conditions: When we do things carelessly or things that are wrong, unpleasant consequences tend to happen. To end the need for punishment, we would have to control everyone's antecedents carefully and monitor their behavior constantly to make sure it is sufficiently reinforced. This is not a scenario that's likely to develop, nor is it one most people would want. Instead, behavior analysts encounter clients whose prior behavior and reinforcement history are unknown. If parents, teachers, or others have tried to influence antecedents and consequences at all, they've generally intervened inconsistently. Haphazardly catching the person doing well and then applying reinforcers isn't usually enough to improve a behavior (Brown, 1982).

Generally speaking, *behavior analysts try to avoid using punishment.* When is using punishment acceptable? We'll look at some issues that can help us judge whether to use punishment and what types of punishers to apply. The first issue to consider is whether *nonaversive methods have been tried*. The methods of manipulating antecedents, extinction, and differential reinforcement are often effective, thereby eliminating the need to use punishment. We can determine which of these approaches to try by conducting a careful functional assessment. If all of the nonpunitive techniques identified with a functional assessment have been tried and have failed to decrease the target behavior, we may want to consider using punishment (Axelrod, 1990; Guess, Turnbull, & Helmstetter, 1990). Unfortunately, not all professionals conduct functional assessments when designing and implementing interventions to change people's behavior.

The second issue we need to examine in deciding whether to use punishment relates to *characteristics of the target person's behavior*. An important characteristic of the behavior is its likelihood of causing injury to the person or others. The greater the likelihood of injury, the more acceptable using punishment becomes (Smith, 1990). Self-injurious behavior, severe aggression, and ruminative vomiting are three kinds of behavior for which punishment typically can be justified. In addition, behaviors that are highly embarrassing or bizarre, such as self-stimulation, have the effect of isolating the individual socially. For that reason, punishment may be an acceptable approach if other behavioral methods have not been successful. Many professionals have substantial reservations about using punishment, even when injury is likely if the behavior is allowed to continue (Donnellan & LaVigna, 1990; Luiselli, 1990). But if other methods have failed to decrease behaviors that are dangerous or severely impair intellectual and social development, professionals who are trying to change the behaviors may find it necessary to consider using punishment.

The third issue in deciding on using punishment entails our ability to *control extraneous, counterproductive reinforcers* of the undesirable behavior. Some behaviors may have automatic, or "built-in," reinforcers, as in cases of self-stimulation and public masturbation (Van Houten, 1983). Other behaviors, such as stealing or speeding when driving, may result in naturally occurring reinforcement. And some behaviors may receive reinforcement from individuals over whom we have little control. When we cannot control extraneous reinforcement, nonpunitive methods may not be sufficient to decrease the behavior very much, and punishment may be necessary.

Our last issue relating to making decisions on using punishment has to do with the *types of punishers* available. Punishers that produce strong pain or tissue damage evoke humanitarian concerns and are often precluded or restricted by professional guidelines or law (Hamilton & Matson, 1992; Singh, Lloyd, & Kendall, 1990). In addition, the general public may have a voice in the choice of punishers that can be applied, particularly in schools. One study had adults rate different types of punishers for use in school and at home (Blampied & Kahan, 1992). Response cost and reprimands were rated as the most acceptable types, followed by time-out; physical punishment was the least acceptable. Although this order of acceptability held for both school and home, physical punishment was rated as more acceptable at home than at school. What's more, these acceptability ratings may be related to the punishers' likelihood of leading to negative side effects. For instance, studies have found relatively few negative side effects in using response cost rather than physical punishment methods (Kazdin, 1972). For these reasons, behavior analysts are more likely to use negative punishment—particularly time-out and response cost—than positive punishment in behavior change programs.

Of course, an important consideration in choosing a punisher is that it must be effective in decreasing the target behavior. Regardless of the type of punisher selected, its degree of severity or restrictiveness should be as mild as possible while still allowing the intervention to succeed in reducing the undesirable behavior. (Go to .)

CONCEPT CHECK 18.1

Check your understanding of the preceding concepts. Remember: The symbol ⇔ means that the answer can vary. Answer the following questions about deciding whether to use punishment.

1. In _____ punishment, a stimulus or condition the target person already has is taken away.
2. Two advantages of using punishment are that it _____ and _____ .
3. If nonaversive methods have been tried without success in decreasing a problem behavior, and that behavior is dangerous or embarrassing, behavior analysts are more _____ to use punishment.
4. Punishment methods that produce _____ are often precluded or restricted by law or professional guidelines.
5. Compared with physical punishment, time-out and response-cost methods are rated by adults in the general public as relatively _____ forms of punishment.
6. An example of a positive punisher that the general public finds acceptable is _____ . ⇔

NEGATIVE PUNISHMENT: TIME-OUT AND RESPONSE COST

Time-out and response cost are the two main procedures that behavior analysts apply as negative punishment to decrease an operant behavior.

USING TIME-OUT

Time-out is a negative punishment procedure in which the target person's access to or opportunity to earn reinforcers is discontinued for a period of time as a consequence of performing a target behavior (Brantner & Doherty, 1983; Van Houten, 1983). This technique is sometimes given the longer name *time-out from positive reinforcement*. The time-out procedure is carried out either by changing the person's environment from one with opportunities for reinforcement (called *time-in*) to one that is much less reinforcing or by ending the person's access to reinforcement within an environment. In Chapter 7, we described three types or levels of time-out (Brantner & Doherty, 1983):

1. **Isolation time-out**—the person who misbehaves is removed from a reinforcing environment to a separate setting, such as a time-out room or cubicle, that offers little or no opportunity for reinforcement.

2. **Exclusion time-out**—the person is cut off from the current opportunities for reinforcement without being isolated, such as by being moved to a separate part of a classroom and not allowed to participate in ongoing reinforcing activities.

3. **Nonexclusion time-out**—the person who misbehaves is not removed from the ongoing activities at all, but receives a signal indicating a period in which he or she cannot earn reinforcers that would have been available if the misbehavior hadn't occurred.

For these approaches to decrease the target behavior, the time-out condition should offer substantially less opportunity for reinforcement than the time-in circumstances. The greater the difference in opportunities for reinforcement between time-out and time-in, the more effective the punishment is likely to be. For instance, a misbehaving student who is put in the hallway as time-out may find as many opportunities for reinforcement there as he or she had in the classroom (time-in), such as by peeking or making funny faces at students in other rooms. As you may suspect, time-out is used often in group settings, particularly classrooms.

Examples of Time-Out Methods

Isolation time-out was used as a component in an intervention to decrease infants' potentially dangerous behaviors, such as touching stoves and electrical cords (Mathews et al., 1987). In each 10-minute baseline session, the infants engaged in free play while their mothers performed other activities, such as washing dishes, and a record was kept of whether a potentially dangerous behavior occurred in each 30-second interval. The target behaviors occurred frequently, in about one third of the intervals. The intervention consisted of three components—the mothers were trained to:

1. Childproof the house (a method for managing antecedents for the behaviors).

2. Praise the child often for appropriate behavior.

3. Implement time-out immediately after a potentially dangerous behavior occurred by firmly saying "no," picking up the child, and putting him or her in a playpen for a short time (until the infant was quiet for 5 to 10 seconds).

This intervention quickly and markedly decreased the target behaviors, and at a follow-up assessment 7 months later, potentially dangerous behaviors occurred at near zero levels in all four of the infants.

An example of *exclusion time-out* comes from an intervention to decrease the spitting and self-injurious behaviors of a boy with autism (Solnick, Rincover, & Peterson, 1977). The study used a time-in condition that was "enriched": The boy was in training sessions with simple prompted tasks he could do easily, thereby allowing him to earn a variety of reinforcers—praise, food, and playing with toys—while recorded music played continuously. When a target behavior occurred, a 90-second time-out was applied immediately: The behavior analyst turned off the music, removed the reinforcers (but not the toys, which the boy didn't play with alone), and moved to the far side of a partition out of view. Thus exclusion time-out can be applied by having the target person stay in the same environment while the materials used for reinforcement are taken away for a short period. This intervention decreased the boy's spitting and self-injurious behaviors from very high levels in baseline to near zero. In another example of the application of exclusion time-out, the tirades of a woman with mental retardation were eliminated (see Figure 3-6) by moving her to a corner of the room when a tirade occurred and leaving her there for 2 minutes (Bostow & Bailey, 1969).

We saw an example of *nonexclusion time-out* in Chapter 7: Students with mental retardation who were eligible to earn reinforcers wore a colored ribbon to signify this status; each time they performed disruptive behavior, such as by yelling, they lost the ribbon for 3 minutes, meaning that they could not receive reinforcers during that time (Foxx & Shapiro, 1978). The percentage of class time they spent in disruptive behavior decreased from 42% in baseline to about 6% when time-out was in force. In another example, nonexclusion time-out was used on a playground to reduce fourth- and fifth-grade students' problem behaviors that included noncompliance and aggression (White & Bailey, 1990). When a student misbehaved, he or she was told what the misbehavior was and required to sit nearby on the ground for 3 minutes and watch the activities; once the time-out ended, the student could rejoin the group and earn reinforcement. In addition, the students lost their usual computer or free-play time, depending on how often they misbehaved in each 10-minute session. This method reduced the number of misbehaviors dramatically.

Combining Differential Reinforcement With Punishment

When using time-out, response cost, or any other punishment method, it's a good idea to apply differential reinforcement methods as well. As punishment decreases the problem behavior, differential reinforcement can help reduce that behavior or increase appropriate behaviors. Some methods of differential reinforcement discussed in Chapter 17 are well suited for this combination, particularly:

* Differential reinforcement of incompatible behavior (DRI), which rewards a competing response
* Differential reinforcement of alternative behavior (DRA), which rewards an alternative behavior that is not necessarily incompatible with the problem behavior
* Differential reinforcement of other behavior (DRO), which reinforces the absence of the problem behavior

In each of these methods, we also extinguish the problem behavior. As you may expect, by combining punishment and differential reinforcement methods we are likely to enhance the intervention's effectiveness in decreasing an operant behavior.

USING RESPONSE COST

In the example described earlier of a nonexclusion time-out method that was carried out on a playground, the consequences for the problem behaviors included the students' loss of their usual computer or free-play time. This technique is an example of **response cost**, a negative punishment method in which misbehavior leads to losing an item or privilege that was probably a reinforcer for an earlier behavior (Rapport & Begolli, 2005; Van Houten, 1983). Examples of items we could take away are money, as with a fine, or a music CD; privileges we could take away are minutes of recess in school or of watching TV. And we can take away an item or privilege temporarily or permanently—for instance, a music CD or favorite article of clothing can be taken away for good or just for a period of time. Although the item or privilege is usually something the person already has, it can also be a reinforcer he or she has earned but not yet received. Like most forms of punishment, response cost decreases a target behavior fairly quickly; but it can be implemented more quickly and conveniently than many other punishers, particularly when used in a program that applies token reinforcers (Musser, Bray, Kehle, & Jenson, 2001).

In the opening story to this chapter, we looked at an example of the application of response cost: charging telephone customers a fee for using directory assistance to find local phone numbers (McSweeny, 1978). After the fee was introduced, directory assistance calls plummeted. Another example of using response cost involved a group contingency in a fourth-grade classroom in which a great deal of disruptive behavior occurred, such as students being out of their seats or talking without permission (Barrish, Saunders, & Wolf, 1969). To reduce these target behaviors, the teacher introduced a competitive game that would apply during math periods in which the class was separated into two groups. Each time a disruptive behavior occurred, a mark was placed on the chalkboard in a column for that student's group; because any group with the *fewest* marks or *fewer than five* marks at the end of the period won privileges, each mark represented a loss of likelihood of winning, thereby serving as response cost. The privileges included lining up first or early for lunch and having free time at the end of the day to engage in special projects. Figure 18-1 presents the data for the math periods, showing that the response-cost method decreased the students' disruptive behaviors dramatically; similar results were found when the same intervention was also applied in another class.

As you can see, response cost is a versatile punishment approach for decreasing operant behavior. The items or privileges a target person can lose are quite broad, and the structure of the contingency for misbehavior is flexible. (Go to 🔍.)

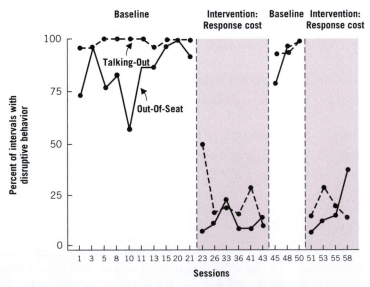

Figure 18-1 Percent of 1-minute intervals containing unauthorized talking and out-of-seat behaviors during fourth-grade math periods with 24 students. In baseline, the teacher tried to use her usual manner; in the intervention, the target behaviors received response-cost punishment that reduced the likelihood of winning privileges for the misbehaving student and his or her team. *Source*: Adapted from H. H. Barrish, M. Saunders, & M. Wolf (1969), Good behavior game: Effects of individual contingencies for group consequences on disruptive behavior in a classroom. *Journal of Applied Behavior Analysis*, 2, 119–124, Figure 1. Copyright © 1969 Society for the Experimental Analysis of Behavior. Used by permission.

CONSIDERATIONS IN USING NEGATIVE PUNISHMENT

To use time-out and response cost effectively and responsibly, a number of issues need to be addressed in planning an intervention to decrease a problem behavior.

ISSUES WITH TIME-OUT

Using time-out has some advantages—for instance, it usually produces large decreases in a behavior quickly, is fairly easy to apply with most target persons, and is considered by professionals and others to be more acceptable than most forms of positive punishment. If you consider using time-out procedures at a school or other institution, be sure to check with supervisors there regarding their acceptability. If the supervisors or target person's parent objects to the use of time-out, you probably won't be able to use it.

Time-out procedures can have some disadvantages and are not advisable in some cases. Here are some examples:

- For isolation time-out, a special room may be needed that is available and safe to use, such as a place having no objects that target persons might injure themselves with. Individuals who might harm themselves if left unattended may require a staff member to monitor their behavior in isolation.
- Isolating children with developmental disabilities may provide them with opportunities to perform undesirable or dangerous self-stimulation or self-injurious behaviors.
- Time-out is appropriate for behaviors maintained by positive reinforcement, but not negative reinforcement, especially escape from training sessions or other essential activities.
- Time-out reduces the target person's instructional time, thereby impairing the learning of other behaviors, such as academic or self-help skills.
- If the target person resists going to isolation or exclusion time-out or being put on nonexclusion time-out, especially if he or she is likely to cause someone injury, we may not be able to use these methods. Similarly, if we can't prevent the person from escaping from the time-out situation, we shouldn't use the method.

CLOSE-UP

Can We Use Response Cost for Behavior Maintained by Negative Reinforcement?

In most of the examples of response cost we've discussed, the studies were done before behavior analysts had developed functional assessment methods, but the punished behaviors were probably maintained by positive reinforcement. For instance, some likely reinforcers for the disruptive fourth-grade classroom behaviors are social attention from classmates and desired tangible items or activities. Is response cost effective when the problem behavior is maintained by negative reinforcement?

Researchers studied this question with 33-year-old Shai, a woman with severe mental retardation who performed frequent destructive acts, including self-injurious behavior, aggression, and throwing and breaking objects (Keeney, Fisher, Adelinis, & Wilder, 2000). A functional analysis of the target behavior revealed that escape (negative reinforcement) from training demands was the strongest reinforcer and social attention was close behind, as the top panel in Figure 18-2 depicts; destructive acts occurred rarely during play and alone conditions. Further assessments determined that attention and listening to music through headphones were strong positive reinforcers for Shai. An experiment was carried out that consisted of five phases—baseline,

(Continued)

(Continued)

noncontingent reinforcement, response cost, baseline, and response cost—that were conducted during training sessions. In each phase, Shai's destructive acts resulted in escape for 30 seconds, negative reinforcement.

Chapter 14 defines noncontingent reinforcement as an antecedent manipulation in which a reinforcer is delivered on a periodic schedule that is independent of the target person's behavior; this method is an abolishing operation that decreases the effectiveness of the reinforcer for the target behavior. In the response-cost phase of the experiment with Shai, music or attention was freely available except when a destructive act occurred, which resulted in the loss of the headphones or attention for 30 seconds. Now look at the bottom panel of Figure 18-2 and notice two things. First, attention and music were manipulated on different days in the noncontingent reinforcement and first response-cost phases, so that their effects could be compared. Second, response cost for music (not attention) reduced Shai's destructive acts essentially to zero, but noncontingent reinforcement had little effect.

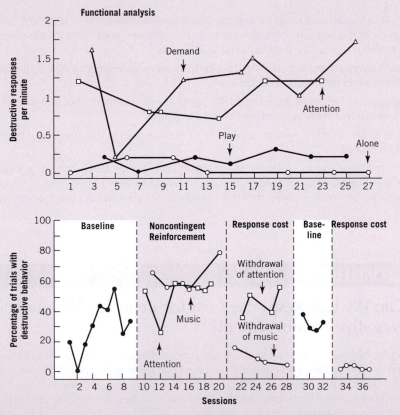

Figure 18-2 Rates of destructive acts during the functional analysis (top panel) and the experiment's five phases: baseline, noncontingent reinforcement, response cost, baseline, and response cost. Music and social attention were the reinforcers given in noncontingent reinforcement and lost in response cost; notice that these reinforcers were manipulated on different days so that their effects could be compared. *Source:* From K. M. Keeney, W. W. Fisher, J. D. Adelinis, & D. A. Wilder (2000), The effects of response cost in the treatment of aberrant behavior maintained by negative reinforcement. *Journal of Applied Behavior Analysis, 33,* 255–258, Figure 1. Copyright © 2000 Society for the Experimental Analysis of Behavior. Used by permission.

If you decide that you can implement time-out, you should inform the target person of the new contingencies and describe the problem behaviors that will result in punishment.

Three additional guidelines should be followed. First, each time-out period should be brief, typically less than 15 minutes. In many cases, periods of 1 to 5 minutes can be effective. Second, the end of any time-out period should be flexible: If the target person is misbehaving as the period is ending, you should extend the time-out until no misbehavior has occurred for a while (Brantner & Doherty, 1983). For example, a study required that a child must be behaving appropriately during the final minute of the period before the time-out could end (Fabiano et al., 2004). Third, be sure to apply the time-out procedure for each instance of the target behavior. (Go to .)

"I CAN'T TALK LONG, JOEY. I'M BETWEEN TIME-OUTS."

Because Dennis seems to get lots of time-outs, we might wonder whether his parents have been carrying out the technique effectively and whether other methods might have a stronger influence on his behavior. *Source:* Reprinted with special permission of King Features Syndicate.

CASE STUDY

Problematic Time-Out? The Cases of Sid and Paul

We saw in Chapter 13 that functional assessments can produce inconclusive outcomes, not identifying the reinforcers that maintain a problem behavior. Researchers examined the effects of using a relatively stringent time-out procedure to punish severe behaviors, such as aggression and self-injury, when a functional analysis produced inconclusive results (Magee & Ellis, 2001). The procedure, called *basket-hold time-out*, consists of physically restraining the target person for a short time in a chair or while facedown on the floor.

The study tested Sid and Paul, 13-year-old boys with mental retardation and other disorders. The functional analysis seemed to suggest initially that attention was the main reinforcer for Sid's problem behavior, but after a few sessions, he performed few of the target behaviors in any condition; the main reinforcer for Paul's behavior seemed to be escape from training demands—a finding that could make time-out inadvisable as a punisher because it might actually reinforce the behavior. The intervention used basket-hold time-out each time the boys performed the target behaviors. For both boys, basket-hold time-out *increased* the problem behaviors markedly across sessions. These findings indicate that using time-out is not appropriate when the functional assessment produces inconclusive results and when the main reinforcer for the target behavior is escape.

ISSUES WITH RESPONSE COST

Using response cost has similar advantages to those of time-out—response cost usually produces large decreases in a behavior quickly, is fairly easy to apply with most target persons, and is considered by professionals and others to be more acceptable than most forms of positive punishment. Some evidence suggests that response cost may be more effective than differential reinforcement of other behavior (DRO) in decreasing behavior (Conyers et al., 2004). Researchers compared the two procedures in reducing preschool students' disruptive classroom behaviors, using each procedure on alternate days across dozens of days. For both procedures, 15-minute sessions were divided into short intervals—for DRO, the students received a token if they did not misbehave during an interval; for response cost, they lost a token if they misbehaved in an interval. The tokens could be redeemed later for candy. The study found that both methods produced substantial reductions in the behaviors quickly and DRO was initially more effective, but response cost became more successful at reducing the behaviors than DRO over time.

If you are thinking about using response-cost punishment to decrease a problem behavior, you should consider several issues. First, response cost can sometimes lead a target person to react negatively, such as by avoiding the situation—for instance, being truant—or by being verbally or physically aggressive. These problems can often be reduced by explaining the new contingencies to the person and why they are needed. Second, you will need to identify the items or privileges and the amounts of them that will be lost when the person misbehaves. Losing the items or privileges is sometimes based on a token system, so tokens are lost at the time the target behavior occurs; but that loss makes it less likely that the person will be able to buy the item or privilege as a backup reinforcer. In any case, you need to make sure that the person values highly the items or privileges that will be lost and that the amount lost, such as the number of tokens, with each instance of misbehavior is large enough to reduce the behavior but not so large that it creates negative reactions.

The third issue to consider is whether the response cost for each instance of misbehavior will be instituted immediately or delayed. Using delayed response cost is appropriate for individuals who can understand the system and remember or keep track of what the misbehavior was and what they lost. Fourth, it's important to check with supervisors at a school or other institution where you may want to apply response-cost procedures regarding the acceptability of such procedures there. For instance, it may be unacceptable to use food as the item the target person will lose for misbehavior. If the supervisors or the target person's parent objects to the use of response cost, you probably won't be able to use it.

TIPS ON USING NEGATIVE PUNISHMENT

The following tips apply to the use of time-out and response-cost punishment methods to decrease problem behaviors.

1. Check with supervisors at a school or other institution where you may want to apply time-out or response-cost methods regarding their acceptability there.

2. If negative punishment will be used, select the weakest level that is likely to be effective. For instance, use time-out periods of short durations.

3. Try to design the procedure for negative punishment so that it can be applied immediately after every instance of the target behavior to be decreased.

4. Instruct the target person in advance and as clearly as possible what the problem behavior is, what the new consequences will be, and why it is important to decrease the behavior.

5. Don't present punishment at about the same time as reinforcement. If this happens, one or both consequences may weaken. This could happen, for example, if you were to comfort the target person soon after a punisher is presented because he or she looks sad.

6. It's a good idea to precede instances of punishment with a warning cue, such as saying, "No!" Doing so may strengthen the ability of the cue to suppress unwanted behavior.

7. Identify and reinforce an alternative behavior or competing response.

8. When using time-out punishment, make sure the time-in is reinforcing.

9. Use time-out for behaviors that are maintained by positive reinforcement, not negative reinforcement, as determined with a functional assessment.

10. When using response-cost punishment, make sure there is always a supply of items or privileges to lose. Without a supply, you've lost the punisher.

11. When using response cost, make sure that the person values highly the items or privileges that will be lost.

(Go to .)

STUDY AND REVIEW

SUMMARY

Although all effective forms of punishment suppress the behavior on which they are contingent, in negative punishment, a valued stimulus or condition is taken away when the behavior occurs. By contrast, in positive punishment, an aversive stimulus or condition is added when the behavior occurs. Two advantages of using punishment are that it suppresses the behavior rapidly and often eliminates it. Behavior analysts generally reserve methods of punishment for behaviors that have received nonaversive procedures unsuccessfully, that are potentially dangerous, and whose reinforcers they can't control.

Time-out is a negative punishment technique that can take one of three forms: isolation time-out, exclusion time-out, and nonexclusion time-out. Response cost is a negative punishment technique in which the occurrence of a problem behavior results in the loss of a valued item or privilege. Time-out can be used to decrease only problem behaviors maintained by positive reinforcement, but response cost can be used for behaviors maintained by positive or negative reinforcement. For both types of negative punishment, a functional assessment should be performed and reveal clear outcomes. For time-out to be very effective, time-in should be

CONCEPT CHECK 18.2

Answer the following questions about time-out and response cost.

1. In the punishment procedure called _____ time-out, the target person is cut off from opportunities for reinforcement but is not removed to a separate setting.

2. In nonexclusion time-out, the person receives a _____ indicating the start of a period when he or she cannot earn reinforcers.

3. An example of signal in nonexclusion time-out is _____ . ⇔

4. In the punishment procedure called _____ , misbehavior results in the loss of an item or privilege.

5. Isolating individuals who are developmentally disabled may provide them with the opportunity to engage in undesirable or dangerous behaviors, such as _____ . ⇔

6. You should check with _____ at schools or institutions for approval and/or restrictions regarding using punishment methods.

very reinforcing; the duration of each time-out period should be short, usually from 1 to 5 minutes; and release from time-out should depend on the person's good behavior at the end of the period. For response cost to be very effective, the items or privileges the person can lose should be ones he or she values highly.

To prepare for exams, use the following key terms and review questions and the online study guide that's available on this book's companion website at www.wiley.com/college/sarafino.

KEY TERMS

punishment
time-out

isolation time-out
exclusion time-out

nonexclusion time-out
response cost

ANSWERS TO CONCEPT CHECKS (CCs)

CC18.1 Answers: **1.** negative **2.** achieves rapid results, eliminates the behavior **3.** likely **4.** strong pain or tissue damage **5.** acceptable **6.** reprimands

CC18.2 Answers: **1.** exclusion **2.** signal **3.** the person cannot wear a ribbon that indicates eligibility for reinforcement **4.** response cost **5.** self-injury **6.** supervisors

REVIEW QUESTIONS

1. Define *positive* and *negative punishment*, and give an example of each that was not presented in this book.
2. What factors should you consider when deciding whether to use punishment?
3. Distinguish among isolation, exclusion, and nonexclusion time-out.
4. Describe the intervention and findings of the research by Solnick, Rincover, and Peterson (1977) on using exclusion time-out methods to decrease a boy's spitting and self-injurious behavior.
5. Describe the research and findings of Barrish, Saunders, and Wolf (1969) on using response-cost punishment to decrease classroom disruptive behaviors.
6. Describe the research and findings of Keeney, Fisher, Adelinis, and Wilder (2000) on using response cost to decrease a woman's destructive acts that were maintained by negative reinforcement.
7. When is using time-out punishment not advisable?
8. Describe the research and findings of Magee and Ellis (2001) on the importance of determining the reinforcers with a functional assessment before using time-out punishment.
9. What issues should you consider before using response-cost punishment?

RELATED READINGS

* Axelrod, S., & Apsche, J. (Eds.). (1983). *The effects of punishment on human behavior.* New York: Academic Press.
* Repp, A. C., & Singh, N. N. (Eds.). (1990). *Perspectives on the use of nonaversive and aversive interventions for persons with developmental disabilities.* Sycamore, IL: Sycamore.
* Walters, G. C., & Grusec, J. E. (1977). *Punishment.* San Francisco: W.H. Freeman.

19

USING POSITIVE PUNISHMENT TO DECREASE A BEHAVIOR

Positive Punishment and Its Problems
Aversive Stimuli
Aversive Activities
Cautions and Ethics in Using Positive Punishment

How to Use Positive Punishment Effectively
Selecting the Best Punishers
Administering Punishers

Tips on Using Positive Punishment

Study and Review

PROLOGUE

"I'm going to step on your face," said 10-year-old Peter to a classmate. As you may have guessed, Peter was an aggressive boy. He was diagnosed as mentally retarded and legally blind, which glasses improved. His aggression was the target behavior in an intervention, and it was manifested in two ways: verbal, such as saying in an angry tone, "I'm going to kill you," and physical, such as kicking or choking another person (Luce, Delquadri, & Hall, 1980). During baseline, Peter performed an average of about 63 aggressive actions and 24 aggressive statements per school day.

The intervention used two methods in separate phases. One method, *contingent exercise*, involved having him perform the sequence of standing up and sitting down on the floor 10 times each time Peter made an aggressive action or statement. When the staff at his school introduced the contingent exercise method, they gave physical guidance and verbal ("stand up" and "sit down") prompts when needed. And he received instructions on the target behaviors and contingencies. The other method used in the intervention was differential reinforcement of other behavior (DRO), which consisted of rewarding his nonaggressive behavior with praise (such as, "Good, Peter, you didn't fight at all this period") and tokens that could be redeemed for privileges or edible items twice a day. For these intervention procedures, contingent exercise was far more effective than DRO in decreasing Peter's aggressive actions and statements, reducing them to fewer than 10 a day. What's more, a follow-up assessment 6 weeks after the intervention ended revealed that his aggressive actions and statements occurred 1.2 and 2.2 times a day, respectively.

We discussed in Chapter 7 that one type of punishment involves having the target person engage in disliked activities. Peter probably didn't like performing the sequence of standing and sitting repeatedly, as used in this contingent exercise method. Regardless of his liking, the critical issue is that the activity was presented after each instance of an aggressive action or statement, and his aggression decreased—given that the behaviors declined, the method qualifies as punishment. In this chapter, we examine techniques of positive punishment for decreasing operant behaviors.

POSITIVE PUNISHMENT AND ITS PROBLEMS

We've seen in earlier chapters that positive punishment methods involve delivering, or *adding*, an aversive stimulus or condition after a target behavior occurs. Positive punishers can be grouped into two categories: *aversive stimuli* and *aversive activities*.

AVERSIVE STIMULI

Stimuli can be aversive in two ways: Some stimuli result in the target person feeling physical discomfort, as spanking a child can do, and some result in psychological discomfort, as a verbal reprimand can do.

Reprimands

Reprimands are harsh verbal criticisms of behavior, such as when a parent says sharply to a misbehaving child, "No. Don't do that!" or "That's bad!" These positive punishers are used very commonly in all sorts of settings because they can be administered easily and quickly, and sometimes they are more effective than other punishers that are more time-consuming to use (Doleys et al., 1976). The effectiveness of reprimands in changing behavior is enhanced when the person receiving them is nearby and the statements are accompanied by a fixed stare and firm grasp, such as of the person's arm or shoulders (Van Houten, 1983; Van Houten et al., 1982). Their effects can also be enhanced by pairing them with other punishers, such as mild, physically aversive stimuli (Dorsey, Iwata, Ong, & McSween, 1980). Pairings of this type are common—for instance, before administering some other punisher, such as time-out, a parent or teacher usually states a reprimand to clarify the contingency: "Taking her toy was bad! Go sit in the corner." Reprimands that suppress responses are conditioned punishers—that is, they gained their ability to suppress behavior by having been paired with other punishers.

Reprimands are often used by themselves to change behavior, but this approach can lead to more variable effects than those of other consequences. For instance, we've seen in earlier chapters that parents' and teachers' reprimands often serve as reinforcers for children's undesirable behavior—that is, they *increase* rather than decrease the target behavior. In fact, a study of children with developmental disabilities found that reprimands given during training sessions after problem behavior, such as aggression and vocalizations, increased that behavior more than other kinds of attention, such as praise or tickles, did (Kodak, Northup, & Kelley, 2007). Also keep in mind that sometimes using reprimands creates an illusion of being effective: The misbehavior stops quickly, but only for a short time, and the frequency of the behavior actually increases later. Still, if periodic assessments are made and show that the reprimands are working, these punishers can be very useful as a part of programs to change behavior.

Physically Aversive Stimuli

We saw in Chapter 7 that **physically aversive stimuli** produce bodily pain, discomfort, or sensations that people generally find unpleasant. When these stimuli are effective as punishers, they are delivered each time the target behavior occurs, and they decrease that behavior. Table 19.1 lists a variety of physically aversive stimuli and the

Table 19.1   *Type of Physically Aversive Stimulus Applied to Target Person as Punisher, Behavior It Decreased, and Reference for the Intervention*

Physically Aversive Stimulus	Behavior Decreased	Reference
Cold (ice cube held briefly against jaw)	Bruxism (grinding teeth)	Blount, Drabman, Wilson, & Stewart (1982)
Facial screening (briefly covering face with cloth or hand)	Self-injurious behavior	Singh, Watson, & Winton (1986)
Noise (loud tone through earphones; stopped when behavior ended)	Finger sucking	Ellingson et al. (2000)
Odor (ammonia fumes contained in capsules held under nose)	Self-injurious behavior	Tanner & Zeiler (1975)
Spray (brief water spray to face)	Self-injurious behavior	Dorsey, Iwata, Ong, & McSween (1980)
Taste (lemon juice squirted into mouth)	Rumination (regurgitating food)	Sajwaj, Libet, & Agras (1974)

target behaviors they have decreased when used as positive punishers in interventions. Notice that most of the listed behaviors were serious problems, and the punishers were not severe. This reflects the professional view in behavior analysis that using physically aversive stimuli should be reserved for very serious behaviors, such as chronic self-injury, and the stimuli should be as mild as possible while still decreasing the behavior.

One type of physically aversive stimulus not listed in the table is electric shock. This stimulus has been studied extensively as a punisher; for instance, dozens of studies have used electric shock to reduce self-injurious behavior in individuals with mental retardation (Duker & Seys, 1996). Studies using electric shock as a punisher have used various shock strengths—the best indicator of strength is amperage (amplitude) measured in milliamperes (mA): The higher the mA, the stronger the shock. People vary in their perceptions of the intensity of shock of the same mA. For example, 3.5 mA indicates fairly mild shock, and people's reports of that shock's strength vary from its being imperceptible to feeling like a rubber band snapped on the arm (Linscheid et al., 1990). Some studies have used shock intensities that were several times stronger, such as 15 to 18 mA. In one of these studies, 5 of the 12 individuals receiving shock punishment reacted initially with "panic and extreme anxiety (i.e., screaming, crying, attack, escape)" when the shock was introduced (Duker & Seys, 1996, p. 298).

Linscheid and his colleagues (1990) have developed and studied a procedure called the Self-Injurious Behavior Inhibiting System (SIBIS) that uses mild electric shock to punish and decrease head banging, a common and dangerous self-injurious behavior. The shock apparatus contains a stimulus module to deliver shock to the arm or leg and a headband that holds an impact detector that senses a hit to the head. When a hit to the head occurs, the impact detector sends a signal to the stimulus module that sounds a tone and delivers a 3.5-mA shock (as an option, the behavior analyst can control delivery of shock with a transmitter). These researchers evaluated the effectiveness of SIBIS in reducing long-term, severe head banging in five individuals with developmental disabilities. The individuals had received various other treatments, such as with other types of punishers and differential reinforcement, that had not succeeded; they were currently being protected from self-injury by being restrained, wearing padded gear, or taking sedating drugs. SIBIS decreased head banging dramatically and quickly, reducing it to zero or near-zero levels in all five cases.

What about long-term effects of SIBIS? On this question, the answers are less clear. One 4-year study followed a man who was treated with SIBIS for head hitting and found that his self-injurious behavior declined to one instance per hour across many months of treatment, but it began to increase after that substantially even though the apparatus was still being used (Ricketts, Goza, & Matese, 1993). This finding suggests that the punishment may lose its effectiveness for some individuals when applied on a long-term basis. But another study found that the effectiveness of SIBIS in reducing self-injury in a teenage boy continued across the 5 years in which it was applied even though the target behavior would reappear quickly when there was a lapse in the treatment, such as when the apparatus broke down (Linscheid & Reichenbach, 2002). There is little evidence to suggest that SIBIS can be discontinued without having the self-injurious behavior come back. Keep in mind that SIBIS has virtually always been applied as a single procedure, without combining it with other methods such as differential reinforcement. A combination of methods might allow a gradual withdrawal of the SIBIS component without having the problem behavior reappear. One difficulty in using other methods is that conducting a functional assessment with individuals who are so severely disordered is problematic and often produces inconclusive results (Duker & Seys, 1996; Linscheid & Reichenbach, 2002). (Go to 🐾.)

AVERSIVE ACTIVITIES

Instead of punishing a problem behavior by following an instance of it with a physically aversive stimulus, we can require the target person to engage in or experience an activity that is a low-probability behavior—in everyday terms, the activity is uncomfortable or unpleasant. As we saw in Chapter 5, the Premack principle states that consequences are reinforcing because they involve performing high-probability behaviors, activities people do frequently when they have a free choice. Low-probability behaviors represent the other side of that coin: **Aversive activities** involve behaviors the person does not do often and does not enjoy doing. Aversive activities are punishers when they are contingent on a target behavior and decrease that behavior.

Contingent Exercise, Physical Restraint, and Response Blocking

In this chapter's opening story about Peter, his aggressive behavior was greatly reduced by having him engage in an activity called **contingent exercise**. In this activity, the person must perform a series of movements repeatedly; usually the movements are unrelated to the problem behavior. In Peter's case, when he performed an aggressive action or statement, he had to stand up and sit down 10 times.

Two other aversive activities that can serve as punishment are physical restraint and response blocking. In **physical restraint**, the behavior analyst holds the part of the target person's body that carries out the problem behavior so that it cannot move for a short period of time, such as 1 minute. Thus a high-probability behavior, such as head hitting or aggression, is followed by a low-probability behavior such as not moving the hands. In **response blocking**, the behavior analyst physically intervenes, preventing completion of the response, as soon as the problem behavior begins to occur. For example, to decrease a child's mouthing of the fingers, you could place the palm of your hand in front of the mouth as soon as the child initiates moving his or her hand toward the face. Response blocking is generally classified as a punishment procedure, but it is unclear whether it may be mainly an *extinction* procedure because it also prevents possible automatic reinforcement of the problem behavior (see, for example, Smith, Russo, & Le, 1999).

Overcorrection

A punishment procedure that uses aversive activities is **overcorrection**, which requires the person to engage in effortful, low-probability behaviors that correct or are the opposite of the problem behavior when that misbehavior occurs (Foxx & Azrin, 1972). As stated in Chapter 7, overcorrection can take and include two forms:

1. **Restitution** involves correcting the effects of the problem behavior and restoring the environment, usually to a condition better than it was before the misbehavior. For example, a boy who repeatedly gets his clothes muddy when playing outside might be required to wash and fold those and other clothes and put them away.

2. **Positive practice**, used when the misbehavior occurs, requires the person to perform repeatedly an appropriate or useful alternative behavior or competing response. For instance, a girl in school who makes many math errors because she rushes through her work might have to do correctly over and over the math problems she got wrong.

Overcorrection can use restitution and positive practice together or separately (Axelrod, Brantner, & Meddock, 1978; Donohue, 2005; Ollendick & Matson, 1978).

An intervention to reduce stealing by institutionalized adults with mental retardation used restitution as punishment for the target behaviors (Azrin & Wesolowski, 1974). These 34 individuals stole from one another

CASE STUDY

Use of SIBIS in Treating Donna's Self-Injurious Behavior

To illustrate the SIBIS approach and evaluation of the intervention, we'll focus on the treatment of one participant: 17-year-old Donna, who was profoundly retarded and had no language (Linscheid et al., 1990). She attended a school but lived with her parents, who reported that she had been hitting her head for at least 10 years and had injured herself frequently. To prevent Donna from injury when she was put to bed at night, her parents would hold her arms until she went to sleep, which sometimes took hours.

The research design to evaluate the intervention consisted of seven phases that included two for baseline, two for SIBIS, and three for SIBIS inactive (that is, Donna wore the apparatus, but the stimulus module was turned off). Each phase had at least four sessions, during which she was not protected from hitting herself; each session lasted a short time (10 minutes or until she hit her head 25 times) to reduce the risk of injury. Figure 19-1 presents her head-banging data—responses per minute—for the seven phases. Notice first that some sessions show more than 25 responses per minute; these sessions were stopped before 1 minute, and the data were prorated to represent a full minute. Now compare the data across phases: Clearly, SIBIS decreased Donna's head banging dramatically and quickly, reducing it to near zero immediately. During the subsequent weeks when she continued to receive SIBIS treatment while in school, her self-injurious behavior stayed at low levels, and her general classroom behavior improved.

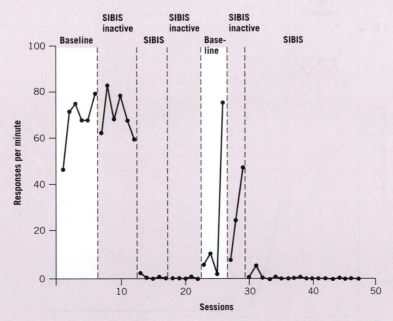

Figure 19-1   Donna's head-hitting responses per minute during seven phases of an experiment to evaluate the effectiveness of an electric shock punishment procedure (SIBIS) in decreasing that behavior. Notice the high rates of hitting in the first two phases: an average of more than one hit per second. Because any session was terminated when 25 head hits occurred, the data showing greater than 25 responses needed to be prorated to represent a full minute. *Source*: From T. R. Linscheid B. A. Iwata, R. W. Ricketts, D. E. Williams, & J. C. Griffen (1990), Clinical evaluation of the self-injurious behavior inhibiting system (SIBIS). *Journal of Applied Behavior Analysis, 23*, 53–78, Figure 8. Copyright © 1990 Society for the Experimental Analysis of Behavior. Used by permission.

very frequently, and one of the main items they would steal was food at mealtimes and at snack times. No baseline assessment was made, because it would require an ethically indefensible condition: The staff would not be able to intervene when they were aware of victims losing their property. Instead, the first few days of the intervention used a "simple correction" procedure in which staff required only that the thief return the food (or the part remaining, if some was already consumed). Because thefts often occurred as a "sudden grasping-biting movement," this procedure often didn't restore the original condition, and thefts continued at a high rate. The intervention used an overcorrection–restitution method that included the simple correction procedure *and* the requirement that the thief go to the food display area with a staff member, get an identical item, and give it to the victim. Nearly 20 thefts occurred each day when simple correction was the only consequence, but the thefts declined rapidly with the restitution method and were completely eliminated in a few days, as Figure 19-2 shows.

Positive practice was used in an intervention to reduce sprawling—that is, sitting or lying about—on floors instead of sitting in available chairs (Azrin & Wesolowski, 1975). The intervention was carried out with adult residents at an institution for mental retardation. The sprawling was not just unsightly; it also created a hazard that had caused injuries. Other methods had been tried without success to change this behavior. Positive practice was conducted in the following way: Individuals who sat on the floor were told they could not do that and were required to get up, go to a nearby chair, sit there for about a minute, and then go and sit for a minute on each of several other chairs. They were left sitting on the last chair. Verbal directions and physical help were given for each step in the sequence. Positive practice eliminated floor sprawling in about 10 days, and a follow-up assessment found that the residents continued to use the chairs 6 months later.

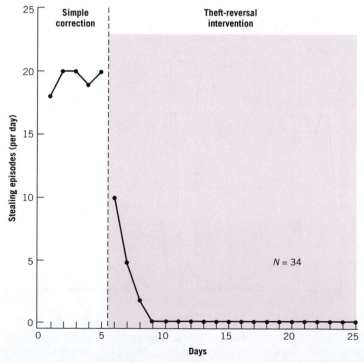

Figure 19-2 Frequency of stealing episodes each day by 34 adults with mental retardation during two phases: simple correction and an overcorrection theft-reversal intervention. *Source:* From N. H. Azrin & M. D. Wesolowski (1974), Theft reversal: An overcorrection procedure for eliminating stealing by retarded persons. *Journal of Applied Behavior Analysis, 7*, 577–581, Figure 1. Copyright © 1974 Society for the Experimental Analysis of Behavior. Used by permission.

Research has shown that overcorrection methods can be effective in reducing a variety of problem behaviors in hospital, classroom, and home settings (Axelrod, Brantner, & Meddock, 1978; Ollendick & Matson, 1978). And some research results indicate that overcorrection may be effective in classrooms even when the positive practice is delayed until a lesson or the class is over (Azrin & Powers, 1975; Barton & Osborne, 1978). An advantage of overcorrection methods is that they have built-in alternative behaviors or competing responses, thereby providing opportunities to learn appropriate behaviors instead of just suppressing misbehavior (Carey & Bucher, 1981). But these methods have some disadvantages as well—for example, they are complicated and very time-consuming to administer (Kelly & Drabman, 1977; MacKenzie-Keating & McDonald, 1990). In addition, problems may arise with any punisher that involves an aversive activity if the person who is being punished refuses to engage in the activity. Suppose the individuals with retardation who were stealing food refused to make the required restitution. What then? Although sometimes using physical guidance can move the person into a given activity, if such measures don't work, other efforts that can help include explaining to the person in advance why an aversive activity is being used and that a more unpleasant backup punisher, such as response cost or a physically aversive stimulus, will be applied if refusal occurs. If these efforts don't work, however, we may have to abandon using the aversive activity as a punisher.

CAUTIONS AND ETHICS IN USING POSITIVE PUNISHMENT

Some organizations, such as The Association for Persons with Severe Handicaps (TASH), as well as individual professionals oppose the application of punishment, particularly physically aversive stimuli, as inhumane and unjustified methods for changing behavior (Donnellan & LaVigna, 1990; TASH, 2011). Most professionals in applied behavior analysis disagree with this view, believing that punishment of all kinds can be humane and justified under certain restricted circumstances. Deciding to use punishment to change a behavior should be made after considering other methods—if all nonpunitive methods are inappropriate or not effective enough, sometimes having already been tried, punishment may be the most appropriate next step. At that point, deciding whether to use a particular form of punishment can be made after considering the following issues.

Safety of the Target Person and Caretakers

One consideration in deciding whether to use punishment is the safety of the target person and other individuals, such as caregivers, behavior analysts, or classmates. Two questions are important. First, *does the punishment procedure pose a safety risk?* Using a very strong physically aversive stimulus, isolation time-out in an unsafe room, or forceful physical guidance could lead to injury—such punishment procedures are not acceptable. Second, *does failing to stop a problem behavior pose a safety risk?* Self-injurious behavior and aggression create danger for the target person and others. Some persons who performed self-injurious behaviors have blinded themselves and produced serious facial injuries and "cauliflower" ears (Duker & Seys, 1996; Smith, Russo, & Le, 1999). When serious injury is likely, punishment methods may be justified if they are liable to stop the behavior. This issue is similar to medical decisions for serious illnesses, such as cancer: Chemotherapy and surgical treatments are difficult and painful experiences, but if they can stop the course of the disease, wouldn't you consider them?

Using the Most Effective but Least Restrictive Treatment

As we've seen here and in Chapters 7 and 18, an advantage of using punishment is that it often decreases the problem behavior quickly, markedly, and to near-zero levels. Nonpunitive methods sometimes have similar effects and should be tried first.

Another issue to consider when deciding whether punishment is an appropriate method to change a problem behavior is the degree to which the procedure restricts the target person's rights. *Restrictive* procedures exert a very high degree of control and manipulation over the person's freedom of action (TASH, 2011). Probably most people would give the following rank order for the techniques we've described in this book for changing operant behavior, from least to most restrictive:

1. Antecedent manipulations and positive reinforcement
2. Negative reinforcement
3. Negative punishment (time-out and response cost)
4. Positive punishment

Within positive punishment, reprimands would be the least restrictive, aversive activities would be next, and physically aversive stimuli would be the most restrictive. In addition, the viewpoint of the target person is important: Linscheid and colleagues noted that "most individuals who have received a shock from SIBIS indicated that they consider the procedure less aversive than tastes (e.g., lemon juice and Tabasco sauce), ammonia odor, overcorrection, or restraint" (1990, p. 75). Our expectations about the restrictiveness of a technique may be wrong.

Generally speaking, behavior analysts should try to use the least restrictive approaches before using more restrictive ones. For example, if a functional assessment can be done and produces conclusive outcomes, there is a good chance that antecedent manipulations and positive reinforcement methods will succeed in changing a problem behavior. Treatment decisions often involve a balancing act of a method's effectiveness and restrictiveness. The ideal situation is when a behavior change technique is low in restrictiveness and high in effectiveness, but this ideal doesn't always exist. Would it be appropriate to use a method that is low in restrictiveness and in effectiveness? Probably not, but most interventions apply a combination of methods, such as extinction of the target behavior, reinforcement of an alternative behavior, and antecedent manipulations. The combination is usually more effective than any of the methods alone.

Obtaining Informed Consent and Peer Review

Before applying aversive activities or physically aversive stimuli on a target person, behavior analysts must seek and receive two forms of approval: informed consent and peer review. In **informed consent**, target persons or their parent or guardian give their *permission in writing* to conduct an intervention after receiving information describing the intervention methods, including all positive and negative features that might affect their willingness to allow the intervention, and are told that they may decline or discontinue the intervention freely at any time. The person giving consent must be an adult with legal authority to give permission and the ability to understand the information about the intervention methods.

In a *peer review*, a panel of professionals, including individuals with expertise in behavior analysis, examines a proposal for the intervention that details how the methods will be carried out and a rationale to justify their application for the target person. This rationale should include information about other methods that have been used in the past to change the behavior. If the panel decides that the methods are well designed, justified for the problem behavior, and likely to be effective in changing the target behavior, its members give their permission in writing. For interventions designed as research projects, the peer review is conducted by a panel of individuals called an institutional review board, which we discuss in Chapter 27.

Training and Supervision of Punishment Procedures

If punishment will be used in an intervention, guidelines must be written describing how it will be implemented: what the procedure will be, who will carry it out, and under what circumstances it will be used. With this detailed information, all personnel—behavior analysts, teachers, or other staff—who will carry out the procedure can be trained to a high level of competence before implementing it. After the punishment procedure begins, data should be collected on the target behavior and supervisory personnel should oversee the application of the punishment and examine the data regularly. These processes ensure that the punishment is being implemented correctly, is reducing the behavior, and is not misused. (Go to 🔍 and then 📖.)

CLOSE-UP

Using Aversive Stimuli as a Last Resort

In the interventions for Peter's aggressive actions and statements in the opening story and Donna's self-injurious behavior in the Case Study, the problem behaviors were severe and posed safety risks, had existed for years, and were treated unsuccessfully in the past with other behavioral methods. These conditions are consistent with recommendations to use physically aversive stimuli as a last resort (Iwata, 1988). Linscheid and his colleagues stated in the article introducing the SIBIS procedure:

> SIBIS is not intended to be used as the first or the only means of treating SIB [self-injurious behavior]. Indeed, the aversive components of SIBIS may be appropriate only as a default technology, to be used with a small percentage of cases involving the treatment of severe self-injurious or aggressive behavior. (1990, p. 77)

Similar statements can be made for using other physically aversive stimuli as punishers. The less restrictive, negative punishment procedures—time-out and response cost—are more acceptable approaches for decreasing problem behaviors and are used much more often than aversive activities and stimuli. And the development of functional assessment methods has enabled behavior analysts to apply antecedent and reinforcement techniques more effectively, negating the need to use punishment.

CONCEPT CHECK 19.1

Check your understanding of the preceding concepts. Remember: The symbol ⇔ means that the answer can vary. Answer the following questions about positive punishment and its problems.

1. Two examples of aversive stimuli are _____ and _____ . ⇔
2. A problem with using reprimands as punishers is that they sometimes _____ the behavior we want to decrease.
3. The SIBIS shock intensity of _____ mA is fairly mild and may feel as strong as a rubber band snapped on the arm.
4. Two examples of aversive activities that can be effective punishers are _____ and _____ . ⇔
5. The target person's having to correct the effects of the problem behavior by restoring the environment to a condition that is as good or better than it was before the misbehavior is called _____ .
6. When target persons or guardians give permission in writing to use intervention methods after being told about the procedures, this is called _____ .

HOW TO USE POSITIVE PUNISHMENT EFFECTIVELY

If we decide to use punishment to change behavior, we should take steps to maximize its effectiveness. The more carefully we apply punishment, the less frequently we'll need to apply it because the behavior will decline faster. In this section, we'll discuss how to select punishers and administer them well.

SELECTING THE BEST PUNISHERS

Included in our Chapter 15 discussion of applying reinforcement methods was the topic of identifying potential reinforcers. One approach to identify reinforcers involved direct assessments—using structured tests to present possibly reinforcing items or activities and observe how the target person reacts to them. Researchers have adapted this approach to identify effective punishers (Fisher et al., 1994). The structured tests used a set of nine commonly used punishers, such as facial screening or contingent exercise; only one of them was used in each session, which lasted about 20 minutes. Each potential punisher was presented 10 times in a session; and for each trial, an observer recorded on a laptop the occurrence of specific types of reaction, two of which were *negative vocalizations*, such as crying or saying "go away," and *avoidance movements*, such as turning away or trying to block implementation of an activity or stimulus. These reactions were used as measures of nonpreference (dislike): The greater the dislike of an activity or stimulus, the more effective a punisher it was likely to be.

A consideration other than the likely effectiveness of a punisher is its degree of restrictiveness. As we saw earlier, choosing methods to use in an intervention involves a balancing of the effectiveness and restrictiveness of possible techniques. A good way to decide on the punishers to use would be to conduct brief tests with different punishers, as was done in designing an intervention to reduce self-injurious behavior (Thompson, Iwata, Conners, & Roscoe, 1999). The researchers tested several punishers, each in a separate AB design; they compared the outcomes and then "chose the least restrictive procedure that resulted in a 75% or greater decrease" in the target behavior (p. 321). Of course, using brief AB designs to compare punishers' effects requires that the methods show maximal effects quickly, which many punishers do.

ADMINISTERING PUNISHERS

The most basic rule in applying consequences is to be *systematic*. To apply punishment well, we'll need to use behavioral criteria consistently to determine when to apply a punisher, instead of waiting until we've "had enough" of the misbehavior (Hall et al., 1971). It is also important to eliminate or reduce as much as possible extraneous reinforcers that maintain the behavioral excess. In the next sections, we'll examine aspects in the application of punishment that can influence how effective it will be.

Reinforcing Alternative Behaviors or Competing Responses

It's rarely a good idea to design an intervention that uses punishment by itself to decrease a problem behavior and does not provide reinforcement for other actions. There are three reasons to reinforce alternative behaviors or competing responses when using punishment. First, punishment teaches only what *not* to do. It doesn't teach new, more appropriate behavior to take the place of the undesirable actions (Brown, 1982). Second, combining reinforcement of alternative behaviors or competing responses with punishment is more effective in decreasing target behaviors than punishment is alone (Van Houten, 1983). This approach can make relatively mild punishers more useful because the alternative behavior or competing response helps suppress the problem behavior (Carey & Bucher, 1986). Third, the occasional negative side effects of punishment are less likely to appear if alternative behaviors or competing responses are reinforced (Van Houten, 1983).

Using Instructions

Punishment appears to work best in suppressing unwanted behavior when the person receives specific instructions describing both the target behavior and the consequences. An intervention that used instructions was conducted to reduce negative social behaviors among unpopular boys in the first to third grades in school (Bierman, Miller, & Stabb, 1987). The program decreased these behaviors by describing the undesirable acts and applying response cost when they occurred. What's more, some of the boys also received instructions on and reinforcement for performing positive social behaviors as alternative behaviors. Only the boys who received instructions on positive and negative behaviors along with consequences for each type of behavior became more popular among their classmates.

Punisher Magnitude

In general and within limits, the more intense a punisher is, the more effective it is likely to be in suppressing the target behavior (Dinsmoor, 1998; Van Houten, 1983). But this relationship doesn't mean that it's a good idea to use highly aversive consequences as punishers. Intense punishers tend to produce more negative side effects than milder ones do, and mild punishment is often quite effective when combined with reinforcement for alternative behaviors or competing responses. To restate the rule presented earlier about applying punishment: Use the mildest level possible to achieve the behavioral goals of the program (Brantner & Doherty, 1983).

The Timing of Punishment

Punishment is most effective in suppressing undesirable behaviors when it is delivered *immediately after every instance* of the behavior (Dinsmoor, 1998; Van Houten, 1983). Its effects are weakened when it is delayed or when it occurs only unsystematically, particularly at the beginning of an intervention. Sometimes after the behavior has declined substantially, the punishment can be *thinned to an intermittent schedule* and eventually eliminated, and this can be a good idea. For instance, studies have found that delivering time-out punishment intermittently after the behavior has been decreased to a low frequency does not lead to an increase in the behavior (Calhoun & Lima, 1977; Clark, Rowbury, Baer, & Baer, 1973). If the behavior involves a chain of responses, it's probably best to punish it as early in the sequence of responses as possible.

Varying the Punishers

We saw in Chapter 15 that reinforcement tends to be more effective when a variety of reinforcers are available to be given for appropriate behavior. A similar effect exists for punishment—that is, varying the punishers applied for misbehavior appears to suppress the behavior more effectively than using the same punisher all the time. This phenomenon was demonstrated with three 5- and 6-year-olds with developmental disabilities in an intervention to decrease specific deviant behaviors, such as aggression and self-stimulation (Charlop, Burgio, Iwata, & Ivancic, 1988). During some training sessions, the children received one of four punishment methods: reprimands, overcorrection, time-out, and a loud noise. During other training sessions, the trainer alternated using three of the four punishers when misbehaviors occurred. The results revealed that each of the punishers suppressed the deviant behaviors when presented singly in the sessions. But the children engaged in deviant behaviors even less often during sessions when the trainer varied the punishers. It may be that people adapt to the same punisher over time and that varying the punishers prevents this adaptation.

TIPS ON USING POSITIVE PUNISHMENT

Here are several tips on using positive punishment methods. These tips can be applied to decrease operant behavior.

1. Check with supervisors at a school or other institution where you may want to apply aversive activities or stimuli as punishers regarding their acceptability and restrictions there. Be sure to consider the ethical issues described in this chapter.

2. Use nonpunitive procedures developed from a functional assessment before resorting to the use of punishment.

3. Make sure the target person is aware of the changes in consequences and exactly what the target behavior is.

4. If at all possible, identify an alternative behavior or competing response to prompt and reinforce when methods are used to decrease the target behavior.

5. Think carefully about the reinforcers that maintain the behavioral excess and what can be done to eliminate them. After the behavior starts to decline, watch for new sources of reinforcement that may cause the behavior to recover.

6. If a positive punisher will be used, select the least restrictive and weakest level that is likely to be effective.

7. Use a variety of punishers, if possible.

8. Make sure a punisher to be used in the intervention can be applied immediately after every instance of the target behavior to be decreased. Gradually thin the schedule to intermittent punishment after the behavior has declined and stabilized at a low level.

9. It's a good idea to precede instances of punishment with a warning cue, such as saying, "No!" By doing this, you may strengthen the ability of the cue to suppress unwanted behavior.

10. Collect data on the target behavior throughout the program, and review them often to see whether the punishment is working.

(Go to .)

CONCEPT CHECK 19.2

Answer the following questions about how to use positive punishment well.

1. The approach of applying structured tests to identify effective punishers used two reactions of the target persons, _____ and _____ , as measures of nonpreference for the stimuli.

2. A good way to balance the effectiveness and restrictiveness of punishers we select would use an AB design for each stimulus or condition and compare the data to choose the least restrictive of those that reduced the behavior by _____ % or more.

3. When using punishment, one reason to reinforce an alternative or competing response to the target behavior is that doing so _____ . ⇔

4. During the process of applying punishment to decrease a problem behavior, the timing of delivering each punisher should be _____ .

5. After punishment has produced a substantial and stabilized decrease in the target behavior, we can gradually _____ the punishment to a(n) _____ schedule.

STUDY AND REVIEW

SUMMARY

Punishment suppresses the behavior on which it is contingent. In positive punishment, an aversive stimulus or condition is added after the person performs the behavior. Some positive punishers are reprimands; others are physically aversive stimuli, such as when a target person receives lemon juice squirted into the mouth or electric shock to an arm or leg. The Self-Injurious Behavior Inhibiting System (SIBIS) is a procedure that delivers mild electric shock when target persons hit their heads.

Other positive punishers involve having to perform aversive activities, which are low-probability behaviors, after the problem behavior occurs. Aversive activities include contingent exercise, physical restraint, response blocking, and overcorrection, which can have two components: restitution and positive practice. One problem that can occur when using aversive activities is that the person may refuse to do them and may be aggressive if the behavior analyst insists.

Due to the nature of positive punishment, ethical issues must be considered before using aversive activities and physically aversive stimuli. Four issues are important. The first is whether the problem behavior poses a safety risk to the target person or others, and whether failing to stop it poses risks. Self-injurious behavior and aggression often pose risks. The second issue is that behavior analysts should strive to use the most effective but least restrictive treatment methods. The third is that we should obtain informed consent and peer-review approval for the methods we plan to apply. Last, we should be certain that the individuals who will apply punishment are well trained and supervised so that they will apply it correctly and not misuse it.

To apply punishment effectively, begin by selecting the most effective and least restrictive procedures, using positive punishment as a last resort. Other methods should be considered first, after conducting a functional assessment to determine the most appropriate ones to apply. If positive punishment is used, we should apply it immediately and consistently, combined with reinforcing an alternative behavior or competing response; what's more, we should instruct the target person in advance of the problem behavior and new consequences. The best approach is to use varied punishers and apply the weakest intensity of each that will be successful.

To study for exams, use the following key terms and review questions and the online study guide that's available on this book's companion website at www.wiley.com/college/sarafino.

KEY TERMS

reprimands	physical restraint	positive practice
physically aversive stimuli	response blocking	informed consent
aversive activities	overcorrection	
contingent exercise	restitution	

ANSWERS TO CONCEPT CHECKS (CCs)

CC19.1 *Answers:* **1.** reprimands, electric shock   **2.** increase   **3.** 3.5   **4.** contingent exercise, physical restraint   **5.** restitution   **6.** informed consent

CC19.2 *Answers:* **1.** negative vocalizations, avoidance movements   **2.** 75   **3.** prevents negative side effects   **4.** immediately after every instance of the behavior   **5.** thin, intermittent

REVIEW QUESTIONS

1. Describe the research by Luce, Delquadri, and Hall (1980) in the opening story on decreasing Peter's aggression.

2. Describe the advantages and problems in using reprimands to decrease a behavior.

3. What kinds of physically aversive stimuli have interventions used as punishers?

4. Describe the SIBIS procedure, how Linscheid and his coworkers (1990) applied it with Donna to reduce her head hitting, and the results of that intervention.

5. Give one example each of contingent punishment, physical restraint, and response blocking using procedures that were not discussed in this book.

6. Describe the procedure and findings of the research by Azrin and Wesolowski (1974) on using restitution as punishment for stealing food.

7. What can be done to have a person perform an aversive activity if he or she might refuse to do so?

8. Discuss the issue of safety for the target person and others in deciding whether to use punishment to decrease a problem behavior.

9. Define the term *restrictive procedures*. Which methods are more restrictive than others? How does this issue relate to the choice of techniques we use to change a behavior?

10. Describe the process of informed consent.

11. Describe the process for selecting the best punishers.

12. What aspects of administering punishment influence its effectiveness in changing a behavior?

RELATED READINGS

- Axelrod, S., & Apsche, J. (Eds.). (1983). *The effects of punishment on human behavior*. New York: Academic Press.
- Repp, A. C., & Singh, N. N. (Eds.). (1990). *Perspectives on the use of nonaversive and aversive interventions for persons with developmental disabilities*. Sycamore, IL: Sycamore.
- Walters, G. C., & Grusec, J. E. (1977). *Punishment*. San Francisco: W.H. Freeman.

20

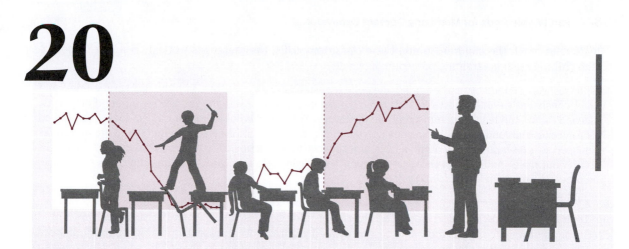

MAXIMIZING AND MAINTAINING OPERANT BEHAVIOR CHANGES

Combining Methods in Designing a Program
Identifying Possible Methods and Deciding Which To Use
Examples of Multidimensional Programs

Checking and Adjusting the Program Design
Assessing a Program's Progress
Improving a Program

Will the Improved Behavior Last?
Regression of Behavior, and Why It Happens
Examples of Relapses

Ways to Maintain Behavior Changes
Promoting Generalization of the Behavior
Fading Prompts and Thinning Reinforcement
Assuring Antecedents and Natural Reinforcement for the Behavior
Booster Programs

Tips on Maximizing and Maintaining Behavior Changes

Study and Review

PROLOGUE

Imagine that you were one of the therapists in the following intervention to train eight 4- to 13-year-old children with autism to perform basic classroom behaviors, such as looking at the teacher and imitating the teacher's actions when requested (Koegel & Rincover, 1974). Children must be able to do these things so they can learn in a classroom. But these children had very poor basic classroom skills. For instance, four of them were mute and the others could only echo words they heard others say. All of them had extremely low IQ scores.

In an effort to teach the children several basic classroom skills, the therapists worked on a one-to-one basis with the children, using a training procedure in which

> responses were shaped by first rewarding the child for establishing eye contact with the teacher until the child would consistently (90% correct trials for three consecutive days) look at the teacher for a period of at least 5 seconds when the teacher commanded, "Look at me." Then, nonverbal imitation was gradually established by prompting and reinforcing copying behaviors until the subject could consistently imitate ... . Imitation was then used as a prompt to teach other nonverbal responses to instructions. For example, the teacher would say, "Touch your nose" and prompt the correct response by saying "Do this" and modeling the correct response. The prompts were then faded. (p. 47)

After 2 to 4 weeks of this training, all of the children were able to perform the skills correctly at least 80% of the time. Then came the crucial test to see if the children would use these skills when the situation was more like a classroom setting—that is, if they were tested with all eight children present in the same room, instead of alone. The average correct responding when alone—nearly 89%—dropped to about 28% when they were tested with other children present.

If you had spent weeks in one-to-one training of basic classroom behaviors, only to have the skills fall apart when the children were tested together, you might be very discouraged. Why didn't these behaviors generalize to the group situation? What can you do to maximize changes in operant behavior and increase the likelihood that the behaviors you train will be maintained in and generalize to other appropriate situations? These are the issues we examine in this chapter.

COMBINING METHODS IN DESIGNING A PROGRAM

Maximizing and maintaining behavior changes starts with the design of the program. In particular, it's important to combine methods in the design to make an intervention more effective—as we've seen, for example, when discussing the value of reinforcing desirable alternative behaviors while using extinction or punishment to reduce a problem behavior. You may have noticed in prior chapters that each technique is useful in addressing one dimension of a problem—the target behavior itself, its antecedents, or its consequences—and they can be combined. **Multidimensional programs** are interventions that include methods to address more than one dimension of a behavior (Friedman, Campbell, & Evans, 1993). To design an effective multidimensional program to change a behavior, we need to consider techniques to address these dimensions:

- *Antecedents*—manipulating antecedent physical or social stimuli to alter the likelihood of the behavior occurring.
- *Behavior*—such as by teaching the person a desirable, competing response.
- *Consequences*—changing the existing consequences of the person's behaviors through reinforcement, extinction, or punishment methods.

This chapter describes how to select from and combine the techniques we've discussed so far to address these three dimensions and design successful programs to change behavior. In addition to designing a multidimensional program, it's important to include procedures to promote the generalization and maintenance of the improved behavior and prevent unwanted behaviors from returning (Friedman, Campbell, & Evans, 1993). Later in this chapter, we examine techniques to maintain behavior changes over long periods of time. These techniques can be added to the program once the intervention is under way.

IDENTIFYING POSSIBLE METHODS AND DECIDING WHICH TO USE

By now, you've learned about all of the basic techniques to consider using in designing a multidimensional program to change operant behavior. The starting point to identify techniques that might be appropriate for a program is conducting a *functional assessment* of the behavior. Then we should ask: Is *the program being designed to change a behavioral excess or a behavioral deficit?* The answer will suggest different techniques to apply. For instance, reinforcement methods are extremely important to correct an operant behavioral deficit or increase an alternative behavior; extinction and punishment procedures might be very useful in decreasing a behavioral excess. With this information, we can consult the checklist in Figure 20-1, which lists methods we've discussed in the preceding chapters and groups them according to the main dimension each one addresses. You can find those discussions by using the index at the end of the book, and most of the terms are defined in the glossary.

How do we decide which techniques to use? The first consideration in designing a program is to decide which techniques are likely to be effective. Whenever possible, of course, choose the most effective methods for the type of problem to be addressed. For instance, when trying to increase an operant behavior, it is essential to include a strong system of reinforcers.

Another consideration in choosing techniques is practicality, especially in the time or effort they require and their financial cost. Some techniques require little time and money. Shortcut methods for shaping or stimulus control are examples of very effective, economical techniques. Other methods are complicated or burdensome to implement, sometimes requiring large amounts of time to carry out well; overcorrection punishment procedures are an example (Kelly & Drabman, 1977). Time-consuming methods may be rejected if they will be implemented by paid staff or therapists, thereby adding to the cost of the intervention, or by friends or relatives, who may be unwilling or unable to give very much of their time. The expense for materials, such as tangible reinforcers, may also influence the specific methods we choose for a particular program.

The decision to use punishment should be made very carefully in designing programs to change behavior. In most cases, aversive activities and physically aversive stimuli are rejected because they are more restrictive

---

CHECKLIST OF BEHAVIOR CHANGE METHODS

This checklist of Behaviour Change Methods can be used to generate and select ideas in designing programs to change operant behavior. Use the index at the end of this book to find descriptions of the techniques listed. The techniques are separated on the basis of whether their *most common uses* are to manage the antecedents, the behavior, or the consequences. But some techniques may be directed toward managing more than one dimension of the behavior change process. If you use the checklist to design a program, you may want to make a photocopy of it and write *yes* or *no* in the spaces preceding the methods to indicate whether you think they may be useful.

Managing the Antecedents
_____ Discrimination learning
_____ Prompting/fading
　　_____ Response prompts
　　_____ Stimulus prompts
_____ Modeling
_____ Instructions
_____ Altering antecedent chains
_____ Managing discriminative stimuli (S^D_s)
_____ Motivating operations
　　_____ Establishing operations
　　_____ Abolishing operations
_____ Noncontingent reinforcement
_____ Response effort

Managing the Behavior
_____ Self-monitoring
_____ Shaping
_____ Shortcuts to shaping
_____ Chaining
_____ Alternative behaviors
_____ Competing responses

Managing the Consequences
_____ Positive reinforcement
　　_____ Tangible/consumable
　　_____ Activities
　　_____ Social reinforcers
　　_____ Feedback
　　_____ Tokens
_____ Intermittent reinforcement/thinning
_____ Negative reinforcement
_____ Extinction (operant)
_____ Controlling counterproductive
　　reinforcers
_____ Lotteries/group contingencies
_____ Punishment
　　_____ Physically aversive stimuli
　　_____ Reprimands
　　_____ Aversive activities
　　_____ Time-out
　　_____ Response cost
_____ Differential reinforcement
　　_____ DRI, DRL, or DRO
　　_____ DRA, functional
　　　　communication training
_____ Habit reversal

Figure 20-1   Checklist of behavior change methods.

than other effective methods. Using aversive methods, especially ones that are moderately or very aversive, should be considered only as a last resort, and only when:

- The target behavior is dangerous or very maladaptive.
- Appropriate, less restrictive methods have been tried and failed.
- The program has gotten written informed consent and ethical approval.
- The program contains safeguards to protect the client.

Punishment procedures that are only mildly unpleasant, such as some forms of time-out or response cost, are usually more acceptable; but a program that includes them should be approved by a supervisor and other appropriate people. Keep in mind that one drawback of using aversive procedures is that they can reduce the person's motivation to participate in the program (Wilson, Leaf, & Nathan, 1975; Wilson & Tracey, 1976).

EXAMPLES OF MULTIDIMENSIONAL PROGRAMS

To see how various techniques to change behavior can be combined, we'll examine a variety of multidimensional programs with very different goals and settings. Some of these programs were designed for specific individuals, and others were designed to apply broad resources with many clients.

Interventions Implemented to Improve an Individual's Behavior

Multidimensional programs have changed many operant behaviors successfully for individual clients. In one example, a program to increase the operant behavior of dental flossing was conducted in the homes of four 7- to 11-year-old boys and girls (Dahlquist & Gil, 1986). The behavior analysts provided each child with training in correct flossing procedures, and the program included the following techniques:

- To *manage the antecedents*, the intervention used prompts of two types: Cards stating "Remember to Floss" were hung in the child's room, and a poster describing the steps in flossing was hung in the bathroom.
- To *manage the consequences*, three methods were used. First, each child received feedback on his or her flossing by recording instances of flossing on a calendar in the bathroom and saving spent floss in a bag. Second, parents were trained to evaluate their child's flossing and give praise or corrective feedback. Third, each child received tangible reinforcers three times a week if his or her record keeping and flossing quality met certain criteria.
- To *manage the behavior*, the intervention used qualitative shaping: The criteria for reinforcement were low initially but were increased periodically during the intervention.

As an independent demonstration of the effects of the intervention, dental plaque levels were assessed and showed a large drop during the several months of the intervention.

Classroom Programs

Multidimensional programs have been applied extensively in classrooms to enhance students' academic learning and improve their social behavior and general conduct. One program was designed to improve the social skills of nine 8- and 9-year-old children who were deaf and had language disabilities (Rasing & Duker, 1992). The program focused on increasing several specific behaviors, such as waiting to speak without interrupting someone; calling a hearing person's name once or twice in a moderate voice to get his or her attention; and providing help, praise, or comfort to someone. It also focused on reducing certain other behaviors—aggression, screaming, and teasing other people, for example. A variety of behavioral methods were included in the program, which the children's teachers were trained to implement. The intervention included methods to:

- *Manage the antecedents*, such as prompts for appropriate social behaviors.
- *Manage the behavior*, using shortcuts to shaping by providing verbal and modeled instruction regarding the specific behaviors to perform.

- *Manage the consequences*, using two methods: (a) negative feedback and corrective instruction for inappropriate behaviors; and (b) rewards for appropriate behaviors by giving praise and tokens, which the children could redeem for tangible and activity reinforcers.

All of the children showed substantial increases in the appropriate social behaviors and decreases in the inappropriate behaviors.

Broad, Community-Based Programs

Community-based programs to change behavior are designed with the view that serious behavior problems, such as alcohol abuse, result from factors that operate in and are affected by the community in which the individual lives. This view suggests that the best way to treat substance abuse is to rearrange these factors in the community rather than trying to correct the problem in a hospital. Using this view, Azrin and his colleagues designed the *community-reinforcement approach* to treat alcoholism (Azrin, 1976; Azrin, Sisson, Meyers, & Godley, 1982; Hunt & Azrin, 1973; Sisson & Azrin, 1989). The program evolved over the years and included the following elements:

- Daily doses of the emetic drug *disulfiram*. Emetics produce nausea; disulfiram has this effect if the target person drinks. Taking the drug is monitored and verbally reinforced by the person's spouse or other intimate individual.
- Marital counseling, job counseling, and a program aimed at getting work
- Reinforcers for taking the disulfiram and attending counseling sessions
- Assistance in developing hobbies and recreational activities in which alcohol is not available
- Training in refusing drinks that are offered to the problem drinker
- Training in ways to promote relaxation and handling social problems that have led to drinking in the past

If you examine this list carefully and with the checklist in Figure 20-1, you'll see that the program includes techniques directed at the antecedents, behavior, and consequences of drinking—for instance, drinking alcohol after taking disulfiram leads to nausea. Several interventions applying the community-reinforcement approach have been used with high rates of success in maintaining sobriety (Smith, Meyers, & Delaney, 1998; Tucker, Vuchinich, & Downey, 1992). Data from one of these interventions showing its success relative to other approaches are presented in Figure 20-2.

CHECKING AND ADJUSTING THE PROGRAM DESIGN

When behavior analysts start applying a program to change behavior, we want to know soon whether it is working, especially if we are using punishment procedures. Applying punishment is usually done on a tentative basis, and it is retained only if it is working well in decreasing a target behavior and the client is dealing with it well. If a program is not working as well as we'd like, we'll want to adjust the design.

ASSESSING A PROGRAM'S PROGRESS

Three approaches can be used to assess how well a program is working. First, we can interview individuals who must deal with the behavioral problem on a day-to-day basis (Baer, Wolf, & Risley, 1968). These people may include the target person himself or herself as well as his or her teachers, parents, or coworkers. Have they noticed any change at all? Are they pleased with the changes they've seen? Second, we can consult experts and research literature on the particular behavioral problem we're trying to change. From these sources, we can try to determine how much change we should expect in the time since the intervention began.

The third and most critical approach is to conduct a *graphic analysis* of the data. We saw in Chapter 3 that a graphic analysis is done by visually inspecting a graph of the data to judge whether it depicts pronounced changes in the behavior that can be attributed to the intervention. A graphic analysis assesses two *trends*—whether the

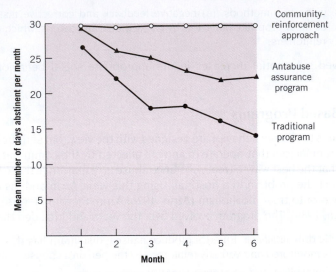

Figure 20-2   Mean number of days per month on which clients with alcoholism who had received treatment with an emetic drug (disulfiram) did not drink during a 6-month follow-up period. Each of the 41 clients received one of three treatments: the *community-based reinforcement approach* (a multidimensional program that included the use of disulfiram), the *antabuse assurance program* (which focused only on having the client take disulfiram in the presence of a significant other at scheduled times and places), and the *traditional program* (which simply provided the client with disulfiram and instructions on how, when, and why it should be administered). *Source:* From N. H. Azrin, R. W. Sisson, R. Meyers, & M. Godley (1982), Alcoholism treatment by disulfiram and community reinforcement therapy. *Journal of Behavior Therapy and Experimental Psychiatry*, 13, 105–112, Figure 2. Copyright © 1982 Elsevier Ltd. Used by permission.

target behavior *improved from baseline to intervention* and whether the behavior has continued to *improve across time during the intervention*. This analysis can be clarified in two ways:

1. *Trend lines*: On the graph, draw a straight line that best "fits" or represents all of the data points for each time period being considered.

2. *Amount of overlap*: Compare the baseline and intervention data points to see how much overlap exists.

With the trend-line method, if the intervention line displays a markedly different level and slope compared to the baseline line, and the level and slope are in the desired direction, the program is working. With the overlap approach, the lower the overlap, the more effective the intervention's effect is (Parker & Hagan-Burke, 2007).

IMPROVING A PROGRAM

When our assessment indicates that the program is not working as well as expected and desired, we'll need to diagnose the shortcomings and correct them.

Diagnosing a Program's Shortcomings

Because conducting a functional assessment is essential before designing a program to change behavior, we'll assume one was done. If you used an unstructured descriptive assessment (see Chapter 13), consider upgrading its rigor by manipulating the suspected antecedents and consequences. Conducting a functional analysis, starting with a brief version, should help determine whether the suspected antecedents and consequences are in fact the controlling factors.

Even when a rigorous functional assessment has been done, design problems can reduce a program's effectiveness. For instance, the intervention's methods may not be the best ones available or as powerful as desired. Using less than optimal techniques is a fairly common problem that can usually be corrected easily. For example, we may have designed a program with reinforcement systems or antecedent manipulations that are not as powerful as needed. Skill in choosing and designing an optimal program with effective techniques improves with experience.

Also, the individuals who administer program techniques may not implement them as carefully or rigorously as they should. This may happen partly because many of the techniques that are used in changing behavior are commonly used in everyday life, but usually in a haphazard manner and for behaviors that have not been carefully defined. Parents and teachers apply reinforcers and punishers to influence children's behavior, but these adults typically do not apply consequences consistently and immediately for every instance of a behavior they want to change. Sometimes individuals carrying out a behavior change program fail to apply consequences consistently or immediately, because the behavior is not well defined. It takes a lot of time, effort, motivation, and training to carry out a behavior change program effectively. (Go to 🔍.)

CLOSE-UP

Diagnostic Questions for Troubleshooting a Program

Improving a program begins with the process of *troubleshooting*—that is, investigating to find problems—for all aspects of the existing program (DeRisi & Butz, 1975; Holmes, 1977). To troubleshoot a program, use the diagnostic questions listed here concerning the program's implementation—answer *only those questions that pertain to the way the program was actually designed or conducted.* The questions are grouped under headings that reflect the dimensions to which the techniques apply or the procedures the program has involved.

Methods of Managing the Antecedents

Answer the following questions about the methods to manage the target behavior's antecedents that the program has been using:

1. Were the prompts, modeling, or instructions used in the intervention (a) noticed by the target person and (b) effective?
2. Were there difficulties in trying to alter chains, manage discriminative stimuli, or use motivating operations?
3. Were noncontingent reinforcers presented independently of the target person's behavior?
4. Was the change in response effort substantially different from normal?

Methods of Managing the Behavior

Answer the following questions about the methods for managing the behavior that the program has been using:

1. Was the target behavior clearly defined for the individuals implementing the program?
2. Were the shaping and chaining steps appropriate to the skills and abilities of the target person?
3. Did the target person lack any prerequisite skills for learning the new behavior?
4. Were the alternative behaviors or competing responses in the program appropriate for the target behavior and reinforced?

(Continued)

(Continued)

Methods of Managing the Consequences

Answer the following questions about the methods to manage the consequences of the target behavior that the program has been using:

1. Did the reinforcers lose some of their appeal or become undermined by external factors, such as other people providing stronger, counterproductive reinforcers?
2. Were some reinforcers provided immediately after appropriate behaviors, and were these rewards given frequently and in small amounts?
3. Were any stimuli that were intended as punishers functioning as reinforcers—that is, did they seem to maintain a behavioral excess instead of decreasing it?
4. Were there difficulties implementing extinction procedures for positive or negative reinforcement in an effort to decrease undesirable behavior?
5. Did lottery or group contingency procedures for administering reinforcers lead to any difficulties?
6. Was the differential reinforcement method used the most appropriate one for the behavioral goal, such as to eliminate the behavior completely? For differential reinforcement of other behavior (DRO), were the initial time interval and its later increases appropriate for the abilities of the target person? Were the response rates for differential reinforcement of low rates (DRL) lowered at an appropriate pace?
7. For a habit reversal procedure, did the person seem to be aware of instances of the target behavior, and was each instance of competing response practice done for a suitable length of time?

Procedural Aspects of the Program

Examine procedural aspects of the program by answering the following questions:

1. Were assessment methods performed correctly and accurately, and were data calculated or charted without errors?
2. Was the data collection process overly difficult, complex, or time-consuming?
3. Were the program's techniques or procedures, such as reinforcement, implemented correctly and as planned?
4. Were all behavior analysts or program administrators using the techniques in the same way?
5. Did some unexpected outside factor interfere with or disrupt the program?

Correcting the Program

Use the written answers to the Diagnostic Questions for Troubleshooting a Program in the box to decide how to correct the problems discovered and stimulate rethinking of decisions made in designing the intervention. Consult also:

- The functional assessment materials
- Relevant sections of this text
- The Checklist of Behavior Change Methods (Figure 20-1) to determine whether our program left out any useful techniques
- The reinforcer selection data, such as from the Preferred Items and Experiences Questionnaire (Figure 15-1), to see whether the program's system of reinforcers was well designed

After deciding how to revise the program's design, we should make sure to have any materials needed to incorporate the new methods into the intervention. We can then begin the revised program and reevaluate the program's progress after several days by conducting another graphic analysis. Revising a program shouldn't suggest a "failure" in your ability—it's a positive and reasonable step to fine-tune the program's effectiveness. (Go to 📄.)

WILL THE IMPROVED BEHAVIOR LAST?

Even when the goal of an intervention is to produce a permanent improvement in a target person's behavior and he or she wants to succeed, the behavior sometimes regresses after the intervention ends. For instance, you surely know individuals who seemed to have succeeded in stopping smoking or reducing their intake of fattening foods, but then went back to their old habits.

REGRESSION OF BEHAVIOR, AND WHY IT HAPPENS

Returning to a former, full-blown pattern of an undesired behavior after having changed is called a **relapse**. Some relapses progress from a *lapse*, an instance of backsliding—a relatively isolated or temporary regression to the former behavior. For example, people who are following a low-calorie diet may "cheat" on occasion but often can bounce back from a lapse fairly easily if they know that backsliding commonly happens and should be expected. Relapses are likely to occur when the person is not very committed to changing the target behavior, especially when it involves changing lifestyle or long-standing habits. Other relapses—probably most—occur for behaviors that were recently acquired and are not yet habitual. These relapses happen because the intervention did not prepare the new behavior for circumstances, particularly antecedents and consequences, that exist in the person's everyday environment. Let's look at a few examples of relapses occurring after the behaviors had improved.

CONCEPT CHECK 20.1

Check your understanding of the preceding concepts. Remember: The symbol ⇔ means that the answer can vary. Answer the following questions about combining methods in an intervention and adjusting the program design.

1. Interventions that contain techniques to address the antecedents, behavior, and consequences are called _____ programs.
2. A technique that could be useful for reducing a behavioral excess but not for changing a behavioral deficit might be _____ . ⇔
3. A component of the community-reinforcement approach for treating alcohol abuse that is directed at managing behavioral consequences is _____ . ⇔
4. The first consideration in deciding to use a technique for a behavior change program is this: Is it likely to be _____ ?
5. Techniques that are moderately or very _____ should be considered for a behavior change program only as a last resort.
6. Answering diagnostic questions to find problems in the way a program was actually conducted is part of the process of _____ .

EXAMPLES OF RELAPSES

The first example of a relapse comes from an intervention to improve the feeding skills of a 6-year-old girl with profound retardation (O'Brien, Bugle, & Azrin, 1972). Before the intervention began, she was eating without utensils, using her hands to grasp some food, crush it, and put it in her mouth. As you might imagine, her feeding was both unsightly and messy. The intervention used two main techniques to teach her to eat with a spoon:

1. Physical guidance prompts, in which the teacher held and moved the girl's hand through the feeding movements.
2. Interruption–extinction, in which the teacher stopped an incorrect response, such as trying to eat with the hands, and prevented reinforcement by cleaning the food from the girl's hands so she couldn't eat it.

When physical guidance was used, the teacher withheld guidance for the next response following a correctly performed, guided response so as to assess her skill in independent feeding with a spoon. Figure 20-3 shows that the girl's performance in using a spoon to eat improved greatly when the interruption–extinction method was added to the physical guidance but dropped sharply when the intervention techniques were withdrawn in the reversal phase. Even though the girl had learned how to eat with a spoon, she did not continue to eat properly when the intervention ended.

Researchers conducted a program in which 20 children with developmental disabilities received intensive individual training to reduce undesirable behaviors, such as engaging in self-stimulation, and to increase desirable behaviors—for example, using speech, playing with other children, and performing self-care activities (Lovaas, Koegel, Simmons, & Long, 1973). The program applied behavioral methods over many months and improved the target behaviors in all of the children; some children showed very large gains. Then, 1 to 4 years after their discharge from the program, follow-up assessments were made on each child. These assessments

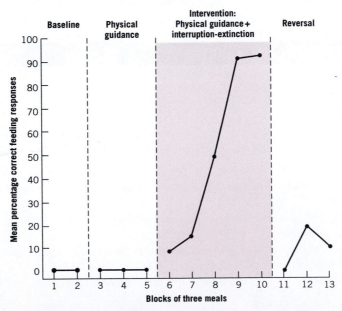

Figure 20-3   Percentage of independently and correctly performed feeding responses by a child with profound retardation during four phases of the program. The mean percentages were calculated across three meals. During phases in which physical guidance was used, the guidance was withheld for some responses to assess independent feeding. *Source:* From F. O'Brien, C. Bugle, & N. H. Azrin (1972), Training and maintaining a retarded child's proper eating. *Journal of Applied Behavior Analysis, 5,* 67–72, Figure 1. Copyright © 1972 Society for the Experimental Analysis of Behavior. Used by permission.

revealed that the environment *after* the intervention is crucial to maintaining the children's behavioral improvements. Some of the children went to live at home upon leaving the program, and their parents received training in behavioral methods. These children's behaviors continued to improve. Those who could not be placed at home went to institutions, where they received basically custodial care with no behavioral methods, and their behavior relapsed.

The third example of relapse comes from interventions to prevent or reduce juvenile delinquency in problem adolescents by using behavioral methods to increase their performance of socially and academically desirable behaviors and decrease their performance of activities that lead to social, academic, and legal problems. These interventions applied a variety of behavioral methods with token reinforcement systems in school, at the youths' homes, or in community-based group homes (Fixsen et al., 1978; Heaton & Safer, 1982; Safer, Heaton, & Parker, 1981; Wolf, Braukmann, & Ramp, 1987). Although each of these programs produced marked improvements in the youths' target behaviors during the many months that the intervention was in effect and for about a year after it ended, the behavioral improvements for many participants were lost after a couple of years. Relapse seems likely if problem adolescents are returned to their original life circumstances without continued treatment or support to encourage them to maintain the improved behaviors.

WAYS TO MAINTAIN BEHAVIOR CHANGES

To promote the persistence of behavior changes, procedures can be applied during the intervention and after. The first approaches we'll consider are used during the program, usually near the end of the training; the remaining approaches occur after the intervention ends.

PROMOTING GENERALIZATION OF THE BEHAVIOR

To increase the chances that an improved behavior will persist after an intervention, behavior change programs should include steps to help the response generalize to the antecedents that are likely to be encountered in everyday life. We saw in Chapter 8 that when we learn to make responses in association with specific antecedents, we also tend to make those responses to stimuli we encounter that are similar to the antecedents we have learned. This phenomenon is called *stimulus generalization*. Although there are many forms of generalization (see Allen et al., 1991), we will focus on eliciting the behavior in a variety of appropriate situations that were not explicitly trained in the intervention.

How well do improved behaviors generalize to everyday appropriate situations? Some behavior change programs have assessed the occurrence of target behaviors in nontrained situations, without having included specific steps to promote generalization. Sometimes the behavior did generalize—that is, it occurred in nontrained settings or with different antecedent cues (Baer, Peterson, & Sherman, 1967; McNeil et al., 1991; Stokes & Baer, 1976). But in other programs, the behavior did not generalize (Guevremont, Osnes, & Stokes, 1988; Hersen, Eisler, & Miller, 1974).

What can be done to enhance generalization of improved behaviors? Interventions can use several techniques to promote generalization (Landrum & Lloyd, 1992; Stokes & Baer, 1976; Stokes & Osnes, 1988, 1989). One simple way to promote generalization is to tell target persons about or demonstrate specific other antecedents, such as other tasks or environments, and ask them to perform the new behavior when in those situations. Studies that have used this approach have found high levels of generalization (Hughes, Harmer, Killian, & Niarhos, 1995; Ninness, Fuerst, Rutherford, & Glenn, 1991). Let's look at some other techniques to improve the generalization of improved behavior.

Training With Everyday Antecedents

Interventions often occur in settings and with antecedent stimuli that are very different from those that will be present in the target person's everyday life when he or she will need to perform the target behavior. For instance, the settings in therapists' offices and psychiatric hospitals are quite different from those clients will encounter in their natural environments. The greater the differences between intervention and natural settings, the less likely it is that the behavior will generalize. As a result, programs to change behavior need to ensure that training occurs under conditions that are as similar as possible to those in the person's usual environment (Favell & Reid, 1988; Landrum & Lloyd, 1992; Stokes & Osnes, 1989). To provide this training, behavior analysts start by *listing all of the everyday antecedent settings and situations* in which the person should perform the target behavior.

There are three ways to make the intervention and natural conditions similar, thereby promoting generalization of the target behavior. One approach involves fading any prompts that are being used in training a behavior that will not be available in the person's everyday environment. The second way involves conducting some or all of the intervention training in the person's natural environment. As an example, a program to improve the strained communication patterns of parents and their adolescent children initially provided training in therapists' offices (Serna, Schumacker, Sherman, & Sheldon, 1991). Although the parents and adolescents learned the skills and could demonstrate them when assessed in the office settings, they didn't use these skills effectively at home until training was moved to the home situation. Other studies with different behaviors and participants have also found that carrying out training in settings like those in which the behavior is intended to occur promotes generalization to those situations (Corte, Wolfe, & Locke, 1971; Stark, Collins, Osnes, & Stokes, 1986).

In the third approach for making the intervention and natural conditions similar to promote generalization of the target behavior, aspects of the everyday environment are brought into the therapy setting. An intervention used this approach to get children with autism to generalize to the classroom situation the basic classroom behaviors they were taught individually in a different room (Koegel & Rincover, 1974). Initial tests showed that the behaviors, such as looking at the teacher and imitating the teacher's actions upon request, did not generalize well. To promote generalization, the training conditions were changed to be more like a classroom by gradually adding other children to intervention sessions. This procedure was very effective in getting the children to generalize the target behaviors to the classroom. (Go to .)

CASE STUDY

Getting Alice to Speak Up in Class

Alice was a very withdrawn 15-year-old girl who was mildly retarded and almost never spoke at a level others could hear (Jackson & Wallace, 1974). A program we described in an earlier chapter was undertaken to increase the loudness of Alice's speech by using tokens to reinforce her when she read words at acceptable loudness levels while sitting inside an enclosed booth in a laboratory. We didn't mention earlier that although the intervention succeeded in the therapy setting, Alice still spoke too softly in the classroom when tested each day of the intervention. To promote generalization of louder, audible speech, the behavior analysts made the therapy setting more and more like the classroom by introducing the following sequence of changes during the next 15 training sessions:

1. Two classmates were brought into the laboratory to study silently several feet away from the booth and out of Alice's view while she read words.
2. The side of Alice's booth was opened partway, thereby reducing her privacy.
3. The side of the booth was removed, exposing Alice to the two classmates who studied silently.
4. The teacher and five students conducted a study period in the laboratory while Alice read words in the booth, still with the side removed.

These steps to promote generalization succeeded. Soon Alice was speaking at normal loudness levels in the classroom.

Widening Stimulus Control

Another reason for the failure of people's improved behaviors to generalize to everyday life is that the behaviors may become associated with too small a range of antecedent stimuli during the intervention. For example, suppose a child receives training in naming objects, and only one teacher and set of materials are used. The stimulus control of that teacher and set of materials may become overly strong because these discriminative stimuli (S^Ds) have been associated with reinforcement frequently and consistently, but other stimuli have not. As a result, the child may respond correctly only when these S^Ds are present and not when other teachers or materials are used. Interventions can avoid this kind of problem and promote generalization of the behavior by taking steps to widen stimulus control.

We can widen stimulus control by including a range of antecedent stimuli in the intervention. The program can use more than one teacher, for example, and a variety of materials, activities, or settings. The effects of using this approach were tested in a study of ways to increase the positive comments students made to one another at a residential home for delinquent and disturbed teenagers (Emshoff, Redd, & Davidson, 1976). All of the students in the study received token and social reinforcers for making positive comments to a peer during seven 30-minute sessions. Half of the students experienced these sessions with varying antecedent stimuli (trainers, locations, time during the day) and activities (at dinner, for instance, or while playing cards, word games, or table tennis). For the remaining students, the sessions always occurred with the same trainer, location, time of day, and activity (table tennis).

To test whether generalization was greater when training was carried out with varied antecedents, positive comments were assessed during other home activities, such as watching TV. Not only did the students who received training with varied antecedents show far more generalization of the behavior to other home activities, but during follow-up assessments in the 3 weeks after the intervention ended, their positive comments continued to occur at higher rates than seen in those students trained with constant antecedents. Other studies with different behaviors and participants have also found high levels of generalization when the interventions used varied antecedent stimuli (Poche, Brouwer, & Swearingen, 1981; Stokes, Baer, & Jackson, 1974).

Teach a Range of Equivalent Responses

In addition to using a range of antecedent stimuli to widen stimulus control, we can teach a range of functionally equivalent responses for those antecedents. With *functionally equivalent responses*, each response the person performs serves the same function—that is, it leads to the same consequences. A procedure called **general case training** combines both approaches: It uses a range of antecedents and responses (Albin & Horner, 1988; Horner, Eberhard, & Sheehan, 1986; Sprague & Horner, 1984). General case training begins with a specification of the exact situations in which the behavior should occur after the program has ended, as well as the extent to which antecedent stimuli and the person's behavior can be allowed to vary. The next step is to identify a series of teaching examples that sample the full range of stimulus and response variations for each situation in which the behavior should be performed—for instance:

- If the general case involved using a variety of vending machines with different displays of snacks and ways to activate the machines, such as pushing a button or pulling a knob, we would train with these variations. In each case, with different antecedents (displays) and responses, the outcomes (getting the snack) would be the same.
- If the general case involved using ballpoint pens of different types, we might use pens that expose the writing tip by taking off a cap, or pushing a button, or twisting the shaft. Once again, the outcomes (being able to write) would be the same.

The last step in this procedure is to provide the general case training, using all of the teaching examples.

Studies that have tested the general case training approach have found that it is effective in promoting the generalization of target behaviors and is more effective in promoting generalization than several other commonly used approaches (Ducharme & Feldman, 1992; Horner, Eberhard, & Sheehan, 1986; Neef et al., 1990).

Probe for Generalization

Generalization probes—that is, trials to check whether the target person performs the behavior with relevant, natural antecedents or contexts—should be carried out:

- Before generalization training to see whether the behavior already occurs in those situations; if it does, we may be able to may reduce the scope of the training.
- During generalization training; if it generalizes, we may be able to cut short the training.
- After generalization training periodically to see whether the behavior is being maintained and decide whether additional training is needed.

A study used generalization probes before, during, and after general case training in the operation of different vending machines by adolescent students with mental retardation (Sprague & Horner, 1984). After general case training,

> all students showed substantial increases in their performance across the 10 nontrained, probe machines. With five of the six students this increase was immediate. Student 3's lack of immediate improvement in probe session 5 may have been the result of a ritualistic pattern of coin insertion which he developed during prior probe sessions. Training sessions for Student 3 between probe sessions 5 and 6 emphasized repeated practice on the step of coin insertion during daily training sessions. (p. 277)

Thus probes can be diagnostic, indicating that certain changes in the training procedures may be useful.

FADING PROMPTS AND THINNING REINFORCEMENT

Two procedures—fading prompts and thinning reinforcement—to promote maintenance of improved behavior are carried out near the end of an intervention to train the target behavior. Fading prompts promotes generalization of the behavior by making stimulus control the same during the intervention and after, and it benefits persistence of the behavior by eliminating the person's reliance on prompts, which are unlikely to occur in the everyday environment. Thinning reinforcement to an intermittent schedule helps maintain the target behavior in two ways. First, it makes the pattern of reinforcement similar during and after the intervention. Second, intermittent reinforcement during the intervention makes the behavior more resistant to extinction after the intervention ends, as we saw in Chapter 16. Thinning reinforcement is important because the target person's everyday life may provide little or inconsistent reinforcement for the behavior.

ASSURING ANTECEDENTS AND NATURAL REINFORCEMENT FOR THE BEHAVIOR

To prevent relapses, we can make sure that the target person's everyday environment provides *appropriate antecedents*—providing opportunities for the improved behavior to occur—and *natural reinforcers* when it does. The choice of specific behaviors to change in an intervention is important in these efforts: The person's everyday environment is likely to have many opportunities to perform and provide rewards for some behaviors more than others, particularly if they improve the person's behavioral and social functioning (Bosch & Fuqua, 2001). For example, we saw in Chapter 2 that *behavioral cusps* are behaviors that have broad benefits because they expose the target person to rich learning opportunities and consequences that would not be available otherwise (Rosales-Ruiz & Baer, 1997). Let's consider other ways to assure that appropriate antecedents and natural reinforcement occur in the person's everyday environment.

Assessing and Promoting Appropriate Antecedents

To make sure a target person's everyday environment provides appropriate antecedents for the improved behavior, the behavior analyst can examine the environment to see whether it already provides them (Horner,

Williams, & Knobbe, 1985). For example, if the target behavior is doing homework, some of the antecedents would be to have a place to work and the needed materials, such as books. Everyday antecedents can be evaluated in a functional assessment conducted near the end of the intervention or soon after (Durand & Carr, 1991; Favell & Reid, 1988; Kohler & Greenwood, 1986).

What if the environment doesn't already provide appropriate antecedents? We'll discuss two ways to make the antecedents available. One way is to provide a "cheat sheet" or other prompts the target person can access. For instance, an intervention to teach 9- to 14-year-old boys with autism domestic skills and recreational behaviors used pictorial prompts as antecedents for these activities at a group home (MacDuff, Krantz, & McClannahan, 1993). Before this intervention, the boys required staff supervision and verbal prompts to perform these activities. After training to use the pictorial prompts to guide their behavior, all of the boys could perform independently the complex activities for an hour with the aid of the pictorial prompts. Other research has shown that audio prompts delivered through earphones could enhance the performance of a man with mild retardation in custodial activities, such as vacuuming and removing office trash (Post, Storey, & Karabin, 2002).

Another way to make appropriate antecedents available is to recruit significant people in the target person's everyday life to provide them. These people can arrange for opportunities for the person to perform the target behavior by setting the occasion for it, such as with cues or prompts. The significant people can be school staff, classmates, or family members—anyone who is willing and conscientious enough to be trained in the tasks and provide them often. For instance, teachers of children whose social behaviors have been improved can schedule classroom activities and provide materials that encourage rather than constrain the desired behaviors.

Assuring Natural Reinforcement for the Target Behavior

We saw in Chapter 5 that **natural reinforcers** are rewards people receive in their usual life situations. In contrast to the programmed reinforcers in interventions, natural reinforcers happen spontaneously as a normal part of our daily lives. Behavior change programs generally try to teach behaviors and skills that are expected to produce natural reinforcers in the person's everyday life. If a person whose behavior has been improved in an intervention is returned to an environment that does not reinforce the improved behavior, the gains will be lost. Because natural reinforcement of improved behavior is so important in maintaining it, behavior change programs should include procedures that promote its occurrence and effects. Let's see how this can be done.

Applying Natural-like Reinforcers

Ending an intervention involves a transition from programmed rewards to naturally occurring reinforcers. A behavior change program can help the target person make this transition by applying natural-like reinforcers in the intervention. For instance, because social reinforcers, such as praise, occur often in daily life, behavior analysts deliberately program and apply social reinforcers in an intervention, even when other types of rewards are used. Doing so is likely to ease the transition to the person's natural environment. For example, programs to improve the social behaviors of children have had more mature classmates model, initiate, and praise appropriate social behavior, such as smiling and inviting another child to play (Cooke & Apolloni, 1976; Strain, Shores, & Timm, 1977). To the extent that these positive social behaviors become part of the mutual interactions of the children in class, the behaviors will be maintained by natural reinforcement (Fowler, 1988).

Assessing and Increasing Natural Reinforcement

One of the first steps in promoting the occurrence of natural reinforcement for improved behavior is to assess the target person's everyday environment (Horner, Williams, & Knobbe, 1985). We can do this by conducting a functional assessment of the behavior near the end of the intervention or soon after (Durand & Carr, 1991; Favell & Reid, 1988; Kohler & Greenwood, 1986). If these assessments indicate that the environment is unlikely to maintain the target person's behavior, efforts should be made to modify the environment.

How can we increase the occurrence of natural reinforcement in the everyday life of someone whose behavior has been changed in an intervention? One way is to train the target person to seek out or *recruit* natural reinforcement. For instance, because people often fail to get the feedback and praise they need to maintain appropriate behavior, it may be useful to train them in ways to elicit the reinforcement they need. This approach was used in an intervention to improve the work skills of three individuals with mental retardation in a sheltered workshop (Hildebrand, Martin, Furer, & Hazen, 1990). Training these workers to recognize when they reached a productivity goal and ask a supervisor to give them feedback increased the production rates of two of the participants. Similarly, children with developmental disabilities have been trained to recruit teacher attention and feedback for their classroom work (Craft, Alber, & Heward, 1998).

Another approach for increasing natural reinforcement after an intervention involves training other people in the target person's everyday life to watch for the behavior and reinforce it. Although these other people are usually family members or teachers, anyone with whom the person has contact regularly can assist in monitoring and reinforcing the behavior. Here are three examples: First, programs to improve classroom conduct have included procedures to train teachers to incorporate token reinforcement in their classrooms on a regular basis (Walker & Buckley, 1972; Walker, Hops, & Johnson, 1975). Second, an intervention to improve speaking and self-care skills in children with autism trained their parents in using rewards (Lovaas, Koegel, Simmons, & Long, 1973). Third, after a man's pain behaviors had been reduced and then relapsed when he returned home, his family was trained to ignore his pain complaints and praise his motor activities (Kallman, Hersen, & O'Toole, 1975). In each of these interventions, training people in the target person's natural environment to apply reinforcement helped the improved behavior persist.

BOOSTER PROGRAMS

A good approach for heading off relapses is having the target person participate in a posttreatment **booster program**—a set of extra intervention phases or sessions carried out to refresh the original program's training. The sessions generally occur periodically, perhaps every few months or whenever the behavior seems to be regressing. As an example, a booster program was applied to refresh the training socially withdrawn school children received that reinforced social behaviors with tokens (Paine et al., 1982). Because the children's improved social behavior tended to decline after the original training, a booster program with the same methods as the intervention was introduced and occurred a few times as separate phases that had reversal (baseline) phases in between. Across successive intervention phases, the children lost less and less of the improved behavior during the reversal phases and continued to show social behaviors that were within the normal range after the booster program ended. Another approach used computer-based instruction with models and prompts to teach 15-year-old students with intellectual disabilities how to perform life skills, such as making a sandwich and using a microwave (Ayres & Cihak, 2010). Using the program periodically as booster sessions helped the students maintain the skills. Other studies have found that booster programs help individuals maintain improvements in assertive behavior, problem drinking, and classroom conduct (Baggs & Spence, 1990; Connors, Tarbox, & Faillace, 1992; Maletzky, 1974).

TIPS ON MAXIMIZING AND MAINTAINING BEHAVIOR CHANGES

This chapter described several ways behavior analysts can help individuals maintain behavior changes after an intervention is over. Here are some tips to consider when designing and carrying out a program:

1. Design multidimensional programs, using methods to address the target behavior itself and, especially, its antecedents and consequences. Use several methods, based on data from a functional assessment.

2. If more than one target behavior is involved in the program, consider using separate reinforcers and behavioral criteria for each behavior to make sure each one improves.

3. Describe to the target person the rules or criteria determining what consequences will apply to the behaviors to be changed.

4. Try to maximize the target person's commitment to the program and motivation for carrying out the tasks and achieving the behavioral goals. One way to do this is to involve the person in designing and implementing the program.

5. Involve significant other people during and after the intervention to provide antecedents and reinforcement for the target behavior.

6. After the intervention has been in force for about a week, do a graphic analysis with trend lines. Troubleshoot and make revisions, if needed.

7. Target behaviors that will be useful in the person's natural environment are likely to be maintained after a program ends because they lead to reinforcement.

8. Train the target behaviors with a variety of antecedent stimuli that are likely to be encountered in the natural environment. If possible, start the training with simple tasks, such as with antecedents that are easy to discriminate, and then progress to harder ones.

9. Monitor the behavior very carefully during an intervention when fading prompts, thinning reinforcement, or introducing other procedural changes. Make sure that fading and thinning are carried out gradually so that the behavior doesn't regress.

10. Conduct generalization probes before, during, and after an intervention.

11. Before the intervention ends, assess the likelihood of appropriate antecedents and natural reinforcement for the target behaviors in the person's everyday life.

12. Introduce techniques to increase the ability of the improved behavior to generalize and persist in appropriate environments after the intervention ends.

(Go to .)

 CONCEPT CHECK 20.2

Answer the following questions about making behavioral improvements last.

1. Regressing into one's former full-blown pattern of unwanted behavior is called a(n) _____ .
2. Figure 20-1 shows that a girl's improved behavior of eating with a spoon did not persist after the intervention ended; this is an example of a(n) _____ .
3. During an intervention, one method we can apply to promote generalization is _____ . ⇔
4. The method of teaching in an intervention a range of antecedents and functionally equivalent responses is called _____ .
5. Checking to see whether a behavior generalizes to specific antecedents is called a(n) _____ .
6. One way to increase the occurrence of natural reinforcement for the improved behavior is to _____ . ⇔
7. If we provided treatment phases or sessions after an intervention ended, we'd be using a(n) _____ to head off a relapse.

STUDY AND REVIEW

SUMMARY

Multidimensional programs address more than one dimension of the problem behavior—the behavior itself, its antecedents, and its consequences. These programs have been applied to improve a wide variety of behaviors, including classroom conduct problems, children's self-help skills, parenting skills, social skills, and excessive alcohol use.

Although interventions designed and implemented by behavior analysts often produce permanent behavior changes, sometimes the behavior regresses and a relapse occurs. Relapses can occur for several reasons. First, the former behavior may have been learned very thoroughly, perhaps being habitual. Second, the target person is likely to encounter the old antecedent cues and behavioral chains again. Third, sometimes the intervention did not teach the behavioral improvements well enough or include procedures to help them generalize to and be reinforced in the person's everyday environment. Graphic analysis methods can determine whether a program is working well—if it is not, troubleshooting can reveal shortcomings, which should be corrected.

We can maintain behavior changes in several ways. First, we can include in our interventions procedures to promote generalization, such as by training with everyday antecedents, widening stimulus control, using general case training with a range of antecedents and functionally equivalent responses, and probing for generalization. Second, during the intervention, we can be sure to fade prompts and thin reinforcement to an intermittent schedule to make the behavior more persistent. Third, we can assess and promote antecedents in the target person's everyday environment and assure that natural reinforcers will be available there. Last, we can provide a posttreatment booster program to shore up or refresh the intervention's methods, thereby helping the behavior persist.

> To prepare for exams, use the following key terms and review questions and the online study guide that's available on this book's companion website at www.wiley.com/college/sarafino.

KEY TERMS

multidimensional programs	general case training	booster program
relapse	natural reinforcers	

ANSWERS TO CONCEPT CHECKS (CCs)

CC20.1 *Answers*: **1.** multidimensional **2.** punishment/extinction **3.** reinforcing taking disulfiram **4.** highly effective **5.** aversive **6.** troubleshooting

CC20.2 *Answers*: **1.** relapse **2.** relapse **3.** train with everyday antecedents **4.** general case training **5.** generalization probe **6.** train the person to recruit it **7.** booster program

REVIEW QUESTIONS

1. Describe the research by Koegel and Rincover (1974) and its outcome regarding teaching students with autism to perform basic classroom behaviors.

2. What is a multidimensional program? Describe two examples from the text.

3. Describe how to identify possible methods to include in an intervention to improve an operant behavior, and decide which ones to use.

4. Describe how to assess a program's progress and improve it. Include the process of troubleshooting.

5. Define the term *relapse*, and give two examples of it you've seen in your life.

6. Describe methods behavior analysts use to promote generalization. Include the approach Koegel and Rincover (1974) used for classroom behaviors of students with autism.

7. Describe the method Jackson and Wallace (1974) used to promote generalization of Alice's louder speaking in a classroom.

8. What is general case training? Give an example of how a teacher could use it with students who have mental retardation.

9. Describe the research of MacDuff, Krantz, and McClannahan (1993) in which they trained boys with autism to use pictorial prompts for behaviors they learned in an intervention.

10. What are natural reinforcers? How can behavior analysts assess and promote their occurrence for a target person's improved behavior?

RELATED READINGS

*   Horner, R. H., Dunlap, G., & Koegel, R. L. (Eds.). (1988). *Generalization and maintenance: Life-style changes in applied settings*. Baltimore, MD: Paul H. Brookes.

*   Landrum, T. J., & Lloyd, J. W. (1992). Generalization in social behavior research with children and youth who have emotional or behavioral disorders. *Behavior Modification*, 16, 593–616.

*   Stokes, T. F., & Osnes, P. G. (1989). An operant pursuit of generalization. *Behavior Therapy*, 20, 337–355.

21

RESPONDENT CONDITIONING

PROLOGUE

Child psychiatrist Michael Rutter (1975) provided therapy for a 6-year-old boy named Martin who seemed to be a generally happy child with no psychological problems other than an extreme fear of dogs. He was so terrified of dogs that he would run into a road, heedless of traffic, to avoid encounters with dogs. If a dog came near,

> he screamed, cried, and ran away. The fear of dogs first started when Martin was a year old when he was repeatedly frightened by two very large and noisy hounds in the adjoining garden. The dogs never attacked Martin, but they would put their paws on top of the fence and snarl and bark at him. Martin would either stand still, screaming and terrified, or would rush into the house in tears. (p. 220)

Although Martin's parents protested, the neighbors did not change the situation, which continued for a couple of years. The intense fear he developed persisted until he received therapy 3 years after the situation with the dogs at home had ended. Martin's case is an example of a learned fear. It had become so maladaptive that it interfered with the boy's general functioning—for instance, it precluded his going shopping or walking with his parents or on family outings. The therapy he received used methods like those we discuss in the next chapter and succeeded in curbing the fear.

Martin learned to fear dogs through respondent conditioning. In Chapter 1, we saw how John Watson and Rosalie Rayner (1920) demonstrated that an infant boy named "Little Albert" could learn to fear a gentle white rat. These researchers paired the rat, an initially *neutral stimulus* (it didn't evoke fear), with a loud noise, an *unconditioned stimulus* (US), that could already elicit in Albert an *unconditioned response* (UR) of fear. This pairing made the rat a *conditioned stimulus* (CS) that could now elicit the CR in the absence of the US. Martin's fear of dogs had become a *conditioned response* (CR) in real life in much the same way as Albert's fear was conditioned in a laboratory. The present chapter examines the process and characteristics of respondent conditioning; the next chapter describes methods based on respondent conditioning that are useful in changing respondent behaviors. We'll start by examining the process and characteristics of respondent conditioning in everyday life.

RESPONDENT CONDITIONING IN EVERYDAY LIFE

Martin's experience provides a good example of people learning respondent behaviors in everyday life. And as we saw in Chapter 1, respondent and operant conditioning usually happen together—for instance, when Martin would run away or scream and cry, chances are his behaviors received reinforcement: escape as a negative reinforcer for running away, and comforting from other people for screaming and crying. One problem with escaping and then avoiding dogs, the feared CS, is that the fear persists because the boy prevents his experiencing friendly dogs (Lovibond et al., 2009). (Go to 🐾.)

CONDITIONED EMOTIONAL RESPONSES

One type of respondent behavior that is of concern in applied behavior analysis is the **conditioned emotional response (CER)**, pronounced by spelling "c-e-r." In this type of behavior, the CR is mainly an emotion, such as fear or anger. Some researchers distinguish between two categories of *fear*, defining **phobia** as an intense and irrational fear of something specific, and **anxiety** as a fear that has a vague or unspecified source. Thus Martin's fear of all dogs would be a phobia, and the fear that something awful might happen in social situations would be an anxiety. But these terms are often used interchangeably, and distinctions among them don't seem to be useful in practice (Davison & Neale, 1994; Sarafino, 1986). This book generally uses the term *fear* interchangeably with *phobia* and *anxiety*, but uses the two latter terms mainly when the specificity or vagueness of the CER is obvious. The processes of experience and biology play important roles in learning CERs.

Role of Direct and Indirect Experience in CERs

Studies have shown that people can acquire CERs through direct or indirect respondent conditioning (Emmelkamp, Bouman, & Scholing, 1992; Poulton & Menzies, 2002; Rachman, 1991). Respondent conditioning is *direct* when the person actually experiences the CS and US, as Martin did; it is *indirect* when the person acquires a CER by observing other people in fearful situations (modeling) or by receiving fearful information about a situation, such as being told that spiders or snakes will bite you.

Evidence from interviews and surveys of people with fears suggests that phobias are common in childhood and that most phobias tend to disappear on their own in months. In perhaps two thirds or more cases,

CASE STUDY

What's What in Martin's Respondent Conditioning?

Some people have difficulty distinguishing among respondent conditioning components, especially the CS and US. A simple procedure can help you figure out what's what in an example of respondent conditioning (Lutz, 1994). Just answer three questions:

1. What *overt or covert response did the individual make* in the example? This response is the UR *and* CR, which are virtually identical. In the story about Martin, these responses were his fearful behaviors, such as distress and escape.

2. What *antecedent stimulus occurred* before the response that *probably had been able to elicit the response before the situation* in the example? This is the US. Although the US is often a stimulus that elicits the response "naturally"—that is, automatically or without learning—it can also be a learned antecedent with sufficient stimulus control to function as a US. For Martin's conditioning, it was the challenging acts of the dogs—paws on the fence, snarling and barking.

3. What *other stimulus* (or more than one) occurred *before the response*, probably did *not* have the ability to elicit the response before being paired with the US, but seems to have *gained the ability* to do so in the example? This is the CS, and the response it now elicits is the CR. The CS usually occurs just before the US in respondent conditioning. In Martin's case, it was his seeing the dogs.

Figure 21-1 diagrams the components in Martin's respondent conditioning for his fear of dogs.

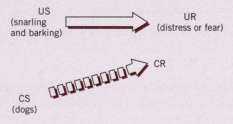

Figure 21-1   Likely elements in the respondent conditioning of Martin's fear of dogs.

fears were acquired mainly through direct respondent conditioning: Most people reported having experienced negative situations with the feared object—say, dentists—before the fear developed (Doogan & Thomas, 1992; Kleinknecht, 1994; Merckelbach, Muris, & Schouten, 1996; Muris, Merckelbach, de Jong, & Ollendick, 2002; Ost, 1987; Ost & Hugdahl, 1981; Wolpe, 1981). But many of these individuals also said that modeling and verbal information they received fostered the development of their fears. Although it's possible that these people's reports were inaccurate because they were based on their recall of past events, some of which happened many years earlier, the proportions of individuals reporting direct and indirect sources of their fears have been similar across studies. And findings from experiments with children strongly support the role of modeling and receiving fearful information from others, such as their parents (Askew & Field, 2007; Muris, van Zwol, Huijding, & Mayer, 2010). Still, the way indirect respondent conditioning leads to CERs is unclear, and direct conditioning processes don't account well for the fact that many people who have extremely frightening experiences, such as in war, do not appear to develop long-lasting, severe fears (Rachman, 1991). Other processes may be involved.

Inborn Processes and CERs

Studies of fear across diverse cultures and within families have found evidence for a role of biological processes in people's development of CERs (Davey et al., 1998; Graham & Gaffan, 1997). The clearest evidence concerns the role of *genetics*. One way to examine the role of genetics is to compare a characteristic, such as the presence of fears, among identical and same-sex fraternal twins. *Identical*, or monozygotic, twins share the same genetic inheritance because they result from the splitting of one fertilized egg. *Fraternal*, or dizygotic, twins arise from two separate eggs, each of which was fertilized by a separate sperm. If genetic factors are involved in the development of fears, researchers should find greater similarities in the fears of pairs of individuals who are identical twins than fraternal twins. Research has generally confirmed this hypothesis (Emmelkamp, Bouman, & Scholing, 1992; Muris, Merckelbach, de Jong, & Ollendick, 2002). Such findings indicate that inborn factors may make some people more vulnerable than others to develop fear reactions from their experiences. Although we don't yet know exactly what these factors are or how they work, they may lead to certain behavioral patterns, such as being very inhibited, that predispose some individuals to develop fears.

PHYSIOLOGICAL REACTIONS

The classic research of Pavlov (1927) demonstrated the respondent conditioning of a physiological response, salivation, in dogs. Salivation is a UR to the US of food in the mouth; through conditioning, almost any *previously neutral stimulus* can become a CS and elicit salivation, now a CR. All physiological reactions can become CRs by way of respondent conditioning, and here are some examples:

- *Asthma* is a condition marked by episodes in which the airways become inflamed and narrowed, causing impaired breathing. Although these episodes are triggered mainly by allergic stimuli, such as pollen (the US), research has found that people can learn through respondent conditioning to make respiratory reactions and have impaired breathing (CR) to a harmless stimulus, which becomes a CS by being paired with the US (De Peuter et al., 2005).

- People with chronic *low back pain* can learn to make specific muscular responses (the CR) to a previously neutral stimulus, which becomes a CS by being presented with pain (US) in the muscle area repeatedly (Schneider, Palomba, & Flor, 2004). Associations of this type have been demonstrated in research and may contribute to episodes of low back pain becoming chronic in everyday life.

- *Immune system functioning* can be altered through respondent conditioning. In the original research (Ader & Cohen, 1975, 1985), rats received sweetened water to drink, which they seemed to like, and then got an injection of a drug (US) that induces nausea and immune suppression (UR). By being paired with the US, the sweetened water became a CS. Continued drinking of the sweetened water (CS) across many days kept their immune functioning low (CR), leading to their falling ill. Similar effects of respondent conditioning have been found in humans, such as cancer patients who receive medications that impair immune function (Kusnecov, 2001).

These examples make it sound like respondent conditioning is bad for our physiological systems, but it isn't necessarily. Respondent conditioning can also operate in the opposite directions, decreasing asthma and pain symptoms and improving immune functioning (Sarafino & Smith, 2011). Chapters 22 and 23 describe behavioral methods that accomplish these outcomes.

SUBSTANCE USE AND ABUSE

Respondent and operant conditioning contribute to one's continued and increasing use of mood-altering *substances*, such as tobacco, alcohol, and illicit drugs (Sarafino & Smith, 2011). With operant conditioning, the effects on substance use occur in two ways:

1. *Positive reinforcement*: Taking substances usually produces pleasant mood states that provide positive reinforcement for the behavior.

2. *Negative reinforcement*: When people stop taking a substance after having taken it for a while, they typically experience unpleasant "withdrawal" symptoms—such as anxiety, headache, and tremors—which go away quickly by taking the substance again.

The consequences of using substances have a major impact on the efforts people will make to acquire and use them.

Respondent conditioning is involved in substance use in two principal ways. First, *it develops* CSs, such as a smoker's seeing a cigarette and lighter, which produce *internal* CRs like the unconditioned reactions of actually using the substance (Cunningham, 1998; Niaura et al., 1988; Rohsenow et al., 1994). These internal CRs include physiological reactions—for instance, the nicotine in cigarette smoke arouses the body, increasing the person's heart rate, blood pressure, and alertness. And people with alcoholism who see their favorite liquor respond with strong cravings to drink and increased salivation and physiological arousal. Cravings for the substance are greater when the CSs occur in real life than when they are presented on TV (Shadel, Niaura, & Abrams, 2001). Individuals who quit using a substance and then encounter associated CSs have a difficult time resisting the temptation to start using it again.

Second, the body adapts to a substance, requiring more and more of it to achieve the same effect—a phenomenon called *tolerance*. Respondent conditioning contributes to increased substance use because the addicts associate CSs, such as the room in which they use it, with the physiological reactions (the URs) that occur with and protect the body from the increased amounts of the substance (USs). The body seems to acquire tolerance by trying to "protect" itself with physiological reactions that counteract the effects of the substance (Hinson, Poulos, & Cappell, 1982). This has an important effect for users of narcotics: Heroin addicts typically take doses of the drug that would ordinarily kill people who had never or rarely used it. Then why do addicts sometimes die from their normal dose (normal, that is, in terms of amount and purity)? Researchers reasoned that these deaths happen when the tolerance effect fails temporarily because the usual CSs that have come to elicit the protective reaction as a CR are not there—if, perhaps, the addict took heroin in a new environment (Siegel, Hinson, Krank, & McCully, 1982). To test this hypothesis, the researchers injected rats with heroin every other day in a particular room until the animals reached a high level of tolerance, taking large doses. On alternate days, the rats were injected with a sugar-water solution in a distinctly different room. Then the animals received a larger than usual dose of heroin; half of the animals received the dose in the room where they had received heroin in the past and half received it in the room where they had gotten the sugar-water. If the "heroin room" had become a CS that would elicit a protective CR, fewer rats would die from the heroin overdose given in this room than in the other room. The results confirmed this expectation: 32% of the "heroin room" rats died, compared with 64% of the other rats.

People voluntarily use many illegal or unhealthful substances, including tobacco, alcohol, and drugs. Partly because of the addictive chemicals in these substances, it's often difficult to stop these behaviors; but evidence indicates that some respondent techniques can help (Sobell, Toneatto, & Sobell, 1990; Tucker, Vuchinich, & Downey, 1992). One respondent method, for example, that is used in treating alcohol abuse is called **emetic therapy** because it has the person take an *emetic*—that is, a drug (US) that produces nausea as a UR when alcohol is consumed. In a typical half-hour session in a hospital, the person first receives an injection of the drug and then repeatedly drinks an alcoholic beverage, each time quickly becoming nauseated and vomiting (Miller & Hester, 1980). After several of these sessions, drinking alcohol is able to elicit nausea without the emetic drug (US): Alcohol is now a CS, and nausea is a CR. The person usually receives occasional "booster" sessions after being discharged from the hospital. Many studies have found that emetic therapy can be effective in treating alcohol abuse (Elkins, 1991). But one critic of this approach has noted that emetic therapy may not be more effective than other behavioral methods that are less costly to implement (Wilson, 1991). Keep in mind also that quitting using a substance is easier to achieve than staying quit for good. Many people return to using tobacco, alcohol, or drugs weeks or months after quitting.

CANCER TREATMENT REACTIONS

Have you ever gotten sick to your stomach after eating something and quickly disliked the food you "blamed"? If so, you probably learned to associate the food as a CS for the US, becoming sick, and your new disliking of the food is the CR. This conditioning is called *taste aversion* learning. Animals learn quickly to associate foods they consumed with becoming sick, too, and avoid those foods in the future (Garcia, Ervin, & Koelling, 1966; Garcia, Hankins, & Rusiniak, 1974; Wilcoxon, Dragoin, & Kral, 1971). Taste aversion relates to a side effect of cancer treatment.

Many cancer patients receive chemotherapy treatment in which powerful drugs are administered orally or by injection to circulate through the body and kill cells that divide rapidly, as cancer cells typically do (Laszlo, 1987; Williams, 1990). A difficult side effect of chemotherapy is the severe nausea (often with vomiting) many patients experience, which often produces two reactions by respondent conditioning. One reaction is called **learned food aversion**, which is like taste aversion learning: A food becomes distasteful because the person associates it as a CS with the US of becoming sick. Taste aversions can develop for foods eaten hours before the chemotherapy treatment and are more likely for foods with strong odors or tastes, such as chocolate and coffee, than for milder foods (Bernstein, 1991). The other reaction is called **anticipatory nausea**, in which the drug is the US and nausea is the UR and CR (Kvale et al., 1991; Taylor et al., 1992). By association, other related events, such as thinking at home about the procedure or seeing the hospital, become CSs and can then elicit nausea in the absence of the drug.

LEARNING POSITIVE REACTIONS

Not all behaviors we learn through respondent conditioning are unpleasant or bad for us. In fact, chances are respondent conditioning was at least partly involved in developing almost all of the positive reactions to events or items you experience in your life. This conditioning occurs by pairing a previously neutral stimulus with a US that already elicits a positive response (UR), such as happiness. A classic demonstration of the respondent conditioning of positive reactions was performed with college students as the participants (Staats, Minke, Martin, & Higa, 1972). Some of the students were food deprived, and others were not. The researchers presented to the students meaningless three-letter items, such as *vup* and *qeh*, paired with food words (US), such as *stew* and *pizza*, and asked them to learn the pairs. This pairing made the meaningless items CSs. Later, the students were asked to rate each of the three-letter items on a pleasant–unpleasant scale: Those who were deprived of food during the pairings rated the items more positively than did those who were not food deprived during the pairings.

Advertisers use respondent conditioning in TV commercials by pairing pleasant images (US), such as celebrities or attractive models that elicit favorable reactions (UR), with a product or name of the manufacturer, which becomes a CS. They hope that the CS in the future will elicit a favorable reaction (CR), leading the viewers to buy the product. (Go to 📑.)

CONCEPT CHECK 21.1

Check your understanding of the preceding concepts. Remember: The symbol ⇔ means that the answer can vary. Answer the following questions about respondent conditioning in everyday life.

1. In Martin's learning to fear dogs, the US, UR, CS, and CR were _____ , _____ , _____ , and _____ , respectively. ⇔
2. When a CR is mainly an emotion, the respondent behavior is called a(n) _____ .
3. The two categories of fear are _____ and _____ .
4. Two examples of physiological reactions that can be modified through respondent conditioning are _____ and _____ . ⇔
5. In the respondent conditioning technique of emetic therapy, what might be the **a.** US, **b.** UR, **c.** CS, and **d.** CR? ⇔
6. A cancer patient who becomes nauseated at the thought of the next chemotherapy treatment is experiencing _____ .

FACTORS AND PHENOMENA IN RESPONDENT CONDITIONING

Several factors and phenomena influence the development of respondent conditioning and the strength of the resulting respondent behavior. One of these factors is how *consistently* the CS and US were paired: CSs that were paired consistently with a US are more likely to elicit the CR than CSs that were paired only sometimes with the US. Another factor is obvious: The greater the *number of times the CS and US were paired*, the greater the ability of the CS to elicit the CR and the stronger the CR is likely to be (Kimble, 1961). In the development of Martin's fear, it's likely that the continued pairing of the dogs with their threatening behavior (the US) of snarling and barking made it more likely that the dogs (now CSs) would elicit the boy's fearful CR and that the response would be intense. Let's look at some other important factors and phenomena in respondent conditioning.

CS–US TIMING AND INTENSITY

In respondent conditioning, as in telling a joke, timing is a critical factor. The neutral stimulus and US typically must occur *close enough in time* to allow the individual to connect the two. This makes sense. Imagine someone shouting to a toddler, "Watch out!" (the eventual CS) just before a ball hits her in the head (the US). It wouldn't take very many such events to teach her to take defensive action, such as ducking, to the CS alone. But she'd have a hard time learning the relationship if the ball hit her, say, 30 minutes after the warning. In general, respondent conditioning develops most quickly and strongly when the eventual CS precedes the US by a fairly short amount of time, usually between a quarter-second and several seconds (Fitzgerald & Martin, 1971; Kehoe & Macrae, 1998; Kimble, 1961).

The *intensities* of the CS and US are also important in conditioning. Shouting "Watch out!" is a more intense CS than saying it in a moderate voice, and being hit hard is a more intense US than being slapped mildly. Respondent conditioning develops more quickly and strongly when either or both of these stimuli are fairly strong rather than weak (Kimble, 1961; Lutz, 1994).

RELEVANCE OF THE CS TO THE US

In our discussion of taste aversion earlier, you may have thought, "It makes sense to develop a dislike of a food that makes you sick." The food and sickness are related conceptually and causally. Chances are, if you've gotten sick to your stomach after eating something, you learned this connection quickly, even though you may not have felt sick for hours after you'd eaten the food. What's more, it's easier to learn to associate the taste of food as a CS with becoming sick (US) than with receiving electric shock (US; Garcia & Koelling, 1966). These findings indicate that some CS–US combinations are more easily related than others.

Why would this be? Some CS–US combinations consist of stimuli that are more "relevant" to each other, either because of prior learning or as a result of some innate tendency to associate them (Davey, 1992; Hollis, 1997; Hugdahl & Öhman, 1977; Seligman, 1971). A study demonstrated the importance of CS–US relevance by presenting college students with an aversive loud noise and vibration just once and telling them this aversive event might occur shortly after some of the pictures that were about to be projected on a screen (Honeybourne, Matchett, & Davey, 1993). When each picture was shown, the students estimated the likelihood that the aversive event would happen, but the aversive event never actually occurred. Their estimates that the aversive event would happen were much higher when the pictures they saw were of fear-relevant objects, such as a snake or handgun, than when the pictures were of fear-irrelevant objects, such as a flower.

OVERSHADOWING, BLOCKING, AND LATENT INHIBITION

In real-life respondent conditioning, the US occurs in a context with many stimuli, any of which could become a CS (Bouton & Nelson, 1998). For example, if you were in deep water and felt like you were drowning, many stimulus elements in this context could become CSs: seeing, feeling, hearing (splashes), smelling, and even tasting the water. Which of these elements will become a CS?

People tend to perceive one or more stimulus elements in a context as relatively prominent or noticeable, particularly when a stimulus is very intense or involves a sensory system the person relies on heavily. For instance, most people rely more on vision than smell. In contexts with many stimuli, two phenomena can occur. First, the most prominent stimulus will probably become the strongest CS, having the greatest control in eliciting the CR. This phenomenon is called **overshadowing** because one stimulus outweighs the others in importance (Kamin, 1969; Pavlov, 1927). In the example of feeling like you're drowning, the CS of *seeing* the water may overshadow the other stimuli, such as smelling it. Second, once a strong CS has been established, it tends to "block" other stimuli from becoming signals (CSs) for that US in the future. So, if at a later time you felt threatened in a large swimming pool, the sight of the water might prevent other features of the situation from becoming CSs. **Blocking** refers to the phenomenon in which an existing CS prevents other stimuli from becoming effective signals of the US (Arcediano, Matute, & Miller, 1997; Halas & Eberhardt, 1987; Kamin, 1969). It may be that blocking occurs because the individual pays attention only to the established CS or because the other stimuli are redundant—they simply offer no added information.

A third phenomenon in respondent conditioning involves prior experience with potential CSs. In **latent inhibition**, prior experience with a potential CS in neutral circumstances—that is, without a US—makes later respondent conditioning involving that stimulus more difficult. For instance, if Martin had had lots of prior experience with neutral or friendly dogs before encountering his neighbor's dogs, his fear would have been more difficult to condition. Two studies of the origins of fears support this view. First, a study found that adults who were afraid of dogs reported having had relatively little contact with dogs before their fear developed (Doogan & Thomas, 1992). Second, an experiment gave neutral exposure to a stimulus for half of the participants (Vervliet, Kindt, Vansteenwegen, & Hermans, 2010). All subjects then received conditioning, pairing the stimulus with electric shock. The participants who had prior experience with the stimulus showed less-fearful reactions to similar stimuli than did the subjects without the pre-exposure. These results and those of other studies suggest that early nonfearful exposure to potentially fearful events, such as dental treatment, can help prevent the development of fears later when aversive encounters happen (Lubow, 1998).

In latent inhibition, children who have pleasant experience with potentially fearful situations—in this case, deep water—are less likely to develop fears of that situation if they have aversive encounters with it later. *Source:* Copyright © Mark A. Johnson/Copyright © Corbis.

CLOSE-UP

Preventing Learned Food Aversions

Cancer patients who develop learned aversions to foods they like can become very demoralized by these experiences, feeling that they have suffered enough. Simply telling the patient why these aversions develop doesn't seem to stop them from occurring. Can behavioral methods be used to prevent cancer patients from learning to dislike foods they normally eat?

A promising approach to prevent a patient's normal foods from becoming disliked uses the phenomenon of *overshadowing*. The procedure is simple: The patient just consumes a strongly flavored, unfamiliar food shortly before the chemotherapy session. Because it has been introduced as a very prominent item in the person's recent diet, the unfamiliar food will probably become the strongest CS if a taste aversion develops. In effect, this procedure makes this food a *scapegoat*, so that it "takes the blame" for the nausea. Studies using scapegoat candies and drinks with unusual, strong flavors, such as plum or coconut, have markedly reduced learned food aversions in adults and children who experienced nausea-producing events (Bernstein, 1991; Okifuji & Friedman, 1992).

One other point should be made. The influence of overshadowing, blocking, and latent inhibition on a given conditioning situation can be complex, and more than one of these phenomena may be playing a role simultaneously (Blaisdell, Bristol, Gunther, & Miller, 1998). (Go to 🔍.)

SECOND-ORDER CONDITIONING

Think back to Martin, the boy in the opening story. Suppose that after his fear was very strong, a relative (Robin) of the people next door came to stay at their house for a while and would take the dogs for a walk, during which they were well behaved. Martin sees this happen. How would Martin feel about Robin? When I've presented this scenario in class, most students answered that Martin probably feels some fear when he sees Robin, even when the dogs are not there. Why? Robin has now been paired with the dogs that evoke fear in Martin.

But the dogs are not a US in the conditioning with Robin, they're CSs. Robin was paired with CSs that functioned like a US. When conditioning occurs with a true US, it is called *first-order conditioning*, the kind of respondent conditioning we've discussed so far in this book. But respondent conditioning can develop by pairing a neutral stimulus (Robin) with a strong CS, too, as Figure 21-2 illustrates. In **second-order conditioning** (also

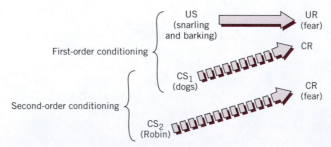

Figure 21-2   A comparison of the first-order and second-order conditioning. Martin's fear (CR) of dogs (CS$_1$) developed in first-order conditioning, with the dogs' snarling and barking as the US. But his fear of Robin (CS$_2$) developed in second-order conditioning, building on his strong fear (CR) of dogs—a strong CS that could function like a US.

called *higher-order conditioning*) a new stimulus (Robin) becomes a CS, eliciting the CR (fear), by being paired with a CS (dogs) that can function as a US to elicit that respondent behavior (Rizley & Rescorla, 1972). Martin's fear at seeing Robin would be a result of second-order conditioning. This is an important phenomenon because it expands the scope of respondent conditioning. A new CS can develop by being paired with a CS, without a true US.

Students sometimes confuse second-order conditioning and blocking, which we discussed earlier, because both phenomena involve pairing an established CS and a potential CS. The difference between the two is subtle, but critical. In blocking, an established CS is paired with a potential CS *in the presence of the* US, and the potential CS *does not* develop the ability to elicit the CR. In second-order conditioning, a strongly established CS and a potential CS are paired *without the original* US, and the potential CS *does* develop the ability to elicit the CR.

DISCRIMINATION, GENERALIZATION, AND EXTINCTION

In earlier chapters, we discussed the processes of discrimination, generalization, and extinction in operant conditioning. These processes occur in respondent conditioning, too. We saw in operant conditioning that people learn to *discriminate* between different antecedent stimuli and respond differently toward them, even though the stimuli may be similar in some respects. In respondent conditioning, the CS is the antecedent, and people learn to discriminate between a particular CS and other potential antecedents (Kimble, 1961). We can see this in Martin's case because he was afraid of dogs but not other animals, such as cats, which also have four legs, furry coats, and tails. He could discriminate among these animals and react fearfully only to dogs.

We also saw earlier that people's reactions to operant antecedents show *stimulus generalization*, whereby we tend to respond to antecedents other than the exact ones we experienced in conditioning, particularly if they are similar. Stimulus generalization occurs with respondent behaviors, too. For instance, Martin was afraid of *all* dogs, not just the ones he encountered at home. The greater the similarity between a new antecedent stimulus and the actual CS the individual experienced in conditioning, the stronger the CR is likely to be (Kimble, 1961). Martin probably showed more fear with dogs that looked like the ones at home than with dogs much different in size and color.

What do you suppose would have happened to Martin's fear of dogs if new neighbors had moved in next door with a very gentle, friendly dog? At first the child would have been very frightened, but eventually he would have learned that the new dog did not snarl and bark at him, and his fear would have begun to diminish. This example illustrates how extinction can happen with respondent behaviors. In respondent conditioning, as in operant conditioning, the term **extinction** has two meanings: (a) a *procedure* or *condition* in which a CS is presented repeatedly *without the* US it had been paired with during conditioning, and (b) a *process* in which the likelihood and vigor of the CR decrease when the US no longer occurs with the CS. Extinction probably plays a substantial role in reducing respondent behaviors in everyday life and is surely part of the reason early fears tend to decline as children get older (Sarafino, 1986).

PREPARING TO CHANGE A RESPONDENT BEHAVIOR

Most procedures in applied behavior analysis are designed and implemented to change operant behaviors because behavior analysts' clients typically have far more problems with operant than respondent behaviors. CERs that impair normal functioning—such as Martin's fear of dogs—are more commonly treated in behavior therapy mainly by clinical psychologists (see Wixted, Bellack, & Hersen, 1990). Designing an intervention to change a respondent behavior requires similar procedures and data-gathering activities to those we've seen for changing operant behaviors. Therapists need to measure the behavior and do a functional assessment of it before deciding exactly which methods to use and how to implement them.

ASSESSING RESPONDENT BEHAVIORS

For the most part, we can assess respondent behaviors by using the strategies and types of data we discussed in Chapter 2. Because most respondent behaviors addressed in interventions are CERs, we'll focus our discussion on measuring fear in two ways: direct and indirect assessment methods (Wixted, Bellack, & Hersen, 1990). With *direct assessment methods*, we observe the person's overt fearful behaviors, such as Martin's reluctance to approach a dog (the CS) or distress when one was present. A commonly used direct method for measuring fear is the **behavioral approach test** (also called the *behavioral avoidance test*) in which the client and feared stimulus, such as an insect or animal, are brought closer together until the client reports discomfort. At that point, the test ends and the distance between the client and the stimulus is measured and recorded. If we are measuring the person's distress, we can observe and record its *frequency* and *duration*, when it's important to know how often the fear CR occurs or how long it lasts when the CS is present, and its *magnitude*—the degree or intensity of the CR. Behavior analysts typically require that some form of direct assessment be made of any behavior we try to change.

Indirect assessment methods use self reports, others' reports, or physiological measures of the person's reactions to the CS. These methods can also measure the frequency, duration, and magnitude of the CR. Assessing the magnitude of fear with indirect assessment methods is most commonly accomplished in two ways:

1. *Physiological measures* assess internal events, such as heart rate, that are known to vary with outward signs and self-reports of fear. The greater the increase in heart rate when the CS appears, the stronger the fear is assumed to be.

2. *Rating scales* assess the person's subjective feelings of fear when in the fearful situation. The higher the rating, the stronger the fear is assumed to be.

A common rating scale to assess fear is the **subjective units of discomfort scale (SUDS)**, which is pronounced as "suds." People use SUDS to rate their fear experiences, usually on a scale ranging from 0 to 100 (Heimberg, 1990; Wolpe, 1973). The highest rating on the scale is defined in words—for instance, "the worst fear you have ever experienced"—and each unit in the scale is called a SUD. Thus a CR the person rates at 70 SUDs is subjectively much stronger than one rated at 20 SUDs. Because these are *subjective* ratings, we cannot assume that the same rating given by different people indicates that all raters experienced the same degree of discomfort. But we can assume that a person who gave the same rating to two CSs, such as taking an exam and giving a speech, experienced the same magnitude of fear in these two situations.

FUNCTIONAL ASSESSMENT OF RESPONDENT BEHAVIORS

Conducting a functional assessment is just as important in changing a respondent behavior as it is in changing an operant behavior (Emmelkamp, Bouman, & Scholing, 1992). By using A-B-C log and summary record forms, we can identify and describe in detail the respondent behavior's antecedents, behaviors, and consequences to address in an intervention.

Antecedents for Respondent Behaviors

The antecedents for a respondent behavior can be of two types: the actual CSs that were conditioned through the person's experiences or stimuli to which the CR has generalized. One approach for identifying problem CERs is to have individuals fill out questionnaires. For example, the *Fear Inventory* has people rate how much they are disturbed by various situations, such as seeing lightning and being criticized (Wolpe, 1973). Some instruments focus on assessing fears in children (Morris & Kratochwill, 1983). Self-reports regarding how the antecedents came to elicit the CR are not necessarily useful in changing the behavior.

To design an effective intervention to change a respondent behavior, we need to know the *specific recent antecedents* for the behavior. A functional assessment of a CER, such as a phobia or anxiety, should try to answer the following three questions about its antecedents (Emmelkamp, Bouman, & Scholing, 1992):

1. *Under what circumstances does the target person's CER tend to occur?* These circumstances should include specific stimuli, such as certain places or people. Try to identify a large number—say, two dozen or so—of CSs that could elicit at least a weak CER.

2. *What factors seem to affect how likely or strongly the CER will be performed when the circumstances above occur?* These factors should be present in the person's general life, such as being unemployed or disabled, when the CER occurs.

3. *What thoughts tend to precede the* CER? We can use interviews to identify these thoughts.

Answers to these three questions about the antecedents can help in deciding which methods we should include in an intervention and how to use them. We'll discuss several of these methods in the next chapter.

The Respondent Behavior

The functional assessment should enable us to determine three characteristics about the respondent behavior we want to change (Emmelkamp, Bouman, & Scholing, 1992). We should try to identify the person's:

1. *Bodily sensations and activities* at the time of the CER. For example, does the person become fidgety, bite his or her nails, or blush when the fear occurs?

2. *Avoidance behaviors* evoked by the CER. For instance, does the person put off doing important behaviors, such as looking for a job, or try to get out of them entirely when the CER occurs? Does he or she use mood-altering substances, such as alcohol, to reduce feelings of fear?

3. *Related problem behaviors.* For example, someone who uses drugs to reduce his or her CER may have social or academic difficulties also.

Consequences for Respondent Behaviors

Chapter 1 described how respondent and operant conditioning occur together in real life. A respondent behavior, such as a CER, often receives consequences—for instance, the person may receive comforting or special treatment when a CER occurs, which may give positive reinforcement for the response. And if the CER involves successful avoidance or escape acts, as in Martin's fear of dogs, those behaviors receive negative reinforcement, maintaining the CER. A functional assessment should allow us to identify the short- and long-term consequences of a CER (Emmelkamp, Bouman, & Scholing, 1992). For example, when escape behavior reduces people's current feelings of fear, the negative reinforcement is a short-term consequence. The long-term consequences of avoidance or escape behavior are problematic when they affect the person's general functioning. For instance, Martin's fear of dogs prevented him from going shopping or on outings with his parents. (Go to 📖.)

STUDY AND REVIEW

SUMMARY

People learn many respondent behaviors, such as fears, from experiences in everyday life. This learning includes an association between an eventual conditioned stimulus (CS) and an unconditioned stimulus (US): The CS gains the ability to elicit a conditioned response (CR) in the absence of the US. An important respondent behavior is the conditioned emotional response (CER), such as fear or anger. Two types of fear are phobias and anxiety. We can learn CERs through direct and indirect conditioning; inborn processes, such as genetics, influence the likelihood that a person will acquire CERs. Other behaviors that are influenced by respondent conditioning include physiological reactions; substance use; cancer treatment reactions, such as learned food aversions and anticipatory nausea; and positive attitudes. Emetic therapy is a respondent procedure that can reduce alcohol use.

Respondent conditioning usually develops most quickly and strongly when the US is intense and the CS and US are conceptually related and are paired consistently, frequently, and close enough in time to permit them to be associated. Three important phenomena in respondent conditioning are (a) overshadowing, in which

CONCEPT CHECK 21.2

Answer the following questions about factors and phenomena in and preparing to change a respondent behavior.

1. The association we learn in respondent conditioning is based largely on the CS and US occurring _____ in time.

2. Respondent conditioning develops most strongly and quickly when the CS precedes the US by _____ seconds.

3. An example of one CS overshadowing another at the time of a car accident (the US) might be _____ . ⇔

4. Parents might use latent inhibition to reduce the likelihood that their child will learn to fear water by _____ . ⇔

5. A person who is fearful of all flying insects after being stung by a bee is showing stimulus _____ .

6. A food that might be a good candidate for a scapegoat to prevent learned food aversions to foods in an adult cancer patient's normal diet would be _____ . ⇔

7. A common rating scale for the assessment of fears is called _____ .

one CS outweighs others in being able to elicit the CR; (b) blocking, whereby an existing CS prevents other stimuli from becoming conditioned to its CR; and (c) latent inhibition, in which past neutral experience with a CS makes it more difficult to associate it with a US in the future.

People can learn respondent behavior through second-order conditioning in which an established CS functions like a US in conditioning a new CS to a CR. Three processes that occur in operant conditioning also occur in respondent conditioning. One process is discrimination learning: People can learn to distinguish among a particular CS and other stimuli that could serve as antecedents. The second process is stimulus generalization: People respond to CSs that are not exactly the same as the one they were conditioned to. The third process is extinction: The strength of the CR declines when the person repeatedly experiences the CS without the US.

The frequency, duration, and magnitude of respondent behaviors can be measured with direct and indirect assessment methods. Direct assessments, such as the behavioral approach test, are preferred. Two indirect assessment methods that are commonly used to measure the magnitude of respondent behaviors are physiological measures and rating scales, especially the subjective units of discomfort scale. By conducting a functional assessment, we can identify and define the respondent behavior and its antecedents and consequences to help in designing an intervention to modify the target behavior, such as a CER.

To prepare for exams, use the following key terms and review questions and the online study guide that's available on this book's companion website at www.wiley.com/college/sarafino.

KEY TERMS

conditioned emotional response   phobia   emetic therapy
   (CER)   anxiety   learned food aversion

anticipatory nausea
overshadowing
blocking

latent inhibition
second-order conditioning
extinction

behavioral approach test
subjective units of discomfort scale
(SUDS)

ANSWERS TO CONCEPT CHECKS (CCs)

CC21.1 *Answers:* **1.** snarling and barking, fear, dogs, fear　**2.** conditioned emotional response　**3.** phobia, anxiety **4.** asthma, low back pain　**5a.** emetic drug **b.** nausea **c.** seeing a bottle of liquor or a drink **d.** nausea **6.** anticipatory nausea

CC21.2 *Answers:* **1.** close together　**2.** $^1\!/_4$ to several　**3.** the sound of a horn being a stronger CS than the rainy weather conditions at the accident　**4.** giving the child pleasant early experiences with water　**5.** generalization　**6.** strong grape-flavored Kool-Aid　**7.** SUDS/subjective units of discomfort scale

REVIEW QUESTIONS

1. Define the term *conditioned emotional response* (CER), and describe how direct and indirect conditioning can be involved in its development.

2. Describe how respondent and operant conditioning can lead to substance use and abuse. What specifically are the CS, US, UR, and CR in emetic therapy for alcohol abuse?

3. Describe the research by Siegel and his colleagues (1982) on tolerance effects and drug overdoses.

4. How are CS–US intensity, pairing consistency, and timing important in respondent conditioning?

5. Why are taste aversions learned so quickly even though the CS and US occur far apart in time?

6. Define the terms *overshadowing*, *blocking*, and *latent inhibition*, and give an example of each phenomenon that happened or might have happened in your own life.

7. How is overshadowing helpful in preventing learned food aversions in cancer patients who receive chemotherapy?

8. Define the term *second-order conditioning*, and describe an example of it from your own life, pointing out the first- and second-order parts of the process.

9. Describe the subjective units of discomfort scale (SUDS), and indicate how it is used in measuring emotion magnitude.

10. Describe how to conduct a functional assessment of a CER and what you would try to determine from it.

RELATED READINGS

- Emmelkamp, P. M. G., Bouman, T. K., & Scholing, A. (1992). *Anxiety disorders: A practitioner's guide.* Chichester, UK: Wiley.

- Morris, R. J., & Kratochwill, T. R. (1983). *Treating children's fears and phobias: A behavioral approach.* New York: Pergamon.

- Rachman, S. (1991). Neo-conditioning and the classical theory of fear acquisition. *Clinical Psychological Review,* 11, 155–173.

- Sarafino, E. P. (1986). *The fears of childhood: A guide to recognizing and reducing fearful states in children.* New York: Human Sciences Press.

- Wolpe, J. (1973). *The practice of behavior therapy.* New York: Pergamon.

22

CHANGING RESPONDENT BEHAVIORS

PROLOGUE

When getting on an escalator, does it ever occur to you that the moving handrail might move too fast and pull you forward, making you trip and fall? This idea formed part of a female college student's phobia when she entered therapy (Nesbitt, 1973). Her fear of riding on escalators had developed several years earlier at a shopping mall: With her relatives, she had ridden on one of these people-movers to an upper floor with no difficulty, but when the family began to board the escalator later to descend, she said she was afraid because of the apparent height. The relatives may have thought she was "being silly," so they forced her onto the escalator, and the ride down was very scary. Ever since that experience, she avoided escalators and always took the stairs or elevator instead. If she was with other people who suggested taking an escalator, she bluntly refused.

On one subsequent occasion, she approached an escalator unexpectedly while shopping and became so overcome by fear that she nearly vomited. Because of the problems she experienced with escalators, she had tried, before entering therapy, to reduce her fear

> by attempting, in the company of friends, to get on an escalator. On those occasions when she could bring herself to stand at the foot of the escalator, she would not step on for fear that by holding on to the handrail she would be pulled downward and so miss her step. (p. 405)

How did the therapist help her overcome her fear? He used one very intense session in which she had to ride on a department store escalator repeatedly with him. Getting her to board the escalator the first time was very difficult and required a great deal of coaxing and "a little physical force." Once on board, she held onto the therapist's shirt tightly, said she felt she'd vomit, and seemed on the verge of crying. The next escalator ride was somewhat easier. After nearly half an hour of riding escalators continuously, she could ride on her own comfortably. Months later, she reported rarely experiencing fear when on escalators.

Most interventions to change respondent behaviors address behavioral excesses, such as when individuals react fearfully or angrily too frequently, too strongly, or for too long. This chapter describes a variety of procedures for changing respondent behaviors, especially fears and other conditioned emotional responses (CERs), with the behavioral goal of eliminating the CER, helping the person function more adaptively. If individuals continue to escape or avoid the conditioned stimulus (CS), their fears tend to persist (Lovibond et al., 2009).

You'll see later in the chapter that the therapy method the therapist used in the opening story is called *flooding*, and you may have thought that it was a good idea to have a therapist with the client on the escalator in case she "freaked out." Experienced therapists usually can gauge how anxious a client is and help prevent the person from feeling overwhelmed. The other procedures for reducing fears that we'll discuss are not as emotionally challenging or risky. Behavior therapists who carry out these procedures must be able to assess the target behavior and would conduct a functional assessment before designing the intervention to decrease the behavior, as we saw in the last chapter. The first two methods we'll examine are respondent extinction and counterconditioning.

EXTINCTION AND COUNTERCONDITIONING

We saw in Chapter 21 that respondent and operant conditioning have several phenomena in common, such as the processes of stimulus discrimination and generalization. We also saw that extinction of a respondent behavior occurs when the CS is presented repeatedly but the unconditioned stimulus (US) no longer occurs. And we noted that the fear of dogs a boy named Martin had developed might have declined without therapy if the old neighbors with the aggressive dogs moved away and the new neighbors had a gentle, friendly dog.

RESPONDENT EXTINCTION

The process of extinguishing a respondent behavior tends to proceed gradually rather than rapidly, just as it does for operant behavior. For instance, an intervention using extinction procedures to reduce people's strong conditioned emotional responses (CERs) to social situations found that ratings on a subjective units of discomfort scale (SUDS) for feared social CSs declined by about 3.2% per treatment session (Turner, Beidel, Long, & Greenhouse, 1992). By the end of the 16 sessions in the intervention, the clients' SUDS ratings had declined by about 50%. When used in respondent therapy, extinction is often called *exposure* because the procedure exposes the person to the CS, or a stimulus like it, without the US.

Another parallel to operant conditioning phenomena is that extinction procedures do not erase the memory of the original respondent learning. We remember at least part of what we learned in the original conditioning and in extinction. As a result, the extinguished CR can reappear, especially if the CS occurs in a context different from the one where extinction was carried out, which may lead to a relapse in a CER (Neumann

& Kitlertsirivatana, 2010). Reappearance of an extinguished CR can occur in three ways—*spontaneous recovery*, *renewal*, and *reinstatement*—which are like the processes we discussed in Chapter 6 for operant behaviors (Bouton, 2000; Thewissen et al., 2006; Vansteenwegen et al., 2006). What's more, if the CS and US are presented together again after extinction has been carried out for a prolonged period, the strength of the CR often returns very rapidly (Bouton & Nelson, 1998; Bouton & Swartzentruber, 1991). So, if the woman in the opening story with the strong fear of escalators were to have a very negative encounter with an escalator after her fear had been eliminated with extinction procedures, her strong fear might return quickly.

Respondent extinction can help in treating substance abuse. You'll recall that when people use mood-altering substances, they develop CSs, such as the sight of liquor or the place where they usually drink, that produce internal conditioned responses (CRs) like the unconditioned reactions of actually taking the substance. Researchers applied extinction procedures with six male problem drinkers by having them repeatedly experience important CSs for their drinking, such as holding a can of beer, while not allowing them to drink (Blakey & Baker, 1980). These sessions were carried out a few times per week for several weeks or months. Self-reports from most of these men suggested that their cravings for alcohol and drinking had decreased. Similar procedures and effects on craving have been found for heavy users of methamphetamine (Price et al., 2010). Several programs have had some success in treating substance abuse by applying respondent extinction alone or combining it with other behavioral or cognitive methods (Drummond & Glautier, 1994; Monti et al., 1994; Sitharthan, Sitharthan, Hough, & Kavanagh, 1997). These programs have provided strong evidence for the usefulness of respondent extinction by assessing substance use in relatively objective ways, such as by having the subjects take breath or urine tests and having family members confirm drinking data.

COUNTERCONDITIONING

Another similarity in respondent and operant methods to change behavior is in the use of alternative behaviors or competing responses to reduce behavioral excesses. To reduce a respondent behavior, a procedure called **counterconditioning** trains the target person to substitute a competing or incompatible behavior for the CR when the CS is present (Wolpe, 1958, 1973). This technique is called *counterconditioning* because it was developed to reverse a person's previous learning of fear. Wolpe proposed that "If a response [that inhibits] anxiety can be made to occur in the presence of anxiety-provoking stimuli, it will weaken the bond between these stimuli and the anxiety" (1973, p. 17). Because the counterconditioning procedure presents the CS without the US, extinction is part of the process.

Chapter 1 presented an example of counterconditioning in which the fear of rabbits a boy named Peter had developed was reduced (Jones, 1924). Before the therapy was conducted, he would cry if he spotted a rabbit, even if it was far away and in a cage. Over the next several weeks, Peter received counterconditioning therapy once or twice a day. The procedure simply involved bringing the rabbit a little closer each time while Peter ate some favorite foods in the presence of an assistant he liked; the boy's eating and being calm were the competing responses. By the end of the intervention, Peter would ask for the rabbit and play with it. Other interventions using counterconditioning had the target persons *imagine* social situations in which a CS occurred. For instance, a female college student who was afraid that she would humiliate herself at a banquet that her ex-boyfriend would also attend was asked to imagine various scenes at the banquet, each ending in a mildly absurd event, such as her ex-boyfriend arriving dressed in leotards (Ventis, 1973). When she heard that last detail, she smiled and looked surprised, but then imagined the scene with a smile on her face. Her jolly reaction was the competing response. After she had actually attended the banquet, she reported having felt only mild apprehension while she was there. A similar approach was applied successfully to decrease a woman's anger toward her husband and child (Smith, 1973).

A study examined whether the effectiveness of using extinction to reduce spider phobias would be improved by adding to it a counterconditioning procedure (de Jong, Vorage, & van den Hout, 2000). The participants were 34 women with strong fears of spiders; they were randomly assigned to two groups, each of which received a 3-hour treatment session: 16 women received exposure (extinction), and 18 received extinction plus counterconditioning. For the extinction treatment, the women were exposed to a spider (the CS) gradually, starting with seeing the spider in a covered glass jar and progressing to actual physical contact with it, such as having it placed on an arm. For the counterconditioning treatment, the last half hour of the session presented two calming features: The women listened to their favorite music and ate tasty foods. The results revealed substantially lowered fears by the end of the session and in follow-up testing a year later for the women in both groups, which did not differ. In this study, extinction was a highly effective treatment, and adding the counterconditioning component didn't increase its success.

RELAXATION TECHNIQUES

If a friend suggested that you "relax" when you are presenting a speech to an audience, would that advice help? Probably not, and because most people don't know how to relax when feeling tense, it might even make your anxiety worse. One indication of tension is blood pressure; researchers used this measure while male participants who had not been trained to relax watched an erotic videotape (Suls, Sanders, & Labrecque, 1986). Some of the men were asked simply to try to relax and keep their blood pressures low while they watched the TV, and others were asked to respond as they normally would. The men who were asked to relax showed greater blood pressure *increases* during the videotape than those subjects who were given no such instructions. Perhaps people who have not been trained to relax try too hard. Individuals who have received training in relaxation methods are able to become psychologically and physiologically relaxed and to react less strongly when they experience arousing stimuli (Lichstein, 1988; Poppen, 1998, 2005).

What does the term *relaxation* mean? **Relaxation** refers to a state of calmness with low psychological and physiological tension or arousal. Tension and arousal accompany and are part of fear reactions and are experienced physically as tense muscles and rapid breathing and heart rate. Techniques to produce relaxation gained wide acceptance in the 1970s as psychological treatments for CERs, especially anxieties and phobias, and a variety of medical problems, such as asthma, high blood pressure, migraine and tension headache, and cancer chemotherapy reactions (Carlson & Hoyle, 1993; Lichstein, 1988; Poppen, 1998).

Several different techniques can be used to achieve relaxation. Regardless of the particular methods the person uses, a few points should be kept in mind (Lichstein, 1988; Moore, 1987; Taylor, 1978):

- *The setting*: The procedure must be carried out in a *comfortable place, free of interruptions and distractions*. The person should be seated or reclining, but not comfortable enough to fall asleep. Tight-fitting clothing should be loosened.

- *Session length and schedule*: Relaxation sessions last between 10 *and* 30 *minutes*, but while the person is learning the technique, sessions usually take more time. It is typically a good idea for the person to *set aside regular times* to practice the relaxation exercises once or twice a day as "homework." Relaxation sessions can leave some people relaxed but *alert* when they are finished, making it hard for them to fall asleep if the session ends an hour or so before bedtime.

Finally, the person should record data rating the magnitude of his or her relaxation during sessions, using a data sheet like the one in Figure 22-1. We'll look at three commonly used relaxation techniques—progressive muscle relaxation, autogenic training, and meditation—in the next sections. Each of them requires that individuals do relaxation exercises for, say, half an hour as they are learning the procedure, which later can be shortened to 10 or 20 minutes. After individuals have mastered the technique, they can develop a *rapid relaxation induction* method that allows them to calm themselves quickly with a set of words, images, and deep breathing (Sarafino, 2011, gives detailed procedures for developing a rapid method).

PROGRESSIVE MUSCLE RELAXATION

The approach called **progressive muscle relaxation** (or just *progressive relaxation*) involves alternately tensing and relaxing separate muscle groups while resting, which leaves the muscles more relaxed than they were before. This technique, developed many years ago by Jacobson (1938), was extremely detailed, sometimes taking dozens of

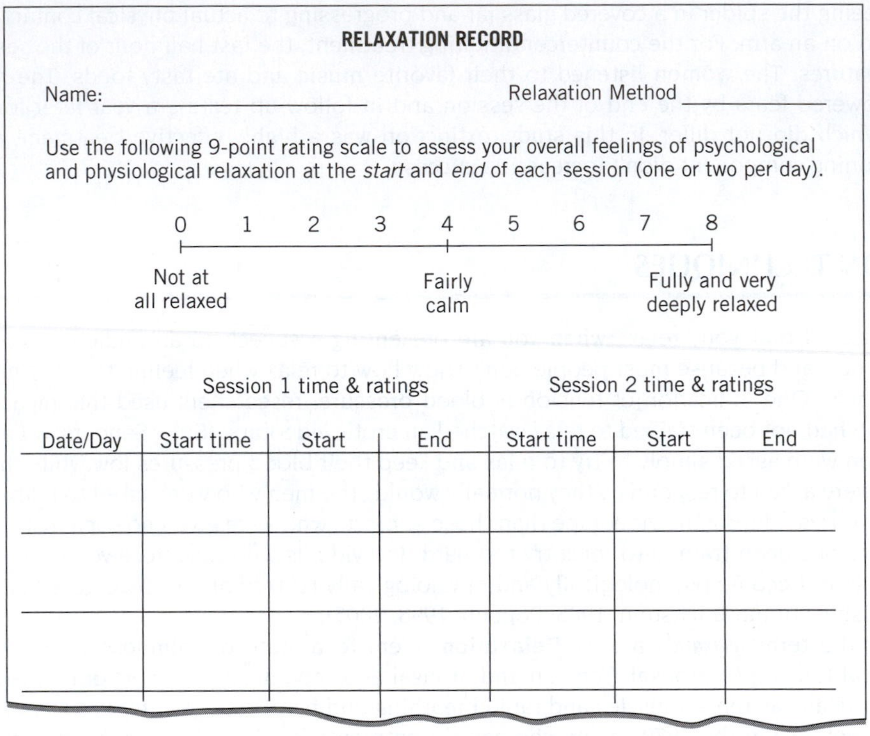

RELAXATION RECORD

Name:_____   Relaxation Method _____

Use the following 9-point rating scale to assess your overall feelings of psychological and physiological relaxation at the *start* and *end* of each session (one or two per day).

```
    0    1    2    3    4    5    6    7    8
    ├────┼────┼────┼────┼────┼────┼────┼────┤
```

| Not at | | Fairly | | Fully and very |
| all relaxed | | calm | | deeply relaxed |

	Session 1 time & ratings			Session 2 time & ratings		
Date/Day	Start time	Start	End	Start time	Start	End

Figure 22-1 A data sheet for keeping relaxation records of progress made in practicing relaxation techniques. For each session, the person records the start time and the start and end ratings of relaxation.

hours for training. As a result, Bernstein and Borkovec (1973) designed a shorter, easier-to-learn version, and this version—or some variation of it—became the standard procedure for progressive muscle relaxation (Lichstein, 1988). Studies with follow-up assessments have shown that the positive psychological and physiological effects of using progressive muscle relaxation continue, and may even get stronger, in the weeks and months after individuals receive training in the procedure (Carlson & Hoyle, 1993). Children at just 3 or 4 years of age can learn muscle relaxation techniques and apply them to reduce their fears during stressful events, such as receiving dental treatment (Siegel & Peterson, 1980).

Two aspects of the progressive muscle relaxation procedure are controversial. First, researchers are not certain whether it is necessary or desirable to *tense* the muscles as part of the process. For instance, one study found evidence that alternating between tensing and relaxing muscle groups may not be as effective in inducing deep physiological relaxation as procedures that omit the tensing phase (Lucic, Steffen, Harrigan, & Stuebing, 1991). But other researchers have reported contradictory results, and it appears that tensing the muscles is helpful *while people are being trained* in the technique (Lehrer, 1982). Tensing probably promotes learning the skill of relaxing by teaching people to discriminate between relaxation and muscular tension. After people have mastered the skill, tensing the muscles can be eliminated (Moore, 1987).

The second controversial aspect of the progressive muscle relaxation procedure involves the value of using audio-recorded *protocols*, or scripts, to guide the process during relaxation sessions. Many therapists provide protocol recordings or advise clients to make recordings of the scripts that are used in relaxation exercises. Although these recordings are generally used for clients to practice relaxation as homework assignments, they have also been tried as a substitute for in-person training with a therapist. Studies have found that using audio-recorded protocols without supervised training can teach the relaxation procedure, but in-person training is more effective (Beiman, Israel, & Johnson, 1978; Lehrer, 1982). It may be that supervised training allows the therapist to notice difficulties and give the person corrective feedback. Other studies have shown that the beneficial effects of relaxation are greater when in-person training is conducted individually rather than in groups and that providing audio-recorded protocols for clients to use in practicing relaxation on their own appears to be very helpful (Carlson & Hoyle, 1993). Although clients tend to overstate the amount of homework practice they do, most appear to practice relaxation about as often as the therapist advises (Taylor, Agras, Schneider, & Allen, 1983).

The next Close-Up box outlines a protocol for progressive muscle relaxation, giving the muscle groups and procedures for tensing and relaxing them (the full protocol is available in Sarafino, 2011). You'll notice that the tensing and relaxing progresses through a series of different muscle groups. Breathing exercises are included, as well. The tensing phase for each muscle group is usually between 5 and 10 seconds long, and relaxation phases are between 20 and 45 seconds. (Go to 🔍.)

CLOSE-UP

An Overview of a Progressive Muscle Relaxation Protocol

The following list gives the name of each body region or function with its *tensing* and *relaxing* procedures, based on information from several sources (Bernstein & Borkovec, 1973; Lichstein, 1988; NJNPI, 1972; Taylor, 1978). Clients would receive instructions telling them to tense quickly and tightly only the muscles in the stated region or function, hold the tension until told to relax, and then let the muscles go completely limp.

1. *Right hand.* Tensing: Make a tight fist; hold tension. Relaxing: Let muscles go limp when told to relax; notice tension flowing out.
2. *Left hand.* Tensing/relaxing: Same as right hand.
3. *Right biceps.* Tensing: Bend arm; make biceps very hard; hold tension. Relaxing: Let arm fall to side; let muscles go limp; notice tension flowing out.
4. *Left biceps.* Tensing/relaxing: Same as right biceps.
5. *Eyebrows.* Tensing: Pull brows together tightly, wrinkling the forehead as much as possible; hold tension. Relaxing: Let forehead muscles go limp; notice tension flowing out.
6. *Face.* Tensing: Scrunch up lower part of face, wrinkling nose and frowning; hold tension. Relaxing: Let face muscles go limp; notice tension flowing out.
7. *Back of neck.* Tensing: Bend head forward to stretch back of neck, pulling chin close to the chest; hold tension. Relaxing: Let neck muscles go limp; notice tension flowing out.
8. *Front of neck.* Tensing: Bend head backward as far as possible; hold tension. Relaxing: Let neck muscles go limp; notice tension flowing out.
9. *Breathing.* Tensing: Take very deep breath; hold tension. Relaxing: Exhale slowly; notice tension flowing out.
10. *Shoulders.* Tensing: Move shoulders upward; hold tension. Relaxing: Let muscles go limp so shoulders sink back down; notice tension flowing out.
11. *Stomach.* Tensing: Arch back backwards and tighten abdominal muscles; hold tension. Relaxing: Let stomach muscles go limp; notice tension flowing out.
12. *Legs/calves.* Tensing: Lift both legs and curl toes so calves are tight; hold tension. Relaxing: Let legs fall; let muscles go limp; notice tension flowing out.
13. *Legs/thighs.* Tensing: Lift both legs; tighten thigh and lower abdominal muscles; hold tension. Relaxing: Let legs fall and muscles go limp; notice tension flowing out.
14. *Breathing—five breaths.* Tensing: Each time, take very deep breath. Relaxing: Each time, exhale slowly; notice tension flowing out.

OTHER RELAXATION PROCEDURES

Some clients find that progressive muscle relaxation methods are not as effective or appropriate for them as other relaxation procedures, such as autogenic training and meditation.

Autogenic Training

The relaxation technique called **autogenic training** has people imagine being in a pleasant and peaceful scene and experiencing specific bodily sensations, such as their arms feeling warm or heavy (Schultz, 1957; Schultz & Luthe, 1969). The term *autogenic* means that the technique's psychological and physiological effects are self-produced.

In the standard autogenic training procedure, the person listens to instructions from a therapist or a recording and tries to imagine the events described. The procedure starts by asking the person to:

1. Adopt a passive and relaxed attitude.
2. Allow changes in his or her bodily processes to evolve naturally.
3. Choose a pleasant, peaceful scene, such as lying on the beach or sitting in a meadow on a beautiful, warm day.

Then the training proceeds through a series of six phases, each with a theme regarding the type of sensation to imagine in the body. Of these themes, the two that are the most commonly used in therapy involve feeling *heaviness* and *warmth* in parts of the body (Lichstein, 1988). The instructions specify the parts of the body to focus on and what to feel—for instance:

> My left arm is heavy .... I'm at peace .... My left arm is heavy .... My left arm is heavy .... I'm at peace .... My left arm is heavy .... My left arm is heavy .... My left arm is heavy.

The therapist reads each instruction very slowly. The target person repeats the instruction while focusing attention on that part of the body and then receives a rest period. This sequence of reading/repeating/resting with the same instruction is repeated three times for a total of about 5 minutes. This same procedure then moves to six other parts of the body for 5 minutes each, still with the same theme. Covering the theme for all seven parts of the body takes about 35 minutes.

The next theme is warmth, and the instructions include phrases like, "My abdomen is warm." Each of the six themes is covered in the same way we've seen, and whole phase takes about 35 minutes. Because the complete, standard procedure for autogenic training is so time-consuming to carry out, researchers have developed shorter versions in which the repetition, the timing of each instruction sequence, or the number of themes is reduced (Lichstein, 1988). These versions take less than half an hour to carry out. One advantage of autogenic training is that it doesn't require the person to tense and relax muscles, which is important for people who suffer from medical conditions, such as severe arthritis or low back pain, that make movement painful or difficult.

Meditation

The third approach for helping people learn to relax uses **meditation**—the process of contemplating or focusing one's attention on an object, event, or idea to help people become detached from their physical states, thoughts, and feelings (de Silva, 1984, 1990; Lane, 2005; Solé-Leris, 1986; Thera, 1979). Meditation derives from Eastern philosophy and religion, mainly Buddhism, and produces relaxation and a *mindful awareness* of the meaning of each experience, unencumbered by cognitive or emotional distortions. An example of the concept and role of mindful awareness comes from interventions to help people cope with chronic pain conditions (Kabat-Zinn, 1982; Kabat-Zinn, Lipworth, & Burney, 1985). By training these patients to focus on painful sensations as they happened, rather than trying to block them out, and to separate the physical sensations from the cognitive and emotional reactions that accompany pain, the patients could become aware of the pain itself, unaffected

Meditation should occur in a quiet setting, and the person should sit upright in a relaxed and comfortable position. *Source:* Masterfile.

by their thoughts or feelings about it. This training reduced the patients' reported physical and psychological discomfort.

We can achieve the relaxation component of meditation by doing exercises to focus attention on a *meditation stimulus*, such as a pleasing and simple *visual object* like a flower or vase; a *mantra*, or word-like sound, such as "om"; or our own slow and deep *breathing*. During meditation, the person's mind may sometimes wander to other thoughts. This is to be expected. When it happens, he or she can simply and gently coax attention back to the meditation stimulus, without getting intellectually or emotionally involved in intrusive thoughts or becoming annoyed. While people are learning to meditate as a relaxation technique, they are instructed to practice it once or twice a day for about 20 minutes a session. Although it isn't clear how well people from Western cultures can reduce their physiological arousal after meditation training (Holmes, 1984; Lichstein, 1988), Buddhist monks in Southeast Asia can dramatically alter their body metabolism and brain electrical activity through meditation (Benson et al., 1990). (Go to ▤.)

SYSTEMATIC DESENSITIZATION

The verb *desensitize* means to make someone less responsive or susceptible to certain stimuli, such as a CS. Wolpe (1958, 1973) used his concept of counterconditioning as the basis for developing a technique to desensitize people's fears, which he described as proceeding in the following way:

A physiological state inhibitory of anxiety is induced in the patient by means of muscle relaxation, and he is then exposed to a weak anxiety-arousing stimulus for a few seconds. If the exposure is repeated several times, the stimulus progressively loses its ability to evoke anxiety. Then successively "stronger" stimuli are introduced and similarly treated. (1973, p. 95)

CONCEPT CHECK 22.1

Check your understanding of the preceding concepts. Remember: The symbol ⇔ means that the answer can vary. Answer the following questions about respondent extinction, counterconditioning, and relaxation.

1. To extinguish the fear of bees a child developed after being stung twice, we would need to present a(n) _____ without _____ . ⇔
2. An alternative or competing response to replace fear or anger might be _____ . ⇔
3. The procedure that substitutes an alternative or competing response for a CR when the CS is present is called _____ .
4. The method of alternately tensing and relaxing separate muscle groups while resting comfortably is called _____ .
5. Saying to oneself, "My right leg is very warm. I'm at peace," is likely to be part of the relaxation procedure of _____ .
6. A procedure that helps people become detached from their physical states, thoughts, and feelings by focusing attention on an object, event, or idea is called _____ .
7. A static visual object you could use as a meditation stimulus in your own residence is _____ . ⇔

This technique, called **systematic desensitization**, is designed to reduce a CER by presenting CSs *that are successively more fear arousing* while the individual remains in a physiologically calm state, which is induced by having the *person perform relaxation exercises* (McGlynn, 2005). Relaxation is a competing response to fear because people almost never feel afraid and relaxed at the same time. The technique is called *systematic* because it is carried out with a gradual, step-by-step procedure: Each CS *is presented briefly* and is *desensitized before advancing to a stronger one*. Let's see how the procedure is designed and carried out.

DEVELOPING A STIMULUS HIERARCHY

After conducting a functional assessment of the respondent target behavior, such as a fear of flying, we should have identified a large number—say, 20 or so—of CSs related to the CER that could elicit at least a weak CR. These stimuli are used to arrange a *hierarchy* of CSs, from the weakest to the strongest stimuli. The CSs can be of three types:

1. *In vivo*, or real-life events, objects, or people. For instance, for people who are very fearful of flying in airplanes, a strong CS might be actually sitting in a plane.
2. *Imaginal*, or mental representations of events, objects, or people, such as imagining being on an airplane.
3. *Symbolic*, or overt representations of events, objects, or people, such as seeing a picture of people sitting in an airplane. Virtual reality technology can make symbolic stimuli more like in vivo presentations (North, North, & Cobble, 1997).

A critical step in using systematic desensitization is to construct a **stimulus hierarchy**—a graded sequence of CSs that are rank-ordered based on the magnitude of the CER they are likely to elicit. Stimulus hierarchies commonly consist of between 10 and 15 rank-ordered stimuli—if the functional assessment identified more than 15, we would delete some.

Let's see how we would construct a stimulus hierarchy for a target person's fear of spiders after having identified 20 in vivo CSs in our functional assessment. We would use five tasks to pare down these stimuli:

1. Write each CS on an index card, giving enough information to picture or create the stimulus in detail.

2. Have the person give each CS a subjective units of discomfort scale (SUDS) rating on a scale of 0 to 100.

3. Set up "anchor points"—a very weak CS and the strongest CS, making sure that all the strong CSs represent reasonable situations that might be encountered in real life and are not very dangerous. In this example, seeing a spider in a covered jar 12 feet away is the weak anchor, rated at 5 SUDs, and seeing a spider crawling on the subject's pants leg is the strongest anchor, rated at 90 SUDs.

4. Rank the remaining index cards on the basis of the SUDS ratings.

5. Cull 5 to 10 CSs, trying to equalize the step "sizes"—that is, the number of SUDs—between adjacent stimuli we retain for the hierarchy.

It's important to make the progression through the hierarchy *gradual* by making the distances separating stimuli fairly consistent and by including not more than 10 SUDs (Wolpe, 1973). If the ratings of the original set of stimuli contain a large gap, the target person should identify an intervening CS. Table 22.1 presents two example stimulus hierarchies, one with all in vivo CSs for a fear of heights and one with a combination of symbolic, imaginal, and in vivo CSs for a fear of dating.

THE SYSTEMATIC DESENSITIZATION PROCEDURE

The systematic desensitization procedure starts by having the individual sit or lie down comfortably and perform the relaxation exercises. If the stimuli are imaginal, the person is asked to picture each one as a scene and signal by raising a finger when the image is clearly formed (Wolpe, 1973). But if the stimuli are in vivo or symbolic, the person actually experiences each one, such as by looking at or approaching it.

Let's see how we would proceed once the target person is completely relaxed and ready for the first CS, the weakest one from the hierarchy. Here is the procedure for any CS:

1. Present the CS for several seconds and then say, "Stop."

2. The person would look away or close his or her eyes and state in SUDs how much discomfort the activity elicited. That rating—say, 5—would end the first "trial" with that CS.

3. We would immediately say "Go back to relaxing," and allow the person to do so for 20 to 30 seconds.

4. We'd start the next trial with the same CS, repeating the same procedure. We'd continue with additional trials until the person reported 0 *on two successive trials.*

Upon reaching this "success criterion," we can advance to the next stimulus in the hierarchy. We would not advance to the next stimulus at any point in the desensitization process until this criterion has been met. We would perform this same procedure for each CS, advancing through the hierarchy in sequence.

Here are some guidelines to follow in desensitization (Sarafino, 1986; Wolpe, 1973). First, each desensitization session usually lasts between 15 and 30 minutes, and only part of the stimulus hierarchy is used in a single session. Second, reducing a moderately strong fear is likely to take several sessions, and stronger fears may require many more. Third, the first stimulus used in each succeeding session should be the last one desensitized in the previous session, and the success criterion should be repeated. Fourth, be flexible and willing to revise the procedure to meet the client's needs. Finally, don't rely only on SUDS ratings to assess treatment progress and success. Periodically apply a behavioral approach test or get corroboration from appropriate people regarding the client's overt behaviors when the CS is present in everyday life.

You may have noticed that systematic desensitization requires that the target person function at a fairly high level. Can desensitization be used with children who are very young or developmentally disabled? No, but a counterconditioning method called *contact desensitization* is available for these individuals. It uses a stimulus hierarchy that a therapist develops and provides reinforcers when the person approaches the feared object more

Table 22.1   *Examples of Stimulus Hierarchies With Hypothetical SUDS Ratings for a Fear of Heights and a Fear of Dating*

Heights: *Stimulus hierarchy using all in vivo CSs:*

1.   Standing at a closed upper-floor window and looking out. (SUDS = 5)
2.   Standing on a stepladder, 3 feet from the floor, to change a light bulb. (SUDS = 12)
3.   Standing on a balcony 2 feet from the railing, several stories above the ground. (SUDS = 22)
4.   Walking on flat ground above a mountain cliff, 15 feet from the edge. (SUDS = 30)
5.   Walking on flat ground above a mountain cliff, 5 feet from the edge. (SUDS = 39)
6.   Hiking on a steep trail. When cliffs are very near, there are guard rails. (SUDS = 58)
7.   Being a passenger in a car traveling at the speed limit on a narrow and winding mountain road. When cliffs occur, there are guardrails. (SUDS = 65)
8.   Standing on a stepladder outside a house, 6 feet from the ground, cleaning debris from a gutter. (SUDS = 71)
9.   Being on an extension ladder outside a house, cleaning a second-story window. (SUDS = 77)
10. Climbing up a 50-foot-high water tower, using a ladder with handrails. (SUDS = 86)
11. Standing on a moderately sloped roof of a house. (SUDS = 95)

Dating: *Stimulus hierarchy using symbolic, imaginal, and in vivo CSs:*

1.   Looking at a photograph of an attractive prospective person to date. (SUDS = 3)
2.   Imagining meeting the person in the photograph (item 1) at a party. (SUDS = 10)
3.   Looking at a photograph of a couple on a date. (SUDS = 17)
4.   Imagining being at a movie with several acquaintances and sitting next to one of them who could be a prospective date. (SUDS = 25)
5.   Imagining exchanging phone numbers with an attractive person who could be a prospective date. (SUDS = 35)
6.   Imagining calling the item 5 person to chat. (SUDS = 40)
7.   Imagining accidentally meeting the item 5 person at a shopping mall and going for coffee together. (SUDS = 48)
8.   Imagining calling the item 5 person for a date. (SUDS = 55)
9.   Imagining being on a date with item 5 person. (SUDS = 65)
10. Imagining a friend talking about helping to arrange a date with an actual mutual acquaintance who is an attractive person. (SUDS = 74)
11. Actually dialing the first several digits of the phone number of the attractive item 10 person, without completing the call. (SUDS = 80)
12. Dialing a number that always has a taped message, such as the phone at a movie theatre, then talking as if the call had gone through to the attractive item 10 person and asking for a date. (SUDS = 85)
13. Imagining an "awkward silence" when conversing on a date with the item 10 person. (SUDS = 92)
14. Actually calling the item 10 person for a date. (SUDS = 98)

and more closely when asked to do so. Contact desensitization has been applied successfully to reduce dog phobias in men with moderate to profound retardation and to reduce a fear of animated toys, such as a dancing doll, in an 8-year-old boy with autism (Erfanian & Miltenberger, 1990; Ricciardi, Luiselli, & Camare, 2006).

HOW EFFECTIVE IS SYSTEMATIC DESENSITIZATION?

Systematic desensitization is a well-documented, highly effective method for helping people overcome fears and other CERs (Borden, 1992; TFPDPP, 1993; Wilson, 1982). What's more, the reductions in fear are durable. Follow-up assessments taken for 2 years after treatment have found few recurrences in the fears (Paul, 1967; Rosen, Glasgow, & Barrera, 1977). And many individuals who succeed in overcoming specific fears in treatment with systematic desensitization often report improvements in other areas of emotional functioning in their lives (Paul, 1967). Desensitization has also been used successfully in treating other anxiety-related problems—for example, people's being unable to urinate in public restrooms and checking compulsively for potentially harmful conditions, such as whether doors are locked (McCracken & Larkin, 1991; Overholser, 1991).

Is desensitization with imaginal CSs effective? Although desensitization with imaginal stimuli can reduce people's fears, several studies have shown that in vivo CSs result in greater fear reduction (Barlow, Leitenberg, Agras, & Wincze, 1969; Crowe, Marks, Agras, & Leitenberg, 1972; Menzies & Clarke, 1993; Sherman, 1972; Wilson, 1982). In the research by Barlow and his colleagues, female college students who were afraid of snakes were pretested for their fear with a "harmless boa constrictor" that was kept in a glass box with a wire mesh cover. Then they were desensitized for their fear and posttested with the snake. The pretests and posttests included assessments of two types: (a) a *behavioral approach test* that contained 17 acts ranging from watching the snake in the cage 15 feet away to picking up the snake, and (b) a *physiological test* that measured the galvanic skin response (GSR) while the snake was in the box at various distances away. Desensitization was carried out with the CSs in the stimulus hierarchy presented by either an imaginal or an in vivo procedure. Posttests conducted with the snake revealed that the individuals desensitized with the in vivo stimuli were able to perform more of the items in the behavioral test and showed much less physiological arousal (GSR) to the snake than did those desensitized with the imaginal stimuli, as depicted in Figure 22-2.

Some controversy exists over the need to include two of the procedural features of systematic desensitization:

1. *Relaxation*: Findings from some studies suggest that relaxation during sessions enhances the desensitization process, but other findings are contradictory (Kazdin & Wilcoxon, 1976).

2. *Relatively weak CSs*: A study compared the use of a full stimulus hierarchy with using only the strongest stimuli for desensitizing college students' math anxieties (Richardson & Suinn, 1973). The two approaches were equally successful in reducing the students' fears. If using a small number of stimuli in a hierarchy produces an overly large "step" between CSs that entails too much discomfort for the target person, an intermediate CS can be added (Sturges & Sturges, 1998).

Although there is some doubt about the importance of these features to the success of desensitization, the evidence against their use is not clear enough to warrant dropping them. Because relaxation exercises and

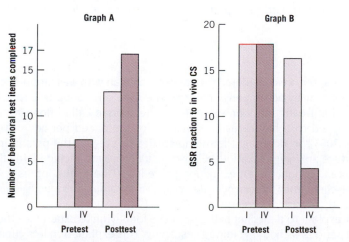

Figure 22-2   Number of items completed in a 17-item behavioral test (graph A) and galvanic skin response (GSR, graph B) with a real CS, a snake. The data are for snake-phobic adults before (pretest) and after (posttest) systematic desensitization to snakes conducted with imaginal (I) or in vivo (IV) CSs. High GSR scores indicate greater fear reactions. *Source*: Data from Barlow, Leitenberg, Agras, & Wincze (1969), Tables 1 and 2.

full stimulus hierarchies don't seem to harm clients and may help the treatment process, it's probably best to include these features in systematic desensitization.

OTHER METHODS FOR TREATING FEAR

In addition to systematic desensitization for treating fear and other CERs, other applied behavior analysis methods have been used and found effective in research for reducing fears in adults and children.

IN VIVO EXPOSURE THERAPIES

In vivo exposure therapies have the target person experience real-life CSs without using relaxation techniques—in other words, they are essentially extinction procedures. Some of these therapies proceed very gradually in exposing the person to fearful situations to minimize the degree of fear experienced. Other techniques take a different approach: They deliberately expose the person to high levels of fear while preventing the possibility of escape or avoidance behaviors (Porter et al., 2006). One purpose of this approach is to extinguish the escape or avoidance behaviors the person has relied on in the past when the fear was aroused. We will discuss both approaches.

Gradual In Vivo Exposure

The procedure for **gradual in vivo exposure** is very similar to systematic desensitization, but it doesn't use relaxation techniques. A stimulus hierarchy is developed based on the target person's SUDS ratings of CSs, and each CS is presented in order from weakest to strongest for the person to experience briefly and rate for its level of discomfort during the presentation. When a particular CS is desensitized, receiving a rating of 0 on two successive trials, the target person advances to the next stimulus, and so on through the hierarchy. Studies have shown that gradual in vivo exposure is a very effective treatment for several types of fear, such as agoraphobia—the fear of being in crowded or open spaces (Kring, Johnson, Davison, & Neale, 2010; Porter et al., 2006). Like contact desensitization, this approach can be used with individuals who are very young or developmentally disabled. In such cases, SUDS ratings are not used to design the stimulus hierarchy, and the clients do not rate their comfort with presentations of CSs during sessions (instead, the therapist monitors clients' overt behaviors).

Flooding

At the beginning of this chapter, we considered the case of a woman who was afraid of escalators. Her therapist helped her overcome that fear by accompanying her as she rode on a department store escalator repeatedly for about half an hour. This treatment is an example of a technique called **flooding** (or *response prevention*) in which the person is exposed to a highly feared situation for prolonged periods of time under a therapist's direction (Emmelkamp, 2005). In flooding, the therapist tries to prevent the person from using avoidance or escape responses to reduce anxiety; relaxation exercises usually are not included. In effect, given that negative reinforcement is prevented, flooding is an extinction procedure. Due to the intensity of the CS and possible emotional difficulty the client may experience, *the application of flooding procedures requires professional supervision*, particularly during the early sessions of treatment (Stanley, 1992).

Therapists typically explain to their clients the rationale for having to experience the highly feared situation intensely for prolonged periods without avoiding or escaping. This explanation lets clients know what to expect, so they can decide whether they are willing to receive this treatment and try hard to tolerate emotionally difficult periods in the treatment. When the source of a fear is fairly specific, such as escalators, it is often possible to complete flooding treatment in one session. But when the source is broad, complex, or vague, as it is with most social anxieties, many sessions may be needed to present a wide range of possible CSs.

In the example we saw of the woman who was afraid of escalators, getting her to board the escalator initially was very difficult. And once she was on board the first time, the woman appeared very frightened. Clients often are highly emotional initially in flooding procedures, but these reactions decrease with exposure. Still, some clients are not able to tolerate extremely intense initial exposures; a therapist may need to present the feared situation somewhat gradually, advancing through a short stimulus hierarchy that contains several fear-arousing situations (Borden, 1992). Being faced with an exposure that is too threatening may lead the client to drop out of treatment and retain the fear. Obviously, the therapist should make certain that exposure to the feared situation (the CS) will *not* be accompanied by an unpleasant US. For instance, a client who is fearful of dogs should not be exposed to a dog that might bite.

Fearful situations in flooding are sometimes presented as imaginal CSs. Research comparing in vivo and imaginal flooding procedures has found that both methods can successfully reduce many different anxieties and phobias, and neither approach is clearly more effective than the other (Borden, 1992; James, 1986; Mathews et al., 1976). Thus imaginal procedures can be used effectively when it is difficult or impossible to present feared situations in their real-life form. For example, it may be difficult to use real-life stimuli when a person is afraid of flying in airplanes, especially if the fear is greatest when turbulence or strange noises occur. And it would be impossible to present in vivo stimuli to reduce the fears individuals develop from experiencing extremely traumatic events, such as in war, natural disasters, or a rape. If imaginal CSs are used, flooding may provide more effective treatment than systematic desensitization, since the latter method is less effective with imaginal than in vivo procedures. (Go to .)

Is Flooding Effective and Safe to Use?

Research has shown that flooding is a highly effective technique for reducing a wide variety of anxiety and phobic conditions (TFPDPP, 1993; Trull, Nietzel, & Main, 1988). Flooding is about as effective as systematic desensitization, but imaginal flooding appears to be more effective than imaginal desensitization (Marshall

CASE STUDY

Imaginal Flooding for War Trauma

Joseph was a 6½-year-old Lebanese boy who was referred for therapy by his teacher because he had developed frequent temper outbursts, memory problems, and inattention behaviors in class after experiencing a bomb blast (Saigh, 1986). Interviews and clinical assessments revealed that he showed similar behavior problems at home, had trauma-related nightmares, and was very depressed. Imaginal flooding was applied to reduce his emotional condition.

The therapy Joseph received combined a flooding procedure with relaxation, using progressive muscle relaxation exercises and a calm scene of being on a beach. (As noted earlier, using relaxation with flooding is unusual.) Each session began with relaxation exercises and then focused mainly on flooding one of several trauma-related scenes, two of which were "hearing a loud explosion and seeing injured people and debris" and "being led away from the site against background calls for help and automobile horns." Joseph had rated in SUDs each of the trauma-related scenes as being extremely uncomfortable to imagine. No mild or moderate CSs were used. During the flooding procedure, he was asked to imagine a traumatic scene in great detail for over 20 minutes and give it a SUDS rating every minute. The rest of the session was spent briefly imagining the other traumatic scenes and doing more relaxation exercises. The SUDS ratings Joseph gave were reduced dramatically in about three sessions for each traumatic scene. Follow-up assessments made during the 6 months after treatment showed only mild discomfort for any of the scenes.

et al., 1977; Wilson, 1982). When flooding and similar therapies were originally described, many therapists were concerned about the possibility of serious side effects that might make their clients' conditions worse rather than better. A survey of therapists who had used these therapies with clients revealed that the procedures are quite safe and that negative outcomes were extremely rare (Shipley & Boudewyns, 1980).

MODELING AND VIRTUAL REALITY EXPOSURE

Two other methods for reducing fear use indirect exposure procedures. One of these methods is modeling, which shows another person adapting to a fearful situation. The other method presents CSs in a virtual reality format.

Modeling

A girl named Keisha was able to overcome her fear of cats by watching her parents play with one and later, with their encouragement, joining in and gradually contacting the cat. Notice that in this example, the parents *modeled* fearless behavior for their child to watch. Modeling can be applied to desensitize fears in a *vicarious* manner. Keisha's parents reduced her fear with a method called **participant modeling**, in which the fearful person watches someone else cope well in real-life, increasingly threatening situations; then the person is encouraged to join in and is guided toward more and more contact with the feared object (Bandura, 1975; Bandura, Jeffery, & Gajdos, 1975). Guiding toward contact usually involves verbal and physical guidance prompts.

Studies of participant modeling have found it to be very successful in reducing fears and more effective than simply watching a filmed model cope with the feared situation (Borden, 1992; Wilson, 1982). Teaching individuals *how* to behave in fearful situations and *actually performing that behavior* in the modeling sessions seem to be critical components to overcoming fears. One study found that children who were asked to practice the coping behaviors they had seen in a video of children undergoing dental treatment were less disruptive in a subsequent dental visit than were other children who merely watched the video (Klingman, Melamed, Cuthbert, & Hermecz, 1984). Other research findings indicate that the fear reduction produced through modeling can be fairly specific. For instance, a girl who was extremely afraid of dogs and cats was treated first for her fear of dogs, which participant modeling decreased (Matson, 1983). But her fear of cats continued until it was specifically addressed.

Videotaped and Computer-Aided Modeling

Videotaped modeling is an effective method for reducing patients' anxieties before, during, and after receiving frightening medical treatments, such as surgery or invasive dental work (Parrish & Babbitt, 1991). Reducing patients' anxieties is important for humane reasons, but it can also increase the likelihood that patients will cooperate with and not disrupt the medical procedures as well as decrease the amount of time patients spend in the hospital to recover and the amount of medication they take while there (Sarafino & Smith, 2011).

The application of videotaped and filmed modeling to reduce anxieties before undergoing surgery has focused mainly on pediatric patients (Parrish & Babbitt, 1991). For example, researchers conducted a study with 4- to 12-year-old patients who were scheduled for elective surgery (Melamed & Siegel, 1975). The children were assigned to two groups, matching the children for age, sex, race, and type of operation. One group saw a film that was relevant to having surgery, and the other group saw a film about a boy who goes on a nature trip in the country. The relevant film, entitled "Ethan Has an Operation," portrays the hospital experience of a 7-year-old boy,

> showing various events that most children encounter when hospitalized for elective surgery from the time of admission to time of discharge including the child's orientation to the hospital ward and medical personnel such as the surgeon and anesthesiologist; having a blood test and exposure to standard hospital equipment;

separation from the mother; and scenes in the operating and recovery rooms .... Both the child's behavior and verbal remarks exemplify the behavior of a coping model so that while he exhibits some anxiety and apprehension, he is able to overcome his initial fears and complete each event in a successful and nonanxious manner. (p. 514)

To assess the emotional adjustment of the children in the two groups the evening before surgery and at a follow-up visit about 3 weeks after the operation, the researchers used measures of three types: the children's hand sweating, questionnaire self-reports of fear, and ratings of their emotional behavior by trained observers.

The results with all three measures revealed that the children who saw the film about Ethan's operation experienced less anxiety before and after surgery than did those who saw the irrelevant film. Video preparations for surgery are usually helpful and appear to be cost effective: A study of children in the hospital for elective surgery found that those who received video preparation recovered more quickly than those who did not get the preparation (Pinto & Hollandsworth, 1989). The savings from being released from the hospital sooner amounted to several times the cost of providing the preparation.

An extension of videotaped modeling is *computer-aided vicarious exposure* in which the target person uses a computer to guide the scenarios—that is, the CSs—a person on a screen experiences. This approach reduced spider-phobic behavior in 10- to 17-year-olds, but it was not as effective as gradual in vivo exposure (Dewis et al., 2001). A follow-up assessment of spider fears 33 months after treatment with gradual in vivo exposure and computer-aided vicarious exposure showed that both methods produced durable reductions in the fears (Gilroy et al., 2003).

Virtual Reality Exposure

Virtual reality computer technology allows a person to experience three-dimensional scenes that rather closely simulate real-life situations, including the sensations of vision, sound, and touch. This process can be used to present CSs to reduce people's fears with *virtual reality exposure* methods. Researchers applied this method to reduce a woman's fear of driving vehicles (Wald & Taylor, 2000). The virtual reality program presented four scenarios; the client ranked them from least to most fear arousing, thus producing a stimulus hierarchy. Here is one moderately fearful scenario:

Highway driving with bridge: flat terrain; straight and curved sections; two lanes; two-way stop sign oncoming cars pass by; uphill onto a two lane bridge; downhill off bridge; two-way stop sign. (p. 252)

The scenarios were presented in order from least to most fearful. At the end of each presentation, the client rated the highest anxiety—from 0 to 100—that she felt during the presentation; when her rating for a scenario dropped to 10 or less, the next scenario was introduced. Virtual reality exposure decreased the woman's fear of driving: She was able to drive in real life with little anxiety, and the reduced fear continued at a follow-up assessment 7 months later.

TIPS ON CHANGING RESPONDENT BEHAVIORS

The following tips on using respondent-based techniques focus on reducing problem CERs.

1. Techniques that do not use a stimulus hierarchy and induce very high levels of fear, as often happens with flooding, should be conducted only by professionals.
2. When deciding which type of relaxation method to use, consider whether any type would be physically uncomfortable for the target person to perform.
3. Mastering a relaxation technique requires practice. The person should stick closely to a planned schedule of practice sessions.

4. Whenever possible, a stimulus hierarchy should be designed based on a functional assessment of the target behavior and the target person's SUDS ratings of all CSs it includes.

5. CSs should be presented in ways that maximize how clearly and fully the target person will experience them.

6. A stimulus hierarchy can contain imaginal CSs, especially for stimuli that cannot be presented in more concrete ways. Although imaginal stimuli can reduce CERs in the procedures we've discussed, in vivo stimuli are usually more effective.

7. If you are using systematic desensitization, don't start the first session until the target person has practiced the relaxation exercises at least five times (preferably about 10) and experiences deep relaxation within several minutes.

8. Make sure each CS in a hierarchy is fully desensitized before moving on to the next. Some sessions may not get beyond one or two stimuli.

9. Periodically use a behavioral approach test or other means to assess overt fear behavior to judge the treatment's progress and success.

10. Don't make sessions too long. Systematic desensitization sessions generally do not exceed half an hour.

11. Systematic desensitization sessions should take place at least once or twice a week.

12. In systematic desensitization, if the target person feels too much discomfort or difficulty relaxing with a newly introduced CS, withdraw the stimulus, practice relaxation for a couple of minutes, and try the CS again for a shorter time. If there are still difficulties, either go back to the previous CS and desensitize it again or identify one or two intervening CSs to insert before the problem CS.

(Go to .)

CONCEPT CHECK 22.2

Answer the following questions about systematic desensitization and other methods for reducing fear.

1. Systematic desensitization is based on Wolpe's concept of _____ .
2. An example of a weak in vivo CS for a fear of flying might be _____ . ⇔
3. An example of a strong imaginal CS for a fear of flying might be _____ . ⇔
4. Rank-ordering CSs in a stimulus hierarchy is based on the target person's _____ ratings of the stimuli.
5. A fear reduction procedure that is very similar to systematic desensitization but does not include relaxation is called _____ .
6. An example of a fear for which in vivo flooding would be difficult or impossible to conduct is the fear of _____ .
7. Having a fearful person gradually contact a feared object or situation while watching someone else cope well with it is called _____ .

STUDY AND REVIEW

SUMMARY

Two processes that can reduce CERs are extinction, the repeated occurrence of a CS without the US, and counterconditioning, in which an alternative or competing response, such as relaxation, replaces the CR. People can learn to relax through the techniques of progressive muscle relaxation, autogenic training, and meditation.

Systematic desensitization involves having the target person become and remain relaxed while experiencing in vivo, imaginal, or symbolic CSs from a stimulus hierarchy. This method is very effective for reducing fears and other emotional behaviors, and using in vivo stimuli is usually more effective in reducing fears than using imaginal or symbolic stimuli. Functional assessment data and SUDS ratings of the target person are used in developing a stimulus hierarchy.

In vivo exposure therapies, such as gradual in vivo exposure and flooding, present CSs but do not include relaxation as part of the process; they basically apply extinction to change a CER. Flooding is a technique in which the target person experiences intense, prolonged exposure to feared situations under the direction of a therapist. This method is designed to arouse high levels of fear while preventing the target person from escaping or avoiding the fearful situations presented. The exposure can be in vivo or imagined, both of which are highly effective in reducing strong fears.

Modeling techniques, such as participant modeling, have been applied to help people reduce strong fears and cope well with frightening or uncomfortable medical procedures. Using videotaped modeling to reduce medical patients' fears regarding surgical procedures increases the likelihood that they will cooperate with and not disrupt the procedures and can decrease patients' recovery time and length of hospital stay. Virtual reality exposure uses computer technology to present feared situations in three dimensions and involves the senses of vision, hearing, and touch.

To prepare for exams, use the following key terms and review questions and the online study guide that's available on this book's companion website at www.wiley.com/college/sarafino.

KEY TERMS

counterconditioning	meditation	flooding
relaxation	systematic desensitization	participant modeling
progressive muscle relaxation	stimulus hierarchy	
autogenic training	gradual in vivo exposure	

ANSWERS TO CONCEPT CHECKS (CCs)

CC22.1 *Answers*: **1.** bee, the sting **2.** calm or laughter **3.** counterconditioning **4.** progressive muscle relaxation **5.** autogenic training **6.** meditation **7.** a bowl or abstract painting

CC22.2 *Answers*: **1.** counterconditioning **2.** calling an airline ticket agent for information **3.** picturing being on a bumpy flight **4.** SUDS **5.** gradual in vivo exposure **6.** being mugged or shot **7.** participant modeling

REVIEW QUESTIONS

1. Define *extinction* in respondent conditioning, and give an example of how it might be used to reduce a person's anger.

2. How are counterconditioning and systematic desensitization related?

3. Describe the guidelines the text gives for the setting, session length, and schedule for applying relaxation techniques.

4. Define *progressive muscle relaxation*, and discuss the pros and cons of including muscle tension in the procedure.

5. What are autogenic training and meditation, and how are they conducted?

6. Describe the steps in constructing a stimulus hierarchy.

7. Describe the procedure for conducting systematic desensitization.

8. What are imaginal and in vivo CSs? Discuss the advisability of using these types of stimuli in reducing fear.

9. Describe the research by Barlow and his colleagues (1969) on desensitizing snake phobias. What do the results mean in designing stimulus hierarchies?

10. Define the methods of gradual in vivo exposure and flooding, indicating how they are similar and different.

11. Describe the flooding procedure Saigh (1986) used to reduce the fears a boy named Joseph developed from war traumas.

12. Describe the research of Melamed and Siegel (1975) on reducing anxiety in children who are awaiting surgery.

RELATED READINGS

- Bandura, A. (1969). *Principles of behavior modification*. New York: Holt, Rinehart & Winston.
- Borden, J. W. (1992). Behavioral treatment of simple phobia. In S. M. Turner, K. S. Calhoun, & H. E. Adams (Eds.), *Handbook of clinical behavior therapy* (2nd ed.). New York: Wiley.
- Emmelkamp, P. M. G., Bouman, T. K., & Scholing, A. (1992). *Anxiety disorders: A practitioner's guide*. Chichester, UK: Wiley.
- Wolpe, J. (1973). *The practice of behavior therapy*. New York: Pergamon.

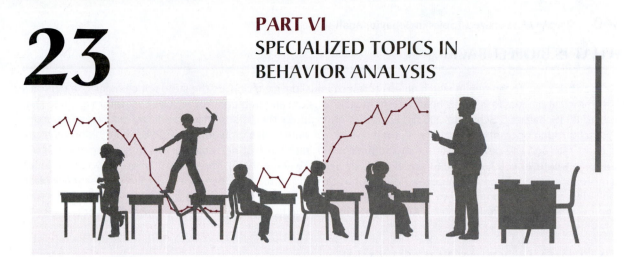

23

BIOFEEDBACK

What Is Biofeedback?
Instrumentation and Measurement
The Importance of Training and Developmental Level
Certification in Biofeedback Treatment

Biofeedback Applications
Treating Hypertension
Treating Seizure Disorders: Epilepsy
Treating Chronic Headache
Treating Anxiety
Treating Asthma
Treating Neuromuscular Disorders

Study and Review

PROLOGUE

Imagine that you have asthma, a respiratory condition with recurrent episodes of impaired breathing that results when tissue inflammation causes the airways to narrow, develop spasms, and produce mucus (AAFA, 2011; Sarafino & Smith, 2011). Now, suppose you had some way to tell that an episode is just starting, and you had learned a skill that helps you keep the airways open. If you could receive feedback about the status of your respiratory processes, you might be able to learn to control them and avoid future asthma episodes, or reduce their severity. Receiving information about the status of our bodily functions is the basis of biofeedback, the topic of this chapter. We discuss the definition and features of biofeedback and examine the methods and evidence for its use in treating six medical and psychological conditions: high blood pressure, epilepsy, chronic headache, anxiety, asthma, and neuromuscular disorders.

WHAT IS BIOFEEDBACK?

Biofeedback is a technique in which an electromechanical device monitors the status or changes of a person's physiological processes, such as heart rate or muscle tension, and immediately reports that information to that individual (Schwartz & Schwartz, 2003). This information allows the person to *gain voluntary control over these bodily processes* through operant conditioning. If, for instance, we were to use biofeedback to lower your blood pressure or heart rate and the device reports that the pressure or rate has just decreased a bit, this information would reinforce whatever you had done to achieve this decrease (Weems, 1998). The phrase "whatever you had done" is more interesting than it may appear: People who learn to control a bodily process through biofeedback often can't describe the responses they make that affect it. Maybe this shouldn't be surprising—think about your singing or whistling different notes. Can you describe exactly the actions you make to emit different tones?

INSTRUMENTATION AND MEASUREMENT

Measuring blood pressure provides a clear and familiar example of how biofeedback devices work. You've surely seen a physician or nurse apply the basic device, called a *sphygmomanometer*, to measure a patient's blood pressure. A cuff on the person's arm is filled with air until it is tight enough to stop the blood from flowing through the main artery in the arm (AMA, 2003). The cuff is then slowly deflated so that the medical worker can hear through a stethoscope the first beat forcing its way along the main artery as the blood flow overcomes the pressure in the cuff. The cuff pressure at that first beat can be seen on a gauge and indicates the person's maximum (that is, systolic) blood pressure at that time, which occurs when the heart contracts to pump the blood. The medical worker continues the procedure by deflating the cuff until the beating sound has disappeared. The pressure shown on the gauge at this time reflects the resting (diastolic) pressure in the artery while the heart chambers fill with blood between contractions. Blood pressure biofeedback sessions can be conducted in several different ways (Olson & Kroon, 1987). In one approach, many sphygmomanometer readings are taken, and the person receives each pressure reading. Some devices can inflate and deflate the cuff and take readings automatically (Goldstein, Jamner, & Shapiro, 1992).

The information individuals receive in a biofeedback procedure can take many different forms. For instance, the level of physiological functioning can be reflected by high or low numbers on a gauge, pitches of tones produced by an audio speaker, degrees of loudness of a tone from a speaker, or degrees of brightness of a light. Status and functioning can be measured for many different physiological processes, enabling the use of biofeedback on each process (Olson, 1987; Peek, 2003). For some body functions, such as heart rate or temperature, measurements can be taken continuously without having to cycle through a complex procedure. Specific names are given for biofeedback techniques for different physiological processes. Here are the names and descriptions of some commonly used techniques:

- **BP biofeedback**. Gives feedback on the person's blood pressure (BP) measured with a sphygmomanometer.
- **HR biofeedback**. Measures and gives feedback on heart rate (HR), or heartbeats per minute.
- **GSR biofeedback**. The galvanic skin response (GSR—also called electrodermal activity, EDA) is a measure of sweat gland activity assessed with a device that tests how readily the skin conducts minute levels of electricity: Sweaty skin conducts more readily than dry skin. GSR level is given as feedback.
- **EEG biofeedback**. An *electroencephalograph* (EEG) assesses electrical activity in the brain, including certain types of brain waves. EEG level is given as feedback.
- **EMG biofeedback**. An *electromyograph* (EMG) measures muscle tension by assessing the electrical activity of muscles when they contract. EMG level is given as feedback.
- **Thermal biofeedback**. Assessments of *skin temperature* in a region of the body measure the flow of blood, which is warm, in that part of the body, such as a foot or hand. Temperature level is given as feedback.

Note that all these measures are indirect. They are taken on the outside of the body or just below the skin to reflect changes deeper in the body, such as brain or heart activity. And sometimes the measure allows us only to *infer* internal changes, as when we assume that skin temperature changes suggest that blood flow changes have occurred—the higher the temperature, the greater the blood flow.

Biofeedback sessions typically begin after the target person has had a period of time to adapt to the situation. The length of the adaptation period depends on the person and his or her familiarity with the procedures and experiences in the preceding minutes (Arena & Schwartz, 2003). Two examples show why adaptation can be important. First, the procedure involves having sensors attached to various parts of the body, and people who are not familiar with this may feel uneasy, thus arousing their physiological function. Second, some individuals may have rushed or climbed stairs to make the appointment, and some of them may have arrived early and had time to adapt physically in the waiting room. Each biofeedback session begins with a baseline assessment of the physical system targeted for biofeedback; this baseline period should usually last at least 15 minutes (Arena & Schwartz, 2003). Once the system appears stabilized, biofeedback can begin.

THE IMPORTANCE OF TRAINING AND DEVELOPMENTAL LEVEL

Learning to regulate one's own bodily processes with biofeedback usually requires training, which is most effectively provided by an experienced professional. The training clients get incorporates a shaping procedure in which tiny physiological changes in the desired direction are reinforced initially; as the training progresses, larger and larger changes are required for reinforcement. Clients are usually encouraged to practice biofeedback techniques at home when they receive training. Home practice appears to enhance the success of biofeedback in certain applications, such as in treating headache (Gauthier, Côté, & French, 1994), but it may not help people learn the methods better or faster during training (Blanchard et al., 1991).

Researchers have proposed that children may be especially good candidates for treatment with biofeedback (Attanasio et al., 1985). Some evidence supports this view: A study combining data from prior research found that biofeedback treatment for headache was more successful in reducing headache pain with children than with adults (Sarafino & Goehring, 2000). Although we aren't sure why children would have greater success with biofeedback treatments, two speculations have been offered (Attanasio et al., 1985). First, children seem to be more interested in and enthusiastic about the equipment and procedure than adults are. Second, adults appear to be more skeptical about their ability to learn to control their physiological function and to benefit from doing so.

CERTIFICATION IN BIOFEEDBACK TREATMENT

The Biofeedback Certification Institute of America (BCIA) provides accreditation for non-university-based training programs in biofeedback and certification for practitioners (Schwartz & Montgomery, 2003). The purpose of certification is to give the public some way to determine that biofeedback individual practitioners are likely to be competent, having met basic requirements for training and experience. You can get additional information about the organization and the accreditation and certification processes at www.bcia.org. (Go to 📄.)

BIOFEEDBACK APPLICATIONS

Because biofeedback techniques have been applied successfully to produce many medical and psychological benefits for people, some biofeedback practitioners and commercial companies have advertised "miracle" cures for all sorts of problems, sometimes even when little or no good evidence has been found that these techniques are effective. For instance, one company advertised, "Let your cancer disappear with image rehearsal and biofeedback," "Image rehearsal and biofeedback to let your joints be normal and comfortable if you have arthritis," and "Feel wonderful without the urge to drink alcohol excessively with image rehearsal and biofeedback" (these quotations from Stern & Ray, 1980, p. v). Beware of opportunists. In the rest of this chapter, we'll discuss several biofeedback applications for which there is at least fairly solid research evidence for their effectiveness. (Go to 🔍.)

CONCEPT CHECK 23.1

Check your understanding of the preceding concepts. Remember: The symbol ⇔ means that the answer can vary. Answer the following questions about biofeedback and its methods.

1. Biofeedback involves giving individuals information about the _____ of their physiological systems.
2. Receiving information about the status or changes in muscle tension is called _____ biofeedback.
3. Receiving information about the status or changes in brain wave activity is called _____ biofeedback.
4. Receiving information about the status or changes in skin temperature is called _____ biofeedback.
5. Biofeedback certification can be obtained through an organization whose name is abbreviated as _____ .

CLOSE-UP

"Mind Control" with EEG Biofeedback?

In the early 1970s, the findings of research on EEG biofeedback seemed to suggest that training to increase a specific type of brain electrical activity, called *alpha brain waves*, enabled individuals to achieve an "alpha experience" of deep relaxation and well-being (Olson & Schwartz, 1987; Stern & Ray, 1980). Alpha waves are a normal component of wakeful brain activity, and they tend to increase during certain conditions, such as daydreaming or meditating. The news media quickly publicized the findings about controlling alpha waves with biofeedback, and many people rushed to get some training or to buy equipment with instructions so they could achieve that experience, and with it, some level of "mind control."

The idea of being able to control one's own brain activity to decrease feelings of anxiety and increase feelings of relaxation through EEG biofeedback is quite intriguing. But research results have not supported this possibility (Olson & Schwartz, 1987; White & Tursky, 1982). For instance, studies have shown that people who receive training to increase alpha activity are likely to report that they have had the alpha experience only if they were told it would happen (Plotkin, 1976). EEG training to increase alpha-wave activity does not seem to help people reduce their anxiety or experience feelings of relaxation and well-being.

TREATING HYPERTENSION

Hypertension is the medical condition of having blood pressure that is consistently high over several weeks or more (AHA, 2011). Medical treatment for hypertension usually starts with having the person make lifestyle changes, such as by exercising and making dietary changes designed to lower weight, and often involves taking prescription drugs. Biofeedback can be a useful supplement to medical treatment, enabling people to control their blood pressure to some degree, achieve lower blood pressure levels, and use less medication (McCaffrey & Blanchard, 1985; McGrady & Linden, 2003; Olson & Kroon, 1987). Drugs used in treating hypertension can cause side effects, such as increased blood sugar levels or feelings of weakness or confusion, that may be difficult for some patients to tolerate. Using biofeedback, sometimes with relaxation techniques, may be especially useful for these people in helping to reduce their blood pressures while minimizing the use of drugs. Research has shown that biofeedback applied with or without relaxation is effective in lowering blood pressure in people with hypertension (McGrady & Linden, 2003).

Some successful biofeedback treatments for hypertension apply BP biofeedback, using a sphygmomanometer that measures blood pressure directly; but other approaches, such as thermal, GSR, or EMG biofeedback, have had success, too (McGrady & Linden, 2003). Patients learn the BP biofeedback method in about 3 months in supervised sessions and are generally asked to practice the procedure at home, particularly at times of the day when their blood pressure tends to be high.

TREATING SEIZURE DISORDERS: EPILEPSY

Epilepsy is a neurological condition marked by recurrent, sudden seizures that result from electrical disturbances in the brain (AMA, 2003; EFA, 2011). Brain-wave examinations of patients with epilepsy have revealed recurring patterns of excessive neuron firing in specific regions of the brain, such as the temporal lobes located above the ears (Monastra, 2003). In the most severe form of epileptic seizure, called a *grand mal* or *tonic-clonic* seizure, the person loses consciousness and has muscle spasms. Biofeedback treatment of epilepsy was developed initially for patients whose seizures were not adequately reduced by medication.

EEG biofeedback has been used successfully with many epilepsy patients in helping them learn to control their brain electrical activity and reduce their seizures (Monastra, 2003; Sterman & Egner, 2006; Strehl, 2003). The general approach in using EEG biofeedback for people with epilepsy involves training them to decrease certain kinds of brain-wave activities and increase others in specific areas of the brain. If they can gain some measure of control over these brain waves in the areas of the brain where the disturbances occur, seizures should diminish. Although not all patients benefit from this approach, most show substantial reductions in the number of seizures. Because the treatment is costly, researchers have examined factors that may predict which patients are likely to benefit from this approach and which are not. Some evidence suggests that the sizes of certain brain waves before beginning biofeedback treatment and the location of abnormal waves are related to the treatment's success (Strehl, 2003).

TREATING CHRONIC HEADACHE

Two biofeedback approaches have been used for treating patients who suffer from severe, recurrent headaches (Andrasik, Blake, & McCarran, 1986). The biofeedback approach used depends on the headache type:

- *Tension-type* (or "muscle-contraction") *headache* seems to result from the combined effects of a central nervous system dysfunction and persistent contraction of the head and neck muscles (AMA, 2003; Holroyd, 2002). Patients with tension-type headaches generally receive EMG biofeedback training to control the tension in specific muscle groups, such as those in the forehead.

- *Migraine headache* seems to result from the combination of dilation of blood vessels surrounding the brain and a dysfunction in the nervous system (AMA, 2003; Holroyd, 2002). Patients with migraine headaches generally receive thermal biofeedback training (usually monitoring the hand) to help them control the constriction and dilation of arteries.

A large number of carefully conducted experiments have shown that biofeedback is an effective treatment for tension-type and migraine headache (Nestoriuc, Martin, Rief, & Andrasik, 2008).

Studies have also shown that biofeedback methods and relaxation methods are about equally effective in reducing chronic headache, and using both methods together can be more effective than using either one alone, at least for some patients (Andrasik, Blake, & McCarran, 1986; Holroyd & Penzien, 1985). What's more, the results of many studies with follow-up periods averaging 14 months have shown that treating chronic headache with relaxation techniques or with relaxation and biofeedback methods together provides durable relief (Blanchard, 1987; Nestoriuc, Martin, Rief, & Andrasik, 2008). The data from one study with five yearly follow-up assessments are presented in Figure 23-1 (Blanchard et al., 1987). The success of biofeedback in reducing headache has been demonstrated in adults and children (Hermann & Blanchard, 2002). Children acquire skills in EMG and thermal

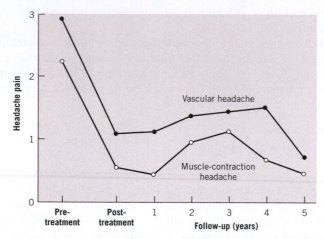

Figure 23-1   Mean ratings of headache pain (0 = no headache; 5 = intense, incapacitating headache) for muscle-contraction (tension-type) and vascular (migraine, often with tension-type) headache patients who completed treatment with either progressive muscle relaxation or both relaxation and biofeedback. The graph plots patients' ratings at pretreatment, posttreatment, and in follow-up years 1 through 5. *Source:* Data from Blanchard et al. (1987), Table 1.

biofeedback as easily as adults, and they appear to get at least as much headache relief from biofeedback procedures as adults do (Sarafino & Goehring, 2000).

TREATING ANXIETY

Two biofeedback approaches have been tested as treatments for anxiety. One approach uses EMG biofeedback. We've seen in earlier chapters that procedures that relax the muscles, particularly progressive muscle relaxation techniques, can reduce anxiety and other conditioned emotional responses. Because EMG biofeedback can help people learn to relax specific muscle groups, studies have investigated and found support for the utility of this form of biofeedback in treating anxiety. Most of these studies applied biofeedback to reduce tension in the *frontalis* region of the head—where rectangular sheets of muscle span the forehead—because some evidence suggested a link between frontalis relaxation and general body relaxation (Surwit & Keefe, 1978). The second approach tested for treating anxiety uses EEG biofeedback, such as by increasing the person's alpha waves; evidence of its effectiveness is not strong (Monastra, 2003).

Although EMG biofeedback appears to reduce anxiety, an important question is whether it is more effective than more easily or cheaply administered methods, such as progressive muscle relaxation. A review of the evidence suggests that biofeedback is not more effective than relaxation (Gatchel, 1982). (Go to 🔍.)

TREATING ASTHMA

Two biofeedback approaches have been applied to reduce the frequency and intensity of asthma episodes (Sarafino, 1997). One approach uses EMG biofeedback, typically for the frontalis muscle, which is of questionable utility. We'll focus on the other approach, *respiratory biofeedback*, in which airflow is measured with an apparatus as the patient breathes and feedback is given on respiratory function so that the person can learn to control airway diameter. One respiratory biofeedback apparatus has the person breathe through a device that varies air pressure and assesses airway resistance to these variations: The greater the resistance, the poorer the airflow. The feedback informs the person when changes occur, such as with numbers on a gauge. After several training sessions, the patient is able to make stronger and stronger airflow improvements and can eventually increase airflow when an asthma episode begins. As an addition to respiratory biofeedback, the person can be trained in relaxation to reduce the role of emotion in initiating an episode or making it worse when one occurs. Studies have generally found that respiratory biofeedback and relaxation are useful supplements to medical treatments for asthma (Nickel et al., 2005; Sarafino, 1997).

CLOSE-UP

Biofeedback and Heart Failure: A Tantalizing Finding

Congestive heart failure is a medical condition in which the heart's capacity to pump can no longer meet the body's needs, reducing physical stamina and making the person short of breath with little exertion (AMA, 2003). This condition occurs most frequently in old age, and its victims often become disabled, having difficulty just climbing a few steps or walking at a moderate pace across a room. Research has found tentative evidence for the utility of biofeedback procedures in improving the energy and functioning of people with heart failure (Swanson et al., 2009). Heart failure patients with relatively strong heart function were assigned to two groups, one of which received six weekly sessions of biofeedback to improve heart and breathing function. A comparison group received sham biofeedback: They had sessions for the same amount of time, but the equipment gave false readings. At the end of the study, the group that received the real biofeedback performed substantially better in tests of exercise stamina taken after treatment than they did in baseline, but participants in the comparison group had not improved. Given that exercise stamina is an important predictor of later functioning and survival, this finding suggests that biofeedback treatment may enable many heart failure patients to live longer and with less heart-related illness.

TREATING NEUROMUSCULAR DISORDERS

Neuromuscular disorders are medical conditions that affect the muscles and the nerves that carry information directing the muscles to move. Some neuromuscular disorders involve paralysis, which may have resulted from a spinal cord injury or a stroke that damages the brain; other disorders cause the muscles to become rigid or have spasms. Such conditions have been treated successfully with EMG biofeedback (Brudny, 1982; Fogel, 1987; Krebs & Fagerson, 2003). This procedure involves monitoring muscles in the affected body parts, such as the legs, with sensitive electronic equipment to detect tiny changes in muscular function. In the case of patients

Woman's leg with EMG biofeedback sensors attached to treat her neuromuscular disorder. Biofeedback is being used to teach her to walk again after a car accident injury. *Source*: Paul Rubiera/NewsCom.

with paralysis of part of the body, the paralysis cannot be total—a condition that happens when the spinal cord is completely severed. Incomplete paralysis can occur if nerves are damaged, but not severed. For patients whose muscles are incompletely paralyzed, EMG biofeedback is conducted by showing the patient that the muscle has tensed a bit and encouraging him or her to tense it more and more, thereby gradually increasing its strength. For patients with rigid muscles, the feedback focuses on relaxing the muscles. Patients with muscle spasms focus on trying to get the EMG pattern to match that of normal muscle action. (Go to 📄.)

STUDY AND REVIEW

SUMMARY

The technique of biofeedback uses an electromechanical device to monitor the status or changes of a person's physiological processes. The device immediately reports that information to the person, enabling him or her to gain voluntary control over those internal processes through operant conditioning. Biofeedback methods can be applied entirely by professionals or taught to individuals so that they can apply it to themselves. Professionals who are certified through the Biofeedback Certification Institute of America (BCIA) are likely to be competent in the needed skills for applying and teaching clients the methods. Biofeedback procedures can monitor a wide variety of physiological functions:

- BP biofeedback monitors blood pressure.
- HR biofeedback monitors heart rate.
- GSR (galvanic skin response) biofeedback monitors skin conductivity as a measure of sweat-gland activity.
- EEG (electroencephalographic) biofeedback assesses brain-wave activity.
- EMG (electromyograph) biofeedback monitors muscle tension.
- Thermal biofeedback assesses skin temperature as an indication of blood flow.

CONCEPT CHECK 23.2

Answer the following questions about biofeedback applications.

1. EEG training to increase _____ wave brain activity does not seem to help people reduce their anxiety.
2. Biofeedback with or without relaxation training is effective in lowering _____ in people with hypertension.
3. The seizure disorder called _____ can be treated effectively with EEG biofeedback.
4. A medical condition other than hypertension and epilepsy for which biofeedback training can be helpful is _____ . ⇔

Biofeedback has been used with some success in treating hypertension, epilepsy, chronic headache, anxiety, asthma, and neuromuscular disorders.

To prepare for exams, use the following key terms and review questions and the online study guide that's available on this book's companion website at www.wiley.com/college/sarafino.

KEY TERMS

biofeedback
BP biofeedback
HR biofeedback

GSR biofeedback
EEG biofeedback
EMG biofeedback

thermal biofeedback

ANSWERS TO CONCEPT CHECKS (CCs)

CC23.1 *Answers:* **1.** status or changes **2.** EMG (electromyograph) **3.** EEG (electroencephalograph) **4.** thermal **5.** BCIA

CC23.2 *Answers:* **1.** alpha **2.** blood pressure **3.** epilepsy **4.** asthma, neuromuscular disorders, or headache

REVIEW QUESTIONS

1. What is biofeedback?

2. How does a sphygmomanometer work, and how is it used to monitor blood pressure in BP biofeedback?

3. Define EEG, EMG, and *thermal biofeedback procedures*. How are they similar to and different from each other?

4. Discuss the importance of the target person's training and developmental level in learning to control a physiological function with biofeedback.

5. Describe the general approach in using BP biofeedback to lower blood pressure and EEG biofeedback to reduce episodes of epilepsy.

6. How are tension-type and migraine headaches treated with biofeedback, and how effective are these methods?

7. Describe the approaches of respiratory biofeedback for treating asthma and EMG biofeedback for treating neuromuscular disorders.

RELATED READINGS

*   Schwartz, M. S., & Andrasik, F. (Eds.) (2003). *Biofeedback: A practitioner's guide* (3rd ed.). New York: Guilford.
*   White, L., & Tursky, B. (Eds.) (1982). *Clinical biofeedback: Efficacy and mechanisms*. New York: Guilford.

24

BEHAVIORAL CONTRACTS AND SELF-MANAGEMENT

Using Behavioral Contracts
Components of Behavioral Contracts
Negotiating the Terms of a Behavioral Contract
Settings for Applying Behavioral Contracts
Benefits of Using Behavioral Contracts

Using Self-Management Methods
Goals in Self-Management
Self-Monitoring and Behavioral Contracts
Managing Antecedents in Self-Management
Managing Consequences in Self-Management
Respondent Methods in Self-Management

Study and Review

PROLOGUE

Jim had enrolled in a wellness program at the large company where he worked, hoping to increase his exercising, lose weight, and stop smoking. In the effort to stop smoking, he and a wellness program representative negotiated and signed a year-long agreement that began on January 2nd. The contract called for substantial amounts of money to be given to charity by Jim or the company, depending on how well he abstained from smoking:

- For each day that he did not smoke, the company would give $10 to the charity.
- For each cigarette he smoked, he would give $25 (maximum of $100 for any day).

Jim knew quitting smoking would not be easy—he had smoked more than a pack a day for the last 20 years, and he had tried to quit a couple of times before.

In the contract, the company could have required that Jim submit to medical tests to verify that he did in fact abstain; but they were willing to trust his word and that of his family, friends, and coworkers. These people were committed to helping him quit, and they agreed to be contacted by someone from the program weekly to give honest reports. Did he succeed? Yes, but he had a few "lapses" that cost him $325. By the end of the year, Jim had not smoked for 8 months continuously.

This chapter examines the use of contracts to structure the process of behavior change and the processes and methods in self-management interventions in which the target person plays an active role in designing and implementing the program.

USING BEHAVIORAL CONTRACTS

A **behavioral contract** (also called a *contingency contract*) is a formal document that describes each target behavior and states when it should or should not be performed as well as what the outcomes will be for performing that behavior. In other words, a behavioral contract describes the behavior, specifies its antecedents, and spells out the consequences that will apply in an intervention to change the behavior (DeRisi & Butz, 1975; Homme, 1971; O'Banion & Whaley, 1981; Reitman, Waguespack, & Valley-Gray, 2005).

COMPONENTS OF BEHAVIORAL CONTRACTS

Behavioral contracts are generally developed and signed by the *target person*, often with at least one *mediator*—an individual who can and will monitor the behavior and dispense the consequences. The mediator can be the target person's therapist, teacher, coworker, friend, or relative. In some cases, more than one mediator is involved; and in self-management programs, the target person and mediator may be the same person. The contract should indicate the roles of all parties, and each one should sign.

A good behavioral contract should contain or clearly describe the following elements:

* *Target behaviors and antecedents*: The agreement should specify the behaviors, the occasions when they should or should not occur, and the behavioral goals, that is, the level of the behavior to be achieved.
* *Monitoring process*: The contract should state who will observe the behavior, the type of data to be collected, and how these data will be recorded and made available to determine the consequences.
* *Consequences*: This information should include immediate and delayed rewards for meeting the terms of the contract. Reinforcers should be chosen carefully, using procedures we examined in Chapter 15. Penalties for not meeting the contract's terms can also be included and usually take the form of time-out or response-cost punishment. The contract should specify who will dispense the consequences, and when. Bonus rewards can be used for high-level, consistent compliance with the terms of the contract.

The agreement should also include a *schedule* for reviewing the target person's progress and the *signatures* of all parties involved. The terms of the contract should be negotiated by the parties, not simply imposed on each person by someone who has power. Figure 24-1 gives a sample of a behavioral contract.

You can see in the figure that agreements can involve more than one behavior, more than one mediator, and several reinforcers. In addition, agreements can designate separate reinforcers for different behaviors. For example, Stuart (1971) helped develop a contract for a delinquent 16-year-old girl named Candy and her parents. It stated that (a) Candy could go out one weekend evening until 11:30 p.m. and not have to account for her whereabouts if she maintained "a weekly average of 'B' in the academic ratings of all her classes" and (b) she could go out in the afternoons on weekend days and holidays if she "completed all household chores *before* leaving" and agreed to call her parents once while she was out.

NEGOTIATING THE TERMS OF A BEHAVIORAL CONTRACT

Behavioral contracts generally provide for outcomes that are wanted by all parties. In Candy's case, she wanted some freedom to socialize with friends, and her parents wanted her delinquent behavior to decrease and her

---

BEHAVIORAL CONTRACT
between Jo and her teacher and mother
Date: _____

1. *Target Behaviors and Antecedents:* Jo has refused to go to school for the past 3 weeks, and when she was going she often failed to do her homework, claiming she "forgot" to take home the books she needed. The five target behaviors she must do are: (a) not fussing at home when getting ready to go to school, (b) arriving at school each day on time, (c) attending all classes as scheduled, (d) taking home all of her books, and (e) submitting an acceptable homework on time.

2. *Monitoring Process:* Jo's mother will observe and keep records of her getting ready for school and bringing home her books. Her teacher will observe the three in-school behaviors and write his initials at the end of each day on a card next to any of the three listed behaviors she performed acceptably.

3. *Consequences:* At the end of each school day that Jo earns two or more initialings on her card, she may feed the class hamster or choose a book for the teacher to read to the class on the next school day. She will take the card home. Jo's mother will review with her each day's card and records regarding Jo's fussing and bringing home books. When Jo has accumulated ten acceptably performed behaviors, she may choose one of the following rewards: (a) have a friend over to play, (b) a candy bar, (c) have first choice of what to watch on TV for an hour that night, (d) help her mother make cookies, (e) take some homemade cookies as a treat for her class. If Jo's records show fewer than three acceptably performed behaviors on any school day, she cannot have her usual snack before bedtime. Rule-release: If Jo is clearly ill (e.g., has a fever) these rules are suspended until she is well.

4. *Bonus Rewards:* If Jo's records show all five behaviors performed acceptably on each of three school days in one calendar week, she may choose a videotape for her mother to rent and watch it that night.

5. *Schedule for Reviewing Progress:* Every day with her teacher at school and mother at home. Her teacher and mother will talk on the phone every Friday.

6. *Signatures:* By signing below, I agree to follow the terms of this contract.

Jo _____

Mother _____

Teacher _____

Figure 24-1   Sample of a moderately complex behavioral contract for an 8-year-old girl with school-related behavior problems. The complexity of behavioral contracts can vary—some are simpler than the sample, and others are more complex.

performance of schoolwork and household chores to improve. Look at the contract presented in Figure 24-1; what outcomes did Jo, her teacher, and her mother want?

Because the conditions of the agreement affect all parties, each should have a say in the contract's provisions (Kanfer & Grimm, 1980; O'Banion & Whaley, 1981). Being a mediator is an imposition: It takes time and effort, and often there is no pay. Thus a mediator's motivation to follow the agreement will depend on provisions the contract contains. Sometimes it's useful to include provisions for reinforcing the mediator's activities. Because the motivation of the target person is also critical to the success of the behavior change program, he or she should have a say in which reinforcers the program will use and the criteria for earning them. Standards that are simply imposed by others lead to smaller changes in behavior than standards the target person has helped to develop (Dickerson & Creedon, 1981; Lovitt & Curtiss, 1969). The parties to a contract usually negotiate among themselves to reach an agreement they think is fair and reasonable for them to follow. Having a therapist supervise the negotiations can help in developing a contract that contains few flaws and will achieve what each party wants.

An intervention to improve the homework performance of four 9- to 11-year-old students employed negotiated behavioral contracts between each child and one of his or her parents (Miller & Kelley, 1994). Two types of negotiation occurred throughout the intervention. First, for each homework assignment, the parent and child negotiated the division of the task into "challenging, yet attainable" goals for the child to complete. Each party would suggest a goal and then negotiate a compromise, which was recorded. For instance, they might agree that the child should complete five math problems in the next 10 minutes. Second, each week the parent and child negotiated the rewards for the child's bringing home the needed homework materials and achieving the goals they agreed upon for each assignment. For these negotiations, the parent was to

> identify several rewards from which the child could choose and to change the rewards occasionally to prevent the child from becoming bored with reward choices. Rewards were different for each child and included special snacks, small amounts of money (e.g., 25 cents), stickers, and late bedtime as daily rewards, and renting a videotape, having a friend spend the night, or a trip to a shopping mall as weekly rewards. (p. 78)

The parents received instructions on listening carefully to the child's views, offering a variety of solutions, avoiding criticism, and being willing to compromise. All four of the children showed substantial improvements in their homework performance during the intervention.

SETTINGS FOR APPLYING BEHAVIORAL CONTRACTS

Behavioral contracts can be applied in a variety of settings. The intervention we just considered on improving homework performance is an example of applying behavioral contracts at *home*, and this chapter's opening story about Jim quitting smoking gives an example of applying behavioral contracts in a *work* setting. We'll consider two other settings where behavioral contracts have been used:

1. *Classrooms*: An intervention used a behavioral contract to reduce a 7-year-old girl's disruptive classroom behavior, such as being off task and fighting with other students (Wilkinson, 2003). The girl, Ana, and her teacher negotiated the contract's behavioral goals and reinforcers for completing classroom assignments, interacting well with other students, and complying with teacher requests and rules. The rewards included teacher attention and engaging in preferred activities. The teacher monitored the target behaviors and dispensed the consequences.

2. *Clinics or institutions*: John was an 11-year-old student with attention-deficit/hyperactivity disorder, a condition in which the person is persistently inattentive and shows high levels of restless and impulsive behaviors. His teacher referred him to a psychology clinic because of his extreme off-task behavior (Flood & Wilder, 2002). Before the treatment was designed, observations were made of John's off-task behavior, and his preferences for reinforcers were assessed. The observations indicated that off-task behavior was most likely when the task was difficult and he was not receiving teacher attention. As a result, John first received functional communication training so he could ask for help and feedback when he needed it. Once he mastered this skill, a behavioral contract was introduced; it provided that he would receive one of his preferred rewards for every instance of getting two math problems or 10 word problems correct by the end of the session. Thus, he could receive multiple rewards after a session. The therapist monitored the target behaviors and dispensed the consequences.

In these interventions with Ana and John, the children's behavior improved markedly. For instance, John's off-task behavior dropped from 86% of the time to 11%, and the percentage of math problems he executed correctly increased from 5% to 24%.

BENEFITS OF USING BEHAVIORAL CONTRACTS

What are the benefits of using a behavioral contract to formalize the procedures to change behavior? We'll consider five. First, having a contract can reduce disagreements and errors in carrying out the program because it ensures that the parties know what their roles are and what the conditions of the program are. Second, the parties to the contract tend to have a greater commitment to fulfilling their roles after they sign the agreement. Third, putting the conditions in writing makes the target person's progress and closeness to meeting the program's goals clearer. Fourth, the process of negotiating the agreement increases the likelihood that the program contains elements that will lead to success. Fifth, negotiating a contract and structuring difficult interpersonal relationships may help improve the way the parties interact. (Go to .)

USING SELF-MANAGEMENT METHODS

We saw in Chapter 4 that **self-management** is the process of applying behavioral and cognitive methods to change one's own behavior. Most of these methods derive from applied behavior analysis and involve managing the antecedents and consequences of a target behavior. A more detailed description of self-management methods can be found in Sarafino (2011).

GOALS IN SELF-MANAGEMENT

Self-management interventions can be conducted with professional supervision, such as in therapy, or entirely by a target person who has been trained in the methods. Most self-management interventions are implemented to achieve four types of *broad goals*: being more effective and efficient in daily life, breaking undesirable habits, developing desired lifestyle behaviors, and mastering difficult skills. I have taught courses for many years in which students were trained in self-management methods and designed and conducted an intervention to change a behavior of their choice. Here are some examples of frequently chosen target behaviors they changed:

- Reducing cigarette smoking
- Decreasing nail biting
- Increasing exercise
- Improving daily organization and time management
- Decreasing calorie and fat consumption
- Decreasing anxiety in taking tests
- Increasing time and concentration in studying
- Reducing feelings of jealousy
- Reducing spending money

CONCEPT CHECK 24.1

Check your understanding of the preceding concepts. Remember: The symbol ⇔ means that the answer can vary. Answer the following questions about behavioral contracts.

1. Two components a behavioral contract should contain are _____ . ⇔
2. In the contract between Jo and her teacher and mother (Figure 24-1), her _____ and _____ monitored her behavior and dispensed consequences.
3. An outcome Jo wanted for her improved behavior was _____ . ⇔
4. A benefit of using a behavioral contract is _____ . ⇔

- Practicing a musical instrument
- Decreasing saying "um" or "like"
- Reducing swearing

In looking at this list, you can see how each target behavior fits into at least one of the broad goals of self-management interventions mentioned earlier.

SELF-MONITORING AND BEHAVIORAL CONTRACTS

Data collection and graphic analysis are important activities in applied behavior analysis, and they are in self-management, too. Before individuals design and conduct a self-management intervention, they *should perform a functional assessment* to determine the exact behavior as well as its antecedents and consequences. This step is followed by data collection in baseline and intervention phases, which enables the individuals to do a graphic analysis to determine whether the target behavior has changed. These activities are very similar to those we've discussed for applied behavior analysis.

Two differences commonly exist between typical self-management and applied behavior analysis methods. First, the data in self-management programs are generally collected by the target person rather than someone else. **Self-monitoring** (also called *self-observation*) is a procedure in which the target person observes his or her own behavior and records each instance of it, most commonly in terms of its frequency, magnitude, or duration (Karoly, 2005). Although self-monitoring was originally introduced as a method for data collection, researchers found that doing it also tends to change the behavior in the desired direction—in other words, self-monitoring is itself a behavior change method in self-management. For instance, researchers found that individuals who bite their nails reduce their biting when they self-monitor the behavior (Harris & McReynolds, 1977). Other studies showed that self-monitoring by itself improved students' on-task behavior and academic performance (Wood et al., 1998) and helped a woman reduce her frequent upsetting thoughts about the possibility of developing cancer (Frederiksen, 1975).

Second, self-management programs typically include a behavioral contract, and the target person almost always has a great deal of control, often total control, over its provisions. This allows the person to estimate the costs of conducting the program in time and money, which adds to the benefits of contracts that we discussed earlier.

MANAGING ANTECEDENTS IN SELF-MANAGEMENT

Earlier chapters have described a variety of antecedent manipulations, such as motivating operations and prompts, that are used in applied behavior analysis. The same methods are used in self-management, along with a few others we've not discussed before that address or utilize cognitive processes. The person who designs a self-management program should choose some of these methods for managing the behavior's antecedents and include them in the behavioral contract. In this section, the examples of using each method come from self-management projects my students have done in classes I have taught.

Applying Motivating Operations

We've seen that **motivating operations (MOs)** are procedures that alter the effectiveness of a reinforcer or punisher on behavior and performance of that behavior. MOs can be of two types. *Establishing operations* (EOs) increase the effectiveness of a consequence—that is, a reinforcer or punisher—on a behavior. For example, students in my classes who used snacks as a reinforcer made sure not to eat for a suitable amount of time, such as a few hours, before they got the snacks as a reward. *Abolishing operations* (AOs) decrease the effectiveness of a consequence on a behavior. For instance, students who were trying to limit their caloric intake to lose weight dealt with the problem of overeating at restaurants by snacking on low-calorie foods before going. Because they weren't very hungry at the restaurant, they tended to eat less. Chapters 9 and 14 provide detailed discussions of MOs and ways to apply them.

Using Prompts

Chapter 11 describes several types of **prompts** that are used as shortcut stimulus control methods to encourage the person to make a desired response that is a behavioral deficit (such as studying) or *not* to make an undesired response that is a behavioral excess (such as smoking cigarettes). Some types of prompts are especially common in self-management programs—they include *verbal prompts*, *pictorial prompts*, and *auditory prompts*. As examples of verbal and pictorial prompts, students in my classes who were following a self-management program to lose weight often put a sticky note or a picture of an obese individual on their food cabinets or refrigerator to remind them not to overeat.

Altering Antecedent Chains

Chapter 14 describes ways to alter chains that lead to a problem behavioral excess or deficit. To alter an antecedent chain that leads to a behavioral excess, we can build pauses into the chain or reorder its links. For instance, students of mine who wanted to quit smoking would pause between reaching for a pack of cigarettes and opening the pack or would reach for a lighter before reaching for the pack of cigarettes.

    Antecedent chains can lead to a behavioral deficit in two ways: The chain doesn't get started, or the chain ends in a response that makes the target behavior unlikely. One way to get a chain started or prevent an undesired response at the end is to provide prompts—for example, some students who wanted to increase their studying would place sticky notes on the TV saying, "No TV until homework done." Sometimes doing the first part of a chain is sufficient to assure that the last links are completed at a later time. For instance, students of mine who wanted to make sure they took the correct books with them to classes would pack their backpacks the night before.

Making Environmental Changes

Our usual environments may encourage undesirable behavior, such as too much snacking on high-calorie, high-fat foods. This may happen in our homes, particularly if members of the household stock a lot of these foods in the kitchen or pantry. Two ways for making environmental changes to manage antecedents are substituting a new environment for the old one and altering the availability of items that encourage the undesired behavior. In the case of snacking at home, for example, my students have used two approaches: spending time away from home in places that don't have snacks, such as a library, or arranging for high-calorie, high-fat snacks to be unavailable at home or kept out of common areas of the residence (the roommate or family member who wanted the snacks kept them in his or her bedroom). Making these environmental changes reduced greatly the likelihood that my students would eat prohibited snacks.

Using Narrowing Methods

The technique of *narrowing* is used to reduce a behavioral excess—it involves restricting an undesirable behavior to a smaller range of antecedents, such as snacking only in your kitchen or smoking only in certain periods of time. Students in my classes who wanted to reduce their TV watching have narrowed their viewing to certain places, such as in their living rooms, or during specific time periods, such as between 9:00 and 11:00 p.m.

Using Cognitive Approaches

Several cognitive approaches can be applied to manage antecedents when we are about to perform a behavioral excess, such as overeating, or trying to convince ourselves not to perform a behavioral deficit, such as studying. For instance, we can:

- *Apply self-instructions*, statements we say to ourselves that describe, direct, or guide the behavior we are to perform or not perform. *Positive self-instructions* lead us to perform appropriate or desirable behaviors; *negative self-instructions* encourage undesirable behavior and prevent us from performing appropriate actions. A student of mine who wanted to reduce her anger in traffic would say to herself when traffic problems appeared, "No need to get upset. Even if this slows me down, I'll get there at about the scheduled time." Self-instructions have been used effectively with children who were hyperactive, getting them to slow down and pay attention to tasks by saying to themselves when trying to copy a picture, "I have to go slowly and carefully. Okay, draw the line down, down, good; and then to the right, that's it; now down some more and then left. Good, I'm doing fine so far … Good. Even if I make an error I can go on slowly and carefully" (Meichenbaum, 1986, p. 351). Children who are hyperactive sometimes fail to use the self-instructions they are taught, but if they are prompted to do so, they apply them effectively and improve their performance (Guevremont, Osnes, & Stokes, 1988).

- *Think about the benefits* of the target behavior, such as eating less and studying. Students in my classes would think about how much better they'd look or feel if they lost weight and the higher grades they'd receive if they studied more.

- *Distract ourselves* from the antecedents that will lead to the undesired behavior, such as eating too much. Students who felt tempted to buy a candy bar in a vending machine would look away from the machine and talk to friends.

- *Re-perceive the antecedents* that will lead to the undesired behavior. When our perceptions of an antecedent, such as seeing a pie, involve "hot" cognitions, such as, "That pie looks so scrumptious," the undesirable behavior of eating restricted foods becomes hard to resist. Students of mine who were trying to watch less TV but were tempted to watch when they were tired or bored would substitute "cool" cognitions: Instead of thinking how exciting watching TV would be, they would think, "Most TV shows just fill time; they're not really fun or interesting."

One thing to keep in mind about using cognitions to manage antecedents is that the thoughts you use must be believable. Thinking that watching TV is "never fun" is extreme and unrealistic, and you won't believe it. (Go to .)

CASE STUDY

Betty's Self-Instructions for Studying

A 19-year-old college student named Betty had a problem with studying (Cohen, De James, Nocera, & Ramberger, 1980). By talking on the phone, snacking, conversing with roommates, or listening to music, she often got sidetracked or distracted from studying. She decided to try to increase the percentage of time she actually studied during her regular study hours simply by using self-instructions. Before starting to study, she would read a card that stated:

> It's important to study to get good grades. I need to study to understand new material. I'm not going to talk to my roommates because it's important that I learn this material …. I will not talk on the phone. I will remain studying even though I feel the urge to eat or drink something. Because listening to music distracts me and it's important that I learn this material I will not play the stereo. (pp. 447–448)

Every 15 minutes during studying, she would read a similar statement.

Betty collected data during baseline and intervention phases using the time-sampling method: Every 5 minutes during her study hours, she recorded whether or not she was studying. The data in her graph showed that her studying increased from about 60% of the time during baseline to over 80% of the time during intervention.

MANAGING CONSEQUENCES IN SELF-MANAGEMENT

Arranging to receive reinforcement and punishment for one's own behavior is a basic and essential strategy in self-management programs. In this section, we discuss ways to self-administer consequences, problems with this method, and ways to prevent or resolve these problems.

Self-Administered Reinforcement and Punishment

The type of consequence that is most commonly applied in self-management programs is positive reinforcement. Almost all of my students who have done a self-management program to change an operant behavior have included reinforcement contingencies. For instance, some of these students who wanted to increase their studying would allow themselves to watch TV or use the Internet for, say, half an hour at night as a reinforcer after having studied for an hour (not including interruptions) earlier in the day. These reinforcement methods were typically *self-administered*—that is, the students monitored their own behavior and provided the reinforcers only when the behavior met previously specified criteria.

We saw in Chapter 15 that the first step in designing a reinforcement system is to identify potential reinforcers. For self-management programs, a good way to identify potential positive reinforcers is to have the target person fill out a survey, such as the Preferred Items and Experiences Questionnaire (PIEQ; Sarafino & Graham, 2006) that we saw in Figure 15-1. The rewards identified can be administered directly or as backup reinforcers when using tokens. Reinforcement systems in self-management often make use of tokens to enable immediate reinforcement and then dispense backup rewards later. The next step after identifying the reinforcers is to determine exchange rates—the level of the behavior that must be performed to receive each reinforcer and, if using tokens, the number of tokens needed to get each backup reinforcer. One way to enhance the value of tokens is for target persons to deposit their own items of value, such as money or favorite articles of clothing, as backup reinforcers that they can buy back with tokens (Dallery, Meredith, & Glenn, 2008).

Negative reinforcement and punishment are sometimes used in self-management programs. In negative reinforcement approaches, an undesired circumstance is reduced or eliminated if the appropriate behavior occurs. For instance, a student of mine who wanted to stop smoking arranged with her roommates that it would be her usual job to clean up the kitchen each evening after dinner; but if she didn't smoke for the entire day, they would clean the kitchen for her. Recall from Chapter 7 that punishment can be of two types: In positive punishment, an aversive stimulus or condition is added as a consequence of the target behavior's occurrence; in negative punishment, a pleasant or valued stimulus or condition is taken away as a consequence for the inappropriate behavior. An example of negative punishment applied in a self-management program was given in the opening story of this chapter: Jim had to give money to a charity for each cigarette he smoked. This example is of response cost, probably the most commonly used type of punishment in self-management programs.

Problems With Self-Administered Consequences

We saw in Chapter 15 that a problem with self-administered reinforcement is that the target person sometimes takes unearned rewards. A similar problem can occur with punishment: Sometimes the person fails to administer an earned punisher, such as by not implementing a fine when an inappropriate behavior occurs. These problems tend to occur when the criteria for receiving a consequence are too rigorous, friends and family are unaware of the effort to change the behavior, and there is no tactic in the program to check the accuracy of administering the consequences. Recall that Jim's family, friends, and coworkers were committed to helping him quit smoking and provided weekly reports of their observations of his smoking. When a self-management program has eliminated the circumstances that encourage failing to self-administer consequences accurately, the best approach usually is to have someone else in charge of delivering the consequences. A student used this approach for a self-management program to increase her fitness (Kau & Fischer, 1974). After finding that she ignored reinforcement rules and didn't exercise as planned, she had her husband monitor her exercise behavior and dispense the rewards, which succeeded.

RESPONDENT METHODS IN SELF-MANAGEMENT

Not all behaviors addressed in self-management are operant; often they are respondent, particularly conditioned emotional responses (CERs), such as anxiety or anger. Some of my students have done self-management programs to reduce their fear of wasps or other insects, anger when driving a car, or anxiety during academic exams. The programs the students designed and carried out typically involved the procedures we saw in Chapter 22—they would:

- Learn and master a relaxation technique, usually progressive muscle relaxation.
- Design a stimulus hierarchy based on their subjective units of discomfort scale (SUDS) ratings of conditioned stimuli related to the CER.
- Apply the systematic desensitization method, gradually exposing themselves to stronger and stronger stimuli in the hierarchy while applying their relaxation techniques.

Although the students tried to use in vivo stimuli in their hierarchies, they often used symbolic or imaginal ones, which can be somewhat less effective. Still, their programs reduced their CERs substantially. Although systematic desensitization procedures can be applied safely and effectively in self-management after training in the methods, keep in mind that *in vivo exposure therapies* (see Chapter 22), especially flooding, should be conducted with professional supervision. (Go to 📄.)

STUDY AND REVIEW

SUMMARY

A behavioral contract is a negotiated, written, and signed agreement describing the target behavior to be addressed in an intervention, the antecedents for when it should or should not be performed, the monitoring process, the consequences for the target behavior's occurrence, and a schedule for reviewing progress in the intervention. The contract is made between the target person and a mediator, who can be the target person or that person's therapist, teacher, coworker, friend, or relative. In some cases, there is more than one mediator. The contract should indicate the roles of all parties, and each party should sign the agreement. Behavioral

CONCEPT CHECK 24.2

Answer the following questions about self-management methods.

1. Two examples of behaviors frequently addressed in self-management programs of students are _____ . ⇔
2. Compared with procedures typical of applied behavior analysis, self-management is more likely to employ the procedures of _____ and _____ .
3. Two methods for managing antecedents in self-management programs are _____ . ⇔
4. The first step in designing a reinforcement system for a self-management program is to _____ , and the best way to do this is to fill out the _____ .
5. Students who have learned the needed skills can apply _____ procedures in a self-management program to reduce a CER.

contracts can be applied at home, at work, in classrooms, and in clinics or institutions. Some benefits of using behavioral contracts are that they can reduce disagreements and errors in carrying out the program and enhance the commitment of the parties to fulfilling their roles, the clarity of the target person's progress, and the likelihood that the program contains methods that will lead to success.

Individuals who are trained in self-management can apply behavioral and cognitive methods to change their own behavior, such as to reduce their smoking or calorie intake, increase their exercise or studying, and decrease their anger or anxiety. Data collection in self-management is usually conducted through the process of self-monitoring, whereby the target person observes and records instances of his or her own behavior. In self-management programs, we manage the antecedents and consequences of the target behavior. To manage antecedents, we can apply motivating operations and prompts, alter antecedent chains, make environmental changes, and use narrowing and cognitive techniques, such as self-instructions and re-perceiving antecedents. To manage the consequences of the target behavior, we can self-administer reinforcers and punishers or have someone else do that. With careful training, people can design and implement systematic desensitization to reduce their conditioned emotional responses.

To prepare for exams, use the following key terms and review questions and the online study guide that's available on this book's companion website at www.wiley.com/college/sarafino.

KEY TERMS

behavioral contract
self-management

self-monitoring
motivating operations (MOs)

prompts

ANSWERS TO CONCEPT CHECKS (CCs)

CC24.1 *Answers*: **1.** monitoring process and consequences **2.** teacher, mother **3.** candy **4.** it reduces disagreements and errors in carrying out the program

CC24.2 *Answers*: **1.** decreasing nail biting and increasing studying **2.** self-monitoring, behavioral contracts **3.** applying motivating operations and using prompts **4.** identify potential reinforcers, PIEQ **5.** systematic desensitization

REVIEW QUESTIONS

1. What is a behavioral contract, and what elements should it contain?
2. Describe how separate reinforcers were specified in the behavioral contract Stuart (1971) helped construct to improve Candy's behavior.
3. Describe the negotiation process Miller and Kelley (1994) used in developing behavioral contracts between each of four children and their parents.
4. Describe how behavioral contracts have been used in various settings.
5. What is self-management, and what are some behavioral excesses and deficits it can correct?
6. Describe how motivating operations and prompts can be used to manage antecedents in self-management programs.
7. Describe cognitive approaches that can be used to manage antecedents in self-management programs.
8. What problem can occur with self-administered consequences, and how can it be prevented or eliminated?
9. If you wanted to reduce a fear you have, what systematic desensitization methods would you need to master so you could design and carry out a self-management program to change the target behavior?

RELATED READINGS

- DeRisi, W. J., & Butz, G. (1975). *Writing behavioral contracts: A case simulation practice manual.* Champaign, IL: Research Press.

- Hamilton, S. B. (1980). Instructionally based training in self-control: Behavior-specific and generalized outcomes resulting from student-implemented self-modification projects. *Teaching of Psychology, 7,* 140–145.

- Heffernan, T., & Richards, C. S. (1981). Self-control of study behavior: Identification and evaluation of natural methods. *Journal of Counseling Psychology, 28,* 361–364.

- Sarafino, E. P. (2011). *Self-management: Using behavioral and cognitive principles to manage your life.* Hoboken, NJ: Wiley.

- Stuart, R. B. (1971). Behavioral contracting within the families of delinquents. *Journal of Behavior Therapy and Experimental Psychiatry, 2,* 1–11.

25

TOKEN ECONOMIES

PROLOGUE

Located in Mexico about 175 miles south of the Arizona border is a private community called Comunidad los Horcones (Los Horcones, 2009; Rohter, 1989). Its several dozen adult and child residents have constructed a set of social rules and consequences to build and maintain a society based on cooperation and equality, rather than competition and discrimination. The community is self-supporting and sustains itself by farming and by providing educational programs for children from a nearby city. The entire community shares the money these activities bring in and engages in discussion and democratic vote to make decisions about how to spend their income.

One of the community's founders, Juan Robinson, had studied psychology and read B. F. Skinner's (1948) *Walden Two*. This novel by the famous behaviorist describes a utopian society that used operant conditioning principles to create an environment that promoted positive social conduct and relationships. To achieve these goals for los Horcones, Juan and his fellow residents used democratic procedures to develop a detailed code of behavior applying to all residents and all major facets of life in their community. The code for children, for instance, had 24 categories of outcome goals with about 150 specific, defined behaviors. By behaving in accordance with the code—for example, by performing the work needed for the community to function—individual residents earn token reinforcers. As you might guess, the token reinforcement system applied at los Horcones is very complex.

We've seen in earlier chapters that using tokens as reinforcers has several advantages over using rewards of some other types. For instance, the tokens can be given immediately after a desirable behavior to bridge the delay between performing the behavior and getting the tangible, consumable, or activity reinforcer that has been earned. Token reinforcers can also be applied more easily than other rewards with groups of individuals, and since tokens can be exchanged for a variety of attractive backup reinforcers, their reward value is likely to remain high. Advantages like these have made token reinforcers popular in behavior change programs. This chapter introduces you to complex systems of token reinforcement called token economies.

THE TOKEN ECONOMY APPROACH

What is a token economy, and what makes it different from the token reinforcement approaches we've seen so far? A **token economy** is a method that uses a complex system of consequences and is typically applied with groups of individuals for a wide range of target behaviors (Ayllon & Azrin, 1968b). Although the terms *token economy* and *token system* are sometimes used interchangeably, the methods differ in three ways. Compared with other token systems, token economies generally:

- Try to change the behaviors of groups of individuals, rather than just one person
- Attempt to change relatively wide ranges of target behaviors
- Use relatively complex systems of consequences for those behaviors

Although these characteristics help define "token economies," there are no definite criteria that determine if a program qualifies as a token economy. The number of target individuals included in the intervention, the range of behaviors to be changed, and the complexity of the system of consequences can vary. Some professionals use the term *token economy* to refer to simple token systems.

USUAL SETTINGS FOR TOKEN ECONOMIES

One of the earliest recorded instances of using a token economy approach occurred in a 19th-century prison (Pitts, 1976). Alexander Meconochie, a captain in the British Royal Navy, was placed in charge of

> one of the worst British penal colonies, Norfolk Island, located about 1000 miles off the coast of Australia. The inmates were two-time losers, having committed major crimes in both England and Australia. (p. 146)

To control the inmates' behavior, the captain implemented a point system by which they could earn their way out of the penal colony by performing appropriate tasks and social behaviors. The number of points the inmates needed depended on the seriousness of the crimes they had committed. Meconochie had a motivational rationale for using this approach: "When a man keeps the key of his own prison, he is soon persuaded to fit it into the lock." Even though his approach seemed to be successful in controlling the behavior of the Norfolk Island prisoners, Meconochie's superiors criticized it and recalled him to England.

Because token economies are usually implemented to change the behaviors of groups of individuals, they are applied mainly in organizational or institutional settings. Token economies have been used in a great variety of settings, including classrooms for typically functioning students of all ages, classrooms and institutions for people with developmental disabilities, hospitals for psychiatric patients and drug abusers, group homes for teenagers who have committed antisocial acts and are at risk of becoming delinquents, and work settings to enhance job performance (Kazdin, 1985). Los Horcones, described at the beginning of this chapter, is one of several similar communities in such locations as Kansas, Michigan, Virginia, and Canada that have been established with token economies to structure their members' social behaviors (Rohter, 1989).

WHAT'S NEEDED TO START A TOKEN ECONOMY

Starting a token economy requires that many complex tasks be completed in advance. One of the main tasks is to decide on the target behaviors that the intervention will try to change. Decisions about which behaviors to include will depend on the types of problems observed, the specific needs of individual group members, and the needs of the organization or institution where the program will be implemented. If the individuals in the group are very similar to one another in their problem behaviors and personal characteristics, the target behaviors and rules about them can apply broadly to all members of the group. Having similar target individuals in the group is a fairly common circumstance, as might be expected from the examples of settings just mentioned.

Once the target behaviors have been identified, they must be defined carefully and in detail so that the members of the group and the staff who administer the program will know exactly what the behaviors are and can determine reliably whether they occurred. At that point, four tasks should be initiated. First, functional assessments should be conducted to determine the antecedents and consequences that seem to be involved in each of the behaviors. Second, because token economies usually require several staff members to administer the program, these individuals must be recruited. Third, the staff must receive extensive training in identifying the target behaviors, using methods to reduce the antecedents and consequences that have promoted inappropriate behaviors in the past, recording data, and administering the token reinforcers. Fourth, the staff must collect baseline data. Let's see what the next steps would be to set up a token economy and implement it.

SETTING UP AND IMPLEMENTING A TOKEN ECONOMY

After the functional assessments have been conducted, all the materials, equipment, and facilities that will be needed to implement the token economy can be set up while the baseline data are being collected. The materials and equipment might include a supply of tokens, data sheets to record each person's behaviors and tokens earned, behavioral contracts, backup reinforcers, timing devices, and so on. Any special facilities that will be needed must be set up in advance. For instance, token economies in large institutions often have a special room, set up like a store, where tokens can be exchanged for tangible or consumable backup reinforcers. In smaller token economies, the store may be kept in a cabinet or large box. To set up all of these prerequisites, it is necessary to plan various features of the program.

Choosing the Tokens and Backup Consequences

Tokens can take many different forms. For instance, they can be poker chips, stars or stamps attached to a chart, check marks in a table, data entries in logs that are like bankbooks, or specially printed paper money. Tokens can be color-coded to reflect some important dimension, such as their value or the type of behavior for which they were earned. Because tokens function like money, they serve as points or credits toward the exchange cost for backup reinforcers. Sometimes tokens are specifically designed to operate timers or automatic dispensers. For example, Jason (1985) used coinlike tokens in a program that had TV watching as an activity backup reinforcer for several behaviors, such as doing chores or homework. A timer was connected to the TV set, and each token activated the timer for 30 minutes.

Ideally, tokens should have certain practical characteristics: They should be durable, convenient to store and handle, easy to carry around and dispense, and difficult to steal or counterfeit. Stealing tokens must be prevented. It is also a good idea to provide some way for each person to store the tokens he or she earns, such as in a purse or wallet. Sometimes tokens are printed on paper to serve as "paper money" receipts that cannot be easily counterfeited or redeemed if stolen—partly because each one had to be filled out by a staff member, as shown in Figure 25-1.

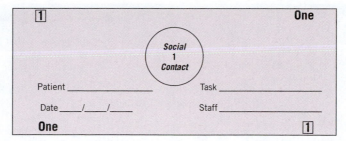

Figure 25-1 Sample of the "paper money" receipts used in a token economy. *Source:* Based on information in Logan (1970).

Making decisions about which backup reinforcers and punishers to include in a token economy program can be accomplished by using the information we discussed in Chapters 15 and 16. We can identify potentially strong backup reinforcers by observing the target persons' preferences in naturalistic or structured tests and by interviewing them or having them fill out a survey, like the Preferred Items and Experiences Questionnaire (PIEQ; see Figure 15-1). Try to have a large variety of reinforcers for exchange in the token system to maintain the tokens' effectiveness and provide strong reinforcement for all individuals under the token economy. A type of punishment that often fits easily into token economy procedures is response cost, in which the target person pays fines, in tokens, for not behaving appropriately.

Managing the Consequences

Perhaps the most basic issue in managing the consequences well is to keep a large supply of tokens and backup reinforcers available and devise a system to administer the rewards and punishers. Chapter 16 described in detail issues we need to decide in advance to manage the consequences well. I've summarized these decisions briefly here:

- *Guidelines for administering tokens*: Everyone involved should (a) know the behavioral criteria for earning tokens and exchange rates for backup reinforcers; (b) award tokens as soon as possible after the desired behavior occurs; (c) use natural reinforcers, such as praise, along with dispensing tokens; (d) keep careful and accurate records of the target behaviors and the reinforcers dispensed; and (e) provide bonus rewards for high-level performance, if possible.

- *Who will administer consequences?* The individuals who will deliver and keep track of the tokens each target person earned or lost and the backup reinforcers or punishers received will need to monitor the target behaviors, record data carefully, and deliver tokens promptly.

- *How many tokens will a behavior earn?* The goal in deciding how many tokens a behavior will earn is to maximize each target person's performance of the target behaviors. Supply and demand can influence these decisions, and so can the relative abilities of different target persons. Also, it can be useful to use more liberal criteria initially and thin the reinforcement to an intermittent schedule later on.

- *What will the exchange rates be?* Decisions about the number of tokens needed to buy each backup reinforcer depend on four factors: the number of tokens target individuals can earn for each behavior, the cost of the backup reinforcers, the degree of demand of different reinforcers, and the therapeutic relevance of different reinforcers.

- *How often will backup reinforcers be available?* How often and when tokens can be redeemed for backup reinforcers depends on the intellectual ability of the target individuals in the token economy: The lower the ability, the more often the backup reinforcers should be available. Very young and low-functioning persons generally have backup reinforcers available at least twice a day, particularly when they first enter the program. After the first few days, reinforcer availability can be reduced gradually toward the goal of allowing them to redeem their tokens much less frequently, in some cases only once a week.

An issue we did not discuss earlier is whether the program will use *group or individual contingencies* for administering reinforcers. When a token economy uses a group contingency, tokens are given on the basis of the group's

After this boy performs well, his teacher gives him a token, which he can exchange later for a backup reinforcer.
Source: Copyright © Christina Kennedy/PhotoEdit.

performance as a whole. With an individual contingency, tokens are given to each person based on his or her own performance. As we discussed in Chapter 16, group contingencies are relatively easy to administer and have built-in incentives to prevent group members from reinforcing one another's inappropriate behaviors. But negative peer-pressure tactics, such as threats, seem more likely to happen with group than with individual contingencies, especially if the consequences include group punishment when behavioral criteria are not met. Some programs combine these approaches, using individual contingencies for some behaviors and group contingencies for other behaviors.

Phasing Out the Program

Although token economies are sometimes used just to maintain appropriate conduct or high performance while people are in organizational and institutional settings, they can also be applied in programs with broader, long-term goals. For instance, the goals of token economies in psychiatric hospitals may involve helping individuals function better in natural environments, outside the institution. The methods we discussed in Chapter 20 for maintaining improved behavior after an intervention ends can help achieve these long-term goals. One of these approaches involved using natural reinforcers, such as praise and feedback, along with tokens. Later in the program, the natural reinforcers can gradually replace the tokens.

Other approaches for maintaining improved behavior after an intervention ends include thinning and delaying reinforcement. These methods can be implemented by:

- Decreasing the number of tokens each target behavior earns
- Decreasing the number of target behaviors that earn tokens
- Increasing the number of tokens required to buy backup reinforcers
- Increasing the delays between receiving tokens and having opportunities to redeem them for backup reinforcers
- Assuring that the person's everyday environment will encourage the improved behavior by providing appropriate antecedents and consequences

These approaches can be used separately or in combination, but it is not yet clear which method or combination of techniques enhances the maintenance of improved behaviors best. (Go to 📖.)

CONCEPT CHECK 25.1

Check your understanding of the preceding concepts. Remember: The symbol ⇔ means that the answer can vary. Answer the following questions about token economy methods.

1. A behavior change program designed to change a wide range of behaviors in groups of individuals by using a complex system of reinforcers is called a _____ .
2. An example of the materials or equipment to be obtained and set up before starting a token economy is _____ . ⇔
3. An example of tokens that could be used in a token reinforcement program is _____ . ⇔
4. A type of punishment that can fit into a token economy especially easily is _____ .
5. People who are likely to need opportunities to exchange tokens for backup reinforcers very frequently are likely to be individuals with lesser _____ abilities.

AN EXAMPLE TOKEN ECONOMY: ACHIEVEMENT PLACE

Now that we have seen the general features of token economies and how they are set up and implemented, we will examine in some detail a fine example of a token economy program to see how one functions. This token economy, called Achievement Place, was developed in Kansas in the 1960s and 1970s (Phillips, 1968; Phillips, Phillips, Fixsen, & Wolf, 1971, 1973).

THE PURPOSE AND STRUCTURE OF ACHIEVEMENT PLACE

Achievement Place was designed as a residential token economy program for juvenile boys who were classified as "pre-delinquent," a term for juveniles whose home lives and records of minor offenses, such as petty thefts and fighting, indicated they are at risk of becoming habitual lawbreakers. The purpose of Achievement Place was to rehabilitate the juveniles who were placed by the courts in the program to prevent them from becoming delinquents. The approach this program developed became a model for over 300 other programs to prevent delinquency in the United States, including Boys Town (Fixsen et al., 1978; Fixsen, Blasé, Timbers, & Wolf, 2007). Although most of these programs have been for boys, many have been for girls. The average age at *entry* is about 14 years; on average, boys spend 11 months and girls 6 months in the programs (Kirigin, Braukmann, Atwater, & Wolf, 1982).

Achievement Place was originally set up in a large house and received pre-delinquent boys from the local community. The house served as the residence for several boys at a time and for a pair of *teaching parents*, who supervised the program. The boys continued to go to their own schools, and their teachers completed brief "report cards" daily. Each day the boys could earn or lose points based on their performing specific social, academic, and everyday living behaviors both at the house and in school. Whenever points were earned or lost, the behavior and number of points were recorded on an index card each boy carried with him. Table 25.1 describes some of the target behaviors in the program and the number of points the behaviors earned or lost. The backup reinforcers—or *privileges*, as they were called—were mainly activities, such as being allowed to go downtown, and consumable items, such as snacks, that would be naturally available in most teenagers' everyday lives.

An important feature of this program was a gradual transition toward self-regulation. The boys made this transition by advancing through three levels or phases of the program. When a boy entered the program, he

Table 25.1   *Some Target Behaviors in the Achievement Place Program and the Number of Points Each One Earned or Lost*

Behaviors That Earned Points	Points
1. Watching news on TV or reading the newspaper	300 per day
2. Cleaning and maintaining neatness in one's room	500 per day
3. Keeping one's person neat and clean	500 per day
4. Reading books	5–10 per page
5. Aiding house-parents in various household tasks	10–1,000 per task
6. Doing dishes	500–1,000 per meal
7. Being well dressed for an evening meal	100–500 per meal
8. Performing homework	500 per day
9. Obtaining desirable grades on school report cards	500–1,000 per grade
10. Turning out lights when not in use	25 per light

Behaviors That Lost Points	Points
1. Failing grades on the report card	500–1,000 per grade
2. Speaking aggressively	25–50 per response
3. Forgetting to wash hands before meals	100–300 per meal
4. Arguing	300 per response
5. Disobeying	100–1,000 per response
6. Being late	10 per minute
7. Displaying poor manners	50–100 per response
8. Engaging in poor posture	50–100 per response
9. Using poor grammar	20–50 per response
10. Stealing, lying, or cheating	10,000 per response

Source: From E. L. Phillips (1968), Achievement Place: Token reinforcement procedures in a home-style rehabilitation setting for "pre-delinquent" boys. *Journal of Applied Behavior Analysis, 1,* 213–223, Table 2. Copyright © 1968 Society for the Experimental Analysis of Behavior. Used by permission.

started on a *daily point system* in which the points he earned were tallied up at the end of each day and could be exchanged for privileges he would receive on the following day. This arrangement allowed him to learn how the system worked and the value of earning tokens. As soon as the boy could function with less structure, he advanced to the second level, the *weekly point system*, in which his points were tallied for a full week and exchanged for reinforcers he would receive for the following week. In the last level of the program, called the *merit system*, the point system was phased out and the privileges became freely available as long as improved social, academic, and everyday living behaviors were maintained with social reinforcement alone. Boys were placed on the merit system only if their behavior was consistently good and they appeared to be almost ready to leave Achievement Place to return home.

The token economy for the daily and weekly point systems was designed so that boys who performed all of the target behaviors and lost few points in fines could expect to earn essentially all of the privileges available. Table 25.2 lists the privileges the boys could earn at Achievement Place and the number of points needed to purchase each one on the daily and weekly point systems. The privileges called *basics* were exchanged as a package that included the use of a telephone, a radio, the recreation room, and tools. The number of points needed to purchase each privilege stayed fairly constant but could change occasionally if the reward value varied. For example, watching TV cost more tokens during the winter than in other seasons. Various "special privileges" could be available. One special privilege the boys could buy at an auction each week was the opportunity to serve as *manager*—the person with authority to assign chores and award tokens to the other boys under his supervision. The manager's behavior earned or lost points for him, depending on how well the other boys performed their household chores and everyday living behaviors, such as brushing their teeth and getting up on time in the morning.

Table 25.2 *Privileges (Backup Reinforcers) That Could Be Earned at Achievement Place and the Numbers of Points Needed to Purchase Them on the Daily and Weekly Point Systems*

Privileges	Price in Points	
	Weekly System	Daily System
Basics (hobbies and games)	3,000	400
Snacks	1,000	150
TV	1,000	150
Allowance (per $1.00)	2,000	300
Permission to leave Achievement Place (home, downtown, sports events)	3,000	*
Bonds (savings for gifts, special clothing, etc.)	1,000	150
Special privileges	Variable	*

*Not available

Source: From E. L. Phillips, E. A. Phillips, D. L. Fixsen, & M. M. Wolf (1971), Achievement Place: Modification of the behaviors of pre-delinquent boys within a token economy. *Journal of Applied Behavior Analysis*, 4, 45–59, Table 1. Copyright © 1971 Society for the Experimental Analysis of Behavior. Used by permission.

A DAY IN ONE'S LIFE AT ACHIEVEMENT PLACE

Because the boys lived in a house with two "teaching parents," and the social structure and activities were like those of a family, the Achievement Place approach came to be known as the *teaching-family model*. The daily routine was designed to be like the routines of most families. The boys got up at a standard time in the morning, showered and dressed, and cleaned their rooms. Then,

> after breakfast, some of the boys had kitchen clean-up duties before leaving for school. After school the boys returned home and prepared their homework, after which they could watch TV, play games, or engage in other recreational activities if these privileges had been earned via the token economy. Some boys were assigned kitchen clean-up duties after the evening meal. (Phillips, 1968, p. 214)

A "family conference" was held each evening to enable the boys and teaching parents to discuss the day's events, the manager's performance, and problems with the token economy program (Phillips, Phillips, Wolf, & Fixsen, 1973). These conferences gave the boys chances to contribute to and learn from the way the program was administered. During the rest of the evening, the boys could engage in individual and group recreational activities before going to bed at a standard time.

HOW EFFECTIVE IS THE ACHIEVEMENT PLACE APPROACH?

Studies have shown that the Achievement Place approach is very effective in improving a wide variety of behaviors while pre-delinquent juveniles are in the program and for a year or so after it ends. For instance, a follow-up study found that, compared with boys who were placed in a large institution for delinquents or on probation, Achievement Place boys had substantially fewer police and court contacts, greater school attendance, and higher grades in the following 2 years (Fixsen et al., 1978). The programs appear to be more effective when the staff is well trained and they have access to experts for advice regarding problems they encounter in implementing the intervention (Fixsen, Blasé, Timbers, & Wolf, 2007).

Another study compared the effects of two types of group homes: 13 homes that followed the teaching-family model and 9 homes that used other approaches to prevent delinquency (Kirigin, Braukmann, Atwater, & Wolf, 1982). The court and police records of each boy or girl were examined for instances of alleged criminal offenses during the intervention period and for 1 year before and after the group home intervention. The *rate* of offenses was then determined by taking the average number of offenses per month. The researchers then compared the rates of offenses for the three periods—before, during, and after intervention. For the juveniles in the homes using the teaching-family model, the rate of offenses dropped by about half during the intervention and did not increase in the subsequent year. For those in the homes using other approaches, the rate of offenses *increased* sharply during the intervention and dropped in the subsequent year to the same rate as that of the teaching-family homes. This means that the teaching-family homes were much more effective in controlling delinquent behaviors while the juveniles were in group homes, but the two types of programs did not differ in being able to prevent delinquency in the subsequent year.

Despite the success of the teaching-family model for improving the behavior of pre-delinquent juveniles while they are in the program and for the year after, it is now clear that these improvements are often lost after a couple of years (Wolf, Braukmann, & Ramp, 1987). In addition, the rate of criminal offenses after completing a teaching-family intervention is, on average, still well above national norms for juveniles of matching ages.

The inability of short-term interventions to prevent delinquency over the long term should not be very surprising. Juveniles who complete a teaching-family program typically are returned to the same environment that reinforced antisocial behavior in the past. Little encouragement exists in that environment for the kinds of behaviors that were reinforced at the group home. Even among teenagers who are receiving group therapy sessions with peers, members of the group often promote deviant behavior in each other (Dishion, McCord, & Poulon, 1999). The solution to the problem of maintaining the gains interventions produce in pre-delinquent juveniles may be to provide longer-term contact with environments that support positive social behavior, perhaps by training parents and foster parents in behavioral methods to help them guide the actions of these teens during adolescence (Wolf, Braukmann, & Ramp, 1987). This possibility has received support in research (Chamberlain & Reid, 1998; Dishion & Andrews, 1995).

OTHER SETTINGS FOR TOKEN ECONOMIES

Three of the many other settings in which token economies have been used successfully are in school classrooms, places of employment, and institutions for psychiatric and developmentally disabled individuals. Here we'll look briefly at some examples and the target behaviors they addressed.

TOKEN ECONOMIES IN CLASSROOMS

The use of rewards to influence classroom behavior has a long history. Your parents and grandparents probably remember teachers who gave "stars" to students for academic achievement and extra recess time to children who had "been good." These reinforcers are still used today—they basically give social reinforcement or feedback, since they are generally not exchanged for backup reinforcers. But using tokens as rewards in schools has a shorter history. It began in the 1960s and has continued in many regular and special education classrooms since then, usually in programs conducted to improve students' general conduct and academic performance. Some of these programs qualify as token economies because they addressed several target behaviors and used fairly complex reinforcement systems.

One early example of a token economy applied in school was carried out in a special education classroom with 8- to 14-year-olds with mild or moderate retardation (Birnbrauer, Wolf, Kidder, & Tague, 1972). Although token and social reinforcement were given mainly for correct performance on academic assignments, such as vocabulary and arithmetic tasks, the students could also earn tokens for being cooperative or doing some extra activity. Reprimands and time-out were used as punishment for disruptive behaviors. The tokens were marks the teacher put in squares that divided up sheets of paper in a student's "mark book" folder. At the end of the daily token economy class, the students could exchange fully marked sheets for backup reinforcers (balloons, trinkets, pencils, etc.). Sheets that had any squares unmarked could be carried over the next day. In some cases a child would save up sheets to buy a special, relatively expensive item that was included as a backup reinforcer specifically for him or her. After the students had spent more than 3 months in the token economy, the token reinforcement was suspended for more than 3 weeks. Only a third of the children continued to perform well during the program suspension, but the higher performance levels returned when the token economy was reinstated.

Another token economy program was applied for a full academic year in an entire elementary school, spanning classes from kindergarten through sixth grade (Boegli & Wasik, 1978). The target behaviors differed somewhat for the younger and older children, but in all cases they called for students to be at assigned areas on time, have needed supplies and books for the day's activities, talk or move about quietly so as not to disturb others, help other individuals, and successfully complete assigned work. All teachers and all other staff of the school, including librarians and aides, were trained in the token economy method and could distribute tokens for appropriate behaviors. Although token exchanges could occur at various times during any day, the child's teacher supervised all exchanges, and children could save their tokens across days if they wished. Sometimes auctions were held in which the children could bid on various items—such as musical recordings, magazines, comic books, toys, and jewelry—donated by parents and merchants. Data analyses revealed decreases in student disruptions and suspensions, and the students' scores on reading and mathematics achievement tests showed greater improvements during the year of the program than during the preceding year.

TOKEN ECONOMIES IN WORKSITES

The owner of a company that manufactures egg cartons in Massachusetts introduced a token economy to improve several behaviors, with a focus on decreasing absenteeism and discipline problems (Nelton, 1988). The point system worked in this way: Each employee would earn 25 points for excellent attendance for an entire year, 20 points for having no formal disciplinary action for a year, and 15 points for having no injuries requiring an absence in a year. They could also earn points for submitting suggestions that improve safety or reduce costs and lose points for being absent from work. When workers accumulated 100 points, they became members of the company's "100 Club" and were awarded a jacket with the name of the club and company logo printed on it. Although the backup reinforcer is limited and may appear a bit corny, individuals who received it seemed quite proud.

A more complex worksite token economy was introduced at two open-pit mines to improve worker safety in the hazardous jobs associated with mining (Fox, Hopkins, & Anger, 1987). Each year in the United States, hundreds of mining workers are killed and many thousands are injured. The two mines that received the intervention had very poor safety records; the numbers of days their workers lost due to work-related injuries was several times higher than the national mining average. The tokens were trading stamps that were awarded monthly with paychecks and could be redeemed at stores for hundreds of different items, such as a spice rack, bowling ball, gas-fired barbecue grill, and microwave oven. Workers received the tokens mainly for not having had any injuries requiring a physician's care in the prior month, but they could also earn tokens for safety suggestions. The token economy divided the workers into four groups based on how hazardous their jobs were. Although injuries had occurred in all job groups, most injuries were in jobs associated with the use and maintenance of heavy machinery. The more hazardous the job, the more tokens workers received for avoiding injury. What's more, a group contingency was added so that all workers under the same supervisor got tokens if none of those workers were injured during a month. As Figure 25-2 depicts, the rates of work-related injuries dropped after the token economies were introduced and remained relatively low at both mines during the many years the interventions remained in effect.

TOKEN ECONOMIES IN INSTITUTIONAL SETTINGS

The structure and usefulness of the token economy approach for changing behavior was first described by Ayllon and Azrin (1968b) based on the program they applied in a psychiatric hospital. In this groundbreaking program, patients could earn tokens for a variety of activities and chores, such as helping to serve meals or clean the kitchen, gathering clothes to be laundered, and performing personal hygiene tasks. After this program provided a model structure for a token economy and demonstrated that this approach could be implemented successfully in psychiatric settings, token economies were applied in other psychiatric hospitals and in institutions of many other types (Glynn, 1990; Welch & Gist, 1974). A subsequent long-term research project compared the effectiveness of a token economy program with two other commonly used approaches in treating middle-aged psychiatric patients who had been in mental institutions most of their adult lives (Paul & Lentz, 1977).

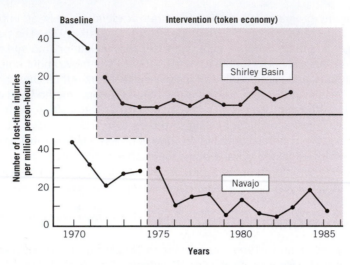

Figure 25-2   Baseline and intervention rates of serious work-related injuries, as reflected in the yearly number of injuries, per million person-hours worked, that resulted in the loss of 1 or more days from work. The token economies were studied with a multiple-baseline format that compared employees at two open-pit mines: the Shirley Basin uranium mine in Wyoming and the Navajo coal mine in Arizona. *Source:* From D. K. Fox, B. L. Hopkins, & W. K. Anger (1987), The long-term effects of a token economy on safety performance in open-pit mining. *Journal of Applied Behavior Analysis, 20,* 215–224, Figure 2. Copyright © 1987 Society for the Experimental Analysis of Behavior. Used by permission.

The researchers randomly assigned a large number of patients to the three treatment approaches and assessed outcomes over several years. Compared to the patients treated with the other approaches, the patients treated with the token economy program showed greater improvements in their behaviors in the institution, used less medication to control their psychological functioning, were released sooner, and adjusted better to living outside the institution.

Despite the clear utility of the token economy approach in treating psychiatric patients, it was not widely adopted in mental hospitals for four reasons (Glynn, 1990). First, mental hospital staff sometimes resist using token economies because of the intensive supervision and monitoring these approaches require and for philosophical reasons, such as viewing reinforcers as "bribes." Second, immediate costs of backup reinforcers and extra staff needed to carry out a token economy may preclude the use of this approach. Third, because of cost-containment policies at most institutions, patients do not remain in hospitals long enough to benefit from the token economy approach; the emphasis is for outpatient treatment. Fourth, legal rulings and ethical concerns have had the effect of restricting the types of backup reinforcers that can be used with psychiatric patients. In some places, for instance, institutions are required to give free access to personal property, cheerful furnishings, television, and so on. Although these constraints do not prevent token economies from being used, they make it more difficult to apply powerful reinforcers to change behavior in institutions.

BENEFITS AND PROBLEMS OF TOKEN ECONOMIES

The token economy has been clearly established as an effective treatment approach for changing problem behaviors (TFPDPP, 1993). Target individuals tend to perform a program's target behaviors at high rates when the token economy is in effect. But these gains are often temporary if the program is discontinued, such as when individuals are released from an institution that uses a token economy. Although the loss of these gains is an important problem, the real question should be whether improved behaviors are maintained better after interventions with token economies than with other approaches. As we have seen in programs with pre-delinquent adolescents and psychiatric patients, token economies are at least as effective, and sometimes more effective, as other approaches in maintaining improved behaviors.

Not all behavioral improvements are likely to be lost when a token economy ends. For instance, children who acquire new academic skills in classroom token economies are likely to retain these skills, especially if the skills are useful—that is, reinforced—in other classes or outside the academic environment. Skills in reading or arithmetic typically are useful in many situations children encounter. In contrast, improvements in people's general conduct or lifestyle behaviors may be harder to maintain after a token economy has ended because the natural environment may not reinforce the new behaviors. Token economies for particular individuals usually can't be continued for many years because of the expense, unless the financial savings of the improved behavior outweigh the costs—as occurred in the token economies that increased workers' safety in mining jobs, discussed earlier. By maintaining safety behaviors year after year, industries with hazardous jobs can save money in the costs of insurance and absenteeism. These savings often can offset the costs of running an effective program to change behavior.

Some people claim token economies are "demeaning" to the individuals in them. But participants in these programs don't seem to agree. For instance, a study assessed the satisfaction of pre-delinquent adolescents for the programs they were in by having them fill out 7-point rating scales, where a 7 reflected high satisfaction. Teenagers who received interventions in group homes gave ratings that averaged 6.5 out of 7 points for the homes using the teaching-family model and only 5.0 points for the homes using other approaches (Kirigin, Braukmann, Atwater, & Wolf, 1982). Perhaps token economy participants realize that the system is not very different from their earning pay for working or grades for studying. Perhaps they also realize that any demeaning aspects to the program, if they exist, are easily offset by the sense of self-esteem and pride to be gained from improving personal problem behaviors. (Go to .)

STUDY AND REVIEW

SUMMARY

A token economy is a complex system of consequences that is usually applied to change a wide range of behaviors in groups of people. Token economies have been used mainly in organizational and institutional settings, such as classrooms for normal students, institutions for people with mental retardation and psychiatric disorders, group homes for pre-delinquent teenagers, and worksites.

CONCEPT CHECK 25.2

Answer the following questions about Achievement Place and other settings for token economies.

1. In the Achievement Place program, the last level toward self-regulation is called the _____ system.
2. A likely task of an Achievement Place manager might be to have other boys _____ . ⇔
3. Although teaching-family interventions reduce teens' problem behaviors, the rate of criminal offenses of juveniles after receiving the intervention is still _____ than the national norms for teens.
4. In the token economy applied at the two mines, workers received token reinforcers mainly for _____ .
5. An improved behavior that might be relatively difficult to maintain after a token economy ends is _____ . ⇔

Setting up a token economy is a complex process. It involves choosing the tokens and the backup reinforcers and punishers to be used. It entails assigning staff to administer consequences as well as deciding the number of tokens a behavior will earn, the exchange availability and rates for reinforcers, and whether individual or group contingencies will be used. Phasing out a token economy can promote the maintenance of the improved behavior by using methods that thin and delay reinforcement and assuring that antecedents and consequences in the target person's everyday life will encourage the improved behavior.

Achievement Place was designed as a residential token economy in which "teaching parents" supervised the behavior of pre-delinquent juveniles. This approach is called the teaching-family model. It features a gradual transition toward self-regulation by requiring the teenagers to progress through three levels: the daily point system, the weekly point system, and the merit system. Although the teaching-family model appears to be more effective in reducing antisocial behavior than other group home approaches while the juveniles are in the program, the gains are often lost within 2 years after the teenagers are returned to their home environments.

Token economies have been applied successfully to improve a wide variety of behaviors, including classroom conduct and academic achievement, job performance and safety, and social behaviors of many types. Because improved behaviors often are not maintained after people leave the program, it may be necessary to continue the program in some form to prevent relapses, particularly if the financial savings from the improved behavior outweigh the costs of providing the program.

To prepare for exams, use the following key terms and review questions and the online study guide that's available on this book's companion website at www.wiley.com/college/sarafino.

KEY TERMS

token economy   Achievement Place

ANSWERS TO CONCEPT CHECKS (CCs)

CC25.1 *Answers:* **1.** token economy **2.** backup reinforcers **3.** poker chips **4.** response cost **5.** cognitive/intellectual
CC25.2 *Answers:* **1.** merit **2.** clean bathrooms **3.** higher **4.** not having injuries **5.** obeying rules

REVIEW QUESTIONS

1. What is a token economy, and how is it different from other token reinforcement systems?

2. Describe the steps that need to be completed before a token economy can start to function.

3. What kinds of tokens are there?

4. Describe the issues we need to decide in advance regarding how to manage the consequences in a token economy.

5. How can token economies be phased out to enhance the likelihood that desirable behaviors are maintained after participants leave the program?

6. What levels of transition does Achievement Place provide toward self-regulation?

7. Describe the study by Kirigin, Braukmann, Atwater, and Wolf (1982) comparing the outcomes of group homes using the teaching-family model with homes using other approaches.

8. Describe the study by Fox, Hopkins, and Anger (1987) on applying token economies to improve worker safety in mining.

9. Describe the research by Paul and Lentz (1977) comparing a token economy with other approaches in treating psychiatric patients. What did they find?

10. Discuss why token economies are not used widely with psychiatric patients.

RELATED READINGS

- Ayllon, T., & Azrin, N. H. (1968b). *The token economy: A motivational system for therapy and rehabilitation*. Englewood Cliffs, NJ: Prentice-Hall.

- Glynn, S. M. (1990). Token economy approaches for psychiatric patients: Progress and pitfalls over 25 years. *Behavior Modification*, 14, 383–407.

- Phillips, E. L. (1968). Achievement Place: Token reinforcement procedures in a home-style rehabilitation setting for "pre-delinquent" boys. *Journal of Applied Behavior Analysis*, 1, 213–223.

- Stainback, W. C., Payne, J. S., Stainback, S. B., & Payne, R. A. (1973). *Establishing a token economy in the classroom*. Columbus, OH: Charles E. Merrill.

- Wolf, M. M., Braukmann, C. J., & Ramp, K. A. (1987). Serious delinquent behavior as part of a significantly handicapping condition: Cures and supportive environments. *Journal of Applied Behavior Analysis*, 20, 347–359.

26

RULE–GOVERNED AND VERBAL BEHAVIOR

Rule-Governed Behavior
How Rules Govern Behavior
When Are Rules Especially Useful?

Verbal Behavior
Types of Verbal Behavior
Training Mands and Tacts

Study and Review

PROLOGUE

"In case of fire, use the stairs to escape," said a sign near the elevator of a hotel where I was staying. This information gives instructions in words about a behavior to perform (go down the stairs) when a specific antecedent (fire) is present, and the consequence (escape) of performing that behavior. In this example, the consequence for using the stairs involves negative reinforcement: escape from the fire and threat of injury. Using words is important for people in many ways—for instance, we can use words to govern or influence our behavior and to express our ideas or desires.

The extent to which humans can use language sets us apart from other animals, most of which have very limited communication abilities. Humans' ability to use words underlies and makes possible our extensive knowledge, understanding, thought and problem-solving processes, and complex social interactions. Because of the central role of language in human life, behavior analysts try to use it effectively in promoting desired behaviors and in helping individuals acquire language skills so that they can function more effectively in life. In this chapter, we examine two topics that involve language. First we'll consider how rules can govern behavior and then we'll discuss several language skills and ways to teach them to individuals who are very young or have intellectual handicaps.

RULE-GOVERNED BEHAVIOR

In applied behavior analysis, a *rule* is a verbal statement of a contingency that involves an antecedent, a behavior, and a consequence. Thus, a rule states that a certain consequence is likely when an individual performs a particular behavior under a specific antecedent condition. "In case of fire, use the stairs to escape" is a rule, and we saw in the opening story that following its suggestion can lead to negative reinforcement. Here are two other rules:

1. "It is two days before the test—if I don't start reading the assignment, I'll flunk." This rule describes punishment (flunking) as the consequence of not reading, and a good way (reading) to avoid that event.

2. The grammatical rule "*i* before *e* except after *c*" is taught in English classes. It implies positive reinforcement as the consequence, such as feedback or praise when you answer *r-e-c-e-i-v-e* (but not *r-e-c-i-e-v-e*) when asked to spell *receive* in class.

For people with sufficient language skills, using rules is efficient in two ways. First, they can respond in accordance with the specified contingencies about an unpleasant consequence, such as flunking a test, and avoid actually experiencing the unpleasantness. Second, they can react appropriately (taking the stairs in a fire) to a situation even though they have never experienced the threatened consequence (being trapped in an elevator in a burning building).

Rule-governed behavior is an action that carries out or is controlled by a prescription given in a stated rule (Biglan, 2005; Hayes, 1989). If we carried out the prescriptions of the rules just described—that is, we used the stairs in a fire, did the assigned reading, and spelled received correctly—we'd be engaging in rule-governed behaviors.

HOW RULES GOVERN BEHAVIOR

In most cases, a rule is a discriminative stimulus (S^D) and serves as an antecedent: Thinking of or being told the rule sets the occasion for performing the prescribed behavior. If a teacher asks students to spell *receive* and states the rule, "Remember, *i* before *e* except after *c*," they'll probably spell the word correctly and receive reinforcement. If a parent says to a child, "If you touch the stove when this light is on, you'll get burned," the child might hold a hand over the stove, feel that it is hot, and see that the rule is correct. In each of these cases, the rule is a verbal prompt, a shortcut stimulus control method we discussed in Chapter 11.

Why do we learn rules? A rule is learned because it specifies the behavior, the consequence it states is confirmed, and following the rule's prescription is reinforced—by positive reinforcement in the case of spelling correctly and negative reinforcement by knowing we can avoid being burned (either in a burning building or a hot stove). In each of these instances, failing to follow the rule is likely to result in punishment. Another way that negative reinforcement may be involved in learning rules is when a rule elicits an aversive emotion. For example, thinking that we will flunk a test if we don't read an assignment may elicit anxiety, and following the rule's prescribed behavior—that is, doing the reading—may reduce that aversive emotion.

WHEN ARE RULES ESPECIALLY USEFUL?

One circumstance when rules are very useful is when they are formalized in a *behavioral contract* in a self-management program. In Chapter 24, we saw that a behavioral contract describes the target behavior, circumstances when it should be performed (antecedents), and consequences that will result when the target person does or does not perform it. In other words, the contract states the rule in writing. For example, a contract for increasing sixth-grader Brad's studying might specify exactly what behaviors qualify as studying, when those behaviors should occur, and the reinforcers he will receive for performing them. Brad's studying when the rule is in force would be an example of rule-governed behavior. Rules are also useful when:

- *The target behavior's consequences will be delayed.* For instance, suppose the parents of a teenaged girl wanted her to clean her room every Sunday and stated the following rule: "If you clean your room to our satisfaction on Sunday by late afternoon, you may watch your favorite TV show that night." The corollary is that if she does not clean her room on Sunday, she can't watch or record the show. Knowing this rule would help bridge the delay, maintaining the girl's motivation to do the cleaning.

- *Natural reinforcers for the target behavior don't occur often enough.* For example, natural reinforcement for an owner-salesperson of a store generally involves making a sale, which adds to the profit he or she will take home. During certain times in any week or even across periods of the year, business may be slow, but keeping the store stocked and looking neat and attractive is important. Having a rule, such as "Keeping the store attractive and well stocked will bring in customers, and some of them are likely to buy," can bridge the delay and maintain motivation.

- *Rapid behavioral change is highly desirable.* This is particularly true in two situations: (a) when performing an undesirable behavior can lead to severe punishment or injury, as in taking an elevator in a burning building; and (b) if overcoming a behavioral deficit can yield reinforcers that are highly desirable, such as passing a course the person is currently flunking or improving a sports skill to a professional level. In the latter instance, the skill might be concentration, and the rule might be, "If I focus on the motions of the pitcher and the ball as it approaches, and don't get distracted by things the other infielders do, I'll swing the bat better and get more hits."

Rules are likely to be most effective in leading to the desired behavior if they are stated clearly. That is, the rule should describe the antecedents, behavior, and consequences specifically, not vaguely. For example, saying to a child, "Be good at the dentist's office," is vague, whereas "If you sit still while the dentist examines your teeth, you may ride your bike when we get home" is much clearer and more complete. Rules are also more effective when they describe consequences that are likely to occur and very important to the target person: Reinforcers should be highly desirable, and punishers should be undesirable. Although rule-governed behavior has many advantages, the person must have sufficient verbal skills to use rules. (Go to 📄.)

VERBAL BEHAVIOR

The dictionary definition of *verbal* is "of, relating to, or consisting of words." In applied behavior analysis, the term **verbal behavior** refers to an action that uses language and results in a consequence—verbal behavior that

CONCEPT CHECK 26.1

Check your understanding of the preceding concepts. Remember: The symbol ⇔ means that the answer can vary. Answer the following questions about rule-governed behavior.

1. A teacher saying to a class, "If you line up quietly, we'll leave for the playground right away and you'll have an extra 5 minutes there," is an example of stating a(n) _____ .
2. In the preceding question, the students lining up quietly would be an example of _____ behavior.
3. Rules are often formalized in writing in a self-management _____ .
4. Rules are very useful when the target behavior's reinforcers will be _____ . ⇔
5. An example of a poorly stated rule parents might give their child is _____ . ⇔

receives reinforcement is strengthened or maintained. Verbal behavior can be *vocal* (spoken) or *nonvocal*, such as written, typed, or gestural acts; an example of gestural acts is using sign language. The focus in behavior analysis on the role of consequences in using and developing language derives from a book by B. F. Skinner (1957) called *Verbal Behavior*. In social interaction, verbal behavior involves a *speaker*, or communicator, and a *listener*, or recipient: The speaker performs the vocal or nonvocal verbal behavior; the listener reacts with a consequence. The term *listener* is used broadly and can involve just reading. (Go to 🔍.)

TYPES OF VERBAL BEHAVIOR

Skinner (1957) identified six types of verbal behavior. We'll discuss two of them, mands and tacts; Table 26.1 describes the remaining four. Our focus will be on mands and tacts because they are among the earliest verbal behaviors children acquire and often form the basis for development of other types of verbal behavior (Bijou & Baer, 1965).

Mands

A **mand** is a verbal behavior that requests something the speaker needs or wants. The strength or clarity of the request can vary: A mand can just imply the desire for an item or act, or it could state it as a demand. For example, 2-year-olds who want to be picked up might use an unclear mand, such as just crying, or a clear mand, such as reaching their arms up and saying, "Up." An important characteristic of mands is that their form or content is determined by a *motivating operation*, such as hunger or discomfort (see Chapters 5 and 9). Here are some examples of vocal mands:

- "Please pass the potatoes."
- "Stop making that noise!"
- "Could you help me measure this?"
- "Do you have this shirt in blue?"
- "Could you get me an aspirin for my headache?"
- "Where's the nearest gas station?"

Receiving the requested item or action reinforces performing the mand, which can involve positive reinforcement, such as receiving the potatoes, or negative reinforcement, as in the noise ending. Mands can be made vocally or nonvocally—for instance, to gain a refund of some money, you could ask for it in person or in a letter. Learning to mand appropriately is very important: When motivating operations are strong, stating a mand enables individuals to obtain what they need or want and prevents them from acquiring undesirable behaviors, such as grabbing another child's toy instead of asking for it. Learning to mand also enables the

Table 26.1 *Definitions and Examples of Four of Skinner's Six Types of Verbal Behaviors*

Type	Definition	Examples
Echoic	Repeating or copying with point-to-point correspondence the words presented vocally or nonvocally.	Saying *hat* when requested to "Say hat"; writing or typing a copy of words from a book.
Intraverbal	Answering a question with words not included in the question.	Answering *Albany* to "What is the capital of New York State?
Textual	Translating words from one mode (e.g., print) to another (e.g., speech).	Reading from a book; signing the words someone spoke.
Transcription	Writing or spelling (vocally or finger spelling) requested words.	Writing *cat* and spelling *d-o-g* when asked vocally to write *cat* and spell *dog*.

CLOSE-UP

Manual "Speaking": Two Nonvocal Verbal Behaviors

Two nonvocal verbal behaviors, used mainly for communication with people who are deaf or unable to talk, are performed manually: sign language and finger spelling. The speaker makes arm and hand movements to communicate with the listener. These movements take the place of and function like speech. In sign language, the arm and hand movements represent words or phrases; in finger spelling, each specific formation of fingers represents a letter of the alphabet. Figure 26-1 depicts a few signed words and finger-spelled letters. Notice that recognizing the word that a sign represents often requires seeing a sequence of movements, as in the signs for *last week* and *read*.

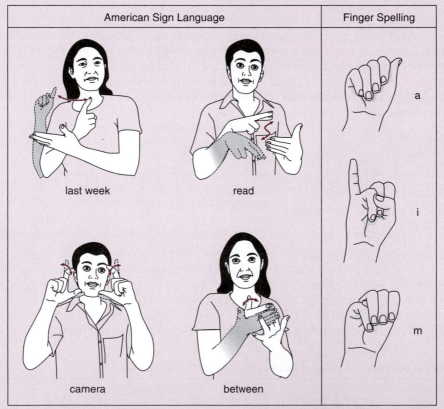

Figure 26-1 Examples of nonvocal verbal behavior: (a) manual signs of American Sign Language and (b) finger-spelled letters that make up the word *aim*. Notice the extensive motion sequence in the signs for *last week* and *read*, but not for *camera* and *between*. Seeing the motion sequence is critical for reading many signs. For complete lists of the manual signs and finger-spelled alphabet, consult www.handspeak.com.

person to experience a variety of reinforcers. Notice the phrase "to mand" in the preceding sentence—the word *mand* can also be used as a verb. For instance, we can say, "She is manding," or "He manded."

Tacts

A **tact** is a verbal behavior that names or identifies an item or event. The form or content of this type of verbal behavior is determined by an S^D, not a motivating operation. An example of a tact is when a child answers, "A coat," when shown a coat (the S^D) and asked, "What is this?" Feedback and praise, such as "That's right" or "Good girl," are common reinforcers for tacts given to answer a question. The S^D can involve any sense modality—for example, we can name or identify a song we hear or the spice we taste. Some other examples of tacts are:

- Naming the correct color when asked, "What color is this truck?"
- Saying, "This is a ripe peach," after gently squeezing several peaches.
- Writing "lower back" on a doctor's form that asks the location of your pain.
- Signing, "Tom's cooking supper," to a friend who's deaf.
- Writing on a postcard, "The picture is of Hyde Park gardens, which we enjoyed."

Like mands, tacts can be vocal or nonvocal, and the word *tact* can also be used as a verb (as in *tacted* or *tacting*).

TRAINING MANDS AND TACTS

At 18 months of age, the average child understands about 200 words and uses about 50 of them in speaking (Sarafino & Armstrong, 1986). About 50% of their vocabulary consists of nouns; conjunctions (*and, or, if*) and prepositions (*in, for, from, with, to*) are almost completely absent. Over the next several years, the average child's vocabulary grows at a huge rate—over 1,700 words a year. By 3 years of age, only about one quarter of the child's speech consists of nouns because the number of verbs, adjectives, conjunctions, and prepositions has increased sharply. Children's first mands and tacts appear during their second year and typically consist of just one word, such as saying "Milk" when they want some milk or "Ball" if they want to call attention to the toy. By 3 years of age, these verbal behaviors become more complex and precise, such as saying "More milk" and "See ball."

Almost all of children's early progress in all six types of verbal behavior occurs not through formal training, but through everyday social interaction. For instance, in children's second year, they frequently engage in echoic behavior with family members. When children enter school, formal training begins in earnest; and if they have handicaps, such as being deaf or intellectually impaired, the training needs to be more structured and intensive. Although teachers provide formal training for all six of the types of verbal behavior Skinner (1957) described, we'll consider just ways to teach mands and tacts.

Mand training is complicated by the requirement that it must be paired with a motivating operation. For children with strong language skills, mands can usually be taught as rules, such as "If you want some more milk, say *more milk please.*" However, the pairing works best when the person experiences the motivating operation, performs the mand, and receives the desired item or event as reinforcement. If the child has learned few mands and has not had milk or other liquids for a couple of hours, it may be useful to prompt performance of the mand—for example, "Would you like some milk? Say *milk please.*" This procedure can work well for unconditioned reinforcers.

For conditioned reinforcers, the motivating operation may need to be constructed, such as by "blocking" performance of a behavioral chain by making one or more links in the chain temporarily impossible to do (Michael, 1988). This situation forms a method called *blocked-response conditioned establishing operation* (recall from Chapter 9 that an establishing operation is a motivating operation that increases the effectiveness of a consequence). If manding will result in the blocking being removed—that is, enabling the link's performance and completion of the chain—being able to perform the link becomes a reinforcer for the mand. This blocked-response procedure was used to train manding in two teenagers, a male and a female, who were deaf and had mental impairments (Hall & Sundberg, 1987). Each teen was trained to perform behavioral chains—for instance, to open and consume a can of fruit, the chain "consisted of taking the can opener, opening the can, pouring the fruit into the bowl, and eating the fruit with a spoon" (p. 46). An example of the mand training after the chain was well learned is as follows: The girl was given all of the objects needed for the canned fruit chain except the can opener, which she had to request by signing "can opener." She learned the mand and could use it even when the request (S^D) for her to open the can was stated differently.

Training in mands appears to have two benefits for the learner beyond being able to ask for and receive something he or she wants. First, a study found that training to make signed mands increases vocal responses in learners with developmental disabilities (Carbone, Sweeney-Kerwin, Attanasio, & Kasper, 2010). Some professionals have assumed that teaching signing to children with minimal verbal skills would impair their learning to talk. Second, teaching children with autism to mand for answers to questions they can't answer, such as having them mand, "I don't know; please tell me," helps them learn to answer questions, such as, "Where do you live?" (Ingvarsson & Hollobaugh, 2010). Similarly, training typically developing (nondisabled) children in tacts helps them learn to answer questions (Petursdóttir, Ólafsdóttir, & Aradóttir, 2008).

Tact training procedures generally involve the teacher asking a question about an item or event and reinforcing the correct response with praise, such as "That's right." We'll consider two studies, each of which provided training in both tacts and mands. The first study pretested nursery school children and identified nine who did not demonstrate the tacts and mands to be trained (Lamarre & Holland, 1985). They were then trained in tacts or mands with two objects, a toy dog and a flower, and the correct answer they would need to give to questions would be saying, "On the left" or "On the right." Four of the children were trained in tacts: On any trial, the dog and flower were placed next to each other on a table, and the child was asked either "Where is the dog?" or "Where is the flower?" The correct answer received praise. While the children were learning to tact, they were assessed occasionally for being able to demonstrate the corresponding mand: They were given the chance to decide where an object would be placed on the table—they were asked, "Where would you like me to put the dog [or flower]?" Answering this question correctly indicated that they had acquired the corresponding mand, even though they had not been specifically trained for it. The remaining five children were trained in mands: The dog or flower was placed where they requested when they were asked, "Where would you like me to put the dog [or flower]?" The teacher's placing the object in the requested position was the reinforcer. While learning the mand, the children were also assessed occasionally for the corresponding tact for which they had received no specific training. The results showed that the children learned the trained tacts and mands but did not acquire the corresponding mands and tacts for which they did not receive training.

The second study trained both tacts and mands to each of six preschool children by having them construct four toys, such as a crane, by assembling three parts (Carroll & Hesse, 1987). Because the children already had some knowledge of some of the parts, the parts were given made-up names, such as "tarmen" and "binkle," during training. Each child received training in tacts for two of the toys and training in both tacts and mands for the two other toys. During tact training, the teacher presented each part for a toy as an S^D and said, "This is a [name of part]. What is this?" and then reinforced each correct answer with praise. During tact-and-mand training, the two types of verbal behavior were alternated: Tact training was carried out with the procedure described in the preceding sentence, and mand training used a blocked-response conditioned establishing operation—for example, a child was asked to "Make a crane [or other toy]," but one part was missing; the child had to request it (make a mand, such as "Give tarmen"). Receiving the part was the reinforcer for manding correctly. The results revealed that the children learned the trained tacts and mands and that learning the mands made it easier to learn the tacts—that is, the children learned the tacts in fewer trials in the tact-and-mand training condition than in the tact-only training condition. These results, and those of others (Petursdóttir, Ólafsdóttir, & Aradóttir, 2008), suggest that learning tacts can be made easier when their training is combined with mand training.

Children with intellectual disabilities—such as autism or mental retardation—typically need extra structure and help in learning mands and tacts. Two examples come from studies of training verbal behaviors in children with autism. One study found that prompting and shaping methods helped such children learn mands (Thomas, Lafasakis, & Sturmey, 2010). Another study found that training in mands and tacts can be enhanced by combining them with echoic training for the same words (Kodak & Clements, 2009). (Go to .)

STUDY AND REVIEW

SUMMARY

A rule describes a contingency for an antecedent, a behavior, and a consequence. It is an S^D and serves as an antecedent, often in the form of a verbal prompt. An action that is performed under the control of a rule is called rule-governed behavior. We learn rules when performing their prescribed behaviors receives positive or negative reinforcement. Rules are useful in several circumstances, such as when they are included in behavioral contracts and the behavior's consequences will be delayed, when natural reinforcers occur infrequently, and when rapid change is desirable. They are particularly effective when stated clearly and the consequences are very important to the target person and are very likely to occur.

A vocal or nonvocal action that uses language and results in a consequence is called verbal behavior. Two examples of nonvocal verbal behavior are communicating through sign language and finger-spelling words. There are six types of verbal behavior: mands, tacts, echoic, intraverbal, textual, and transcription. Mands request an item or action, and receiving the item or action reinforces the mand. The form and content of mands are determined by motivating operations. Tacts name or identify items or events; receiving feedback, such as with praise, usually reinforces it.

Children's vocabulary increases at an astounding rate during the several years after 18 months of age, and so does their verbal behavior. These increases generally occur through social interactions, without formal training. Mand training is most effective when it pairs the mand, such as "Water please," with its motivating operation (being thirsty). A useful approach for constructing a motivating operation for conditioned reinforcers in mand training is called the blocked-response conditioned establishing operation. In tact training, a teacher asks a question about an item or event (such as "What are you eating for breakfast?"), the individual answers, and the teacher provides praise as a reinforcer. Tact training appears to be easier when it is combined with mand training.

CONCEPT CHECK 26.2

Answer the following questions about verbal behavior.

1. Copying material word for word from a book is an example of _____ verbal behavior.
2. Saying "May I have some juice please" is an example of a(n) _____ .
3. An example of a tact an airplane passenger might use is _____ . ⇔
4. A type of verbal behavior in addition to mands, tacts, and echoic is _____ . ⇔
5. Asking "This is a ball. What is this?" might be used in _____ training.

> To prepare for exams, use the following key terms and review questions and the online study guide that's available on this book's companion website at www.wiley.com/college/sarafino.

KEY TERMS

rule-governed behavior   mand
verbal behavior   tact

ANSWERS TO CONCEPT CHECKS (CCs)

CC26.1 *Answers:* **1.** rule **2.** rule-governed **3.** behavioral contract **4.** delayed (or infrequent) **5.** "Be nice when Granny is here."

CC26.2 *Answers:* **1.** echoic **2.** mand **3.** "This seat is 27A" **5.** intraverbal tact

REVIEW QUESTIONS

1. Define the term *verbal behavior*, and describe how it can include vocal and nonvocal acts.
2. Define the term *mand*, and describe three examples of it that were not included in this book. What determines its form or content?
3. What is the reinforcer for performing a mand?
4. Define the term *tact*, and describe three examples of it that were not included in this book.
5. Describe the language development of typical children from $1\frac{1}{2}$ to 5 years of age.
6. Describe how you would teach a young child to mand a request for help in buttoning a shirt.
7. Define the procedure called *blocked-response conditioned establishing operation*, and describe when it is useful in teaching mands.
8. Describe the research procedure and findings of Lamarre and Holland (1985) on training mands and tacts.
9. Describe the research procedure and findings of Carroll and Hesse (1987) on training mands and tacts.

RELATED READINGS

- Hayes, S. C. (1989). *Rule-governed behavior: Cognition, contingencies, and instructional control.* New York: Plenum Press.
- Partington, J. W., & Sundberg, M. L. (1998). *The assessment of basic language and learning skills (The ABLLS).* Pleasant Hill, CA: Behavior Analysts, Inc.
- Skinner, B. F. (1957). *Verbal behavior.* New York: Appleton-Century-Crofts.

27

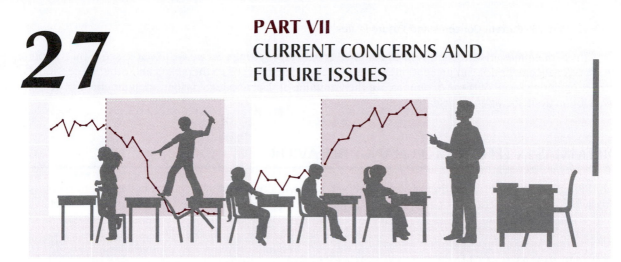

DILEMMAS AND ETHICS

PROLOGUE

Cory, an 11-year-old boy with mental retardation, was a student in a school that permitted the use of restrictive punishment procedures only when a pupil performed an extreme act of aggression or property destruction, which he did often (Grace, Kahng, & Fisher, 1994). To test the effects of following the school's rules, researchers applied a nonpainful punishment technique. The punishment consisted of crossing Cory's arms across his chest, guiding him to a seated position on the floor, and holding him there for 3 minutes. We saw in Chapter 18 that this method is called *basket-hold time-out*.

During some phases of the intervention, the therapist applied this punishment technique only after Cory performed very severe aggressive or destructive acts, such as forcefully striking another person or throwing furniture. In other phases, the therapist used the technique after very severe acts *and* moderately severe acts, such as shoving someone or pushing objects off a table. Cory's aggressive and destructive behaviors in these different phases were compared. Punishing *both* the very severe and moderately severe acts resulted in an almost total elimination of Cory's aggressive and destructive behaviors. Punishing only the very severe acts was much less successful in decreasing his aggressive and destructive behaviors. These findings present a dilemma: Should the school change its policy about the use of punishment?

Ethical dilemmas arise frequently in educational and therapy settings. As we are about to see in this chapter, efforts to change behavior can present dilemmas of many different types to therapists and other professionals. After considering some of these dilemmas, we then examine ethical and legal issues and guidelines in applied behavior analysis therapy and research.

DILEMMAS IN EFFORTS TO CHANGE BEHAVIOR

The dilemmas therapists and other professionals often face in their efforts to change behavior can be placed into two categories: those that pertain to the behavior change *goals* and those that pertain to the behavior change *methods* of the intervention.

ARE THE BEHAVIOR CHANGE GOALS ACCEPTABLE?

Most interventions involve target behaviors and behavioral goals that almost everyone would agree are appropriate and useful for a behavior change intervention. Few people would disagree with the goals of improving children's academic performance, reducing excessively disruptive classroom conduct, decreasing severely aggressive behavior, reducing serious anxiety problems, eliminating self-injurious behavior among children with developmental disabilities, and increasing behaviors that promote health and fitness. **Goal acceptability** refers to the degree to which the outcome or behavioral goals are fair, appropriate, and reasonable. What factors determine the acceptability of behavior change goals?

Deciding If Behavior Change Goals Are Acceptable

We are likely to think the goals of a behavior change program are acceptable if they meet two broad *goal acceptability criteria*: First, the goals should have a high degree of *social validity*—that is, they should be desired by society and appropriate for the target person's life (Wolf, 1978). Second, the goals should involve a *clinically significant* (see Chapter 3) improvement that we can realistically hope to achieve. We can evaluate whether the goals of a behavior change program meet these acceptability criteria by answering several relevant questions, each starting with the phrase, "Would achieving the goals":

- Be a likely prospect, given research evidence on the success of the planned methods with similar behavior problems?
- Greatly improve the target person's general adaptive functioning—by, for example, enabling him or her to socialize more effectively?
- Substantially decrease the likelihood of physical or psychological harm to oneself, such as from self-injurious behavior?
- Markedly reduce the likelihood that the client will physically or psychologically harm someone else—for instance, a teacher or classmate?
- Greatly decrease reasonable difficulties that other people experience with the target person's behavior?
- Bring the target behavior to a normal level for the target person's age and gender?

Although an affirmative answer to at least one of these questions suggests that the behavior change goals might be acceptable, a *no* answer to the first question severely limits goal acceptability. Keep in mind that these are not the only criteria societies have invoked in deciding whether a program's behavior change goals were acceptable—and sometimes these other criteria have led to strong controversies. (Go to 🔍.)

CLOSE-UP

Trying to Make Gays Straight

Society's criteria for the acceptability of behavior change goals are profoundly affected by current beliefs. We can see this in the history of efforts to alter the sexual orientation of gay males and females (lesbians), based on the belief that being a homosexual is a "wrong," learned "choice" that can be changed.

What Causes Homosexuality?

Two of the most widely held views on the development of homosexuality propose that people become gay because of the experiences they have. One theory is based on respondent conditioning: Homosexual preference is learned through conditioning. This view proposes that a person might acquire such conditioning if a same-sex person (the conditioned stimulus, CS) were paired with the individual's sexual arousal (the unconditioned stimulus, US), perhaps through seduction or sexual exploration. The other theory is based on the Freudian psychodynamic view that parent–child relationships determine sexual orientation—for instance, males become gay because their fathers are detached and ineffectual, providing a poor role model, and their mothers are dominating and overprotective. But extensive research on the upbringing and experiences of homosexuals has failed to find much support for either of these theories (Bell, Weinberg, & Hammersmith, 1981; Garnets & Kimmel, 1991; O'Donohue & Plaud, 1994; Storms, 1983).

   Rather, this research has revealed three critical findings. First, the parent–child relationships experienced by homosexuals and heterosexuals while growing up are not very different. Second, although siblings share the same parents, who might in fact consist of an ineffectual father and dominating mother, the siblings of a child who turns out to be gay will not necessarily be gay, too. Third, gay men and women very often report being able to trace their homosexual feelings to their childhood years, long before they ever had sexual relations or even knew what sex was. What's more, some evidence suggests a substantial influence of biological factors, such as genetics, in the development of homosexuality (Angier, 1995; Byne, 1994; LeVay & Hamer, 1994).

The Failure of "Conversion" Therapies

Many different *conversion* (or "reparative") *therapies* have been designed and applied to change clients' sexual preferences from gay to heterosexual (Haldeman, 1994). Some of these therapies have followed psychodynamic procedures; others use behavioral methods, mainly involving aversive methods; and others use fundamentalist Christian programs of "reorientation counseling." In aversion therapy methods, electric shock or other aversive stimuli have been paired with sexually arousing photographs or thoughts (Barlow, 1978). Research on conversion therapies has shown that *none of these therapies is effective in changing sexual orientation*, even among individuals who want very much to change (Crary, 2009; Haldeman, 1994). Perhaps this should not be surprising. After all, would you expect conversion therapy to be effective in changing people's sexual preferences from heterosexual to homosexual?

   In clinical practice years ago, Gerald Davison was a prominent psychologist who pioneered the use of behavioral methods to try to change sexual orientation. In 1976, three years after the American Psychiatric Association had declared that homosexuality would no longer be considered an "illness," he wrote an article questioning the effectiveness of conversion therapy and detailing ethical objections to applying those therapies. Other professional organizations—including the American Medical Association, American Psychological Association, and National Association of Social Workers—have arrived at similar conclusions and recommend against the use of these forms of therapy. Conversion therapies clearly do not meet the goal acceptability criteria outlined earlier.

Examples of Dilemmas in Behavior Change Goals

Occasionally, social and moral questions regarding the behavior change goals in therapy make the choice of goals controversial. Here we look at two very different examples in which choosing the goals of therapy might present dilemmas for many people. Each example begins by expressing the dilemma with a question.

The first dilemma is, *Should a therapy program pursue the goal of helping obese individuals achieve normal weight levels by dieting?* Considerable evidence indicates that being obese—that is, being more than 20% overweight for one's gender, height, and frame size—puts individuals at high risk of developing and dying from heart disease, hypertension, and diabetes (Sarafino & Smith, 2011). This evidence has provided the basis for the development of weight control programs in many nations to promote health, and some employers have introduced policies that overweight workers must lose weight or lose their jobs. But a controversy about the value of dieting developed around 1990, when an anti-dieting movement formed (Brownell & Rodin, 1994). Leaders of this movement claimed that (a) diets almost always fail, (b) genetic factors make permanent weight reduction impossible for many people, and (c) obese people who do manage to lose weight and keep it off do not necessarily live longer. These claims are extreme, but they are not entirely wrong. For instance, although most people who lose weight do not keep it off for more than a year, many maintain their weight loss for years. Behavioral methods are more effective than other treatments in helping people lose weight and keep it off. Is the goal of losing weight worth pursuing in therapy if many people fail? Would the goal be worth pursuing if people who kept the weight off didn't live very much longer than they otherwise would have?

The second dilemma is, *Should a therapy program pursue the goal of decreasing children's extremely oppositional and aggressive behavior if doing so requires getting them to play alone much of the time?* Wahler and Fox (1980) applied behavioral methods with four 5- to 8-year-old boys to reduce their problem behaviors, which included failing to comply with requests, temper tantrums, destroying property, fighting, and hitting their parents. After the baseline phase, each child experienced solitary and cooperative play interventions in separate phases of a few weeks each. In the *solitary play* intervention, being reinforced required that the child play alone, quietly, and without interacting with others in any way. In the *cooperative play* intervention, being reinforced required that the child play with family members in a cooperative manner with no rule violations. Observations revealed that the children's oppositional behavior decreased during solitary play phases, but not during cooperative play phases, and that all other social interactions decreased during solitary play phases, too. The researchers

This couple has chosen to exercise as part of a weight-loss program. Although most dieters regain the lost weight within a year, many succeed in keeping it off for years. *Source:* Masterfile.

concluded that treatments emphasizing solitary behaviors may be more effective in reducing oppositional behavior than approaches stressing appropriate social interaction. They also pointed out that critics might feel that encouraging children with high levels of oppositional behavior simply to become less sociable would not be an acceptable way of correcting the behavior problem.

Dilemmas are often hard to resolve. When we arrive at a resolution, we tend to base our judgment on our value systems. For example, you may believe that making a child less sociable is too high a "price to pay" for being able to decrease oppositional behavior as effectively as possible. But other people, such as parents and teachers who must deal with that behavior, may have different value systems and not agree with you.

ARE THE BEHAVIOR CHANGE METHODS ACCEPTABLE?

Another issue of importance in therapy is popular acceptability of the behavior change treatments. **Treatment acceptability** refers to the extent to which the client and community consider the methods of a behavior change program to be *fair, appropriate, and reasonable* for the circumstances (Kazdin, French, & Sherick, 1981; Wolf, 1978). Treatment acceptability is part of the assessment of social validity (see Chapter 3), in which the goals, procedures, and outcomes of interventions are evaluated. Evaluating treatment acceptability is important for two principal reasons: to protect clients' rights and to make the intervention agreeable to clients so they will participate fully in the treatment (Singh, Lloyd, & Kendall, 1990; Wacker et al., 1990).

Treatments Involving Aversive Stimuli

Probably the greatest concerns regarding treatment acceptability relate to methods that apply physically aversive stimuli, either as punishers or as USs in aversion therapy. As we have seen in earlier chapters, there are compelling reasons to avoid procedures that use physically aversive stimuli and reserve them for cases in which all other methods derived from careful functional assessments have failed to change the behavior. When aversive stimuli are used as punishers, their severity or restrictiveness should be as mild as possible while still allowing the intervention to succeed in reducing the unwanted behavior. Two useful procedures covered in earlier chapters can be used to protect clients from harm and safeguard their rights (Green, 1990). First, the therapist should identify an appropriate professional committee that can review the plan to use aversive methods and seek their approval. Second, the therapist should fully describe the aversive methods to the client or guardian and seek their consent to use those methods.

Careful scrutiny regarding the use of aversive stimuli has been applied to programs for improving the behaviors and skills of children, particularly those who are developmentally disabled (Singh, Lloyd, & Kendall, 1990). In some cases, advocacy groups and professional organizations have issued policy statements to guide or restrict the use of punishment techniques of certain types. Unfortunately, the recommendations these organizations have developed are often contradictory. Some organizations oppose the use of all painful stimuli, but others take the position that painful stimuli may be used under very restricted circumstances. An example of such circumstances is when the target behavior is harmful to the client or others and has not been reduced by other methods. When contradictory recommendations exist, which ones should therapists follow? Should they simply follow the recommendations of the organization whose value system or beliefs most closely match their own?

Dilemmas often arise when therapists recognize that alternative treatments have failed to decrease a potentially harmful behavior and physically aversive punishment may be the only alternative to doing nothing. In such instances, it is helpful to consider whether the ends justify the means. Goldiamond (1974) has described a thought-provoking case. A little girl in an institution was being made to wear a padded football helmet and had her hands tied to her crib to protect her from self-injurious head-banging behavior. In her efforts to take off the helmet, the child tossed her head violently and pulled out her hair whenever she got the chance. Her head was constantly bruised and bald. Eventually the child was placed in a different program, in which punishment was introduced for her self-injurious behaviors. The punishment consisted of the therapist shouting, "Don't!" and administering a sharp slap on the cheek. After fewer than a dozen instances of this punishment method, the self-injurious behavior stopped, the helmet was removed, her hair began to grow back, and her social behaviors began to improve. When the original institution and the girl's parents learned of the slapping, however, they removed her from the new program and returned her to the institution, where her behavior regressed and she was again restrained in her crib and required to wear a helmet. We can now ask ourselves two questions: Was using physical punishment acceptable in this case? Was it acceptable to return her to the original treatment conditions?

Sometimes schools and psychiatric institutions restrict the use of punishment procedures that are not painful, but are *intrusive*, or forced on individuals without their permission. For instance, the institutions may not allow under any circumstance the use of time-out or response cost procedures. We've seen in earlier chapters that most behavior analysts would disagree with these policies and take the view that some circumstances can justify using almost any type of punisher, even physically aversive stimuli.

Assessing Treatment Acceptability

The procedure used in assessing treatment acceptability involves having individuals fill out rating scales to evaluate the methods applied in interventions (Elliott, 1988). Several rating instruments have been developed for this purpose and are becoming more and more widely used. The instruments can be filled out by clients, relatives or friends of clients, teachers or coworkers of clients, hospital staff, and members of the general community (Schwartz & Baer, 1991). Because the assessments can serve various purposes, the intended purpose determines whose judgments would be sought. Thus we would have clients rate the treatment methods if we wanted to know whether they would participate fully in their own therapy, and we would have teachers or hospital staff rate the treatment methods if we wanted to know how motivated they would be to learn the techniques and administer them carefully.

The idea of assessing treatment acceptability may seem simple on the surface, but the factors affecting the ratings are actually very complex. The ratings people give depend on the exact wording used in describing the treatments and tend to be higher if a rationale for the method is given and the rater has a good understanding of the treatment procedures (Elliott, 1988). Ratings of treatment acceptability also tend to be higher when the client's behavior problem is very severe, there are few undesirable side effects from the treatment, the methods involve reinforcement rather than punishment, and the cost in time and effort is low (Jones, Singh, & Kendall, 1998; O'Brien & Karsh, 1990; Wacker et al., 1990). Acceptability ratings also tend to be higher if the therapist has obtained the consent of the client or guardian and approval from an appropriate committee (discussed later) to use the techniques. (Go to ▤.)

ETHICAL AND LEGAL ISSUES IN THERAPY AND RESEARCH

Many different ethical concerns and issues can emerge when psychology professionals conduct therapy, diagnostic assessments, and research; and improper actions regarding some ethical issues can make the professional subject to legal action. Professionals who are engaged in therapy, assessments, and research are expected to carry out these activities at a high level of competence and take measures to protect the rights and safety of clients and subjects.

An important mechanism that is available to protect clients and participants in research is the *institutional review board* (IRB) or other review committee. In the United States, the Department of Health and Human Services introduced the requirement that all institutions receiving direct or indirect funding from the government establish an IRB for the evaluation of proposals for conducting research, to assure that clients and subjects are protected from harm. These committees consist of at least five individuals who are not connected to the therapy or research in question and who can represent the views of significant and relevant elements of society, such as the general community, child welfare groups, and the fields of medicine and law. What's more, major professional organizations have developed guidelines as standards of general professional conduct and as rules

CONCEPT CHECK 27.1

Check your understanding of the preceding concepts. Remember: The symbol ⇔ means that the answer can vary. Answer the following questions about dilemmas in efforts to change behavior.

1. When behavior change goals involve clinically significant improvement and have a high degree of social validity, they meet the two main _____ criteria.
2. A finding that disconfirms a widely held view of homosexuality is that the parent–child relationships homosexuals and heterosexuals have when growing up are _____ .
3. All types of _____ therapies to change clients' sexual preferences appear to be ineffective.
4. A claim that the anti-dieting movement makes to argue against dieting is that _____ . ⇔
5. The extent to which the client and community consider the methods of a behavior change program to be fair, appropriate, and reasonable is called _____ .
6. Treatment acceptability is commonly assessed with _____ scales.

to guide the process of conducting therapy and research. We'll examine some guidelines that currently exist for professionals who study or apply principles of behavior change.

GENERAL PRINCIPLES FOR PSYCHOLOGISTS

Because psychologists work in many settings and roles, the American Psychological Association (APA, 2002) has developed a detailed set of ethical principles and codes of conduct to guide the behavior of psychologists in nearly all facets of their work. For instance, there are specific standards for explaining to the client the results of diagnostic assessments and for maintaining confidentiality. This code of ethics is divided into two sets of guidelines: general principles and ethical standards. The *general principles* are aspirations that psychologists should strive toward; the *ethical standards* constitute specific guidelines that the APA can enforce with sanctions. Five general principles apply broadly:

1. *Beneficence and non-malfeasance.* Psychologists try to benefit and do no harm to the individuals they work with or provide services for.
2. *Fidelity and responsibility.* Psychologists strive to establish trusting and consultative relationships with colleagues, clients, and others they work with in an effort to serve the best interests of those individuals and to prevent unethical conduct.
3. *Integrity.* Psychologists strive to be honest and fair toward others and in presenting descriptions of their qualifications and activities.
4. *Justice.* Psychologists oppose injustice in the distribution and quality of psychological services and procedures for all individuals.
5. *Respect for people's rights and dignity.* Psychologists respect people's rights to privacy, confidentiality, and autonomy and try to be aware of and sensitive to cultural and individual differences, particularly those related to "age, gender, gender identity, race, ethnicity, culture, national origin, religion, sexual orientation, disability, language, and socioeconomic status." (p. 1063)

The rest of this chapter describes more specific guidelines from relevant organizations to guide the manner in which professionals, including behavior analysts and behavior therapists, conduct therapy and research.

COMPETENCE AND TRAINING OF PROFESSIONALS IN APPLIED BEHAVIOR ANALYSIS

The Behavior Analyst Certification Board (BACB, 2011a) has outlined more than 100 specific tasks that all behavior analysts are expected to master. The tasks are separated into the 10 content areas described in Table 27.1. These content areas and tasks form the basis for an examination that the organization administers to professionals who want to receive certification as behavior analysts or associate behavior analysts (see Chapter 28). The content areas and tasks are also used in evaluating whether the BACB will provide accreditation for training programs in applied behavior analysis—for instance, the BACB specifies the number of contact hours the program must provide students for each of the content areas. For the BACB's full lists of tasks, detailed information of requirements for certification, and training programs with approved sequences of courses, visit the website at www.bacb.com.

ETHICAL SAFEGUARDS IN TREATMENT SETTINGS

The Association for Behavior Analysis International (ABAI, 2011) adopted in 1989 and continues to advance a set of positions called the Statement on the Right to Effective Behavioral Treatment. This statement lists six client rights to:

1. A *therapeutic environment* that includes opportunities for training, stimulation, and social interaction.
2. Services with the client's *personal welfare as the overriding goal*. This includes an assessment of treatment and goal acceptability.
3. Treatment administered by a *competent behavior analyst* who has had appropriate training and experience.
4. Interventions that *reduce behaviors that are dangerous or problematic and teach skills that are functional* in everyday life.

Table 27.1   *Behavior Analyst Task List, Third Edition*

Content Areas	Example Tasks to Be Mastered
1. Ethical considerations	Participate in professional development activities to update competence; protect clients' confidentiality; use the most effective treatment methods, consistent with applicable ethical standards.
2. Definition and characteristics	Be able to interpret behavior analysis journal articles and use behavior analytic terms to describe and explain behavior.
3. Principles, processes, and concepts	Be able to define and give examples of behavior analytic methods, such as positive and negative reinforcement and punishment, stimulus control, establishing operations, and mands.
4. Behavioral assessment	Be able to collect, organize, and interpret behavioral data and conduct functional analyses.
5. Experimental evaluation of interventions	Be able to use reversal, alternating treatment, multiple-baseline, and changing-criterion designs.
6. Measurement of behavior	Be able to use a variety of measures of behavior (for example, frequency, duration, and latency) and methods to evaluate data reliability and accuracy.
7. Displaying and interpreting behavioral data	Be able to select and use appropriate graphical displays, such as line graphs (with axes marked in equal intervals) and cumulative graphs, and interpret data from them.
8. Selecting intervention outcomes and strategies	Be able to conduct task analyses, recommend methods to clients, and select appropriate alternative responses.
9. Behavior change procedures	Be able to identify and apply positive and negative reinforcers and punishers, use and fade prompts, and use shaping and chaining procedures.
10. Systems support	Be able to design and apply strategies to monitor the integrity of intervention procedures and obtain support from people in the target person's natural environment to maintain the changed behavior.

Source: BACB (2011a). The full version of these tasks is available at www.bacb.com via the Site Contents page.

5. Objective *assessments of behavior* and its antecedents and consequences before and during treatment, and an ongoing evaluation of the treatment.

6. The *most effective treatments* available, considering the scientific evidence, the degree of restrictiveness of the methods, and the importance of producing quick, clinically significant behavior changes.

In addition, several organizations have issued specific guidelines to protect clients from harm in psychological therapy and to promote effective behavior change. One guideline commonly included in these codes is to obtain **informed consent** from the client or other legally authorized individual if the target person is too young or otherwise unable to give consent.

Two organizations with specific ethical guidelines are the BACB and the APA. The BACB adopted in 2004 the BACB Guidelines for Responsible Conduct, an extensive and detailed code of conduct that is divided into 10 topic areas, such as behavior analysts' professional conduct as a teacher or in research (BACB, 2011b). You can access the full document online at www.bacb.com. The APA has published ethics codes since 1953 and updates the codes periodically. The current version is in an article entitled *Ethical Principles of Psychologists and Code of Conduct* (APA, 2002), which details the standards of conduct for 10 topic areas, such as professional competence, privacy and confidentiality, and ways to resolve ethical issues.

To give you a sense of the issues involved in protecting clients from harm and promoting effective treatment, we'll examine the guidelines for therapy developed by the Association for the Advancement of Behavior Therapy (AABT, 1977). The AABT has published an extensive set of questions that therapists and other individuals can consider in evaluating the ethical standards of an intervention. Table 27.2 paraphrases these questions and gives an introductory explanation by the committee that developed them. Keep in mind that the questions were designed to apply broadly to professionals who provide all types of human services, not just those who conduct behavior therapy. As you examine these questions, you may notice that some touch on topics we have considered at various points in this book. Other questions cover issues we've not discussed before but are also important, such as the possibility of coercion to participate in therapy. If a therapist is planning or conducting an intervention, he or she should try to answer each question in the list. Answering *no* to any of these questions suggests that the program contains one or more features that may be ethically questionable. In such a case, revisions may be in order.

ETHICAL SAFEGUARDS IN RESEARCH

The APA has also developed guidelines to safeguard individuals' rights and protect from harm those who serve as participants, or subjects, in research (APA, 1982, 2002). These guidelines parallel and are similar to those used in therapy. The ethical safeguards in research include the following principles:

1. All individuals, regardless of their ages or other characteristics, have rights that supersede those of the researcher.

2. The researcher should (a) inform the participant of all features of the research that may affect his or her willingness to participate, and (b) answer the subject's questions in terms that are appropriate to his or her abilities to comprehend.

3. *Informed consent* should be obtained from the participant, if possible. If the participant is a child or an adult unable to give consent, it should be obtained in writing from his or her parents or individuals who have the legal authority or can reasonably act in loco parentis (teachers or directors of institutions, for example). Individuals giving consent should be informed of all features of the research that may affect their willingness to consent.

4. The researcher should respect the subject's freedom to choose *not* to participate in the research or to discontinue participation at any time without undue coercion to reconsider such decisions.

5. The researcher should not use any procedure that may harm the participant physically or psychologically. When harm seems possible, the researcher must consult an IRB for guidance and approval. This often means that the research will need to be postponed and redesigned or abandoned.

6. Concealing important information from participants or deceiving them should be avoided whenever possible. If such procedures are contemplated, the researcher must consult an IRB, demonstrate that alternative procedures are not feasible, and show that the research outcome will have considerable scientific or applied value. If the use of concealment or deception is allowed, the researcher must debrief the subjects to correct misconceptions

Table 27.2 *Questions for Evaluating Interventions*

The eight questions listed here were developed by a committee of the AABT for professionals to consider when evaluating therapeutic interventions in all types of human service. In the questions, the term *client* refers to the individual whose behavior is to be changed, but a guardian may be substituted if the client cannot understand the issues to be considered; *therapist* refers to the professional in charge of providing the treatment. Ideal interventions generally allow clients maximum involvement in planning and carrying out the treatment while taking into account societal pressures on the clients, the therapists, and the therapists' employers. Although ideal interventions would receive *yes* answers for all eight questions, exceptions to this rule are possible while still maintaining high ethical standards. As you examine these questions, assume that the evaluation is made continuously, both before and during the intervention.

1. *Have the client and therapist considered the goals of treatment adequately?* An answer of *yes* is based on whether (a) the goals were made explicit to the client, preferably in writing; (b) the therapist had the client restate the goals orally or in writing; (c) the therapist and client agreed on the goals; (d) the immediate interests of or benefits for the client are consistent with his or her long-term interests; and (e) the interests of the client are compatible with those of other relevant individuals.

2. *Has the therapist examined the choice of treatment methods adequately?* A *yes* answer is based on whether (a) the published literature indicates that the methods in the intervention are the best ones for treating the client's problem, (b) the methods used are consistent with accepted therapeutic practice, (c) the client was informed of alternative methods and their relative advantages and disadvantages, and (d) for treatment methods that are professionally, legally, or societally controversial, the therapist obtained approval through an ethical review by independent professionals.

3. *Is the client participating in treatment voluntarily?* To answer *yes*, the therapist should consider whether the client (a) is being coerced to participate, (b) was offered a choice of methods and therapists if the treatment was legally mandated, and (c) can withdraw from therapy without penalties beyond the loss of costs incurred for the treatment received.

4. *If some person or agency is legally empowered to arrange for treatment, have the interests of the client been considered adequately?* An answer of *yes* is based on whether (a) the client, although subordinated legally, was told of the treatment objectives and has had some input into the choices of treatment methods; (b) the empowered person or agency has discussed the goals and methods with the therapist and approved them; and (c) efforts were undertaken to make the interests of the client and those of the empowered person or agency compatible when their interests were in conflict.

5. *Does the intervention include procedures to assess treatment effectiveness?* A *yes* answer is based on whether (a) the intervention includes methods to assess the client's problem quantitatively and chart its progress, and (b) the client has access to these assessments during treatment.

6. *Is the confidentiality of the therapeutic relationship adequately protected?* An answer of *yes* is based on whether (a) the client's records are accessible only to authorized individuals, and (b) the client knows who has access to those records.

7. *Has the therapist referred the client to other professionals when necessary?* A *yes* answer is based on whether the client (a) was informed that he or she would receive a referral to another therapist if dissatisfied with the treatment, and (b) received an appropriate referral if the treatment was unsuccessful.

8. *Is the therapist qualified to perform the treatment?* Answering *yes* depends on whether (a) the therapist has had appropriate training or experience in treating problems like those of the client, (b) the client was informed of any deficits in the therapist's qualifications, (c) an unqualified professional has referred the client to or obtained careful supervision from a therapist who is qualified, and (d) the client was informed that a professional providing treatment is doing so under the supervision of a qualified therapist if such a circumstance exists.

Source: Based on AABT (1977).

preferably as soon as their participation has been completed. Debriefing entails describing the purpose of the research and explaining the need for deception (which may then be self-evident).

7. The researcher should keep confidential all information obtained about participants, unless the participants had agreed in advance to the open use of the information.

8. When research procedures result in unforeseen and undesirable circumstances for the participant, the researcher should take immediate action to correct the circumstances, including any long-term effects they may have on the subject.

(Go to 📖.)

CONCEPT CHECK 27.2

Answer the following questions about ethical and legal issues in therapy and research.

1. Committees mandated by the U.S. Department of Health and Human Services to review the ethics of research are called _____ .
2. The APA recommendation that psychologists should be aware of and sensitive to individual differences in culture, gender, sexual orientation, and religion is part of the general principle called _____ .
3. A client's or guardian's approval for therapy to proceed after learning what the procedures will be is called _____ .
4. A question the AABT recommends that professionals ask in evaluating the ethics of an intervention is _____ . ⟺
5. Whenever possible, researchers should avoid using _____ . ⟺

STUDY AND REVIEW

SUMMARY

Although most behavior change interventions involve outcome and behavioral goals that are generally acknowledged as being desirable, sometimes questions arise about the acceptability of certain goals for behavior change programs. An intervention's goals are likely to be viewed favorably if they meet two goal acceptability criteria: The goals should have a high degree of social validity, and they should propose achieving a clinically significant improvement. As an application of these criteria, we saw that although psychologists have used conversion therapies in attempts to change the sexual orientation of homosexuals, these efforts have not been successful, their behavioral goals do not meet acceptability criteria, and major professional organizations recommend against using them. Value systems play a large role in people's acceptance of the goals of an intervention.

Treatment acceptability refers to assessments of the fairness, appropriateness, and reasonableness of the behavior change methods. Using physically aversive stimuli in interventions presents problems for treatment acceptability and should be avoided whenever possible. If aversive stimuli are used, their severity and restrictiveness should be as mild as possible while still allowing the program to succeed in changing the target behavior. The acceptability of treatment methods can be assessed by having individuals fill out rating scales.

Because many ethical concerns can arise in conducting psychological therapy and research, institutional review boards or other review committees can be used to examine the plans and protect the rights of clients and research participants. Several professional organizations have developed principles to guide the behavior of psychologists and behavior analysts in research and therapy activities. These organizations include:

- American Psychological Association (APA)
- Behavior Analyst Certification Board (BACB)
- Association for Behavior Analysis International (ABAI)
- Association for Advancement of Behavior Therapy (AABT)

The guidelines they developed discuss broad issues, such as competence and integrity, and outline codes of conduct in very specific activities, such as selecting intervention methods and maintaining confidentiality.

Clients' rights in therapy and research can be protected with three mechanisms: (a) using institutional review boards, (b) assessing the social validity of the treatment, and (c) obtaining informed consent from the client or guardian. Ethical safeguards specific to research are also applied to protect the rights of participants.

> To prepare for exams, use the following key terms and review questions and the online study guide that's available on this book's companion website at www.wiley.com/college/sarafino.

KEY TERMS

goal acceptability   treatment acceptability   informed consent

ANSWERS TO CONCEPT CHECKS (CCs)

CC27.1 *Answers*: **1.** acceptability **2.** not very different **3.** conversion **4.** diets almost always fail **5.** treatment acceptability **6.** rating

CC27.2 *Answers*: **1.** institutional review boards **2.** respect for people's rights and dignity **3.** informed consent **4.** Is the client's participation voluntary? **5.** deception

REVIEW QUESTIONS

1. Describe the case study of Cory, and discuss the meaning of the outcome of the intervention for policies on using punishment.

2. What two acceptability criteria apply in deciding whether behavior change goals are acceptable?

3. Describe the questions one should ask in deciding if behavior change goals are acceptable.

4. Describe the evidence against the view that homosexuality is caused by children's experiences with their parents.

5. Pick one of the two dilemmas in behavior change goals discussed in the chapter, and present two arguments for and against the goals.

6. Define the term *treatment acceptability*.

7. What is an institutional review board (IRB)?

8. Describe four of the APA's general principles of ethics for psychologists.

9. Describe five of the BACB content areas presented in Table 27.1 that behavior analysts are expected to master.

10. Describe how you might use the AABT questions in Table 27.2 to judge the ethics of therapy.

11. Describe the ethical guidelines for doing psychological research.

RELATED READINGS

- APA (American Psychological Association). (1982). *Ethical principles in the conduct of research with human participants.* Washington, DC: Author.

- APA (American Psychological Association). (2002). Ethical principles of psychologists and code of conduct. *American Psychologist*, 57, 1061–1073.

- BACB (Behavior Analyst Certification Board). (2011a). BCBA® & BCBA® *Behavior Analyst Task List, Third Edition.* This document is available at www.bacb.com.

- BACB (Behavior Analyst Certification Board). (2011b). *Behavior Analyst Certification Board Guidelines for Responsible Conduct.* This document is available at www.bacb.com.

- Stolz, S. B., & Associates (1978). *Ethical issues in behavior modification.* San Francisco: Jossey-Bass.

28

FUTURE CHALLENGES FOR THE FIELD AND YOU

Challenges for Behavior Analysis
Improving the Field of Applied Behavior Analysis
Integrating Therapy Approaches
Enhancing the Image of Applied Behavior Analysis

Careers and Training in Behavior Analysis
Careers in Applied Behavior Analysis
Training in Applied Behavior Analysis

Study and Review

PROLOGUE

 A student of mine named Greg worked at an institution for children with autism while he took my course. After graduating, he completed graduate work and continued to work at the same institution, applying behavior analysis techniques and conducting research. In his career, he has contributed to the growth of the field and improved the lives of the children he has treated and those of their families. If you are impressed with the effectiveness of the behavior analysis approach and want to apply its methods and contribute to its growth, this chapter may help you plan your next steps and your long-term future.

   We've covered a lot of ground in this book as we examined principles of applied behavior analysis, and we've seen that these principles have great potential for benefiting individuals and societies. You now have a clear picture of what these principles are and how to apply them successfully. In this last chapter, we look at some challenges the discipline faces for the future, the career goals you may have that involve the application of behavior analysis techniques, and how you can pursue those goals.

CHALLENGES FOR BEHAVIOR ANALYSIS

We've seen that the techniques of applied behavior analysis are highly effective; often produce obvious improvements in behavior quickly, sometimes in just a few sessions; and can be applied in a wide variety of settings to change almost any behavioral deficit or excess. These techniques are generally at least as effective as other methods in changing behavior. Although the techniques of applied behavior analysis possess significant strengths, they have some limitations, too (Goldfried & Castonguay, 1993). The field has some important challenges for the future.

IMPROVING THE FIELD OF APPLIED BEHAVIOR ANALYSIS

Despite the success of applied behavior analysis methods, sometimes behavior change programs fail or don't correct the target behavior as quickly as desired or expected. We'll consider two reasons for these difficulties. First, although functional assessments are widely used today, some professionals who design behavior change programs probably still use "intuitive" processes instead of functional assessments in choosing treatment methods. Functional assessment is one of the most important advances in treatment with applied behavior analysis techniques since the 1980s and has made these techniques more effective and efficient (Ervin et al., 2001). Second, behavior analysis techniques are not always implemented correctly. For instance, staff members who administer interventions may become lax in applying the techniques if they are not carefully and periodically trained and monitored in their efforts (Harchik, Sherman, Sheldon, & Strouse, 1992).

These difficulties suggest that we can improve the field of applied behavior analysis by enhancing the care with which interventions are designed and implemented. In the remainder of this section, we consider how the effectiveness and cost–benefit documentation of behavior change methods can be improved.

Improving the Effectiveness of Applied Behavior Analysis

In Chapter 15 we discussed a study with a boy named Walsh, whose aggressive behaviors were maintained by more than one reinforcer (Borrero & Vollmer, 2006). To decrease his aggression, the researchers addressed each of the reinforcers in sequence—for example, by eliminating one reinforcer at a time and rewarding alternative behaviors. Using a multiple-baseline design, they were able to show systematic decreases in the problem behavior as each reinforcer was addressed. These results indicate that addressing all reinforcers for a behavior problem improves the success of the program and enables behavior analysts to apply behavior analysis methods more effectively.

Not only are behavior analysis techniques useful in correcting behavior problems that already exist, they have shown some promise in the *prevention* of human suffering and problem behaviors, too. For example, interventions have been conducted with some degree of success in preventing teenagers from developing unhealthful addictive behaviors, such as smoking cigarettes or using drugs (Botvin et al., 1990; Flay et al., 1989; Murray, Pirie, Leupker, & Pallonen, 1989). Some methods in these studies were designed specifically to prevent future behavior problems by training individuals in self-management skills to help them function better in everyday life. Although some tentative evidence suggests that behavioral methods may be useful in efforts to prevent medical and psychological problems, much more research is needed to improve the methods and demonstrate their effects convincingly.

We have seen that *relapse* is an important problem in the success of programs to change behavior. In many cases, behavioral methods change problem behaviors while the programs are in effect, but the behavior sometimes regresses after the programs have ended. Although some progress has been made in developing methods to reduce the likelihood of relapse, this problem remains as a critical challenge for the future and needs to be addressed more fully in research.

Documenting Cost–Benefit Ratios

Another challenge for the future of applied behavior analysis will be to justify conducting its interventions in relation to their financial costs (Baer, Wolf, & Risley, 1987; Yates, 1994). More research is needed to demonstrate *cost–benefit ratios*—that is, the extent to which providing the intervention saves more money in the long run than it costs (Jospe, Shueman, & Troy, 1991; Kaplan, 1989). These bottom-line issues often are used in deciding whether to apply certain procedures or whether insurance will pay for an intervention. Many applied behavior analysis interventions have the potential to produce far more financial benefits than costs. For instance, we considered research findings earlier in this book that hospital patients who receive help in coping with medical procedures recover more quickly and use less medication than those who don't receive such help. But most therapy techniques that we know are effective have not yet been subjected to cost–benefit analyses (Yates, 1994).

Two promising approaches for reducing costs involve using the mass media and the Internet to deliver interventions. For instance, an intervention that used TV and radio to provide training in behavioral techniques, such as progressive muscle relaxation, greatly reduced the headaches and medication usage of people with chronic headaches (de Bruijn-Kofman et al., 1997). Other interventions have used the Internet to monitor behavior and address the antecedents and consequences of behaviors, such as to increase novelists' writing (Porritt, Burt, & Polling, 2006) and to help people quit smoking (Glenn & Dallery, 2007). These approaches are likely to be cost effective because they reach large numbers of people at low cost.

Increasing the Scope of Behavior Analysis Application

In looking at the history of applied behavior analysis, we can see that the types of behavior and the settings for its application have expanded greatly over the years. In the 1960s, behavioral methods were applied mainly in institutional settings with special populations, such as individuals who were developmentally disabled or delinquent. In the intervening decades, the scope of behavior analysis application has expanded greatly. In this book, we've discussed the application of behavior analysis methods with nurses in hospitals, students in regular classrooms, workers in industries, athletes on sports teams, and the general population to improve their health and energy conservation behaviors. Almost all of these applications occurred between 1970 and today.

INTEGRATING THERAPY APPROACHES

Due to the central role of research and data in applied behavior analysis, many professionals who use its methods have been willing to consider using new techniques that research has demonstrated are effective in changing behavior. For instance, in the first decade or so after behavior therapy was introduced as a discipline, its therapists tended to apply a single technique, such as reinforcement, by itself. Then the discipline began to combine different behavioral methods, and soon behavioral and cognitive methods were used in the same interventions (Linden & Pasatu, 1998; Wilson, Hayes, & Gifford, 1997).

By the 1970s, behavior therapists had become increasingly eclectic in their orientations (Swan & MacDonald, 1978). These changes marked the beginning of a movement to integrate therapy approaches from widely different theoretical bases (Wilson, 1990). A chief argument that has led to an integration of therapy approaches is that research has found support for the effectiveness of many different methods of therapy (Beitman, Goldfried, & Norcross, 1989; Smith & Glass, 1977). A common form of integration with behavior therapy is the use of medication—for example, in treating anxiety disorders, depression, and hyperactivity (Emmelkamp, Bouman, & Scholing, 1992; Roth et al., 1982; Satterfield, Satterfield, & Cantwell, 1981; Simons, Murphy, Levine, & Wetzel, 1986). Although psychologists cannot prescribe medication, they often provide therapy in conjunction with professionals who can—that is, medical doctors (physicians or psychiatrists). One benefit of this type of combination is that medication dosages often can be reduced or eliminated. In treating depression, for instance, research indicates that cognitive-behavioral therapy is at least as effective as medication, and it costs less, too (Antonuccio, Danton, & DeNelsky, 1996; Antonuccio, Thomas, & Danton, 1997). The value of integrating therapy approaches is controversial, and the speed and direction it will take are currently unclear.

ENHANCING THE IMAGE OF APPLIED BEHAVIOR ANALYSIS

We saw in Chapter 1 that the terms *applied behavior analysis* and *behavior modification* have similar meanings, and some professionals see little difference between them. There is great overlap in the techniques these disciplines use to change behavior. *Behavior modification* was the first label applied to these techniques, and the field got off to a rocky start in terms of public and professional acceptance of its approach. It received very sharp criticism for two of its defining characteristics. First, its philosophical foundations seemed to reject the role of cognitive and biological processes in behavior. Second, the techniques it used seemed simplistic, cold, and impersonal. For instance, much early research and application involved punishment, sometimes using intense, physically aversive stimuli with children who were developmentally disabled. We have seen in this book that the field has evolved, discarding and replacing unacceptable and untenable features with perspectives and methods that are more consistent with mainstream psychological views.

The negative impact of the early characteristics of behavior modification on its image continued at least until the 1980s (O'Leary, 1984). The extent of people's biases against the use of behavioral methods was shown in a fascinating study (Woolfolk, Woolfolk, & Wilson, 1977). Undergraduate and graduate students at a university watched a videotape in which a teacher of children in a special education class used reinforcement techniques, including social and token reinforcers. Before watching the tape, the subjects were separated into two groups: one was told they would see a teacher using *behavior modification* techniques with her class; the other was told they would see a teacher using *humanistic psychology* teaching methods. The participants were then asked to rate the teacher and her methods. As you may suspect, the subjects who were told the techniques were humanistic rated the teacher much more favorably than the subjects who were told the techniques were behavioral. What's more, the participants rated the "humanistic" teacher's methods as being more likely to promote academic and emotional growth than the "behavioral" teacher's methods.

Assessments of the image of applied behavior analysis generally still use the term *behavior modification*. Since 1980, professionals who use behavioral methods have been working to correct the negative image of the field. One way they've tried to achieve this goal has been to challenge incorrect statements and misconceptions about the field that have appeared in the news media (O'Leary, 1984). Another way to enhance the image of behavioral methods has been to publicize how widely accepted and used the techniques are within the field of psychology. As the field of applied behavior analysis, or behavior modification, has evolved since the 1970s, the image of the field seems to have improved (Axelrod, 1996). A newer study of university students' views of behavior modification, conducted like the one we just considered, found no difference in the students' ratings of teaching methods labeled "behavior modification" and "humanistic" (Katz, Cacciapaglia, & Cabral, 2000).

CAREERS AND TRAINING IN BEHAVIOR ANALYSIS

Like Greg in this chapter's opening story, many students who learn about techniques in applied behavior analysis want to get more training in its methods, experience applying them with people who need help improving their behavior, and consider careers that use these methods. If you are among those students, the remainder of this chapter should provide helpful information.

CAREERS IN APPLIED BEHAVIOR ANALYSIS

Several careers that students commonly enter can enable you to apply the knowledge you gain in behavior analysis methods. Each of the following activities represents a different career field that applies behavior analysis:

- Teaching special education in public or private schools
- Training individuals with developmental disabilities in institutions
- Providing clinical psychotherapy with cognitive and behavioral techniques
- Teaching and conducting research in behavior analysis in colleges
- Improving work and safety behaviors in industry
- Improving health-related behaviors of medical patients

Entry-level positions with the first two careers in the list can be obtained with a BA or BS degree, such as in special education or in psychology with extensive training in behavior analysis; an MA degree is often preferred, usually commands a higher salary, and offers more opportunities for advancement. Many students find that the MA degree gives the optimum level of training for their careers in applied behavior analysis. For the remaining career fields in the list, the PhD degree is usually needed or preferred, but an MA degree is sometimes acceptable.

After you have received sufficient training in behavior analysis and completed the needed academic degree, two good sources can help you find the type of job you want. These sources are the Association for Behavior Analysis International (ABAI) and the American Psychological Association (APA), each of which offers job placement services and provides information about these services at their websites (see list in Related Readings).

TRAINING IN APPLIED BEHAVIOR ANALYSIS

What kind of training should you seek in applied behavior analysis, and how can you find out which colleges or universities provide good programs in it? First of all, it's a good idea for new professionals in applied behavior analysis to become certified through the Behavior Analyst Certification Board (BACB). The process and requirements to gain this certification are given at the BACB website (see Related Readings). The requirements include having received training that meets specific standards and passing an examination that the BACB administers. To become certified as a Board Certified Behavior Analyst, you must have completed a master's degree that meets the BACB standards; to be certified as a Board Certified Associate Behavior Analyst, you must have completed a bachelor's degree with appropriate coursework.

How to Find Good Training Programs in Applied Behavior Analysis

Here are five ways to find high-quality programs in applied behavior analysis, to which you can then apply for admission:

1. The BACB gives an alphabetical list of approved programs ("course sequences") at their website (see Related Readings). The list contains many dozens of programs, most of them in the United States; some of them can be completed through distance learning.

2. At the ABAI website (see Related Readings), there is a Graduate Training Directory that you can search using several restrictions, such as location, grade point average requirements, and whether the program is accredited through ABAI. You can also see a list of all accredited programs and get detailed information about them by clicking on each link.

3. As you read this book, you may have come across research you found particularly interesting. Look in PsychInfo for recent research by that author and to learn if he or she is affiliated with a university. Check whether that university has an MA or PhD program in applied behavior analysis, particularly one that is approved by the ABAI or BACB. If so, send that researcher an e-mail discussing the research that interests you.

4. Check an article by Shabani and colleagues (2004), which lists 56 institutions that are the most prolific in producing behavior analysis research. If these institutions offer graduate programs in applied behavior analysis that are approved by ABAI or BACB, they would be good choices for you to consider further.

5. Ask the instructor in the course that uses this textbook.

The approaches listed here for finding training programs in applied behavior analysis focus on graduate programs; this is partly because you probably are already matriculated at a college and will complete a bachelor's degree there.

A Schedule for Gaining Admission for Graduate Training

The process of acquiring graduate training requires you to start early and make continuous progress in taking needed entrance exams and finding and applying to graduate programs. You should start this process as you are completing your *junior* year as an undergraduate. The tasks you need to complete can be organized chronologically by grouping them into upcoming seasons:

- *Summer* (at end of junior year): Begin preparing for the Graduate Record Examination (GRE), *which you should take in the fall*. Get GRE preparation manuals, and study them intensively and consistently all summer. By midsummer, identify several graduate programs that look appealing to you and determine their admission requirements, particularly the undergraduate grade point average (GPA) and GRE performance cutoff scores (often a 3.0 GPA and a 500 on the verbal and quantitative areas of the GRE). By August, request program application materials and apply to take the GREs in the fall. Near the end of the summer, take a GRE practice test; if you score well, you'll be in good shape to take the exam in the fall; if you score lower than you'll need, study some more.

- *Fall*: Take the GREs; if you don't score well enough, you can retake them. Ask instructors who know you well to write letters of recommendation for graduate schools. Check the dates when applications are due and make sure yours get there on time, including recommendations.

- *Spring*: This is cross-your-fingers time. When you receive acceptance notifications from graduate schools, let your instructors know and thank them for the letters.

The summer of this year can be more laid back than the last one. In a couple of years when you have nearly completed the graduate program, find out when the BACB exams are given and what you need to do to prepare for one. Hundreds of candidates take the exams for the Board Certified Behavior Analyst (BCBA) or Board Certified Associate Behavior Analyst (BCABA) status each year. From 2000 to 2010, about 74% and 65% of individuals taking, respectively, the BCBA and BCABA exams passed (BACB, 2011c).

As the final chapter comes to a close, I want to say that I hope you have enjoyed reading this book. You may find it useful to refer to in the future when and if you are working as a professional. If you pursue a career in applied behavior analysis, I hope you find it rewarding, and that you can help to advance the knowledge we have and our success in helping to enhance people's functioning. Regardless of your career path, I hope you enjoy your life and benefit society. (Go to .)

STUDY AND REVIEW

SUMMARY

Several challenges remain for the future of applied behavior analysis. These challenges include improving the effectiveness of behavior change methods, particularly in preventing problem behaviors and relapses;

CONCEPT CHECK 28.1

Check your understanding of the concepts in this chapter. Remember: The symbol ⇔ means that the answer can vary. Answer the following questions about challenges and careers in applied behavior analysis.

1. One way to improve the effectiveness of applied behavior analysis methods is to _____ . ⇔
2. More research is needed to document the _____ ratios for methods in applied behavior analysis.
3. The Internet has been used successfully to deliver behavioral interventions to help people _____ . ⇔
4. Behavior analysts can become certified as practitioners through an organization whose name is abbreviated as _____ .
5. Becoming a Board Certified Behavior Analyst requires a(n) _____ degree; becoming a Board Certified Associate Behavior Analyst requires a(n) _____ degree.

integrating effective approaches from other disciplines into the field; and enhancing the image of applied behavior analysis (behavior modification). The field also needs to document cost–benefit ratios and increase the scope of behaviors and settings in which behavior analysis is applied.

Several career fields can enable you to apply behavior analysis techniques. Entry-level positions in some of these fields are available with a bachelor's degree, but an MA degree offers important advantages; for some positions, a PhD may be required or preferred. Achieving the status of Board Certified Behavior Analyst or Board Certified Associate Behavior Analyst gives job applicants an advantage. There are several ways to identify programs that offer high-quality training in applied behavior analysis.

> To prepare for exams, use the following review questions and the online study guide that's available on this book's companion website at www.wiley.com/college/sarafino.

ANSWERS TO CONCEPT CHECKS (CCs)

CC28.1 *Answers*: **1.** identify and address all reinforcers of problem behaviors **2.** cost-benefit **3.** quit smoking **4.** BACB **5.** M.A., B.A.

REVIEW QUESTIONS

1. Describe two reasons that some applied behavior analysis interventions may not work as well as they should.
2. Explain why more research is needed on cost–benefit ratios for using applied behavior analysis methods.
3. Describe the research by Woolfolk, Woolfolk, and Wilson (1977) on the public image of behavior modification. How are these results different from a similar study done more than 20 years later by Katz, Cacciapaglia, and Cabral (2000)?
4. Describe the ways to find high-quality training programs in applied behavior analysis.
5. Describe the schedule you should follow to gain admission to a graduate school.
6. Describe the procedure for becoming certified in the practice of applied behavior analysis.

RELATED READINGS

This section on related readings focuses on online sources. I have listed the names of organizations with information on applied behavior analysis and their websites that you can access.

Organization	Website
American Psychological Association Division 25 (Behavior Analysis)	www.auburn.edu/~newlamc/apa_div25
American Psychological Association Online Job Search	jobs.psyccareers.com/search
Association for Behavior Analysis	www.abainternational.org
Association for Behavioral and Cognitive Therapies	www.abct.org
Behavior Analysis Certification Board	www.bacb.com
Berkshire Association for Behavior Analysis and Therapy	www.babat.org
California Association for Behavior Analysis	www.calaba.org
Florida Association for Behavior Analysis	fabaworld.org
Texas Association for Behavior Analysis	txaba.org

GLOSSARY

The chapter abbreviations in parentheses indicate where major discussions of the term occur and/or where it is listed as a key term in the Study and Review section.

A-B-C Log (Ch. 13)   A chronological record of the target behavior, describing each instance along with the antecedents and consequences that accompanied it.

AB design (Ch. 3)   Research involving one baseline phase and one intervention phase.

ABA design (Ch. 3)   Research design that uses three phases: baseline, intervention, and reversal (baseline).

ABAB design (Ch. 3)   A reversal design consisting of four phases: baseline, intervention, reversal (baseline), and intervention.

abative effect (Ch. 9)   A decrease in a behavior resulting from a motivating operation, an establishing operation applied to a punisher, or an abolishing operation applied to a reinforcer.

abolishing operations (AOs, Ch. 9)   Motivating operations that decrease the effectiveness of a reinforcer or punisher and produce corresponding alterations in behavior.

Achievement Place (Ch. 25)   A residential token economy program for pre-delinquent teenagers in which live-in teaching parents supervise the behavior and administration of reinforcers.

alternating-treatment designs (Ch. 3)   A research design in which two or more treatments are conducted during the same intervention phase to compare their effectiveness. Also called *simultaneous-treatment* or *multi-element designs.*

alternative behavior (Ch. 6)   A response that is dissimilar to the target behavior and can replace it if reinforced regularly.

antecedents (Ch. 1 & 8)   Stimuli that exist or occur before and set the occasion for particular behaviors.

anticipatory nausea (Ch. 21)   In cancer patients, nausea in reaction to a conditioned stimulus related to their chemotherapy procedures or setting; develops through respondent conditioning.

anxiety (Ch. 21)   A fear with vague or unspecified sources.

applied behavior analysis (Ch. 1)   A field that applies principles of learning, mainly operant conditioning, to change behavior.

auditory prompts (Ch. 11)   Stimulus prompts that are composed of sounds other than words.

autism (Ch. 4)   A developmental disability characterized by an early onset, severely impaired social and language behaviors, and frequent disruptive and inattentive acts.

autogenic training (Ch. 22)   A technique designed to induce psychological and physical calm by having the person imagine being in a pleasant scene and experiencing certain calming body sensations.

automatic reinforcement (Ch. 5)   A type of natural reinforcement in which a behavior produces a reinforcer itself, independent of the actions of other people.

aversive activities (Ch. 19)   Behaviors that a person does not enjoy and performs very infrequently.

avoidance conditioning (Ch. 5)   Learning a behavior that prevents an aversive event or circumstance from occurring.

backward chaining (Ch. 12)   A method for teaching a chain of behavior by having the person master one link at a time, starting with the last link and adding each new one in the reverse sequence of the chain.

bar graphs (Ch. 3)   Diagrams that use rectangles to represent data points to show how one variable changes with another.

baseline (Ch. 3)   A term referring to a period of time when an intervention is absent, *or* to the data collected during a baseline period.

behavior (Ch. 1)   Any measurable response or action a person makes.

behavior-altering effects (Ch. 9)   The influence that implementing motivating operations has on behavior.

behavior analysts (Ch. 1)   Professionals who study or practice applied behavior analysis.

behavioral approach test (Ch. 21)   A procedure for assessing fear in which the person and feared object are brought closer and closer until he or she reports discomfort; the distance between the two is measured. Also called the *behavioral avoidance test.*

behavioral chain (Ch. 12)   A sequence of operant responses, each of which produces a stimulus that functions as its reinforcer and as a discriminative stimulus for the next response; completion of the chain leads to a consequence.

behavioral contract (Ch. 24)   A written agreement in a behavior change program that specifies the target behavior and states where and when it should or should not occur and the consequences for doing so.

behavioral deficit (Ch. 1)   An appropriate behavior that is not performed often enough, long enough, well enough, or strongly enough.

behavioral excess (Ch. 1)   An inappropriate response that is performed too often, too strongly, or for too long.

behavioral goal (Ch. 2)   The level of the target behavior that is to be achieved by the end of a behavior change program.

behavioral methods (Ch. 1)   Techniques that apply principles of operant conditioning, respondent conditioning, and modeling toward modifying behavior.

behaviorism (Ch. 1)   The school of thought that stresses the study of observable, measurable responses and proposes that behavior can be explained mainly by principles of learning, especially operant and respondent conditioning.

biofeedback (Ch. 23)   A technique that enables individuals to regulate the functioning of their physiological systems by providing moment-to-moment information about the status of each system.

blocking (Ch. 21)   A respondent conditioning phenomenon in which having learned a CS as a signal for a particular US makes it difficult to learn a new CS for that US.

booster program (Ch. 20)   An extension after an intervention, consisting of periodic sessions of intervention methods to refresh their original effects, with the purpose of maintaining improved behaviors after the intervention has ended.

BP biofeedback (Ch. 23)   A biofeedback procedure in which the information provided on the status of a physiological system is for blood pressure (BP), which enables the person to regulate its level.

changing-criterion designs (Ch. 3)   Research designs in which the effect of an intervention is examined by altering the standards for correct performance periodically and seeing if the behavior matches the new standards.

clinical significance (Ch. 3)   An evaluation of an intervention's success in terms of how meaningful the change in behavior is to the person's everyday life. A highly meaningful change is one that is large and brings the behavior into the normal range.

cognition (Ch. 1)   Covert actions, such as thinking, reasoning, and imagining.

competing response (Ch. 6)   An action that is incompatible or conflicts with performance of a target behavior.

computer-assisted instruction (CAI, Ch. 4)   A form of programmed instruction in which a series of questions or problems is presented on a computer, which can provide immediate feedback for the individual's answers and give examples and explanations of concepts.

concept (Ch. 8)   A cognitive category that groups objects, events, activities, or ideas that share characteristics; stimulus generalization applies to items within a concept, and discrimination can apply to items within and across categories.

conditioned emotional response (CER, Ch. 21)   A respondent behavior that reflects an emotion, such as fear and anger.

conditioned motivating operations (CMOs, Ch. 9)   Motivating operations that developed their ability to alter a consequence's effectiveness through learning.

conditioned reinforcers (Ch. 5)   Stimuli that gained the ability to strengthen behavior by way of conditioning, typically by being associated with established reinforcers. Also called *secondary reinforcers*.

conditioned response (CR, Ch. 1 & 21)   A specific respondent behavior that can be elicited by a conditioned stimulus as a result of prior learning.

conditioned stimulus (CS, Ch. 1 & 21)   An event that has gained the ability to elicit a specific response through the respondent conditioning procedure of repeated pairing with a stimulus that already elicits that response.

contingent exercise (Ch. 19)   An aversive activities type of punishment in which the person must perform motor acts repeatedly.

continuous recording (Ch. 2)   A measurement strategy of keeping data records of a target behavior for all instances of its occurrence in a specified time period.

continuous reinforcement (CRF, Ch. 6 & 15)   A reinforcement schedule in which each instance of the target behavior is reinforced.

cost–benefit ratio (Ch. 3)   A financial assessment of the extent to which the costs of providing an intervention are offset by the savings over time.

counterconditioning (Ch. 22)   A respondent learning process in which repeated pairing of a previously learned CR, usually an emotion, with a competing or incompatible response, usually being calm, when the CS is present leads to the substitution of the calm response for the emotion.

cumulative graphs (Ch. 3)   Line graphs in which the measure of one variable accumulates across units scaled along the horizontal axis. Also called *cumulative records*.

differential reinforcement of alternative behavior (DRA, Ch. 17)   Delivering reinforcers contingent on the individual performing an alternative behavior to an undesirable target behavior.

differential reinforcement of incompatible behavior (DRI, Ch. 17)   Delivering reinforcers contingent on the individual performing a competing response to an undesirable target behavior.

differential reinforcement of low rates (DRL, Ch. 17)   Delivering reinforcers contingent on the individual performing an undesirable target behavior at a rate that is below a certain level.

differential reinforcement of other behavior (DRO, Ch. 17)   Delivering reinforcers contingent on the individual not performing an undesirable target behavior at all during a certain time period.

direct assessment methods (Ch. 2)   Straightforward procedures for measuring behavior, usually by observing and recording it directly.

discrimination training (Ch. 8)   Learning to distinguish between and respond differently toward different stimuli.

discriminative stimulus (S^D, Ch. 8)   A stimulus that has been associated as an antecedent for a specific reinforced response.

duration (Ch. 2)   A measure of behavior in which the length of time an instance of it lasts is observed and recorded.

EEG biofeedback (Ch. 23)   A biofeedback procedure in which the information provided on the status of a physiological system is for brain electrical activity (measured with an electroencephalograph, EEG), which enables the person to regulate its functioning.

emetic therapy (Ch. 21)   A behavior modification approach for reducing alcohol abuse by having clients take a drug that makes them become nauseated if they then drink alcohol.

EMG biofeedback (Ch. 23)   A biofeedback procedure in which the information provided on the status of a physiological system is for muscle tension (measured with an electromyograph, EMG), which enables the person to regulate its functioning.

environmental prompts (Ch. 11)   Changing or moving the normal environment to make it likely that the target behavior will occur when the S^D is presented.

escape conditioning (Ch. 5)   Learning a behavior that can serve to reduce or eliminate an existing aversive circumstance.

establishing operations (Ch. 8 & 9)   Motivating operations that increase the effectiveness of a reinforcer or punisher and produce corresponding alterations in behavior.

evocative effect (Ch. 9)   An increase in a behavior resulting from a motivating operation, an establishing operation applied to a reinforcer, or an abolishing operation applied to a punisher.

exclusion time-out (Ch. 18)   A time-out punishment procedure that removes misbehaving individuals from reinforcing situations without isolating them, such as by placing them in a separate part of the room.

extinction (Ch. 6, & 17)   In operant conditioning, the process or procedure in which reinforcement is terminated for a previously reinforced behavior, making it less likely to occur in the future.

extinction (Ch. 6 & 21)   In respondent conditioning, the process or procedure in which the CS occurs repeatedly without the US it was paired with, making the CR less likely to occur in the future.

extinction burst (Ch. 6)   A temporary increase that sometimes occurs in the frequency or magnitude of a response soon after an extinction procedure is introduced.

fading (Ch. 11)   Process of removing or changing a prompt gradually across instances of the behavior that occur in the presence of the discriminative stimulus; the purpose is to decrease the person's reliance on the prompt.

fixed interval (FI, Ch. 16)   A type of interval reinforcement schedule in which the time period after each reinforcer is given when reinforcement is no longer available remains constant from one instance of reward to the next. The first correct response made after that period of time has elapsed is reinforced.

fixed ratio (FR, Ch. 16)   A reinforcement schedule in which the ratio of the number of correct responses that must be made for each instance of reward remains constant.

flooding (Ch. 22)   A treatment in which the client receives intense, prolonged exposure to one or more CSs based on a real-life feared situation; exposure can be in vivo or imaginal. Also called *response prevention*.

forward chaining (Ch. 12)   A method for teaching a behavioral chain by having the person master one link at a time, starting with the first link and adding each new one in the sequence.

frequency (Ch. 2)   A measure of how often a target behavior occurs in a specific time period.

full-session DRL (Ch. 17)   A variation in the procedure of differential reinforcement of low rates of responding (DRL) in which reinforcement is given if the number of responses is below a specific level for an entire session.

functional analysis (Ch. 13)   A functional assessment procedure that uses controlled conditions and manipulates antecedents and consequences to identify functional relations between them and the target behavior.

functional assessment (Ch. 13)   A procedure to determine the factors in a behavior's occurrence by examining connections between the behavior and its antecedents and consequences.

functional communication training (Ch. 17)   A procedure that teaches mands (ways to communicate needs) as alternative behaviors for problem behaviors.

general case training (Ch. 20)   An approach that trains with a range of antecedents and responses to enhance maintenance of behavior changes after an intervention ends.

gestural prompts (Ch. 11)   Response prompts that consist of physical motions that have meanings the client already knows and that make performing the target behavior likely.

goal acceptability (Ch. 27)   The extent to which the outcome or purposes of a behavior change program are fair, appropriate, and reasonable.

gradual in vivo exposure (Ch. 22)   A fear reduction procedure that presents CSs in a stimulus hierarchy, like systematic desensitization, but does not use relaxation exercises.

graph (Ch. 3)   A diagram for displaying data, generally showing how one variable, such as a behavior, changes as a function of another variable.

graphic analysis (Ch. 3)   A visual inspection procedure for graphs of data from behavior change programs to evaluate whether the program succeeded in producing a substantial change in the behavior.

group contingency (Ch. 16)   A procedure for administering reinforcers in which the behavior of some or all members of a group determines the consequences they receive.

GSR biofeedback (Ch. 23)   A biofeedback procedure in which the information provided on the status of a physiological system is skin electrical conductivity (measured as a galvanic skin response, GSR), which enables the person to regulate its functioning.

habit reversal (Ch. 17)   An array of techniques designed to decrease operant behaviors, especially ones that are habitual or automatic. The methods include competing response practice and training to make the person aware of the behavior's occurrence.

health psychology (Ch. 4)   A field of psychology introduced to study psychosocial processes in the development, prevention, and treatment of illness.

HR biofeedback (Ch. 23)   A biofeedback procedure in which the information provided on the status of a physiological system is for heart rate (HR), which enables the person to regulate its level.

indirect assessment methods (Ch. 2)   Measuring behavior with abstract or roundabout procedures, such as self-report, rather than observing it directly.

informed consent (Ch. 19 & 27)   Approval by the participants and/or their guardians to the planned procedures in therapy or research after being told what the procedures will be and any negative effects they may have.

intermittent reinforcement (Ch. 6 & 15)   The condition in which some, but not all, instances of a behavior receive reinforcement. Also called *partial reinforcement*.

intermittent reinforcement schedule (Ch. 16)   A reinforcement pattern in which only some instances of a behavior receive a reinforcer.

interobserver agreement (IOA, Ch. 2)   An assessment of the degree to which the data from two or more observers agree regarding the occurrence of a target behavior. Also called *interrater reliability* or *interobserver agreement*.

interval DRL (Ch. 17)   A variation in the procedure of differential reinforcement of low rates of responding (DRL) in which a session is divided into equal intervals and reinforcement is given at the end of each interval if the number of responses in that period was below a specific level.

interval recording (Ch. 2)   A measurement strategy in which observation periods are divided into fairly short intervals of equal length and a record is kept of whether the target behavior occurred in each interval.

interval schedules (Ch. 16)   Schedules of reinforcement in which delivery of each instance of reward is based on a rule that involves a period of time after each reinforcer is given when reinforcement is no longer available. The first correct response made after that period of time has elapsed is reinforced.

intervention (Ch. 3)   A program or period of time in which an effort is made to produce a change, such as in a person's behavior.

isolation time-out (Ch. 18)   A time-out punishment procedure that removes misbehaving individuals from reinforcing situations to a separate setting that offers little access to rewards.

latent inhibition (Ch. 21)   A respondent conditioning phenomenon in which prior experience with a specific stimulus in neutral circumstances retards the subsequent learning of that stimulus as a CS for a US.

learned food aversions (Ch. 21)   A respondent conditioning phenomenon in which a patient who receives cancer treatment that produces the unconditioned stimulus (US) of nausea comes to dislike (a conditioned response, CR) foods associated with that treatment, such as a food eaten a few hours before.

learning (Ch. 1)   A relatively permanent change in behavioral tendency as a result of experience.

line graphs (Ch. 3)   Diagrams that display data points connected with straight lines that show changes of one variable, such as behavior, in relation to another variable.

lottery (Ch. 16)   A procedure for administering reinforcers by entering all eligible individuals in a drawing to win one or more prizes.

magnitude (Ch. 2)   A measure that assesses the intensity, degree, or size of a behavior.

mands (Ch. 26)   Verbal behaviors in which people request things they need or want.

meditation (Ch. 22)   A relaxation technique to induce psychological and physical calm by having the person focus attention on a meditation stimulus, such as an object, event, or idea.

modeling (Ch. 1 & 4)   The process of learning a behavior by observing someone perform it. Also called *observational learning*, *social learning*, and *vicarious learning*.

modeling prompts (Ch. 11)   Response prompts that involve modeled actions.

motivating operations (MOs, Ch. 5, 9, & 24)   Procedures that alter the effectiveness of a consequence and performance of behaviors that usually produce that reinforcer or punisher.

multidimensional programs (Ch. 20)   Programs that combine several methods, mainly to alter antecedents or consequences, in order to change a target behavior.

multiple-baseline designs (Ch. 3)   Research designs in which two or more AB designs are conducted, with all baseline phases starting simultaneously but continuing for different lengths of time.

natural reinforcers (Ch. 5 & 20)   Unprogrammed rewards people receive as a natural part of their everyday lives.

negative punishment (Ch. 7)   A process in which subtracting or reducing a stimulus or condition suppresses the behavior on which it is contingent.

negative reinforcement (Ch. 5)   A process in which decreasing or removing an aversive stimulus as a consequence of a behavior strengthens that behavior.

noncontingent reinforcement (Ch. 14)   A procedure in which an established reinforcer is provided periodically, independent of the person's performing a behavior.

nonexclusion time-out (Ch. 18)   A time-out punishment procedure that keeps individuals who misbehaved in the same environment where reinforcers are being earned but identifies them as ineligible for participation or rewards for a period of time.

operant conditioning (Ch. 1)   A form of learning in which behavior is affected by its consequences: reinforcement increases the behavior, and punishment decreases it.

overcorrection (Ch. 7 & 19)   A punishment procedure that has the person engage in activities that correct (see *restitution*) and/or are the opposite of the undesirable behavior (see *positive practice*) when the misbehavior occurs.

overshadowing (Ch. 21)   A respondent conditioning phenomenon in which one of multiple CSs outweighs the others in the ability to elicit the CR.

participant modeling (Ch. 22)   A fear reduction technique in which a fearful individual watches a therapist or other person engage in a feared activity and is encouraged and guided to join in the activity.

personalized system of instruction (PSI, Ch. 4)   A teaching structure in which the content to be learned is divided into modules that students study independently and are tested when they think they are ready.

phobia (Ch. 21)   Intense and irrational fears, usually of something specific.

physical guidance prompt (Ch. 11)   Response prompts that involve manually moving the person's body through the desired behavior.

physical restraint (Ch. 19)   A punishment method in which the body part that makes a problem behavior is held in place for a period of time, preventing the unwanted action.

physically aversive stimuli (Ch. 7 & 19)   Punishers that cause physical discomfort, pain, or other unpleasant sensations.

pictorial prompts (Ch. 11)   Stimulus prompts that are composed of pictures, such as a drawing or video.

positive practice (Ch. 19)   A component of the overcorrection method of punishment in which the misbehaving person must engage repeatedly in a response that is the opposite of the misbehavior.

positive punishment (Ch. 7)   A process in which adding or introducing an aversive event suppresses the behavior on which it is contingent.

positive reinforcement (Ch. 5)   A process in which adding or introducing an item or experience as a consequence of a behavior strengthens that behavior.

positive reinforcer (Ch. 5)   An item or experience that is added or introduced as a consequence of a behavior and strengthens that action.

post-reinforcement pauses (Ch. 16)   Brief pauses in responding that individuals often show after each instance of reward when they are reinforced on a fixed-ratio schedule.

Premack principle (Ch. 5)   The view that activities can reinforce a response that occurs infrequently for a particular person because they are high-probability behaviors for that individual.

programmed instruction (Ch. 4)   A self-teaching process in which individuals learn material by working at their own pace through a series of questions or problems and receive immediate feedback for their answers.

programmed reinforcers (Ch. 5)   Rewards that are deliberately applied with the intention of strengthening specific behaviors.

progressive muscle relaxation (Ch. 22)   A technique for inducing psychological and physical calm by having the person tense and relax separate muscle groups and pay attention to those sensations. Also called *progressive relaxation*.

prompts (Ch. 11 & 24)   Antecedents that supplement the everyday discriminative stimuli for a behavior, thereby reminding the person to perform a behavior or helping the person learn how to perform it.

punishment (Ch. 1, 7, & 18)   A process in which a consequence of a behavior decreases the future performance of that behavior.

ratio schedules (Ch. 16)   Schedules of reinforcement in which delivery of each instance of reward is determined by a rule that specifies the number of correct responses that must have been made since the last reinforcer was given.

ratio strain (Ch. 16)   Deterioration of a behavior when the number of responses required in a ratio schedule of reinforcement becomes too large.

reactivity (Ch. 2)   A phenomenon in which people's behavior tends to change when they know they are being observed.

reinforcement (Ch. 1 & 5)   A process whereby a consequence of an operant response strengthens that behavior, increasing its future performance.

reinforcer (Ch. 5)   An item or experience that strengthens a behavior on which its delivery is contingent.

relapse (Ch. 20)   A falling back to one's former level of an unwanted behavior.

relaxation (Ch. 22)   A psychological and physical state of calm and a procedure to produce it.

reprimands (Ch. 7 & 19)   Verbal statements expressing strong criticism of one's behavior.

resistance to extinction (Ch. 6)   The tendency of a behavior to continue after the reinforcement that had maintained it is discontinued when extinction is in effect.

respondent conditioning (Ch. 1, 21, & 22)   A learning process in which a previously neutral stimulus gains the ability to elicit a particular response by its repeated pairing with an unconditioned stimulus that already elicits that response. Also called *classical conditioning*.

response blocking (Ch. 19)   Physically intervening to prevent a person's performance of an unwanted target behavior.

response cost (Ch. 7 & 18)   A punishment procedure in which the misbehaving person loses a valued item or privilege as a consequence of performing that behavior.

response effort (Ch. 14)   The amount of work in time or exertion for an individual to perform a behavior.

response prompts (Ch. 11)   Shortcut stimulus control methods in which a teacher or behavior analyst performs an action as a supplement to the normal S^D to set the occasion for the learner to perform the target behavior.

restitution (Ch. 19)   A component of the overcorrection method of punishment in which the misbehaving person must correct or restore the environmental situation, often to a condition that is better than it was previously.

reversal designs (Ch. 3)   Research designs with a series of phases in which an intervention is alternately absent (baseline) and present.

rule-governed behavior (Ch. 26)   An action that is controlled by an antecedent rule that describes the contingency between performance of the behavior and specific consequences.

S-delta (S^Δ, Ch. 8)   A stimulus that has been associated consistently with the absence of reinforcement of a specific response.

schedule of reinforcement (Ch. 15)   A rule that specifies which instances of a behavior will be rewarded.

second-order conditioning (Ch. 21)   A respondent conditioning phenomenon in which a new CS gains the ability to produce a CR by becoming associated with an existing CS that already elicits that response.

self-management (Ch. 4 & 24)   Applying behavioral or cognitive methods to change one's own behavior.

self-monitoring (Ch. 24)   Observing and keeping records of one's own target behaviors.

shaping (Ch. 10)   A process or procedure of requiring successively better instances of a new behavior to receive reinforcement, thereby making the behavior increasingly well developed.

single-subject designs (Ch. 3)   A research approach that examines changes in behavior for one individual at a time while an intervention is either in effect or absent. Also called *intrasubject designs*.

social validity (Ch. 3)   An evaluation by the client and individuals in his or her life of the social utility and adaptiveness of the change in behavior produced by an intervention.

spaced-responding DRL (Ch. 17)   A variation in the procedure of differential reinforcement of low rates of responding (DRL) in which reinforcement is given if responses are separated by a predetermined interval of time.

spontaneous recovery (Ch. 6)   The reappearance of a previously extinguished behavior; the response tends to be weak and is temporary if extinction conditions continue.

sport psychology (Ch. 4)   A discipline that studies and applies behavior analytic methods to improve athletic skills.

stimulus control (Ch. 8)   The degree of control an antecedent stimulus has on performing a specific behavior; it develops through discrimination training.

stimulus generalization (Ch. 8)   The tendency to perform a learned behavior in response to an antecedent stimulus or condition that is similar but not identical to the actual discriminative stimulus for that behavior.

stimulus hierarchy (Ch. 22)   A series of CSs that are rank-ordered in terms of the degree of emotion, usually fear, each one arouses.

stimulus prompts (Ch. 11)   Procedures that physically change the normal antecedent for a behavior by altering the S^D or supplementing it with another stimulus, such as pictures or sounds.

structured descriptive assessment (Ch. 13)   A functional assessment approach in which observations of a behavior are made in the natural environment while antecedents are manipulated to determine their effect.

subjective units of discomfort scale (SUDS, Ch. 21)   A rating scale for assessing the degree of fear aroused by particular CSs.

successive approximations (Ch. 10)   A sequence of actions that resemble more and more the well-performed target behavior in form and quantity.

summary record (Ch. 13)   A form used in a functional assessment that organizes and summarizes data from an A-B-C Log to allow relationships to be seen between a target behavior and its antecedents and consequences.

systematic desensitization (Ch. 22)   A respondent conditioning method for reducing fear by presenting increasingly strong fear CSs while the person engages in relaxation, thereby enabling the calm response to replace the CR of fear.

table (Ch. 3)   A chart that arranges a set of data systematically in rows and columns.

tacts (Ch. 26)   Verbal behavior in which individuals name or identify items or events.

target behaviors (Ch. 1)   The responses to be changed in an applied behavior analysis intervention.

task analysis (Ch. 12)   A process used in identifying discriminative stimuli and responses as required components in a sequence that makes up a complex action.

thermal biofeedback (Ch. 23)   A biofeedback procedure in which the information provided on the status of a physiological system is for skin temperature, which enables the person to regulate its level.

thinning (Ch. 15)   A procedure of gradually reducing the rate at which a behavior is reinforced.

time-out (Ch. 7 & 18)   A punishment method in which, contingent on misbehavior, the person's reinforcing environment is converted or moved, generally for a brief period, to one that is less reinforcing.

time sampling (Ch. 2)   A measurement strategy in which the occurrence or absence of a behavior is recorded; observation periods are divided into subperiods of equal length, and a record is kept of the occurrence of the target behavior during a short interval at the start of each subperiod.

token economy (Ch. 25)   A method that uses a complex system of consequences with tokens as reinforcers to modify a wide range of behaviors in groups of individuals.

token reinforcement system (Ch. 16)   A reward system in which token reinforcers and backup rewards are chosen and applied with specific rules to change a target behavior.

tokens (Ch. 5)   Rewards that serve as conditioned reinforcers by virtue of their being traded for and paired with already established, backup reinforcers.

total-task presentation (Ch. 12)   A method for teaching a chain of behavior by having the person learn all of the links together as a complete sequence.

treatment acceptability (Ch. 27)   The extent to which the treatment methods in a behavior change program are considered fair, appropriate, and reasonable by the client and community.

trend line (Ch. 3)   A straight line applied in a graph to "fit" or represent a set of data and show overall changes in one variable, such as behavior, as a function of another variable.

unconditioned motivating operations (UMOs, Ch. 9)   Motivating operations with an ability to alter a consequence's effectiveness that is inborn to the person; these effects are not learned.

unconditioned reinforcers (Ch. 5)   Consequences that require little or no learning for them to have the ability to strengthen behavior. Also called *primary reinforcers*.

unconditioned response (UR, Ch. 1 & 21)   An inborn specific behavior made reflexively to a particular stimulus, the unconditioned stimulus (US).

unconditioned stimulus (US, Ch. 1 & 21)   A specific event that elicits a particular response reflexively, without having been learned.

unstructured descriptive assessment (Ch. 13)   A functional assessment approach in which observations of a behavior are made in the natural environment without intervening in any way to identify its antecedents and consequences.

urine alarm apparatus (Ch. 4)   A liquid-sensitive sheet that a bed-wetting child sleeps on; the apparatus sounds an alarm when urination begins, and wakes the child.

value-altering effect (Ch. 9)   The influence that implementing motivating operations has on the effectiveness of a consequence.

variable interval (VI, Ch. 16)   An interval reinforcement schedule in which the time period when reinforcement is no longer available changes and is unspecified from one instance of reward to the next. The first correct response made after each period of time has elapsed is reinforced.

variable ratio (VR, Ch. 16)   A ratio reinforcement schedule in which the number of correct responses that must be made for each instance of reward changes and is unspecified from one instance to the next.

verbal behavior (Ch. 26)   Actions that use language and lead to a consequence.

verbal prompts (Ch. 11)   Response prompts that are composed of words, such as directions.

REFERENCES

Note: Authorship listed for references with more than six authors is cited with the format: first five authors et al. In the chapters, citations give all authors' names when there are four or fewer authors; with five or more authors, citations use the format: first author et al.

AABT (Association for Advancement of Behavior Therapy). (1977). Ethical issues for human services. *Behavior Therapy*, 8, v–vi.

AAFA (Asthma and Allergy Foundation of America). (2011). *Asthma facts and figures*. Retrieved (1-5-2011) from http://www.aafa.org.

AAIDD (American Association on Intellectual and Developmental Disabilities). (2011). *Definition of Intellectual Disability*. Retrieved (1-3-2011) from http://www.aaidd.org.

ABAI (Association for Behavior Analysis International). (2011). *Statement on the Right to Effective Behavioral Treatment, 1989*. Retrieved (1-3-2011) from http://www.abainternational.org.

Acker, L. E., Goldwater, B. C., & Agnew, J. L. (1990). Sidney Slug: A computer simulation for teaching shaping without an animal laboratory. *Teaching of Psychology*, 17, 130–132.

Ackerman, M. D., & Carey, M. P. (1995). Psychology's role on the assessment of erectile dysfunction: Historical precedents, current knowledge, and methods. *Journal of Consulting and Clinical Psychology*, 63, 862–876.

Ader, R., & Cohen, N. (1975). Behaviorally conditioned immunosuppression. *Psychosomatic Medicine*, 37, 333–340.

Ader, R., & Cohen, N. (1985). CNS-immune system interactions: Conditioning phenomena. *Behavioral and Brain Sciences*, 8, 379–395.

AHA (American Heart Association). (2011). *About high blood pressure*. Retrieved (1-3-2011) from http://www.americanheart.org.

Ahearn, W. H., Kerwin, M. E., Eicher, P. S., Shantz, J., & Swearingin, W. (1996). An alternating treatments comparison of two intensive interventions for food refusal. *Journal of Applied Behavior Analysis*, 29, 321–332.

Alavosius, M. P., & Sulzer-Azaroff, B. (1986). The effects of performance feedback on the safety of client lifting and transfer. *Journal of Applied Behavior Analysis*, 19, 261–267.

Alberto, P. A., & Troutman, A. C. (1990). *Applied behavior analysis for teachers* (3rd ed.). Columbus, OH: Merrill.

Albin, R. W., & Horner, R. H. (1988). Generalization with precision. In R. H. Horner, G. Dunlap, & R. L. Koegel (Eds.), *Generalization and maintenance: Life-style changes in applied settings* (pp. 99–120). Baltimore, MD: Paul H. Brookes.

Alexander, R. N., Corbett, T. F., & Smigel, J. (1976). The effects of individual and group consequences on school attendance and curfew violations with predelinquent adolescents. *Journal of Applied Behavior Analysis*, 9, 221–226.

Allen, J. S., Tarnowski, K. J., Simonian, S. J., Elliott, D., & Drabman, R. S. (1991). The generalization map revisited: Assessment of generalized treatment effects in child and adolescent behavior therapy. *Behavior Therapy*, 22, 393–405.

Allen, K. D., Loiben, T., Allen, S. J., & Stanley, R. T. (1992). Dentist-implemented contingent escape for management of disruptive child behavior. *Journal of Applied Behavior Analysis*, 25, 629–636.

Allen, K. D., & Stokes, T. F. (1987). Use of escape and reward in the management of young children during dental treatment. *Journal of Applied Behavior Analysis*, 20, 381–390.

Allen, L. D., & Iwata, B. A. (1980). Reinforcing exercise maintenance: Using existing high-rate activities. *Behavior Modification*, 4, 337–354.

Allan, R. W. (1998). Operant-respondent interactions. In W. O'Donohue (Ed.), *Learning and behavior therapy* (pp. 146–168). Boston: Allyn & Bacon.

Allison, J. (1989). The nature of reinforcement. In S. B. Klein & R. R. Mowrer (Eds.), *Contemporary learning theories: Instrumental conditioning and the impact of biological constraints on learning* (pp. 13–39). Hillsdale, NJ: Erlbaum.

Alterman, A. I., Gariti, P., & Mulvaney, F. (2001). Short- and long-term smoking cessation for three levels of intensity of behavioral treatment. *Psychology of Addictive Behaviors*, 15, 261–264.

Altman, K., Haavik, S., & Cook, J. W. (1978). Punishment of self-injurious behavior in natural settings using contingent aromatic ammonia. *Behaviour Research and Therapy*, 16, 85–96.

Alvero, A. M., & Austin, J. (2004). The effects of conducting behavioral observations on the behavior of the observer. *Journal of Applied Behavior Analysis, 37,* 457–468.

AMA (American Medical Association). (2003). *American Medical Association complete medical encyclopedia.* New York: Random House.

Anderson, C. M., & Long, E. S. (2002). Use of a structured descriptive assessment methodology to identify variables affecting problem behavior. *Journal of Applied Behavior Analysis, 35,* 137–154.

Anderson, K. O., & Masur, F. T. (1983). Psychological preparation for invasive medical and dental procedures. *Journal of Behavioral Medicine, 6,* 1–40.

Andrasik, F., Blake, D. D., & McCarran, M. S. (1986). A biobehavioral analysis of pediatric headache. In N. A. Krasnegor, J. D. Arasteh, & M. F. Cataldo (Eds.), *Child health behavior: A behavioral pediatrics perspective* (pp. 394–434). New York: Wiley.

Angier, N. (1995). Gene hunters pursue elusive and complex traits of mind. *New York Times,* pp. C1, C3.

Antonuccio, D. O., Danton, W. G., & DeNelsky, G. Y. (1996). Psychotherapy versus medication for depression: Challenging the conventional wisdom with data. *Professional Psychology Research and Practice, 26,* 574–585.

Antonuccio, D. O., Thomas, M., & Danton, W. G. (1997). A cost-effectiveness analysis of cognitive behavior therapy and fluoxetine (Prozac) in the treatment of depression. *Behavior Therapy, 28,* 187–210.

APA (American Psychological Association). (1982). *Ethical principles in the conduct of research with human participants.* Washington, DC: Author.

APA (American Psychological Association). (2002). Ethical principles of psychologists and code of conduct. *American Psychologist, 57,* 1061–1073.

Arcediano, F., Matute, H., & Miller, R. R. (1997). Blocking of Pavlovian conditioning in humans. *Learning and Motivation, 28,* 188–199.

Arena, J. G., & Schwartz, M. S. (2003). Psychophysiological assessment and biofeedback baselines. In M. S. Schwartz & F. Andrasik (Eds.), *Biofeedback: A practitioner's guide* (3rd ed., pp. 128–158). New York: Guilford.

Arndorfer, R. E., Miltenberger, R. G., Woster, S. H., Rortvedt, A. K., & Gaffaney, T. (1994). Home-based descriptive and experimental analysis of problem behaviors in children. *Topics in Early Childhood Special Education, 14,* 64–87.

Asbell, B. (1984). Writers' workshop at age 5. *New York Times Magazine,* pp. 55–72.

Ash, D. W., & Holding, D. H. (1990). Backward versus forward chaining in the acquisition of a keyboard skill. *Human Factors, 32,* 139–146.

Askew, C., & Field, A. P. (2007). Vicarious learning and the development of fears in childhood. *Behaviour Research and Therapy, 45,* 2616–2627.

Athens, E. S., & Vollmer, T. R. (2010). An investigation of differential reinforcement of alternative behavior without extinction. *Journal of Applied Behavior Analysis, 43,* 569–589.

Athens, E. S., Vollmer, T. R., & St. Peter Pipkin, C. C. (2007). Shaping academic task engagement with percentile schedules. *Journal of Applied Behavior Analysis, 40,* 475–488.

Attanasio, V., Andrasik, F., Burke, E. J., Blake, D. D., Kabela, E., & McCarran, M. S. (1985). Clinical issues in using biofeedback with children. *Clinical Biofeedback and Health, 8,* 134–141.

Axelrod, S. (1990). Myths that (mis)guide our profession. In A. C. Repp & N. N. Singh (Eds.), *Perspectives on the use of nonaversive and aversive interventions for persons with developmental disabilities* (pp. 59–72). Sycamore, IL: Sycamore.

Axelrod, S. (1996). What's wrong with behavior analysis? *Journal of Behavioral Education, 6,* 247–256.

Axelrod, S., Brantner, J. P., & Meddock, T. D. (1978). Overcorrection: A review and critical analysis. *Journal of Special Education, 12,* 367–391.

Axelrod, S., Hall, R. V., Weis, L., & Rohrer, S. (1974). Use of self-imposed contingencies to reduce the frequency of smoking behavior. In M. J. Mahoney & C. E. Thoresen (Eds.), *Self-control: Power to the person* (pp. 77–85). Monterey, CA: Brooks/Cole.

Ayllon, T., & Azrin, N. H. (1968a). Reinforcer sampling: A technique for increasing the behavior of mental patients. *Journal of Applied Behavior Analysis, 1,* 13–20.

Ayllon, T., & Azrin, N. H. (1968b). *The token economy: A motivational system for therapy and rehabilitation.* Englewood Cliffs, NJ: Prentice-Hall.

Ayllon, T., & Michael, J. (1959). The psychiatric nurse as a behavioral engineer. *Journal of the Experimental Analysis of Behavior, 2,* 323–334.

Ayres, J. J. B. (1998). Fear conditioning and avoidance. In W. O'Donohue (Ed.), *Learning and behavior therapy* (pp. 122–145). Boston: Allyn & Bacon.

Ayres, K., & Cihak, D. (2010). Computer- and video-based instruction of food preparation skills: Acquisition, generalization, and maintenance. *Intellectual and Developmental Disabilities*, 48, 195–208.

Azrin, N. H. (1976). Improvements in the community-reinforcement approach to alcoholism. *Behaviour Research and Therapy*, 14, 339–348.

Azrin, N. H., & Foxx, R. M. (1971). A rapid method of toilet training the institutionalized retarded. *Journal of Applied Behavior Analysis*, 4, 89–99.

Azrin, N. H., & Holz, W. C. (1966). Punishment. In W. K. Honig (Ed.), *Operant behavior: Areas of research and application* (pp. 380–447). New York: Appleton.

Azrin, N. H., Hontos, P. T., & Besalel-Azrin, V. (1979). Elimination of enuresis without a conditioning apparatus: An extension by office instruction of the child and parents. *Behavior Therapy*, 10, 14–19.

Azrin, N. H., & Nunn, R. G. (1973). Habit-reversal: A method of eliminating nervous habits and tics. *Behaviour Research and Therapy*, 11, 619–628.

Azrin, N. H., Nunn, R. G., & Frantz, S. E. (1980). Habit reversal vs. negative practice treatment of nervous tics. *Behavior Therapy*, 11, 169–178.

Azrin, N. H., & Peterson, A. L. (1990). Treatment of Tourette syndrome by habit reversal: A waiting-list control group comparison. *Behavior Therapy*, 21, 305–318.

Azrin, N. H., & Powell, J. (1969). Behavioral engineering: The use of response priming to improve prescribed self-medication. *Journal of Applied Behavior Analysis*, 2, 39–42.

Azrin, N. H., & Powers, M. A. (1975). Eliminating classroom disturbances of emotionally disturbed children by positive practice procedures. *Behavior Therapy*, 6, 525–534.

Azrin, N. H., Sisson, R. W., Meyers, R., & Godley, M. (1982). Alcoholism treatment by disulfiram and community reinforcement therapy. *Journal of Behavior Therapy and Experimental Psychiatry*, 13, 105–112.

Azrin, N. H., & Thienes, P. M. (1978). Rapid elimination of enuresis by intensive learning without a conditioning apparatus. *Behavior Therapy*, 9, 342–354.

Azrin, N. H., & Wesolowski, M. D. (1974). Theft reversal: An overcorrection procedure for eliminating stealing by retarded persons. *Journal of Applied Behavior Analysis*, 7, 577–581.

Azrin, N. H., & Wesolowski, M. D. (1975). The use of positive practice to eliminate persistent floor sprawling by profoundly retarded adults. *Behavior Therapy*, 6, 627–631.

BACB (Behavior Analyst Certification Board). (2011a). BCBA® & BCBA® *Behavior Analyst Task List*, Third Edition, and *Third Edition Task List contact hour requirement per content area*. Retrieved (1-3-2011) from http://www.bacb.com.

BACB (Behavior Analyst Certification Board). (2011b). *Behavior Analyst Certification Board Guidelines for Responsible Conduct*. Retrieved (1-3-2011) from http://www.bacb.com.

BACB (Behavior Analyst Certification Board). (2011c). *Examination administration results*. Retrieved (1-3-2011) from http://www.bacb.com.

Baer, D. M., Peterson, R. F., & Sherman, J. A. (1967). The development of imitation by reinforcing behavioral similarity to a model. *Journal of the Experimental Analysis of Behavior*, 10, 405–416.

Baer, D. M., Wolf, M. M., & Risley, T. R. (1968). Some current dimensions of applied behavior analysis. *Journal of Applied Behavior Analysis*, 1, 91–97.

Baer, D. M., Wolf, M. M., & Risley, T. R. (1987). Some still-current dimensions of applied behavior analysis. *Journal of Applied Behavior Analysis*, 20, 313–327.

Baer, R. A., Blount, R. L., Detrich, R., & Stokes, T. F. (1987). Using intermittent reinforcement to program maintenance of verbal/nonverbal correspondence. *Journal of Applied Behavior Analysis*, 20, 179–184.

Baggs, K., & Spence, S. H. (1990). Effectiveness of booster sessions in the maintenance and enhancement of treatment gains following assertion training. *Journal of Consulting and Clinical Psychology*, 58, 845–854.

Bailey, J. S., Timbers, G. D., Phillips, E. L., & Wolf, M. M. (1971). Modification of articulation errors of pre-delinquents by their peers. *Journal of Applied Behavior Analysis*, 4, 265–281.

Baker, T. B., Piper, M. E., McCarthy, D. E., Majeskie, M. R., & Fiore, M. C. (2004). Addiction motivation reformulated: An affective processing model of negative reinforcement. *Psychological Review*, 111, 33–51.

Baldwin, J. D., & Baldwin, J. I. (1981). *Beyond sociobiology*. New York: Elsevier.

Ballard, K. D., & Glynn, T. (1975). Behavioral management in story writing with elementary school children. *Journal of Applied Behavior Analysis*, 8, 387–398.

Bancroft, S. L., & Bourret, J. C. (2008). Generating variable and random schedules of reinforcement using Microsoft Excel macros. *Journal of Applied Behavior Analysis, 41,* 227–235.

Bandura, A. (1965). Vicarious processes: A case of no-trial learning. In L. Berkowitz (Ed.), *Advances in experimental social psychology* (Vol. 2, pp. 3–55). New York: Academic Press.

Bandura, A. (1969). *Principles of behavior modification.* New York: Holt, Rinehart & Winston.

Bandura, A. (1975). Effecting change through participant modeling. In J. D. Krumboltz & C. E. Thoresen (Eds.), *Counseling methods* (pp. 248–265). New York: Holt, Rinehart, & Winston.

Bandura, A., Jeffery, R. W., & Gajdos, E. (1975). Generalizing change through participant modeling with self-directed mastery. *Behaviour Research and Therapy, 13,* 141–152.

Bangert-Drowns, R. (1988). The effects of school-based substance abuse education—a meta-analysis. *Journal of Drug Education, 18,* 243–264.

Bank, L., Marlowe, J. H., Reid, J. B., Patterson, G. R., & Weinrott, M. R. (1991). A comparative evaluation of parent-training interventions for families of chronic delinquents. *Journal of Abnormal Child Psychology, 19,* 15–33.

Barker, M. R., Bailey, J. S., & Lee, N. (2004). The impact of verbal prompts on child safety-belt use in shopping carts. *Journal of Applied Behavior Analysis, 37,* 527–530.

Barlow, D. H. (1978). Aversive procedures. In W. S. Agras (Ed.), *Behavior modification: Principles and clinical applications* (2nd ed., 86–133). Boston: Little, Brown.

Barlow, D. H., & Hayes, S. C. (1979). Alternating treatments design: One strategy for comparing the effects of two treatments in a single subject. *Journal of Applied Behavior Analysis, 12,* 199–210.

Barlow, D. H., Leitenberg, H., Agras, W. S., & Wincze, J. P. (1969). The transfer gap in systematic desensitization: An analogue study. *Behaviour Research and Therapy, 7,* 191–196.

Barrera, F. J., & Teodoro, G. M. (1990). Flash bonding or cold fusion? A case analysis of Gentle Teaching. In A. C. Repp & N. N. Singh (Eds.), *Perspectives on the use of nonaversive and aversive interventions for persons with developmental disabilities* (pp. 199–214). Sycamore, IL: Sycamore.

Barrera, M., & Glasgow, R. E. (1976). Design and evaluation of a personalized instruction course in behavioral self-control. *Teaching of Psychology, 3,* 81–84.

Barrish, H. H., Saunders, M., & Wolf, M. M. (1969). Good behavior game: Effects of individual contingencies for group consequences on disruptive behavior in a classroom. *Journal of Applied Behavior Analysis, 2,* 119–124.

Barton, E. J., & Osborne, J. G. (1978). The development of classroom sharing by a teacher using positive practice. *Behavior Modification, 2,* 231–250.

Barton, E. S., Guess, D., Garcia, E., & Baer, D. M. (1970). Improvement of retardates' mealtime behaviors by timeout procedures using multiple-baseline techniques. *Journal of Applied Behavior Analysis, 3,* 77–84.

Bauers, S. (2009, December 3). Recycling pays, literally, under new city effort. *The Philadelphia Inquirer,* pp. A1, 14.

Baum, W. M. (1994). *Understanding behaviorism: Science, behavior, and culture.* New York: HarperCollins.

Bear, G. G. (1998). School discipline in the United States: Prevention, correction, and long-term social development. *Educational and Child Psychology, 15,* 15–39.

Beck, A. T., Ward, C. H., Mendelson, M., Mock, J. E., & Erbaugh, J. K. (1961). An inventory for measuring depression. *Archives of General Psychiatry, 4,* 561–571.

Beck, H. P., Levinson, S., & Irons, G. (2009). Finding Little Albert: A journey to John B. Watson's infant laboratory. *American Psychologist, 64,* 605–614.

Becker, L. J., Rabinowitz, V. C., & Seligman, C. (1980). Evaluating the impact of utility company billing plans on residential energy consumption. *Evaluation and Program Planning, 3,* 159–164.

Becker, W. C., Madsen, C. H., Arnold, C. R., & Thomas, D. R. (1972). The contingent use of teacher attention and praise in reducing classroom behavior problems. In K. D. O'Leary & S. G. O'Leary (Eds.), *Classroom management: The successful use of behavior modification* (pp. 91–114). New York: Pergamon.

Beiman, I., Israel, E., & Johnson, S. A. (1978). During training and posttraining effects of live and taped extended progressive relaxation, self-relaxation, and electromyogram biofeedback. *Journal of Consulting and Clinical Psychology, 46,* 314–321.

Beitman, B. D., Goldfried, M. R., & Norcross, J. C. (1989). The movement toward integrating the psychotherapies: An overview. *American Journal of Psychiatry, 146,* 138–147.

Bell, A. P., Weinberg, M. S., & Hammersmith, S. K. (1981). *Sexual preference: Its development in men and women.* Bloomington, IN: Indiana University Press.

Belles, D., & Bradlyn, A. S. (1987). The use of the changing criterion design in achieving controlled smoking in a heavy smoker: A controlled case study. *Journal of Behavior Therapy and Experimental Psychiatry, 18,* 77–82.

Beneke, W. M., & Vander Tuig, J. G. (1996). Improving eating habits: A stimulus-control approach to lifestyle change. In J. R. Cautela & W. Ishaq (Eds.), *Contemporary issues in behavior therapy: Improving the human condition* (pp. 105–121). New York: Plenum Press.

Benson, H., Malhotra, M. S., Goldman, R. F., Jacobs, G. D., & Hopkins, P. J. (1990). Three case reports of the metabolic and electroencephalographic changes during advanced Buddhist meditation techniques. *Behavioral Medicine, 16,* 90–94.

Bernstein, D. A., & Borkovec, T. D. (1973). *Progressive relaxation training: A manual for the helping professions.* Champaign, IL: Research Press.

Bernstein, D. A., Borkovec, T. D., & Coles, M. G. H. (1986). Assessment of anxiety. In A. R. Ciminero, K. S. Calhoun, & H. E. Adams (Eds.), *Handbook of behavioral assessment* (2nd ed., pp. 353–403). New York: Wiley.

Bernstein, I. L. (1991). Aversion conditioning in response to cancer and cancer treatment. *Clinical Psychology Review, 11,* 185–191.

Bierman, K. L., Miller, C. L., & Stabb, S. D. (1987). Improving the social behavior and peer acceptance of rejected boys: Effects of social skill training with instructions and prohibitions. *Journal of Consulting and Clinical Psychology, 55,* 194–200.

Biglan, A. (2005). Rule-governed behavior. In G. Sugai & R. Horner (Eds.; M. Hersen, Ed. in Chief). *Encyclopedia of behavior modification and cognitive behavior therapy: Educational applications* (Vol. 3, pp. 1483–1487). Thousand Oaks, CA: Sage.

Bijou, S. W., & Baer, D. M. (1965). *Child development. Vol. 2: Universal stage of infancy.* New York: Appleton-Century-Crofts.

Birnbrauer, J. S., Wolf, M. M., Kidder, J. D., & Tague, C. E. (1972). Classroom behavior of retarded pupils with token reinforcement. In K. D. O'Leary & S. G. O'Leary (Eds.), *Classroom management: The successful use of behavior modification* (pp. 293–311). New York: Pergamon.

Blaisdell, A. P., Bristol, A. S., Gunther, L. M., & Miller, R. R. (1998). Overshadowing and latent inhibition counteract each other: Support for the comparator hypothesis. *Journal of Experimental Psychology: Animal Behavior Processes, 24,* 335–351.

Blakey, R., & Baker, R. (1980). An exposure approach to alcohol abuse. *Behaviour Research and Therapy, 18,* 319–325.

Blampied, N. M., & Kahan, E. (1992). Acceptability of alternative punishments. *Behavior Modification, 16,* 400–413.

Blanchard, E. B. (1987). Long-term effects of behavioral treatment of chronic headache. *Behavior Therapy, 18,* 375–385.

Blanchard, E. B., Applebaum, K. A., Guarnieri, P., Morrill, B., & Dentinger, M. P. (1987). Five year prospective follow-up on the treatment of chronic headache with biofeedback and/or relaxation. *Headache, 27,* 580–583.

Blanchard, E. B., Nicholson, N. L., Radnitz, C. L., Steffek, B. D., Applebaum, K. A., & Dentinger, M. P. (1991). The role of home practice in thermal biofeedback. *Journal of Consulting and Clinical Psychology, 59,* 507–512.

Bloom, K. (1979). Evaluation of infant vocal conditioning. *Journal of Experimental Child Psychology, 27,* 60–70.

Blount, R. L., Drabman, R. S., Wilson, N., & Stewart, D. (1982). Reducing severe diurnal bruxism in two profoundly retarded females. *Journal of Applied Behavior Analysis, 15,* 565–571.

Blum, K., Cull, J. C., Braverman, E. R., & Comings, D. E. (1996). Reward deficiency syndrome. *American Scientist, 84,* 132–145.

Boegli, R. G., & Wasik, B. H. (1978). Use of the token economy system to intervene on a school-wide level. *Psychology in the Schools, 15,* 72–78.

Bonem, E. (2005). Differential reinforcement of low rates of responding. In A. M. Gross & R. S. Drabman (Eds.; M. Hersen, Ed. in Chief), *Encyclopedia of behavior modification and cognitive behavior therapy: Child clinical applications* (Vol. 2, pp. 803–804). Thousand Oaks, CA: Sage.

Bonem, M. K. (2005). Differential reinforcement of incompatible behavior. In A. M. Gross & R. S. Drabman (Eds.; M. Hersen, Ed. in Chief). *Encyclopedia of behavior modification and cognitive behavior therapy: Child clinical applications* (Vol. 2, pp. 801–802). Thousand Oaks, CA: Sage.

Borden, J. W. (1992). Behavioral treatment of simple phobia. In S. M. Turner, K. S. Calhoun, & H. E. Adams (Eds.), *Handbook of clinical behavior therapy* (2nd ed., pp. 3–12). New York: Wiley.

Borkovec, T. D., Wilkinson, L., Folensbee, R., & Lerman, C. (1983). Stimulus control applications to the treatment of worry. *Behaviour Research and Therapy, 21,* 247–251.

Bornstein, P. H., Hamilton, S. B., & Bornstein, M. T. (1986). Self-monitoring procedures. In A. R. Ciminero, K. S. Calhoun, & H. E. Adams (Eds.), *Handbook of behavioral assessment* (2nd ed., 176–222). New York: Wiley.

Borrero, C. S. W., & Vollmer, T. R. (2006). Experimental analysis and treatment of multiply controlled problem behavior: A systematic replication and extension. *Journal of Applied Behavior Analysis, 39,* 375–379.

Borrero, J. C., Vollmer, T. R., Wright, C. S., Lerman, D. C., & Kelley, M. E. (2002). Further evaluation of the role of protective equipment in the functional analysis of self-injurious behavior. *Journal of Applied Behavior Analysis, 35,* 65–72.

Bosch, S., & Fuqua, W. (2001). Behavioral cusps: A model for selecting target behaviors. *Journal of Applied Behavior Analysis, 34,* 123–125.

Bostow, D. E., & Bailey, J. B. (1969). Modification of severe disruptive and aggressive behavior using brief timeout and reinforcement procedures. *Journal of Applied Behavior Analysis, 2,* 31–37.

Botvin, G. J., Baker, E., Dusenbury, L., Tortu, S., & Botvin, E. M. (1990). Preventing adolescent drug use through a multimodal cognitive-behavioral approach: Results of a 3-year study. *Journal of Consulting and Clinical Psychology, 58,* 437–446.

Bouton, M. E. (2000). A learning theory perspective on lapse, relapse, and the maintenance of behavior change. *Health Psychology, 19*(Suppl.), S57–S63.

Bouton, M. E., & Nelson, J. B. (1998). The role of context in classical conditioning: Some implications for cognitive behavior therapy. In W. O'Donohue (Ed.), *Learning and behavior therapy* (pp. 59–84). Boston: Allyn & Bacon.

Bouton, M. E., & Swartzentruber, D. (1991). Sources of relapse after extinction in Pavlovian and instrumental learning. *Clinical Psychology Review, 11,* 123–140.

Brantner, J. P., & Doherty, M. A. (1983). A review of timeout: A conceptual and methodological analysis. In S. Axelrod & J. Apsche (Eds.), *The effects of punishment on human behavior* (pp. 87–132). New York: Academic Press.

Brothers, K. J., Krantz, P. J., & McClannahan, L. E. (1994). Office paper recycling: A function of container proximity. *Journal of Applied Behavior Analysis, 27,* 153–160.

Broussard, C., & Northup, J. (1997). The use of functional analysis to develop peer interventions for disruptive classroom behavior. *School Psychology Quarterly, 12,* 65–76.

Brown, P. L. (1982). *Managing behavior on the job.* New York: Wiley.

Brownell, K. D., & Rodin, J. (1994). The dieting maelstrom: Is it possible and advisable to lose weight? *American Psychologist, 49,* 781–791.

Brudny, J. (1982). Biofeedback in chronic neurological cases: Therapeutic electromyography. In L. White & B. Tursky (Eds.), *Clinical biofeedback: Efficacy and mechanisms* (pp. 249–275). New York: Guilford.

Butler, R. A. (1954). Incentive conditions which influence visual exploration. *Journal of Experimental Psychology, 48,* 19–23.

Byne, W. (1994). The biological evidence challenged. *Scientific American, 270*(5), 50–55.

Calhoun, K. S., & Lima, P. P. (1977). Effects of varying schedules of timeout on high- and low-rate behaviors. *Journal of Behavior Therapy and Experimental Psychiatry, 8,* 189–194.

Call, N. A., Wacker, D. P., Ringdahl, J. E., Cooper-Brown, L. J., & Boelter, E. W. (2004). An assessment of antecedent events influencing noncompliance in an outpatient clinic. *Journal of Applied Behavior Analysis, 37,* 147–157.

Cammilleri, A. P., Tiger, J. H., & Hanley, G. P. (2008). Developing stimulus control of young children's requests to teachers: Classwide applications of multiple schedules. *Journal of Applied Behavior Analysis, 41,* 299–303.

Campbell, B. A., & Kraeling, D. (1953). Response strength as a function of drive level and amount of drive reduction. *Journal of Experimental Psychology, 45,* 97–101.

Cannella, H. I., O'Reilly, M. F., & Lancioni, G. E. (2006). Treatment of hand mouthing in individuals with severe to profound developmental disabilities: A review of the literature. *Research in Developmental Disabilities, 27,* 529–544.

Cantwell, D. P., & Baker, L. (1984). Research concerning families of children with autism. In E. Schopler & G. B. Mesibov (Eds.), *The effects of autism on the family* (pp. 41–63). New York: Plenum.

Carbone, V. J., Sweeney-Kerwin, E. J., Attanasio, V., & Kasper, T. (2010). Increasing the vocal responses of children with autism and developmental disabilities using manual sign mand training and prompt delay. *Journal of Applied Behavior Analysis, 43,* 705–709.

Carey, R. G., & Bucher, B. (1981). Identifying the educative and suppressive effects of positive practice and restitutional overcorrection. *Journal of Applied Behavioral Analysis, 14,* 71–80.

Carey, R. G., & Bucher, B. D. (1986). Positive practice overcorrection: Effects of reinforcing correct performance. *Behavior Modification, 10,* 73–92.

Carlson, C. R., & Hoyle, R. H. (1993). Efficacy of abbreviated progressive muscle relaxation training: A quantitative review of behavioral medicine research. *Journal of Consulting and Clinical Psychology, 61,* 1059–1067.

Carlson, C. S., Arnold, C. R., Becker, W. C., & Madsen, C. H. (1968). The elimination of tantrum behavior in a child in an elementary classroom. *Behaviour Research and Therapy, 6,* 117–119.

Carr, E. G. (1988). Functional equivalence as a mechanism of response generalization. In R. H. Horner, G. Dunlap, & R. L. Koegel (Eds.), *Generalization and maintenance: Life-style changes in applied settings* (pp. 221–241). Baltimore, MD: Paul H. Brookes.

Carr, E. G., & Carlson, J. I. (1993) Reduction of severe behavior problems in the community using a multicomponent treatment approach. *Journal of Applied Behavior Analysis, 26,* 157–172.

Carr, E. G., & Durand, V. M. (1985). Reducing behavior problems through functional communication training. *Journal of Applied Behavior Analysis, 18,* 111–126.

Carr, E. G., Taylor, J. C., & Robinson, S. (1991). The effects of severe behavior problems in children on the teaching behavior of adults. *Journal of Applied Behavior Analysis, 24,* 523–525.

Carr, J. E., & Burkholder, E. O. (1998). Creating single-subject design graphs with Microsoft Excel™. *Journal of Applied Behavior Analysis, 31,* 245–251.

Carroll, R. J., & Hesse, B. E. (1987). The effects of alternating mand and tact training on the acquisition of tacts. *The Analysis of Verbal Behavior, 5,* 55–65.

Carson, T. P. (1986). Assessment of depression. In A. R. Ciminero, K. S. Calhoun, & H. E. Adams (Eds.), *Handbook of behavioral assessment* (2nd ed., pp. 404–445). New York: Wiley.

Carter, N., Holmström, A., Simpanen, M., & Melin, L. (1988). Theft reduction in a grocery store through product identification and graphing of losses for employees. *Journal of Applied Behavior Analysis, 21,* 385–389.

Caudill, B. D., & Lipscomb, T. R. (1980). Modeling influences on alcoholics' rates of alcohol consumption. *Journal of Applied Behavior Analysis, 13,* 355–365.

Cautela, J. R. (1981). *Behavior analysis forms for clinical intervention* (Vol.2). Champaign, IL: Research Press.

Cautela, J. R., & Upper, D. (1975). The process of individual behavior therapy. In M. Hersen & R. M. Miller (Eds.), *Progress in behavior modification* (Vol. 1, pp. 276–305). New York: Academic Press.

Chamberlain, P., & Reid, J. B. (1998). Comparison of two community alternatives to incarceration for chronic juvenile offenders. *Journal of Consulting and Clinical Psychology, 66,* 624–633.

Chapman, A. L., Gratz, K. L., & Brown, M. Z. (2006). Solving the puzzle of deliberate self-harm: The experiential avoidance model. *Behaviour Research and Therapy, 44,* 371–394.

Charlop, M. H., Burgio, L. D., Iwata, B. A., & Ivancic, M. T. (1988). Stimulus variation as a means of enhancing punishment effects. *Journal of Applied Behavior Analysis, 21,* 89–95.

Christophersen, E. R., Arnold, C. M., Hill, D. W., & Quilitch, H. R. (1972). The home point system: Token reinforcement procedures for application by parents of children with behavior problems. *Journal of Applied Behavior Analysis, 5,* 485–497.

Chung, S.-H. (1965). Effects of delayed reinforcement in a concurrent situation. *Journal of the Experimental Analysis of Behavior, 8,* 439–444.

Ciminero, A. R. (1986). Behavioral assessment: An overview. In A. R. Ciminero, K. S. Calhoun, & H. E. Adams (Eds.), *Handbook of behavioral assessment* (2nd ed., pp. 3–11). New York: Wiley.

Clark, H. B., Greene, B. F., Macrae, J. W., McNees, M. P., Davis, J. L., & Risley, T. R. (1977). A parent advice package for family shopping trips: Development and evaluation. *Journal of Applied Behavior Analysis, 10,* 605–624.

Clark, H. B., Rowbury, T., Baer, A. M., & Baer, D. M. (1973). Timeout as a punishing stimulus in continuous and intermittent schedules. *Journal of Applied Behavior Analysis, 6,* 443–455.

Clayton, M., Helms, B., & Simpson, C. (2006). Active prompting to decrease cell phone use and increase seat belt use while driving. *Journal of Applied Behavior Analysis, 39,* 341–349.

Cohen, R., De James, P., Nocera, B., & Ramberger, M. (1980). Application of a simple self-instruction procedure on adults' exercise and studying: Two case reports. *Psychological Reports, 46,* 443–451.

Cone, J. D. (1997). Issues in functional analysis in behavioral assessment. *Behaviour Research and Therapy, 35,* 259–275.

Connors, G. J., Tarbox, A. R., & Faillace, L. A. (1992). Achieving and maintaining gains among problem drinkers: Process and outcome results. *Behavior Therapy, 23,* 449–474.

Conyers, D., Miltenberger, R., Maki, A., Barenz, R., Jurgens, M., et al. (2004). A comparison of response cost and differential reinforcement of other behavior to reduce disruptive behavior in a preschool classroom. *Journal of Applied Behavior Analysis, 37,* 411–415.

Cook, J. W., Altman, K., Shaw, J., & Blaylock, M. (1978). Use of contingent lemon juice to eliminate public masturbation. *Behaviour Research and Therapy*, 16, 131–134.

Cooke, T. P., & Apolloni, T. (1976). Developing positive social-emotional behaviors: A study of training and generalization effects. *Journal of Applied Behavior Analysis*, 9, 65–78.

Cooper, L. J., Wacker, D. P., Thursby, D., Plagmann, L. A., Harding, J., Millard, T., & Derby, M. (1992). Analysis of the effects of task preferences, task demands, and adult attention on child behavior in outpatient and classroom settings. *Journal of Applied Behavior Analysis*, 25, 823–840.

Correa, E. I., & Sutker, P. B. (1986). Assessment of alcohol and drug behaviors. In A. R. Ciminero, K. S. Calhoun, & H. E. Adams (Eds.), *Handbook of behavioral assessment* (2nd ed., pp. 446–495). New York: Wiley.

Corte, H. E., Wolfe, M. M., & Locke, B. J. (1971). A comparison of procedures for eliminating self-injurious behavior of retarded adolescents. *Journal of Applied Behavior Analysis*, 4, 201–213.

Craft, M. A., Alber, S. R., & Heward, W. L. (1998). Teaching elementary students with developmental disabilities to recruit teacher attention in a general education classroom: Effects on teacher praise and academic productivity. *Journal of Applied Behavior Analysis*, 31, 399–415.

Crary, D. (2009). *Psychologists repudiate gay-to-straight therapy*. Retrieved (8-5-2009) from http://news.yahoo.com/s/ap/20090 805/ap_on_re_us/us_psychologists_gays.

Creer, T. L., Chai, H., & Hoffman, A. (1977). A single application of an aversive stimulus to eliminate chronic cough. *Journal of Behavior Therapy and Experimental Psychiatry*, 8, 107–109.

Crespi, L. P. (1942). Quantitative variation of incentive and performance in the white rat. *American Journal of Psychology*, 55, 467–517.

Critchfield, T. S., Haley, R., Sabo, B., Colbert, J., & Macropoulis, G. (2003). A half century of scalloping in the work habits of the United States Congress. *Journal of Applied Behavior Analysis*, 36, 465–486.

Crowe, M. J., Marks, I. M., Agras, W. S., & Leitenberg, H. (1972). Time-limited desensitization, implosion and shaping for phobic patients: A crossover study. *Behaviour Research and Therapy*, 10, 319–328.

Cunningham, C. E., & Linscheid, T. R. (1976). Elimination of chronic infant ruminating by electric shock. *Behavior Therapy*, 7, 231–234.

Cunningham, C. L. (1998). Drug conditioning and drug-seeking behavior. In W. O'Donohue (Ed.), *Learning and behavior therapy* (pp. 518–544). Boston: Allyn & Bacon.

Cuvo, A. J., Davis, P. K., O'Reilly, M. F., Mooney, B. M., & Crowley, R. (1992). Promoting stimulus control with textual prompts and performance feedback for persons with mild disabilities. *Journal of Applied Behavior Analysis*, 25, 477–489.

Cuvo, A. J., Leaf, R. B., & Borakove, L. S. (1978). Teaching janitorial skills to the mentally retarded: Acquisition, generalization, and maintenance. *Journal of Applied Behavior Analysis*, 11, 345–355.

Dahlquist, L. M., & Gil, K. M. (1986). Using parents to maintain improved dental flossing skills in children. *Journal of Applied Behavior Analysis*, 19, 255–260.

Dallery, J., Meredith, S., & Glenn, I. M. (2008). A deposit contract method to deliver abstinence reinforcement for cigarette smoking. *Journal of Applied Behavioral Analysis*, 41, 609–615.

Danforth, J. S. (2005). Fading. In A. M. Gross & R. S. Drabman (Eds.; M. Hersen, Ed. in Chief), *Encyclopedia of behavior modification and cognitive behavior therapy: Child clinical applications* (Vol. 2, pp. 836–837). Thousand Oaks, CA: Sage.

Davey, G. C. L. (1992). An expectancy model of laboratory preparedness effects. *Journal of Experimental Psychology: General*, 121, 24–40.

Davey, G. C. L., McDonald, A. S., Hirisave, U., Prabhu, G. G., Iwawaki, S., et al. (1998). A cross-cultural study of animal fears. *Behaviour Research and Therapy*, 36, 735–750.

Davison, G. C. (1976). Homosexuality: The ethical challenge. *Journal of Consulting and Clinical Psychology*, 44, 157–162.

Davison, G. C., & Neale, J. A. (1994). *Abnormal psychology* (6th ed.). New York: Wiley.

de Bruijn-Kofman, A. T., van de Wiel, H., Groenman, N. H., Sorbi, M. J., & Klip, E. (1997). Effects of a mass media behavioral treatment for chronic headache: A pilot study. *Headache*, 37, 415–420.

Deitz, S. M. (1977). An analysis of programming DRL schedules in educational settings. *Behaviour Research and Therapy*, 15, 103–111.

Deitz, S. M., & Malone, L. W. (1985). On terms: Stimulus control terminology. *Behavior Analyst*, 8, 259–264.

Deitz, S. M., & Repp, A. C. (1973). Decreasing classroom misbehavior through the use of DRL schedules of reinforcement. *Journal of Applied Behavior Analysis*, 6, 457–463.

Deitz, S. M., Repp, A. C., & Deitz, D. E. D. (1976). Reducing inappropriate classroom behaviour of retarded students through three procedures of differential reinforcement. *Journal of Mental Deficiency Research*, 20, 155–170.

Deitz, S. M., Slack, D. J., Schwarzmueller, E. B., Wilander, A. P., Weatherly, T. J., & Hilliard, G. (1978). Reducing inappropriate behavior in special classrooms by reinforcing average interresponse times: Interval DRL. *Behavior Therapy*, 9, 37–46.

de Jong, P. J., Vorage, I., & van den Hout, M. A. (2000). Counterconditioning in the treatment of spider phobia: Effects on disgust, fear, and valence. *Behaviour Research and Therapy*, 38, 1055–1069.

de Kinkelder, M., & Boelens, H. (1998). Habit-reversal treatment for children's stuttering: Assessment in three settings. *Journal of Behavior Therapy and Experimental Psychiatry*, 29, 261–265.

Delfs, C. H., & Campbell, J. M. (2010). A quantitative synthesis of developmental disability research: The impact of functional assessment methodology on treatment effectiveness. *Behavior Analyst Today*, 11, 4–19.

De Luca, R. V., & Holborn, S. W. (1992). Effects of a variable-ratio reinforcement schedule with changing criteria on exercise in obese and nonobese boys. *Journal of Applied Behavior Analysis*, 25, 671–679.

Demchak, M. (1990). Response prompting and fading methods: A review. *American Journal on Mental Retardation*, 6, 603–615.

De Peuter, S., Van Diest, I., Lemaigre, V., Li, W., Verleden, G., et al. (2005). Can subjective asthma symptoms be learned? *Psychosomatic Medicine*, 67, 454–461.

DeRicco, D. A., & Niemann, J. E. (1980). In vivo effects of peer modeling on drinking rate. *Journal of Applied Behavior Analysis*, 13, 149–152.

DeRisi, W. J., & Butz, G. (1975). *Writing behavioral contracts: A case simulation practice manual*. Champaign, IL: Research Press.

de Silva, P. (1984). Buddhism and behavior modification. *Behaviour Research and Therapy*, 6, 661–678.

de Silva, P. (1990). Buddhist psychology: A review of theory and practice. *Current Psychology: Research and Reviews*, 9, 236–254.

DeVries, J. E., Burnette, M. M., & Redmon, W. K. (1991). AIDS prevention: Improving nurses' compliance with glove wearing through performance feedback. *Journal of Applied Behavior Analysis*, 24, 705–711.

Dewis, L. M., Kirkby, K. C., Martin, F., Daniels, B. A., Gilroy, L. J., & Menzies, R. G. (2001). Computer-aided vicarious exposure versus live graded exposure for spider phobia in children. *Journal of Behavior Therapy and Experimental Psychiatry*, 32, 17–27.

Dicesare, A., McAdam, D. B., Toner, A., & Varrell, J. (2005). The effects of methylphenidate on a functional analysis of disruptive behavior: A replication and extension. *Journal of Applied Behavior Analysis*, 38, 125–128.

Dickerson, E. A., & Creedon, C. F. (1981). Self-selection of standards by children: The relative effectiveness of pupil-selected and teacher-selected standards of performance. *Journal of Applied Behavior Analysis*, 14, 425–433.

Didden, R., Duker, P. C., & Korzilius, H. (1997). Meta-analytic study on treatment effectiveness for problem behaviors with individuals who have mental retardation. *American Journal on Mental Retardation*, 101, 387–399.

Didden, R., Prinsen, H., & Sigafoos, J. (2000). The blocking effect of pictorial prompts on sight-word reading. *Journal of Applied Behavior Analysis*, 33, 317–320.

Dinsmoor, J. A. (1998). Punishment. In W. O'Donohue (Ed.), *Learning and behavior therapy* (pp. 188–204). Boston: Allyn & Bacon.

Dishion, T. J., & Andrews, D. W. (1995). Preventing escalation in problem behaviors with high-risk young adolescents: Immediate and 1-year outcomes. *Journal of Consulting and Clinical Psychology*, 63, 538–548.

Dishion, T. J., McCord, J., & Poulin, F. (1999). When interventions harm: Peer groups and problem behavior. *American Psychologist*, 54, 755–764.

Dixon, M. R., Jackson, J. W., Small, S. L., Horner-King, M. J., Mui Ker Lik, N., et al. (2009). Creating single-subject design graphs in Microsoft Excel™ 2007. *Journal of Applied Behavior Analysis*, 42, 277–293.

Doleys, D. M. (1977). Behavioral treatments for nocturnal enuresis in children: A review of the recent literature. *Psychological Bulletin*, 84, 30–54.

Doleys, D. M., Wells, K. C., Hobbs, S. A., Roberts, M. W., & Cartelli, L. M. (1976). The effects of social punishment on noncompliance: A comparison with timeout and positive practice. *Journal of Applied Behavior Analysis*, 9, 471–482.

Donahue, J. A., Gillis, J. H., & King, K. (1980). Behavior modification in sport and physical education: A review. *Journal of Sport Psychology*, 2, 311–328.

Donnellan, A. M., & LaVigna, G. W. (1990). Myths about punishment. In A. C. Repp & N. N. Singh (Eds.), *Perspectives on the use of nonaversive and aversive interventions for persons with developmental disabilities* (pp. 33–58). Sycamore, IL: Sycamore.

Donohue, B. C. (2005). Overcorrection. In M. Hersen & J. Rosqvist (Eds.; M. Hersen, Ed. in Chief). *Encyclopedia of behavior modification and cognitive behavior therapy: Adult clinical applications* (Vol. 1, pp. 417–417). Thousand Oaks, CA: Sage.

Donohue, B. C., & Farley, A. (2005). Habit reversal. In M. Hersen & J. Rosqvist (Eds.; M. Hersen, Ed. in Chief). *Encyclopedia of behavior modification and cognitive behavior therapy: Adult clinical applications* (Vol. 1, pp. 325–328). Thousand Oaks, CA: Sage.

Doogan, S., & Thomas, G. V. (1992). Origins of fear of dogs in adults and children: The role of conditioning processes and prior familiarity with dogs. *Behaviour Research and Therapy, 30,* 387–394.

Dorsey, M. F., Iwata, B. A., Ong, P., & McSween, T. E. (1980). Treatment of self-injurious behavior using a water mist: Initial response suppression and generalization. *Journal of Applied Behavior Analysis, 13,* 343–353.

Dougherty, B. S., Fowler, S. A., & Paine, S. C. (1985). The use of peer monitors to reduce negative interaction during recess. *Journal of Applied Behavior Analysis, 18,* 141–153.

Dowrick, P. W. (1991). Analyzing and documenting. In P. W. Dowrick (Ed.), *Practical guide to using video in the behavioral sciences* (pp. 30–48). New York: Wiley.

Drummond, D. C., & Glautier, S. (1994). A controlled trial of cue-exposure treatment in alcohol dependence. *Journal of Consulting and Clinical Psychology, 62,* 809–818.

Ducharme, J. M., & Feldman, M. A. (1992). Comparison of staff training strategies to promote generalized teaching skills. *Journal of Applied Behavior Analysis, 25,* 165–179.

Duker, P. C., & Seys, D. M. (1996). Long-term use of electrical aversion treatment with self-injurious behavior. *Research in Developmental Disabilities, 17,* 293–301.

Durand, V. M., & Carr, E. G. (1987). Social influences on "self-stimulatory" behavior: Analysis and treatment application. *Journal of Applied Behavior Analysis, 20,* 119–132.

Durand, V. M., & Carr, E. G. (1991). Functional communication training to reduce challenging behavior: Maintenance and application in new settings. *Journal of Applied Behavior Analysis, 24,* 251–264.

Durand, V. M., & Crimmins, D. B. (1988). Identifying the variables maintaining self-injurious behavior. *Journal of Autism and Developmental Disorders, 18,* 99–117.

Dush, D. M., Hirt, M. L., & Schroeder, H. (1983). Self-statement modification with adults: A meta-analysis. *Psychological Bulletin, 94,* 408–422.

Dweck, C. S., & Elliott, E. S. (1983). Achievement motivation. In P. H. Mussen (Ed.) & E. M. Hetherington (Vol. IV Ed.), *Handbook of child psychology* (4th ed., pp. 643–691). New York: Wiley.

Dyer, K., Dunlap, G., & Winterling, V. (1990). Effects of choice making on the serious problem behaviors of students with severe handicaps. *Journal of Applied Behavior Analysis, 23,* 515–524.

Edelbrock, C. (1984). Developmental considerations. In T. H. Ollendick & M. Hersen (Eds.), *Child behavioral assessment: Principles and procedures* (pp. 20–37). New York: Pergamon.

EFA (Epilepsy Foundation of America). (2011). *About epilepsy.* Retrieved (1-3-2011) from http://www.efa.org.

Elkins, R. L. (1991). An appraisal of chemical aversion (emetic therapy) approaches to alcoholism treatment. *Behaviour Research and Therapy, 29,* 387–413.

Ellingson, S. A., Miltenberger, R. G., Stricker, J. M., Garlinghouse, M. A., Roberts, J., & Galensky, T. I. (2000). Analysis and treatment of finger sucking. *Journal of Applied Behavior Analysis, 33,* 41–52.

Elliott, S. N. (1988). Acceptability of behavioral treatments: Review of variables that influence treatment selection. *Professional Psychology: Research and Practice, 19,* 68–80.

Emmelkamp, P. M. G. (2005). Flooding. In M. Hersen & J. Rosqvist (Eds.; M. Hersen, Ed. in Chief). *Encyclopedia of behavior modification and cognitive behavior therapy: Adult clinical applications* (Vol. 1, pp. 303–306). Thousand Oaks, CA: Sage.

Emmelkamp, P. M. G., Bouman, T. K., & Scholing, A. (1992). *Anxiety disorders: A practitioner's guide.* Chichester, UK: Wiley.

Emshoff, J. G., Redd, W. H., & Davidson, W. S. (1976). Generalization training and the transfer of prosocial behavior in delinquent adolescents. *Journal of Behavior Therapy and Experimental Psychiatry, 7,* 141–144.

Engel, G. L. (1977). The need for a new medical model: A challenge for biomedicine. *Science, 196,* 129–136.

Engel, G. L. (1980). The clinical application of the biopsychosocial model. *American Journal of Psychiatry, 137,* 535–544.

English, C. L., & Anderson, C. M. (2006). Evaluation of the treatment utility of the analog functional analysis and the structured descriptive assessment. *Journal of Positive Behavior Interventions, 8,* 212–229.

Erfanian, N., & Miltenberger, R. G. (1990). Contact desensitization in the treatment of dog phobias in persons who have mental retardation. *Behavioral Residential Treatment, 5,* 55–60.

Erhardt, D., & Baker, B. L. (1990). The effects of behavioral parent training on families with young hyperactive children. *Journal of Behavior Therapy and Experimental Psychiatry*, 21, 121–132.

Ervin, R. A., Radford, P. M., Bertsch, K., Piper, A. L., Ehrhardt, K. E., & Poling, A. (2001). A descriptive analysis and critique of the empirical literature on school-based functional assessment. *School Psychology Review*, 30, 193–210.

Evans, I. M., & Nelson, R. O. (1986). Assessment of children. In A. R. Ciminero, K. S. Calhoun, & H. E. Adams (Eds.), *Handbook of behavioral assessment* (2nd ed., pp. 601–630). New York: Wiley.

Eyre, H. L. (2007). Keller's Personalized System of Instruction: Was it a fleeting fancy or is there a revival on the horizon? *Behavior Analyst Today*, 8, 317–324.

Eysenck, H. J. (1952). The effects of psychotherapy: An evaluation. *Journal of Consulting Psychology*, 16, 319–324.

Fabiano, G. A., Pelham, W. E., Manos, M. J., Gnagy, E. M., Chronis, A. M., et al. (2004). An evaluation of three time-out procedures for children with attention deficit/hyperactivity disorder. *Behavior Therapy*, 35, 449–469.

Fantuzzo, J. W., & Clement, P. W. (1981). Generalization of the effects of teacher- and self-administered token reinforcers to nontreated students. *Journal of Applied Behavior Analysis*, 14, 435–447.

Fantuzzo, J. W., Rohrbeck, C. A., Hightower, A. D., & Work, W. C. (1991). Teachers' use and children's preferences of rewards in elementary school. *Psychology in the Schools*, 28, 175–181.

Favell, J. E., McGimsey, J. F., & Jones, M. L. (1978). The use of physical restraint in the treatment of self-injury and as positive reinforcement. *Journal of Applied Behavior Analysis*, 11, 225–241.

Favell, J. E., & Reid, D. H. (1988). Generalizing and maintaining improvement in problem behavior. In R. H. Horner, G. Dunlap, & R. L. Koegel (Eds.), *Generalization and maintenance: Life-style changes in applied settings* (pp. 171–196). Baltimore, MD: Paul H. Brooks.

Fawcett, S. B., & Miller, L. K. (1975). Training public-speaking behavior: An experimental analysis and social validation. *Journal of Applied Behavior Analysis*, 8, 125–135.

Feeney, E. J. (1972). Performance audit, feedback and positive reinforcement. *Training and Development Journal*, pp. 8–13.

Feldman, M. A., Case, L., Garrick, M., MacIntyre-Grande, W., Carnwell, J., & Sparks, B. (1992). Teaching child-care skills to mothers with developmental disabilities. *Journal of Applied Behavior Analysis*, 25, 205–215.

Field, A. P., & Lawson, J. (2003). Fear information and the development of fears during childhood: Effects on implicit fear responses and behavioural avoidance. *Behaviour Research and Therapy*, 41, 1277–1293.

Finney, J. W., Rapoff, M. A., Hall, C. L., & Christophersen, E. R. (1983). Replication and social validation of habit reversal for tics. *Behavior Therapy*, 14, 116–126.

Fischer, J., & Nehs, R. (1978). Use of a commonly available chore to reduce a boy's rate of swearing. *Journal of Behavior Therapy and Experimental Psychiatry*, 9, 81–83.

Fisher, W. W., Kelley, M. E., & Lomas, J. E. (2003). Visual aids and structured criteria for improving visual inspection and interpretation of single-case designs. *Journal of Applied Behavior Analysis*, 36, 387–406.

Fisher, W. W., Piazza, C. C., Bowman, L. G., Hagopian, L. P., Owens, J. C., & Slevin, I. (1992). A comparison of two approaches for identifying reinforcers for persons with severe and profound disabilities. *Journal of Applied Behavior Analysis*, 25, 491–498.

Fisher, W. W., Piazza, C. C., Bowman, L. G., Kurtz, P. F., Sherer, M. R., & Lachman, S. R. (1994). A preliminary evaluation of empirically derived consequences for the treatment of pica. *Journal of Applied Behavior Analysis*, 27, 447–457.

Fiske, D. W., & Maddi, S. R. (1961). A conceptual framework. In D. W. Fiske & S. R. Maddi (Eds.), *Functions of varied experience*. Homewood, IL: Dorsey.

Fitzgerald, R. D., & Martin, G. K. (1971). Heart-rate conditioning in rats as a function of interstimulus interval. *Psychological Reports*, 29, 1103–1110.

Fixsen, D. L., Blasé, K. A., Timbers, G. D., & Wolf, M. M. (2007). In search of program implementation: 792 replications of the teaching-family model. *Behavior Analyst Today*, 8, 96–110.

Fixsen, D. L., Phillips, E. L., Baron, R. L., Coughlin, D. D., Daly, D. L., & Daly, P. B. (1978, November). The Boy's Town revolution. *Human Nature*, pp. 54–61.

Flaherty, C. F., & Caprio, M. (1976). Dissociation between instrumental and consummatory measures of incentive contrast. *American Journal of Psychology*, 89, 485–498.

Flay, B. R., Koepke, D., Thomson, S. J., Santi, S., Best, A., & Brown, K. S. (1989). Six-year follow-up of the first Waterloo school smoking prevention trial. *American Journal of Public Health*, 79, 1371–1376.

Fleece, L., Gross, A., O'Brien, T., Kistner, J., Rothblum, E., & Drabman, R. (1981). Elevation of voice volume in young developmentally delayed children via an operant shaping procedure. *Journal of Applied Behavior Analysis*, 14, 351–355.

Flood, W. A., & Wilder, D. A. (2002). Antecedent assessment and assessment-based treatment of off-task behavior in a child diagnosed with attention deficit-hyperactivity disorder (ADHD). *Education and Treatment of Children*, 25, 331–338.

Flood, W. A., Wilder, D. A., Flood, A. L., & Masuda, A. (2002). Peer-mediated reinforcement plus prompting as treatment for off-task behavior in children with attention deficit hyperactivity disorder. *Journal of Applied Behavior Analysis*, 35, 199–204.

Fogel, E. R. (1987). Biofeedback-assisted musculoskeletal therapy and neuromuscular re-education. In M. S. Schwartz (Ed.), *Biofeedback: A practitioner's guide* (pp. 377–409). New York: Guilford.

Foster, S. L., & Cone, J. D. (1986). Design and use of direct observation procedures. In A. R. Ciminero, K. S. Calhoun, & H. E. Adams (Eds.), *Handbook of behavioral assessment* (2nd ed., pp. 253–324). New York: Wiley.

Foster, S. L., & Mash, E. J. (1999). Assessing social validity in clinical treatment research: Issues and procedures. *Journal of Consulting and Clinical Psychology*, 67, 309–319.

Fowler, S. A. (1988). The effects of peer-mediated interventions on establishing, maintaining, and generalizing children's behavior changes. In R. H. Horner, G. Dunlap, & R. L. Koegel (Eds.), *Generalization and maintenance: Life-style changes in applied settings* (pp. 143–170). Baltimore, MD: Paul H. Brookes.

Fowler, S. A., Dougherty, B. S., Kirby, K. C., & Kohler, F. W. (1986). Role reversals: An analysis of therapeutic effects achieved with disruptive boys during their appointments as peer monitors. *Journal of Applied Behavior Analysis*, 19, 437–444.

Fox, D. K., Hopkins, B. L., & Anger, W. K. (1987). The long-term effects of a token economy on safety performance in open-pit mining. *Journal of Applied Behavior Analysis*, 20, 215–224.

Foxx, R. M., & Azrin, N. H. (1972). Restitution: A method of eliminating aggressive-disruptive behaviors of retarded and brain damaged patients. *Behaviour Research and Therapy*, 10, 15–27.

Foxx, R. M., & Schaeffer, M. H. (1981). A company-based lottery to reduce the personal driving of employees. *Journal of Applied Behavior Analysis*, 14, 273–285.

Foxx, R. M., & Shapiro, S. T. (1978). The timeout ribbon: A nonexclusionary timeout procedure. *Journal of Applied Behavior Analysis*, 11, 125–136.

France, K. G., & Hudson, S. M. (1990). Behavior management of infant sleep disturbance. *Journal of Applied Behavior Analysis*, 23, 91–98.

Frank, A. R., Wacker, D. P., Berg, W. K., & McMahon, C. M. (1985). Teaching selected microcomputer skills to retarded students via picture prompts. *Journal of Applied Behavior Analysis*, 18, 179–185.

Frankel, F. (1993). A brief test of parental behavioral skills. *Journal of Behavior Therapy and Experimental Psychiatry*, 24, 227–231.

Franks, I. M., & Maile, L. J. (1991). The use of video in sport skill acquisition. In P. W. Dowrick (Ed.), *Practical guide to using video in the behavioral sciences* (pp. 231–243). New York: Wiley.

Frederiksen, L. W. (1975). Treatment of ruminative thinking by self-monitoring. *Journal of Behavior Therapy and Experimental Psychiatry*, 6, 258–259.

Frederiksen, L. W., Jenkins, J. O., Foy, D. W., & Eisler, R. M. (1976). Social skills training to modify abusive verbal outbursts in adults. *Journal of Applied Behavior Analysis*, 9, 117–125.

Frederiksen, L. W., & Lovett, S. B. (1980). Inside organizational behavior management: Perspectives on an emerging field. *Journal of Organizational Management*, 2, 193–203.

Freeman, K. A., Anderson, C. M., & Scotti, J. R. (2000). A structured descriptive methodology: Increasing agreement between descriptive and experimental analyses. *Education and Training in Mental Retardation and Developmental Disabilities*, 35, 55–66.

Freud, S. (1933). *New introductory lectures in psychoanalysis* (W. J. H. Sprott, trans.). New York: Norton.

Freud, S. (1949). *An outline of psychoanalysis* (J. Strachey, trans.). New York: Norton.

Friedman, A. G., Campbell, T. A., & Evans, I. M. (1993). Multi-dimensional child behavior therapy in the treatment of medically related anxiety: A practical illustration. *Journal of Behavior Therapy and Experimental Psychiatry*, 24, 241–247.

Friedrich-Cofer, L., & Huston, A. C. (1986). Television violence and aggression: The debate continues. *Psychological Bulletin*, 100, 364–371.

Friman, P. C., & Altman, K. (1990). Parent use of DRI on high rate disruptive behavior: direct and collateral benefits. *Research in Developmental Disabilities*, 11, 249–254.

Gagné, R. M. (1985). *The conditions of learning and theory of instruction* (4th ed.). New York: Holt, Rinehart & Winston.

Gagnon, M., & Ladouceur, R. (1992) Behavioral treatment of child stutterers: Replication and extension. *Behavior Therapy, 23,* 113–129.

Galbicka, G. (1994). Shaping in the 21st century: Moving percentile schedules into applied settings. *Journal of Applied Behavior Analysis, 27,* 739–760.

Garcia, J., Ervin, F. R., & Koelling, R. A. (1966). Learning with prolonged delay of reinforcement. *Psychonomic Science, 5,* 121–122.

Garcia, J., Hankins, W. G., & Rusiniak, K. W. (1974). Behavioral regulation on the milieu interne in man and rat. *Science, 185,* 824–831.

Garcia, J., & Koelling, R. A. (1966). Relation of cue to consequence in avoidance learning. *Psychonomic Science, 4,* 123–124.

Garnets, L., & Kimmel, D. (1991). Lesbian and gay male dimensions in the psychological study of human diversity. In J. D. Goodchilds (Ed.), *Psychological perspectives on human diversity in America* (pp. 143–189). Washington, DC: American Psychological Association.

Gatchel, R. J. (1982). EMG biofeedback in anxiety reduction. In L. White & B. Tursky (Eds.), *Clinical biofeedback: Efficacy and mechanisms* (pp. 372–396). New York: Guilford.

Gauthier, J., Coté, G., & French, D. (1994). The role of home practice in the thermal biofeedback treatment of migraine headache. *Journal of Consulting and Clinical Psychology, 62,* 180–184.

Gaynor, S. T., & Clore, J. (2005). Shaping. In A. M. Gross & R. S. Drabman (Eds.; M. Hersen, Ed. in Chief). *Encyclopedia of behavior modification and cognitive behavior therapy: Child clinical applications* (Vol. 2, pp. 1031–1036). Thousand Oaks, CA: Sage.

Gee, C. (2010). How does sport psychology actually improve athletic performance? A framework to facilitate athletes' and coaches' understanding. *Behavior Modification, 34,* 386–402.

Gelfand, D. M., Hartmann, D. P., Lamb, A. K., Smith, C. L., Mahan, M. A., & Paul, S. C. (1974). The effects of adult models and described alternatives on children's choice of behavior management techniques. *Child Development, 45,* 585–593.

Geller, E. S., Bruff, C. D., & Nimmer, J. G. (1985). "Flash for Life": Community-based prompting for safety belt promotion. *Journal of Applied Behavior Analysis, 18,* 309–314.

Ghitza, U. E., Epstein, D. H., Schmittner, J., Nahabzadeh, M., Lin, J.-L., & Preston, K. L. (2008). Effect of reinforcement probability and prize size on cocaine and heroin abstinence in prize-based contingency management. *Journal of Applied Behavior Analysis, 41,* 539–549.

Gibson, E. J., & Levin, H. (1975). *The psychology of reading.* Cambridge, MA: MIT Press.

Gilroy, L. J., Kirkby, K. C., Daniels, B. A., Menzies, R. G., & Montgomery, I. M. (2003). Long-term follow-up of computer-aided vicarious exposure versus live graded exposure in the treatment of spider phobia. *Behavior Therapy, 34,* 65–76.

Glenn, I. M., & Dallery, J. (2007). Effects of Internet-based voucher reinforcement and a transdermal nicotine patch on cigarette smoking. *Journal of Applied Behavior Analysis, 40,* 1–13.

Glynn, S. M. (1990). Token economy approaches for psychiatric patients: Progress and pitfalls over 25 years. *Behavior Modification, 14,* 383–407.

Goetz, E. M., & Baer, D. M. (1973). Social control of form diversity and the emergence of new forms in children's blockbuilding. *Journal of Applied Behavior Analysis, 6,* 209–217.

Goh, H.-L., & Iwata, B. A. (1994). Behavioral persistence and variability during extinction of self-injury maintained by escape. *Journal of Applied Behavior Analysis, 27,* 173–174.

Goldiamond, I. (1965). Self-control procedures in personal behavior problems. *Psychological Reports, 17,* 851–868.

Goldiamond, I. (1974). Toward a constructional approach to social problems: Ethical and constitutional issues raised by applied behavior analysis. *Behaviorism, 2,* 1–84.

Goldfried, M. R., & Castonguay, L. G. (1993). Behavior therapy: Redefining strengths and limitations. *Behavior Therapy, 24,* 505–526.

Goldstein, I. B., Jamner, L. D., & Shapiro, D. (1992). Ambulatory blood pressure and heart rate in healthy male paramedics during a workday and a nonworkday. *Health Psychology, 11,* 48–54.

Goodman, W. (1994). A few scary pictures can go a long way. *New York Times,* pp. 28, 34.

Goodwin, D. W. (1986). Heredity and alcoholism. *Annals of Behavioral Medicine, 8*(2–3), 3–6.

Gottschalk, J. M., Libby, M. E., & Graff, R. B. (2000). The effects of establishing operations on preference assessment outcomes. *Journal of Applied Behavior Analysis, 33,* 85–88.

Grace, N. C., Kahng, S. W., & Fisher, W. W. (1994). Balancing social acceptability with treatment effectiveness of an intrusive procedure: A case report. *Journal of Applied Behavior Analysis, 27,* 171–172.

Graham, J., & Gaffan, E. A. (1997). Fear of water in children and adults: Etiology and familial effects. *Behaviour Research and Therapy, 35,* 91–108.

Graham, K. A. (2010, October 9). "Structured recess" tried at school to cut bullying. *Philadelphia Inquirer,* p. B5.

Gras, M. E., Cunill, M., Planes, M., Sullman, M. J. M., & Oliveras, C. (2003). Increasing safety-belt use in Spanish drivers: A field test of personal prompts. *Journal of Applied Behavior Analysis, 36,* 249–251.

Green, C. W., Reid, D. H., Canipe, V. S., & Gardner, S. M. (1991). A comprehensive evaluation of reinforcer identification processes for persons with profound multiple handicaps. *Journal of Applied Behavior Analysis, 24,* 537–552.

Green, C. W., Reid, D. H., White, L. K., Halford, R. C., Brittain, D. P., & Gardner, S. M. (1988). Identifying reinforcers for persons with profound handicaps: Staff opinion versus systematic assessment of preferences. *Journal of Applied Behavior Analysis, 21,* 31–43.

Green, G. (1990). Least restrictive use of reductive procedures: Guidelines and competencies. In A. C. Repp & N. N. Singh (Eds.), *Perspectives on the use of nonaversive and aversive interventions for persons with developmental disabilities* (pp. 479–494). Sycamore, IL: Sycamore.

Greenspoon, J. (1955). The reinforcing effect of two spoken sounds on the frequency of two responses. *American Journal of Psychology, 68,* 409–416.

Greenwood, C. R., Carta, J. J., & Kamps, D. (1990). Teacher-mediated versus peer-mediated instruction: A review of educational advantages and disadvantages. In H. C. Foot, M. J. Morgan, & R. H. Shute (Eds.), *Children helping children* (pp. 177–205). Chichester, UK: Wiley.

Greenwood, C. R., & Hops, H. (1981). Group-oriented contingencies and peer behavior change. In P. S. Strain (Ed.), *The utilization of classroom peers as behavior change agents* (pp. 189–259). New York: Plenum.

Greenwood, C. R., Hops, H., Delquadri, J., & Guild, J. (1974). Group contingencies for group consequences in classroom management: A further analysis. *Journal of Applied Behavior Analysis, 7,* 413–425.

Greer, R. D., & Polirstok, S. R. (1982). Collateral gains and short-term maintenance in reading and on-task responses by inner-city adolescents as a function of their use of social reinforcement while tutoring. *Journal of Applied Behavior Analysis, 15,* 123–139.

Greer, R. D., & Singer-Dudek, J. (2008). The emergence of conditioned reinforcement from observation. *Journal of the Experimental Analysis of Behavior, 89,* 15–29.

Griffen, A. K., Wolery, M., & Schuster, J. W. (1992). Triadic instruction of chained food preparation responses: Acquisition and observational learning. *Journal of Applied Behavior Analysis, 25,* 193–204.

Groden, G. (1989). A guide for conducting a comprehensive behavioral analysis of a target behavior. *Journal of Behavior Therapy and Experimental Psychiatry, 20,* 163–169.

Groden, G., Stevenson, S., & Groden, J. (1996). *Understanding challenging behavior: A step-by-step behavior analysis guide.* Worthington, OH: IDS Publishing.

Gross, A. M. (1984). Behavioral interviewing. In T. H. Ollendick & M. Hersen (Eds.), *Child behavioral assessment: Principles and procedures* (pp. 61–79). New York: Pergamon.

Gross, A. M., & Drabman, R. S. (1982). Teaching self-recording, self-evaluation, and self-reward to nonclinic children and adolescents. In P. Karoly & F. H. Kanfer (Eds.), *Self-management and behavior change: From theory to practice* (pp. 285–314). New York: Pergamon.

Guess, D., Sailor, W., Rutherford, G., & Baer, D. M. (1968). An experimental analysis of linguistic development: The productive use of the plural morpheme. *Journal of Applied Behavior Analysis, 1,* 297–306.

Guess, D., Turnbull, H. R., & Helmstetter, E. (1990). Science, paradigms, and values: A response to Mulick. *American Journal on Mental Retardation, 95,* 157–163.

Guevremont, D. C., Osnes, P. G., & Stokes, T. F. (1988). The functional role of preschoolers' verbalizations in the generalization of self-instructional training. *Journal of Applied Behavior Analysis, 21,* 45–55.

Guttman, N., & Kalish, H. I. (1956). Discriminability and stimulus generalization. *Journal of Experimental Psychology, 51,* 79–88.

Hains, A. H., & Baer, D. M. (1989). Interaction effects in multi-element designs: Inevitable, desirable, and ignorable. *Journal of Applied Behavior Analysis, 22,* 57–69.

Hake, D. F., & Azrin, N. H. (1965). Conditioned punishment. *Journal of the Experimental Analysis of Behavior, 6,* 297–298.

Halas, E. S., & Eberhardt, M. J. (1987). Blocking and appetitive reinforcement. *Bulletin of the Psychonomic Society*, 25, 121–123.

Haldeman, D. C. (1994). The practice and ethics of sexual orientation conversion therapy. *Journal of Consulting and Clinical Psychology*, 62, 221–227.

Hall, G., & Sundberg, M. L. (1987). Teaching mands by manipulating conditioned establishing operations. *The Analysis of Verbal Behavior*, 5, 41–53.

Hall, R. V., Axelrod, S., Foundopoulos, M., Shellman, J., Campbell, R. A., & Cranston, S. S. (1971). The effective use of punishment to modify behavior in the classroom. *Educational Technology*, 11, 24–26.

Hamilton, M., & Matson, J. L. (1992). Mental retardation. In S. M. Turner, K. S. Calhoun, & H. E. Adams (Eds.), *Handbook of clinical behavior therapy* (2nd ed., pp. 317–336). New York: Wiley.

Hamilton, S. B. (1980). Instructionally based training in self-control: Behavior-specific and generalized outcomes resulting from student-implemented self-modification projects. *Teaching of Psychology*, 7, 140–145.

Hanley, G. P., Iwata, B. A., & McCord, B. E. (2003). Functional analysis of problem behavior: A review. *Journal of Applied Behavior Analysis*, 36, 147–185.

Harchik, A. E., Sherman, J. A., Sheldon, J. B., & Strouse, M. C. (1992). Ongoing consultation as a method of improving performance of staff members in a group home. *Journal of Applied Behavior Analysis*, 25, 599–610.

Harding, J. W., Wacker, D. P., Berg, W. K., Rick, G., & Lee, J. F. (2004). Promoting response variability and stimulus generalization in martial arts training. *Journal of Applied Behavior Analysis*, 37, 185–195.

Haring, T. G., & Kennedy, C. H. (1990). Contextual control of problem behavior in students with severe disabilities. *Journal of Applied Behavior Analysis*, 23, 235–243.

Harris, C. L., & McReynolds, W. T. (1977). Semantic cues and response contingencies in self-instructional control. *Journal of Behavior Therapy and Experimental Psychiatry*, 8, 15–17.

Harris, F. R., Wolf, M. M., & Baer, D. M. (1964). Effects of adult social reinforcement on child behavior. *Young Children*, 20, 8–17.

Harris, V. W., & Sherman, J. A. (1973). Use and analysis of the "good behavior game" to reduce disruptive classroom behavior. *Journal of Applied Behavior Analysis*, 6, 405–417.

Hasazi, J. E., & Hasazi, S. E. (1972). Effects of teacher attention on digit-reversal behavior in an elementary school child. *Journal of Applied Behavior Analysis*, 5, 157–162.

Hawkins, R. C., & Clement, P. F. (1980). Development and construct validation of a self-report measure of binge eating tendencies. *Addictive Behaviors*, 5, 219–226.

Hawkins, R. P. (1991). Is social validity what we are interested in? Argument for a functional approach. *Journal of Applied Behavior Analysis*, 24, 205–213.

Hawkins, R. P., & Dotson, V. A. (1975). Reliability scores that delude: An Alice in Wonderland trip through the misleading characteristics of interobserver agreement scores in interval recording. In E. Ramp & G. Semb (Eds.), *Behavior analysis: Areas of research application* (pp. 359–376). Englewood Cliffs, NJ: Prentice-Hall.

Hayes, S. C. (1989). *Rule-governed behavior: Cognition, contingencies, and instructional control*. New York: Plenum Press.

Hayes, S. C., Rosenfarb, I., Wulfert, E., Munt, E. D., Korn, Z., & Zettle, R. D. (1985). Self-reinforcement effects: Artifact of social standard setting? *Journal of Applied Behavior Analysis*, 18, 201–214.

Heaton, R. C., & Safer, D. J. (1982). Secondary school outcome following a junior high school behavioral program. *Behavior Therapy*, 13, 226–231.

Hegel, M. T., Ayllon, T., VanderPlate, C., & Spiro-Hawkins, H. (1986). A behavioral procedure for increasing compliance with self-exercise regimens in severely burn-injured patients. *Behaviour Research and Therapy*, 24, 521–528.

Heimberg, R. G. (1990). Cognitive behavior therapy. In A. S. Bellack & M. Hersen (Eds.), *Handbook of comparative treatments for adult disorders* (pp. 203–218). New York: Wiley.

Herbert, B. (1997, December 14). The success taboo. *New York Times*, p. WK13.

Hermann, C., & Blanchard, E. B. (2002). Biofeedback in the treatment of headache and other childhood pain. *Applied Psychophysiology and Biofeedback*, 27, 143–162.

Hermann, J. A., de Montes, A. I., Dominquez, B., Montes, F., & Hopkins, B. L. (1973). Effects of bonuses for punctuality on the tardiness of industrial workers. *Journal of Applied Behavior Analysis*, 6, 563–570.

Herrnstein, R. J. (1969). Method and theory in the study of avoidance. *Psychological Review*, 76, 49–69.

Hersen, M., Eisler, R. M., & Miller, P. M. (1974). An experimental analysis of generalization in assertive training. *Behaviour Research and Therapy*, 12, 295–310.

Higgins, S. T., Heil, S. H., & Lussier, J. P. (2004). Clinical implications of reinforcement as a determinant of substance abuse disorders. *Annual Review of Psychology*, 55, 431–461.

Hildebrand, R. G., Martin, G. L., Furer, P., & Hazen, A. (1990). A recruitment-of-praise package to increase productivity levels of developmentally handicapped workers. *Behavior Modification*, 14, 97–113.

Hilgard, E. R. (1962). *Introduction to psychology* (3rd ed.). New York: Harcourt, Brace & World.

Hilliard, R. B. (1993). Single-case methodology in psychotherapy process and outcome research. *Journal of Consulting and Clinical Psychology*, 61, 373–380.

Hinson, R. E., Poulos, C. X., & Cappell, H. (1982). Effects of pentobarbital and cocaine in rats expecting pentobarbital. *Pharmacology Biochemistry and Behavior*, 16, 661–666.

Hollis, K. L. (1997). Contemporary research on Pavlovian conditioning: A "new" functional analysis. *American Psychologist*, 52, 956–965.

Holmes, D. L. (1977). *Troubleshooting checklist and procedure*. (Materials produced by Eden Institute, Princeton, NJ.)

Holmes, D. S. (1984). Meditation and somatic arousal reduction. *American Psychologist*, 39, 1–10.

Holroyd, K. A. (2002). Assessment and psychological management of recurrent headache disorders. *Journal of Consulting and Clinical Psychology*, 70, 656–677.

Holroyd, K. A., & Penzien, D. B. (1985). Client variables and the behavioral treatment of recurrent tension headache: A meta-analytic review. *Journal of Behavioral Medicine*, 9, 515–536.

Homme, L. E. (1965). Perspectives in psychology: XXIV. Control of coverants, the operants of the mind. *Psychological Record*, 15, 501–511.

Homme, L. E. (1971). *How to use contingency contracting in the classroom*. Champaign, IL: Research Press.

Honeybourne, C., Matchett, G., & Davey, G. C. L. (1993). Expectancy models of laboratory preparedness effects: A UCS-expectancy bias in phylogenetic and ontogenetic fear-relevant stimuli. *Behavior Therapy*, 24, 253–264.

Hopkins, B. L., Conrad, R. J., Dangel, R. F., Fitch, H. G., Smith, M. J., & Anger, W. K. (1986). Behavioral technology for reducing occupational exposures to styrene. *Journal of Applied Behavior Analysis*, 19, 3–11.

Horner, R. A., Williams, J. A., & Knobbe, C. A. (1985). The effect of "opportunity to perform" on the maintenance of skills learned by high school students with severe handicaps. *Journal of the Association for Persons with Severe Handicaps*, 10, 172–175.

Horner, R. D., & Keilitz, I. (1975). Training mentally retarded adolescents to brush their teeth. *Journal of Applied Behavior Analysis*, 8, 301–309.

Horner, R. H., Eberhard, J. M., & Sheenan, M. R. (1986). Teaching generalized table bussing: The importance of negative teaching examples. *Behavior Modification*, 10, 457–471.

Houts, A. C. (2003). Behavioral treatment for enuresis. In A. E. Kazdin & J. R. Weisz (Eds.), *Evidence-based psychotherapies for children and adolescents* (pp. 389–406). New York: Guilford.

Houts, A. C., Berman, J. S., & Abramson, H. (1994). Effectiveness of psychological and pharmacological treatments for nocturnal enuresis. *Journal of Consulting and Clinical Psychology*, 62, 737–745.

Huffman, K. (2002). *Psychology in action* (6th ed.). New York: Wiley.

Hugdahl, K., & Öhman, A. (1977). Effects of instruction on acquisition and extinction of electrodermal responses to fear-relevant stimuli. *Journal of Experimental Psychology: Human Learning and Memory*, 3, 608–618.

Hughes, D., Harmer, M. L., Killian, D. J., & Niarhos, F. (1995). The effects of multiple-exemplar self-instructional training on high school students' generalized conversational interactions. *Journal of Applied Behavior Analysis*, 28, 201–218.

Hull, C. L. (1943). *Principles of behavior*. New York: Appleton-Century-Crofts.

Hulse, S. H., Deese, J., & Egeth, H. (1975). *The psychology of learning* (5th ed.). New York: McGraw-Hill.

Hundert, J., & Batstone, D. (1978). A practical procedure to maintain pupil's accurate self-rating in a classroom token program. *Behavior Modification*, 2, 93–112.

Hunt, G. M., & Azrin, N. H. (1973). A community-reinforcement approach to alcoholism. *Behaviour Research and Therapy*, 11, 91–104.

Hutchinson, R. R. (1977). By-products of aversive control. In W. K. Honig & J. E. R. Staddon (Eds.), *Handbook of operant behavior* (pp. 415–431). Englewood Cliffs, NJ: Prentice-Hall.

Ingvarsson, E. T., & Hollobaugh, T. (2010). Acquisition of intraverbal behavior: Teaching children with autism to mand for answers to questions. *Journal of Applied Behavior Analysis*, 43, 1–17.

Isaacs, W., Thomas, J., & Goldiamond, I. (1960). Application of operant conditioning to reinstate verbal behavior in psychotics. *Journal of Speech and Hearing Disorders*, 25, 8–12.

Ishuin, T. (2009). Linking brief functional analysis to intervention design in general education settings. *Behavior Analyst Today*, 10, 47–53.

Iwata, B. A. (1988). The development and adoption of controversial default technologies. *Behavior Analyst*, 11, 149–157.

Iwata, B. A., Dorsey, M. F., Slifer, K. J., Bauman, K. E., & Richman, G. S. (1982). Toward a functional analysis of self-injury. *Analysis and Intervention of Developmental Disabilities*, 2, 3–20.

Iwata, B. A., Pace, G. M., Cowdery, G. E., & Miltenberger, R. G. (1994). What makes extinction work: An analysis of procedural form and function. *Journal of Applied Behavior Analysis*, 27, 131–144.

Iwata, B. A., Pace, G. M., Kalsher, M. J., Cowdery, G. E., & Cataldo, M. F. (1990). Experimental analysis and extinction of self-injurious escape behavior. *Journal of Applied Behavior Analysis*, 23, 11–27.

Iwata, B. A., Smith, R. G., & Michael, J. (2000). Current research on the influence of establishing operations on behavior in applied settings. *Journal of Applied Behavior Analysis*, 33, 411–418.

Iwata, B. A., Wallace, M. D., Kahng, S. W., Lindberg, J. S., Roscoe, E. M., et al. (2000). Skill acquisition in the implementation of functional analysis methodology. *Journal of Applied Behavior Analysis*, 33, 181–194.

Jackson, D. A., & Wallace, R. F. (1974). The modification and generalization of voice loudness in a fifteen-year-old retarded girl. *Journal of Applied Behavior Analysis*, 7, 461–471.

Jacobson, E. (1938). *Progressive relaxation* (2nd ed.). Chicago: University of Chicago Press.

Jacobson, N. S., Follette, W. C., & Revenstorf, D. (1984). Psychotherapy outcome research: Methods for reporting variability and evaluating clinical significance. *Behavior Therapy*, 15, 336–352.

Jacobson, N. S., Roberts, L. J., Berns, S. B., & McGlinchey, J. B. (1999). Methods for defining and determining the clinical significance of treatment effects: Description, application, and alternatives. *Journal of Consulting and Clinical Psychology*, 67, 300–307.

James, J. E. (1981). Behavioral self-control of stuttering using time-out from speaking. *Journal of Applied Behavior Analysis*, 14, 25–37.

James, J. E. (1986). Review of the relative efficacy of imaginal and *in vivo* flooding in the treatment of clinical fear. *Behavioural Psychotherapy*, 14, 183–191.

Jason, L. A. (1985). Using a token-actuated timer to reduce television viewing. *Journal of Applied Behavior Analysis*, 18, 269–272.

Jason, L. A., Neal, A. M., & Marinakis, G. (1985). Altering contingencies to facilitate compliance with traffic light systems. *Journal of Applied Behavior Analysis*, 18, 95–100.

Jensen, B. J., & Haynes, S. N. (1986). Self-report questionnaires and inventories. In A. R. Ciminero, K. S. Calhoun, & H. E. Adams (Eds.), *Handbook of behavioral assessment* (2nd ed., pp. 150–175). New York: Wiley.

Jerome, J., Frantino, E. P., & Sturmey, P. (2007). The effects of errorless learning and backward chaining on the acquisition of Internet skills in adults with developmental disabilities. *Journal of Applied Behavior Analysis*, 40, 185–189.

Johnson, M. D., & Fawcett, S. B. (1994). Courteous service: Its assessment and modification in a human service organization. *Journal of Applied Behavior Analysis*, 27, 145–152.

Johnson, S. P., Welsh, T. M., Miller, L. K., & Altus, D. E. (1991). Participatory management: Maintaining staff performance in a university housing cooperative. *Journal of Applied Behavior Analysis*, 24, 119–127.

Johnson, W. G., Schlundt, D. G., Barclay, D. R., Carr-Nangle, R. E., & Engler, L. B. (1995). A naturalistic functional analysis of binge eating. *Behavior Therapy*, 26, 101–118.

Jones, L. J., Singh, N. N., & Kendall, K. A. (1990). Effects of Gentle Teaching and alternative treatments on self-injury. In A. C. Repp & N. N. Singh (Eds.), *Perspectives on the use of nonaversive and aversive interventions for persons with developmental disabilities* (pp. 215–230). Sycamore, IL: Sycamore.

Jones, M. C. (1924). The elimination of children's fears. *Journal of Experimental Psychology*, 7, 382–390.

Jones, R. T., Nelson, R. E., & Kazdin, A. E. (1977). The role of external variables in self-reinforcement. *Behavior Modification*, 1, 147–178.

Jordan, J., Singh, N. N., & Repp, A. C. (1989). An evaluation of gentle teaching and visual screening in the reduction of stereotypy. *Journal of Applied Behavior Analysis*, 22, 9–22.

Jospe, M., Shueman, S. A., & Troy, W. G. (1991). Quality assurance and the clinical health psychologist: A programmatic approach. In J. J. Sweet, R. H. Rozensky, & S. M. Tovian (Eds.), *Handbook of clinical psychology in medical settings* (pp. 95–112). New York: Plenum.

Kabat-Zinn, J. (1982). An outpatient program in behavioral medicine for chronic pain patients based on the practice of mindfulness meditation: Theoretical considerations and preliminary results. *General Hospital Psychiatry*, 4, 33–47.

Kabat-Zinn, J., Lipworth, L., & Burney, R. (1985). The clinical use of mindfulness meditation for the self-regulation of chronic pain. *Journal of Behavioral Medicine*, 8, 163–190.

Kahng, S. W., Chung, K. M., Guttshall, K., Pitts, S. C., Kao, J., & Girolami, K. (2010). Consistent visual analyses of intrasubject data. *Journal of Applied Behavior Analysis*, 43, 35–45.

Kahng, S. W., & Iwata, B. A. (1999). Correspondence between outcomes of brief and extended functional analyses. *Journal of Applied Behavior Analysis*, 32, 149–159.

Kallman, W. M., & Feuerstein, M. J. (1986). Psychophysiological procedures. In A. R. Ciminero, K. S. Calhoun, & H. E. Adams (Eds.), *Handbook of behavioral assessment* (2nd ed., pp. 325–352). New York: Wiley.

Kallman, W. M., Hersen, M., & O'Toole, D. H. (1975). The use of social reinforcement in a case of conversion reaction. *Behavior Therapy*, 6, 411–413.

Kamin, L. J. (1969). Predictability, surprise, attention, and conditioning. In B. A. Campbell & R. M. Church (Eds.), *Punishment and aversive behavior* (pp. 279–296). New York: Appleton-Century-Crofts.

Kanfer, F. H., & Grimm, L. G. (1980). Managing clinical change: A process model of therapy. *Behavior Modification*, 4, 419–444.

Kaplan, R. M. (1989). Health outcome models for policy analysis. *Health Psychology*, 8, 723–735.

Karlsson, T., & Chase, P. N. (1996). A comparison of three prompting methods for training software use. *Journal of Organizational Behavior Management*, 16, 27–44.

Karoly, P. (2005). Self-monitoring. In M. Hersen & J. Rosqvist (Eds.; M. Hersen, Ed. in Chief), *Encyclopedia of behavior modification and cognitive behavior therapy: Adult clinical applications* (Vol. 1, pp. 521–526). Thousand Oaks, CA: Sage.

Karraker, R. J. (1977). Self versus teacher selected reinforcers in a token economy. *Exceptional Children*, 43, 454–455.

Katz, R. C., Cacciapaglia, H., & Cabral, K. (2000). Labeling bias and attitudes toward behavior modification revisited. *Journal of Behavior Therapy and Experimental Psychiatry*, 31, 67–72.

Kau, M. L., & Fischer, J. (1974). Self-modification of exercise behavior. *Journal of Behavior Therapy and Experimental Psychiatry*, 5, 213–214.

Kayser, J. E., Billingsley, F. F., & Neel, R. S. (1986). A comparison of in-context and traditional instruction approaches: Total task, single trial versus backward chaining, multiple trials. *Journal of the Association for Persons with Severe Handicaps*, 11, 28–38.

Kazdin, A. E. (1971). The effect of response cost in suppressing behavior in a pre-psychotic retardate. *Journal of Behavior Therapy and Experimental Psychiatry*, 2, 137–140.

Kazdin, A. E. (1972). Response cost: The removal of conditioned reinforcers for therapeutic change. *Behavior Therapy*, 3, 533–546.

Kazdin, A. E. (1973). The effect of vicarious reinforcement on attentive behavior in the classroom. *Journal of Applied Behavior Analysis*, 6, 71–78.

Kazdin, A. E. (1978). *History of behavior modification: Experimental foundations of contemporary research*. Baltimore, MD: University Park Press.

Kazdin, A. E. (1985). The token economy. In R. Turner & L. M. Asher (Eds.), *Evaluating behavior therapy outcome* (pp. 225–253). New York: Springer.

Kazdin, A. E., & Erickson, L. M. (1975). Developing responsiveness to instructions in severely and profoundly retarded residents. *Journal of Behavior Therapy and Experimental Psychiatry*, 6, 17–21.

Kazdin, A. E., French, N. H., & Sherick, R. B. (1981). Acceptability of alternative treatments for children: Evaluations by inpatient children, parents, and staff. *Journal of Consulting and Clinical Psychology*, 49, 900–907.

Kazdin, A. E., & Geesey, S. (1977). Simultaneous-treatment design comparisons of the effects of earning reinforcers for one's peers versus oneself. *Behavior Therapy*, 8, 682–693.

Kazdin, A. E., & Polster, R. (1973). Intermittent token reinforcement and response maintenance in extinction. *Behavior Therapy*, 4, 386–391.

Kazdin, A. E., & Wilcoxon, L. A. (1976). Systematic desensitization and nonspecific treatment effects: A methodological evaluation. *Psychological Bulletin*, 83, 729–758.

Keeney, K. M., Fisher, W. W., Adelinis, J. D., & Wilder, D. A. (2000). The effects of response cost in the treatment of aberrant behavior maintained by negative reinforcement. *Journal of Applied Behavior Analysis*, 33, 255–258.

Kehoe, E. J., & Macrae, M. (1998). Classical conditioning. In W. O'Donohue (Ed.), *Learning and behavior therapy* (pp. 36–58). Boston: Allyn & Bacon.

Keller, F. S. (1968). "Good-bye teacher . . ." *Journal of Applied Behavior Analysis*, 1, 79–89.

Kelly, J. A., & Drabman, R. S. (1977). Overcorrection: An effective procedure that failed. *Journal of Clinical Child Psychology,* 6, 38–40.

Kelly, J. F., & Hake, D. F. (1970). An extinction-induced increase in an aggressive response in humans. *Journal of the Experimental Analysis of Behavior,* 14, 153–164.

Kempe, C. H. (1976). Child abuse and neglect. In N. B. Talbot (Ed.), *Raising children in modern America: Problems and prospective solutions* (pp. 173–188). Boston: Little, Brown.

Kendall, P. C., Marrs-Garcia, A., Nath, S. R., & Sheldrick, R. C. (1999). Normative comparisons for the evaluation of clinical significance. *Journal of Consulting and Clinical Psychology,* 67, 285–299.

Kennedy, C. H. (1994). Manipulating antecedent conditions to alter the stimulus control of problem behavior. *Journal of Applied Behavior Analysis,* 27, 161–170.

Kern, L., Childs, K. E., Dunlap, G., Clarke, S., & Falk, G. D. (1994). Using assessment-based curricular intervention to improve the classroom behavior of a student with emotional and behavioral challenges. *Journal of Applied Behavior Analysis,* 27, 7–19.

Kimble, G. A. (1961). *Hilgard and Marquis' conditioning and learning* (2nd ed.). New York: Appleton-Century-Crofts.

Kirby, F. D., & Shields, F. (1972). Modification of arithmetic response rate and attending behavior in a seventh-grade student. *Journal of Applied Behavior Analysis,* 5, 79–84.

Kirigin, K. A., Braukmann, C. J., Atwater, J. D., & Wolf, M. M. (1982). An evaluation of teaching-family (Achievement Place) group homes for juvenile offenders. *Journal of Applied Behavior Analysis,* 15, 1–16.

Kladopoulos, C. N., & McComas, J. J. (2001). The effects of form training on foul-shooting performance in members of a women's college basketball team. *Journal of Applied Behavior Analysis,* 34, 329–332.

Kleinknecht, R. A. (1994). Acquisition of blood, injury, and needle fears and phobias. *Behaviour Research and Therapy,* 32, 817–823.

Klingman, A., Melamed, B. G., Cuthbert, M. I., & Hermecz, D. A. (1984). Effects of participant modeling on information acquisition and skill utilization. *Journal of Consulting and Clinical Psychology,* 52, 414–422.

Kodak, T., & Clements, A. (2009). Acquisition of mands and tacts with concurrent echoic training. *Journal of Applied Behavior Analysis,* 42, 839–843.

Kodak, T., Lerman, D. C., Volkert, V. M., & Trosclair, N. (2007). Further examination of factors that influence preference for positive versus negative reinforcement. *Journal of Applied Behavior Analysis,* 40, 25–44.

Kodak, T., Northup, J., & Kelley, M. E. (2007). An evaluation of the types of attention that maintain problem behavior. *Journal of Applied Behavior Analysis,* 40, 167–171.

Koegel, R. L., & Rincover, A. (1974). Treatment of psychotic children in a classroom environment: 1. Learning in a large group. *Journal of Applied Behavior Analysis,* 7, 45–59.

Kohler, F. W., & Greenwood, C. R. (1986). Toward a technology of generalization: The identification of natural contingencies of reinforcement. *Behavior Analyst,* 9, 19–26.

Kohler, F. W., & Greenwood, C. R. (1990). Effects of collateral peer supportive behaviors within the classwide peer tutoring program. *Journal of Applied Behavior Analysis,* 23, 307–322.

Kohler, F. W., & Strain, P. S. (1990). Peer assisted interventions: Early promises, notable achievements, and future aspirations. *Clinical Psychology Review,* 10, 441–452.

Komaki, J., & Barnett, F. T. (1977). A behavioral approach to coaching football: Improving the play execution of the offensive backfield on a youth football team. *Journal of Applied Behavior Analysis,* 10, 657–664.

Komaki, J., Barwick, K. D., & Scott, L. R. (1978). A behavioral approach to occupational safety: Pinpointing and reinforcing safe performance in a food manufacturing plant. *Journal of Applied Psychology,* 63, 435–445.

Konarski, E. A., Johnson, M. R., Crowell, C. R., & Whitman, T. L. (1981). An alternative approach to reinforcement for applied researchers: Response deprivation. *Behavior Therapy,* 12, 653–666.

Kortick, S. A., & O'Brien, R. M. (1996). The World Series of quality control: A case study in the package delivery industry. *Journal of Organizational Behavior Management,* 16, 77–93.

Krantz, P. J., & McClannahan, L. E. (1998). Social interaction skills for children with autism: A script-fading procedure for beginning readers. *Journal of Applied Behavior Analysis,* 31, 191–202.

Krantz, P. J., & Risley, T. R. (1977). Behavioral ecology in the classroom. In K. D. O'Leary & S. G. O'Leary (Eds.), *Classroom management: The successful use of behavior modification* (2nd ed., pp. 349–366). New York: Pergamon.

Krebs, D. E., & Fagerson, T. L. (2003). Biofeedback in neuromuscular reeducation and gait training. In M. S. Schwartz & F. Andrasik (Eds.), *Biofeedback: A practitioner's guide* (3rd ed., pp. 485–514). New York: Guilford.

Kring, A. M., Johnson, S. L., Davison, G. C., & Neale, J. M. (2010). *Abnormal psychology* (11th ed.). New York: Wiley.

Kritch, K. M., & Bostow, D. E. (1998). Degree of constricted-response interaction in computer-based programmed instruction. *Journal of Applied Behavior Analysis*, 31, 387–398.

Krumboltz, J. D., & Krumboltz, H. B. (1972). *Changing children's behavior*. Englewood Cliffs, NJ: Prentice-Hall.

Kurtz, P. F., Chin, M. D., Huete, J. M., Tarbox, R. S. F., O'Connor, J. T., et al. (2003). Functional analysis and treatment of self-injurious behavior in young children: A summary of 30 cases. *Journal of Applied Behavior Analysis*, 36, 205–219.

Kusnecov, A. W. (2001). Behavioral conditioning of the immune system. In A. Baum, T. A. Revenson, & J. E. Singer (Eds.), *Handbook of health psychology* (pp. 105–115). Mahwah, NJ: Erlbaum.

Kvale, G., Hugdahl, K., Asbjørnsen, A., Rosengren, B., & Lote, K. (1991). Anticipatory nausea and vomiting in cancer patients. *Journal of Consulting and Clinical Psychology*, 59, 894–898.

Lalli, J. S., & Kates, K. (1998). The effect of reinforcer preference on functional analysis outcomes. *Journal of Applied Behavior Analysis*, 31, 79–90.

Lalli, J. S., Mace, F. C., Livezey, K., & Kates, K. (1998). Assessment of stimulus generalization gradients in the treatment of self-injurious behavior. *Journal of Applied Behavior Analysis*, 31, 479–483.

Lam, K.-N., Marra, D., & Salzinger, K. (2005). Social reinforcement of somatic versus psychological description of depressive events. *Behaviour Research and Therapy*, 43, 1203–1218.

Lamarre, J., & Holland, J. G. (1985). The functional independence of mands and tacts. *Journal of the Experimental Analysis of Behavior*, 43, 5–19.

Lancioni, G. E. (1982). Normal children as tutors to teach social responses to withdrawn mentally retarded schoolmates: Training, maintenance, and generalization. *Journal of Applied Behavior Analysis*, 15, 17–40.

Landrum, T. J., & Lloyd, J. W. (1992). Generalization in social behavior research with children and youth who have emotional or behavioral disorders. *Behavior Modification*, 16, 593–616.

Lane, J. B. (2005). Mindfulness meditation. In M. Hersen & J. Rosqvist (Eds.; M. Hersen, Ed. in Chief). *Encyclopedia of behavior modification and cognitive behavior therapy: Adult clinical applications* (Vol. 1, pp. 372–375). Thousand Oaks, CA: Sage.

Lang, R., O'Reilly, M., Machalicek, W., Lancioni, G., Rispoli, M., & Chan, J. M. (2008). A preliminary comparison of functional analysis results when conducted in contrived versus natural settings. *Journal of Applied Behavior Analysis*, 41, 441–445.

Laraway, S., Snycerski, S., Michael, J., & Poling, A. (2003). Motivating operations and terms to describe them: Some further refinements. *Journal of Applied Behavior Analysis*, 36, 407–414.

Laszlo, J. (1987). *Understanding cancer*. New York: Harper & Row.

Lattal, K. A. (1969). Contingency management of toothbrushing behavior in a summer camp for children. *Journal of Applied Behavior Analysis*, 2, 195–198.

LaVigna, G. W., & Willis, T. J. (2005). Differential reinforcement of other behavior. In M. Hersen & J. Rosqvist (Eds.; M. Hersen, Ed. in Chief). *Encyclopedia of behavior modification and cognitive behavior therapy: Adult clinical applications* (Vol. 1, pp. 261–262). Thousand Oaks, CA: Sage.

LeGray, M., Dufrene, B., Sterling-Turner, H., Olmi, D. J., & Bellone, K. (2010). A comparison of function-based differential reinforcement interventions for children engaging in disruptive classroom behavior. *Journal of Behavioral Education*, 19, 185–204.

Lehrer, P. M. (1982). How to relax and how not to relax: A re-evaluation of the work of Edmund Jacobson—I. *Behaviour Research and Therapy*, 20, 417–428.

Leitenberg, H., Burchard, J. D., Burchard, S. N., Fuller, E. J., & Lysaght, T. V. (1977). Using positive reinforcement to suppress behavior: Some experimental comparisons with sibling conflict. *Behavior Therapy*, 8, 168–182.

Lennox, D. B., Miltenberger, R. G., & Donnelly, D. R. (1987). Response interruption and DRL for the reduction of rapid eating. *Journal of Applied Behavior Analysis*, 20, 279–284.

Lerman, D. C., & Iwata, B. A. (1996). Developing a technology for the use of operant extinction in clinical settings: An examination of basic and applied research. *Journal of Applied Behavior Analysis*, 29, 345–382.

Lerman, D. C., Iwata, B. A., & Wallace, M. D. (1999). Side effects of extinction: Prevalence of bursting and aggression during the treatment of self-injurious behavior. *Journal of Applied Behavior Analysis*, 32, 1–8.

Lerman, D. C., Kelley, M. E., Van Camp, C. M., & Roane, H. S. (1999). Effects of reinforcement magnitude on spontaneous recovery. *Journal of Applied Behavior Analysis*, 32, 197–200.

LeVay, S., & Hamer, D. H. (1994). Evidence for a biological influence in male homosexuals. *Scientific American*, 270(5), 44–49.

Lewis, D. J. (1960). Partial reinforcement: A selective review of the literature since 1950. *Psychological Bulletin*, 57, 1–28.

Lewis, D. J., & Duncan, D. P. (1956). Effect of different percentages of money reward on extinction of a lever-pulling response. *Journal of Experimental Psychology*, 52, 23–27.

Lewis, D. J., & Duncan, D. P. (1957). Expectation and resistance to extinction of a lever-pulling response as functions of percentage of reinforcement and amount of reward. *Journal of Experimental Psychology*, 54, 115–120.

Lichstein, K. L. (1988). *Clinical relaxation strategies*. New York: Wiley.

Lindberg, J. S., Iwata, B. A., Kahng, S. W., & DeLeon, I. G. (1999). DRO contingencies: An analysis of variable-momentary schedules. *Journal of Applied Behavior Analysis*, 32, 123–136.

Linden, M., & Pasatu, J. (1998). The integration of cognitive and behavioral interventions in routine behavior therapy. *Journal of Cognitive Psychotherapy: An International Quarterly*, 12, 27–38.

Lindsay, J. (2008). Teaching fish to swim—into a net, on command. *Philadelphia Inquirer*, p. A15.

Linscheid, T. R., Iwata, B. A., Ricketts, R. W., Williams, D. E., & Griffen, J. C. (1990). Clinical evaluation of the self-injurious behavior inhibiting system (SIBIS). *Journal of Applied Behavior Analysis*, 23, 53–78.

Linscheid, T. R., & Meinhold, P. (1990). The controversy over aversives: Basic operant research and the side effects of punishment. In A. C. Repp & N. N. Singh (Eds.), *Perspectives on the use of nonaversive and aversive interventions for persons with developmental disabilities* (pp. 435–450). Sycamore, IL: Sycamore.

Linscheid, T. R., & Reichenbach, H. (2002). Multiple factors in the long-term effectiveness of contingent electric shock treatment for self-injurious behavior: A case example. *Research in Developmental Disabilities*, 23, 161–177.

Litow, L., & Pumroy, D. K. (1975). A brief review of classroom group-oriented contingencies. *Journal of Applied Behavior Analysis*, 8, 341–347.

Logan, D. L. (1970). A "paper money" token system as a recording aid in institutional settings. *Journal of Applied Behavior Analysis*, 3, 183–184.

Long, P., Forehand, R., Wierson, M., & Morgan, A. (1993). Does parent training with young noncompliant children have long term effects? *Behaviour Research and Therapy*, 32, 101–107.

Los Horcones (2009). *Los Horcones: Walden Two Community*. Retrieved (8-6-2009) from http://loshorcones.org.

Lovaas, O. I. (1977). *The autistic child: Language development through behavior modification*. New York: Irvington.

Lovaas, O. I., Koegel, R., Simmons, J. Q., & Long, J. S. (1973). Some generalization and follow-up measures on autistic children in behavior therapy. *Journal of Applied Behavior Analysis*, 6, 131–166.

Lovaas, O. I., Newsom, C., & Hickman, C. (1987). Self-stimulatory behavior and perceptual reinforcement. *Journal of Applied Behavior Analysis*, 20, 45–68.

Lovaas, O. I., Schaeffer, B., & Simmons, J. Q. (1965). Building social behavior in autistic children by using electric shock. *Journal of Experimental Research in Personality*, 1, 99–109.

Lovaas, O. I., & Simmons, J. Q. (1969). Manipulation of self-destruction in three retarded children. *Journal of Applied Behavior Analysis*, 2, 143–157.

Lovaas, O. I., & Smith, T. (2003). Early and intensive behavioral intervention with autism. In A. E. Kazdin & J. R. Weisz (Eds.), *Evidence-based psychotherapies for children and adolescents* (pp. 325–340). New York: Guilford.

Lovibond, P. F., Mitchell, C. J., Minard, E., Brady, A., & Menzies, R. G. (2009). Safety behaviors preserve threat beliefs: Protection from extinction of human fear conditioning by an avoidance response. *Behaviour Research and Therapy*, 47, 716–720.

Lovitt, T. C., & Curtiss, K. A. (1969). Academic response rate as a function of teacher- and self-imposed contingencies. *Journal of Applied Behavior Analysis*, 2, 49–53.

Lowe, C. F., & Chadwick, P. D. J. (1990). Verbal control of delusions. *Behavior Therapy*, 21, 461–479.

Lowe, K., & Lutzker, J. R. (1979). Increasing compliance to a medical regimen with a juvenile diabetic. *Behavior Therapy*, 10, 57–64.

Lubow, R. E. (1998). Latent inhibition and behavior pathology: Prophylactic and other possible effects of stimulus preexposure. In W. O'Donohue (Ed.), *Learning and behavior therapy* (pp. 107–121). Boston: Allyn & Bacon.

Luce, S. C., Delquadri, J., & Hall, R. V. (1980). Contingent exercise: A mild but powerful procedure for suppressing inappropriate verbal and aggressive behavior. *Journal of Applied Behavior Analysis*, 13, 583–594.

Lucic, K. S., Steffen, J. J., Harrigan, J. A., & Stuebing, R. C. (1991). Progressive relaxation training: Muscle contraction before relaxation? *Behavior Therapy*, 22, 249–256.

Ludwig, T. D., & Geller, E. S. (1991). Improving the driving practices of pizza deliverers: Response generalization and moderating effects of driving history. *Journal of Applied Behavior Analysis*, 24, 31–44.

Luiselli, J. K. (1990). Recent developments in nonaversive treatment: A review of rationale, methods, and recommendations. In A. C. Repp & N. N. Singh (Eds.), *Perspectives on the use of nonaversive and aversive interventions for persons with developmental disabilities* (pp. 73–86). Sycamore, IL: Sycamore.

Luiselli, J. K. (2005). Stimulus control. In G. Sugai & R. Horner (Eds.; M. Hersen, Ed. in Chief). *Encyclopedia of behavior modification and cognitive behavior therapy: Educational applications* (Vol. 3, pp. 1548–1552). Thousand Oaks, CA: Sage.

Luthans, F., & Kreitner, R. (1985). *Organizational behavior modification and beyond: An operant and social learning approach*. Glenview, IL: Scott, Foresman.

Lutz, J. (1994). *Introduction to learning and memory*. Pacific Grove, CA: Brooks/Cole.

MacDuff, G. S., Krantz, P. J., & McClannahan, L. E. (1993). Teaching children with autism to use photographic activity schedules: Maintenance and generalization of complex response chains. *Journal of Applied Behavior Analysis, 26*, 89–97.

MacKenzie-Keating, S. E., & McDonald, L. (1990). Overcorrection: Reviewed, revisited and revised. *Behavior Analyst, 13*, 39–48.

Maddi, S. R. (1996). *Personality theories: A comparative analysis* (6th ed.). Prospect Heights, IL: Waveland.

Madsen, C. H., Becker, W. C., & Thomas, D. R. (1968). Rules, praise, and ignoring: Elements of elementary classroom control. *Journal of Applied Behavior Analysis, 1*, 139–150.

Madsen, C. H., Becker, W. C., Thomas, D. R., Koser, L., & Plager, E. (1970). An analysis of the reinforcing function of "sit down" commands. In R. K. Parker (Ed.), *Readings in educational psychology* (pp. 265–278). Boston: Allyn & Bacon.

Magee, S. K., & Ellis, J. (2001). The detrimental effects of physical restraint as a consequence for inappropriate classroom behavior. *Journal of Applied Behavior Analysis, 34*, 501–504.

Mahoney, K., Van Wagenen, & Meyerson, L. (1971). Toilet training of normal and retarded children. *Journal of Applied Behavior Analysis, 4*, 173–181.

Main, M., & George, C. (1985). Responses of abused and disadvantaged toddlers to distress in age-mates: A study in the day care setting. *Developmental Psychology, 21*, 407–412.

Malatesta, V. J., & Adams, H. E. (1986). Assessment of sexual behavior. In A. R. Ciminero, K. S. Calhoun, & H. E. Adams (Eds.), *Handbook of behavioral assessment* (2nd ed., pp. 496–525). New York: Wiley.

Maletzky, B. M. (1974). Behavior recording as treatment: A brief note. *Behavior Therapy, 5*, 107–111.

Malott, R. W. (2005). Self-management. In M. Hersen & J. Rosqvist (Eds.; M. Hersen, Ed. in Chief). *Encyclopedia of behavior modification and cognitive behavior therapy: Adult clinical applications* (Vol. 1, pp. 516–521). Thousand Oaks, CA: Sage.

Marholin, D., & Gray, D. (1976). Effects of group response-cost procedures on cash shortages in a small business. *Journal of Applied Behavior Analysis, 9*, 25–30.

Marholin, D., & Townsend, N. M. (1978). An experimental analysis of side effects and response maintenance of a modified overcorrection procedure: The case of the persistent twiddler. *Behavior Therapy, 9*, 383–390.

Marshall, W. L., Gauthier, J., Christie, M. M., Currie, D. W., & Gordon, A. (1977). Flooding therapy: Effectiveness, stimulus characteristics, and the value of brief *in vivo* exposure. *Behaviour Research and Therapy, 15*, 79–87.

Marshall, W. L., Presse, L., & Andrews, W. R. (1976). A self-administered program for public speaking anxiety. *Behaviour Research and Therapy, 14*, 33–39.

Martens, B. K., Ardoin, S. P., Hilt, A. M., Lannie, A. L., Panahon, C. J., & Wolfe, L. A. (2002). Sensitivity of children's behavior to probabilistic reward: Effects of a decreasing-ratio lottery system on math performance. *Journal of Applied Behavior Analysis, 35*, 403–406.

Massetti, G. M., & Fabiano, G. A. (2005). Group contingency. In A. M. Gross & R. S. Drabman (Eds.; M. Hersen, Ed. in Chief). *Encyclopedia of behavior modification and cognitive behavior therapy: Child clinical applications* (Vol. 2, pp. 870–872). Thousand Oaks, CA: Sage.

Mathews, A. M., Johnston, D. W., Lancashire, M., Munby, M., Shaw, P. M., & Gelder, M. G. (1976). Imaginal flooding and exposure to real phobic situations: Treatment outcome with agoraphobic patients. *British Journal of Psychiatry, 129*, 362–371.

Mathews, J. R., Friman, P. C., Barone, V. J., Ross, L. V., & Christophersen, E. R. (1987). Decreasing dangerous infant behaviors through parent instruction. *Journal of Applied Behavior Analysis, 20*, 165–169.

Mathews, R. M., & Dix, M. (1992). Behavior change in the funny papers: Feedback to cartoonists on safety belt use. *Journal of Applied Behavior Analysis, 25*, 769–775.

Matson, J. L. (1983). Exploration of phobic behavior in a small child. *Journal of Behavior Therapy and Experimental Psychiatry, 14*, 257–259.

Matson, J. L., & Taras, M. E. (1989). A 20-year review of punishment and alternative methods to treat problem behaviors in developmentally delayed persons. *Research in Developmental Disabilities*, 10, 85–104.

Matson, J. L., & Vollmer, T. R. (1995). *User's guide: Questions About Behavioral Function (QABF)*. Baton Rouge, LA: Scientific Publishers.

Mattick, R. P., Kimber, J., Breen, C., & Davoli, M. (2003). Buprenorphine maintenance versus placebo or methadone maintenance for opioid dependence. *Cochrane Database of Systematic Reviews*, Issue 2. Retrieved 10-5-2006 from http://mrw.interscience.wiley.com. DOI: 10.1002/14651858.CD002207.pub2.

May, R. K., & Meyers, A. W. (2004). Sport psychology. In W. E. Craighead & C. B. Nemeroff (Eds.), *The concise Corsini encyclopedia of psychology and behavioral science* (pp. 937–938). New York: Wiley.

Mayhew, G. L., & Harris, F. (1978). Some negative side effects of a punishment procedure for stereotyped behavior. *Journal of Behavior Therapy and Experimental Psychiatry*, 9, 245–251.

McAdam, D. B., Klatt, K. P., Koffarnus, M., Dicesare, A., Solberg, K., et al. (2005). The effects of establishing operations on preferences for tangible items. *Journal of Applied Behavior Analysis*, 38, 107–110.

McAlister, W. R., & McAlister, D. E. (1995). Two factor theory: Implications for understanding anxiety based clinical phenomena. In W. O'Donohue & L. Krasner (Eds.), *Theories of behavior therapy: Exploring behavior change* (pp. 145–171). Washington, DC: American Psychological Association.

McCaffrey, R. J., & Blanchard, E. B. (1985). Stress management approaches to the treatment of essential hypertension. *Annals of Behavioral Medicine*, 7(1), 5–12.

McClannahan, L. E., McGee, G. G., MacDuff, G. S., & Krantz, P. J. (1990). Assessing and improving child care: A personal appearance index for children with autism. *Journal of Applied Behavior Analysis*, 23, 469–482.

McClannahan, L. E., & Risley, T. R. (1975). Design of living environments for nursing-home residents: Increasing participation in recreational activities. *Journal of Applied Behavior Analysis*, 8, 261–268.

McClelland, D. C., Atkinson, M. W., Clark, R. A., & Lowell, E. L. (1953). *The achievement motive*. New York: Appleton-Century-Crofts.

McComas, J., Hock, H., Paone, D., & El-Roy, D. (2000). Escape behavior during academic tasks: A preliminary analysis of idiosyncratic establishing operations. *Journal of Applied Behavior Analysis*, 33, 479–493.

McConnell, M. E., Cox, C. J., Thomas, D. D., & Hilvitz, P. B. (2001). *Functional behavioral assessment*. Denver, CO: Love Publishing.

McCracken, L. M., & Larkin, K. T. (1991). Treatment of paruresis with *in vivo* desensitization: A case report. *Journal of Behavior Therapy and Experimental Psychiatry*, 22, 57–62.

McGee, G. G., Almeida, M. C., Sulzer-Azaroff, B., & Feldman, R. S. (1992). Promoting reciprocal interactions via peer incidental teaching. *Journal of Applied Behavior Analysis*, 25, 117–126.

McGee, J. J., & Gonzalez, L. (1990). Gentle Teaching and the practice of human interdependence: A preliminary group study of 15 persons with severe behavioral disorders and their caregivers. In A. C. Repp & N. N. Singh (Eds.), *Perspectives on the use of nonaversive and aversive interventions for persons with developmental disabilities* (pp. 237–254). Sycamore, IL: Sycamore.

McGee, J. J., Menolascino, F. J., Hobbs, D. C., & Menousek, P. E. (1987). *Gentle Teaching: A nonaversive approach for helping persons with mental retardation*. New York: Human Sciences Press.

McGlynn, F. D. (2005). Systematic desensitization. In M. Hersen & J. Rosqvist (Eds.; M. Hersen, Ed. in Chief). *Encyclopedia of behavior modification and cognitive behavior therapy: Adult clinical applications* (Vol. 1, pp. 574–582). Thousand Oaks, CA: Sage.

McGrady, A., & Linden, W. (2003). Biobehavioral treatment of essential hypertension. In M. S. Schwartz & F. Andrasik (Eds.), *Biofeedback: A practitioner's guide* (3rd ed., pp. 382–405). New York: Guilford.

McLaughlin, T. F., Burgess, N., & Sackville-West, L. (1982). Effects of self-recording and self-recording + matching on academic performance. *Child Behavior Therapy*, 3, 17–27.

McMahon, R. J. (1984). Behavioral checklists and ratings scales. In T. H. Ollendick & M. Hersen (Eds.), *Child behavioral assessment: Principles and procedures* (pp. 80–105). New York: Pergamon.

McNeil, C. B., Eyberg, S., Eisenstadt, T. H., Newcomb, K., & Funderburk, B. (1991). Parent-child interaction therapy with behavior problem children: Generalization of treatment effects to the school setting. *Journal of Clinical Child Psychology*, 20, 140–151.

McReynolds, W. T., & Church, A. (1973). Self-control, study skills development and counseling approaches to the improvement of study behavior. *Behaviour Research and Therapy*, 11, 233–235.

McSweeny, A. J. (1978). Effects of response cost on the behavior of a million persons: Charging for directory assistance in Cincinnati. *Journal of Applied Behavior Analysis*, 11, 47–51.

McWilliams, R., Nietupski, J., & Hamre-Nietupski, S. (1990). Teaching complex activities to students with moderate handicaps through the forward chaining of shorter total cycle response sequences. *Education and Training in Mental Retardation & Developmental Disabilities*, 25, 292–298.

Meichenbaum, D. (1986). Cognitive-behavior modification. In F. H. Kanfer & A. P. Goldstein (Eds.), *Helping people change: A textbook of methods* (3rd ed., pp. 346–380). New York: Pergamon.

Melamed, B. G., & Siegel, L. J. (1975). Reduction of anxiety in children facing hospitalization and surgery by use of filmed modeling. *Journal of Consulting and Clinical Psychology*, 43, 511–521.

Melin, L., & Götestam, K. G. (1981). The effects of rearranging ward routines on communication and eating behaviors of psychogeriatric patients. *Journal of Applied Behavior Analysis*, 14, 47–51.

Menzies, R. G., & Clarke, J. C. (1993). A comparison of *in vivo* and vicarious exposure in the treatment of childhood water phobia. *Behaviour Research and Therapy*, 31, 9–15.

Merckelbach, H., Muris, P., & Schouten, E. (1996). Pathways to fear in spider phobic children. *Behaviour Research and Therapy*, 34, 935–938.

Michael, J. (1982). Distinguishing between discriminative and motivational functions of stimuli. *Journal of the Experimental Analysis of Behavior*, 37, 149–155.

Michael, J. (1986). Repertoire-altering effects of remote contingencies. *Analysis of Verbal Behavior*, 4, 10–18.

Michael, J. (1988). Establishing operations and the mand. *The Analysis of Verbal Behavior*, 6, 3–9.

Michael, J. (2000). Implications and refinements of the establishing operation concept. *Journal of Applied Behavior Analysis*, 33, 401–410.

Miller, D. L., & Kelley, M. L. (1994). The use of goal setting and contingency contracting for improving children's homework performance. *Journal of Applied Behavior Analysis*, 27, 73–84.

Miller, L. K. (1980). *Principles of everyday behavior analysis* (2nd ed.). Pacific Grove, CA: Brooks/Cole.

Miller, P. W. (1972). The use of behavioral contracting in the treatment of alcoholism: A case report. *Behavior Therapy*, 3, 593–596.

Miller, W. R., & Hester, R. K. (1980). Treating the problem drinker: Modern approaches. In W. R. Miller (Ed.), *The addictive behaviors: Treatment of alcoholism, drug abuse, smoking, and obesity* (pp. 11–141). New York: Pergamon.

Miltenberger, R. G. (2005). The role of automatic negative reinforcement in clinical problems. *International Journal of Behavioral Consultation and Therapy*, 1, 1–11.

Miltenberger, R. G., Fuqua, R. W., & Woods, D. W. (1998). Applying behavior analysis to clinical problems: Review and analysis of habit reversal. *Journal of Applied Behavior Analysis*, 31, 447–469.

Miltenberger, R. G., Redlin, J., Crosby, R., Stickney, M., Mitchell, J., et al. (2003). Direct and retrospective assessment of factors contributing to compulsive buying. *Journal of Behavior Therapy and Experimental Psychiatry*, 34, 1–9.

Minton, L. (1999). Who controls your money? Our teen survey results. *Parade Magazine*, p. 10.

Monastra, V. J. (2003). Clinical applications of electroencephalographic biofeedback. In M. S. Schwartz & F. Andrasik (Eds.), *Biofeedback: A practitioner's guide* (3rd ed., pp. 438–463). New York: Guilford.

Monette, D. R., Sullivan, T. J., & DeJong, C. R. (1990). *Applied social research: Tool for the human services* (2nd ed.). Fort Worth, TX: Holt, Rinehart & Winston.

Monti, P. M., Rohsenow, D. J., Rubonis, A. V., Naiura, R. S., Sirota, A. D., Colby, S. M., Goddard, P., & Abrams, D. B. (1994). Cue exposure with coping skills treatment for male alcoholics: A preliminary investigation. *Journal of Consulting and Clinical Psychology*, 61, 1011–1019.

Moore, S. (1987). Relaxation training. In R. J. Corsini (Ed.), *Concise encyclopedia of psychology* (pp. 969–970). New York: Wiley.

Morin, C. M., Culbert, J. P., & Schwartz, S. M. (1994). Nonpharmacological interventions for insomnia: A meta-analysis of treatment efficacy. *American Journal of Psychiatry*, 151, 1172–1180.

Morris, E. K., & Redd, W. H. (1975). Children's performance and social preference for positive, negative, and mixed adult-child interactions. *Child Development*, 46, 525–531.

Morris, R. J., & Kratochwill, T. R. (1983). *Treating children's fears and phobias: A behavioral approach*. New York: Pergamon.

Mowrer, O. H. (1938). Apparatus for the study and treatment of enuresis. *American Journal of Psychology*, 51, 163–165.

Mowrer, O. H. (1947). On the dual nature of learning—A reinterpretation of "conditioning" and "problem solving." *Harvard Educational Review*, 17, 102–148.

Mueller, M. M., Sterling-Turner, H. E., & Scattone, D. (2001). Functional assessment of hand flapping in a general education classroom. *Journal of Applied Behavior Analysis*, 34, 233–236.

Muris, P., Merckelbach, H., de Jong, P. J., & Ollendick, T. H. (2002). The etiology of specific fears and phobias in children: A critique of the non-associative account. *Behaviour Research and Therapy*, 40, 185–195.

Muris, P., van Zwol, L., Huijding, J., & Mayer, B. (2010). Mom told me scary things about this animal: Parents installing fear beliefs in the children via the verbal information pathway. *Behaviour Research and Therapy*, 48, 341–346.

Murphy, E. S., McSweeney, F. K., Smith, R. G., & McComas, J. J. (2003). Dynamic changes in reinforcer effectiveness: Theoretical, methodological, and practical implications for applied research. *Journal of Applied Behavior Analysis*, 36, 421–438.

Murphy, H. A., Hutchison, J. M., & Bailey, J. S. (1983). Behavioral school psychology goes outdoors: The effects of organized games on playground aggression. *Journal of Applied Behavior Analysis*, 16, 29–35.

Murray, D. M., Pirie, P., Leupker, R. V., & Pallonen, U. (1989). Five- and six-year follow-up results from four seventh-grade smoking prevention strategies. *Journal of Behavioral Medicine*, 12, 207–218.

Murrell, M., Hardy, M., & Martin, G. L. (1974). Danny learns to match digits with the number of objects. *Special Education in Canada*, 49, 20–22.

Musser, E. H., Bray, M. A., Kehle, T. J., & Jenson, W. R. (2001). Reducing disruptive behaviors in students with serious emotional disturbance. *School Psychology Review*, 30, 294–304.

Myers, D. G. (1998). *Psychology* (5th ed.). New York: Worth.

Najdowski, A. C., Wallace, M. D., Doney, J. K., & Ghezzi, P. M. (2003). Parental assessment and treatment of food selectivity in natural settings. *Journal of Applied Behavior Analysis*, 36, 383–386.

Najdowski, A. C., Wallace, M. D., Ellsworth, C. L., MacAleese, A. N., & Cleveland, J. M. (2008). Functional analyses and treatment of precursor behavior. *Journal of Applied Behavior Analysis*, 41, 97–105.

Nakano, K. (1990). Operant self-control procedure in modifying Type A behavior. *Journal of Behavior Therapy and Experimental Psychiatry*, 21, 249–255.

Neef, N. A., Lensbower, J., Hockersmith, I., DePalma, V., & Gray, K. (1990). In vivo versus simulation training: An interactional analysis of range and type of training exemplars. *Journal of Applied Behavior Analysis*, 23, 447–458.

Nelton, S. (1988). Motivating for success. *Nation's Business*, pp. 18–26.

Nesbitt, E. B. (1973). An escalator phobia overcome in one session of flooding *in vivo*. *Journal of Behavior Therapy and Experimental Psychiatry*, 4, 405–406.

Nestoriuc, Y., Martin, A., Rief, W., & Andrasik, F. (2008). Biofeedback treatment for headache disorders: A comprehensive efficacy review. *Applied Psychophysiology and Biofeedback*, 33, 125–140.

Neumann, D. L., & Kitlertsirivatana, E. (2010). Exposure to a novel context after extinction causes a renewal of extinguished conditioned responses: Implications for the treatment of fear. *Behaviour Research and Therapy*, 48, 565–570.

Nevin, J. A. (1988). Behavioral momentum and the partial reinforcement effect. *Psychological Bulletin*, 103, 44–56.

NHTSA (National Highway Traffic Safety Administration). (2004). *Vehicle-based countermeasures for signal and stop sign violation*. Retrieved (1-21-2009) from http://nhtsa.dot.gov.

Niaura, R. S., Rohsenow, D. J., Binkoff, J. A., Monti, P. M., Pedraza, M., & Abrams, D. B. (1988). Relevance of cue reactivity to understanding alcohol and smoking relapse. *Journal of Abnormal Psychology*, 97, 133–152.

Nickel, C., Kettler, C., Muehlbacher, M., Lahmann, C., Tritt, K., et al. (2005). Effect of progressive muscle relaxation in adolescent female bronchial asthma patients: A randomized, double-blind, controlled study. *Journal of Psychosomatic Research*, 59, 393–398.

Nielsen, D., Sigurdsson, S. O., & Austin, J. (2009). Preventing back injuries in hospital settings: The effects of video modeling on safe patient lifting by nurses. *Journal of Applied Behavior Analysis*, 42, 551–561.

Ninness, H. A. C., Fuerst, J., Rutherford, R. D., & Glenn, S. S. (1991). Effects of self-management training and reinforcement on the transfer of improved conduct in the absence of supervision. *Journal of Applied Behavior Analysis*, 24, 499–508.

NJNPI (New Jersey Neuro-Psychiatric Institute). (1972). *Behavior modification training program: Drug staff*. Princeton, NJ: Author.

NLM (National Library of Medicine: MedlinePlus, Drug Information). (2011). *Varenicline*. Retrieved (1-3-2011) from http://www.nlm.nih.gov.

Noell, G. H., VanDerHeyden, A. M., Gatti, S. L., & Whitmarsh, E. L. (2001). Functional assessment of the effects of escape and attention on students' compliance during instruction. *School Psychology Quarterly, 16,* 253–269.

Nordquist, V. M. (1971). The modification of a child's enuresis: Some response-response relationships. *Journal of Applied Behavior Analysis, 4,* 241–247.

North, M. M., North, S. M., & Coble, J. R. (1997). Virtual reality therapy for fear of flying. *American Journal of Psychiatry, 154,* 130.

Northup, J. (2000). Further evaluation of the accuracy of reinforcer surveys: A systematic replication. *Journal of Applied Behavior Analysis, 33,* 335–338.

Northup, J., Wacker, D., Sasso, G., Steege, M., Cigrand, K., et al. (1991). A brief functional analysis of aggressive and alternative behavior in an outclinic setting. *Journal of Applied Behavior Analysis, 24,* 509–522.

Novaco, R. W. (1976). The functions and regulation of the arousal of anger. *American Journal of Psychiatry, 133,* 1124–1128.

O'Banion, D. R., & Whaley, D. L. (1981). *Behavior contracting: Arranging contingencies of reinforcement.* New York: Springer.

O'Brien, F., Bugle, C., & Azrin, N. H. (1972). Training and maintaining a retarded child's proper eating. *Journal of Applied Behavior Analysis, 5,* 67–72.

O'Brien, S., & Karsh, K. G. (1990). Treatment acceptability: Consumer, therapist, and society. In A. C. Repp & N. N. Singh (Eds.), *Perspectives on the use of nonaversive and aversive interventions for persons with developmental disabilities* (pp. 503–516). Sycamore, IL: Sycamore.

O'Brien, T. P., Riner, L. S., & Budd, K. S. (1983). The effects of a child's self-evaluation program on compliance with parental instructions in the home. *Journal of Applied Behavior Analysis, 16,* 69–79.

O'Callahan, P. M., Allen, K. D., Powell, S., & Salama, F. (2006). The efficacy of noncontingent escape for decreasing children's disruptive behavior during restorative dental treatment. *Journal of Applied Behavior Analysis, 39,* 161–171.

O'Donnell, J. (2001). The discriminative stimulus for punishment or SD^p. *Behavior Analyst, 24,* 261–262.

O'Donnell, J., Crosbie, J., Williams, D. C., & Saunders, K. J. (2000). Stimulus control and generalization of point-loss punishment with humans. *Journal of the Experimental Analysis of Behavior, 73,* 261–274.

O'Donohue, W., & Plaud, J. J. (1994). The conditioning of human sexual arousal. *Archives of Sexual Behavior, 23,* 321–344.

Okifuji, A., & Friedman, A. G., (1992). Experimentally induced taste aversions in humans: Effects of overshadowing on acquisition. *Behaviour Research and Therapy, 30,* 23–32.

Olds, J., & Milner, P. (1954). Positive reinforcement produced by electrical stimulation of the septal area and other regions of the rat brain. *Journal of Comparative and Physiological Psychology, 47,* 419–427.

O'Leary, K. D. (1984). The image of behavior therapy: It is time to take a stand. *Behavior Therapy, 15,* 219–233.

Oliver, S. D., West, R. C., & Sloane, H. N. (1974). Some effects on human behavior of aversive events. *Behavior Therapy, 5,* 481–493.

Ollendick, T. H. (1983). Reliability and validity of the Revised Fear Survey Schedule for Children (FSSC-R). *Behaviour Research and Therapy, 21,* 685–692.

Ollendick, T. H., & Hersen, M. (1984). An overview of child behavioral assessment. In T. H. Ollendick & M. Hersen (Eds.), *Child behavioral assessment: Principles and procedures* (pp. 3–19). New York: Pergamon.

Ollendick, T. H., & Matson, J. L. (1978). Overcorrection: An overview. *Behavior Therapy, 9,* 830–842.

Olson, R. P. (1987). Definitions of biofeedback. In M. S. Schwartz (Ed.), *Biofeedback: A practitioner's guide* (pp. 33–38). New York: Guilford.

Olson, R. P., & Kroon, J. S. (1987). Biobehavioral treatments of essential hypertension. In M. S. Schwartz (Ed.), *Biofeedback: A practitioner's guide* (pp. 316–339). New York: Guilford.

Olson, R. P., & Schwartz, M. S. (1987). An historical perspective on the biofeedback field. In M. S. Schwartz (Ed.), *Biofeedback: A practitioner's guide* (pp. 3–18). New York: Guilford.

Oltmanns, T. F., Neale, J. M., & Davison, G. C. (1991). *Case studies in abnormal psychology* (3rd ed.). New York: Wiley.

O'Neill, R. E., Horner, R. H., Albin, R. W., Sprague, J. R., Storey, K., & Newton, J. S. (1997). *Functional assessment and program development for problem behavior: A practical handbook* (2nd ed.). Pacific Grove, CA: Brooks/Cole.

O'Reilly, M. F., Green, G., & Braunling-McMorrow, D. (1990). Self-administered written prompts to teach home accident prevention skills to adults with brain injuries. *Journal of Applied Behavior Analysis, 23,* 431–446.

Ormrod, J. E. (1990). *Human learning: Theories, principles, and educational applications.* New York: Macmillan.

Ost, L. G. (1987). Age of onset in different phobias. *Journal of Abnormal Psychology, 96,* 223–229.

Ost, L. G., & Hugdahl, K. (1981). Acquisition of phobias and anxiety response patterns in clinical patients. *Behaviour Research and Therapy, 19,* 439–447.

Overholser, J. C. (1991). Prompting and fading in the exposure treatment of compulsive checking. *Journal of Behavior Therapy and Experimental Psychiatry, 22,* 271–279.

Pace, G. M., Ivancic, M. T., Edwards, G. L., Iwata, B. A., & Page, T. J. (1985). Assessment of stimulus preference and reinforcer value with profoundly retarded individuals. *Journal of Applied Behavior Analysis, 18,* 249–255.

Paclawskyj, T. R., Matson, J. L., Rush, K. S., Smalls, Y., & Vollmer, T. R. (2000). Questions About Behavioral Function (QABF): A behavioral checklist for functional assessment of aberrant behavior. *Research in Developmental Disabilities, 21,* 223–229.

Page, T. J., Iwata, B. A., & Neef, N. A. (1976). Teaching pedestrian skills to retarded persons: Generalization from the classroom to the natural environment. *Journal of Applied Behavior Analysis, 9,* 433–444.

Paine, S. C., Hops, H., Walker, H. M., Greenwood, C. R., Fleischman, D. H., & Guild, J. J. (1982). Repeated treatment effects: A study of maintaining behavior change in socially withdrawn children. *Behavior Modification, 6,* 171–199.

Parker, R. I, & Hagan-Burke, S. (2007). Useful effect size interpretations for single case research. *Behavior Therapy, 38,* 95–105.

Parker, R. I., & Vannest, K. (2009). An improved effect size for single-case research: Nonoverlap of all pairs. *Behavior Therapy, 40,* 357–367.

Parrish, J. M., & Babbitt, R. L. (1991). Video-mediated instruction in medical settings. In P. W. Dowrick (Ed.), *Practical guide to using video in the behavioral sciences* (pp. 166–185). New York: Wiley.

Patterson, C. J., & Mischel, W. (1975). Plans to resist temptation. *Developmental Psychology, 11,* 369–378.

Patterson, G. R. (1982). *Coercive family processes.* Eugene, OR: Castalia Press.

Patterson, G. R. (2005). Coercive cycles in families. In G. Sugai & R. Horner (Eds.; M. Hersen, Ed. in Chief), *Encyclopedia of behavior modification and cognitive behavior therapy, Volume 3: Educational applications* (pp. 1224–1225). Pacific Grove, CA: Sage.

Paul, G. L. (1967). Insight versus desensitization in psychotherapy two years after termination. *Journal of Consulting Psychology, 31,* 333–348.

Paul, G. L., & Lentz, R. J. (1977). *Psychosocial treatment of chronic mental patients: Milieu vs. social-learning programs.* Cambridge, MA: Harvard University Press.

Pavlov, I. P. (1927). *Conditioned reflexes.* (G. V. Anrep, trans.). New York: Oxford University Press.

Pawlicki, R. E., & Galotti, N. (1978). A tic-like behavior case study emanating from a self-directed behavior modification course. *Behavior Therapy, 9,* 671–672.

Pedalino, E., & Gamboa, V. U. (1974). Behavior modification and absenteeism: Intervention in one industrial setting. *Journal of Applied Psychology, 59,* 694–698.

Pellecchia, M., & Hineline, P. N. (2007). Generalization of mands in children with autism from adults to peers. *Behavior Analyst Today, 8,* 483–491.

Pellegrino, L. (2007). Patterns of development and disability. In M. L. Batshaw, L. Pellegrino, & N. J. Roizen (Eds.), *Children with disabilities* (6th ed., pp. 217–228). Baltimore, MD: Paul H. Brookes.

Peek, C. J. (2003). A primer of biofeedback instrumentation. In M. S. Schwartz & F. Andrasik (Eds.), *Biofeedback: A practitioner's guide* (3rd ed., pp. 73–127). New York: Guilford.

Pelios, L., Morren, J., Tesch, D., & Axelrod, S. (1999). The impact of functional analysis methodology on treatment choice for self-injurious and aggressive behavior. *Journal of Applied Behavior Analysis, 32,* 185–195.

Perri, M. G., & Richards, C. S. (1977). An investigation of naturally occurring episodes of self-controlled behaviors. *Journal of Counseling Psychology, 24,* 178–183.

Petursdóttir, A. I., Ólafsdóttir, A. R., & Aradóttir, B. (2008). The effects of tact and listener training on the emergence of bidirectional intraverbal relations. *Journal of Applied Behavior Analysis, 41,* 411–415.

Phillips, E. L. (1968). Achievement Place: Token reinforcement procedures in a home-style rehabilitation setting for "pre-delinquent" boys. *Journal of Applied Behavior Analysis, 1,* 213–223.

Phillips, E. L., Phillips, E. A., Fixsen, D. L., & Wolf, M. M. (1971). Achievement Place: Modification of the behaviors of pre-delinquent boys within a token economy. *Journal of Applied Behavior Analysis, 4,* 45–59.

Phillips, E. L., Phillips, E. A., Fixsen, D. L., & Wolf, M. M. (1973). Achievement Place: Behavior shaping works for delinquents. *Psychology Today,* pp. 75–79.

Phillips, E. L., Phillips, E. A., Wolf, M. M., & Fixsen, D. L. (1973). Achievement Place: Development of the elected manager system. *Journal of Applied Behavior Analysis, 6,* 541–561.

Piazza, C. C., Fisher, W. W., Brown, K. A., Shore, B. A., Patel, M. R., et al. (2003). Functional analysis of inappropriate mealtime behaviors. *Journal of Applied Behavior Analysis, 36,* 187–204.

Piazza, C. C., Fisher, W. W., Hanley, G. P., LeBlanc, L. A., Worsdell, A. S., et al. (1998). Treatment of pica through multiple analyses of its reinforcing functions. *Journal of Applied Behavior Analysis, 31,* 165–189.

Piazza, C. C., Roane, H. , S., Keeney, K. M., Boney, B. R., & Abt, K. A. (2002). Varying response effort in the treatment of pica maintained by automatic reinforcement. *Journal of Applied Behavior Analysis, 35,* 233–246.

Pigott, H. E., Fantuzzo, J. W., & Clement, P. W. (1986). The effects of reciprocal peer tutoring and group contingencies on the academic performance of elementary school children. *Journal of Applied Behavior Analysis, 19,* 93–98.

Piliavin, J. A., Dovidio, J. F., Gaertner, S. L., & Clark, R. D. (1981). Responsive bystanders: The process on intervention. In J. Grzelak & V. Derlega (Eds.), *Living with other people: Theory and research on cooperation and helping.* New York: Academic Press.

Pinto, R. P., & Hollandsworth, J. G. (1989). Using videotaped modeling to prepare children psychologically for surgery: Influence of parents and costs versus benefits of providing preparation services. *Health Psychology, 8,* 79–95.

Pitts, C. E. (1976). Behavior modification—1787. *Journal of Applied Behavior Analysis, 9,* 146.

Plotkin, W. B. (1976). On the self-regulation of the occipital alpha rhythm: Control strategies, states of consciousness, and the role of physiological feedback. *Journal of Experimental Psychology, 105,* 66–99.

Poche, C., Brouwer, R., & Swearingen, M. (1981). Teaching self-protection to young children. *Journal of Applied Behavior Analysis, 14,* 169–176.

Poling, A. D., & Ehrhardt, K. (2005). Noncontingent reinforcement. In M. Hersen & J. Rosqvist (Eds.; M. Hersen, Ed. in Chief). *Encyclopedia of behavior modification and cognitive behavior therapy: Adult clinical applications* (Vol. 1, pp. 399–401). Thousand Oaks, CA: Sage.

Pomerleau, O. F., & Pomerleau, C. S. (1989). A biobehavioral perspective on smoking. In T. Ney & A. Gale (Eds.), *Smoking and human behavior* (pp. 69–90). New York: Wiley.

Popkin, J., & Skinner, C. H. (2003). Enhancing academic performance in a classroom serving students with serious emotional disturbance: Interdependent group contingencies with randomly selected components. *School Psychology Review, 32,* 282–295.

Poppen, R. (1998). *Behavioral relaxation training and assessment* (2nd ed.). Thousand Oaks, CA: Sage.

Poppen, R. (2005). Relaxation strategies. In M. Hersen & J. Rosqvist (Eds.; M. Hersen, Ed. in Chief). *Encyclopedia of behavior modification and cognitive behavior therapy: Adult clinical applications* (Vol. 1, pp. 485–489). Thousand Oaks, CA: Sage.

Porritt, M., Burt, A., & Poling, A. (2006). Increasing fiction writers' productivity through an Internet-based intervention. *Journal of Applied Behavior Analysis, 39,* 393–397.

Porter, K., Porcari, C., Koch, E. I., Fons, C., & Spates, C. R. (2006). In vivo exposure treatment for agoraphobia. *Behavior Analyst Today, 7,* 434–439.

Porterfield, J. K., Herbert-Jackson, E., & Risley, T. R. (1976). Contingent observation: An effective and acceptable procedure for reducing disruptive behavior of young children in a group setting. *Journal of Applied Behavior Analysis, 9,* 55–64.

Post, M., Storey, K., & Karabin, M. (2002). Cool headphones for effective prompts: Supporting students and adults in work and community environments. *Teaching Exceptional Children, 34,* 60–65.

Potoczak, K., Carr, J. E., & Michael, J. (2007). The effects of consequence manipulation during functional analysis of problem behavior maintained by negative reinforcement. *Journal of Applied Behavior Analysis, 40,* 719–724.

Poulton, R., & Menzies, R. G. (2002). Non-associative fear acquisition: A review of the evidence from retrospective and longitudinal research. *Behaviour Research and Therapy, 40,* 127–149.

Powell, J., Martindale, A., & Kulp, S. (1975). An evaluation of time-sampled measures of behavior. *Journal of Applied Behavior Analysis, 8,* 463–469.

Premack, D. (1959). Toward empirical behavior laws: I. Positive reinforcement. *Psychological Review, 66,* 219–233.

Premack, D. (1965). Reinforcement theory. In D. Levine (Ed.), *Nebraska Symposium on motivation* (pp. 123–180). Lincoln: University of Nebraska Press.

Price, K. L., Saladin, M. E., Baker, N. L., Tolliver, B. K., DeSantis, S. M., et al. (2010). Extinction of drug cue reactivity in methamphetamine-dependent individuals. *Behaviour Research and Therapy, 48,* 860–865.

Prochaska, J. O., & DiClemente, C. C. (1984). *The transtheoretical approach: Crossing traditional boundaries of therapy.* Homewood, IL: Dow Jones/Irwin.

Prochaska, J. O., DiClemente, C. C., & Norcross, J. C. (1992). In search of how people change: Applications to addictive behaviors. *American Psychologist, 47*, 1102–1114.

Puder, R., Lacks, P., Bertelson, A. D., & Storandt, M. (1983). Short-term stimulus control treatment of insomnia in older adults. *Behavior Therapy, 14*, 424–429.

Rachman, S. (1991). Neo-conditioning and the classical theory of fear acquisition. *Clinical Psychological Review, 11*, 155–173.

Rapp, J. T., Miltenberger, R. G., Galensky, T. L., Ellingson, S. A., & Long, E. S. (1999). A functional analysis of hair pulling. *Journal of Applied Behavior Analysis, 32*, 329–337.

Rapport, M. D., & Begolli, G. (2005). Response cost. In A. M. Gross & R. S. Drabman (Eds.; M. Hersen, Ed. in Chief). *Encyclopedia of behavior modification and cognitive behavior therapy: Child clinical applications* (Vol. 2, pp. 1002–1006). Thousand Oaks, CA: Sage.

Rapport, M. D., Murphy, H. A., & Bailey, J. S. (1982). Ritalin vs. response cost in the control of hyperactive children: A within-subject comparison. *Journal of Applied Behavior Analysis, 15*, 205–216.

Rasey, H. W., & Iversen, I. H. (1993). An experimental acquisition of maladaptive behavior by shaping. *Journal of Behavior Therapy and Experimental Psychiatry, 24*, 37–43.

Rasing, E. J., & Duker, P. C. (1992). Effects of a multifaceted training procedure on the acquisition and generalization of social behaviors in language-disabled deaf children. *Journal of Applied Behavior Analysis, 25*, 723–734.

Rasmussen, E. B., & Newland, M. C. (2008). Asymmetry of reinforcement and punishment in human choice. *Journal of the Experimental Analysis of Behavior, 89*, 157–167.

Rathus, S. A. (1973). A 30-item schedule for assessing assertive behavior. *Behavior Therapy, 4*, 398–406.

Redd, W. H., & Birnbrauer, J. S. (1969). Adults as discriminative stimuli for different reinforcement contingencies with retarded children. *Journal of Experimental Child Psychology, 7*, 440–447.

Reitman, D. (2005). Applied behavior analysis. In M. Hersen & J. Rosqvist (Eds.; M. Hersen, Ed. in Chief). *Encyclopedia of behavior modification and cognitive behavior therapy: Adult clinical applications* (Vol. 1, pp. 14–23). Thousand Oaks, CA: Sage.

Reitman, D., Waguespack, A., & Valley-Gray, S. (2005). Behavioral contracting. In A. M. Gross & R. S. Drabman (Eds.; M. Hersen, Ed. in Chief). *Encyclopedia of behavior modification and cognitive behavior therapy: Child clinical applications* (Vol. 2, pp. 715–719). Thousand Oaks, CA: Sage.

Renne, C. M., & Creer, T. L. (1976). Training children with asthma to use inhalation therapy equipment. *Journal of Applied Behavior Analysis, 9*, 1–11.

Repp, A. C., Deitz, S. M., & Deitz, D. E. D. (1976). Reducing inappropriate behaviors in classrooms and in individual sessions through DRO schedules of reinforcement. *Mental Retardation, 14*, 11–15.

Repp, A. C., Felce, D., & Barton, L. E. (1988). Basing the treatment of stereotypic and self-injurious behaviors on hypotheses of their causes. *Journal of Applied Behavior Analysis, 21*, 281–289.

Ricciardi, J. N., Luiselli, J. K., & Camare, M. (2006). Shaping approach responses as intervention for specific phobia in a child with autism. *Journal of Applied Behavior Analysis, 39*, 445–448.

Richardson, F. C., & Suinn, R. M. (1973). A comparison of traditional systematic desensitization, accelerated massed desensitization, and anxiety management training in the treatment of mathematics anxiety. *Behavior Therapy, 4*, 212–218.

Richman, D. M., Wacker, D. P., & Winborn, L. (2001). Response efficiency during functional communication training: Effects of effort on response allocation. *Journal of Applied Behavior Analysis, 34*, 73–76.

Richman, G. S., Reiss, M. L., Bauman, K. E., & Bailey, J. S. (1984). Teaching menstrual care to mentally retarded women: Acquisition, generalization, and maintenance. *Journal of Applied Behavior Analysis, 17*, 441–451.

Ricketts, R. W., Goza, A. B., & Matese, M. (1993). A 4-year follow-up of self-injury. *Journal of Behavior Therapy and Experimental Psychiatry, 24*, 57–62.

Rilling, M. (1977). Stimulus control and inhibitory processes. In W. K. Honig & J. E. R. Staddon (Eds.), *Handbook of operant behavior* (pp. 432–480). Englewood Cliffs, NJ: Prentice-Hall.

Rincover, A., Cook, R., Peoples, A., & Packard, D. (1979). Sensory extinction and sensory reinforcement principles for programming multiple adaptive behavior change. *Journal of Applied Behavior Analysis, 12*, 221–233.

Riordan, M. M., Iwata, B. A., Finney, J. W., Wohl, M. K., & Stanley, A. E. (1984). Behavioral assessment and treatment of chronic food refusal in handicapped children. *Journal of Applied Behavior Analysis, 17*, 327–341.

Rizley, R. C., & Rescorla, R. A. (1972). Associations in second-order conditioning and sensory preconditioning. *Journal of Comparative and Physiological Psychology, 81*, 1–11.

Roane, H. S., Lerman, D. C., & Vorndran, C. M. (2001). Assessing reinforcers under progressive schedule requirements. *Journal of Applied Behavior Analysis, 34*, 145–167.

Roberts, M. W., Hatzenbuehler, L. C., & Bean, A. W. (1981). The effects of differential attention and time out on child noncompliance. *Behavior Therapy, 12*, 93–99.

Rohsenow, D. J., Monti, P. M., Rubonis, A. V., Sirota, A. D., Niaura, R. S., Colby, S. M., Winschel, S. M., & Abrams, D. B. (1994). Cue reactivity as a predictor of drinking among male alcoholics. *Journal of Consulting and Clinical Psychology, 62*, 620–626.

Rohter, L. (1989). Isolated desert community lives by Skinner's precepts. *New York Times*, pp. C1, 8.

Rolider, A., Cummings, A., & Van Houten, R. (1991). Side effects of therapeutic punishment on academic performance and eye contact. *Journal of Applied Behavior Analysis, 24*, 763–773.

Rollins, H. A., McCandless, B. R., Thompson, M., & Brassell, W. R. (1974). Project Success Environment: An extended application of contingency management in inner-city schools. *Journal of Educational Psychology, 66*, 167–178.

Romeo, F. F. (1998). The negative effects of using a group contingency system of classroom management. *Journal of Instructional Psychology, 25*, 130–133.

Ronen, T. (1991). Intervention package for treating sleep disorders in a four-year-old girl. *Journal of Behavior Therapy and Experimental Psychiatry, 22*, 141–148.

Rosales-Ruiz, J., & Baer, D. M. (1997). Behavioral cusps: A developmental and pragmatic concept for behavior analysis. *Journal of Applied Behavior Analysis, 30*, 533–544.

Rosen, G. M., Glasgow, R. E., & Barrera, M. (1977). A two-year follow-up on systematic desensitization with data pertaining to the external validity of laboratory fear assessment. *Journal of Consulting and Clinical Psychology, 45*, 1188–1189.

Rosen, H. S., & Rosen, L. A. (1983). Eliminating stealing: Use of stimulus control with an elementary student. *Behavior Modification, 7*, 56–63.

Roth, D., Bielski, R., Jones, M., Parker, W., & Osborn, G. (1982). A comparison of self-control therapy and combined self-control therapy and antidepressant medication in the treatment of depression. *Behavior Therapy, 13*, 133–144.

Routh, D. K. (1969). Conditioning of vocal response differentiation in infants. *Developmental Psychology, 1*, 219–226.

Roy-Byrne, P. (2004). Anxiety. In W. E. Craighead & C. B. Nemeroff (Eds.), *The concise Corsini encyclopedia of psychology and behavioral science* (3rd ed., pp. 70–72). New York: Wiley.

Rusch, F. R., & Kazdin, A. E. (1981). Toward a methodology of withdrawal designs for the assessment of response maintenance. *Journal of Applied Behavior Analysis, 14*, 131–140.

Rutter, M. (1975). *Helping troubled children*. New York: Plenum.

Rutter, M., & Garmezy, N. (1983). Developmental psychopathology. In P. H. Mussen (Ed.), *Handbook of child psychology* (4th ed., Vol. IV, pp. 775–911). New York: Wiley.

Safer, D. J., Heaton, R. C., & Parker, F. C. (1981). A behavioral program for disruptive junior high school students: Results and follow-up. *Journal of Abnormal Child Psychology, 9*, 483–494.

Saigh, P. A. (1986). Invitro flooding in the treatment of a 6-year-old boy's posttraumatic stress disorder. *Behaviour Research and Therapy, 6*, 685–688.

Sajwaj, T., Libet, J., & Agras, S. (1974). Lemon-juice therapy: The control of life-threatening rumination in a six-month-old infant. *Journal of Applied Behavior Analysis, 7*, 557–563.

Salend, S. J., Ellis, L. L., & Reynolds, C. J. (1989). Using self-instruction to teach vocational skills to individuals who are severely retarded. *Education and Training in Mental Retardation and Developmental Disabilities, 24*, 248–254.

Sallis, J. F., & Owen, N. (1999). *Physical activity and behavioral medicine*. Thousand Oaks, CA: Sage.

Sanders, M. R., & Glynn, T. (1977). Functional analysis of a program for training high and low preference peers to modify disruptive classroom behavior. *Journal of Applied Behavior Analysis, 10*, 503.

Santogrossi, D. A., O'Leary, K. D., Romanczyk, R. G., & Kaufman, K. F. (1973). Self-evaluation by adolescents in a psychiatric hospital school token program. *Journal of Applied Behavior Analysis, 6*, 277–287.

Sarafino, E. P. (1977). LotPACA: A lottery procedure for administering competitive awards. *Journal of Behavior Therapy and Experimental Psychiatry, 8*, 449–450.

Sarafino, E. P. (1985). Peer-peer interaction among infants and toddlers with extensive daycare experience. *Journal of Applied Developmental Psychology, 6*, 17–29.

Sarafino, E. P. (1986). *The fears of childhood: A guide to recognizing and reducing fearful states in children*. New York: Human Sciences Press.

Sarafino, E. P. (1997). *Behavioral treatments for asthma: Biofeedback-, respondent-, and relaxation-based approaches.* Lewiston, NY: Edwin Mellen Press.

Sarafino, E. P. (2001). *Behavior modification: Principles of behavior change* (2nd ed.). Mountain View, CA: Mayfield.

Sarafino, E. P. (2005). *Research methods: Using processes and procedures of science to understand behavior.* Upper Saddle River, NJ: Prentice-Hall.

Sarafino, E. P. (2011). *Self-management: Using behavioral and cognitive principles to manage your life.* Hoboken, NJ: Wiley.

Sarafino, E. P., & Armstrong, J. W. (1986). *Child and adolescent development* (2nd ed.). St. Paul, MN: West.

Sarafino, E. P., & Ewing, M. (1999). The Hassles Assessment Scale for Students in College: Measuring the frequency and unpleasantness of and dwelling on stressful events. *Journal of American College Health, 48,* 75–83.

Sarafino, E. P., & Goehring, P. (2000). Age comparisons in acquiring biofeedback control and success in reducing headache pain. *Annals of Behavioral Medicine, 22,* 10–16.

Sarafino, E. P., & Graham, J. A. (2006). Development and psychometric evaluation of an instrument to assess reinforcer preferences: The Preferred Items and Experiences Questionnaire. *Behavior Modification, 30,* 835–847.

Sarafino, E. P., & Smith, T. W. (2011). *Health psychology: Biopsychosocial interactions* (7th ed.). Hoboken, NJ: Wiley.

Sarason, I. G., Johnson, J. H., & Siegel, J. M. (1978). Assessing the impact of life changes: Development of the Life Experiences Survey. *Journal of Consulting and Clinical Psychology, 46,* 932–946.

Sasso, G. M., Reimers, T. M., Cooper, L. J., Wacker, D., Berg, W., et al. (1992). Use of descriptive and experimental analyses to identify the functional properties of aberrant behavior in school settings. *Journal of Applied Behavior Analysis, 25,* 809–821.

Satterfield, J. H., Satterfield, B. T., & Cantwell, D. P. (1981). Three-year multimodality treatment study of 100 hyperactive boys. *Journal of Pediatrics, 98,* 650–655.

Scarr, S., & Kidd, K. K. (1983). Developmental behavior genetics. In P. H. Mussen (Ed.), *Handbook of child psychology* (4th ed., Vol. 2, pp. 345–434). New York: Wiley.

Schaefer, H. H. (1970). Self-injurious behavior: Shaping "head-banging" in monkeys. *Journal of Applied Behavior Analysis, 3,* 111–116.

Schepis, M. M., Reid, D. H., & Fitzgerald, J. R. (1987). Group instruction with profoundly retarded persons: Acquisition, generalization, and maintenance of a remunerative work skill. *Journal of Applied Behavior Analysis, 20,* 97–105.

Schlinger, H. D., Derenne, A., & Baron, A. (2008). What 50 years of research tell us about pausing under ratio schedules of reinforcement. *Behavior Analyst, 31,* 39–60.

Schneider, C., Palomba, D., & Flor, H. (2004). Pavlovian conditioning of muscular responses in chronic pain patients: Central and peripheral correlates. *Pain, 112,* 239–247.

Schreibman, L., Charlop, M. H., & Kurtz, P. F. (1992). Behavioral treatment for children with autism. In S. M. Turner, K. S. Calhoun, & H. E. Adams (Eds.), *Handbook of clinical behavior therapy* (2nd ed., pp. 337–351). New York: Wiley.

Schreibman, L., & Koegel, R. L. (2005). Training for parents of children with autism: Pivotal responses, generalization, and individualization of interventions. In E. D. Hibbs & P. S. Jensen (Eds.), *Psychosocial treatments for child and adolescent disorders: Empirically based strategies for clinical practice* (2nd ed., pp. 507–555). Washington, DC: American Psychological Association.

Schroeder, S. R. (1972). Parametric effects of reinforcement frequency, amount of reinforcement, and required response force on sheltered workshop behavior. *Journal of Applied Behavior Analysis, 5,* 431–441.

Schultz, D. D. (1965). *Sensory restriction: Effects on behavior.* New York: Academic Press.

Schultz, J. H. (1957). Autogenous training. In J. H. Masserman & J. L. Moreno (Eds.), *Progress in psychotherapy* (Vol. 2, pp. 173–176). New York: Grune & Stratton.

Schultz, J. H., & Luthe, W. (1969). *Autogenic therapy: 1. Autogenic methods.* New York: Grune & Stratton.

Schwartz, I. S., & Baer, D. M. (1991). Social validity assessments: Is current practice state of the art? *Journal of Applied Behavior Analysis, 24,* 189–204.

Schwartz, N. M., & Schwartz, M. S. (2003). Definitions of biofeedback and applied psychophysiology. In M. S. Schwartz & F. Andrasik (Eds.), *Biofeedback: A practitioner's guide* (3rd ed., pp. 27–39). New York: Guilford.

Schwartz, M. S., & Montgomery, D. D. (2003). Entering the field and assuring competence. In M. S. Schwartz & F. Andrasik (Eds.), *Biofeedback: A practitioner's guide* (3rd ed., pp. 20–26). New York: Guilford.

Scott, D., Scott, L. M., & Howe, B. L. (1998). Training anticipation for intermediate tennis players. *Behavior Modification, 22,* 243–261.

Scott, R. W., Peters, R. D., Gillespie, W. J., Blanchard, E. B., Edmunson, E. D., & Young, L. D. (1973). The use of shaping and reinforcement in the operant acceleration and deceleration of heart rate. *Behaviour Research and Therapy*, 11, 179–185.

Seaver, W. B., & Patterson, A. H. (1976). Decreasing fuel-oil consumption through feedback and social commendation. *Journal of Applied Behavior Analysis*, 9, 147–152.

Seligman, M. E. P. (1971). Phobias and preparedness. *Behavior Therapy*, 2, 307–320.

Seligmann, J., Namuth, T., & Miller, M. (1994). Drowning on dry land. *Newsweek*, pp. 64–66.

Serna, L. A., Schumacker, J. B., Sherman, J. A., & Sheldon, J. B. (1991). In-home generalization of social interactions in families of adolescents with behavior problems. *Journal of Applied Behavior Analysis*, 24, 733–746.

Shabani, D. B., Carr, J. E., Petursdóttir, A. I., Esch, B. E., & Gillett, J. N. (2004). Scholarly productivity in behavior analysis: The most prolific authors and institutions from 1992 to 2001. *Behavior Analyst Today*, 5, 235–243.

Shadel, W. G., Niaura, R., & Abrams, D. B. (2001). Effect of different cue stimulus delivery channels on craving reactivity: Comparing *in vivo* and video cues in regular cigarette smokers. *Journal of Behavior Therapy and Experimental Psychiatry*, 32, 203–209.

Shaw, R. A. (1987). Reinforcement schedules. In R. J. Corsini (Ed.), *Concise encyclopedia of psychology* (p. 968). New York: Wiley.

Sheffield, F. D., Roby, T. B., & Campbell, B. A. (1954). Drive reduction versus consummatory behavior as determinants of reinforcement. *Journal of Comparative and Physiological Psychology*, 47, 349–354.

Sherman, A. R. (1972). Real-life exposure as a primary therapeutic factor in the desensitization treatment of fear. *Journal of Abnormal Psychology*, 79, 19–28.

Shimoff, E., & Catania, A. C. (1995). Using computers to teach behavior analysis. *Behavior Analyst*, 18, 307–316.

Shipley, R. H., & Boudewyns, P. A. (1980). Flooding and implosive therapy: Are they harmful? *Behavior Therapy*, 11, 503–508.

Sidman, M., & Tailby, W. (1982). Conditional discrimination vs. matching to sample: An expansion of the testing paradigm. *Journal of the Experimental Analysis of Behavior*, 37, 5–22.

Siegel, L. J., & Peterson, L. (1980). Stress reduction in young dental patients through coping skills and sensory information. *Journal of Consulting and Clinical Psychology*, 48, 785–787.

Siegel, P. S., & Foshee, J. G. (1953). The law of primary reinforcement in children. *Journal of Experimental Psychology*, 45, 12–14.

Siegel, S., Hinson, R. E., Krank, M. D., & McCully, J. (1982). Heroin "overdose" death: The contribution of drug-associated environmental cues. *Science*, 216, 436–437.

Simons, A. D., Murphy, G. E., Levine, J. L., & Wetzel, R. D. (1986). Cognitive therapy and pharmacotherapy for depression: Sustained improvement over one year. *Archives of General Psychiatry*, 43, 43–48.

Singh, N. N., Dawson, M. J., & Manning, P. (1981). Effects of spaced responding DRL on the stereotyped behavior of profoundly retarded persons. *Journal of Applied Behavior Analysis*, 14, 521–526.

Singh, N. N., Lloyd, J. W., & Kendall, K. A. (1990). Nonaversive and aversive interventions: Issues. In A. C. Repp & N. N. Singh (Eds.), *Perspectives on the use of nonaversive and aversive interventions for persons with developmental disabilities* (pp. 3–16). Sycamore, IL: Sycamore.

Singh, N. N., Watson, J. E., & Winton, A. S. W. (1986). Treating self-injury: Water mist spray versus facial screening or forced arm exercise. *Journal of Applied Behavior Analysis*, 19, 403–410.

Sisson, R. W., & Azrin, N. H. (1989). The community reinforcement approach. In R. K. Hester & W. R. Miller (Eds.), *Handbook of alcoholism treatment approaches: Effective alternatives* (pp. 242–259). New York: Pergamon.

Sitharthan, T., Sitharthan, G., Hough, M. J., & Kavanagh, D. J. (1997). Cue exposure in moderation drinking: A comparison with cognitive–behavior therapy. *Journal of Consulting and Clinical Psychology*, 65, 878–882.

Skinner, B. F. (1938). *The behavior of organisms*. New York: Appleton-Century-Crofts.

Skinner, B. F. (1948). *Walden two*. New York: Macmillan.

Skinner, B. F. (1953). *Science and human behavior*. New York: Macmillan.

Skinner, B. F. (1954). The science of learning and the art of teaching. *Harvard Educational Review*, 24, 86–97.

Skinner, B. F. (1957). *Verbal behavior*. New York: Appleton-Century-Crofts.

Skinner, B. F. (1974). *About behaviorism*. New York: Knopf.

Slifer, K. J., Koontz, K. L., & Cataldo, M. F. (2002). Operant-contingency-based preparation of children for functional magnetic imagining. *Journal of Applied Behavior Analysis*, 35, 191–194.

Smith, B. M., Schumaker, J. B., Schaeffer, J., & Sherman, J. A. (1982). Increasing participation and improving the quality of discussions in seventh-grade social studies classes. *Journal of Applied Behavior Analysis, 15*, 97–110.

Smith, G. J. (1999). Teaching a long sequence of a behavior using whole task training, forward chaining, and backward chaining. *Perceptual & Motor Skills, 89*, 951–965.

Smith, J. E., Meyers, R. J., & Delaney, H. D. (1998). The community reinforcement approach with homeless alcohol-dependent individuals. *Journal of Consulting and Clinical Psychology, 66*, 541–548.

Smith, L. K. C., & Fowler, S. A. (1984). Positive peer pressure: The effects of peer monitoring on children's disruptive behavior. *Journal of Applied Behavior Analysis, 17*, 213–227.

Smith, M. L., & Glass, G. V. (1977). Meta-analysis of psychotherapy outcome studies. *American Psychologist, 32*, 752–760.

Smith, R. E. (1973). The use of humor in the counterconditioning of anger responses: A case study. *Behavior Therapy, 4*, 576–580.

Smith, R. G., Russo, L., & Le, D. D. (1999). Distinguishing between extinction and punishment effects of response blocking: A replication. *Journal of Applied Behavior Analysis, 32*, 367–370.

Smith, S. L., & Ward, P. (2006). Behavioral interventions to improve performance in collegiate football. *Journal of Applied Behavior Analysis, 39*, 385–391.

Smith, T. (1990). When and when not to consider the use of aversive interventions in the behavioral treatment of autistic children. In A. C. Repp & N. N. Singh (Eds.), *Perspectives on the use of nonaversive and aversive interventions for persons with developmental disabilities* (pp. 287–297). Sycamore, IL: Sycamore.

Sobell, L. C., Toneatto, A., & Sobell, M. B. (1990). Behavior therapy. In A. S. Bellack & M. Hersen (Eds.), *Handbook of comparative treatments for adult disorders* (pp. 479–505). New York: Wiley.

Solé-Leris, A. (1986). *Tranquility and insight.* Boston: Shambhala.

Solnick, J. V., Rincover, A., & Peterson, C. R. (1977). Some determinants of the reinforcing and punishing effects of timeout. *Journal of Applied Behavior Analysis, 10*, 415–424.

Solomon, R. L., Kamin, L. J., & Wynne, L. C. (1953). Traumatic avoidance learning: The outcomes of several extinction procedures with dogs. *Journal of Abnormal and Social Psychology, 48*, 291–302.

Speer, D. C. (1992). Clinically significant change: Jacobson and Truax (1991) revisited. *Journal of Consulting and Clinical Psychology, 60*, 402–408.

Spencer, L., Pagell, F., Hallion, M. E., & Adams, T. B. (2002). Applying the transtheoretical model to tobacco cessation and prevention: A review of the literature. *American Journal of Health Promotion, 17*, 7–71.

Spiegel, T. A., Wadden, T. A., & Foster, G. D. (1991). Objective measurement of eating rate during behavioral treatment of obesity. *Behavior Therapy, 22*, 61–67.

Spooner, F. (1984). Comparisons of backward chaining and total task presentation in training severely handicapped persons. *Education and Training of the Mentally Retarded, 19*, 15–22.

Spooner, F., Weber, L. H., & Spooner, D. (1983). The effects of backward chaining and total task presentation on the acquisition of complex tasks by severely retarded adolescents and adults. *Education and Treatment of Children, 6*, 401–420.

Sprague, J. R., & Horner, R. H. (1984). The effects of single instance, multiple instance, and general case training on generalized vending machine use by moderately and severely handicapped students. *Journal of Applied Behavior Analysis, 17*, 273–278.

St. Peter Pipkin, C., & Vollmer, T. R. (2009). Applied implications of reinforcement history effects. *Journal of Applied Behavior Analysis, 42*, 83–103.

Staats, A. W., Minke, K. A., Martin, C. H., & Higa, W. R. (1972). Deprivation–satiation and strength of attitude conditioning: A test of attitude-reinforcer-discriminative theory. *Journal of Personality and Social Psychology, 24*, 178–185.

Stainback, W. C., Payne, J. S., Stainback, S. B., & Payne, R. A. (1973). *Establishing a token economy in the classroom.* Columbus, OH: Merrill.

Stanley, M. A. (1992). Obsessive-compulsive disorder. In S. M. Turner, K. S. Calhoun, & H. E. Adams (Eds.), *Handbook of clinical behavior therapy* (2nd ed., pp. 67–86). New York: Wiley.

Stark, L. J., Collins, F. L., Osnes, P. G., & Stokes, T. F. (1986). Using reinforcement and cueing to increase healthy snack food choices in preschoolers. *Journal of Applied Behavior Analysis, 19*, 367–379.

Stasiewicz, P. R., & Maisto, S. A. (1993). Two-factor avoidance theory: The role of negative affect in the maintenance of substance use and substance use disorder. *Behavior Therapy, 24*, 337–356.

Steege, M. W., Wacker, D. P., Cigrand, K. C., Berg, W. K., Novak, C. G., et al. (1990). Use of negative reinforcement in the treatment of self-injurious behavior. *Journal of Applied Behavior Analysis, 23,* 459–467.

Stephens, C. E., Pear, J. J., Wray, L. D., & Jackson, G. C. (1975). Some effects of reinforcement schedules in teaching picture names to retarded children. *Journal of Applied Behavior Analysis, 8,* 435–447.

Sterman, M. B., & Egner, T. (2006). Foundation and practice of neurofeedback for the treatment of epilepsy. *Applied Psychophysiology and Biofeedback, 31,* 21–35.

Stern, R. M., & Ray, W. J. (1980). *Biofeedback: Potential and limits.* Lincoln, NB: University of Nebraska Press.

Stewart, K. K., Carr, J. E., Brandt, C. W., & McHenry, M. M. (2007). An evaluation of the conservative dual-criterion method for teaching university students to visually inspect AB-design graphs. *Journal of Applied Behavior Analysis, 40,* 713–718.

Stokes, T. F., & Baer, D. M. (1976). Preschool peers as mutual generalization-facilitating agents. *Behavior Therapy, 7,* 549–556.

Stokes, T. F., Baer, D. M., & Jackson, R. L. (1974). Programming the generalization of a greeting response in four retarded children. *Journal of Applied Behavior Analysis, 7,* 599–610.

Stokes, T. F., & Osnes, P. G. (1988). The developing applied technology of generalization and maintenance. In R. H. Horner, G. Dunlap, & R. L. Koegel (Eds.), *Generalization and maintenance: Life-style changes in applied settings* (pp. 5–20). Baltimore, MD: Paul H. Brookes.

Stokes, T. F., & Osnes, P. G. (1989). An operant pursuit of generalization. *Behavior Therapy, 20,* 337–355.

Storms, M. D. (1983). *Development of sexual orientation.* Washington, DC: American Psychological Association.

Strain, P. S., Shores, R. E., & Kerr, M. M. (1976). An experimental analysis of "spillover" effects on the social interaction of behaviorally handicapped preschool children. *Journal of Applied Behavior Analysis, 9,* 31–40.

Strain, P. S., Shores, R. E., & Timm, M. A. (1977). Effects of peer social initiations on the behavior of withdrawn preschool children. *Journal of Applied Behavior Analysis, 10,* 289–298.

Strand, P. S. (2005). Discrimination training. In A. M. Gross & R. S. Drabman (Eds.; M. Hersen, Ed. in Chief), *Encyclopedia of behavior modification and cognitive behavior therapy: Child clinical applications* (Vol. 2, pp. 810–812). Thousand Oaks, CA: Sage.

Strehl, U. (2003). Biofeedback of slow cortical potentials in epilepsy. In M. S. Schwartz & F. Andrasik (Eds.), *Biofeedback: A practitioner's guide* (3rd ed., pp. 464–470). New York: Guilford.

Stromer, R., McComas, J. J., & Rehfeldt, R. A. (2000). Designing interventions that include delayed reinforcement: Implications of recent laboratory research. *Journal of Applied Behavior Analysis, 33,* 359–371.

Stuart, R. B. (1971). Behavioral contracting within the families of delinquents. *Journal of Behavior Therapy and Experimental Psychiatry, 2,* 1–11.

Sturges, J. W., & Sturges, L. V. (1998). In vivo systematic desensitization in a single-session treatment of an 11-year-old girl's elevator phobia. *Child and Family Behavior Therapy, 20,* 55–62.

Sullivan, M. A., & O'Leary, S. G. (1990). Maintenance following reward and cost token programs. *Behavior Therapy, 21,* 139–149.

Suls, J., Sanders, G. S., & Labrecque, M. S. (1986). Attempting to control blood pressure without systematic instruction: When advice is counterproductive. *Journal of Behavioral Medicine, 9,* 567–576.

Sulzer, B., & Mayer, G. R. (1972). *Behavior modification procedures for school personnel.* Hinsdale, IL: Dryden.

Surwit, R. S., & Keefe, F. J. (1978). Frontalis EMG feedback training: An electronic panacea? *Behavior Therapy, 9,* 779–792.

Swain, J. C., & McLaughlin, T. F. (1998). The effects of bonus contingencies in a classwide token program on math accuracy with middle-school students with behavioral disorders. *Behavioral Interventions, 13,* 11–19.

Swain, J. J., Allard, G. B., & Holborn, S. W. (1982). The Good Toothbrushing Game: A school-based dental hygiene program for increasing the toothbrushing effectiveness of children. *Journal of Applied Behavior Analysis, 15,* 171–176.

Swan, G. E., & MacDonald, M. L. (1978). Behavior therapy in practice: A national survey of behavior therapists. *Behavior Therapy, 9,* 799–807.

Swanson, K. S., Gevirtz, R. N., Brown, M., Spira, J., Guarneri, E., & Stoletniy, L. (2009). The effect of biofeedback on function in patients with heart failure. *Applied Psychophysiology and Biofeedback, 34,* 71–91.

Sweet, A. A., & Loizeaux, A. L. (1991). Behavioral and cognitive treatment methods: A critical comparative review. *Journal of Behavior Therapy and Experimental Psychiatry, 22,* 159–185.

Switzer, E. B., Deal, T. E., & Bailey, J. S. (1977). The reduction of stealing in second graders using a group contingency. *Journal of Applied Behavior Analysis, 10,* 267–272.

Tanner, B. A., & Zeiler, M. (1975). Punishment of self-injurious behavior using aromatic ammonia as the aversive stimulus. *Journal of Applied Behavior Analysis, 8,* 53–57.

Tarbox, R. S. F., Wallace, M. D., Penrod, B., & Tarbox, J. (2007). Effects of three-step prompting on compliance with caregiver requests. *Journal of Applied Behavior Analysis, 40,* 703–706.

TASH (The Association for Persons with Severe Handicaps). (2011). TASH *resolution opposing the use of aversive and restrictive procedures.* Retrieved (1-3-2011) from http://www.tash.org/resolutions.

Taylor, C. B. (1978). Relaxation training and related techniques. In W. S. Agras (Ed.), *Behavior modification: Principles and clinical applications* (2nd ed., pp. 134–162). Boston: Little, Brown.

Taylor, C. B., Agras, W. S., Schneider, J. A., & Allen, R. A. (1983). Adherence to instructions to practice relaxation exercises. *Journal of Consulting and Clinical Psychology, 51,* 952–953.

Taylor, K. L., Bovbjerg, D. H., Jacobsen, P. B., Redd, W. H., & Manne, S. L. (1992, March). An *experimental model of classically conditioned nausea during cancer chemotherapy.* Paper presented at the meeting of the Society of Behavioral Medicine, New York, NY.

Test, D. W., Spooner, F., Keul, P. K., & Grossi, T. (1990). Teaching adolescents with severe disabilities to use the public telephone. *Behavior Modification, 14,* 157–171.

TFPDPP (Task Force on Promotion and Dissemination of Psychological Procedures). (1993). A *report to the Division* 12 *Board, October* 1993. Washington, DC: American Psychological Association Division of Clinical Psychology.

Thera, P. (1979). *Buddhist meditation: The way to inner calm and clarity.* Kandy, Sri Lanka: Buddhist Publication Society.

Thewissen, R., Snijders, S. J. B. D., Havermans, R. D., van den Hout, M., & Jensen, A. (2006). Renewal of cue-elicited urge to smoke: Implications for cue exposure treatment. *Behaviour Research and Therapy, 44,* 1141–1149.

Thomas, B. R., Lafasakis, M., & Sturmey, P. (2010). The effects of prompting, fading, and differential reinforcement on vocal mands in nonverbal preschool children with autism spectrum disorders. *Behavioral Interventions, 25,* 157–168.

Thomas, J. D., Presland, I. E., Grant, M. D., & Glynn, T. L. (1978). Natural rates of teacher approval and disapproval in grade-7 classrooms. *Journal of Applied Behavior Analysis, 11,* 91–94.

Thompson, R. H., & Iwata, B. A. (2005). A review of reinforcement control procedures. *Journal of Applied Behavior Analysis, 38,* 257–278.

Thompson, R. H., & Iwata, B. A. (2007). A comparison of outcomes from descriptive and functional analyses of problem behavior. *Journal of Applied Behavior Analysis, 40,* 333–338.

Thompson, R. H., Iwata, B. A., Conners, J., & Roscoe, E. M. (1999). Effects of reinforcement for alternative behavior during punishment of self-injury. *Journal of Applied Behavior Analysis, 32,* 317–328.

Thorndike, E. L. (1898). Animal intelligence: An experimental study of the associative processes in animals. *Psychological Monographs, 2*(4), 1–109.

Thorndike, E. L. (1911). *Animal intelligence, experimental studies.* New York: Macmillan.

Thorndike, E. L. (1931). *Human learning.* New York: Century.

Tierney, K. J., & Bracken, M. (1998). Stimulus equivalence and behavior therapy. In W. O'Donohue (Ed.), *Learning and behavior therapy* (pp. 392–402). Boston: Allyn & Bacon.

Tiger, J. H., Hanley, G. P., & Hernandez, E. (2006). An evaluation of the value of choice with preschool children. *Journal of Applied Behavior Analysis, 39,* 1–16.

Timberlake, W., & Allison, J. (1974). Response deprivation: An empirical approach to instrumental performance. *Psychological Review, 81,* 146–164.

Tincani, M. J., Castrogiavanni, A., & Axelrod, S. (1999). A comparison of the effectiveness of brief versus traditional functional analyses. *Research in Developmental Disabilities, 20,* 327–338.

Todd, J. T., Morris, E. K., & Fenza, K. M. (1989). Temporal organization of extinction-induced responding in preschool children. *Psychological Record, 39,* 117–130.

Torgersen, S. (1983). Genetic factors in anxiety disorders. *Archives of General Psychiatry, 40,* 1085–1089.

Touchette, P. E., & Howard, J. S. (1984). Errorless learning: Reinforcement contingencies and stimulus control transfer in delayed prompting. *Journal of Applied Behavior Analysis, 17,* 175–188.

Townsend, D., Nicholson, R. A., Buenaver, L., Bush, F., & Gramling, S. (2001). Use of habit reversal treatment for temporomandibular pain in a minimal therapist contact format. *Journal of Behavior Therapy and Experimental Psychiatry, 32,* 221–239.

Trosclair-Lasserre, N. M., Lerman, D. C., Call, N. A., Addison, L. R., & Kodak, T. (2008). Reinforcement magnitude: An evaluation of preference and reinforcer efficacy. *Journal of Applied Behavior Analysis, 41,* 203–220.

Truax, P. (2005). Descriptive and functional analysis. In M. Hersen & J. Rosqvist (Eds.; M. Hersen, Ed. in Chief). *Encyclopedia of behavior modification and cognitive behavior therapy: Adult clinical applications* (Vol. 1, pp. 250–256). Thousand Oaks, CA: Sage.

Truchlicka, M., McLaughlin, T. F., & Swain, J. C. (1998). Effects of token reinforcement and response cost on the accuracy of spelling performance with middle-school special education students with behavior disorders. *Behavioral Interventions, 13,* 1–10.

Trull, T. J., Nietzel, M. T., & Main, A. (1988). The use of meta-analysis to assess the clinical significance of behavior therapy for agoraphobia. *Behavior Therapy, 19,* 527–538.

Tucker, J. A., Vuchinich, R. E., & Downey, K. K. (1992). Substance abuse. In S. M. Turner, K. S. Calhoun, & H. E. Adams (Eds.), *Handbook of clinical behavior therapy* (2nd ed., pp. 203–223). New York: Wiley.

Turkat, I. D. (1986). The behavioral interview. In A. R. Ciminero, K. S. Calhoun, & H. E. Adams (Eds.), *Handbook of behavioral assessment* (2nd ed., pp. 109–149). New York: Wiley.

Turner, S. M., Beidel, D. C., Long, P. J., & Greenhouse, J. (1992). Reduction of fear in social phobics: An examination of extinction patterns. *Behavior Therapy, 23,* 389–403.

Twohig, M. P., & Woods, D. W. (2001a). Evaluating the duration of the competing response in habit reversal: A parametric analysis. *Journal of Applied Behavior Analysis, 34,* 517–520.

Twohig, M. P., & Woods, D. W. (2001b). Habit reversal as a treatment for chronic skin picking in typically developing adult male siblings. *Journal of Applied Behavior Analysis, 34,* 217–220.

Van Houten, R. (1983). Punishment: From the animal laboratory to the applied setting. In S. Axelrod & J. Apsche (Eds.), *The effects of punishment on human behavior* (pp. 13–44). New York: Academic Press.

Van Houten, R., Nau, P. A., MacKenzie-Keating, S. E., Sameoto, D., & Colavecchia, B. (1982). An analysis of some variables influencing the effectiveness of reprimands. *Journal of Applied Behavior Analysis, 15,* 65–83.

Van Houten, R., Nau, P., & Marini, Z. (1980). An analysis of public posting in reducing speeding behavior on an urban highway. *Journal of Applied Behavior Analysis, 13,* 383–395.

Van Houten, R., & Retting, R. A. (2001). Increasing motorist compliance and caution at stop signs. *Journal of Applied Behavior Analysis, 34,* 185–193.

Vansteenwegen, D., Vervliet, B., Hermans, D., Beckers, T., Baeyens, F., & Eelen, P. (2006). Stronger renewal in human fear conditioning when tested with an acquisition retrieval cue than with an extinction retrieval cue. *Behaviour Research and Therapy, 44,* 1717–1725.

Venn, J. R., & Short, J. G. (1973). Vicarious classical conditioning of emotional responses in nursery school children. *Journal of Personality and Social Psychology, 28,* 249–255.

Ventis, W. L. (1973). Case history: The use of laughter as an alternative response in systematic desensitization. *Behavior Therapy, 4,* 120–122.

Vervliet, B., Kindt, M., Vansteenwegen, D., & Hermans, D. (2010). Fear generalization in humans: Impact of prior non-fearful experiences. *Behaviour Research and Therapy, 48,* 1078–1084.

Vincent, J.-L. (2003). Nosocomial infections in adult intensive-care units. *Lancet, 361,* 2068–2077.

Volkert, V. M., Lerman, D. C., Call, N. A., & Trosclair-Lasserre, N. (2009). An evaluation of resurgence during treatment with functional communication training. *Journal of Applied Behavior Analysis, 42,* 145–160.

Vollmer, T. R. (1994). The concept of automatic reinforcement: Implications for behavioral research in developmental disabilities. *Research in Developmental Disabilities, 15,* 187–207.

Vollmer, T. R. (2002). Punishment happens: Some comments on Lerman and Vorndran's review. *Journal of Applied Behavior Analysis, 35,* 469–473.

Vollmer, T. R., & Iwata, B. A. (1991). Establishing operations and reinforcement effects. *Journal of Applied Behavior Analysis, 24,* 279–291.

Vollmer, T. R., Iwata, B. A., Zarcone, J. R., Smith, R. G., & Mazaleski, J. L. (1993). The role of attention in the treatment of attention-maintained self-injurious behavior: Noncontingent reinforcement and differential reinforcement of other behavior. *Journal of Applied Behavior Analysis, 26,* 9–21.

Vollmer, T. R., Marcus, B. A., & Ringdahl, J. E. (1995). Noncontingent escape as treatment for self-injurious behavior maintained by negative reinforcement. *Journal of Applied Behavior Analysis, 28,* 15–26.

Vollmer, T. R., Marcus, B. A., Ringdahl, J. E., & Roane, H. S. (1995). Progressing from brief assessments to extended experimental analyses in th evaluation of aberrant behavior. *Journal of Applied Behavior Analysis, 28,* 561–576.

Wacker, D., Steege, M., Northup, J., Reimers, T., Berg, W., & Sasso, G. (1990). Use of functional analysis and acceptability measures to assess and treat severe behavior problems: An outpatient clinic model. In A. C. Repp & N. N. Singh (Eds.), *Perspectives on the use of nonaversive and aversive interventions for persons with developmental disabilities* (pp. 349–360). Sycamore, IL: Sycamore.

Wacker, D. P., Berg, W. K., & Harding, J. W. (2005). Functional relation. In G. Sugai & R. Horner (Eds.; M. Hersen, Ed. in Chief), *Encyclopedia of behavior modification and cognitive behavior therapy, Volume 3: Educational applications* (pp. 1332–1333). Pacific Grove, CA: Sage.

Wahler, R. G. (1969). Infant social development: Some experimental analyses of an infant–mother interaction during the first year of life. *Journal of Experimental Child Psychology, 7,* 101–113.

Wahler, R. G., & Dumas, J. E. (1984). Changing the observational coding styles of insular and noninsular mothers: A step toward maintenance of parent training effects. In R. F. Dangel & R. A. Polster (Eds.), *Parent training: Foundations of research and practice* (pp. 379–416). New York: Guilford.

Wahler, R. G., & Fox, J. J. (1980). Solitary toy play and time out: A family treatment package for children with aggressive and oppositional behavior. *Journal of Applied Behavior Analysis, 13,* 23–39.

Wahler, R. G., & Fox, J. J. (1981). Setting events in applied behavior analysis: Toward a conceptual and methodological expansion. *Journal of Applied Behavior Analysis, 14,* 327–338.

Wahler, R. G., Winkel, G. H., Peterson, R. F., & Morrison, D. C. (1965). Mothers as behavior therapists for their own children. *Behaviour Research and Therapy, 3,* 113–124.

Wald, J., & Taylor, S. (2000). Efficacy of virtual reality exposure therapy to treat driving phobia: A case report. *Journal of Behavior Therapy and Experimental Psychiatry, 31,* 249–257.

Walker, H. M., & Buckley, N. K. (1972). Programming generalization and maintenance of treatment effects across time and across settings. *Journal of Applied Behavior Analysis, 5,* 209–224.

Walker, H. M., Hops, H., & Johnson, S. M. (1975). Generalization and maintenance of classroom treatment effects. *Behavior Therapy, 6,* 188–200.

Wallace, I., & Pear, J. J. (1977). Self-control techniques of famous novelists. *Journal of Applied Behavior Analysis, 10,* 515–525.

Wallin, J. A., & Johnson, R. D. (1976). The positive reinforcement approach to controlling employee absenteeism. *Personnel Journal,* pp. 390–392.

Walters, G. C., & Grusec, J. E. (1977). *Punishment.* San Francisco: W. H. Freeman.

Walters, R. H., & Brown, M. (1963). Studies of reinforcement of aggression: III. Transfer of responses to an interpersonal situation. *Child Development, 34,* 563–571.

Ward, P., & Carnes, M. (2002). Effects of posting self-set goals on collegiate football players' skill execution during practice and games. *Journal of Applied Behavior Analysis, 35,* 1–12.

Wasik, B. H. (1970). The application of Premack's generalization on reinforcement to the management of classroom behavior. *Journal of Experimental Child Psychology, 10,* 33–43.

Watson, J. B. (1913). Psychology as the behaviorist views it. *Psychological Review, 20,* 158–177.

Watson, J. B. (1930). *Behaviorism.* New York: Norton.

Watson, J. B., & Rayner, R. (1920). Conditioned emotional reactions. *Journal of Experimental Psychology, 3,* 1–14.

Watson, T. S., & Sterling, H. E. (1998). Brief functional analysis and treatment of a vocal tic. *Journal of Applied Behavioral Analysis, 31,* 471–474.

Webster-Stratton, C. (1982a). The long-term effects of a videotape modeling parent-training program: Comparison of immediate and 1-year follow-up results. *Behavior Therapy, 13,* 702–714.

Webster-Stratton, C. (1982b). Teaching mothers through videotape modeling to change their children's behavior. *Journal of Pediatric Psychology, 7,* 279–294.

Webster-Stratton, C. (2005). The Incredible Years: A training series for the prevention and treatment of conduct problems in young children. In E. D. Hibbs & P. S. Jensen (Eds.), *Psychosocial treatments for child and adolescent disorders: Empirically based strategies for clinical practice* (2nd ed., pp. 507–555). Washington, DC: American Psychological Association.

Weems, C. F. (1998). The evaluation of heart rate biofeedback using a multi-element design. *Journal of Behavior Therapy and Experimental Psychiatry, 29,* 157–162.

Weiner, H. (1970). Instructional control of human operant responding during extinction following fixed-ratio conditioning. *Journal of the Experimental Analysis of Behavior, 13,* 391–394.

Weiss, R. F., Cecil, J. S., & Frank, M. J. (1973). Steep delay of reinforcement gradient in escape conditioning with altruistic reinforcement. *Bulletin of the Psychonomic Society*, 2, 372–374.

Welch, M. W., & Gist, J. W. (1974). *The open token economy system: A handbook for a behavioral approach to rehabilitation.* Springfield, IL: Charles C. Thomas.

Weld, E. M., & Evans, I. M. (1990). Effects of part versus whole instructional strategies on skill acquisition and excess behavior. *American Journal on Mental Retardation*, 94, 377–386.

Whelan, J. P., Mahoney, M. J., & Meyers, A. W. (1991). Performance enhancement in sport: A cognitive behavioral domain. *Behavior Therapy*, 22, 307–327.

Whitaker, S. (1996). A review of DRO: The influence of the degree of intellectual disability and the frequency of the target behavior. *Journal of Applied Research in Intellectual Disabilities*, 9, 61–79.

White, A. G., & Bailey, J. S. (1990). Reducing disruptive behaviors of elementary physical education students with sit and watch. *Journal of Applied Behavior Analysis*, 23, 353–359.

White, G. D., Nielsen, G., & Johnson, S. M. (1972). Timeout duration and the suppression of deviant behavior in children. *Journal of Applied Behavior Analysis*, 5, 111–120.

White, L., & Tursky, B. (1982). Stress and anxiety. In L. White & B. Tursky (Eds.), *Clinical biofeedback: Efficacy and mechanisms* (pp. 335–337). New York: Guilford.

White, M. A. (1975). Natural rates of teacher approval and disapproval in the classroom. *Journal of Applied Behavior Analysis*, 8, 367–372.

White, N. M., & Milner, P. M. (1992). The psychobiology of reinforcers. In M. R. Rosenzweig & L. W. Porter (Eds.), *Annual review of psychology* (Vol. 43, pp. 443–471). Palo Alto, CA: Annual Reviews.

White, O. R. (2005). Trend lines. In G. Sugai & R. Horner (Eds.; M. Hersen, Ed. in Chief), *Encyclopedia of behavior modification and cognitive behavior therapy, Volume 3: Educational applications* (pp. 1589–1593). Pacific Grove, CA: Sage.

Whitman, T. L., Mercurio, J. R., & Caponigri, V. (1970). Development of social responses in two severely retarded children. *Journal of Applied Behavior Analysis*, 3, 133–138.

Wilcoxon, H. C., Dragoin, W. B., & Kral, P. A. (1966). Illness-induced aversions in rat and quail: Relative salience of visual and gustatory cues. *Science*, 171, 826–828.

Wilder, D. A., Chen, L., Atwell, J., Pritchard, J., & Weinstein, P. (2006). Brief functional analysis and treatment of tantrums associated with transitions in preschool children. *Journal of Applied Behavior Analysis*, 39, 103–107.

Wilkinson, L. A. (2003). Using behavioral consultation to reduce challenging behavior in the classroom. *Preventing School Failure*, 47, 100–105.

Williams, B. A. (2001). Two-factor theory has strong empirical evidence of validity. *Journal of the Experimental Analysis of Behavior*, 75, 362–365.

Williams, C. J. (1990). *Cancer biology and management: An introduction.* New York: Wiley.

Williams, G. E., & Cuvo, A. J. (1986). Training apartment upkeep skills to rehabilitation clients: A comparison of task analytic strategies. *Journal of Applied Behavior Analysis*, 19, 39–51.

Williams, T. I., Rose, R., & Chisholm, S. (2006). What is the function of nail biting: An analog assessment study. *Behaviour Research and Therapy*, 45, 989–995.

Williamson, D. A., Williamson, S. H., Watkins, P. C., & Hughes, H. H. (1992). Increasing cooperation among children using dependent group-oriented reinforcement contingencies. *Behavior Modification*, 16, 414–425.

Wilson, C. C., Robertson, S. J., Herlong, L. H., & Haynes, S. N. (1979). Vicarious effects of time-out in the modification of aggression in the classroom. *Behavior Modification*, 3, 97–111.

Wilson, G. T. (1982). Adult disorders. In G. T. Wilson & C. M. Franks (Eds.), *Contemporary behavior therapy: Conceptual and empirical foundations* (pp. 505–562). New York: Guilford.

Wilson, G. T. (1990). Clinical issues and strategies in the practice of behavior therapy. In C. M. Franks, G. T. Wilson, P. C. Kendall, & J. P. Foreyt (Eds.), *Review of behavior therapy: Theory and practice* (Vol. 2, pp. 271–301). New York: Guilford.

Wilson, G. T. (1991). Chemical aversion conditioning in the treatment of alcoholism: Further comments. *Behaviour Research and Therapy*, 29, 415–419.

Wilson, G. T., Leaf, R. C., & Nathan, P. E. (1975). The aversive control of excessive alcohol consumption by chronic alcoholics in the laboratory setting. *Journal of Applied Behavior Analysis*, 8, 13–26.

Wilson, G. T., & Tracey, D. A. (1976). An experimental analysis of aversive imagery versus electrical aversive conditioning in the treatment of chronic alcoholics. *Behaviour Research and Therapy*, 14, 41–51.

Wilson, K. G., Hayes, S. C., & Gifford, E. V. (1997). Cognition in behavior therapy: Agreements and differences. *Journal of Behavior Therapy and Experimental Psychiatry, 28,* 53–63.

Wilson, W. H., & Simpson, G. M. (1990). Pharmacotherapy. In A. S. Bellack & M. Hersen (Eds.), *Handbook of comparative treatments for adult disorders* (pp. 34–47). New York: Wiley.

Wincze, J. P. (1977). Sexual deviance and dysfunction. In D. C. Rimm & J. W. Somervill (Eds.), *Abnormal psychology* (pp. 343–379). New York: Academic Press.

Witryol, S. L. (1971). Incentives and learning in children. In H. W. Reese (Ed.), *Advances in child development and behavior* (Vol. 6, pp. 2–61). New York: Academic Press.

Wixted, J. T., Bellack, A. S., & Hersen, M. (1990). Behavior therapy. In A. S. Bellack & M. Hersen (Eds.), *Handbook of comparative treatments for adult disorders* (pp. 17–33). New York: Wiley.

Wolf, M. M. (1978). Social validity: The case for subjective measurement *or* how applied behavior analysis is finding its heart. *Journal of Applied Behavior Analysis, 11,* 203–214.

Wolf, M. M., Braukmann, C. J., & Ramp, K. A. (1987). Serious delinquent behavior as part of a significantly handicapping condition: Cures and supportive environments. *Journal of Applied Behavior Analysis, 20,* 347–359.

Wolf, M. M., Hanley, E. L., King, L. A., Lachowicz, J., & Giles, D. K. (1970). The timer-game: A variable interval contingency for the management of out-of-seat behavior. *Exceptional Children, 37,* 113–117.

Wolf, M. M., Risley, T., & Mees, H. L. (1964). Application of operant conditioning to the behaviour problems of an autistic child. *Behaviour Research and Therapy, 1,* 305–312.

Wolfe, D. A., Mendes, M. G., & Factor, D. (1984). A parent-administered program to reduce children's television viewing. *Journal of Applied Behavior Analysis, 17,* 267–272.

Wolpe, J. (1958). *Psychotherapy by reciprocal inhibition.* Stanford, CA: Stanford University Press.

Wolpe, J. (1973). *The practice of behavior therapy.* New York: Pergamon.

Wolpe, J. (1981). The dichotomy between directly conditioned and cognitively learned anxiety. *Journal of Behavior Therapy and Experimental Psychiatry, 12,* 35–42.

Wong, S. E., Terranova, M. D., Bowen, L., Zarate, R., Massel, H. K., & Liberman, R. P. (1987). Providing independent recreational activities to reduce stereotypic vocalizations in chronic schizophrenics. *Journal of Applied Behavior Analysis, 20,* 77–81.

Wood, S. J., Murdock, J. Y., Cronin, M. E., Dawson, N. M., & Kirby, P. C. (1998). Effects of self-monitoring on on-task behaviors of at-risk middle school students. *Journal of Behavioral Education, 8,* 263–279.

Woolfolk, A. E., Woolfolk, R. L., & Wilson, G. T. (1977). A rose by any other name . . . : Labeling bias and attitudes toward behavior modification. *Journal of Consulting and Clinical Psychology, 45,* 184–191.

Wysocki, T., Hall, G., Iwata, B., & Riordan, M. (1979). Behavioral management of exercise: Contracting for aerobic points. *Journal of Applied Behavior Analysis, 12,* 55–64.

Yates, B. T. (1994). Toward the incorporation of costs, cost-effectiveness analysis, and cost-benefit analysis into clinical research. *Journal of Consulting and Clinical Psychology, 62,* 729–736.

Yu, D., Martin, G. L., Suthons, E., Koop, S., & Pallotta-Cornick, A. (1980). Comparisons of forward chaining and total task presentation formats to teach vocational skills to the retarded. *International Journal of Rehabilitation Research, 3,* 77–79.

Zhou, L., Goff, G. A., & Iwata, B. A. (2000). Effects of increased response effort on self-injury and object manipulation as competing responses. *Journal of Applied Behavior Analysis, 33,* 29–40.

Ziegler, S. G. (1987). Effects of stimulus cueing on the acquisition of groundstrokes by beginning tennis players. *Journal of Applied Behavior Analysis, 20,* 405–411.

Zifferblatt, S. M., Wilbur, C. S., & Pinsky, J. L. (1980). Changing cafeteria eating habits. *Journal of the American Dietetic Association, 76,* 15–20.

Zimbardo, P. G. (1985). *Psychology and life* (12th ed.). Glenview, IL: Scott, Foresman.

Zimmerman, E. H., & Zimmerman, J. (1962). The alteration of behavior in a special classroom situation. *Journal of the Experimental Analysis of Behavior, 5,* 59–60.

Zohn, C. J., & Bornstein, P. H. (1980). Self-monitoring of work performance with mentally retarded adults: Effects upon work productivity, work quality, and on-task behavior. *Mental Retardation, 18,* 19–25.

AUTHOR INDEX

SUBJECT INDEX